Master c

Master of Sea Power

A Biography of Fleet Admiral Ernest J. King

Thomas B. Buell

With an Introduction
by John B. Lundstrom

NAVAL INSTITUTE PRESS
Annapolis, Maryland

Naval Institute Press
291 Wood Road
Annapolis, MD 21402

This book was originally published in 1980 by Little, Brown and Company, Boston.

First Naval Institute Press paperback edition published in 2012.
ISBN: 978-1-59114-042-9

The Library of Congress has cataloged the hardcover edition as follows:
Buell, Thomas B.
Master of sea power : a biography of Fleet Admiral Ernest J. King / Thomas B. Buell ; with an introduction by John B. Lundstrom.
p. cm. — (Classics of naval literature)
Originally published: 1st ed. Boston : Little, Brown, 1980. With new introd.
Includes bibliographical references (p.) and index.
ISBN 1-55750-092-4 (alk. paper)
1. King, Ernest Joseph, 1878–1956. 2. Admirals—United States—Biography. 3. United States. Navy—Biography. 4. World War, 1939–1945—Naval operations, American. I. Title. II. Series.
V63.K56B83 1995
359'.0092—dc20
[B] 95-3308

∞ This paper meets the requirements of ANSI/NISO z39.48-1992 (Permanence of Paper).
Printed in the United States of America.

Frontispiece: Fleet Admiral Ernest J. King, Commander in Chief U.S. Fleet, and Chief of Naval Operations, 1945 (National Archives 80-G-416886)

20 19 18 17 16 15 14 13 12 9 8 7 6 5 4 3 2 1
First printing

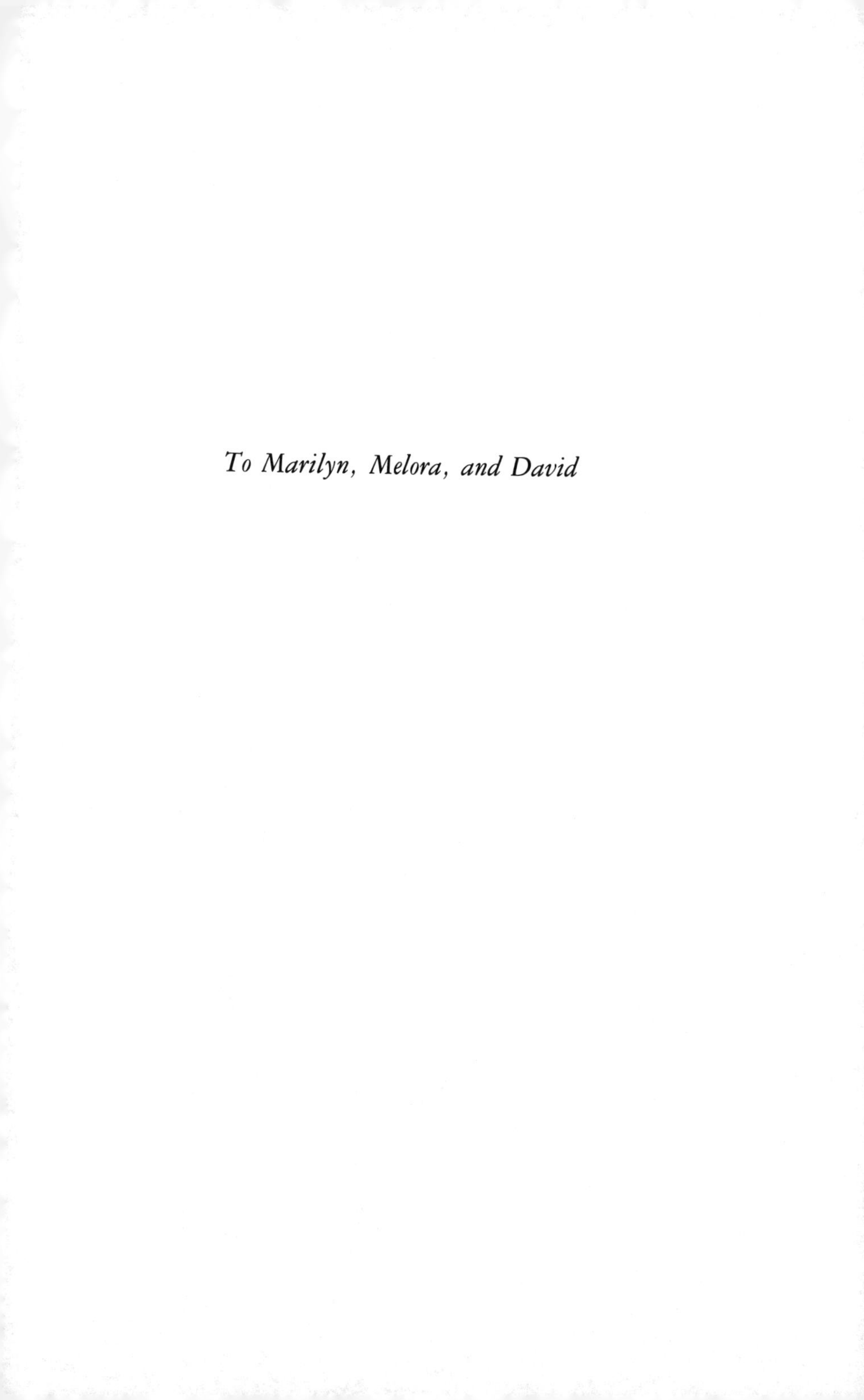

To Marilyn, Melora, and David

Contents

II: The Second World War

III: After the War

Illustrations

Introduction to the Classics of Naval Literature Edition

Current historiography exhibits a fashionable bias toward determinism and dotes on social history. Its practitioners tend to disparage the very real impact that individuals can exert on the broad course of events, particularly at times of great crisis. In contrast, the study of warfare often flirts with a Carlylean interpretation of history that emphasizes the importance of individual commanders. Given the nature of the subject, the actual process of deciding strategy during a campaign or fighting a battle can be analyzed minutely, and the role of specific leaders carefully assessed. Obviously, the institutions that nurtured these commanders to a large extent fashioned their basic philosophy and created the weapons they wielded in battle. Yet at crucial times the particular man or woman placed on the spot can have a great influence on how an entire nation will respond to a crisis.

Following this approach, it is fascinating to contemplate how different the course of World War II might have been without the unique contribution of Fleet Admiral Ernest Joseph King, U.S. Navy, to the strategy employed by the United States in particular and the Allies in general.

On 7 December 1941, Admiral King was serving as commander in chief of the Atlantic Fleet. Thus he was free of the taint of the debacle of the Pacific Fleet at Pearl Harbor. Respected for his ability and toughness, King was the logical choice to revitalize the U.S. Navy and lead it to victory. On 30 December 1941 he was elevated to the restored billet of commander in chief of the United States Fleet, whose official abbreviation he insisted on changing from the uninspiring CinCUS (pronounced "sink us") to CominCh.

Soon after, King acquired more control over the Navy. On 26 March 1942, while still remaining CominCh, he replaced Adm. Harold R. Stark as Chief of Naval Operations (CNO) and became the first individual to hold both posts simultaneously. In addition, a presidential order gave him unprecedented control over the Navy's administrative apparatus. Especially during the tenure of Secretary of the Navy Frank Knox (who died in 1944), King enjoyed relatively little interference from his civilian superiors. Thus he became the most powerful naval officer in the history of the United States and likely the entire world. Certainly no one else has ever commanded more ships, naval aircraft, or sailors.

In addition to running the Navy, King took his rightful place on the newly established U.S. Joint Chiefs of Staff and concurrently on the Allied Combined Chiefs of Staff. There he joined in the often stormy counsels that put together the grand strategy employed by the Allied coalition to defeat the Axis powers.

During 1941 while the United States was still at peace, planners from the U.S. Army and U.S. Navy worked in concert with their British counterparts. Following the lead of President Franklin D. Roosevelt and his key strategists, they determined it was necessary to concentrate forces to defeat Germany and Italy before dealing extensively with any threat Japan might present. Their resulting war plan, Rainbow Five, prescribed future offensive operations in Europe and dictated a strict defensive posture in the Pacific. This was in line with Roosevelt's policy of supporting Britain against Germany. He significantly weakened the Pacific Fleet (the principal deterrent against Japan) in order to fight what was essentially an undeclared war between King's Atlantic Fleet and the German Navy. The desperate plight of the Soviet Union in its savage war with Germany gave even more urgency to this approach.

In the first months of the Pacific War, Japan blitzed through Southeast Asia, the Dutch East Indies, and the western Pacific. The stunned Allies withdrew into the Indian Ocean, the environs of Australia, and eastward halfway across the Pacific. In early 1942 despite these terrible blows, U.S. Army planners, looking always toward Europe, continued to advocate remaining on the defensive in the Pacific Theater, even accepting the loss of Australia if otherwise unavoidable given the meager forces allocated. Conversely, Army chief of staff Gen. George C. Marshall pressed for a massive buildup in England to conduct in the summer of 1942 an amphibious offensive across the English Channel into France.

To King, such passivity in the face of the surging Japanese was totally unacceptable. His long experience as a naval strategist argued that the best defense was a good offense. He knew that it was imperative to seize the initiative from the Japanese and attack before they could advance further or consolidate their hold on their newly gained territories. King also felt that the strident calls for a general European offensive were premature, given the time needed for the United States to mobilize its military strength. Therefore, during this long, unavoidable buildup, some of the massive resources earmarked for eventual use in Europe would be much more effective if used immediately in the Pacific.

King's reasoning compelled him to oppose the prevailing Germany-first strategy. To the president and his fellow American service chiefs, Marshall and Gen. Henry H. Arnold of the U.S. Army Air Forces, King forcefully and tirelessly championed an early offensive in the Pacific. Remarkably, he got his way, and the invasion in August 1942 of Guadalcanal was the result. Thereafter, he followed the Navy's traditional Pacific doctrine based on the old War Plan Orange (the color designated the opponent, in this case Japan). This strategy dictated a general advance from one island group to another all the way across the Pacific Ocean to the Japanese homeland.

At times, King's inflexible stance brought him into direct conflict with the British allies. Yet he showed the perseverance and ability to demonstrate the wisdom of his position. If he did not win over his objectors, at least he secured their general compliance. The astounding war production of the United States in particular gave the Allies the matériel superiority to conduct simultaneous offensives in the European and Pacific theaters and fully vindicated King's audacious strategy.

In December 1944 King became the first officer to be promoted to the new five-star rank of Fleet Admiral. When he finally stepped down in December 1945 (fleet admirals were considered on active duty for life), he had won the greatest naval war in history.

In 1980 Thomas B. Buell published *Master of Sea Power: A Biography of Fleet Admiral Ernest J. King,* the first book-length study of this superb naval officer. It is the second of Buell's highly acclaimed lives of prominent U.S. naval officers. In 1974 he wrote the prize-winning *Quiet Warrior: A Biography of Admiral Raymond A. Spruance,* which in 1987 became the first of his books to be reissued in the U.S. Naval Institute series Classics of Naval Literature.

Circumstances forced Buell to adopt a considerably different approach and focus to research and write the life of Ernie King than he employed for the biography of Ray Spruance. The modest, reclusive Spruance disliked writing anything down, kept few personal papers, and talked little about himself. Much of what he thought and the specific reasons behind many of his actions had to be inferred from events and the testimony of others.

In contrast, King's conduct often bordered on the immodest, and he was certainly far from reclusive. As Buell relates, King developed a strong awareness of history and while still a lowly ensign deliberately preserved his correspondence. His long career and tenure in the Navy's highest commands generated vast amounts of documents, both official and personal, which now repose in numerous archives, including the Library of Congress, the Naval Historical Center, and the Naval War College. After World War II, King himself dictated a lengthy memoir that served as the basis of a massive 1952 autobiography *(Fleet Admiral King: A Naval Record).* It was written in the third person by Walter Muir Whitehill in close collaboration with the admiral. The book's style is somewhat self-conscious and stilted, but withal it appears sincere and frank.

Given the tremendous mass of available source material on King, Buell faced an especially difficult task of selection in order to distill the essence of King's life, career, and personality, what he thought, why he did what he did, and what he was really like. With Spruance, Buell profited from the opportunity to meet the man whose life he would later chronicle. However, he was not so fortunate with King, who died in 1956 while Buell was still a midshipman at the Naval Academy.

The key for Buell became the wholehearted cooperation of Whitehill, King's amanuensis, who had gotten to know the man and his career so well. As with the Spruance opus, Buell searched far and wide to secure the recollections and papers of persons who knew King or had personal dealings with him. King's family and close friends provided especially valuable insights. As a consequence, Buell assembled many revealing accounts and anecdotes that cast new light on the thoughts and complex personality of his subject.

Born in 1878 in Lorain, Ohio, near Cleveland, Ernest King earned an appointment in 1897 to the U.S. Naval Academy. The next April during the commotion attendant to the war with Spain, King showed characteristic personal initiative by managing on his own to go to war on the protected cruiser *San Francisco* (Cruiser No. 5), no mean accomplishment for a plebe. Back at the Academy that fall he excelled in academics and leadership, and in 1901 he graduated fourth in his class. Tall, handsome, and supremely confident, the young naval officer (nicknamed "Rey," Spanish for "king," by his classmates) was encouraged by President Theodore Roosevelt's vast expansion of the U.S. Navy and anticipated a naval career that would bring him to the top of his profession.

By 1932 Captain King was poised to don the gold braid and single sleeve stripe of a rear admiral. In the thirty-one years that had elapsed since his graduation from Annapolis he had seen a wide variety of duties—as junior officer, gunnery expert, and destroyer skipper—and an introduction to higher command by serving on staffs. Going further afield after World War I, he led a division of submarines (but never qualified to wear the submarine dolphins) and commanded the submarine base at New London. Although not a salvage expert, he greatly distinguished himself by raising the sunken submarine *S-51* in 1926 and the *S-4* two years later.

In the meantime, King had found in the growing power of naval aviation a more congenial specialty than submarines. He became a protégé of Rear Adm. William A. Moffett, the politically astute chief of the Bureau of Aeronautics. In 1927 at the advanced age of forty-nine, King learned to fly and was designated a naval aviator. He considered earning the right to wear the golden wings one of the most memorable events in his long career. After a stormy tour in Washington as Moffett's assistant, he happily went to sea as captain of the huge new aircraft carrier *Lexington* (CV-2), one of the most prestigious commands in the Navy.

During the summer of 1932 King advanced another important rung on the ladder of command. He attended the senior course of the Naval War College, where instructors and students examined the strategy to be employed in the event of war. Japan was thought to be the most likely opponent, and the advantages and disadvantages of the many routes across the Pacific were endlessly debated. King's performance during World War II amply demonstrates that he learned his lessons well. That fall, King was selected for future promotion to rear admiral.

After Moffett's untimely death in 1933, Rear Admiral King took over the Bureau of Aeronautics, to the disdain of the career aviators who distrusted the senior "Johnny Come Lately" opportunists who had come to aviation to further their careers. They had hoped that one of their own, Capt. John H. Towers (Naval Aviator No. 3), would have succeeded Moffett. In 1936 King became commander of the Navy's patrol planes and greatly improved their search capability and readiness for war. He reprised this success in 1938 and 1939 while vice admiral in charge of the carriers themselves as Commander, Aircraft, Battle Force, U.S. Fleet.

King had always thought that his naval career would culminate with the post of chief of naval operations. Unwilling to ingratiate himself with the president, he felt his record of command would speak for him. Thus he was crushed in 1939 when Roosevelt reached far down the Navy List to choose Rear Adm. Harold R. Stark instead. Reverting to his permanent rank of rear admiral, King feared as he neared statutory retirement at age sixty-four that his pursuit of the top prize was over.

Ironically, the worsening world situation gave new life to a passed-over admiral considered to be a fighter. In December 1940, King assumed command of the so-called Patrol Force, a rather insignificant collection of mostly elderly naval vessels in the Atlantic. However, bigger things were in the offing. Mirroring Roosevelt's increasing support for Britain against

Nazi Germany, King in February 1941 fleeted up to four stars and command of the newly created Atlantic Fleet. In that role he directed America's response to the growing conflict in the Atlantic and readied his steadily reinforced fleet for the war he knew to be inevitable. During World War II, King's appointment to the top commands of the Navy redounded not only in great credit to himself but added glory to the U.S. Navy.

How can one begin to take the measure of Ernie King? In *Master of Sea Power,* Buell notes how in 1933 King put forward his name as a candidate to succeed Moffett as chief of the Bureau of Aeronautics. Adm. William V. Pratt, the Chief of Naval Operations, forwarded King's letter to Secretary of the Navy Claude A. Swanson and added his own perceptive evaluation of the candidate's qualities:

(a) He is highly intelligent.
(b) He is extremely active and energetic.
(c) He is very forceful.
(d) He is a flyer and a pilot.
(e) He is a man of great decision of character.
(f) He is a good strategist and tactician.
(g) He is not as tactful as some men but he is very direct.
(h) He is trustworthy.

Pratt's list of King's personal attributes provides a useful starting point for taking a closer look at some of the main facets of King's personality, his many strengths and occasional weaknesses, as revealed with discerning insight by Buell in *Master of Sea Power.*

Many of King's words and deeds testify to his acute intelligence and clear thinking. He always liked to say that he could master any job in six months and over the years accumulated vast practical knowledge of his profession. Even more important than his intellectual brilliance, however, was his contempt for the status quo. Buell described King's "perpetual struggle to improve the Navy through the stimulus of change and new ideas." He demanded clarity and brevity and warred against excessive paperwork. While CominCh he usually refused to read any memorandum longer than a single page. Whether he himself was a good administrator is another question, but he chose and closely supervised surrogates who were.

King's forte was strategy, and soon after he took command of the Navy, he articulated to President Roosevelt the need to go over to the offensive in the Pacific. Buell called King's efforts in this regard "the most important contribution he would make to victory in the Second World War" and later added: "In a period of one month—March 1942—King had inspired and advocated the plans and strategy that would govern the entire course of the war in the Pacific." Just over three years of hard fighting across the broad expanse of the Pacific placed the Allies at the gates of Japan.

Throughout the Pacific War King stayed close to the planning process, conferring often with Adm. Chester W. Nimitz, the commander in chief of the Pacific Fleet and Pacific Ocean Areas. Once the Japanese advance had been halted in the South Pacific, King initiated a direct advance across the Central Pacific through the Marianas toward Taiwan (Formosa) to isolate the Japanese homeland from its southern conquests. With varying degrees of success, he attempted to keep Nimitz's chief rival, Gen. Douglas MacArthur, supreme commander of the Southwest Pacific Area, on a short leash. King tried but failed to advance the capture of Taiwan over MacArthur's much-stated aim to return to the Philippines, which he considered a useless diversion of forces. In the one major reversal of his basic strategy he agreed with Nimitz and Vice Admiral Spruance to substitute the invasions of Okinawa and Iwo Jima for his long-advocated landings on Taiwan.

King retained a hands-on approach in dealing with the German U-boat scourge in his old command, the Atlantic Ocean. Shortly after the outbreak of the war, Adm. Karl Doenitz's submarines found easy pickings among unescorted ships plying the East Coast. The Navy's antisubmarine effort was too weak and ill prepared to deal with the onslaught that one recent book, Michael Gannon's *Operation Drumbeat* (New York: Harper & Row, 1990), described, with harsh criticism of King, as worse than the Pearl Harbor disaster. If King failed at the beginning, he learned quickly. To coordinate the U.S. Navy's efforts against the U-boats, he created the Tenth Fleet, nominally under his direct command but run by its chief of staff, Rear Adm. Francis C. Low. The Tenth Fleet contributed mightily to victory in the Battle of the Atlantic.

Imperious, arrogant, supremely confident in his own abilities, and pushing to the limit his powers and prerogatives, King was always a difficult man to serve under. Also, for superiors he did not respect he was on occasion an unruly subordinate. His theoretical concept of leadership involved the selection and training of subordinates who could exercise initiative. He thought it should be sufficient for good commanders to tell their junior officers what needed to be done and let them decide how best to do it.

Of course, King, like anyone else, often failed to practice what he preached. When aroused he could be fiery. While captain of the *Lexington,* "if something went wrong, King's voice rose and his arms flailed like a windmill," but Buell also added, "although King lost his temper he rarely lost his self-control." He was always aware of the effect his outbursts would create. Every subordinate seemed to have a favorite King story with which to horrify friends.

The key to getting along with King was demonstration of unremitting competence and results. He respected those few who had the courage to stand up to him when they, not he, were in the right. However, heaven help any subordinates whom he decided were weak or slack. King hounded such unfortunates unmercifully and never relented, even if they later proved themselves under different circumstances. To him, superior performance was routinely expected and not something deserving of special praise. King led by example as well as by rank and never shirked responsibility, nor did he send others to do what he himself would not do. He pushed his commands to the limit of endurance, but he made them far better for all of their suffering.

Professional experience accrued during a naval career and a broad personal knowledge of naval history have both contributed to award-winning author Thomas Bingham Buell's manifest ability to research and write the lives of naval officers. A 1958 graduate of the U.S. Naval Academy, he served in a wide variety of assignments afloat and ashore. Drawn by inclination to the study of naval history and strategy, he was both a student and an instructor at the Naval War College and also taught at the U.S. Military Academy. He considers a high point of his naval career to be his command of the *Joseph Hewes* (FF-1078), an Atlantic Fleet frigate. That was a sentiment he shared with Ernest King, who treasured the memories of his first command, the destroyer *Terry* (DD-25). Commander Buell retired from the Navy in 1979 and now lives in Chapel Hill, North Carolina.

This student of naval history hopes that Tom Buell will chronicle the life and career of yet another influential American naval officer, with the full expectation that this effort, too, will be another Classic of Naval Literature.

JOHN B. LUNDSTROM

Introduction

THE SECOND WORLD WAR had been over for ten months when Fleet Admiral Ernest J. King boarded a Navy transport plane in Washington, D.C., on a June day in 1946. He was on his way to England, to receive an honorary Doctor of Civil Law degree from Oxford University. King was retired now, after four years of wartime service as Commander in Chief, U.S. Fleet, and Chief of Naval Operations. He had commanded the largest Navy in the world: more than eight thousand ships, nearly twenty-four thousand aircraft, over three million naval officers and sailors, and a half million Marines.

But King was as much thinker as active leader. He had directed the war together with his colleagues on the Joint Chiefs of Staff: Fleet Admiral William D. Leahy, General of the Army George C. Marshall, and General of the Army Henry H. Arnold. Armed forces officers would never again exert the power these four men had wielded in defeating Germany, Japan, and Italy. Civilians would henceforth run wars.

Great Britain had been America's ally. The wartime coalition had succeeded in large measure because the Combined Chiefs of Staff (the Joint Chiefs of Staff and the British Chiefs of Staff) had worked so well together. Yet the British had regarded King more as adversary than ally. Perhaps some of their mutual hostility stemmed from their divergent heritages. King's family had been working-class Scots and Englishmen who had immigrated to northern Ohio in the late nineteenth century. King had been born in a laborer's cottage, reared in a railroad yard, and educated in a small-town school. His British colleagues were aristocrats by inheritance or by inclination, defenders of the British Empire who perpetuated the 1672 injunction of Charles II to Louis XIV: "It is the custom of the British to command at sea."

How they had fought! Field Marshal Lord Alanbrooke, Chief of the Imperial General Staff, had clashed repeatedly with King over questions of strategy when they had met in war councils at Washington, London, Quebec, Casablanca, Malta, and Cairo. General Lord Ismay, chief of staff to Winston Churchill, wrote that King was tough, blunt, rude, intolerant, and suspicious of all things British. Admiral of the Fleet Andrew B. Cunningham, Britain's First Sea Lord, thought King ill mannered, ruthless, and arrogant.

It had been King who had insisted upon fighting hard against Japan, over British protests that the Allies had to beat Germany first. Shipping controlled Allied strategy, and King controlled Allied shipping. He used this advantage to coerce the British into acquiescing to King's war in the Pacific—or so it seemed to the British. Most galling of all, the Royal Navy had become second best to King's Navy. King would not let them forget it.

With victory came goodwill. Discords were forgotten or forgiven. Now the British would honor King. King, too, had mellowed. His aircraft carried several crates of fresh citrus fruit, gifts from the Admiral for the King of England, for Winston Churchill, and for Lord Halifax, the Chancellor of Oxford University. They would be glad to get them. Food was still scarce in England.

On the twenty-sixth of June, King prepared to receive his

King in his crimson robes at Oxford (Courtesy Walter Muir Whitehill)

degree. The past few days had been pleasant—luncheon with Averell Harriman, drives through the countryside, dinner at Claridge's Hotel in London with senior American naval officers, and finally a formal dinner the night before at the residence of the Dean of Wadham College. Now it was time for the grand procession with the other honorary graduates (including Lady Churchill) into Sheldonian Theatre. King wore a crimson robe in a noble gathering of British pomp and pageantry. The most distinguished leaders of Great Britain were in the audience. The ceremony began.

The Public Orator presented King. "Si robur illi atque aes triplex circa pectus erat . . ." Those who were unfamiliar with Latin read the English translation in their programs: "Solid oak and triple bronze, if Horace is right, enclosed the heart of the first man who put to sea. What armor plate, then, must be worn by this brave soul, whose love for his profession taught him to sail *on* the seas as a boy, to sail *under* them as a young man, and to fly *above* them in his later years—the commander in turn of surface craft, submarines, and air arm. . . . The example of his tireless devotion to duty, combining with his peculiar gift of pungent expression, served to tighten naval discipline. . . . It was no surprise to hear of his appointment as Chief of Naval Operations, with supreme command in both the Atlantic and Pacific Oceans. The vastness of that war area and the huge scale of the necessary preparations were not more remarkable than his readiness of mind and speed in execution. I present to you . . . our Ally of the Trident, Admiral Ernest J. King, whose threefold knowledge was a prime factor in our triple victory."

After the ceremony King returned to the United States and obscurity. A stroke slowed him the following year, his health worsened, and he lived in hospitals until he died in 1956.

A destroyer and two minor buildings in King's name are his only commemoration by the Navy. Some say that during his career King antagonized too many people who later wanted his name forgotten. King had but one aim in life during his first forty years of naval service: to become the Chief of Naval Operations. He sought that goal with zealous, single-minded determination. He made no secret of it. He would tell anyone who would listen, and his ambition was common knowledge throughout the Navy.

By 1939 he had risen to the temporary rank of vice admiral for a year and a half before reverting to his permanent rank of rear admiral. Many other flag officers had achieved that much, and more. His career would have been no different from that of other prewar officers who strove for the top, failed to make it, and then retired into anonymity. Yet retirement was incomprehensible. The Navy was his only life.

There were those who said that King failed on his first try—despite his ambition and professionalism—because he had too many enemies, he chased men's wives, and he drank too much. Indeed, his entire career was a series of contradictions. He could be both cruel and loving, both immoral and ethical. His temper was as quick as lightning and as terrible as a volcano. Yet his fearlessness and perseverance steadied the Navy and the nation through the worst crises of the war. Above all, he was a fighter.

People fight in wars for different reasons, some because they are forced to fight, others for self-defense, and still others from patriotism. Dwight D. Eisenhower wrote of the war in Europe as a crusade "bound together by common love of liberty and a refusal to submit to enslavement." Winston Churchill loathed Hitler and the Nazis as a monstrous evil that threatened to destroy civilization. Yet King seemed without emotion or patriotic motivation. Not once did he write about his feelings toward the German nation. Japan was simply an adversary that finally justified his forty years of preparing for war. Italy was a nuisance.

King was, in fact, a dispassionate professional warrior who held his own political system in contempt and spurned all civilian authority except that of his commander in chief—the President. The Axis Powers happened to be the enemy that he had to destroy. A few years earlier King had considered Great Britain as one of America's greatest potential enemies, and we may assume he would have fought the British as ruthlessly as he had Japan and Germany.

One summer as a midshipman in the Class of 1958 at the Naval Academy, I noticed unusual activity near the cemetery. "What is happening?" I asked. "It's Admiral King's funeral," a friend replied. His name meant so little to me then that I thought no more about it. Several years later I helped commission the USS *King* at Puget Sound Naval Shipyard. She was the most beautiful warship I have ever known. By then I had read King's memoirs, *Fleet Admiral King: A Naval Record.* I remember admiring his candor and forthrightness and wanting to be that way myself.

At the Naval War College in the early 1970s I was writing my biography of Admiral Raymond A. Spruance. While I was there my good friend Henry E. Eccles introduced me to the late Walter Muir Whitehill, who had collaborated in writing King's memoirs. I accepted Dr. Whitehill's invitation to visit his North Andover home outside Boston, where King had stayed off and on twenty years before. I slept in King's bed, sat in his chair, ate at his table, and talked for hours with Walter and his lovely wife, Jane, about Fleet Admiral King. That Sunday afternoon, in the Whitehills' converted barn behind their home, I read the files Whitehill had used in writing *Fleet Admiral King: A Naval Record,* published in 1952. There was magic in those papers. King's soul and spirit permeated every page that I read. I was fascinated. That afternoon I decided that I wanted to write a biography of Ernest J. King.

My research began, even though I soon went to sea to command a destroyer. Two years later I came ashore to teach history at the U.S. Military Academy at West Point. Walter Whitehill lent me his papers, and with them as my foundation, my writing began.

And now my work is finished. I offer my readers this story of the most powerful naval officer in the history of the world, on the centennial anniversary of his birth.

Thomas B. Buell

West Point, New York
November 1978

Chronology

23 November 1878	Ernest Joseph King born to James Clydesdale King and Elizabeth Keam King in Lorain, Ohio
6 September 1897	Sworn as Naval Cadet, U.S. Naval Academy, from the fourteenth Congressional District of Ohio
July–August 1898	Temporary duty aboard USS *San Francisco* during Spanish-American War
7 June 1901	Graduates from the Naval Academy with distinction
7 June 1903	Promoted to Ensign
10 October 1905	Marries Martha Lamkin Egerton in the Cadet Chapel, U.S. Military Academy
7 June 1906	Promoted to Lieutenant
1 July 1913	Promoted to Lieutenant Commander
30 April 1914	First command, USS *Terry*
18 July 1914	Second command, USS *Cassin*

6 April 1917	United States enters First World War
1 July 1917	Promoted to Commander
21 September 1918	Promoted to Captain
11 November 1918	First World War ends
7 July 1921	Third command, USS *Bridge*
20 November 1922	Fourth command, Submarine Division Eleven, with additional duty as Commander, Submarine Division Three, in April 1923
4 September 1923	Fifth command, U.S. Submarine Base, New London, Connecticut
25 September 1925	USS *S-51* sunk off Block Island, Rhode Island. King awarded Distinguished Service Medal for directing salvage
28 July 1926	Sixth command, USS *Wright*
26 May 1927	Designated Naval Aviator #3368
17 December 1927	USS *S-4* sunk off Provincetown, Massachusetts. King awarded Gold Star in lieu of second Distinguished Service Medal for directing salvage
1 June 1928	Seventh command, Aircraft Squadrons, Scouting Fleet
24 May 1929	Eighth command, U.S. Naval Air Station, Norfolk, Virginia
20 June 1930	Ninth command, USS *Lexington*
26 April 1933	Promoted to Rear Admiral. Chief of the U.S. Navy Bureau of Aeronautics
15 June 1936	Commander Aircraft, Base Force
1 October 1937	Commander Aircraft, Scouting Force
29 January 1938	Promoted to Vice Admiral. Commander Aircraft, Battle Force

1 July 1939	Reverted to permanent rank of Rear Admiral. Ordered to General Board
17 December 1940	Commander Patrol Force, U.S. Fleet
1 February 1941	Promoted to Admiral. Commander in Chief, U.S. Atlantic Fleet
9–12 August 1941	Atlantic Charter Conference, Argentia, Newfoundland
7 December 1941	United States enters Second World War
22 December 1941	First Washington Conference (ARCADIA) begins, leading to the creation of the Combined Chiefs of Staff and Joint Chiefs of Staff
30 December 1941	Commander in Chief, U.S. Fleet
18 March 1942	Appointed to concurrent duty as Chief of Naval Operations
7 August 1942	Marines assault Guadalcanal
8 November 1942	Allies assault North Africa
14 January 1943	Casablanca Conference (SYMBOL) begins
12 May 1943	Second Washington Conference (TRIDENT) begins
10 July 1943	Allies assault Sicily
17 August 1943	First Quebec Conference (QUADRANT) begins
20 November 1943	American forces assault Gilbert Islands
22 November 1943	Cairo Conference (SEXTANT) begins
27 November 1943	Teheran Conference (EUREKA) begins
28 April 1944	Secretary of the Navy Frank Knox dies

19 May 1944	James V. Forrestal becomes Secretary of the Navy
6 June 1944	Allies assault Normandy
11 September 1944	Second Quebec Conference (OCTAGON) begins
20 October 1944	Army forces assault Leyte
17 December 1944	Promoted to Fleet Admiral
4 February 1945	Yalta Conference (ARGONAUT) begins
12 April 1945	President Franklin D. Roosevelt dies. Vice President Harry S Truman succeeds to the presidency
7 May 1945	Germany surrenders unconditionally
16 July 1945	Potsdam Conference (TERMINAL) begins
2 September 1945	Second World War ends
15 December 1945	Relieved by Fleet Admiral Nimitz
25 June 1956	Ernest J. King dies at the Naval Hospital, Portsmouth, New Hampshire

I

Before the War

I had a proper ambition to get to the top, either Commander in Chief of the United States Fleet, or even to become Chief of Naval Operations.

I believe that my record will speak for itself.

— Ernest J. King

1

In the Beginning

ERNEST J. KING'S PARENTS, James Clydesdale King and Elizabeth Keam, were Scottish and English emigrants. James was nine when his father died in the small Scottish town of Bridge-of-Weir, in Renfrewshire. An improverished widow with five sons and a daughter, James's mother gratefully accepted her brother's offer for her to join him in Cleveland. There James King was naturalized and later became a merchant seaman aboard sailing ships on the Great Lakes.

When the lakes froze and ice immobilized the ships, the mariners were unemployed. James wanted regular work and switched to bridge building. It was a dangerous trade that, not unlike sailing, demanded courage and stamina, especially during fall storms. Since sailing and bridge building both were nomadic, the transition was simple. And the pay was better in bridge building.

When Elizabeth — Bessie — met James she saw in his character strength, self-reliance, and industry, the virtues in her own family. Her father, Joseph Keam, had been a master woodworker — a top sawyer — in a Plymouth, England, dockyard. The shift from sail and wood to steam and steel forced the Keam family to emigrate from England to America. Father, mother and four marriageable daughters settled in Cleveland in 1872. Joseph Keam found work in an emerging petroleum industry, eventually rising to foreman in a refinery.

James King married Bessie Keam in 1876. They left Cleveland, and James resumed his rough-and-tumble life of going where bridges were building. Bessie was separated from her family, living with a husband she scarcely knew, and fearing for his life. After losing her first child, Bessie craved a permanent home, a safer job for James, and the nearness of her kin. James King agreed. He found work in a railroad repair shop in

Lorain, Ohio, a Lake Erie port near Cleveland, and he bought a cottage near the shore. Their luck improved. A second son, Ernest Joseph King, was born in their home on 23 November 1878.

Ernest King's boyhood was largely influenced by his father. The boy loved to visit James King in the shops, noisy, murky, and smelling of smoke and grease. The workers liked young Ernest and taught him the intricacies of steam-driven machinery, the precision of the lathe, and the interrelationship of valves and pistons and gears. Engineers hoisted him into their cabs as they moved about the railyard. Ernest King admired such men. Like his father and grandfather, they were rudimentary, honest, blunt, and outspoken. They also could be profane, opinionated, stubborn, and self-righteous, disdaining equivocation and scorning pretention.

As early as age six or seven the boy's character was becoming evident. On one occasion he accompanied his mother to visit a family named Rawley. Following dinner the hostess served a pumpkin pie overseasoned with pepper. King tasted it.

"I don't like Mrs. Rawley's pie," said young King.

"Ernest!" his mother replied. "You shouldn't say that."

"It's true," King insisted; "I don't like it."

Reminiscing years later, King remarked, "If I didn't agree, I said so." But just as early King recognized the distinction between candor and disobedience. Skipping school or coming home late justifiably deserved punishment.

James King restlessly began moving his family again, seeking better jobs near Cleveland. More children were born, two daughters and two sons. Ernest completed the eighth grade, then declared that he wanted to quit school. His father grudgingly consented, with the provision that Ernest would have to work at least a year. "By the time school came along," King later wrote, "I hinted about going back to school. But my father was deaf, and he remained deaf until the next year when the school year opened." King meanwhile was laid off, and finding work was difficult. "Finally," King later said, "my father said I could have a job down in the railroad shops [where his father was foreman], but I had to understand that I had to do more than anyone else — which was his way of doing things."

After King entered high school his mother fell ill and returned to Cleveland with her other children to live with a sister. King and his father remained in Lorain with a housekeeper. In the summer of 1894 — when King was sixteen — typhoid fever nearly killed him. "My nurse was an old German woman who took very good care of me," he later wrote. "She always called me 'Yonny.' I came to see her many times, especially when I was on leave from the Naval Academy. Until the day she died she still called me 'Yonny.' "

King's mother died in Cleveland the following spring, as King was finishing his sophomore year. King mentions this matter-of-factly in his memoirs without a hint of grief. Living alone with his father evidently suited him. King's memoirs recall his last years in high school with a sense of happiness, especially when his father allowed him increasing independence. "My father once arranged for passes on the railroad from Lorain to Uhrichsville to visit a friend," King later wrote. "I did not ride in the coaches, but on the Engine!"

Still, his teenage years — working in the shops during the summer, living in a house without a mother and other children — perhaps forced him to be a man too early. Throughout his life he would regress to boyish behavior. Once as a houseguest of close friends he mischievously threw newspapers on the floor. "Ernest, pick those papers up!" commanded the hostess, and the Fleet Admiral meekly obeyed. As a father he delighted in playing parlor games with his children, especially Monopoly, but he was a poor loser and would petulantly demand that the game continue late into the night despite his wife's protest that the children had to go to bed. Later she hid the games.

As a young boy King was intellectually stimulated despite his working-class environment. His family — like many Scottish-English immigrants — were literate and politically active, the kind of people who support libraries and value education. (Many of these immigrants' ideas were later embraced by the British and Canadian Labor Parties.) King's grandfather, Joseph Keam, for example, incessantly lectured family and friends with his opinions on government and economics, provoked perhaps by the prevailing political climate: Lorain was surrounded by a rural population in the most abolitionist and radical Republican county in Ohio.

King's Grandmother Keam shared a different kind of intellectualism. "She was a very educated woman," King recalled. "I remember sitting down with her while she read to me about the stars." Then there was a neighbor, a Civil War veteran, who owned a set of books about the men and the battles fought less than twenty-five years earlier. "I used to pore over that from the time I could read," King later said. "I didn't understand about it, but I turned the pages over."

King was attracted to women, of all ages. He attended Sunday school as a teenager solely because he admired the teacher. Older women liked to mother him. He cherished their affection, retained a lifelong gratitude

Ernest J. King as a boy in Lorain
(Courtesy Walter Muir Whitehill)

King's first love, Leona Doane. Photo taken by King and given to Leona with the caption *What do you think of this?*
(Courtesy Lucy K. Hatch)

for their kindness, wrote to them periodically through the years, faithfully called on them whenever he visited Lorain, and remembered their funerals.

He also had several girl friends. By high school graduation a classmate named Leona Doane had become special. When King went to the Naval Academy they parted with an apparent "understanding," which lasted for several years. Then Leona wrote that she would marry someone else.

"Dear Friend," King replied from Annapolis. "Suffice it to say that, for my part, I wish that your life may be as long as I am confident it will be *good*. I think too, that perhaps our lives were better apart, as they are destined to be; for I am sure that you were far, far too *good* for a naval officer. God grant that the man of your choice may be as good as you are. A long and happy life to you both. And now a last farewell to our former friendship. Good bye — Most sincerely, Ernest J. King."

King's high school studies (except for German) came easily — he would graduate as valedictorian. Popular with his classmates and a natural leader, he developed an attitude that he had been "born to manage things." It was an inherited family characteristic, he reasoned, because both his father and his Grandfather Keam were themselves foremen.

An article in the magazine *Youth's Companion* describing the Naval Academy had aroused King's interest as a boy of ten. He sustained his interest in the Academy even though he once had been seasick on Lake Erie. "I thought I would like to go there," King later explained. "My father thought well of it and kept it in mind." James King undoubtedly recognized that the Academy would educate his son at government expense, and besides, he once had been a sailor himself. The elder King contacted Congressman W. S. Kerr when the politician visited Lorain seeking reelection in the summer of 1896. (He had one leg, King recalled, from a railroad accident and not the Civil War.) "My father told him I would like to go to the Naval Academy," King later said. "Mr. Kerr said that the usual arrangement was to make the appointment by competitive exams. My father said that would be fine because he didn't want any favors."

King crammed in the last months of his senior year, tutored by the school superintendent, who advised King to give up German. "He told me I was in for a big job," King later said, "and to go right after it." King's high school, although small (he had only thirteen classmates), was undoubtedly the equivalent of college to the people of Lorain. King's hopes for Annapolis comprised the height of ambition. He had become a celebrity with a host of admirers who wished him well.

Several weeks after graduation the eighteen-year-old King journeyed fifty miles to Congressman Kerr's hometown of Mansfield to compete for the Academy appointment. It was the first time he had ever been away from home by himself. A physician examined King and said he was exceptionally fit. The written examination was next. King followed his tutor's advice to answer each question two or three different ways.

He returned to Lorain with mixed emotions. It was Sunday, and his father was home. "After a while," King later said, "I asked my father to come down to the lake, so we stayed there until dark."

He received his Annapolis appointment, having competed and won against thirty applicants.

James King insisted that his son relax during the remainder of the summer rather than working in the railroad shops, as he customarily had done in summers past. When the time came to leave for Annapolis, the father gave his son a round-trip railroad pass. Ernest King kept that pass for years, perhaps as a symbolic bond between him and Lorain, for he maintained a lifetime affection for its people and they for him. Although the town grew into a large industrial city, King never lost touch and returned to Lorain again and again.

King arrived in Annapolis on 15 August 1897, a slumbering, decaying little fishing port where the Severn River flows into the Chesapeake Bay. Colonial homes, still lovely, and the graceful state capitol emanated a dignity and charm that reflected a once prosperous past. And there was a smell in the air that was new to King. It was salt water from the Atlantic Ocean.

King entered the Naval Academy grounds through the Maryland Avenue gate and walked through the Yard toward the station ship, a sailing hulk named *Santee*. The *Santee* — called simply "the ship" — served as temporary quarters for cadets arriving, leaving, on probation, or being severely punished. It typified the Naval Academy nearing the turn of the century: decrepit, disgraceful, and neglected by Congress. The armory was so near collapse that shoring had to support the outer walls. The principal cadet barracks, constructed of wood during the Civil War and still habitually called "New Quarters" thirty-five years later, was a fire trap. The "Old Quarters," housing a fourth of the 290-member student body, had been built when the Academy had been founded — half a century before King arrived at Annapolis.

"Plebe Summer" was a period of transition, a time for King and his eighty-seven new classmates to learn military discipline and the rudiments of seamanship under sail. Despite regional origins, the young men were socially homogeneous — white middle-class, predominantly Protestant, and sharing similar values. Their motivations for entering Annapolis ranged from patriotism and a fancied romance with the sea to lack of family money and a desire for a free education.

Soon after the academic year began, a well-remembered instructor snarled that many of the plebes would need a return ticket home. The academic department was quickly recognized for what it was: an adversary. Attrition was so severe during the first two years that King and his classmates decided to match good and poor students as roommates. The tutoring scheme worked. Not one failed during the final two years.

Another adversary was the Commandant of Cadets and his staff of lieutenants in the Department of Discipline. There were harsh rules for young men accustomed to the freedom of home life. Plebes were denied a Christmas vacation and their visits to Annapolis were limited to Saturday afternoons. Smoking was forbidden. The naval cadets naturally sought ways and means to beat the system, leading to various conspiracies against Academy authority.

King established his personal goals soon after arriving at the Naval Academy. A drunken upperclassman accused King of bragging that he would be first in his class. King denied it. King's classmate Adolphus Andrews, however, was in the room also, and Andrews boldly confirmed that *he* intended to be number one. The upperclassman berated Andrews for his presumptuousness, and King was impressed. He began to think about the implications. If he graduated first in his class, he reasoned, from then on he would be too visible for comfort throughout his naval career. As too much would probably be expected of him, King concluded that it would be best if he graduated about third or fourth, which would still confer prestige but was not nearly as conspicuous.

A high class standing was easy for King. Most of the instructors were junior naval officers with few academic credentials, fresh from sea duty. Teaching and learning were by rote. This suited King because he was gifted with a prodigious memory. In later years he could remember names of people he had met only briefly many years earlier. (King was also addicted to crossword puzzles, the more difficult the better, which he customarily completed without using a dictionary.) Technical subjects, whether steam engineering or mechanics, were simple after years in the Ohio railroad repair shops.

"Of course, I was not an athlete," King later wrote, and he had begun smoking. Still he tried out for the crew team, failed, then switched to football, where he labored with the scrubs (called the "Hustlers") throughout his senior year. But he could skate and skate well, and his body remained lean and fit. As a plebe he was a slender 135 pounds, but by his senior year he had grown to just over 6 feet and 165 pounds, the heaviest he would ever weigh. His vigorous constitution was reflected in his rosy complexion. Just like the cheeks of a doll, thought his classmates, and King's nickname became "Dolly," which he detested. Indeed, he had become so handsome by his senior year that "Beauty" became another nickname. He liked that even less. "Rey," the Spanish word for king, was more suitable. That he liked.*

King was gregarious, active in class activities, a go-getter and a team player projecting the image of a popular yet respected and responsible leader. His ambition was to achieve the top leadership position within the student hierarchy, that of Battalion Commander. The holder of that position was the sole cadet privileged to wear the four gold stripes of a cadet lieutenant commander. King needed both support from his classmates and approval from the Naval Academy administration. As the two groups were natural adversaries, King had to be many things to many men. He was popular with his classmates, who appreciated his class loyalty and his forthrightness in representing their best interests. On the other hand, the administration recognized King's respect for law and authority and capitalized upon his ability to influence others to obey the regulations. King got the job.

In April of King's plebe year the United States went to war with Spain. Excitement swept the Academy. Junior officers were needed immediately in the fleet, so the first classmen (seniors) were hastily commissioned. The second classmen (juniors) were promised sea duty for the war's duration following their annual exams in May.

The two lower classes besought permission to fight, as well. "We were told to go home and stay there," King later said. Some did. Some fifteen others, including King, finagled orders. King happily joined four classmates aboard the cruiser *San Francisco* at Provincetown, Massachusetts. He was off to his first war. He got there slowly. In response to civilian hysteria, *San Francisco* was assigned to New England waters to protect the coast from an illusory threat from the Spanish fleet. As radio had not entered the fleet, the ship remained near Provincetown in order to communicate by telegraph line with the Navy Department.

Early in the morning following his arrival, King was ordered to take charge of a four-oared dinghy and to go ashore in order to pick up market supplies. King clambered aboard, grasped the tiller ropes, stared

* Nicknames, some rather bizarre, were customary (indeed mandatory) among Naval Aacademy graduates for many decades before the Second World War.

at the sailors impassively gazing at him in return, and wondered what to do next.

"Shove off," he croaked, and with difficulty the dinghy cleared the accommodation ladder. "Someway," King later recalled, "I managed to keep the boat pointed toward the shore." Coming alongside the landing float was complicated by King's inexperience and a treacherous current. Twice he tried and twice he failed, humiliating himself before the sailors and the waterfront loungers.

"Mr. King," said an old seaman from the crew, "maybe I can help you." King gratefully accepted his advice, and the boat was landed and made fast. It was King's introduction to what he regarded as the courtesy of the "Old Navy," manifested by savvy enlisted men who patiently instructed young officers in the ways of the ship and the sea.

Yet King could reject advice just as quickly once he had confidence in his own ability, which was most of the time. He soon fancied himself a boathandler, so much so that as boat officer he ordered a protesting enlisted coxswain to make an unorthodox landing alongside an anchored ship. King's method worked, but it still merited a rebuke from the quarterdeck watch officer. King was undisturbed. His way was obviously the best, and, yet, during a stormy passage by boat several nights later, King deferred entirely to an enlisted coxswain's judgment in making a perilous landing.

These early experiences were the first symptoms of King's internal conflicts when making judgments. He was an egoist, intellectually arrogant and supremely confident in his ability to distinguish truth and righteousness and to reduce the complex to the simplest terms. Subconsciously he sought to be omnipotent and infallible. There were few men whom he regarded as his equal as to brains; he would acknowledge no mind as superior to his own. Yet he also realized that there were things he did not know and things he could not do, and in such matters he would have to depend upon others. But once convinced he had the right answer, he was unyielding toward any suggestion that he might possibly be wrong. Unyielding may be too mild an adjective. Stubborn. Adamant. Tenacious. And fortified with a violent temper — in the words of Walter Muir Whitehill, like an Olympian Zeus returned with lightning flashes and roaring thunder.

Eventually *San Francisco* steamed south to Cuba. She joined the blockade force, came under fire from the forts of Havana for a few exciting minutes, and then the war was over. King and his classmates no longer were needed and were dumped ashore in Florida. King returned to Lorain a hero. "I must say I had a fine time on that leave," he later said.

"I had been to sea and I had been shot at!" Then he returned to Annapolis, an anchor tattooed on his left arm and a small dagger on his right.

When King began his final year at the Naval Academy, his four stripes marked him as a cadet "of some consequence in the battalion." Still, smiles and laughter came easily; he could be one of the boys, even as he exercised an unquestioned authority that awed the younger cadets. "I suppose every plebe looks up to his first class as the best ever," wrote a former cadet to King years later, "perhaps because it is his first standard of measurement. Your class has always seemed the best I've seen go through the Academy; and you are still my 'four striper,' with four stars."

Attracted by the glamour of the Naval Academy, young women came to Annapolis with chaperones and took rooms in Carvel Hall just beyond the Yard. Two effervescent, fun-loving sisters from Baltimore, Mattie and Florrie Egerton, were frequent visitors. Mattie so charmed and dazzled the cadets that they swarmed about her, coveting her attention. She was the most beautiful, the most sought-after young woman at Annapolis. King wanted her for himself. She in turn was attracted to the virile, smiling, self-assured cadet who loved to dance. Mattie decided she would marry Ernest King.

By spring of his senior year King's immediate ambitions had been achieved. He enjoyed the prestige and responsibility of commanding the battalion, and he and Mattie were the most popular, most handsome couple at the Academy, admired and envied by everyone. They had agreed to marriage, but they would have to wait. An Annapolis graduate did not marry immediately, because he first had to learn to become an officer at sea. A new wife would be a distraction.

Graduation was on a warm and rainy June morning in 1901. Four years earlier Annapolis had been a sleepy old village. The call of the soft-crab man and his green-covered tray was heard in season, Jimmy Feldmeyer's was a gathering place, and the Academy grounds reflected somnolence and decay. But now as the class was about to leave, the streets had been paved, clattering trolley cars had appeared, and workmen swarmed over the Yard erecting magnificent new buildings of steel and granite.

James King saw his son graduate fourth in his class. Vice President Theodore Roosevelt was the featured speaker and presented the diplomas. It was the last time the Class of 1901 would ever be assembled as a body. They had begun their Academy careers as strangers, but by graduation they had developed an extraordinary class loyalty. King left

Midshipman King, 1901. Note the stars on his collar, signifying academic excellence. (Courtesy Naval Historical Center)

King and Mattie Egerton, his future wife, in Annapolis, 1901 (Courtesy Ernest J. King, Jr.)

his classmates with a feeling of profound friendship, so much so that he later dedicated his autobiography to them.

King recognized that most Annapolis men were proud to have graduated but would not want to have repeated the experience. "But," said King afterward, "I should say that I had a very good time myself." His graduation, he would later say, was one of the four most important events of his career.

2

Learning

KING LEFT THE Naval Academy in June 1901 as a passed midshipman, a rank he would retain for two years until examined for promotion.* He entered a navy in transition. After years of decay and neglect following the Civil War it had finally come to life, and replacement ships were entering the fleet. In the fall of 1901 there was a new impetus: Theodore Roosevelt became President after McKinley's assassination. Influenced by Alfred Thayer Mahan, Roosevelt was determined to transform the United States into a great sea power. In December 1901 he began his crusade. Within the next four years Congress authorized ten battleships, four armored cruisers, and seventeen other ships. Naval appropriations increased from $85 million to $118 million per year. Despite its increasing generosity with construction appropriations, Congress was reluctant to authorize the numbers of men needed to operate the ships. The expedient of using midshipmen in the Spanish-American War was the most recent example of the Navy's manpower shortage.

The naval officer corps was stagnant. Promotions were based upon seniority rather than merit. An officer, however mediocre, was assured of slow but sure promotion unless he left the service for cause. When King still was a naval cadet an officer could expect to be an ensign for ten years and a lieutenant for twenty years. By the time he was a lieutenant commander he would have been over fifty years old.† As a commander and captain he would be approaching retirement and physically past his prime. Rear admirals were over sixty and could serve but a few years. Small wonder that American flag officers, although older men, were in-

* The rank of naval cadet had been changed to midshipman.
† Today a naval officer normally is promoted to lieutenant commander in his early thirties.

experienced in serving as admirals. By comparison, flag officers in the Royal Navy were younger but far senior in experience and time in rank.

Following graduation King went to a short course in torpedo design and operation at the Naval Torpedo Station in Newport, Rhode Island. Afterwards he reported to the USS *Eagle*, formerly a private wooden yacht, now converted to a geodetic survey ship. Cruising in remote regions gathering data for navigation charts, King would be isolated from the bustle of the Regular Navy and its new steel warships. It was an inexplicable assignment for so promising an Academy graduate.

The wardroom contained six officers: the commanding officer, the executive officer, King and two classmates, and a warrant officer * as chief engineer. King would be the navigator.

It was a good job. The art of navigation is one of the prize skills of a naval officer. King had no less responsibility than those more senior officers who were navigators on large warships. Their common task was to fix the ship's position and to avoid grounding. Their common tools were sextant, chronometer, magnetic compass, a lead to measure water depth, a pitlog to measure the ship's speed, and navigation charts of varying accuracy. Given his Naval Academy training, King was prepared as well as could be expected.

Several days after King reported aboard in Portsmouth, New Hampshire, *Eagle* went to sea and shaped course for southern waters. The next morning King wakened to stand his first watch as officer of the deck (OOD). A long, rolling sea rocked *Eagle* from side to side. King became violently seasick in the predawn darkness but remained on the bridge. With sunrise came fog and overcast, obscuring the stars and landmarks that King needed for navigating.

Eagle moved slowly ahead into the gloom. The boatswain's mate broke out the lead and took station in the chains.† Thrice he whirled the lead in a wide arc to gain momentum. The lead flew forward, hit the water, sank, and touched bottom. The boatswain hauled the line taut, read the marking, and sang out the water depth to King in the chart house. King searched his chart for a similar depth near his estimated position. The soundings were endlessly repeated. After a day of groping through thick weather King could only estimate the ship's position. But if his calculations were correct, he announced to the captain, *Eagle* should cross a shoal at a certain time. "Such came to pass," King subsequently re-

* A rank prescribed for a commissioned technical specialist who was formerly a senior enlisted man.

† A small platform on the forecastle that projects over the water.

called. "Later, we were able to check again with soundings and then we knew where we were. After that the captain told me I was becoming quite able as a navigator."

Encouraged by his captain's praise, King devised a new method of piloting along the Florida Keys. "Perhaps I was born with many ideas," King later wrote. "Since I was quite a young officer I liked to find out what seemed to be the better way." Captains, however, are conservative navigators. Although King theoretically proved he could do it, the captain ordered King to stick to conventional methods.

King came to regard himself as a master navigator and enforced exacting standards for his subordinates. Thirty years later he commanded the aircraft carrier *Lexington* and became notorious for firing his navigators. Forty years later, commanding the Atlantic Fleet, he pressed his captains to use potentially treacherous routes instead of main thoroughfares. If the water was deep enough, insisted King, then a captain should be able to get through "if proper attention were paid to currents, times and tides." King was testing their mettle, but his critics said that King unnecessarily hazarded his ships. If the ship went aground, the captain and not King would be accountable.

Eagle arrived at Cienfuegos Bay, Cuba, and swung at anchor while King and his shipmates worked ashore. Surveying was tedious, and inferior equipment made the job even harder. King tried to improve conditions by using his mechanical skills to modify a theodolite, but he could not eliminate the boredom. In time, sun glare and poor medical treatment so damaged King's eyes that he transferred to the Brooklyn Naval Hospital. When his eyes healed, King sought a new assignment.

King visited Mattie in Baltimore after he was released from the hospital, and their courtship resumed. It followed the pattern of many romances of young naval officers: long months and sometimes years at sea, followed by brief, intense reunions ashore, then again to sea. Reluctantly he left Mattie to report aboard USS *Illinois*, a new battleship berthed in Brooklyn.

Illinois was King's first modern warship. Hundreds of sailors kept her beautiful. In the mornings the deck force holystoned the teak deck, scrubbed the paintwork, and shined the brass fittings to a deep luster. Everything topside — lines, canvas, rigging, and crew — was taut and seaman-like. At full speed her ornate bow plowed a huge wake, and her stacks belched impressive clouds of heavy smoke visible for miles. Ponderous and beamy, with white hull and buff superstructure, *Illinois* epitomized the emerging new power of the United States Navy.

Passed Midshipman King, sitting second from left, with junior officers' mess aboard USS *Illinois* (Courtesy Ernest J. King, Jr.)

A principal function of a navy at peace is showing the flag, the practice of naval diplomacy. Naval reviews — the gathering and grand displays of warships from many nations seeking recognition and international prestige — were particularly popular in the years before the First World War. *Illinois* visited dozens of northern European and Mediterranean ports for ceremonies and parties that never seemed to cease. King became surfeited with the indulgences of prewar Europe.

Under the circumstances, combat readiness suffered. Pomp and appearance came first. Naval guns, although visually imposing, were inaccurate beyond a half mile. Gunfire control instruments were hardly more than crude gunsights unable to compensate for moving ships in a tossing sea. A mood began pervading the fleet that improvements were needed; aboard *Illinois* the more enlightened officers experimented with ways and means to enhance gunnery. King listened, and he watched. "That was the first time," he later said, "that I knew very much about the changes that were being brought about in the U.S. Navy."

King continued to experiment. On *Illinois* he served as aide to the admiral and handled visual communications. To simplify signaling he fashioned a mechanical device to transmit semaphore messages between ships. "There was nothing startling about the arrangement," he later explained, "but it was very handy and useful, so the admiral and captain commended me."

Machinery, especially when complex or finely engineered, continued to fascinate King. It was typical of him that when he bought his first automobile he immediately disassembled the engine to discover how it worked. King could, had he chosen, have been a splendid scientist or engineer. But King did not want to become a technical specialist. He wanted to be a line officer. He had much to learn. King's experience at the Naval Academy had taught him little about conduct in the fleet, and the informality aboard *Eagle* hardly typified a naval officer's normal behavior. *Illinois* was another matter. A new battleship rated the best officers. At last King could see how the real Navy operated.

The wardroom officers, perhaps forty all told, varied from the aloof, remote captain to the rambunctious midshipmen. Nearly all were Naval Academy graduates, but they were different people with different personalities and philosophies. King studied them carefully. Some he admired, others he disliked. The executive officer particularly offended King because of his undignified exuberance. After a successful seamanship maneuver, for example, the exec slapped the captain on the back. ("Believe it or not!" King later exclaimed in his memoirs. "I knew that the captain's gray beard bristled. I will always believe that he shot sparks, because the captain was not one to be slapped on the back!")

Eventually King established his own personal standards. He lacked toughness, he decided. He had been too "soft." He never would progress in the Navy unless he got a grip on himself, or so he reasoned. His concept of softness probably included the admirable traits of sympathy, understanding, and tolerance — all part of King's character. He decided he would have to suppress such compassionate emotions. Despite his best efforts, his humanity sometimes slipped through his stern facade as the years passed.

Ambition now drove King, and he knew he would need assignments that were regarded within the naval service as "career enhancing." On *Illinois* he was an errand boy to Rear Admiral A. S. Crowninshield, so he began to look elsewhere, first toward the torpedo boats that accompanied *Illinois.* The flotilla commander told King he would take him, but he advised King to speak to the *Illinois* commanding officer, Captain

George A. Converse. Stay aboard to gain experience, counseled Converse. King would be commissioned ensign in about six months; then Converse would help find King a good job. King agreed to stay in *Illinois.*

Crowninshield's staff had come to know and like King. Shortly after King's talk with his captain, the flag lieutenant told King that a division and watch officer billet was available on the cruiser *Cincinnati.* It was a top assignment for aspiring junior officers. The incumbent would supervise a deck division of forty sailors, stand OOD watches underway, and quarterdeck watches in port. Crowninshield could reassign officers within his squadron, and his staff wanted to nominate King. Would King accept the job?

Of course he would. He was not even an ensign, and officers normally assigned had several years of commissioned experience. Furthermore, *Cincinnati* was going overseas, while *Illinois* would stay in the United States. But what was King to do about his promise to Converse to remain in *Illinois*? He compromised by being noncommittal, neither accepting nor refusing the offer.

Several days later King received orders from Crowninshield to report to *Cincinnati* and a summons from Converse to report to his cabin. "I was doing some very fast thinking," King later said, "but since I did not ask for my orders to the *Cincinnati* I decided to say nothing." After a perfunctory exchange and a strained silence, Converse dismissed King.

Cincinnati got underway. King would not return to the United States for two-and-a-half years.

By today's standards *Cincinnati* would not be a cruiser. At 3,500 tons displacement and 300 feet long, she was smaller than a modern destroyer or frigate. She was obsolete even though she was only eight years old, owing to the rapid expansion of technology. But she was still good for showing the flag, becoming destined for years of solitary passages from one foreign port to another. *Cincinnati*'s crew of 300 sailors typified the 30,000 enlisted men in the Navy. About a fourth were foreigners, especially the older petty officers. Many were boys. (The minimum enlistment age was fourteen.) Together there never were enough of them. It was not that recruiting was difficult. Retention afterward was the problem.

Many naval officers perpetuated a caste system by their failure to understand the psychology of the enlisted man. The officers were accustomed to discipline and regimentation, the young sailors to independence and freedom of choice; the officers to comfort, privilege, and authority (albeit responsibility), the sailors to subservience and demeaning hardship. The officers all too often regarded sailors with contempt, suspicion, and mistrust, or on the other hand, with condescension and patronization. The sailors, in return, resented and envied the linen and silver of the wardroom, the enlisted servants, and the cabins and beds and sheets that seemed so sumptuous in contrast to their hammocks and sea bags. Passed midshipmen in particular were sarcastically referred to as the "young gentlemen."

Consequently the sailors deserted at a rate of 14 percent a year, for reasons including poor food, crowded living conditions, or restrictions on liberty. It was a vicious circle. Officers were reluctant to allow men ashore because too many would either desert or get drunk and into trouble. Yet one of the chief reasons that sailors did misbehave was to relieve the tension of prolonged confinement and an inflexible routine. Another reason for misbehavior ashore was their reaction to the public's view of enlisted men as picturesque but unwelcome troublemakers. Others — whores, thieves, bar owners, and dishonest merchants — ruthlessly exploited the sailor ashore. No wonder they rebelled.

King's division of forty *Cincinnati* sailors was his first real responsibility and would test his new resolve to be "stern yet just." Searching for a model, King admired those officers who could talk in the sailors' vernacular without loss of dignity. One in particular, King later recalled, "had a way of telling enlisted men what he really thought, and he would use the same expressions the enlisted men used. For myself, I couldn't talk to them that way, and very few officers would try it."

Theodore Roosevelt's advocacy of more accurate shooting had stimulated formal gunnery competition between ships. As winning meant professional recognition and advancement, King decided that his guns would be supreme. (It was the first of many fleet competitions that King would play to win.) First he tinkered unsuccessfully with the *Cincinnati*'s range finder, which had been designed by one of the Navy's most celebrated inventors, Rear Admiral Bradley A. Fiske. It might have worked in a calm, King finally decided, "but the sea has a mind of its own." King next tried to improve his guns' accuracy by altering their sights, telescopes, and gears, even drawing complex blueprints for Japanese shipyard workers.

King's men responded to King's enthusiasm as the firing day approached. "We went out on the range to win," recalled a *Cincinnati* sailor seventy years later. "After all, it really meant so much for us men in the gun crews, as we were out to make records." When the shooting ended, King's sailors had received the highest scores on the ship. Everyone was jubilant. A delighted King praised his sailors for their superb performance. "He was a wonderful man," reminisced one of his sailors, who once had been a teenager in King's division, away from home for the first time. "He always appreciated something you did for him, or that he benefited by. And if you were in his division, 'you were in.' He always stuck to the men of the First Division."

The division later asked King to arrange for a group photograph. King hired a Shanghai cameraman to come aboard on a Sunday afternoon, following the weekly inspection when the men were well turned out. After posing his men King walked away, but his sailors insisted that he join them for the picture. It was a compliment that King savored. Although he would never admit it, King cared how people felt about him. When he later was about to leave *Cincinnati,* King mused to a chief petty officer that he would not be missed. The chief quickly assured King that his men would always remember him because he had been "strict but fair." That was what King wanted to hear.

King and his men cherished their triumph over the intervening years. Thirty-eight years later many of his sailors, by then retired, wrote letters of congratulation when King became Commander in Chief, Atlantic Fleet. Their letters contained a common theme, the happiness and pride of having served with King on *Cincinnati.*

King was then, in 1941, fighting an undeclared war at sea against Germany. Still he took time to answer their every letter. They brought back memories. He asked one of his well-wishers for a copy of the picture of King posing with his division in Shanghai. "I still recall with pleasure and satisfaction," King wrote with nostalgia, "the good work that we did in the First Division — and the part that the forecastle 5-inch played in winning the ship's prize." And to another he closed:

> "Your old shipmate,
> /s/ E. J. King
> Admiral, U.S. Navy (ex-Ensign)"

King's cruise on *Cincinnati* was not without personal problems, however. Alcohol nearly ruined his career. His problem was not unique. Liquor was legal aboard ship, and heavy drinking ashore was common among naval officers on distant station.

At first King enjoyed daytime sightseeing in the Mediterranean ports, but he tired of it after *Cincinnati* passed through the Suez Canal into the Indian Ocean and finally took station in the Far East. When *Cincinnati* stopped in Singapore to replenish coal, King went ashore with a classmate known for his hell-raising revelry. After a night of carousing, the two sodden officers returned to the waterfront at dawn. Already late for quarters, they wrangled over paying the boatman's fare and finally

USS *Cincinnati,* which took King around the world (Courtesy Walter Muir Whitehill)

Ensign King and his division (Courtesy Walter Muir Whitehill)

returned to *Cincinnati* by separate boats. By coincidence they arrived simultaneously at the ship's ladder and resumed their drunken arguing as they clambered aboard in view of their colleagues assembled on the quarterdeck.

Although the commanding officer, Commander Newton E. Mason, gave King an appropriate warning, more trouble came in Shanghai. King again was late returning. This time Mason restricted King to quarters* for five days. When Mason recorded the punishment in King's next fitness report, King shamelessly argued whether the statement should read "few" or "several" hours late. Two months later King was late again. His new captain, Commander Hugo Osterhaus, was unforgiving. "Ensign King is a young and promising officer," reported Osterhaus in King's next fitness report, "and it would be unjust to him to overlook an offense of this nature." King went under hatches for six days.

It was the last time King was late for anything, even though he continued to love parties, gambling, drinking, dancing, and the pursuit of women. On the mornings after, King always would be the first to work, aloof and sober, disdaining anyone with a hangover.

In addition to his drinking, King's tempestuous behavior repeatedly provoked his senior officers. What King regarded as forthrightness they regarded as stubbornness, belligerence, and arrogant insubordination. King's outbursts usually began when he felt that he was right and another wrong. When King was OOD, for example, he resented the navigator's practice of ordering the helmsman to change course behind King's back. King's complaints finally reached Commander Mason.

"What is the trouble between you and the navigator?" asked the captain. King explained that it was intolerable for the navigator (a lieutenant commander) to change course without his knowledge.

"King, the navigator is a much older and more experienced officer than you," said Mason, reminding King that he was still a passed midshipman. "I think you were out of order." King acknowledged his youth but reminded the captain that as OOD he was responsible for the entire ship while he was on watch. Mason said no more and went below.

"I think I was *too* smart," King said in retrospect, because when he later applied for ordnance postgraduate schooling, the Chief of the Bureau of Ordnance disapproved King's application. The bureau chief was Rear Admiral Newton E. Mason.

Early one afternoon King was napping in his bunk, a time of day when the executive officer thought he should have been on deck drill-

* A punishment called "under hatches" in King's day and "in hack" today.

ing his division. The exec (a lieutenant commander) stormed into King's room. Both men started to yell. "Knock on my door before you open it," said King. "And get the hell out of my room. I've already finished training my people."

The exec left, leaving King to wait apprehensively for a summons from Osterhaus. It came several hours later. Osterhaus wanted an explanation. Had King been provoked? He had not, King replied. He had been wrong and he apologized. King said no more despite Osterhaus's searching questions.

"Mr. King," the captain finally said, "I'll have to put you under hatches for ten days." King went to his room. Next morning Osterhaus suspended punishment. "However," King later said, "it naturally was included in my next fitness report."

King went in hack one more time, eighteen months later, following a misunderstanding with an irascible flag officer whom King provoked one time too many. That too entered his fitness report. By then King's service record had collected far too many adverse statements for someone striving for admiral. King resolved never again to be put under hatches.

The Russo-Japanese War of 1904 created excitement and diversion for the neutral warships stationed in the Far East. King saw war at sea for the second time. Battered Russian ships sought refuge in Chinese ports, pursued by Japanese warships boldly violating Chinese territorial waters. *Cincinnati* sometimes was more than a spectator. After Port Arthur fell, she steamed through a blizzard to deliver food and medical aid to several shiploads of Russian refugees. Far East duty thus alternated between adventure and tedium. Radio equipment arrived; King was of course fascinated by its intricacies and potential. The ships of the Asiatic Squadron now could communicate with one another beyond visual range up to 125 miles.

By the spring of 1905 *Cincinnati* had her third commanding officer, a reminder that King had not seen the United States for three years. He wanted to go home and asked for orders. Several months later he boarded a transport, left the Far East, and never again returned.

3

Maturing

WHEN KING RETURNED to the United States he was ready for marriage. Mattie was living at West Point with her sister Florrie, who had wed an Army officer. Ernest J. King and Martha Rankin Egerton were married in the Cadet Chapel on 10 October 1905. After a brief honeymoon in New York City, they traveled to Hampton Roads, Virginia, where King reported to the battleship USS *Alabama*. Mattie returned to her family home in Baltimore.

After several months of sea duty King longed for his wife. Wangling an overnight pass, he took a wearisome, circuitous train trip from Norfolk through North Carolina to Baltimore and returned the next night. It was worth it. "I saw my bride!" he later said.

When winter descends upon Atlantic coast naval bases, the fleet steams south to the Caribbean as predictably as the migration of birds. With King aboard, *Alabama* joined the fleet in its journey to warm waters for the annual training exercises. Lieutenant Frank H. Clark, Jr., the same benefactor who had gotten King aboard *Cincinnati*, was now gunnery officer on *Alabama*. Clark arranged for King to take charge of the huge forward thirteen-inch gun turret as well as several smaller guns. Although King was too junior for the job, Clark recognized that King could make the gunnery department look good. It was a smart decision. Just before a major target practice King's big guns went haywire. King worked on repairs for thirty-six hours without sleep, aided with a stimulant from the doctor. The guns fired on schedule.

King also plunged into shipboard organization and leadership, for years popular subjects of debate. Steam-driven steel warships still were organized like three-masted sailing ships, whose deck crews had been divided into four divisions, each responsible for its one-quarter of the ship, the three boundary lines running athwartships through each mast. As the warships became more complicated, new skills were needed to operate and maintain the equipment. Sailors became trained in sophisticated specialties, but the old four-division organization remained unchanged. Another anomaly was the Powder Division, formerly a conglomeration of landsmen, idlers, boys, midshipmen, and Marines who fetched gunpowder from the magazines during battle. By King's day the system was absurd. The Navy, it seemed, had no standard shipboard organizational doctrine. So it was every ship for itself, each organized and administered at the whim of its respective executive officers, who largely retained the outmoded practices.

The United States Naval Institute offered a way to change the system. In 1873 a group of naval officers had founded the Institute as a means to advance professional and scientific knowledge in the Navy. In time the Institute published a monthly journal, the *Proceedings*, which provided a free and open forum for advanced naval thinking and writing. One of its greatest values was that it allowed junior officers to express thoughts that otherwise would have been stifled.

Organizational reform had a special appeal to King. He studied the *Proceedings*, read from other sources, and reflected upon his own experience as a watch and division officer. In time King asked the *Alabama* exec to allow him to reorganize his division in order to test his theories. The exec at first agreed but then regarded King's experiment as too radical, so he ordered King to resume doing things as before.

King lost the argument but not his interest. Several years later he wrote his first article for the *Proceedings*, and it won the annual essay contest. Entitled "Some Ideas About Organization Aboard Ship," it was the first of many papers he would write during his career. Although his prose was ponderous, his ideas were emphatically, sometimes scathingly, stated — early examples of his blunt and simple method of verbal expresson. "There has never been any logical system, founded on principles, on which to base anything," he wrote in his essay. "The result is that the navy personnel has no semblance of organization, other than what exists temporarily; in the matter of personnel the service leads a 'hand-to-mouth' existence."

Such declarations were bound to offend, and King knew it. "The writer fully realizes the possible opposition," he continued, "for if there is anything more characteristic of the navy than its fighting ability, it is its inertia to change, or conservatism, or the clinging to things that are old because they are old. It must be admitted that this characteristic has

The newlyweds (Courtesy Ernest J. King, Jr.)

Mrs. Ernest J. King (Courtesy Ernest J. King, Jr.)

been in many things a safeguard; it is also true that in quite as many it has been a drag to progress."

This was King's declaration of what became his perpetual struggle to improve the Navy through the stimulus of change and new ideas. Sometimes he won. More often he lost. Yet nothing seemed to deter him, even though many of his schemes were either so radical or so eccentric that they aroused universal opposition. (His program during the Second World War to introduce gray naval uniforms is a striking example.) One of his more commendable long-term crusades was against the bureaucracy of the Navy Department, which was notorious for its special-interest groups and its unresponsiveness to the needs of the fleet. King would try again and again — unsuccessfully — to reorganize the Department during the Second World War. Despite the unprecedented power and prestige of his position as Commander in Chief, U.S. Fleet, and Chief of Naval Operations, he would be frustrated first by President Roosevelt and then by the civilian Navy Secretaries and the Congress. King did win some bureaucratic battles, but despite his best efforts he was unable to win the bureaucratic war.

King's *Proceedings* essay of 1909 criticized another common practice of naval leadership. Junior officers in King's early years had little authority over their men. Instead it was the executive officer who dealt directly with the sailors while bypassing the division officers. (The engineer officer was the exception. His men toiled below decks beyond the sight of the executive officer.) This was wrong, King argued. Junior officers should train for eventual command by learning to exercise authority and responsibility. King advocated the principle of telling a subordinate *what* had to be done but not telling him *how* to do it: the subordinate should use his initiative without interference from the superior. Naval officers would then learn to think for themselves and to act independently, King maintained, while still being accountable to their superiors for the final results. The superior, meanwhile, would not become involved in details and could concentrate on the larger aspects of his responsibilities.

King's article contained nothing original in its statement about delegating authority. How well King later practiced it is another matter. It is, within the Navy, a principle that too often receives lip service. King would be no exception.

Congress finally had authorized more officers for the ships of Roosevelt's new Navy. It was good news for King. After only three years as an ensign he suddenly became eligible for promotion to lieutenant. King went to Washington to go before a selection board that would determine his fitness for promotion. The ten-day examination would be in three parts: a physical examination, an examination of professional knowledge, and finally a review of his performance. King was confident that he easily could pass the first two, but he dreaded the board's reaction to the "spots" in his service record.

Brooding over lunch one day, King met his former *Cincinnati* commanding officer, Commander Hugo Osterhaus, who asked about the exams. Touched by the older officer's sympathetic interest, King confessed his misgivings. Osterhaus tried to reassure King by reminding him that he could rebut the bad reports (Osterhaus had written two of them), and saying that if necessary he would testify in King's behalf. A grateful but still apprehensive King returned to continue his exams.

The final ordeal began. A member of the board, a captain, summoned King. In a dispassionate voice he criticized King's past behavior but was otherwise noncommittal. Finally King came before the full board sitting in formal session to pass judgment on his worthiness to continue his naval career.

"Mr. King," said the senior member, a rear admiral, "you have passed your physical exam and did very well on your professional exam. The board would like you now to read your service record."

"I already am familiar with it," King replied.

"Read it, Mr. King," commanded the admiral.

King read for several minutes and returned his record to the board.

The admiral resumed speaking. "Mr. King, we must make sure that you understand the action of the board." He opened King's record and began to read aloud. Every aspect of King's three years as an ensign received comment. The admiral gave his most critical attention to King's frequent drinking, failures to report for duty, insubordination, and subsequent punishments under the hatches. The other board members silently stared at King.

King prayed for the inquisition to end.

The admiral finished reading and looked up. "Mr. King, the board is happy to congratulate you on your promotion."

Naval service in King's lifetime alternated between sea duty and shore duty. Performance at sea was the more important for promotion, while shore duty provided the opportunity to recuperate from the rigors of duty afloat. If a naval officer had a family, it was also a time to compensate for the prolonged separations of distant cruises.

King returned to the Naval Academy in the fall of 1906. It was a happy time for Mattie. She was near her family and friends in Baltimore, and Annapolis evoked happy memories as an Academy belle. After six years of waiting she finally was with Ernest King, and they rented an apartment at 22 State Circle, just a short walk from the Academy. Mattie's sole ambition was to have children. Soon she was pregnant with the first of six consecutive daughters.

The Naval Academy had changed dramatically. Great granite buildings had replaced the ramshackle wooden structures that King remembered. The student body had quadrupled to more than a thousand midshipmen to provide more officers to the expanding Navy. King's primary duty was as instructor of ordnance, gunnery, and seamanship. In the afternoons he went outside to teach marching and infantry maneuvers in his collateral duty as battalion drillmaster. When King had the watch he slept in the dormitory, Bancroft Hall. Late one night he dreamed he had heard shots, then awakened to discover a flustered Marine orderly. The midshipmen, he reported, were throwing light bulbs at him. King wakened fully half the regiment and stood them at attention, then mustered the midshipmen officers. Investigate for possible drinking, King ordered, and find the cause of the disturbance. Nothing was found. The midshipmen remained in ranks. Finally King allowed them to return to bed, the plebes first and the first classmen much later. It was the last time that King's sleep was ever disturbed.

The Regiment of Midshipmen would provide the flag and senior officers who would fight the Second World War. King drove them ferociously, with forced marches, amphibious landings from whaleboats, rifle and artillery exercises, and interminable parades in the soaking heat of Annapolis. They hated it. After two years King transferred to the Executive Department as an officer-in-charge and enforcer of discipline in Bancroft Hall. There his reputation was even more firmly established.

King's resolve to avoid marks on his fitness reports began to falter despite his experience before the lieutenant selection board. His head of department was Commander A. W. Grant, an able and respected officer who had served at the Naval Academy when King had been a cadet. He had tolerated King's temper then, but his patience with King as a lieutenant had limits. The blowup began when King received a memorandum from Grant, accusing him of ignoring an order. King became furious. His immediate impulse was to rush from the classroom, but he decided to wait until the end of the period. After class he confronted Grant, seated at his desk within sight and sound of the other instructors.

"I'm tired of you ignoring my orders," said Grant. King protested that he had not seen Grant's order. "You might be right this time," said Grant, "but usually you are wrong." Still King would not shut up. The other instructors, uncomfortable yet fascinated, watched from the sidelines. Suddenly aware of his audience, Grant admonished them that they were witnesses to King's insubordination. King countered that they were witnessing his innocence. At least one instructor supported King. Trying to end the spectacle, Grant became conciliatory and ended the argument.

Several days later the superintendent's aide telephoned King. He was to appear before the superintendent the next morning.

"For what reason?" asked King.

"Commander Grant has reported you for being impudent and for ignoring his orders," replied the aide. King entered the admiral's office the next morning. He could have predicted what would follow from past experience. First, the question as to "what was the trouble" between King and his boss. Then King's explanation. Next the lecture about learning to get along with one's superiors. Then the admiral got specific.

"Mr. King," he said, "I want you to apologize to Commander Grant."

King protested that Grant had been wrong. Why should King be the one to apologize? The admiral persisted. King still refused. "Mr. King," said the admiral, "if you do not apologize to Commander Grant I shall have you detached from the Naval Academy. I hope you will do what I have asked."

King left, thought things over, and finally went to see Grant. "I have come," said King in an official voice, "because the admiral has told me that I was impertinent. If you think I was wrong, then I am sorry."

"Oh, that's all right," replied Grant. "Let's forget about it."

King rejected Grant's peace offering because Grant — he felt — had betrayed their friendship. King was so unforgiving that he later snubbed the senior officer at social gatherings. Grant persisted. "Damn it, King," he finally said, "I want you to take a drink with me. Let's forget about our little trouble." King relented. The two men drank together. "We were very good friends until he died," King later said.

Such was King's nature. When King had been on China station, an admiral's aide had attempted to prevent King's return to the United States. "I wouldn't speak to him for many years," King later said, "although I must say that he didn't remember. But I remembered."

Political events, meanwhile, were beginning to affect King's career. Racial antipathy toward Orientals and distrust of Japanese intentions

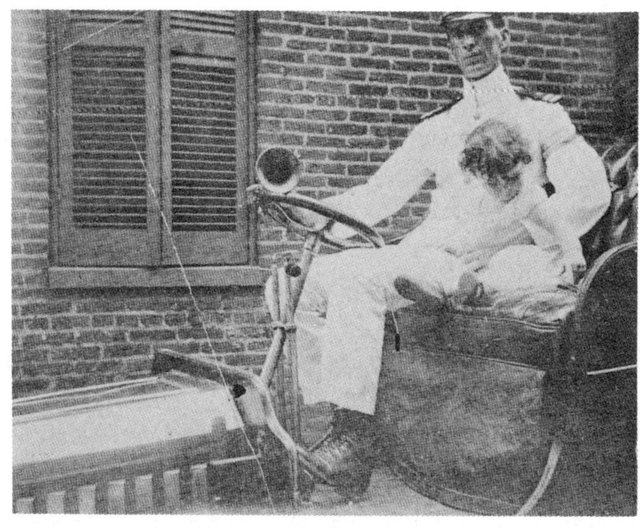

King with his first daughter, Elizabeth, and his first car, Annapolis, 1909 (Courtesy Ernest J. King, Jr.)

had created a war fever in America, focusing public attention on whether the United States Navy was strong enough to fight Japan. In Britain a superior new battleship, HMS *Dreadnaught*, had been commissioned, so advanced in design that all others — including Roosevelt's expensive new battleships — became obsolescent. Roosevelt exploited these events by appealing for four new battleships. Strong congressional forces opposed the President's request, precipitating a protracted contest for public support. The brawl on Capitol Hill evoked questions of national policy, naval strategy, and the role of the United States in foreign affairs, all influencing the size and mission of the United States Navy.

Aroused and excited by the strident national debate, the naval officer corps became intellectually active, and King's own interests began to extend beyond the technical aspects of shipboard operations. He was, after all, a professional warrior. There was more to warfare than the view from the bridge. One day he intended to command a *fleet*, and that ambition required a knowledge of sea power. King began to read military and naval works and became absorbed in the literature of warfare. Some books were about the theories and principles of war, including those of Alfred Thayer Mahan and Sir Edward Hamley. Others were histories of past wars and battles. Still others were biographies.

The spirit of enlightenment enlivened other officers at the Naval Academy. A cerebral classmate, William S. Pye, organized a Naval War College correspondence course. It was hard work: heavy reading, written solutions to complicated problems of strategy and tactics, and long hours of study. "The officers were glad to see it started," King later wrote, "but as usual it petered out in four or five weeks until there was only the usual 'corporal's guard' that was on the job at the end of the program."

It was an Army officer, however, who most stimulated King's pursuit of professional knowledge. Brother-in-law Walter D. Smith, himself a student of military doctrine and history, expanded King's interests beyond Mahan into Napoleon and the Civil War. When their families visited, the two men fled the noise to talk about the art of war. Later they walked the battlefields of Antietam and Gettysburg. Given his exposure to the history of land warfare, in time King fancied himself as the one naval officer most knowledgeable in the work of generals and their armies.

Great leaders intrigued King. He admired Napoleon and studied each of his marshals. Louis Nicolas Davout and Jean Lannes were his favorites. But it seemed to King that the Napoleonic system suffered because Napoleon had personally issued detailed plans for every battle. The marshals, however brave, were not allowed to use their initiative. When by necessity marshals exercised independent command, reflected King, "they got messed up."

Through his intensive reading King developed a respect for authors. Mahan, for example, was exalted everywhere. Writing for publication, King believed, was an important professional achievement. When he won the 1909 prize essay on shipboard organization, King was proud and pleased. "Not only was it a great credit to me with a gold medal from the Naval Institute," King said afterward, "but I also got a life membership and five hundred dollars. I might add that before I got this prize essay, I had been just another officer. But after the prize essay I became noted in the whole naval service, and this probably helped me in my career."

In addition to reading and writing, King continued his interests in mechanical engineering. It will be recalled that when King served in *Cincinnati* the optical range finders were erratic and inaccurate. Another problem was that the range between the firing ship and its target constantly changed, because both were moving through the water at varying courses and speeds. Bill Pye had a theory that if one were to plot a large number of continuous range-finder measurements, then it would be possible to calculate an average range that would open or close at a predictable rate. The gun would then be given a smooth range order rather than a series of jerky orders that changed fitfully with each new range measurement.

Another problem was that the current method of range finding indicated where the target had been rather than predicting where it would be. Therefore naval guns tended to fire behind the target. If Pye's theory was valid, and if the target did not radically change course, the ship's guns would be able to lead the target, much as a hunter leads a bird in flight. Better yet, Pye's theory would compensate for any changes in range when the firing ship changed course.

Pye discussed his ideas with King. Together they decided to design a "range machine." King drew the detailed plans on linen paper, using red and black ink. They were beautifully done, with the skill of a professional draftsman. Then King and Pye began to build their complex assembly of finely machined gears, cams, levers, and dials.

In time the Bureau of Ordnance adopted their design for Navy-wide use. But when King and Pye applied for a patent, the bureau objected. Perhaps the bureau reasoned that the inventors had worked on Navy time using Navy facilities. Therefore the government — not King and Pye — owned the patent rights. Or perhaps the bureau considered the range machine to be a secret weapon. For whatever reasons, Pye and King withdrew their application.

King and Pye were incensed. Not only did they want credit for their invention, they wanted to get paid for it. The bureau, they argued, should petition Congress to authorize a payment of from $50,000 to $100,000 as a reward. After all, they reasoned, their range machine probably would save millions of dollars, especially if it saved an expensive warship from being sunk during a war. The bureau rejected their pleas but continued to use their invention. King finally consoled himself by rationalizing that it was enough that he and Pye had helped improve naval gunnery.

In later years his attitude changed. He came to regard exceptional performances as simply doing one's job. His praise would always be rare and grudgingly given.

King's energy and diverse interests while at the Naval Academy are striking. If he had wanted to rest while on shore duty, it would have been understandable. After all, he had been at sea for five years and was newly married. The Naval Academy would have been satisfied had King concentrated solely on teaching midshipmen. But ambition drove King. He took not one day of leave in almost three years.

He had by then begun losing his hair, to his great chagrin, for he was vain about his appearance. In his early years he deliberately wore undersize uniform caps, which he eventually concluded had restricted circulation to his scalp. "I decided to wear caps that were at least one or two sizes larger," he later said, "but it was too late." In later years he always tried to wear a cap during photographs, although with children he could joke about his baldness.

It also was a time of discovery for King and Mattie. The glamour of their courtship disappeared. The dances and parties were over. Mattie's transformation from belle to matron had begun. Her interests narrowed to her Victorian pursuit of home and children. King's naval career did not interest her; regardless of what her husband did, she was going to have a family. They bought a home on Franklin Street, and Mattie became a permanent resident of Annapolis. When her husband returned to sea, he could visit her during leave.

Their decision was not uncommon. The Navy did not pay for moving costs as it does today. Husbands were away for such long periods that it was customary for wives to stay in one place. So Annapolis was perfect for Mattie. She was among friends who understood about absent husbands at sea, and she was near her family in Baltimore.

King and Mattie had adjusted to circumstances. There had been, however, an unsettling revelation. King discovered that Mattie, for all her beauty and vivaciousness, had not been graced with an equivalent intellect. Educated women, she said, were vulgar. Marriage, children, and domestic affairs were a woman's only valid concerns, Mattie would say, and her conversation rarely ventured elsewhere.

Mattie's intellect had been neither apparent nor important to King during their courtship. But after marriage a person's intelligence began to mean something to him. But Mattie was indifferent to King's achievements — they simply were beyond her range of interests. King came to realize that their attraction had been entirely physical. They were otherwise without anything in common. He would have to adjust his personal life accordingly.

4

Versatility

It was 1909 and time for King to return to sea. His mentor and former *Cincinnati* commanding officer, Hugo Osterhaus, recently had been selected for rear admiral. He asked King to join his staff as flag secretary. Although King had asked for destroyer duty, he immediately accepted.

There were mixed feelings about staff duty. It usually was accepted reluctantly, for it meant absence from the more rewarding shipboard duty and subjugation to the flag officer. It was pro forma for any conscientious staff officer to seem eager to return to shipboard duty at the earliest opportunity.

Not that staff duty was without benefits. An influential flag officer often advanced the career of a favorite staffer. An extreme example was the great champion of gunnery reform, William S. Sims. Having served as naval aide to President Theodore Roosevelt, he was given command of a first-class battleship as a commander, normally a captain's assignment. Such "careerism" bred resentment and jealousy. Thus staff duty generally was taken in small doses, like a bad-tasting medicine that might or might not be good for one's health.

The Navy was so small and reputations were so well known that many admirals chose their own staffs. It was customary, however, to ask an officer if he would be willing to serve. (When King became a flag officer he too would ask rather than order people to his staff.) King's decision to go with Osterhaus was not made precipitately. King chose his admirals carefully, seeking only those whose influence would benefit King. Before Osterhaus he had declined two other offers because he felt they "would not lead anywhere."

King's initial staff experience was brief — less than a year — because Osterhaus went to shore duty. King transferred to the engineering department of a new battleship, USS *New Hampshire.* Within several months King "fleeted up" * to engineer officer.

New Hampshire was a magnificent warship of 16,000 tons, with white hull, gilt trim, polished brass, and imposing guns. But King was not a part of the topside pomp. His domain was below decks in the nether regions of boilers and engines, pumps and dynamos. It was a world by itself, hot, dirty, noisy, and avoided by most naval officers, so King was alone. Only three warrant officers helped him to supervise 250 enlisted engineers. So long as the engines could answer bells, and the dynamos could provide electrical power, and the evaporators could distill fresh water for the captain's bath, then the engineer officer was his own boss.

Roosevelt's legacy of fleet exercises had endured after he had left office. Competition was intense, and to the winners went prestige and promotions. King decided to try for the engineering trophy. It would require gamesmanship. The engineering competition was so new that the rules were ambiguous. Coal, for example, varied in quality, which affected fuel economy; engineer officers fought over which ships would get the best supplies. There were other potentially unfair advantages. *New Hampshire* normally followed in the wake of the three other battleships of her division. King argued that their water turbulence increased *New Hampshire*'s fuel consumption. The division commander's flagship always headed the column, so it benefited from smooth waters. King kept griping until the division commander finally slapped him down for fussing about "trivial matters." But it wasn't trivial to King. He persisted. Finally the Commander in Chief, Atlantic Fleet, gave everyone an equal opportunity to steam through undisturbed water.

King battled anyone who hindered his engineers. It took coal to distill fresh water, so wasting fresh water increased fuel consumption. King borrowed several ensigns and incited them to exhort the crew to conserve water. (It became a popular joke that a man needed a bucket of coal to get a bucket of water.) The officers too were scrutinized; they were wasting water in the showers, reported King's ensigns. King appealed to the executive officer for everyone's cooperation. The ensigns soon reported that the wardroom had received the message.

Except the chaplain, who wallowed like a hippopotamus. He was one person whom the executive officer would not confront. King searched for a remedy. He liked the chaplain and was as reluctant as the exec to discuss the chaplain's bathing habits. King finally hit upon a solution one day at lunch.

* A naval term meaning advancement to a more responsible job.

"Chaplain," said King, "have you heard about the new invention in shower valves?" No, replied the chaplain, he had not.

"Well," said King, "when you remove the soap from the soap dish to lather yourself, the valve automatically turns off."

The chaplain listened intently.

"Then," King continued, "when you are ready to rinse yourself off, you put the soap back in the soap dish and the shower turns back on."

King's ensigns watched the shower room for the remainder of the day and reported in the morning. "Chief," * said his informer, "it didn't work."

There was only one thing left to do. "I told the chaplain about the whole matter," King later explained, "and after that he took care not to use too much water."

As the competition intensified, King sought support from his captain and exec to encourage his men. It was hopeless. His commanding officer, Captain Thomas S. Rodgers, hated engineering. King got him into the engineroom only once, during a full-power trial. The huge triple-expansion reciprocating steam engine thrashed and clattered with thunderous noise and vibration, splattering water, steam, and lubricating oil in all directions.

"It's too dirty down here," said Rodgers. Then he left.

Despite the captain's indifference, King was pleased that his engineering plant had passed the full-power test. King was ready to run for the record and cinch the trophy. Then news came that two battleships had lost their propellers while at high speed. As a precaution the Navy Department forbade further full-power operations. King could not believe it. *New Hampshire* was perfectly safe, he insisted, but no one listened. King never forgave his captain, division commander, and fleet commander for submitting to what King regarded as an unjustified restriction on fleet operations. The trials were canceled, King's trophy went a-glimmering, and that was that.

When Rear Admiral Osterhaus returned to sea several months later as Commander in Chief, Atlantic Fleet, King accepted his offer to again serve as flag secretary. He had been aboard *New Hampshire* for a year. She no longer held any attraction.

King quickly developed a knack as a staff administrator. Prescribing the format and content of documents requiring Osterhaus's signature, King also tried to anticipate the admiral's wants. Everything was so well prepared that Osterhaus felt obliged to sign whatever King put

* The informal title for the engineer officer aboard ship.

before him. At first Osterhaus protested that he was not a rubber stamp, but he soon succumbed to King's efficiency.

The small staff was extraordinarily able. Dudley Knox, later the Director of Naval History, was the fleet gunnery officer, and the fleet engineer was Harry E. Yarnell, later a flag officer of great distinction. Together with King, the two officers established an intellectual rapport. Stimulated by the great military writers and biographers, they constantly shared their own thoughts on the art and science of warfare.

Otherwise staff duty under Osterhaus became routine: fleet exercises, inspections, visits to ports, and an international naval review. A medical officer discovered that King had a hernia; surgery followed, then a month's recuperation. King returned to the staff in time for a lengthy cruise. "The flag lieutenant and I agreed to stop smoking during the cruise," King later wrote, "and each of us put up twenty dollars. But the first time that he came to see me he gave me a tin of a hundred cigarettes and said that the bet was off. I didn't feel like smoking, but in a few days I started again."

After three years at sea King returned to Annapolis in May 1912. He would serve as executive officer of the Naval Engineering Experiment Station, testing materials and equipment for possible marine engineering use. A small but adequate staff of graduate engineers made King's job easy. Given King's interest in new ideas and technology, it was an agreeable assignment. Life in Annapolis provided even more variety when he was appointed Secretary-Treasurer of the Naval Institute, a job that allowed him to edit and publish professional papers in the *Proceedings*.

At the same time King discovered that aviation had entered the Navy. It was not too impressive. Based at a makeshift air station adjacent to King's bailiwick, the fragile, primitive aircraft flew at sixty knots, landed on the water, and frequently crashed. The leader of the airmen was Lieutenant John H. Towers, with whom King would have a long and stormy association. It was Towers who took King for his first airplane ride. There were no cockpits. One simply held on in a chair without seat belts, amidst fabric-covered wings, wooden frames, wire struts, and roaring engine.

Towers was a zealot crusading to establish naval aviation as the strongest arm of the Navy. King listened to Towers talk. The flimsy aircraft lining the banks of the Severn River seemed a ludicrous threat to battleships. But Towers believed in them. It would be a long and bitter struggle.

In the evenings King went to his family, which now included three daughters: Elizabeth, Eleanor, and Martha. During his three years of sea duty King had been home only during brief leave periods. Now that he was ashore the girls gradually became accustomed to having a father. There was no hugging and kissing between father and daughters. Mattie was the disciplinarian; she spanked. King might send a daughter to her room; anything harsher, never.

The girls always wore new clothes, often made by Mattie. Hand-me-downs were forbidden, to impress the neighbors that the Kings could afford to dress well. A family friend, Phoebe Levely, lived in for twenty-five years helping Mattie with the children. And there always were cooks and maids.

Mattie ruled the home. King never argued with her, at least not when the children were present. When he entered Mattie's domain, he conformed to her way of life. Occasionally Mattie needed help — like the day that Elizabeth barricaded herself in the coal bin. Her arm, once broken, had since healed, and the doctor had come to remove the cast. Elizabeth balked. She wanted to keep the cast because she had been receiving so much attention. Now she was heaving coal at anyone who tried to approach her. Quietly and gently, King reasoned with Elizabeth. She went meekly to her room and the cast came off.

Everyone considered Mattie as a wonderful mother, but for all her domestic skills she could not manage money. "It just magically appeared," explained one of her children. King gave Mattie an allowance, which she frequently exceeded. If she asked for more, King would stall. Eventually Mattie resorted to putting written requests on King's dresser. That got results.

King himself was a successful investor. "I'm one-quarter Scotch," he liked to brag, and over the years he created a large estate. Eventually he used a professional trust officer to manage his investments, contingent upon King's approval. King's fiscal decisions were usually prolonged and deliberate, but he would make a snap judgment if necessary. Yet, although King was thrifty, he was generous with his family. He gave Elizabeth a thousand-dollar bond as a marriage gift and gave similar gifts to his other daughters when they married. Every new grandchild received a hundred-dollar bond, and some an education at their grandfather's expense, yet without their knowing the source. King wanted it that way.

To all appearances, then, King was a family man, even raising chickens. The children enjoyed a full-time father. And Mattie became pregnant with a fourth daughter.

In the late winter of 1913 the United States threatened war with Mexico. King wanted to be in it and to hell with shore duty. He went to Washington to lobby for orders.

King wanted a destroyer. Thirteen years after the Naval Academy he was a thirty-five-year-old lieutenant commander who had never commanded. He wanted to prove himself. A destroyer command was the best job in the Navy, he began to tell his classmates. You had to use your own judgment. There was no one else who could tell you what to do.

King got his orders. In the early spring of 1914 he went to Galveston, Texas, to take command of an 800-ton reserve destroyer, the USS *Terry*. With half a crew and one ensign, King's first assignment was to escort a mule transport. When the threat of war fizzled, *Terry* and her flotilla were ordered to Charleston, South Carolina.

Destroyers are the greyhounds of the maritime world, graceful, maneuverable, fast, and powerful. Skippers were expected to conn them with smartness and authority. Some did, especially King's flotilla commander, Franck Taylor ("Kid") Evans, a renowned shiphandler and destroyerman.* It was all new to King. His primary conning experience had been aboard lumbering, sluggish capital ships.

It came time for the flotilla to get underway. King climbed atop his tiny pilothouse, peered at the signals fluttering from Evans's flagship USS *Monaghan*, and maneuvered *Terry* into her station astern. It was a stormy day, and when she reached the open sea *Terry* bucked and rolled. King became drenched. More signals snapped from the halyard, ordering *Terry* closer astern of the *Monaghan*. King refused to move; *Terry* was close enough and would stay where she was. Then another signal ordered *Terry* close alongside.

King was apprehensive. A large swell could slam the ships together without warning, but there was no alternative. Evans was testing him. King increased speed and pulled alongside *Monaghan*. It was not good enough. Evans yelled at King through a megaphone to get closer.

"Aye, aye, sir," responded King. He was learning something about destroyers. An hour later Evans hoisted "well done."

The shiphandling lessons continued until the flotilla arrived in Charleston. Docking at the navy yard would be difficult. The piers were perpendicular to the Cooper River, and the current was so strong that an approaching destroyer would be swept downstream. Evans showed how it was done. *Monaghan* dashed into the narrow slip before the current

* And son of Robley D. ("Fighting Bob") Evans.

could take effect, backed full to avoid going aground, then stopped engines so that she was exactly alongside her assigned pier space. That done, Evans turned to watch King bring in *Terry*. King made it.

In his memoirs King regarded command of *Terry* as one of the four most important achievements of his career.

King moved up to a new thousand-ton destroyer, USS *Cassin*. En route he received further orders as aide to the legendary Captain William S. Sims, who commanded the Atlantic Fleet Destroyer Flotilla. The dual orders were a dilemma, posing a choice between command at sea or more staff duty. The solution was a curious compromise. King served as Sims's aide in the mornings and commanded in the afternoons, taking *Cassin* out for a daily spin in local waters.

Sims was probably the most influential naval officer of his day. Brilliant, innovative, and unconventional, he had led the naval reformers at the turn of the century and had become a favorite of President Theodore Roosevelt. He was accustomed to beating bureaucracies and dealing with Congress and the press. After first improving naval gunnery, Sims had studied tactics and strategy while serving at the Naval War College. With a carefully selected staff (including a future Chief of Naval Operations, William V. Pratt), Sims had accepted the flotilla command in 1913 specifically to test his theories on destroyers. He also intended to improve the flotilla's flagging combat readiness.

Sims encouraged free-wheeling discussions with his subordinates, something new in a hierarchical Navy. What he wanted was mutual trust and free communication between him and his captains: Nelson's band of brothers in steel ships. Having listened to everyone, Sims would pronounce his decision. Presumably no one would beef because every viewpoint had been heard. Then the discussion ended. "Dissent and argument became the rule of the conference until consensus occurred," wrote historian Gerald E. Wheeler. "Then all were expected to give complete loyalty to the operating plan and the guiding doctrine." But skeptical officers suspected that Sims often subtly guided the conferees to the view he already had in mind.

One day Sims assembled his captains to discuss an optimum hypothetical destroyer. King said nothing. After two hours of pros and cons the other captains agreed upon a proposed design that King considered absurd. When Sims predictably agreed with the consensus, King belatedly spoke out. The others were stunned. *No one* opposed Sims after a decision. Sims exploded and King left humiliated.

Next morning King met Sims to walk with him to his office, as was their custom. For several weeks they had been discussing a relief for King so he could be a full-time skipper. King now handed him a list of candidates.

"Which of these officers do you want for your aide?" asked King.

"What's the rush?" responded Sims.

"I think you should get another aide immediately," said King.

"But what's the rush to do it right now?" persisted Sims.

"Well," said King, "I'm sure you don't want me as an aide after what you said to me yesterday afternoon. I think you should ask the Navy Department to order my relief."

And Sims did. The two men never again discussed the episode. Several months later Sims elevated King to the command of a four-ship division in addition to his duties of commanding *Cassin.* As far as King was concerned, he and Sims remained good friends. Sims might not have agreed.

The First World War had begun in Europe, and the United States Navy began to stir even though America was still at peace. *Cassin* became involved in long assignments at sea. King now considered himself a destroyerman, and, like any competent destroyerman, he docked without tugboats and became expert in finding his way through fog and weather in New England waters. He barely went below — perhaps not trusting his OODs — living on the bridge day and night. *Cassin* sometimes passed British warships searching outside American seaports for German merchantmen. "The British were very nice to us," King later wrote, "to let us use the high seas."

King could not take a senior officer's wrath, but he freely blew up at his own subordinates. For example, King wanted his exacting painting standards enforced by his exec, Robert A. ("Fuzzy") Theobald, a man of quick mind, quick temper, and vociferous stubbornness. When King accused Theobald of not doing his job, their silly argument became a question whether the paint on a bulkhead was still wet. King forced Theobald to press the bulkhead. "Of course, it was the wrong thing to do," King later admitted. Theobald stared at his hand smeared with paint, then left in a rage. For several days he brooded how to retaliate but eventually calmed down on the advice of friends. "I liked Theobald," said King, and Theobald years later agreed to be King's exec ashore.

King's anger was indiscriminate. A crack developed in a *Cassin* boiler, which the Brooklyn Navy Yard tried to repair. King inspected the work, declared it a botch, and refused to accept it. After the yard workmen left, King entered the boiler with his own sailors. Throughout the night the fireroom reverberated with clatter and banging. In the morning

USS *Cassin* (Courtesy Walter Muir Whitehill)

King triumphantly announced to the yard workmen that the boiler now had been repaired to his satisfaction. "Thank God," said the shipyard officer-in-charge.

Her boiler again steaming, *Cassin* returned to sea in time for the January 1915 naval migration to the Caribbean. Once underway, King had to rely upon his primitive radio for orders. The last message King had received directed him south from Charleston toward the Caribbean. Hours passed, then days. King obediently held course and speed. The radio was silent.

King's last order also had been to darken ship, so at night *Cassin* was buttoned up, making her interior unbearable. The two radio operators became exhausted and begged for sleep. King kept them awake, hoping for orders. When St. Thomas Island came over the horizon, King finally came right and headed for the fleet rendezvous in Guantánamo Bay, Cuba. He broke radio silence and asked for instructions, but nothing was heard, even after he found the fleet.

Sims's staff solved the mystery. Rear Admiral Clifford J. Boush, a kindly old gentleman mystified by the invention of radio, had not known how to send instructions and had simply allowed his ships to wander southward. At the critique, the fleet commander, Admiral Frank Friday Fletcher, asked King where he had been. It was a touchy question because a naval officer normally is reluctant to criticize his boss in the presence of others. On the other hand, King would look foolish if he took the blame for his solitary passage to St. Thomas. "Sir," replied King, "the last order that I received from Admiral Boush was to steer course one-six-zero, and the order hasn't been altered since." There were smiles around the room, and nothing more was said.

Friends were working for King. One was the chief of staff to Vice Admiral Henry T. Mayo, then Commander, Battleship Force, Atlantic Fleet. Mayo had become famous the year before during the so-called Tampico Incident, in which he had involved the United States in a brief war with Mexico. Mayo and his staff thought King had done well as a division commander, and, in the still small Navy, they knew of King's professional reputation as well. King received an invitation to call on Mayo.

Mayo came to the point. Would King like to serve on his staff? King hedged. He was honored, of course, by the invitation, but he preferred to retain his destroyer command. But Sims soon would be relieved, and the new flotilla commander might not want King around. In that case, said King, he would be glad to join Mayo's staff. Mayo seemed sympathetic and asked King to think it over.

King took leave and asked advice from senior officers whom he liked and respected. They were nearly unanimous in their counsel. Mayo was a "comer," they said, and he was slated to become Commander in Chief, Atlantic Fleet, the following summer. Mayo would certainly help King's career.

King phoned the chief of staff. He would be happy to serve if Mayo still wanted him. King was continuing to choose his admirals carefully.

5

The First World War

THE FIRST WORLD WAR had been raging in Europe for sixteen months when King reported for duty in Mayo's staff in December 1915. In another sixteen months the United States would enter the war. Although King was assigned as staff engineer, he preferred operational planning. Under Sims he had completed several Naval War College correspondence courses in strategy and tactics, a remarkable achievement given the other demands on his time. Now King wanted to practice what he had studied.

He intruded almost immediately. Mayo's staff had developed a scouting plan that mandated each destroyer's course and speed. King, fresh from his own destroyer command, abhorred that kind of oversupervision. Certainly, argued King, the destroyer captains could devise their own plans. Next morning King was summoned before Mayo and the chief of staff, Commander Orton P. Jackson. After a long discussion Mayo agreed with King; then he watched how well the captains could do on their own. He was delighted. King had passed his first test with the admiral.

Several of King's staff colleagues were destined for flag rank and many future associations with King. Foremost was his close friend and classmate, deep-thinking Bill Pye. Another was Russell Willson, whom King would summon as his chief of staff when the Second World War began. Leigh Noyes was yet another future admiral. King was working day by day with some of the finest officers in the Navy, a precious experience.

A former junior officer, Leo H. Thebaud, later recalled his impression of King as a staff officer. "He was always most spotlessly and smartly turned out," said Thebaud. "I admired him. His uniforms were all from Brooks Brothers in New York and the best money could buy. So were mine, and I frankly imitated him and believed that he and I were the best turned out officers on the ship."

King was an opinionated man on the subject of flag officers. Sims and Henry B. Wilson, he believed, were "show-offs." Mayo was wonderfully different, King discovered, modest and restrained, and blessed with integrity and common sense. Mayo also trusted his subordinates. "He had the idea," King later said, "that they were competent until proven otherwise." But those who needed help from Mayo were out of luck. Flag officers, especially, were expected to help themselves.

Mayo's ability to use his staff impressed King. Mayo never wrote anything himself. "It was his habit," King later said, "to talk things over and discuss them, but it was the staff that did the work." In later years King frequently asserted that he venerated Mayo, learned from him, and tried to be like him. These are puzzling statements, because when King became a flag officer his way of doing things did not resemble Mayo's style of command.

When the United States went to war in March 1917, the Navy moved timidly into action. Expecting an attack against the East Coast and fearing submarines as well, the American battle fleet withdrew to protected anchorages and waited for the Germans to cross the Atlantic.

Naval mobilization was chaotic because of Woodrow Wilson's prohibition against any talk of war during the 1916 presidential campaign. When war came shortly after Wilson's inaugural, the Navy was not ready. The unpopular Secretary of the Navy, Josephus Daniels, was a procrastinator incapable of managing in crises. The Chief of Naval Operations, Rear Admiral William S. Benson, had no real authority owing to Daniels's insistence upon civilian control.* And the Navy Department bureaus, hobbled by lethargy and inertia, were unable to satisfy the demands of the fleet commanders. Like the rest of America, the Navy was unprepared for war. It was an atmosphere in which King thrived.

To complicate mobilization, the fleet was converting from coal to oil. King scheduled the work and wrote the instructions for operating the new oil-fired propulsion plants. Meanwhile thousands of recruits had to be trained for the warships being commissioned and the auxiliary ships being acquired from private owners. King and a board of officers in one day found a way that would work, and King received most of the official credit.

* Over Daniels's objections Congress had created the Office of the Chief of Naval Operations two years before. Benson was the first incumbent.

The greatest problem was to decide how the Royal Navy and the United States Navy would combine forces and work as allies. The Navy Department had sent Sims to Great Britain for liaison just before the United States had entered the war. As the fortuitous man on the spot, Sims promptly established himself as the Commander, United States Naval Forces Operating in Europe, with a commensurate promotion to vice admiral. Thinking he knew more about the war than the distant Navy Department did, Sims became infuriated when his advice seemed to be ignored at home. Wondering what Sims was shouting about, Mayo decided to go to Great Britain to see things for himself.

In August 1917 Mayo, King, and key members of the staff arrived in England. Sims was apprehensive. If Mayo decided to stay in Europe, Sims could lose his job. Consequently Sims was suspicious when King and Pye arrived to inspect his headquarters. Perhaps deliberately, King tweaked Sims for not complying with the fleet organization manual. King and Pye gave higher priority to paperwork, Sims later complained, than to fighting the war. He was understandably relieved when Mayo and the staff continued their junket elsewhere.

Mayo's rank and prestige attracted the special attention of European leaders seeking Ameircan favors, so King became a privileged sightseer in a world at war. The role could be deceptive. Abundant food and wine at elaborate luncheons and dinners belied the austerity of the fourth year of conflict. King was lucky enough to attend many of the high-level conferences between Mayo and the Europeans. It was then that King formed his first impressions of British diplomats and their way of doing business. Later — at Casablanca and Teheran — King would remember. . . .

King and Pye were frequent guests of the Royal Navy. Aboard the flagship of Admiral Sir David Beatty, King accompanied the Grand Fleet into the North Sea for war games. Beatty, of course, had commanded at Jutland. The opposing commander was Admiral Sir Doveton Sturdee, who had beaten the Germans at the Battle of the Falkland Islands. It would be a good match.

Fog reduced the visibility as the two British forces closed for the simulated fight. Beatty left the chart house for the bridge and paced apprehensively. "Yes, I'm sure what Sturdee is trying to do," said Beatty, thinking aloud, "since he's always been a fox. I know what I should do, but I can't maneuver in this fog." Beatty obviously feared the risks of collision and held course. When the fog lifted, everyone could see that Sturdee had embarrassed Beatty. His only hope was a complicated

King and Mayo at sea . . . (Courtesy Ernest J. King, Jr.)

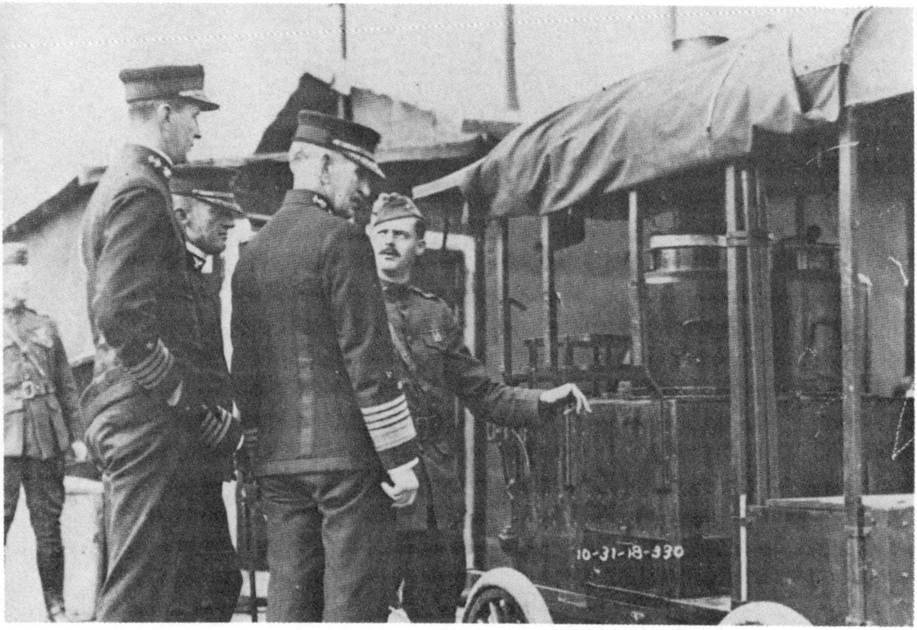

. . . and inspecting a field kitchen ashore (Courtesy Naval Historical Center)

series of maneuvers to save face. Beatty did not want to try it and signaled an end to the exercise.

Afterward Beatty complained to Mayo that King and Pye had made snide remarks. Actually they had remained tactfully silent. Perhaps Beatty had read their minds. "I must say that we thought a lot," said King later.

Occasionally King came under enemy fire from aircraft or shore batteries. King had joined Admiral Sir John Jellicoe, the First Sea Lord, as a fellow spectator aboard the destroyer HMS *Broke*, escorting a monitor bombarding German fortifications at Oostende, Belgium. The Germans shot back. A large projectile exploded close aboard, forcing *Broke* to maneuver evasively.

Jellicoe turned to King. "There is something for you to tell your grandchildren about," he said.

"Yes, Admiral," King replied. "I think that in later years that shot will get closer, and then really close."

King was in Europe with Mayo and his staff on a second trip when the Armistice ended the war in November 1918. Owing to his special intimacy with Admiral Mayo, he had learned much about war. He had dealt with the Navy Department and Washington politicians, mobilized a fleet, and attended conferences with Allied civilian and military leaders. While touring battlefields, bases, airfields, and fleets he had also drafted reports, minutes, and policy papers. Few naval officers of King's relatively junior rank had had an equivalent education in the art of war.

King's duty also had exposed him to flag officers in command. Apparently he did not think much of them. In his memoirs King wrote of his anger with the opposition of influential admirals to postgraduate education. Their reactionary philosophies were stifling intellectual growth in the Navy, King believed, and Rear Admirals Henry B. Wilson and Hugh Rodman where the worst offenders. King, a disciple of Luce and Mahan, thought it was mandatory to study strategy and tactics, and his March 1919 *Proceedings* paper on battleship design was an example. A naval officer must not let his mind stagnate. Go to the Naval War College. Read. Think. Write.

King also disliked flag officers whose behavior was a facade, who blustered to disguise shortcomings in character or competence. Similarly he disapproved of those who exaggerated or publicized their deeds for self-aggrandizement. King could barely conceal his contempt in their presence and he showed it: hostile, arrogant, sometimes disrespectful and even insubordinate. They in turn resented King's supercilious attitude and his infuriating persistence in arguing when they wanted the last word.

Perhaps King was comparing them to past heroes. King pored over *Types of Naval Officers*, Mahan's biographical essays of famous British admirals in the eighteenth century. King's favorite was John Jervis, the Earl of St. Vincent, whose character and discipline had restored the Royal Navy after a fleetwide mutiny. Jervis had chosen outstanding subordinates (Nelson for one) and had allowed them free rein in defeating the French. Nelson, Farragut, Van Tromp, and Suffren were also among King's heroes.

Not all were naval officers. King also esteemed Napoleon and his marshals, as well as generals of the Civil War. King knew them all, and they were his personal inspiration. The mortals of King's era did not have a chance, except for Mayo, whom he worshiped. Or a bold, confident seaman like Kid Evans. But they were a minority.

The war over, Mayo went ashore and King sought a new job. He now was a captain at only forty. Promotions had been rapid during the war, and he sported the Navy Cross, a reward from Mayo. The Navy Department offered King the opportunity to reopen the Naval Postgraduate School in Annapolis, and he was delighted to accept. He had not taken leave in over three years. It was time to go home to Mattie.

6

Peace and Command

THE NAVAL POSTGRADUATE SCHOOL, established as a department of the Naval Academy in 1909, provided the Navy with technically trained officers. It had closed during the war because most officers had gone to sea, but the school reopened after the Armistice. King was given command.

Given his beliefs on education, King was the perfect choice. He presented his budget to Secretary Josephus Daniels in Washington, and together they went by car to appear before Congress. Daniels questioned King's figures.

"Can't you do with less?" asked Daniels.

"There's no velvet," said King. He got what he wanted.

King chose Fuzzy Theobald of the great painting incident as his executive officer. Two other staff officers and seven civilian engineering professors completed the faculty. The 1919–1920 academic year began with fifty-one students.

The Navy had changed drastically during the war, especially in the officer corps swollen by rapid promotions, larger academy classes, and an influx of reserves. A long period of peace and demobilization lay ahead, and the Navy Department wondered how it would train and promote its wartime acquisitions. Prewar career patterns had been overtaken by events.

As King, Dudley Knox, and Bill Pye were stationed in and near Washington, the Chief of the Bureau of Navigation * in the summer of 1919 appointed the three as a board to study the problem and to submit recommendations. They were a good team: service on Osterhaus's staff,

* Later known as the Bureau of Naval Personnel, responsible for the training, education, and assignment of naval personnel.

while King and Pye were intellectual collaborators of long standing, most recently as staff officers for Mayo.

They met periodically for about nine months. "After much deliberation," Knox later recalled, "King suggested that we write a report. He sat down at a desk and wrote that report in the course of perhaps a day, following the details through in his logical way. Although there was a great deal of groundwork by Pye, the report primarily came out of King's head. The stringing together and the argument that you make in such cases was all King's. Scarcely any change was made from the preliminary draft. No one without outstanding ability could have done what he did there."

The gist of the Knox-Pye-King (KPK) report was that a naval officer's training should proceed through four phases.

- Naval Academy. Prepares midshipmen for division officer assignments.
- General Line School. Prepares lieutenants for department head assignments.
- Junior War College Course. Prepares lieutenant commanders for command and staff assignments.
- Senior War College Course. Prepares captains for flag officer assignment.

The report also recommended that line officers acquire a subspecialty (their specialty, of course, being naval warfare) so that the Navy would have experts in technical fields and management. Another recommendation was systematic assignments from ensign to admiral, so that an aspiring officer could chart his course to the top. Heretofore career planning had been largely guesswork and hearsay.

Reports urging change and innovation often become lost and forgotten in the Navy Department. As a precaution King published the report in the August 1920 *U.S. Naval Institute Proceedings*, giving it wide circulation and gaining recognition for himself. Most of its recommendations ended as official policy; by 1928 the Navy Department established both a General Line course and a Junior War College course. The report's basic ideas have since been refined, but naval training and career management today still conform to the concepts and principles that King set down in one day over half a century ago.

King's writing and editing extended beyond the KPK report. He rejoined the Naval Institute Board of Control and judged manuscripts that naval officers submitted for publication. His 1920 essay on battleships won the first honorable mention in a contest sponsored by Walter Lippincott of Philadelphia. Its style, like that of the KPK report, was

Mattie and her first five daughters, l. to r., Claire, Elizabeth, Florie, Martha, and Eleanor (Courtesy Ernest J. King, Jr.)

Joe and Martha (Courtesy J. King, Jr.)

well organized, methodical, and analytical. King's papers were always simple, clear, precise and brief. The KPK report contained twenty-eight pages and one chart, his battleship paper a scant twenty pages. Reports generated within the Department of Defense today on similar topics would be measured in pounds rather than pages. King hated verboseness. In the Second World War he carried succinctness to the extreme. Any letter or memorandum submitted to him for his signature, regardless of its complexity, had to be limited to one typed page.

After he had had a year at Annapolis an attack of shingles drove King to sick bay. The doctor diagnosed overwork as the cause and prescribed outdoor exercise and shorter hours as the cure. (Ironically, King had worried that his students worked too hard, and he had told them to exercise, relax, and get enough sleep.) King took up golf. "Although I wasn't very good at it," he later said, "I persisted and could play a fair game in the middle nineties." A second hernia operation in 1940 and the Second World War finally ended his golf, which was his only athletic activity other than walking. King's nervous energy kept him trim and tough, and he could eat well without gaining weight. Occasionally he tried to quit smoking, but without success.

The King home by now was filled with daughters of all ages and their friends. A son was finally born in the summer of 1922. A woman dinner companion later asked King about the size of his family.

"Six daughters and a son," said King.

"What is your son's name?" she asked.

"Ernest Joseph King, Junior," he replied.

"It should have been 'Ernest Endeavor,'" she twitted. Her joke became King folklore.

As the daughters matured into attractive young women, Mattie encouraged dating and wanted boys to feel welcome. But King was a bear. A midshipman once called upon two girls who were Mattie's guests. King gruffly ordered him away. Mattie was furious. How could he be so rude? King justified himself by citing regulations, chapter and verse. It was a typical King sea-lawyer tactic. Outside his home he delighted in compelling flag officers to concede they were wrong by quoting a regulation in King's favor. But Mattie could not be intimidated.

So King was forced to tolerate the hordes of young men, especially midshipmen, that inundated his home. But he demanded formal introductions. A nervous daughter would begin the ceremony.

"Captain King, I would like you to meet Midshipman Jones."

"What is his name?" King would bellow. One daughter would become so flustered that she usually forgot the name of the terrified midshipman beside her. Then King would hide behind his newspaper. But the young men were unfazed. The King women were too popular.

King could be hospitable to the people he liked. Midshipman Boynton L. Braun from Lorain was one of his favorites. He once told Braun to expect a dinner invitation from Mrs. King. King carefully instructed Braun about proper dinner etiquette, to stay no longer than an hour after the meal, and to write a thank-you note. Everything proceeded as briefed. Braun was enchanted.

The Postgraduate School was running smoothly in its second year when King heard that Rear Admiral Henry B. Wilson would become the new Superintendent of the Naval Academy. King was appalled. In addition to their mutual dislike, King regarded Wilson as the bane of postgraduate education. It was time to seek orders at the Bureau of Navigation.

"What's the rush?" teased the detail officer, Captain William D. Leahy. "You rate a third year at Annapolis."

"You know damn well why I want to go to sea," said King.

"You're too junior for a captain's command," said Leahy. "There's nothing available." King would not give up. After a long discussion King agreed to take the USS *Bridge*, a plodding 9,500-ton supply ship known as a "beef boat." In July 1921, King returned to sea.

Bridge belonged to the Fleet Train, the motley auxiliaries providing mobile logistical support to the warships. Under King's command *Bridge* chugged from port to port, replenishing the Atlantic Fleet and carrying occasional passengers. Although necessary, it was dull work avoided by aspiring officers. King stuck it out. After a year of tedium King revisited Leahy to ask again for a division or flotilla. Leahy iterated that there were no such billets available. King refused to leave. Leahy finally asked if King would be interested in submarines. Simply attend submarine school in New London, Connecticut, for three or four months, said Leahy, and King could learn to command a submarine division. King took the job.

Submarines were new to the fleet. Although the first models had appeared in 1880, they did not become prominent until the First World War's U-boat campaign against Allied shipping. During the war the U.S. Navy accelerated its submarine building program and established a major submarine base at New London. Immediately following the war the submarine force had continued to grow in size and prestige.

THE BEAUTY OF THE KING DAUGHTERS

Florie (Courtesy Ernest J. King, Jr.)

Mildred (Courtesy Ernest J. King, Jr.)

Claire and her daughter (Courtesy Ernest J. King, Jr.)

The elite crews were mostly volunteers, proud, competent, and remote from the mainstream of naval service. Their submarines were small, cramped, uncomfortable, mechanically unreliable, and frequently unseaworthy; still they attracted some of the finest officers and sailors in the Navy. Most submarine officers, however, were too young to command the increased numbers of submarine divisions. Senior officers either had to be drafted or induced to volunteer; accustomed to the comforts of surface ships, they shied from submarines. King was an exception.

King entered submarine school as a curiosity, a captain among some fifty very junior student officers. His earlier experience had been a few demonstration cruises, including one in the Navy's original submarine, USS *Holland.* King admittedly was not a "good" student, but he learned what he felt he had to know. Oddly, he never did take the necessary examinations for qualifying in submarines. He had plenty of opportunities; perhaps he did not want to chance failure. In any event, he time and again in later years emphatically stressed that he was not qualified to wear the submariner's dolphin breast insignia.

How were submarines to be used? World opinion regarded Germany's recent unrestricted submarine warfare as immoral and repugnant. The postwar mood of pacifism generated proposals to outlaw submarine attacks against unarmed merchantmen, and even to abolish submarines altogether. The thinking at New London was that submarines should be limited to defending American ports and overseas possessions.

This concept of local defense was apparent in the daily routine. Everyone wanted to stay close to home. Habitability was so wretched that the crews lived aboard submarine tenders when in port. "As usual," said King later, "I had ideas of my own." King insisted that the submariners should live aboard and stay at sea. King argued tactics, as well. In his opinion submarines should work together — like surface ships — for coordinated attacks against enemy fleets. The submarine officers disagreed. Submarines could not be handled in close-order drill like destroyers, they said. There was danger of collision, especially underwater. King was not listening. He urged the submariners to be more aggressive, to outwit rather than outdive the enemy fleet. The more cautious submariners preferred operating independently with stealth and finesse.

Attacking an enemy's merchant marine was rarely discussed.

King had the last word. With school finished, he took command of a four-submarine division. His first order was for everyone to get off the tender and go back to the submarines — permanently. When the crews protested, King had a logical answer. "Those submarines are really ships," he said. "They displace more tonnage than a destroyer, and all hands live permanently aboard a destroyer." His order stuck.

King would discover that there were few other similarities between destroyers and submarines. In early January 1923 it was time again for the annual cruise to the Caribbean. King hoisted his commodore's pennant in submarine *S-20* and led his division to sea. A northeast gale smashed King's force as it entered the open ocean, forcing *S-20* to break down and wallow helplessly. King ordered the others to press on; *S-20* would rejoin later.

Next morning the sea was empty. The storm continued. King, seasick and miserable, his head and knees bruised from cramped quarters, despaired of finding his scattered flock. None would answer the radio. Several days later he discovered one of his submarines adrift, her engines swamped. Finally one by one, King's division straggled into St. Thomas. King sadly concluded that it would be a long time before submarines would become seaworthy.

King shepherded his reconstituted armada to the Panama Canal Zone to rendezvous with the fleet, still hoping to test his theories. Disappointment followed disappointment. His greatest problem was mechanical casualties that crippled his submarines. "I had very little to do with the fleet maneuvers that I can remember," he later said.

King was partially to blame for being ostracized from the fleet. His immediate boss was Vice Admiral John D. ("Long John") McDonald, commanding the scouting forces that included King's submarines. It was a normal courtesy to ask permission from the senior officer present to get underway, but King decided to ignore precedent because he already had written orders. A signal lamp began flashing from McDonald's flagship.

"Why are you underway without my permission?" asked McDonald.

"I am underway in accordance with your operation order," King replied. King proceeded to sea, with the flagship's signal light still blinking as it faded into the distance.

"The correspondence carried on for months," King said afterward, "until the file was at least half an inch thick. Finally, Long John stated that the incident was closed, which was the usual way of saying that I had won."

Months later King and his submarines returned to New London. The crews were sick to death of their submarines and wanted to move back to the tender. King refused to allow it. The complaints reached King's superior, Rear Admiral Montgomery M. Taylor, who finally ordered

King to give in. King's ignoble experiments in submarine warfare had ended.

In September 1923 King left the boats for command of the Submarine Base at New London. He was delighted with the prestige and opportunities of his new assignment. New London was a large base, several hundreds of acres, employing some five hundred sailors and perhaps a hundred civilians. Its most important function was training officers and men for duty in submarines. King had become the most influential officer in the submarine service.

The mid-1920s were rough for the Navy. Congressional appropriations were meager, reflecting the nation's mood of economy and pacifism. The peacetime Navy suffered from austere budgets, and it was tempting at naval stations to drift into a comfortable, undemanding routine—unless the commanding officer was ambitious.

King was on his way to becoming a rear admiral. "On two occasions," a young aide, Bruce P. Hood, later said, "he told me he was going to the top. No braggadocio, just extreme confidence." To the perceptive aide it appeared that King had "consuming ambition" and "the ability to sell himself to the boys on top."

King established two principal objectives. One was to enforce discipline and efficiency. It would not be easy. King admired the young submariners as adventurous and daring, willing to tackle anything. But they were also free spirits who needed restraint. Work was to begin promptly, King announced, and he glared from his office window to spot any stragglers. When white scarves became a required accessory, King lurked at the main gate to nab junior officers without them. "You will find," he later wrote his relief, "that I have run what is commonly called a 'taut' ship in regard to salutes, uniform, working hours, watches, and in fact everything that requires people to do what they are supposed to do."

King's other great objective was good public relations. He would accept almost any invitation to put the naval service before the public. These included providing spectator launches for the annual Harvard-Yale crew race or taking the MIT Class of 1914 to sea aboard four submarines. (He expected some MIT assistance on technical problems in return.) But his willingness to please had limits. A sharp letter went to any public official who had maligned the Navy.

His major public dispute erupted over alleged naval participation in Ku Klux Klan activities. The controversy grew when a Roman Catholic priest charged that King had attended a Klan meeting. When a newspaper called, King told the reporter that it was "a damned lie" and hung up. Furious at the priest, whom he didn't know, King asked his Roman Catholic executive officer to brief him on the Church's chain of command. The priest's superior, it turned out, was the Bishop of Hartford, who defended the priest's freedom of speech. A short time later one of King's daughters was asked to serve as a maid of honor at a Roman Catholic wedding. King said no. "You'll be blessed with holy water and come back smelling of incense," he said.*

King was punctilious as the principal U.S. Navy representative in Connecticut. He once bawled out a young officer who had almost run into the Connecticut State Commissioner of Motor Vehicles (who was a friend of King's). The officer boldly suggested that the accident was outside King's jurisdiction. "Young man," said King, "when anything happens that reflects on the Navy, it *is* my business."

One night the local police raided an off-base officers' party and confiscated their illegal liquor. In the morning the offenders came before King. He could have convened a court-martial. Instead he struck a bargain. If the story did not get into the newspapers, he told them, King would not punish them. The officers talked to the judge and paid a fine. "The newspapers never caught on," said one of the participants afterward, "and we never had another welcoming party."

But there were plenty of other parties. Social life on base had been dull until King arrived. King wanted some action. His astute executive officer soon was organizing dances, which the King family always attended. King also availed himself of the many invitations he received outside the base. Once he returned by tugboat about midnight. "He was considerably under the weather and carrying his shoes in his hand," recalled the duty officer, Kenneth A. Knowles. "He apparently had had a very good time. He was on the job at 8 A.M. though."

King cared for his sailors by fixing their barracks and improving their food. But most of all, he supported the base athletic teams. Competition between naval commands was intense. King always wanted to win, and he recruited good players as assiduously as a college coach would. Repercussions followed. Rear Admiral Taylor, King's boss, believing that King was unduly emphasizing athletics, ordered King's championship baseball team to sea duty.

"That sowed a small whirlwind," said a Taylor aide afterward. "Early

* King and Mattie themselves were nominal Episcopalians, and their children were confirmed in the Episcopal Church. Although he attended services infrequently, he was well versed in Bible studies and once used a passage from the Book of Common Prayer in a wartime operations order.

One of King's many visitors, who was impressed by the submarine base. Secretary of the Navy Curtis D. Wilbur reviews the Marine honor guard. (Courtesy Naval Historical Center)

the next morning along came Captain King, breathing fire. He brushed me aside when I met him at the gangway and practically ran up to Admiral Taylor's cabin. He emerged in about half an hour, and exited as he had entered. The order stood."

King could shrug off such setbacks. He was the master of the realm. His growing accomplishments impressed important Navy Department visitors and enhanced his professional reputation. Commanding the New London base allowed King a luxurious style of living that his naval pay never could have afforded: a mansion for his family, whom he brought from Annapolis, and four enlisted servants on the household staff. The Navy provided a massive old Marmon car and an enlisted chauffeur, who remained with King for years. Gig and crew stood ready at the waterfront.

King's aide once made the mistake of putting King's driver on report for a minor offense. When the case came to King for official action—captain's mast—King turned and focused upon the officer. "I'll never forget that look to my dying day," Hood later said. The case was dismissed and Hood summoned to King's office for a lecture on the sanctity of King's retinue.

King's evenings, when he was not entertaining or being entertained, were devoted to still another Naval War College correspondence course. In three months he completed the entire twelve installments and received congratulations from the college president. It was an extraordinary achievement in so short a time.

In mid-September 1925 King had been base commander for two years. He and Mattie decided to take a vacation by themselves and to drive through New England. They neither listened to the radio nor read newspapers but simply enjoyed the scenery. The children clustered excitedly in front of the house when their parents returned. In the midst of the confusion Elizabeth spoke to her father. "Daddy," she said, "wasn't it just awful about the loss of the *S-51?*"

The submarine *S-51* had been based in New London, and King knew her well. While he and Mattie were away, *S-51* had put to sea for engineering trials on 24 September. The next day a steamer rammed her near Block Island, south of Rhode Island. The submarine sank, killing thirty-four crewmen. Following a memorial service at New London, King's indirect involvement with *S-51* ended.

Several weeks after the sinking, King returned to his home after a Sunday afternoon of golf. There was a message to phone Rear Admiral Charles P. Plunkett, the Commandant of the Third Naval District in New York. How strange, thought King. He had known Plunkett for years and had always liked him. But why was he calling on a weekend? After many tries King finally got him on the phone.

"You're to be in command of the raising of the *S-51*," said Plunkett.

King was flabbergasted. It was the first time in his career that he had received orders without negotiating in advance and without weighing how they would affect his career. King knew nothing about salvage operations nor had he known that he had been under consideration.

Plunkett was a man of action who wanted an answer. For once in his life King was at a loss for words. To Plunkett's annoyance King stalled for time, trying to organize his thoughts. "Since you don't seem interested in the job," said Plunkett, "I'll try to find someone else to do it."

"Why, Admiral," said King, "of course I'd like to have the job. I just didn't believe my ears. Of course I'll take the job and welcome it."

What King had not known was that the Navy Department, for reasons of public opinion, had decided to salvage *S-51*. As civilian salvage companies had refused to get involved, the Navy decided to proceed on its own. It became a matter of prestige. "The Department cannot afford to take any chance on failure as there are too many critics still around," an admiral later warned King.

An engineering specialist stationed at the Brooklyn Navy Yard, Lieutenant Commander Edward Ellsberg, was behind the Navy's decision. Ambitious and persuasive, Ellsberg convinced first Plunkett and then the Navy Department that he could salvage *S-51* — given the necessary resources. The Navy was reluctant, however, to entrust full responsibility to so junior an officer. Someone more senior was needed to manage and coordinate the entire operation, which entailed a number of ships, complex logistical support, and dealing with senior officials and the press. King was both available and nearby, Plunkett knew him, so King was the perfect choice.

The task seemed overwhelming. *S-51* lay 130 feet below the surface, filled with water, a gash in her port side. Navy divers were not accustomed to working at depths beyond 90 feet. Somehow she had to be raised and towed 175 miles to the Brooklyn Navy Yard. Although Plunkett and the Navy Department had promised unlimited support, the unprecedented salvage would be perilous. King's men would have to work in open sea, and winter was approaching.

Ellsberg would direct the on-site salvage, assisted by a civilian naval architect from the Brooklyn yard named John C. Niedermair. Lieutenant Harry Hartley commanded USS *Falcon*, the principal salvage ship, and Warrant Boatswain Richard E. Hawes supervised the boats and moorings. Together they formed a superb team. Ellsberg was brave, almost reckless, and indefatigable. Hartley and Hawes were superb seamen, experts in anchoring, mooring, towing, and shipbuilding. Niederman was the group's theoretician, calculating weights, pressures, and volumes.

Without previous salvaging experience to guide them, everyone realized that their plans would be guesswork. *Falcon* would moor directly above *S-51*. Divers would close as many of the submarine's watertight fittings as possible, displacing water with compressed air to make the submarine partially bouyant. Finally, eight massive pontoons would lift *S-51* from below and hold her on the surface during the tow to New York.

Three weeks after the sinking, *Falcon* began work. Seven weeks of diving followed, principally to investigate the submarine's condition and to begin pumping water from her after compartments. The diving conditions were brutal. There were many volunteers, but some gave out at the greater depths. Those who were able to tolerate the pressure willingly risked their lives, groping about the submarine's wrecked interior and exposing themselves to extreme cold and to swift currents. King regarded them as the bravest men he had ever known.

December storms made further diving impossible, and King wanted to quit until spring. The Navy Department insisted that he continue, but when ice plugged the air hoses, the salvage flotilla went home.

King returned in mid-April 1926. After trial and error the salvors learned how to raise and lower the pontoons and how to fasten them to the submarine's hull. By 21 June everything was ready to lift *S-51* the next morning. Newsmen would be witnesses.

A storm hit at daybreak. King decided to delay raising the submarine, even though some of the pontoons already were in place. But *S-51* had a mind of her own. To everyone's horror she rose to the surface in a tangle of pontoons, wires, lines, and air hoses. Hartley's tugs grabbed hold, but the submarine was in extremis. After a quick discussion King decided to attempt to tow her into shallow water before she sank.

The storm worsened. Several pontoons broke away, one leaping from the water like a startled whale. To avoid further damage King decided that *S-51* had to be sunk again, this time gently and evenly, by sinking the supporting pontoons. It seemed impossible. Thunderous waves swept over the pontoons, crashing them into each other and into the submarine. Someone — someone very brave — had to leap aboard those pontoons and open their air vents. Incredibly, Boatswain Hawes and his men got the job done. *S-51* sank for a second time.

When the storm abated, King returned to try again, but there was trouble with the divers. The chief diver had finally lost his nerve. Ellsberg was ruining morale, he said, and any more diving would be too hazardous. King said there could be no thought of quitting.

"In that case," said the chief diver, "I will no longer accept responsibility for the divers' safety."

King stared at him intently. "You are sick," said King. "Go ashore and turn yourself in."

The other divers agreed to carry on. Their bravery was beyond description. This time they succeeded. The flotilla, flags at half-mast, entered New York harbor with *S-51* carefully suspended beneath her eight pontoons. With thirty-four bodies entombed in the submarine, it was indeed a funeral cortege. Throngs lined the bank of the East River to watch the procession. To everyone's dismay a bumbling civilian harbor pilot ran *S-51* aground within sight of the Navy Yard. (King had asked for the best available but got instead "an old man who didn't relish the job.")

One final effort, then *S-51* again floated. The tugs gently eased her toward the shipyard. A great crowd had gathered to watch the arrival. King dispatched a sailor to raise a symbolic flag on the submarine's superstructure, barely awash. The man's weight caused the submarine to begin sinking, and he hurriedly jumped clear. After some last-minute maneuvering crises in a strong ebbtide current, the *S-51* finally came to rest at midnight.

King was out on his feet. He went to a friend's home, had a drink, and slept.

Rewards and recognition followed. King, Ellsberg, and Hartley received Distinguished Service Medals, Hawes and seven sailors the Navy Cross; others received promotions or letters of commendation. Ellsberg wrote a book on his experience and resigned from the Navy to go into business.

Given the nationwide publicity of the *S-51* drama, King's service reputation soared. By chance he had been given an incredible opportunity to become famous, but the risks had been terribly high. When King brought *S-51* into harbor he had proven himself in the toughest imaginable job in time of peace, and everyone knew it. Commendably, King generously shared the credit. His progress to flag rank accelerated; he had risen head and shoulders above the crowd of captains.

7

Aviation Begins

When King accepted Plunkett's offer to command the *S-51* salvage, he may have had an earlier letter on his mind. It had been written several months before the sinking by Admiral Charles F. Hughes, the Chief of Naval Operations. "A friendly hint," wrote Hughes, "take it or leave it, but ask no questions." Hughes explained that King's service reputation was in trouble. The talk was that King had had too many glamour jobs and rarely had put his career on the line. "You are sure to be compared with others that have taken the hard knocks of the service and have come through with credit," Hughes continued. "You would be surprised how your record of service is looked upon." Hughes offered some straightforward advice: "Get a job at sea where you can do some of the drudgery of the service."

King, the careful, calculating careerist, was shocked. "I have always been looking to the future," he replied defensively on 17 June 1925, "and have so far felt myself fully able and qualified to do any job that any of my contemporaries, at least, might be called upon to do. I have never, in any degree, knowingly avoided or shirked any duty of any kind. I came into submarines chiefly for my own professional benefit and had hoped to do some work with aircraft in the next five years." King went on to admit that his earlier staff duty might have hurt him. "I can only say," he continued, "that never have I requested such duty nor have I ever sought it." King then reviewed his career, found it satisfactory, and concluded that he was "not unfitting for future usefulness." Nevertheless, King promised to heed Hughes's friendly warning.

Before *S-51* King had expected to return to sea duty in the summer of 1926, but Leahy at the Bureau of Navigation was pessimistic about the availability of the cruiser command that King wanted. There were too many captains senior to King on the waiting list. Then came *S-51* to complicate matters. When salvage efforts paused for the winter, King had time to brood about his future. A letter in mid-February 1927 from Leahy deepened King's anguish.

Leahy wanted King to return to sea duty in June in command of a prosaic naval transport, the USS *Henderson*, regardless of whether King had finished with *S-51*. "It seems to me that I am in a dilemma," King wrote in reply, "chiefly on account of the job of raising the S-51. . . . I wish to make it as clear as I can that I do *not* feel that the success of the work is dependent upon my connection with it—but—I have carried the job about halfway to completion, am thoroughly familiar with all the problems involved, and feel that I should finish it, both as a matter of professional pride and for the good of my service reputation, in the spirit of *finishing* what you have begun. . . . I may as well be frank and say that I now feel that my obligations as to the S-51 appear likely to penalize me in regard to the sea billet that I get. Hence the dilemma—if I by-pass the S-51 job, I get the sea billet, but if I complete the S-51 job, it seems that I have to take whatever sea billet may be available after it is completed. . . . I realize that it is for the Bureau to say when and where I shall go to sea, but am reluctant to be 'penalized' when the reason therefor is that I am doing professional work of the character of salvaging the S-51."

King became even more discouraged when he visited Washington in early April. Leahy confirmed that King would be without a decent job after salvaging *S-51*. Depressed and wondering what next, King was invited to see Rear Admiral William A. Moffett, the first Chief of the Bureau of Aeronautics. Moffett explained that Congress soon would legislate that aviation commands would require either naval aviators or naval aviation observers. Naval aviation was so new, however, that most of the aviators were still youngsters. The Navy's forthcoming aircraft carriers, as well as the naval air stations, needed senior officers. The only solution was to make fliers out of older surface officers. Would King be willing to learn how to fly even though he was almost fifty? If King qualified, Moffett promised him an aircraft carrier.

King asked time to think it over and returned to *S-51*. Several months later he wrote Moffett to accept. "It seemed to me," King later said, "that aviation was the coming thing in the Navy." Perhaps so, but until the last moment King would have forsaken aviation for a light cruiser. In a 13 May 1926 letter to a classmate in the Bureau of Navigation, King wrote, "I suppose that Bill Leahy has told you of my strenuous desires to get command of one of the scouts—I hope that you will keep me in mind for that duty."

King's transition into aviation was hectic. Moffett wavered between having King enter flight training or first command the seaplane tender USS *Wright*. Moffett finally chose the latter since her commanding officer, King's classmate John V. Babcock, wanted a relief. Feeling the pressure, King begged Moffett to leave him alone until *S-51* was safely in New York. Afterward King was "dead tired" and asked for leave before going to *Wright*. Moffett was unsympathetic. King had to take command immediately.

Babcock had written King that *Wright* was loosely run and removed from the mainstream of fleet activities. Her main task was acting as a mobile support base for seaplanes. "Certainly under my regime," wrote Babcock, "she is what the men would call an easy ship." Thus forewarned, King arrived in June and followed the standard relieving procedure, including a cursory inspection of the ship. After relieving, he saw Babcock over the side and then assembled the ship's officers. "And now, gentlemen," said King, "we are going to have an inspection that is an inspection." King tore the ship apart.

A young aviator, H. S. Duckworth, recalled his first encounter with the new captain. "I was talking to the aviation supply officer on the *Wright* one Saturday morning," Duckworth later wrote, "leaning over the rail and idly spitting into the water. Suddenly a tremendous *stand at attention* almost blew us overboard. E. J. was just holding Saturday morning inspection, and we had very carelessly allowed him to come up behind us."

King announced that he would learn how to fly and the *Wright*'s aviators would teach him. His first indoctrination flight was in an open-air rear cockpit of a two-man seaplane. The nimble plane skipped along the surface of Narragansett Bay and then was airborne, the wind whistling through its wire struts. The pilot signaled King to take the controls. "I went to work and tried to pilot the plane in a straight-way flight," King later remembered, "but I didn't do too well since I was weaving the plane and was not in a level flight." King continued to fly at every opportunity, and within a month he could do routine airborne maneuvers. By fall he considered himself so advanced that he requested Moffett to designate him as a student aviator. Moffett replied that he still wanted King to go through formal flight training at Pensacola. In early 1927 King obediently left *Wright* and went to Florida.

The late nineteen twenties were hard times for the Navy. The United States was at peace, the armed forces were unpopular, and congressional appropriations were correspondingly meager. Pensacola reflected the lack of money. When King arrived he found the patchwork training aircraft literally held together by glue and baling wire. The ramshackle buildings and hangars were firetraps. Cattle wandered across the airfields for want of fences, an additional hazard to student pilots.

The training program was an awkward combination of youth and age in reverse roles. The flight instructors kept open minds about the influx of old fuds and tried to be realistic about what they could contribute. Naval aviation needed their seniority and prestige, and the converts were potentially influential spokesmen. Consequently everyone was treated fairly yet impartially. Favors were neither sought nor given, and pulling rank was forbidden. "Although I was a captain," King recalled, "I was merely a student aviator and nothing more." Others like him included Richmond Kelly Turner and Alva D. Bernhard, both future admirals. But most students were recent graduates of the Naval Academy.

King's reputation had preceded him. Submariners had written the flight instructors urging them to flunk King, warning that King would upset naval aviation. But the instructors stuck to their solemn agreement to give the old-timers a fair shake regardless of their notoriety.

King was aloof during his early training so he could concentrate on learning to fly. He went on the wagon, preached abstention for all students, and badgered the base commander to enforce the prohibition laws. When word of King's feelings became known, no one would tell King that nearly every officer's bunk concealed a three-gallon jug of "shinny."

One Saturday noon King stumbled upon a drinking party that had just begun in officers' quarters. The startled host impetuously offered King a drink. A bystander, George van Deurs, remembered King's reaction. "Ernie was just standing there looking silly with a glass in his hand before he realized what had happened. Then he said he might as well taste it. And then he wanted to know how long this had been going on. Hell, he'd been missing something for months, and from then on you couldn't hold him. He was the damnedest party man in the place. He'd been spending Saturday nights in his room studying while everybody else was down at the country club or the hotel just raising hell with a big dance. Ernie was the first guy there on Saturdays from then on. He joined the club because actually he was a great guy with the ladies and with liquor both."

Poker was another diversion. "I never counted King's drinks," recalled one player, Robert W. Bockius, "but he took them well and got extremely relaxed in the midst of a wild poker game. He had at the time the privilege to call the rules. That was all right, but then he did change

DEPARTMENT OF THE NAVY

Date 8 December, 1927

NAVAL AVIATOR NO. 3368

This Certifies that

Captain Ernest J. King, U.S.N.

born 23 *day of* November, 1878 *having fulfilled the conditions prescribed by the United States Navy Department, was appointed a*

NAVAL AVIATOR

on 26 May, 1927.

Chief of Bureau of Navigation.

U. S. GOVERNMENT PRINTING OFFICE J35636

(Seal)

Received E. J. King

Captain, U.S.N.

(Rank and Service)

U. S. GOVERNMENT PRINTING OFFICE J35635

The new naval aviator (National Archives 80-G-705578)

the rules in the middle and thereby caused undue confusion. But no pistols were drawn. . . ."

King soloed soon after arriving in Pensacola, a benefit of his instruction aboard *Wright*. His first solo was one of the most exciting events of his life. "I must say that that was a great day for me," he later wrote. "After thinking over all my instructions, I took the plane on the beach and taxied and got ready to take off and *did*. I was told to take it easy on a straight course and climb steadily to about a thousand feet and then slowly turn about the bay and then land. So I *did*. Eureka!! I certainly thought that this is the life!!!"

In time it became apparent that King was not a natural pilot who flew instinctively. Instead he flew by the numbers, remembering every procedure, always safe, calculating, and careful. His instructors felt that King treated flying as a professional requirement, something he had to master but did not enjoy. One instructor suspected that King avoided unnecessary risks because of his large family. King himself admitted his discomfort during a difficult maneuver. In the end he did the necessary minimum to win his wings and left Pensacola with rudimentary flying skills. He never again flew alone (a safety pilot always accompanied King), but he would still take the controls for routine maneuvers aloft. King had no fear of flying; indeed, he often insisted upon flying as a passenger under conditions that scared his pilots. "Senior naval aviators," King told Congress in 1933, "will not let it be said of them that they send their junior officers in places and under circumstances where they do not go. They must go."

Moffett had been anxiously monitoring King's progress in Pensacola. When he learned that King had achieved the minimum hours to qualify for wings (200, including 75 solo), Moffett ended King's training. King's five months at Pensacola had been exhilarating, "a very fine time," he later wrote, an experience he had "liked very much indeed." On 26 May 1927 King received the coveted breast insigne of a naval aviator. It was, he said, one of the four most important events of his naval career.

King took ten days to visit his family in Annapolis before resuming command of *Wright*. The next several months were routine. King had a collateral duty as chief of staff to Rear Admiral James F. Raby, Commander Air Divisions, Scouting Fleet, who flew his flag in *Wright*. This required extra work, but King did not mind. "I liked to be around when things were being arranged or thought over," King later said, "which gave me the feeling of learning to be an admiral."

One rainy mid-December afternoon, King returned to *Wright* after shopping in Norfolk. His executive officer met him. The CNO, Admiral Hughes, had been on the phone all afternoon asking for King. King returned the call.

Hughes was distressed. Another submarine, the USS *S-4*, had sunk after colliding with a Coast Guard ship near Provincetown on Cape Cod, Massachusetts. Some of the crew might still be alive. King was to go to their rescue.

The race began. As the weather was too foul for flying, King went by overnight train to New York City. A police escort with wailing sirens whisked him from Pennsylvania Station to the Brooklyn Navy Yard, where the battleship USS *New York* had a seaplane and pilot waiting to fly him north. Fortified with coffee and heavy clothing, King settled into the cockpit and the ship's crane hoisted the seaplane over the side. After several hours of frigid flight, King arrived at Provincetown and reported to Rear Admiral Frank H. Brumby, commanding the Atlantic Fleet submarines. To King's relief, he saw that the familiar *Falcon* and her skipper, Harry Hartley, were on the scene. The *S-4* was below, under a hundred feet of water.

There was not much time. The divers reported they had heard tapping inside the hull; some of the crewmen were apparently still alive, but their air was dwindling. Approaching darkness and worsening weather threatened further diving. In later years submarine crewmen could have escaped using the Momsen Lung or the McCann Rescue Chamber. But in 1928 there was no way for them to leave a sunken submarine.

Those on *Falcon* were desperate. Someone suggested that if the ballast tanks were undamaged perhaps *S-4* could be blown to the surface. A diver went below and attached a high-pressure air hose to the tanks. Air bubbles broke the surface: the tanks were too damaged to hold air. The gamble had failed.

The last hope was to provide fresh air to keep the men alive until something else could be tried. In that wild and stormy night two divers nearly killed themselves trying in vain to rig an air hose. Finally Brumby ordered *Falcon* into Provincetown Harbor to ride out the winter gale that lasted for days. The submarine crewmen died of suffocation.

Reporters by the dozens came to Provincetown. Their stories began to imply that the Navy somehow had been negligent, had somehow bungled trying to save the crewmen. Soon Brumby and King had the additional unaccustomed burden of press involvement during a dangerous operation. The newsmen's most insistent demand was permission to go to sea to watch. Brumby agreed upon a two-man pool and asked King how to select them. King, recalling the *S-51* salvage, recommended that the reporters decide. Then there would be no arguments.

Brumby became overwhelmed by the publicity. Conscientious to a fault, the admiral answered letters and telegrams, some so abusive that King advised Brumby to ignore them. Brumby urged reporters to be fair, to avoid distortion and sensationalism. It seemed futile. In King's mind the newsmen became adversaries pressured by editors to write whatever would sell newspapers. Truth, King concluded, was compromised. Although he sympathized with honest reporters, King came to mistrust the press in general. Months afterward, following an acrimonious press conference, King refused to shake hands with a muckraking reporter. "Why, King," Brumby exclaimed later, "if I had known it was that son-of-a-bitch, I would not have shaken hands with him either."

On Christmas Eve, Secretary of the Navy Curtis D. Wilbur and Admiral Hughes came aboard *Falcon*. The Navy had announced that everyone inside *S-4* was dead. Could diving operations continue during the winter? they asked. The consensus was that it would be too dangerous as well as pointless. No matter. Public opinion was so strong that Wilbur and Hughes decided to press on. Brumby left, giving King sole responsibility. With everyone dead, the rescue became a salvage.

People would not leave King alone. In February 1928 Moffett offered him command of the USS *Langley*, the Navy's first aircraft carrier.* "I hardly know how to reply at this time," King wrote in response. "In the first place I have been given this job of salvaging the *S-4*, which I now hope to finish 'some time in April,' but you never can tell. In the second place, developments regarding the Lexington and Saratoga [two splendid new supercarriers] commands may, in June or thereabouts, be of interest and importance to me. In the third place, I don't know when my present cruise began nor when it is supposed to end, although that really doesn't matter to me *if* I can get a good job! All in all, it looks as if I had best ask to let matters stand as they are for a time, if that can be done.

After a three-month struggle in brutal weather, King raised *S-4* with the same pontoon method used earlier with *S-51*. In late afternoon of 17 March 1928 King's flotilla shaped course for Boston with *S-4* in tow. That night a northeast gale hit. King asked his civilian pilots to take a shortcut to escape the storm. Both refused. The South Channel approach, they said, was too treacherous. "There was nothing to be done," King later said, "except to carry on and hope—and pray—that we might make it."

The seas continued to pound *S-4* and her supporting pontoons. The salvors listened helplessly to steel smashing steel, and chains grinding and snapping against the submarine's hull. Even intrepid Harry Hartley, the *Falcon* skipper, began to despair. "I told him," said King afterward, "to please not give up since the matter was on the knee of the gods, and to try to help me to be more cheerful about it."

They made it.

King returned to the *Wright* in May 1928 and a reward of a second Distinguished Service Medal. Several months later Admiral Hughes told King that he had received several votes from the most recent flag officer selection board. King was delighted, because his class would not be considered for another four years. Still, he was realistic. He was, he later said, "too young (50 years old) to be promoted at that time." Nevertheless it was reassuring that the Navy considered him a future admiral.

Shortly after King returned to *Wright*, Rear Admiral Raby went

* Old and slow, she had been converted from a collier and nicknamed the "Covered Wagon."

ashore without relief. King became the temporary Commander, Aircraft Squadrons, Atlantic. He loved it. He was a captain doing an admiral's job.

Things got even better. On 18 June Moffett recommended to the Bureau of Navigation that King take command of the USS *Lexington.* King must have been overjoyed when his orders arrived in early July. *Lexington* was brand new, the premier aviation command in the Navy. She would be King's ticket to rear admiral.

A week later the Bureau of Navigation canceled his orders. A subsequent letter from a friend in the Bureau explained that Moffett wanted King as his assistant in the Bureau of Aeronautics. Bitter and disappointed, King went to Washington in August 1928 for his first permanent duty in the Navy Department. *Lexington* would have to wait.

Moffett had erred in making King his assistant under duress. The champion and organizer of naval aviation, Moffett was energetic and resourceful, combative and yet diplomatic, and he had whipped formidable opposition to establish his bureau in 1921. Moffett was used to having his way. So was King. Arguments became inevitable and increasingly frequent. It took nine months for the showdown.

Moffett used several protégés to popularize naval aviation, including polar explorer Commander Richard E. Byrd and Lieutenant Alford J. Williams, Jr., a famous racing pilot. King resented them. Moffett's "prima donnas," he grumbled, shirking their duty as naval officers. Both King and the Bureau of Navigation agreed that they belonged on sea duty. King also believed that the Bureau of Navigation should control aviation assignments, a prerogative jealously retained by Moffett. King's opposition seemed to Moffett to smack of disloyalty.

"It seems to me you want to be chief of the Bureau," said Moffett finally. "Maybe you want me to quit so you can have my job."

"Admiral," replied King, "I request a change of duty so you can have a different assistant."

In quick time King had orders to command the Air Base at Norfolk, Virginia. It was a large and important aviation shore station, so King had by no means been banished. King marked time there for a year, waiting for sea duty.

After some months Moffett told King that *Saratoga* would be his in the summer of 1930. She was not what King wanted. He would prefer the *Lexington,* he said, because she normally would not have an admiral aboard looking over his shoulder. King got the *Lexington.*

"That was what I wanted," he later said. "I had the finest ship command in the world!"

8

Lexington

Lexington was a magnificent ship, originally intended as a battle cruiser following the First World War. The Washington Naval Treaty of 1922 had scrapped big-gun warships but allowed several aircraft carriers. The United States subsequently converted *Lexington* and her sister ship *Saratoga*,* commissioning both in late 1927.

The *Lexington* was huge, 33,000 tons and a 900-foot flight deck, a streamlined hull and 180,000-horsepower turbo-electric engines. She was fast, more than 30 knots. Her crew averaged about 2,000 men, with more than a hundred officers in the ship's company. When the aircraft squadrons came aboard another 60 or so aviators would swell the wardroom, and the crew would increase by many hundreds.

Lexington was so new and radically different that she intimidated her officers and crew. There was little experience to draw upon (save what had been learned from primitive *Langley*), and the Navy struggled to master *Lexington*'s size and complexity. Her crew was so large and diverse that Lex's senior officers frequently despaired of enforcing the organization and discipline common to other large warships. A mood of laissez-faire had grown by default, and when King took command *Lexington* was generally regarded as a loose ship.

King's reign began in June 1930. The story goes that the new captain assembled his officers, hoisted a copy of Navy Regulations, and announced that henceforth they would be obeyed. King next charged his executive officer and department heads to bring order to the amorphous crew — or else. The exec, Commander John H. Hoover (nicknamed "Genial John" because of his dour personality), suited King perfectly. A capable enforcer of King's policies, Hoover respected King but could

* Fondly nicknamed "Lex" and "Sara."

not be browbeaten. Sometimes the two men would not speak for days, yet they worked well together, each in his own domain.

King established exacting standards for his department heads. Those that faltered went under hatches. If they did not improve, King fired them. As senior officers they were supposed to know their stuff. Some did. The first lieutenant, Mahlon S. Tisdale, was a future admiral and one of the few who could win an argument with King. Those who did not measure up included retread aviators whom the Bureau of Navigation considered still fit for shipboard duty. Several who tried to serve as navigator did not survive. King threw them off the ship.

Another unfortunate pawned on King was a notorious aircraft squadron commander who had been relieved for torpedoing his own ships in a training exercise. Despite King's protests he came to *Lexington* as a department head. It was agony for the officer and the end of his career. Later someone asked King why his right hand always was more tanned than his left. "It's from standing on the wing of the bridge," King is said to have replied, "and shaking my fist at that god-damned air officer on the flight deck." King was much more tolerant of the younger officers. "I suppose he felt that an ensign didn't know much anyway," a *Lexington* officer later remarked, "and he was supposed to learn by making mistakes."

King snapped the crew into an awareness that he was their new captain by announcing the uniform for their first personnel inspection at the last moment. As each uniform was different for each division, many were embarrassed by a limited wardrobe. By the following week every man was prepared with a full sea bag. The Saturday morning inspections were invariable. Even if the ship was in a midwinter overhaul, the inspection would proceed midst snow, rain, and shipyard debris.

King transformed *Lexington* into a clean, smart, glistening man o' war. "It is probable that he inspected every compartment not less than once monthly," a former *Lexington* officer, Charles E. Earl, later said, "and King made it his business to know everything that was happening on the ship." Another officer remembered the sailors using wet rags and sand to polish the paintwork, making it look like fine enamel.

While King enforced most other regulations, he paradoxically violated uniform regulations. An officer normally wore blue service with shirt and tie in the winter and the high-collared white service in summer. Despite the ship's general cleanliness, white trousers and white shoes became scuffed on the ladders. King solved the problem by prescribing a working uniform of white jacket, blue trousers, and black shoes. "Our Russian uniform," the officers gibed, but the laundry bills went down.

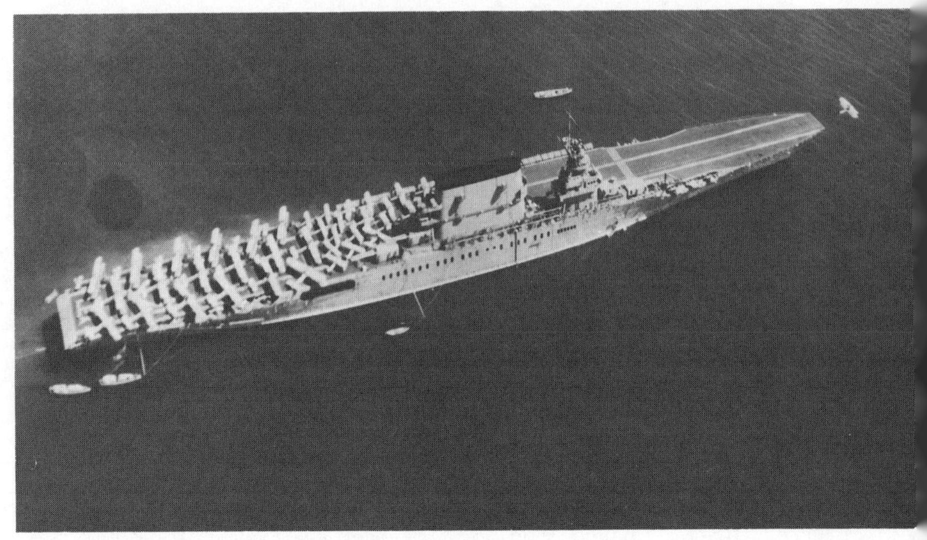

USS *Lexington.* Note aircraft taking off from the bow even though the carrier is anchored. (Courtesy Walter Muir Whitehill)

King and his exec, John H. Hoove
(Courtesy Ernest J. King, Jr.)

Lexington had been commissioned but two-and-one-half years when King had taken command, so doctrine was still largely experimental. King gave himself six months to learn all he could about carrier operations — he claimed it was all he needed to master any new job.

The relationship between the captain of a carrier and the commanding officers of his embarked aircraft squadrons was contentious and ill defined. The squadron skippers resented being told how to fly and often regarded the carrier as no more than a temporary airfield for their convenience. Such attitudes were anathema to King. His first priority was to subdue the semi-independent squadrons assigned to *Lexington.* King began by inspecting them at their headquarters at North Island, San Diego, before they even came aboard. They were a mess, said King. Then the ultimatum. The squadrons would be under *his* command and would conform to *his* standards of smartness and discipline. Their carefree attitude and ragtag appearance at North Island would not be tolerated aboard the *Lexington.*

Four squadrons of sixty-five planes embarked in February 1931. King exerted his authority immediately. Each aviator, King ordered, would thoroughly inspect his aircraft both before and after every flight. The aviators balked. "Some few of these aviators," King later said, "seemed to be what I came to call the 'gentlemen jockeys' who thought that they had only to take off and later land, and then their jobs were over." King "kept hammering" that he was trying to save their necks. In his mind the carrier pilots were too cocky and given to unnecessary risks. He prevailed, of course. "They still had to do what I said."

Once at sea *Lexington* would be expected to test and develop new tactics and procedures. "King was always eager to try anything new," remembered Hoover. But it would be hell to work for him. Every operation would have to be done on the double. "Still, he got results," Hoover later said. "He always did."

Fleet Problem XII off Panama provided King's first chance to operate his squadrons. It got off to a bad start. The carrier division commander, Rear Admiral Joseph M. Reeves, first sent King on a useless chase toward the Galápagos Islands. King fumed. He was missing the main action by charging toward the equator. Some did not mind. Below decks the delighted shellbacks prepared to initiate the pollywogs. Just short of the equator *Lexington* suddenly wheeled about and thundered northward. The shellbacks were furious. Could not King have steamed a few more miles south before reversing course?

Crossing the line and Neptune's Court could be damned. Just as

King had predicted, his scouts had reported empty ocean at the Galápagos. The enemy was to the north. At midday a dirigible reported an enemy carrier, the USS *Langley*, to the northeast. King increased speed to close the distance and planned his attack. The usual practice was to launch scouts to locate the target. After they had made contact, bombers and torpedo planes would follow. But that way would take too long; it would soon be dark. King made a risky decision to launch everything at once, hoping to find and attack *Langley* in time to recover his aircraft before sunset, as required by fleet regulations. *Lexington* turned into the wind and launched forty-six aircraft.

As *Lexington* receded behind them the pilots lost their only visual reference. Navigation over the featureless ocean was crude: a small plotting board on the pilot's knee, a magnetic compass, an estimate of the wind, and guesswork. Even if the pilots found *Langley* their problem was not alleviated. They still had to get back. *Lexington* was a moving airfield tough to find in the gathering darkness. Although a few aircraft carried crude radios, King had imposed radio silence. Many things could go wrong. Many things did.

The scouting squadron returned on schedule. They had seen neither *Langley* nor the attack aircraft whom they had preceded. More time passed. King was about to lose thirty-one aircraft on his first big operation. He tried everything to find them, including radio, smoke, and searchlights. Just before dark the aircraft came into view. The emergency still was not over, for the aviators never before had landed on a carrier at night. That night they did. The flight commander went to the bridge. "Where in the hell have you been?" asked King.

It had been a near thing. The aviators blamed King. Another few minutes and they all would have crashed at sea for lack of fuel. The *Lexington*, they said, was not where she was supposed to have been. "King was loud and profane in his declaration that the plane commanders had misunderstood his briefing," said one of the aviators, Peter A. Wyckoff, afterward. "Everyone was out of step but him!"

The aviators went to bed, but King went sleepless to carry on his war. In the morning he launched again, this time against an enemy cruiser. As a follow-up King told his communications officer to order two nearby cruisers to the attack.

"Captain, you can't do that," said the communicator. "There's an *admiral* in one of those cruisers."

"Goddammit," snapped King. "Don't you think I know what I'm doing?"

The order went out. The two cruisers went straightway toward the enemy.

King's aircraft continued to land, launch, and reattack throughout the remainder of the day, experimenting with tactics for future wars. One such innovation was an airborne combat air patrol circling overhead to protect *Lexington* from enemy air attacks. Escort ships dashed to and fro in response to King's flashing light and flaghoist. It was a magnificent show. That night it was over. "*Lexington* entered Panama Harbor ready to carry on with anything that had to be done," King proudly said afterward.

A visiting journalist, too nervous earlier to watch the night landings, later had asked King about his feelings when the planes had been missing. "I was too busy to worry about how I felt," replied King. "What I had to do was just to arrange how to get those damned planes back aboard."

Another question. How was King after so little sleep and the pressure of the fleet problem? "I've been up since dawn," said King, "and I expect to carry on throughout the day. I might get some little sleep tonight, but it is the way of the Navy to do whatever has to be done. In due time the fleet problem will pass, as everything will pass."

Despite frustrations, King never let up driving his ship and aircraft. One morning *Lexington* headed into the wind for a launch that would begin an important fleet problem. There was immediate trouble. The second plane at the head of the line could not start its engine, blocking the flight deck. All the aircraft would have to be respotted, an ordeal that would delay King's cherished surprise attack. The crew panicked. Relays of sweating sailors frantically cranked the engine while squadron officers yelled advice to the pilot.

"King's boiling point, which was normally low, early in this mess had become very manifest to all hands on board," said the pilot, Fitzhugh Lee, years later. "It ended up with King coming down and personally cranking up the airplane to show us how it could be done, and still it didn't start. We had to unscramble all the airplanes, and the sun was well up when the first plane took off."

Bewildering things could go wrong before King's eyes. A flight of aircraft had just landed after a smoke screen exercise, the still smoking pots strapped beneath their wings. The ventilation system sucked the fumes inside the ship, provoking complaints to the bridge from below.

"Get those smoke pots overboard," ordered King, but the flight deck crew failed to get the message. The complaints became more insistent.

Suddenly King grabbed his junior watch officer, a 210-pound football player, and flung him around. "Goddammit," said King. "You get down on deck and personally throw those pots overboard." The officer, Oscar W. Hagberg, ran to the flight deck. "By this time quite a few men were disposing of the pots," he later said. "I went over among them and spurred them on, meanwhile putting my hand on most of the pots in an assisting gesture — personally disposing of the pots as ordered."

Everyone topside knew that King was always watching; the public address system endlessly summoned offenders to the bridge. Other times King simply yelled. "He didn't need a megaphone," recalled one *Lexington* officer, Kleber H. Masterson. "He'd just stand on the edge of that bridge, and they could hear him from one end to the other of the flight deck, even in a high wind, because he could really bellow when he was mad."

Few could withstand King. Those who did could earn his respect. A torpedo plane one day landed in the after starboard gun gallery. The pilot was summoned to the bridge, his squadron commanding officer, John J. Ballentine, one step ahead.

"Ballentine," asked King, "what is wrong with your pilots?"

"Nothing," replied Ballentine. "Your ship is not into the wind, and until it is, I will not let any more of my pilots land."

Ballentine left the bridge; King adjusted *Lexington*'s course. When King was promoted to flag rank and returned to sea, Ballentine became his operations officer.

King was once proven wrong when *Lexington* carried extra aircraft. After considerable effort the flight deck officer had squeezed them as far aft as possible to allow adequate takeoff distance. King decided that the lead plane was still too near the bow and ordered Air Control to try again. The flight deck officer refused. He had used all available space — nothing more could be done, he said, and there was enough deck to take off.

"Goddamn farmers," snarled King. "I'll show them." King stomped down to the flight deck and took charge. Sailors pushed and shoved the aircraft. When King had finished he had lost ten feet.

King returned to the bridge. "Launch aircraft," he commanded. The lead plane got airborne without difficulty.

Destroyer captains dreaded working with *Lexington*, especially when they had to refuel, a procedure King begrudged as meaning time lost from flight operations. After a missed approach a destroyer finally settled alongside, then sent a signal. "Good morning, captain."

King read the message and crumpled it in his hand. "Good morning, hell," he grumbled. He was even more nettled when they asked for ice cream. In his day sailors had been content with corned beef and hardtack.

Another destroyer once came alongside incorrectly because her captain had not read the most current instructions. A *Lexington* officer, Gerald F. Bogan, passed them across by highline. King then ordered the skipper to break off, read the instructions, and try again.

"You shouldn't have bawled him out," Bogan later said. "He didn't have those instructions before he came alongside the first time."

"I don't care how good they are," King replied. "Unless they get a kick in the ass every six weeks, they slack off."

A destroyer once maneuvered inexplicably after King had ordered her to take station on his port bow. King told a watch officer to find out what the destroyer was doing. Someone quickly composed a message and handed it to King.

> YOUR MOVEMENTS NOT UNDERSTOOD. REPORT REASON COURSE CHANGES AND LOCATION NEW STATION YOU ARE MANEUVERING TO REACH.

King grabbed a pencil, slashed across the draft, then wrote,

> WHERE ARE YOU GOING?

King tolerated the destroyers because they were lifeguards for aviators crashing at sea. One dark and stormy night a destroyer retrieved a pilot and reported the rescue to *Lexington.* The flight operations continued. Another plane crashed. This time the destroyer not only saved the crew but salvaged the plane as well. The destroyer captain, John L. McCrea, by now hoped for a "well done." Instead he got a curt order to cancel night exercises and return to port. Next day McCrea met King ashore. "Hello, John," said King. It was the first time King had ever addressed him by his first name. The rescues were never mentioned during the subsequent quarter-century of their close personal contact.

King conned *Lexington* with imperious disdain for nearby ships. With the Secretary of the Navy aboard, King arrogantly disregarded the rules of the road in order to show off *Lexington*'s speed and maneuverability — as well as his own shiphandling. A year later *Lexington* was operating with the fleet off Long Beach. At day's end the Commander in Chief, U.S. Fleet, hoisted the signal, "Ships proceed independently to assigned anchorages." Conforming with custom, the warships fell in astern of the senior flagship to steam leisurely homeward. Except *Lexington.* Still recovering aircraft, the carrier roared through the formation, scattering ships right and left, then disappeared over the horizon. When the fleet arrived in Long Beach, *Lexington* was at anchor flying King's absentee pennant. The flag officers were enraged.

Next day Admiral Reeves called King on the carpet. King resorted to his sea-lawyer tactics. "The signal said to proceed independently," King argued, "so I did."

"When the Commander in Chief issues an operation order," said Reeves, "he doesn't have to include in it the rules of etiquette at sea."

King apologized and promised it would not happen again.

Not that King was without a sense of propriety. One evening he departed in his gig to attend a boxing match aboard a nearby battleship. When King arrived on the quarterdeck he was properly recognized by the OOD. Then he waited for the host captain to welcome him aboard. No one arrived. King turned to the OOD.

"Call my gig alongside."

King returned to the *Lexington.*

Once in port, King sought entertainment. "I liked parties, lots of them," he once said. "Play time," he called it. It was his way of relaxing, of relieving the tension created by the responsibility of command. The longer King had to remain at sea between parties, the more disagreeable he became.

His stamina was astounding. After Fleet Problem XII in Panama, King had been days without sleep, yet the moment *Lexington* anchored, his gig splashed and sped him ashore. King parked in the back lounge of Marie Kelly's Ritz Bar, buying drinks for his officers while nursing his private bottle of scotch. After a time an officer might excuse himself. "Certainly," King would say. "Stir around and have fun. We go back to work in a couple of days."

At dawn King returned to his gig with Hoover in tow, picked up several junior officers at the landing, and proceeded to the ship. It was a long ride. King was alert and chatted amiably; Hoover tried to stay awake.

"This comedy went on the whole time," recalled one of the passengers, Robert A. Heinlein. "I felt sorry for Hoover. If I fell asleep, only my pride would suffer; the Captain would neither mention it nor hold it against me. But Hoover had face to maintain, being in the presence of both his boss and his juniors. He managed — just barely."

Despite Prohibition, most *Lexington* officers stashed liquor in their staterooms. At first they wondered what King's attitude would be. When *Lexington* arrived in San Francisco very early in his command, King invited some junior officers to join him in his gig. They ended up at a party, and soon King pulled a hip flask from his back pocket and poured drinks. "This word soon got around," said one of the young officers.

Such fraternizing created problems. Aboard ship King was stern, aloof, and austere. Ashore he was one of the boys and was nicknamed "Uncle Ernie." It was inevitable that some of King's officers, emboldened by drink, would become insulting, belligerent, or maudlin toward their captain. Regardless of who said what to him, however (and there were some extreme cases), King never retaliated, much to the relief of terrified junior officers who, when sober, realized their indiscretions of the night before.

"You ought to be very suspicious of anyone who won't take a drink or doesn't like women," King once told a friend. King's interest in women was common knowledge aboard *Lexington*. Sometimes it was innocent, as when he danced and socialized with officers' wives. Women liked his virility. And King had a way of talking that made a woman feel that she was very special, that he understood her, and that he appreciated and admired her wit and her beauty. *She* became the focus of his attention.

But King could also become downright lecherous. Women avoided sitting near him at dinner parties because his hands were too often beneath the table. King's interest in women led him into a number of extramarital affairs. Did Mattie know? No one could tell. King perhaps thought that he was discreet, but his reputation was notorious.

At home King was a family man. A daughter would customarily drive him from the fleet landing to their home in Long Beach, where Mattie reigned as the family matriarch. "Mrs. King was a gracious and motherly hostess to all the junior officers' wives," recalled a *Lexington* officer, James A. Morrison. Other junior officers were, with Mattie's encouragement, actively dating the King daughters.

Some of the girls had already married. Elizabeth had been the first, in the spring of 1927. On the day of the wedding she had been nervous, but her father had been serene. Elizabeth always was grateful for the way he got her through the ceremony. He became, indeed, an expert at these rites, eventually escorting five of his daughters to the altar.

Mattie herself was aging. There had been great excitement in the family when she finally had bobbed her hair, but that could not disguise the fact that she was heavier now. Still, her young visitors regarded her as a handsome woman who had been a beauty in her day, and her daughters obviously had inherited her features.

When the ship returned after a long absence, King and Mattie took one of their periodic vacations into the country. After driving through Yosemite they decided to explore the Mojave Desert. "Mattie," he said, "let's go so far out that we can't see any buildings, but just the desert and the sky and the mountains."

Mattie was not that interested, so instead they simply walked a few hundred yards off the desert highway. It seemed then — at least momentarily — that they were alone in the wilderness. The air had a pristine freshness which King loved, and he wanted to share his euphoria with Mattie. "Yes, Ernest," she finally said, "I must agree that the desert air has a certain tang." Then they returned to their car. "We arrived in Long Beach before dark," King later reminisced, "thinking and believing that this trip had been rather a good leave."

King commanded *Lexington* during the first years of the Depression, when appropriations were austere and Navy morale low. King gave his men little opportunity to think about such things. They were too busy. King was at war. "The *Lexington*," King later said, "was ready to go into battle." He intended that *Lexington* would "serve notice to the people of the United States that the Navy always has been ready to work and fight and play."

War scares with Japan were reason to be alert. After the Japanese invaded Manchuria, *Lexington* sped into San Francisco under tight security, loaded planes and ammunition, then headed toward Hawaii. The alarm subsided, but *Lexington* had been ready.

She had also been ready earlier, in late March 1931, for a different kind of emergency. Anchored in Guantánamo Bay following a fleet exercise, King received orders on short notice to proceed at best speed to Managua, Nicaragua. Upon arrival he was to fly relief supplies ashore to aid earthquake victims. King left harbor the minute enough steam was raised to make steerageway. A boatload of newsreel cameramen chased *Lexington* across the anchorage, but King refused to stop. However, *Lexington* did not yet have enough boilers on the line to outrun their boat. King's profanity filled the air as the cameramen scrambled aboard.

Lexington's great engines increased to full power, consuming boiler water in such quantity that King secured the showers. As *Lexington* was scheduled for an admiral's inspection, the sailors still drew buckets of water to scrub paintwork. King did not feel he had to explain the apparent contradiction. It was certainly no hardship to go without bathing — and *Lexington* would be kept clean regardless of extraordinary circumstances.

When within range of Managua, King launched his first flight with orders to return immediately. The pilots flew the dangerous relief mission through clouds over high mountains. The flight commander, disregarding orders, decided to remain overnight in Managua because of worsening weather and delays in refueling. At noon the next day the overdue flight returned. As the flight commander's plane taxied past the bridge, King leaned over the bulwark with a megaphone. His voice roared above the engines: "Smith, go to your room!"

To emphasize that aviators were naval officers first, King made the pilots stand bridge watches and practice celestial navigation. When they did fly, King pushed them to the limit. To his credit, he never had a fatality. But there were close calls. One aviator ran out of gas just before landing and ditched astern of *Lexington*. The ship circled, came alongside the still-floating aircraft, and hoisted it and the pilot aboard. The pilot went to the bridge to face King. "The next time you decide to land in the water," said King, "do it ahead of the ship so I won't have to turn around to pick you up."

Another aviator survived a spectacular flight-deck crash with no more than a broken nose. As he climbed down on shaky legs from his demolished aircraft, the loudspeaker blared the inevitable summons. Blood streaming down his face, the pilot stood at attention and saluted King. King stared at the pilot, then allowed a flickering smile to dart across his face. "That was the funniest thing I've ever seen," said King.

King lived on the bridge but rarely took the conn. The atmosphere hummed with tension, punctuated by outbursts from King. He spoke, recalled Bob Heinlein, with a voice of command that was instinctively obeyed. One night Heinlein, who had yet to meet King, was standing watch on the bridge. A voice, just loud enough to be heard, came out of the darkness.

"Get out of my way."

Heinlein leaped to stand aside for the new captain.

If something went wrong, King's voice rose and his arms flailed like a windmill. Once in exasperation he even grabbed the steering wheel when the OOD failed to react. Praise was given grudgingly and then only in private. Censure was swift, devastating, and before a cloud of witnesses. "The object of his wrath was unlikely to forget the occasion," recalled one officer, "nor would anyone else within earshot."

Although King lost his temper he rarely lost his self-control. No one has recalled his endangering the *Lexington*. And King was fair — in his own way. "I believe he was probably fair so long as he achieved the results he personally felt he had a right to expect," said Charles Earl in retrospect. "If one did his job properly and conscientiously, it is likely that he would never get into trouble, but the path was very narrow." Under King the fit survived and developed into some of the Navy's finest captains and admirals. The unfit were eliminated.

King could be extraordinarily kind to his junior officers. He counseled them and wrote glowing endorsements when his best ones requested special assignments. In those days a naval officer rarely was shown his fitness report, but every officer under King could read his, could discuss it with King if he desired, and so knew exactly where he stood. It was King's system of reward, reflected where it counted the most.

King treated many of his officers like sons. The *Lexington* football coach, former Annapolis star Oscar Hagberg, is one example. In that era, fleet athletic competition was a serious matter. King fervently wanted to beat *Saratoga* and rooted from the sidelines. The game ended in a frustrating scoreless tie. King entered the dressing room and went to the young officer-coach. "Come with me," said King. They walked to King's car and got inside.

"Are you tired?" asked King.

"Yes," replied Hagberg. "I am tired, disgusted, and banged up from the game."

They went to King's home and sat quietly over drinks. "I gathered that he, too, was disappointed in the game," Hagberg later said, "but he appreciated my efforts."

King, like an indulgent father, tolerated the excesses of youth. Gambling was rife in the junior officers' mess, contrary to all regulations, yet King never interfered. If he was inspecting he gave fair warning, and the poker chips, crap tables, and roulette wheels were out of sight when King entered.

While *Lexington* was in Bremerton for overhaul, a number of the bachelor officers rented a secluded farmhouse, which became notorious for its debauchery. The parents of two Seattle debutantes discovered that their daughters had stayed there for over a week and demanded that King act. King investigated and decided to do nothing. "So King quenched it," said a *Lexington* officer afterward, "kept it from becoming an open scandal." King did not punish the officers, although they had violated Prohibition laws as well as state blue laws. "But these do not in themselves affect an officer's professional fitness to tread a quarterdeck or bridge," reasoned the *Lexington* officer.

King treated his sailors with paternalism of another sort. During reenlistment ceremonies he reminded them that the way of the naval service was that you could argue for hours but in due time you had to obey orders. Just before the sailor recited the enlistment oath, King would issue a final warning. "After you have taken the oath," King would say, "you must understand that you will have to do what you are told to do whether you like it or not — and to go where you will be sent whether you like it or not — and to work at whatever you are given to do. Now, if you understand these things, please hold your hand on 'the Book' and repeat after me . . ."

King's closest contact with sailors was during captain's mast. "Men were frequently so taken by his evidently sincere interest in their problems," said one officer, Francis S. Stich, later, "that they often blurted out secrets that their division officers would much rather have kept hidden." King's initial punishments often were severe, but he invariably reduced them afterward. "I disliked being forced to see him right after he had held mast," remembered one of King's administrative officers. "It was painful to me to see how hard he took it. No loss of sleep, no grueling physical ordeal, ever seemed to affect him. But holding mast — punishing his own children — always wrung him out."

When King was about to leave *Lexington* the officers and crew treated him to a magnificent farewell party, and King was reduced to tears when he finally relinquished command after two years.

Lexington had been King's final test for future flag rank. The opinion of his superiors was that King had done well. His ship, they reported, was exceptionally clean and well maintained. King's service record became filled with letters commending *Lexington*'s superlative performance (although Admiral Reeves marked King down for tact and cooperation). Both Reeves and Rear Admiral Harry E. Yarnell recommended that King be promoted to rear admiral.

9

The New Admiral

REAR AMIRAL STEPHEN B. LUCE and Captain Alfred Thayer Mahan had established the Naval War College in the late nineteenth century to inspire naval officers to study the broader aspects of war, strategy, and tactics. Many senior officers, mistrusting formal education ashore, had opposed the college. Sea duty, they advocated, was the best method of professional development. Nevertheless, the college survived and grew in prestige. Students read, wrote research papers, attended lectures, and played war games — all with a view of preparing themselves for high command and eventual flag rank. Thus it became de rigueur for aspiring naval officers to attend the ten-month course, offered in a relaxed academic atmosphere free of administrative demands or phones ringing in the night.

King had always wanted to attend the college, but an assignment there had never materialized. When he left *Lexington* the time finally seemed propitious. It was a good place to wait until the next selection board convened, and King genuinely wanted to study the art of war without distraction. He also wanted to leave nothing to chance when it was time for promotion. A college certificate would provide that extra plus. The Bureau of Navigation obliged with orders to Newport.

King attacked his studies in August 1932 with his typical zeal, in contrast to some others who regarded assignment to the college as a time to rest. King's prolific solutions to strategic and tactical problems represented an enormous amount of study, work, detail, and thought. Such writing had become second nature after thirty years of experience in the fleet.

King's magnum opus was his thesis, entitled "The Influence of the National Policy on the Strategy of a War." The title was not original; all students had the same subject, and they tended to use the same bibliography and to write similar papers. King's paper certainly reflected the then current naval attitudes: to wit, Japan was America's most likely enemy and America would be unprepared for war.

Most of King's paper was pedantic, but occasionally he expressed feelings about American society and government. "Historically," he began, "despite Washington's (and others) experienced and cogent advice to make due preparations for war it is traditional (and habitual) for us to be inadequately prepared. This is the combined result of a number of factors, the character of which is here only indicated: democracy, which tends to make everyone believe he knows it all; the preponderance (inherent in democracy) of people whose real interest is in their own welfare as individuals; the glorification of our victories in war and the corresponding ignorance of our defeats (and disgraces) and of their basic causes; the inability of the average individual (the man in the street) to understand the interplay of cause and effect not only in foreign but in domestic affairs, as well as his lack of interest in such matters."

Written during the 1932 presidential elections, King's paper simplistically defined Republicans and Democrats as "conservatives and radicals." In King's mind, democracies "put a premium on mediocrity and tend to emphasize the defects of the electorate, already mentioned." Then, after condemning both the electorate and their representatives for pork-barrel politics, he wrote, "When to these attitudes are added our national altruism, our belief in our own capacity to do well at anything we undertake, together with a child-like trust and faith in our destiny, we appear unable to appreciate preparedness [for war] even when, as individuals, we carry fire insurance on our houses and collision insurance on our cars."

King concluded his paper by damning the pacifism that was inhibiting the readiness of the United States Navy for war. "In short," he wrote, "we can expect to become engaged in a war with the initial handicap of inadequate 'ways and means,' to expend much blood and treasure to overcome this handicap (if we can finally overcome it) and gain the victory. We may take what consolation we can from the fact that we have always done this and have, so far, been fortunate in the outcome."

The flag selection board convened in mid-November 1932 to consider the captains in the Naval Academy Class of 1900. King had heard that the top members of his Class of 1901 might be considered for early promotion, but he was fatalistic. Lightning might strike, but his class was not due until 1933. "So I didn't worry," he later wrote. "What was the use?"

So King waited. One day, at lunch, he was called to the phone. It was Captain Charles R. Train of the Class of 1900.

"I've been selected for admiral," said Train.

King responded with appropriate congratulations.

"Well," said Train, "aren't you interested in the other names on the list?"

King was noncommittal.

"You," Train finally said, "are the last man on the list."

After thirty-five years of relentless striving, twenty-two of them at sea, King had made it. He had just passed his fifty-fourth birthday. He could look forward to ten years of service as a flag officer before mandatory retirement. For some, selection to rear admiral was a culmination. To King, it was a beginning. "Some day," said King to his favorite Newport bartender, "I am going to be the Chief of Naval Operations."

New rear admirals normally went to shore duty for seasoning before being allowed to fly their flags at sea. As King wanted to remain in aviation, he concluded that the best job would be Chief of the Bureau of Aeronautics. He knew it would be available because Moffett had told King that he intended to retire in the summer of 1933. King had replied that he would like to be Moffett's relief. Moffett was evasive; rumor had it that he favored Captain John H. Towers, the pioneer naval aviator. The best Moffett would do was a promise not to oppose King.

Reasoning "that you never get a job unless you ask for it," King wrote to influential people in Washington, enclosing a résumé for good measure. The replies generally were friendly but noncommittal. There were too many uncertainties. Franklin D. Roosevelt would soon become the new President, he would bring in a new Secretary of the Navy, and no one could predict whom they would choose to head the bureau. The issue was forced when Moffett died in the crash of the dirigible *Akron* on 4 April 1933, a month after FDR's inaugural. King went to Washington for the funeral and — more to the point — to lobby to become Moffett's replacement.

King's friends already had been working for him, probably without his knowledge. Windor R. Harris, whom King had known for several years, was managing editor of the Norfolk *Virginian-Pilot*. On 15 March 1933 Harris wrote to the new President recommending King to head the bureau. Not coincidentally, Senator Harry F. Byrd of Virginia wrote a similar letter to the President on 23 March. The new Secretary of the Navy, Claude A. Swanson, also had been both a senator and the governor of Virginia, so it is reasonable to assume that Harris spoke to him as well.

Quite unaware of these events, King called on the CNO, Admiral William V. Pratt, following Moffett's funeral. As King proclaimed his qualifications, Pratt seemed impressed. He put King in an adjacent room to write a letter to the Secretary of the Navy. Next he sent King to Swanson (whom King knew slightly), followed by calls on several key senators and representatives. "After having done that," King later said, "it seemed to me the best thing to do was to get out of town and wait for the result."

Pratt endorsed King's letter and sent it on to Swanson. "Captain King has certain characteristics which make him an outstanding officer," wrote Pratt.

"(a) He is highly intelligent.
(b) He is extremely active and energetic.
(c) He is very forceful.
(d) He is a flyer and pilot.
(e) He is a man of great decision of character.
(f) He is a good strategist and tactician.
(g) He is not as tactful as some men but he is very direct.
(h) He is trustworthy.
(i) He is due for promotion to the position of Rear Admiral."

Although King had left with the impression that he had won Pratt's support, Pratt had only been trying to be fair. Ostensibly his endorsement had been commendatory, but King had been only Pratt's fourth choice, after Rear Admirals Joseph W. Reeves, Harry E. Yarnell, and John Halligan.

Less than a week later Swanson recommended King to FDR.* The President concurred. King received the news in a telegram from Windor Harris. A flood of congratulatory letters and telegrams began the next day. Towers never had a chance.

"After I got that appointment," said King years later, "I should think that at least a dozen people came to see me telling what they, themselves, had done to make sure that I'd get the job. . . . I had no way to tell whether they were telling the exact truth or trying to help themselves just as people usually do!"

The Bureau of Aeronautics was twelve years old when King became its second chief in April 1933. The bureau occupied two floors of one

* Swanson later told King he had gotten the job because Swanson had been impressed by his salvaging of *S-51* and *S-4*—which Pratt had not even mentioned.

wing of the Navy Department headquarters on Constitution Avenue, an ugly, blocky building constructed on the Washington Mall during the First World War.* The staff comprised about fifty naval officers and a hundred civilians. It was a grim period for naval aviation owing to the hardships of the Depression. Naval officers had taken a 15 percent pay cut, but at least they were employed. Officers in Washington wore civilian clothes in order to remain inconspicuous—too many people wanted to lower federal expenditures by further reducing naval appropriations.

King was without experience on Capitol Hill, compounding his problems with a new Congress, a new Administration, and a depression that people at first hoped to alleviate by spending less rather than by spending more. By law the Navy was restricted to a thousand aircraft, and the New Deal Congress was reluctant to authorize any additional money for the new carrier *Ranger*, due to be commissioned in 1934. Congress also sought to economize by lowering flight pay; one of King's first tasks was to defend the system before Chairman Carl Vinson's House Naval Affairs Committee.

King himself was fatalistic about the chronic shortage of money, after years of peacetime austerity. After King had tried to justify flight pay retention, Vinson asked about the effect of a pay cut on aviation morale. "I do not wish to be thought facetious, Mr. Chairman," said King, "but to be perfectly straightforward, as I wish to be, we are becoming so accustomed to these matters that I really think we could muster up another grin and bear it."

King's naïveté became apparent in his first appearance before Congressman William A. Ayers's appropriations subcommittee. King could not understand why such an experienced legislator asked such rudimentary questions. When King's annoyance showed, Ayers recessed the hearings. Calling King aside, Ayers explained that his questions were intended to educate committee members unfamiliar with the Navy. King agreed to be patient.

One of the most controversial public issues of the day was the charge that unscrupulous aircraft manufacturers were making excess profits while millions were unemployed. As one of the aviation industry's largest customers, King was summoned before Ayers's subcommittee to explain his bureau's contractual relationship with Pratt and Whitney. The company was the sole source for an aircraft engine that the Navy desperately needed. The engine was also popular with commercial aviation companies, so the Navy had to compete for the limited supply. King's

* Known as "Main Navy," since demolished under order of President Nixon.

The Chief of the Bureau of Aeronautics visits the Naval Air Station, San Diego, October 1933. Left to right: Rear Admiral A. W. Johnson, King, Hoover, and Rear Admiral John Halligan (National Archives 80-G-416403)

staff — especially Arthur W. Radford — pleaded with him not to volunteer information and simply to answer questions; a careless public statement could embarrass Pratt and Whitney. As retaliation the company might refuse to sell to the Navy.

King disregarded his staff's advice and decided to follow his instinct of speaking forthrightly, regardless of the consequences. In late 1933 he sat once again before the Ayers subcommittee. Ayers began the questioning. Is it true, he asked King, that aircraft engine manufacturers were making profits of 45 percent?

"I have a general statement to make on that," replied King. The floodgates opened. King's testimony precipitated a sensational congressional investigation of Pratt and Whitney. Among the repercussions was a provision in the Vinson-Trammel Bill of 27 March 1934 that limited aviation industry net profits to 10 percent. Relations between the company and King's bureau became strained, but the threat of losing the supply of engines apparently never materialized.

King improved slightly as a committee witness during his three-year tenure as chief of the bureau. He learned the rules but suffered from awkward public speaking. His appearances on Capitol Hill must have been an ordeal. He controlled his temper despite occasional flare-ups with hostile members of Congress. Normally he was respectful and responsive, was well briefed on the matters before the various committees, and worked well in private with Vinson. By such means King successfully obtained those appropriations necessary to keep naval aviation alive during those economically depressed years.

Within the Navy Department itself King learned to cope with the bureaucracy. He used his skill as an administrator to husband his resources. There were feuds with the Bureau of Ordnance over money, but he worked well with Rear Admiral William D. Leahy, the Chief of the Bureau of Navigation. Together they established the Naval Aviation Cadet program, recruiting college graduates to augment the inadequate numbers of Naval Academy aviators. Secretary Swanson was usually too ill to become involved with the bureau, although he and King were on good terms. On the other hand, King warred with the CNO, Admiral William H. Standley. (Their relationship grew increasingly sour and acrimonious.) King apparently rarely met with President Roosevelt, despite FDR's great interest in the Navy Department.

Promotions had so stagnated during the Depression that most of the bureau's officers were stuck as lieutenants and lieutenant commanders. But they were among the finest aviators in the Navy, exercising responsibility far beyond their nominal rank. Many later became famous admirals, among them Radford, Marc A. Mitscher, Donald Duncan, and Felix B. Stump. It was a time of experimentation and innovation, and of discovering new and better ways to design and build naval aircraft. King reflected the spirit of that era. "I was always trying something," he later said. Naval aviation progressed despite the Depression.

"I had a proper ambition to get to the top," King once wrote, "either Commander in Chief of the United States Fleet or even to become Chief of Naval Operations." Three years in the bureau was the limit, he reasoned, for he needed to fly his flag at sea to move ahead. Secretary Swanson, a perpetual invalid, wanted King to remain for a normal four-year tour to support him in running the Navy Department. King insisted that he had to leave.

There were only two seagoing billets available for aviation flag officers: Commander, Aircraft, Battle Force, a vice admiral who commanded the Navy's four carriers and their aircraft squadrons; and Commander,

Aircraft, Base Force, a rear admiral who commanded the Navy's seaplane patrol squadrons. King had a great advantage because he was the only flag aviator. His only competitors, seven aviation observer flag officers, were nearing retirement.

Well before King was scheduled to leave the bureau in June 1936, he had campaigned in the Navy Department for the three-star Battle Force assignment, whose incumbent was Vice Admiral Frederick J. Horne, an aviation observer with a year in the job. King was at first optimistic, but he was not among friends. With Swanson incapacitated, Standley became the acting secretary. His grudge against King was shared by King's classmate, Rear Admiral Adolphus Andrews, the Chief of the Bureau of Navigation. The Class of 1901 had long before ostracized Andrews because of his unscrupulous ambition and his shameless courting of powerful politicians, especially Presidents. Andrews had no intention of allowing King to get three stars before he did.

The President reserved final approval of flag officer assignments. The Navy had been his private domain since he had been Assistant Secretary of the Navy during Woodrow Wilson's administration. Roosevelt maintained a well-worn Naval Register and could comment on the merits and deficiencies of nearly every senior officer in the service. "Some were remembered favorably," wrote historian Robert G. Albion, "a few unfavorably, and some, who had not happened to be around the Department in his time, were . . . not remembered at all."

Normally the Navy Department nominated a "slate" of perhaps three candidates for each flag vacancy, expecting Roosevelt to make the final selection. Usually he picked those he knew best. At times Roosevelt selected a personal favorite, even though the officer might not have been nominated. The President was cool toward strangers, no matter how well qualified.

So King had a disadvantage. He never had been within the President's inner, intimate circle, Standley and Andrews opposed him, and Swanson was too sick to lend support. King received the disappointing news that it was contrary to departmental "policy" to give a rear admiral a vice admiral's billet for his first sea assignment. "It was a view in which I could not but acquiesce," wrote a disgruntled King.

And so, essentially by default, King received orders to the Navy's only other aviation flag sea assignment. Commander, Aircraft, Base Force, commanded perhaps a dozen squadrons of land- and sea-based patrol planes, totaling more than a hundred aircraft, located variously at San Diego, Seattle, Honolulu, and Panama. King had a special interest in patrol seaplanes; his bureau had developed the prototype Consolidated PBY

"Catalina," one of the most famous aircraft of the Second World War. The first production models were just entering service. Lieutenant Commander Paul E. Pihl had supervised the aircraft's design and procurement at the bureau, so King brought him along to integrate the new Catalinas into King's patrol squadrons. Most of the remainder of King's staff, some dozen others, had been his choices as well. Among them was his chief of staff, Charles A. ("Baldy") Pownall, later an important flag officer during the Second World War, and John J. Ballentine, the intrepid squadron commander from the *Lexington.*

Fifty years earlier Alfred Thayer Mahan had written a passage that presaged King's philosophy of command in those last years of peace. By their very nature, wrote Mahan, democracies are rarely prepared for war. He used as an example the victory of the French and Spanish fleet over the Royal Navy in the 1744 Battle of Toulon. The British naval officers, said Mahan, had lost the fight by their ineptness. "There is not in modern naval history," wrote Mahan, "a more striking warning to the officers of every era, than this battle of Toulon. Coming as it did after a generation of comparative naval inactivity, it tried men's reputations by fire. The lesson, in the judgment of the author, is the danger of disgraceful failure to men who have neglected to keep themselves prepared, not only in knowledge of their profession, but in the sentiment of what war requires. The average man is not a coward; but neither is he endowed by nature only with the rare faculty of seizing intuitively the proper course at a given moment. He gains it, some more, some less, by experience or by reflection. If both have been lacking to him, indecision will follow; either from not knowing what to do, or from failure to realize that utter self-devotion of himself and his command are required." *

Mahan's thesis appeared to be repeated for the United States in the summer of 1936. War seemed remote to most; the economy and domestic politics were the nation's greatest concern. King was one of the few who instinctively sensed the Navy's peacetime lethargy and resolved to whip it. He established three priorities. One was to train his aviators to fly under wartime conditions. Another was to establish doctrine for the patrol seaplanes, particularly the Catalina, which was superior to the obsolescent aircraft it was replacing. Finally, King wanted to establish bases throughout the Pacific from which his seaplanes could operate.

The seaplane had great promise. The ocean surface afforded an infinite number of runways. The plane's endurance permitted it to stay

* *The Influence of Sea Power Upon History,* chap. 7, fn. 2.

aloft for hours, reconnoitering for the fleet over vast areas. The bases that King sought needed only shelter from the wind and shallow water where the seaplane tender USS *Wright* and the seaplanes could anchor. A usable base need be no more than a coral reef in the center of the Pacific — as it often was. For two years King and his nomadic forces roamed from Alaska to Panama to the Central Pacific, exploring any site that showed promise.

King ordered his seaplanes to fly under conditions that terrified the pilots: taking off in fog or high seas, flying at night in heavy weather, or traveling extreme distances with little fuel reserve. That is what they would have to do in war, King reasoned, and his pilots had to learn before war began. As the aircraft were not equipped with automatic pilots or sophisticated navigation and communication equipment, flying for King became an exhausting and frequently frightening ordeal. Many quit. That suited King. He was getting rid of the weaklings.

King shared the same perils faced by his aviators. At first his staff tried to dissuade him from taking unnecessary risks. "Anyone who won't take a chance now and then," King told them, "isn't worth a damn." Throughout his entire career King was involved in but one serious accident, the crash of his personal seaplane during takeoff in Acapulco Harbor en route to the Canal Zone. King and the crew were promptly rescued by the *Wright*'s lifeboat. Having ascertained that the water was too deep for salvage, King without comment continued his journey aboard *Wright*. Drew Pearson later publicized the accident, claiming that King had been at the controls and that the crash had been his fault. King actually had been riding aft as a passenger. "Although I wrote a letter to the S.O.B.," said King afterward, "he didn't even reply, which is just like them."

After arriving in the Canal Zone King went to the air station at Coco Solo, looking for a plane to fly him to a nearby Albrook Field, where his son-in-law, Army Lieutenant Frederick H. Smith, was stationed. He and his aide, Lieutenant Stanton B. Dunlap, found Lieutenant (junior grade) John T. Hayward standing beside a new Douglas aricraft and reading its instruction manual. When King announced that they were going to fly to Albrook Field, Hayward warned that he had never flown the plane.

"Son," said King, "are you a naval aviator?"

"Yes, sir," said Hayward.

"Get in the plane," said King. "We are going."

Once airborne, King flew until the final approach. Coming in high and fast, he gave the controls to Hayward, who gunned the throttle and

USS *Wright*, King's flagship, which wandered about the Pacific looking for seaplane bases (U.S. Navy photograph)

King and Captain Kenneth Whiting at French Frigate Shoals (U.S. Navy photograph)

made a second approach, to King's obvious annoyance. "When I bring the plane in to land," said King afterward, "you land it."

"If you do, you're crazy," said Dunlap sotto voce.

King routinely accompanied the most hazardous missions. Frequently he flew co-pilot, but he was not much help because his erratic flying complicated the navigation. He seemed so unconcerned about danger that the younger aviators wondered if King comprehended the risks he was imposing on everyone, himself included. After a hair-raising flight from Alaska to Seattle in fog, ice, and clouds, King joined the pilots that evening over drinks. "What were you thinking about?" he asked them.

"Do you really want to know?" asked the squadron commander, William G. ("Red") Tomlinson. (King earlier had overruled him when Tomlinson had advised against the flight).

"Yes," said King.

"I was wondering," said Tomlinson, "whether you knew enough to be scared." *

And there were others who questioned King's judgment. One stormy day at French Frigate Shoals, King ordered the squadron commander, Walter F. Boone, to get his twelve seaplanes underway for remote Kingman's Reef. Boone protested. A Bureau of Aeronautics Technical Order forbade takeoff in the kind of waves pounding the seaplanes at their moorings.

"Boone, you have made your point," said King. "Now return to your plane and take off your squadron." The aircraft somehow got airborne. It became apparent they would never reach Kingman's Reef, once they had been aloft for several hours. Boone got King's permission by radio to divert to Honolulu, which they almost missed in the weather and darkness. The airmen were happy simply to have survived. King was delighted for other reasons: it was the first time a change in mission had been ordered by radio with the flight far at sea. A subsequent inspection revealed that eleven of the seaplanes had so strained their hulls during takeoff that they required repairs. "King never mentioned the bent hulls," Boone remembered.

King's staff and subordinate commanders soon realized that the Admiral had fixed ideas. Consequently he was reluctant to delegate author-

* A staff officer related that the only time he saw King concerned was during the first Catalina flight nonstop from San Diego to Honolulu. The seaplanes were bucking headwinds. King monitored the flight from his headquarters in San Diego, and he was tense when he had to decide whether to allow the seaplanes to proceed beyond the point of no return. His decision to let them proceed was based upon the advice of his aerological officer, whom he later fired for alcoholism.

ity or to accept advice. Recalled Ballentine, "He really felt that no one else could tell these units what to do as well as he could."

"King usually worked alone," Boone later said. "I do not recall of his holding a staff conference or calling a meeting of his principal subordinate commanders to discuss operations, tactics, or schedules. King was an exacting and demanding boss. His treatment of a subordinate depended largely on how well the subordinate knew his job and stood his ground. He could be ruthless toward a subordinate whom he considered incompetent, not hesitating to humiliate an officer before his juniors when that officer failed to perform up to King's high standards. On the other hand, a subordinate who knew his business, did his job well, and was not afraid to stand up to King when he knew he was right got along very well with him. But I have seen King unmercifully browbeat certain staff officers who showed fear of his wrath."

Another observer, J. J. ("Jocko") Clark, later wrote, "King was the only naval officer I ever knew who would actually curse his subordinates."

Yet King must have seemed a paradox to those who knew him. He condemned some mistakes and tolerated others. Sometimes he was ruthless, other times kind. When a seaplane sank overnight at its moorings at French Frigate Shoals because of high winds, King was furious. The entire squadron would remain there, said King, weeks if necessary, until the sunken aircraft had been salvaged. After days of futile efforts King relented and allowed the squadron to return to Honolulu.

On the other hand, his flagship, USS *Wright*, unavoidably ran aground in Seattle shortly after King had taken command. Afterward the commanding officer was too scared to face King, so he sent John Ballentine, whom King personally had selected as *Wright*'s navigator. Ballentine asked King what he wanted to do about the grounding.

"Grounding?" asked King. "I was up here and I didn't see any grounding."

When Japan went to war against China in 1937, the United States government worried that the conflict might spread to America. King's seaplanes began searching for the Japanese fleet. Inevitably, one of them failed to return. King ordered a massive search, and his squadrons flew without respite. Several days later Ballentine phoned a squadron commander and praised the superb search efforts of his aircraft. King overheard the conversation.

"I don't think they're doing a good job," said King. "They didn't do any more than they're supposed to. Anyhow, who's running this force? Are you running it, or am I?"

"Admiral, I think if you go ask some of the people around," Ballentine replied, "there wouldn't be any question that they all think you're running it."

A young seaplane aviator, C. E. Robertson, vividly remembered that period. "During the days of anxiety and search," he later said, "Admiral King more than once personally went to the home of the plane commander to comfort the wife and family. I think he also went to the homes of other crewmen. . . ."

Robertson recalled another incident of King's concern for his subordinates. "At about the same time, my squadron commander was passed over for selection to commander. The news could not have been minutes old when the Admiral made a personal trip from his headquarters to our squadron and called on my squadron commander to express his dismay and regrets."

During this period King "adopted" two young sisters, Abby Dunlap, wife of his aide, Lieutenant Stan Dunlap, and Betsy Matter, wife of Lieutenant (junior grade) Alfred R. ("Dick") Matter, a naval aviator. Both women were bright, attractive, vivacious, and delightfully ingenuous. King loved them like daughters. He in turn was like a father, for they had lost their real father as children.

One early morning in Coronado, Betsy waited near the hangars with other squadron wives to meet their husbands, who were flying ashore after a six-week cruise on the *Lexington.* (The Matters had only recently been married, following an elopement.) Betsy was surprised to see King standing nearby. The planes, at first delayed, eventually appeared one by one and landed. Dick Matter's plane would be the last to arrive.

Suddenly Betsy became scared, and she began to run. Someone grabbed her shoulders and turned her around. It was King.

"Why are you running?" he asked.

"I'm afraid Dick might not love me anymore," said Betsy.

"Now you go back there," said King, "and wait for your husband."

It was then, Betsy later said, that she first recognized King's humanity. Some months later her husband went on a long cruise. "As I was alone," she later said, "Admiral King would frequently stop by and see me and make sure that everything was all right. I was very pregnant at the time. Every time he was in the area he would stop by, have a drink, and then leave. This was the sweetness that I knew."

King regarded his tour in command of seaplanes as only temporary. Before leaving Washington, King later related, there had been "an understanding — no promise was made or asked for" — that King would receive the Aircraft, Battle Force, assignment after a year with the seaplanes. But King heard rumors in late 1936 that he again would be denied the job. In January 1937 King visited the Navy Department, six months after taking the seaplane command. Both Swanson and Andrews told King he would remain in his present assignment because his "services were needed to continue with the expansion, organization and development of patrol squadrons," or so he was told. King's contempt for those in the Bureau of Navigation grew and hardened. "Fixers," he called them.

So King remained with the seaplanes a second year. His force had proven itself as mobile as the fleet; now it was called Aircraft, Scouting Force. King's influence extended throughout naval aviation. He corresponded extensively with his successor at the Bureau of Aeronautics, Rear Admiral Arthur B. Cook, on every conceivable subject. Having sponsored naval aviation cadets, he inspected them intently and asked questions. He could forgive their appearance, but the Regular Navy had higher standards. Pausing before a straining junior officer from the Academy, King carefully rotated a detachable gold uniform button on the officer's dress white uniform. "The eagle should be right-side-up," said King. "You wouldn't wear your cap device upside down, would you?"

King relished the fleet maneuvers. In early 1937 Vice Admiral Horne and his carriers were scheduled to raid San Diego; King was to defend the city with his seaplanes and several squadrons of bombers and fighters. King's seaplane pilots discovered the carriers at night, despite a heavy fog, which prevented Horne from launching. "From daylight on," wrote Jocko Clark, "we launched heavy bombing attacks with our shore-based airplanes and 'sank' the *Saratoga* and *Ranger* before 10 o'clock, which was the end of the problem. But canny King, who was calling the shots — his own and others — kept the attack going until noon. As usual, he covered himself with glory as the undisputed winner of the exercise."

After two years of waiting, King finally fleeted up to Commander, Aircraft, Battle Force. The assignment was inevitable. Horne could not keep the job forever, and King was the only eligible replacement. On 26 November 1937 Swanson sent a letter to FDR for the President's signature, assigning King to the carrier command with a concurrent promotion to vice admiral. King relieved Horne in January 1938. As Horne's new assignment was the General Board — a twilight cruise for flag officers awaiting retirement — the Battle Force job was obviously not on the main road for advancement to CNO.

10

Home Stretch

King's Aircraft, Battle Force, command contained three aircraft carriers: *Saratoga*, *Lexington*, and *Ranger*. Two would be added later: *Yorktown*, which had just been commissioned in Norfolk, and *Enterprise*, which would be commissioned in the spring of 1939. The three Pacific Fleet carriers were commanded respectively by Captains John H. Towers, John H. Hoover, and John S. McCain, all distinguished flag officers during the Second World War.

A few weeks after taking command, King sent a curious letter to Adolphus Andrews, still serving as Chief of the Bureau of Navigation. "I have always assumed that you would wish to know the views and desires of flag officers," King wrote, "as to their own personal preferences where their professional prospects are concerned — even when it may seem that there is a tinge of 'ambition' or even of 'selfishness.' For myself, I think it is up to each of us to do the best he can for himself! I acquainted you, quite fully and frankly, with my personal 'objectives' shortly before you came into office — They are now some six months 'behind schedule' — and 'age 64' looms just that much nearer!"

King then proposed that he be assigned as Commander, Scouting Force, which comprised light cruisers, destroyers, and patrol planes. Furthermore, suggested King, the aircraft carriers should be transferred from the Battle Force to the Scouting Force. The effect would be to release the 33-knot carriers from the 21-knot battleships in order to combine the carriers, cruisers, and destroyers for fast-moving and far-ranging independent operations. Accordingly, King proposed to combine two vice admiral commands into one command — under Ernest J. King.

Andrews must have been astounded at King's audacity. It was incredible that King assumed that Andrews, a battleship advocate jealous of every rival, would have helped King's career by increasing the importance of King's aviation command. Yet King's tactical reasoning was sound. During the Second World War carriers did operate precisely as King had foreseen in 1938. Yet Andrews, searching for an ostensible reason to say no, settled upon King's tactical arguments. His response is important primarily because it clearly reveals the conservative naval thinking of most senior flag officers of the late 1930s.

"The Carriers are extremely vulnerable," wrote Andrews. "But as long as they remain in proximity to the battleships they draw their protection from the latter and need no further protection except against submarines. When, however, carrier operations are projected to areas distant from the battleships, strong protection must be afforded. It requires no great imagination to visualize distant carrier operations which may begin as minor operations, but which turn into major operations by reason of carriers being intercepted by strong, fast surface ships and requiring the active support of battleships — perhaps at some expense to the general plan."

Andrews then concluded that the carriers should remain in the Battle Force, and that King should remain status quo. "I do not feel justified in recommending your detachment from your specialty where you are greatly needed," wrote Andrews, "and ordering you to a command [Scouting Force] where the requirement is not aviation qualification."

Several weeks later Andrews received orders to command the Scouting Force, together with an unprecedented promotion to vice admiral. The "policy" that initial sea assignments had to be a rear admiral's billet obviously did not apply to Andrews.

King's boss was Admiral Edward C. Kalbfus, Commander, Battle Force. They had been shipmates as ensigns on USS *Cincinnati* and had remained friends. Kalbfus was ignorant about naval aviation, he trusted King, so he gave King a free hand. "I won't have to worry about the aircraft of this force," said Kalbfus to his staff, "as long as Ernie King is down in San Diego."

King broke his three-star flag in *Saratoga* and began planning for Fleet Problem XIX, which was to begin in mid-March. In the interim his carriers began intensive training, especially night flying. "Many of the squadrons used to do their night flying by taking off at sunset and coming back in an hour," naval aviator Robert P. Beebe recalled. "King stopped that. The night he made the two air groups of Lex and Sara take off together from their ships is a real legend . . . a mist moved in, getting back aboard was real scary and lots of the people just flew ashore. Scores of the aviators declared they would quit flying if that wasn't stopped, and quite a few did."

King's preparations for the fleet problem went on concurrently. His operations officer, Donald B. Duncan, prepared the basic plan, which included a carrier attack on Pearl Harbor. After considerable effort Duncan submitted the plan to King. King scanned the document and returned it. "Commander, this is not satisfactory," said King. "Have a satisfactory plan on my desk by Monday morning." It would become typical of King to offer no reason for his rejection.

"We saw nothing of Duncan," a fellow staff officer, Cecil E. Blount, later said, "except for brief pop ins, until Monday. Each day he looked tired and drawn and grim, but Monday the new plan was ready, delivered, and accepted."

One by one the staff officers came to know King, one way or the other. Communications watch officer Arthur R. Manning, having decoded a message, groped across the darkened flag bridge. He bumped into someone. "Sir, are you on duty?" he asked the darkened figure.

"Young man," came the reply, "this is the Admiral. I am always on duty."

"One thing for sure was that he let you know he was the Admiral," staff officer Harbert V. Burkart recalled. "You could be two rungs from the top of a ladder when he decided that he wanted to go down. You did not finish your ascent but turned around and ran down. You could be halfway through a haircut and he decided that he wanted a shave. You got out of the barber chair and waited until he was shaved. However, that was his privilege, and he probably had more to do than you did, so you waited."

Given King's fixed ideas on carrier employment, he rarely solicited staff suggestions. And, unlike Mayo, he normally did not delegate important writing tasks (Duncan being an exception). "He had a tendency to jump in and write his own letters or dispatches," Manning later said, "instead of waiting for a staff initiative."

"King wrote out his dispatches and orders in his precise, clear handwriting," staff officer Walter Boone remembered. "He sometimes distributed drafts to staff officers for comment, but seldom made changes as the result of their submissions. His directives were the ultimate in clarity, brevity, and incisiveness, the meaning and intent of every word unmistakable. The exact wording of every dispatch was thought out before putting pencil to paper, so that the first draft rarely contained an erasure."

During a fleet problem King suspected his opposition of decrypting his coded messages, contrary to rules. King countered by inventing his own code, even though his communicators protested he was violating regulations. King's messages also broke encryption rules because they cramped his writing style. Communication security became a joke, but the staff felt that arguing with King was futile. Ensign Blount was an exception. With his superior's permission he rewrote one of King's messages and confronted the Admiral.

"Sir! I have rewritten the dispatch so that it can be encoded according to regulations," said Blount.

"Young man," King replied, "I have been working on that dispatch since three A.M. Send it as it is."

"Admiral, at least look at the revised version." King read it briefly, then returned it with a grim smile.

"Young man, you have done your duty," said King. "Now — *go send the dispatch as I wrote it*."

The communicators began to believe that King held a grudge against them. As they were "attached to the staff" and not "on the staff," they were even excluded from the staff photograph. But they persevered. King gave his communications officer, Henry L. Pitts, an official letter of commendation following Fleet Problem XIX.

The relationship between an admiral and his flagship can be tricky. As a captain, King had preferred *Lexington* because she had no admiral aboard to interfere. Now that he was an admiral, King's practice was to send an official letter advising the captain to act as if King were not aboard. King and his staff would be secluded in the flag bridge, one level above the ship's bridge. All communications would be written.

King's written intentions were often obscure to Captain Towers of the *Saratoga*, a close friend of King's chief of staff, Patrick N. L. Bellinger. In the early hours of the morning Towers frequently asked Bellinger what King would spring on them at the last moment. Bellinger was usually no help because King did not confide in his staff. "Bellinger would go up to the flag bridge," recalled *Saratoga* officer George van Deurs, "and he'd come back like a licked puppy with his tail between his legs. . . . King's staff at that time was nothing but a bunch of messenger boys. Everything that was going on was right inside King's head. He never put it out, I think possibly because he didn't want it to leak out to the ship. But you could bet that half an hour before sunrise, there would be a message come down to the air plot to launch planes in ten minutes. . . ."

In late 1938 King shifted his flag to *Lexington*, under Hoover's command. "Whenever Captain Hoover handled the flagship in a manner that did not please King," Boone later said, "the Admiral would lean over the flag bridge railing and loudly berate the skipper before the two bridge crews. Hoover refused to be perturbed, however. Without looking up he would simply raise his hand in acknowledgment and go on doing what he was doing. Hoover was never afraid of King."

Fleet Problem XIX was a smashing success for King. Contrary to conventional doctrine, Kalbfus allowed King to operate independently without the encumbrance of battleships. "Give Ernie King plenty to do during the exercises," Kalbfus had said. King began with a successful attack on Pearl Harbor, having used a weather front as cover. Several weeks later his carrier aircraft attacked Mare Island Naval Shipyard near San Francisco. King had reached the launch point undetected, again by skillfully evading searching ships and aircraft.

The remainder of 1938 was a series of training exercises and occasional business trips to Washington. King's future and his approaching retirement were frequently on his mind. "I have now been at sea since June 1936," he wrote a close friend, "nearly 2½ years — and expect a change of duty next Spring — which I hope will be in the nature of a 'step up' for I am still as 'ambitious' as ever. . . . I don't let myself think of what I shall — or can — do after I retire in 1942."

King and Mattie celebrated that New Year's Eve at the Coronado Hotel in San Diego. As midnight arrived King was dancing with a young Navy wife, and the racket of horns, bells, and whistles erupted. "Encouraged by champagne and years of custom of my hometown of Omaha," his dancing partner fondly recalled, "I pulled Admiral King down to my level and kissed him properly. Several other gals got the idea. . . . The following morning (Sunday) he walked into church with lipstick smears still showing, his usual austere reserve daring anyone to comment."

In January 1939 King got underway for Fleet Problem XX in the Caribbean. Hitler was threatening war in Europe and in nine months would invade Poland. In the Far East, Japan rampaged through China and Chiang Kai-shek's government had retreated to Chungking on the Yangtze River. The tremors spread across the Pacific. While King's flagship, *Lexington,* headed south from San Diego to the Panama Canal, another of the many Japanese war scares put the United States fleet on wartime alert. King ordered darken ship and gun batteries at the ready, which on *Lexington* meant rearranging deck gratings outside King's cabin. As he was walking in the darkness, King's leg struck one of the gratings. The blow was so painful that he could not walk. Dragging himself into his cabin, King summoned a doctor, who ordered King to bed for at least several days.

King dared not remain in his cabin despite the pain and damage to his leg. He had been hearing rumors that he was drinking at sea. If he stayed below during a wartime alert, people would say he was drunk in his cabin. Barely able to walk, King went to the bridge.

Through it all, King continued to plan the rendezvous of four of his carriers on the Atlantic side of the Panama Canal. King had brought *Lexington* and *Ranger* (Carrier Division One) from the Pacific. Rear Admiral William F. Halsey, in response to the war alert, scurried south from Norfolk with Carrier Division Two, the new carriers *Yorktown* and *Enterprise*. There would be problems when they joined. Never before had four carriers operated as a group. In practice, carriers operated independently with their own screen. King, however, wanted them to work together. "The rules were really vague and sketchy," King later said "but now some order had to be taken, or else the carrier command would be scattered throughout the seven seas."

King wrote every word of the instructions he intended to use. He did not want advice or suggestions from anyone, not his staff, not even Halsey. He regarded Halsey as a competent naval officer but inexperienced in carrier division tactics. Not only did King ignore Halsey, he persecuted him. He began by ruthlessly detaching three of Halsey's officers because he thought Halsey's staff was too large.

King wanted to practice with the four carriers before joining the remainder of the fleet. He started with close-order maneuvering, using signal flags and semaphore — he rarely used a signal light or radio. "King always tried to impress those around him with his knowledge of the General Signal Book," Boone recalled. "While below for breakfast or lunch, he would look up the series of maneuvering signals he intended to use during the exercise period to follow. He would jot them down on a card, memorize them, and put the card in his side pocket. Later on the bridge, he would bark out the actual signal letters in a way to give the impression that he knew the signal book by heart."

Halsey's division was ill prepared for its first encounter with King. "As *Lexington* and *Ranger* came over the horizon," *Yorktown* officer James S. Russell remembered, "*Lexington* blossomed with an unbelievably large display of signal flags. In *Yorktown* our signalmen were hard put to bend the flags on the many hoists, yet they were intent on speed and smartness. In the intense activity on the signal bridge, one signalman failed to get a snap hook in to the ring on the downhaul of a hoist. This hoist of four flags, therefore, took off and flew horizontally from our yard as if it were a clothesline of dirty linen . . . an opportunity did not arrive for at least a half hour for us to haul down the offending flag hoist which was thus adrift and advertising our ineptness."

King shoved the four carriers into a column, which to his mind "made quite an impressive show for the Fleet." Their work had just begun. "I would not allow any ships of my command to be idle and just pass the time," King later said, "so there were busy days ahead for all hands throughout this cruise in the Caribbean." It often got confounding. King was always impatient with his own signal gang (a "bunch of farmers," he called them). During a complicated maneuvering drill King evicted his flag lieutenant and chief signalman from the bridge and took personal charge of all signal hoists. He confused everyone. The carriers nearly collided and the formation degenerated into chaos. "They should have known what I mean," rationalized King. That ended the tactical maneuvers for the day.

The lifeguard destroyers changed frequently and rarely satisfied King. One of the few destroyer captains who succeeded was Arleigh A. Burke (later Admiral and CNO), commanding USS *Mugford*. On their first encounter Burke anticipated King. Lighting off four boilers, Burke conned *Mugford* close aboard King's flagship, narrowly missing the carrier but arriving promptly on station with a destroyerman's dash. "Admiral King himself was an expert seaman and he expected everybody else to be the same," Burke later said. "If some poor destroyer captain was a poor shiphandler, he would really raise hell."

"Let me say that working for Admiral King was not always a pleasant pastime," Russell later said. "We on *Yorktown* felt sorry for Admiral Halsey because he seemed to be along for the ride. We would watch these various maneuvers and never have a hand in them. Finally came the great day. . . . Things quieted down immediately, every evolution was in accordance with tactical doctrine, and the signal flags all made good sense."

As Fleet Problem XX approached, King's disposition worsened. His leg still hurt, he could not get ashore to unwind, and he was obsessed with planning how to use his carriers. He went without sleep (claiming five hours a night was all he needed) and catnapped by jackknifing his long frame on a short transom in flag plot. His only entertainment was the evening movie. He was frequently late and kept the crew waiting.

A movie officer once started the show, thinking that King was not coming. He was wrong. King returned to his cabin in a rage, ordered that the film be stopped and rewound, and that he be informed when it was ready for him to watch.

His second chief of staff, Leigh Noyes, caught most of King's wrath. A mild and meticulous person, Noyes habitually arranged his dispatches into neat little piles on a narrow shelf in flag plot. Still nursing his sore leg, King one day hobbled in after lunch. "King planted himself gloweringly in front of this row of loosely stacked dispatches," Boone recalled, "and with one sweep of his hand sent them flying all over flag plot. Then, without saying a word to Noyes or anyone else, he sat down on his transom."

The fleet problem got underway in the Caribbean in February 1939. It was King's final chance to show his stuff. At first he was frustrated because Kalbfus personally directed everything. King was reduced to following orders, his carriers once again tethered to the lumbering battleships.

After King chafed for several days, Kalbfus finally gave him an independent mission. The "enemy," fittingly enough, was Adolphus Andrews and his Scouting Force of surface ships, over a hundred seaplanes, and the carrier *Ranger*. The crux of the exercise was to neutralize the seaplanes so they could not find the Battle Force. A Kalbfus staff officer, Charles J. Moore, originated the idea of night destroyer raids against the seaplane tenders in their anchorages. King was delighted with the plan's audacity and charged off in *Lexington* and *Enterprise* to make war. King's destroyer raid was only partially successful. USS *Porter* crept into San Juan under cover of darkness and "sank" *Wright*, eliminating the fuel supply for almost half the seaplanes. Because of misunderstandings, however, *Porter* failed to attack *Langley* in nearby Samana Bay.

In the predawn darkness King planned his final battle. After a complicated exchange of aircraft between the two carriers, *Enterprise* would attack *Langley* at Samana Bay, while King in the *Lexington* would get Adolphus Andrews. A great melee erupted as the day wore on. By evening King was convinced that his strategy, his tactics, and his forces had won. "We were hard put to it to counter the great seaplane menace but did it!" he wrote a friend.

Others disagreed. Moore recalled the reaction of Marc Mitscher, who had commanded the seaplanes: "Mitscher was furious because King . . . had ruled an attack by patrol planes on the carrier as ineffective and

King and his chief of staff, Leigh Noyes (National Archives 80-G-457422)

that all the patrol planes were shot down and the carrier wasn't hurt. Mitscher's reaction was that it was the God-damnedest thing he ever heard of, outrageous — his patrol planes had sunk that carrier — damn King, and so forth. He was furious about the thing."

The problem concluded with a dreary performance of the battle line that discredited Kalbfus. King was again a spectator, and his carriers were not given adequate sea room for flight operations. President Roosevelt watched the finale from USS *Houston.* Afterward *Houston* streaked to the anchorage in Culebra with the remainder of the fleet close behind.

With *Houston* at anchor, some twenty or so admirals called on the President. One by one the flag officers approached their commander in chief, made small talk, and then withdrew. Then it was King's turn. King hoped, he said, that the President was pleased with the progress in naval aviation. Yes, the President was pleased, but look out for the Japanese and Germans. King then departed for the fringes of the crowd.

William D. Leahy would retire as CNO that summer, precipitating flag officer reassignments throughout the fleet and Navy Department. The hopeful candidates aboard *Houston* were on their best behavior.

Some sought a favorable word or gesture from the President, while others were shamelessly self-serving. Roosevelt must have been amused. Despite his own ambition, King refused to compete for Roosevelt's attention. He would rely solely on his record.

Not that King was reticent. He wrote on his fitness reports, for example, that his next duty preference was either CNO or Commander in Chief, U.S. Fleet, the top flag command at sea. Throughout the remainder of the spring he remained cautiously optimistic. After all, he reasoned, his service record was filled with letters of commendation gathered during forty years of what he considered to be outstanding performance. Furthermore, he had served in all three branches of the naval service — surface ships, submarines, and aviation. And then there was extensive duty on staffs, as well as the bureau job in Washington. Why not me? he thought.

Rumors and speculation continued to circulate throughout the fleet after Roosevelt returned to Washington. Then it was learned that the President's decision would be announced by Secretary Swanson when he visited the fleet in the Caribbean several weeks after Roosevelt's earlier stay.

Swanson returned to Washington on 14 March, and still King had heard nothing. He went ashore at Guantánamo Bay, Cuba, the following day to find out *something*. As he disembarked at fleet landing, Rear Admiral Harold R. Stark and several other flag officers were about to board Stark's barge. One of the admirals walked over to King. Stark, he said, was the new CNO.

King suppressed his emotions and walked over to Stark to offer congratulations.

King had never had a chance. Secretary Swanson, together with Admiral Leahy and the Chief of the Bureau of Navigation, Rear Admiral J. O. Richardson, had submitted their recommended slate to the President on 24 January 1939. King's name was not included.

One can speculate why King was passed over. His friends told him it was because of his drinking. A more probable reason is that of the seventy-four flag officers then in the Navy, only three were naval aviators: King, Halsey, and Charles A. Blakely. Clearly, the surface ship hierarchy would select one of its own. Fnally, King was not an intimate of Roosevelt. And then there was the ill will that King had aroused despite his professional competence. King's hopes to become CNO had been wishful thinking.

Late that spring King received word that he would be ordered to the General Board. His career was over. He was in tears when he visited a friend at a Sunday afternoon cocktail party. King left for Washington in July 1939, a tired and discouraged naval officer sixty years of age.

II

The Second World War

If one can only hold on for a little time longer, things will be eased up and in due time the trouble will iron out. That has been my own belief, not to say creed, but it works out for me.

No fighter ever won by covering up — by merely fending off the other fellow's blows. The winner hits and keeps on hitting even though he has to take some stiff blows in order to be able to keep on hitting.

— Ernest J. King

11

Resurrection

THE SECRETARY of the Navy had established the General Board as an advisory body in 1900, and its head for many years had been Admiral of the Navy George Dewey. In the passage of time it counseled the Secretary of the Navy on everything from strategy to ships' characteristics. The board that King joined (having reverted to his permanent rank of rear admiral) in August 1939 comprised nine other senior rear admirals and a small staff of officers secretaries and recorders. King's colleagues were the Navy's elder statesmen on their twilight cruise, nearing the retirement age of sixty-four and without hope of advancement; presumably they would deliberate selflessly and objectively, unencumbered with ambition. Service on the board was an honorable conclusion to a career, and the board's studies and recommendations reflected several centuries of collective wisdom and experience. Nevertheless, its advice was frequently rejected or ignored, for those in authority in the Navy Department usually had their own ideas.

The war in Europe erupted within days of King's arrival. Poland fell, then Norway. Japan continued to ravage China. Such events had little effect on the board. Most members followed a leisurely routine of study and meditation, arriving late and leaving early, free from the pressure of administrative responsibility. King was the iconoclast. He threw himself into his work, toiling long hours and attacking a series of complex studies. His attitude about his future varied. When a former subordinate made a courtesy call in the summer of 1940, King was dejected and referred to himself as a "has-been." Yet when another junior officer acquaintance met King in a Navy Department corridor, King looked him in the eye. "They're not done with me yet," said King. "I will have another chance."

It came in late March 1940, when he was summoned to the office of Secretary of the Navy Charles Edison.

Edison, the son of the inventor Thomas Edison, was an excellent business administrator who had entered the Roosevelt Administration as the Assistant Secretary of the Navy in 1936. When Claude Swanson died in July 1939, Edison became the acting secretary. His status remained uncertain until January 1940, when Roosevelt asked Edison to run for governor in Edison's home state of New Jersey. A Republican would replace Edison that summer, explained the President, because Roosevelt wanted a coalition cabinet with war approaching. The President finally did make Edison the "permanent" Secretary of the Navy, almost as an afterthought. But senior line officers continued to disdain Edison because they felt — correctly — that he was still a temporary Secretary who knew nothing about the fleet.

Having concentrated by choice on naval industrial affairs, Edison had learned little about the seagoing Navy during his years in the Department. Now, despite his impending departure, it was somehow decided it was time for his education. A six-week visit to the fleet was proposed, and Edison acceded. At the last minute Roosevelt phoned Edison and suggested he include King as a tour guide. King got the news when he arrived at the Secretary's office. King had other commitments, so it was arranged that he would join the Secretary's party en route to California.

The Secretary's companions included two naval aides, Captain Morton L. Deyo and Lieutenant Robert H. Rice, and his old friend Arthur Walsh, executive vice president of Edison Industries, an irreverent, irrepressible extrovert. The three older men speculated about King's reputation during the train trip from Washington to Kansas City, where King would meet them. Rice remained discreetly silent.

King came aboard about midnight and joined the others for a nightcap. "Admiral, we've been shaking in our boots," said Walsh. "I understand from Bob Rice [Rice winced] that you're so tough that you shave with a blowtorch."

King smiled. That was an exaggeration, he replied. A responsible officer sometimes had to be ruthless. There was no pleasure in it, but one did not flinch when sternness was needed.*

"This set the tone for the next six weeks," Rice later recalled. "King spoke softly, had a sweet smile, took the kidding with good grace, all without loss of dignity."

The first stop was Hollywood to preview an MGM film about

* Walsh later sent King a miniature blowtorch from Tiffany's.

Thomas Edison. The entertainment was lavish, with movie stars in profusion. King loved it. At last Edison's party got down to business, joining the fleet at San Pedro. Admiral J. O. Richardson, Commander in Chief, Pacific Fleet, was the host at a dinner for the Secretary aboard the fleet flagship, USS *Pennsylvania*. The flag officers cornered Rice to find out why King was along. "There was no doubt," Rice later said, "that some of them smelled something." King remembered their reaction. "Richardson wondered what the hell I was doing there," said King. "I went along for the ride."

The fleet, with the Secretary embarked, proceeded to Pearl Harbor. Betsy Matter greeted King there with a lei necklace and took him home. He returned to Betsy every day for a week, burdened with sadness. "The people here think I'm all through," he told the Matters. "I haven't even started yet."

When the trip ended, King resumed his labors on the board. Hitler had invaded the Low Countries, France was collapsing, and England would be alone. No one could predict how Japan would react; the Japanese foreign minister had hinted ominously of designs on the Netherlands East Indies. Roosevelt ordered Richardson and the fleet to remain in Pearl Harbor as a precaution.

Edison gave King carte blanche to increase the fleet's antiaircraft armament, which had been revealed as dangerously inadequate. King recommended a $300 million appropriation, which Vinson's committee took up as first priority in January 1941. "King cut completely across the usual channels and got the job started in about three months instead of the usual two or three years," recalled Francis C. ("Frog") Low, one of King's officer assistants. "This was immensely upsetting to those who had been for so many years in the habit of advising, suggesting, and vetoing, but rarely doing anything quickly." King studied the plans of every type of ship in the fleet, decided where the antiaircraft guns would be installed, and declared what would have to be removed to make room. "It was ruthless surgery and no one liked it," said Low. But King's authority was absolute. "While these improvements were 'quick and dirty,'" said Low, "they were absolutely essential and greatly improved our antiaircraft readiness."

Others noticed King's industry, especially Edison in a final memorandum to Roosevelt on 24 June 1940. "In leaving the Navy," wrote Edison, "I take the liberty of bringing to your attention the need for shaking the service out of a peace-time psychology. Certain fundamental

King as a tour guide for Secretary Edison. Admiral J. O. Richardson stands between them. *Richardson wondered what the hell I was doing there. I went along for the ride.* (U.S. Navy photograph)

weaknesses are freely admitted by most thinking Naval officers, but to quickly throw off a routine state of mind requires leadership of the Jervis type. [King probably had told him about Jervis.] I believe that Rear Admiral E. J. King, USN, is outstandingly of this type and that his appointment as Commander in Chief of the United States Fleet would do wonders for the fleet and the service. I earnestly recommend his appointment."

The President did nothing. Rumors were that Roosevelt felt that King drank too much. Such accusations were "cruel," brooded King. The CNO, Admiral Harold R. ("Betty") Stark, compensated for Roosevelt's coolness. Stark knew that King's talents were being wasted and tried to get him an active command. Meanwhile King would remain stuck in Washington.

By September 1940 King had served on the General Board for more than a year. Events seemed to be passing him by. A month earlier, American naval and military representatives had gone to England to discuss combined operations in the event that America went to war against Germany. France had fallen and the British were fighting for survival in the Battle of Britain. The British desperately needed ships to counteract the U-boats that were sinking her merchantmen. Roosevelt had helped by transferring fifty old destroyers in exchange for the use of Britain's bases in the Western Hemisphere.

One September day Stark asked King into his office, together with Rear Admiral Chester W. Nimitz, the Chief of the Bureau of Navigation. Stark told King that command of the Atlantic Squadron * was available if King wanted it. The squadron was inferior in size and prestige to King's earlier carrier command, since most of the fleet was in the Pacific. Then there was the sensitive matter of rank. When last at sea King had been a vice admiral, but Nimitz interjected that he would have to remain as a rear admiral. A third star might be arranged later. King replied that the rank made no difference. He wanted to go to sea and accepted the offer.

A subsequent physical examination revealed that King first needed a hernia operation. After a month's recuperation he was ready for sea duty. He had heard meanwhile that the new Secretary of the Navy, Frank Knox, would inspect the Navy's Caribbean bases and would watch the Patrol Force train. King asked if he could come, and Knox assented. King was pleased. He could familiarize himself with his new command before he relieved the incumbent, Rear Admiral Hayne Ellis. Equally important, King and Knox could get to know one another.

* Title changed to Patrol Force on 1 November 1940.

Knox's appointment in July 1940 had created a political uproar. Knox had been the Republican vice presidential candidate in 1936, and his newspaper, the Chicago *Daily News*, had consistently opposed the New Deal. Henry Stimson, another Republican stalwart, came aboard as Secretary of War. Roosevelt announced both appointments just before the Republican National Convention met to select a presidential candidate for the national election. The convention predictably condemned both Knox and Stimson as defectors. Roosevelt was delighted. He had his coalition cabinet and had embarrassed the Republicans.

A man of wide and varied interests, Knox had become wealthy both as an industrialist and as a publisher. He was compassionate, generous, and rugged, a patriotic activist who patterned his behavior after Theodore Roosevelt, with whom he had served in the Spanish-American War. (Knox was addressed as "colonel" because of his service in the First World War and a reserve commission.) Roosevelt had reasoned that Knox would support Roosevelt's foreign policy and military preparedness programs; perhaps he would even stop criticizing Roosevelt's domestic programs. And his political experience would help in dealing with Congress, one of the primary functions of the Secretary of the Navy.

Knox had forced concessions from the President before taking the job. The most important was that Knox would run the Navy Department without interference from Roosevelt. All things considered, he was probably one of the most experienced men ever to become Secretary of the Navy. Nevertheless, naval customs and bureaucracy often baffled Knox — much to the amusement of Roosevelt and the senior flag officers.

The inspection trip lasted for several weeks, much of it sightseeing by air. King never left the Secretary's side and controlled the itinerary. In the Canal Zone King ordered a substitute aircraft when the primary transport was damaged on takeoff. The standby pilot did not even know where he was going until King told him after they were aloft.

King still enjoyed parties and drinking. He devised a devastating cocktail which he called "The King's Peg," a combination of brandy and champagne which he mixed himself and poured into tall glasses over a small amount of ice. At the Key West Naval Station King caroused with Rawleigh Warner, Knox's friend and traveling companion. "Admiral King embarrassed all of us with his intoxicated behavior," recalled the station's commanding officer, Fort H. Callahan. When Warner and King returned to their aircraft for an early morning departure, the crew had arranged bunks, assuming both men would need sleep. Warner succumbed, but King remained awake to show Knox the Florida Keys. That evening in Miami King was so bushed that he tried to avoid attending a ceremonial dinner with Knox. "All of us have been together throughout this cruise," insisted Knox, "and we have to keep together until we return to Washington." King went.

King relieved Ellis as Commander, Patrol Force, in Norfolk on 17 December 1940 and broke his two-star flag on the ancient battleship USS *Texas.* Given King's stature, many officers in the force were astonished at his assignment. Once he had commanded huge carriers; now he had old, worn-out ships isolated from fleet operations. The war plans safe, King discovered, contained a single plan: a war with Mexico.

As usual, King had carefully selected his staff. Many of them had worked for King on the General Board; most subsequently became flag officers. The staff was small — eleven officers — on King's theory that fewer numbers increased efficiency. Given the competence of the staff, King was right. The working hours were long and hard. A staff officer could expect a call at any time, except when King napped in the afternoon.

Lieutenant Bob Rice, commanding the Secretary's yacht *Sequoia,* received a letter from King, who remembered Rice as the efficient aide during the Edison expedition. "I have always prized the letter," Rice later said, "as a fine example of his way of doing things and putting *first* things *first.* He asked two things of me:

(1) my chief steward

(2) my services as his flag lieutenant.

My steward I sent off to him the very day I received his letter. As he so courteously invited me to do, I declined the assignment to his staff because I had every reason to expect a fleet submarine command, a better spot, it seemed to me, since war seemed imminent." Rice got his submarine.

Even before taking command, King had issued a directive to his prospective staff, defining his policies and their individual duties. "There was no doubt about what was expected," staff officer James R. Topper recalled. Work was either accepted or rejected with King's cryptic notations "OK-K" or "No-K." Exclamation and question marks sometimes added emphasis. There were rarely amplifying comments. King did not have the time to explain his rejection of a written document. The staff would have to read King's mind and keep trying until he was satisfied.

King still did much of his own writing. "I worked with the whole staff many a week and weekend to prepare a war plan to submit to him," recalled staff officer Dashiell L. Madeira, "only to have him say 'no,' tear it up and then set down and write a complete plan out of his head, with forces located all over the world." King sometimes circulated his own drafts for comment, but customarily he seldom changed anything. Occasionally King dictated to a yeoman but usually used pencil and paper. "His writing was as legible as type," recalled another staff officer, Harry Sanders. "He told me he had practiced writing for the preceding twelve years with a view to easy legibility and the unmistakable identity of each letter."

King knew his priorities. The first was to get ready to fight. Three days after taking command he issued "Measures Suited to the Existence of an Emergency," the first of his many famous Atlantic Fleet orders. It said that war was imminent and to prepare accordingly. The force would darken ship, remove combustible material, increase alertness, and intensify training.

King also reinstituted his notorious white-topped, blue-bottomed uniform. The day after issuing the order he spoke with Harry Sanders, his watch officer on the flag bridge.

"How do you like my Cossack uniform?" asked King.

"It's too hot in the legs, where you want to be cool," replied Sanders, "and too cold above, where you want to be warm."

"Well," said King, "it shows who can prescribe the uniform." He went below, obviously amused.

King rescinded that order several weeks later, but other experiments persisted. King wanted to camouflage the sailors' white uniforms and decided to color them brown. Each sailor on the *Texas* sacrificed one white uniform, which was submerged in a huge cauldron of coffee. "At the first morning quarters after the completion of the task," recalled ship's officer David C. S. Kline, "the *Texas* crew had uniforms ranging in color from ecru to chocolate brown. Needless to say, this plan was dropped and never mentioned again."

King led his motley force from Norfolk shortly before New Year's Day, 1941, on the way to the Caribbean for amphibious training with Marine Corps and Army troops. At sunset the force tried to darken ship but could not overcome twenty years of peacetime habits. As the night wore on, the last light finally went out. They would show no lights until the Second World War was over.

With everything dark topside, King's bony hand thrust an encoded maneuvering signal through the light-tight slot into the flag radio room.

"Send it and let me know when you receive their rogers," said King's voice through the door. One by one the ships acknowledged. When only half had responded King whispered, "Execute." The ships, most without radar, groped through the darkness. "Amazingly, there were no collisions," recalled staff communicator Alfred R. Taylor.

After several hours of scary maneuvers, King ordered a cruising formation and left the bridge. During the midwatch Frog Low, the watch officer, routinely changed course and reported it to King. The Admiral stormed to the bridge.

"Who made that signal?" he asked.

"I did, sir," said Low.

King's temper snapped, and he raged at Low for usurping King's authority. Hurt and stunned, Low retreated to the opposite side of the bridge. After several minutes King came over and patted Low's shoulder. "Don't feel too badly about this," said King.

Low angrily wheeled toward King. "Admiral, aside from asking for my immediate detachment, there is not one goddamn thing you can do to me that I can't take."

Flag officers who are secure within customarily allow their staffs to plan and execute tactical maneuvers, while retaining general supervision. But King once again had failed to allow his subordinates to use their initiative. He still wanted to do everything. Nothing had changed from the days of his carrier command in 1938.

After his outburst against Low, King finally recognized that he had to start trusting others. Hitherto he had commanded small task groups in the Pacific operating near his flagship under his direct control. But his new command encompassed the entire Atlantic Ocean; his ships would be scattered everywhere on any number of independent assignments. As King could not be everywhere, he would have to allow his flag and commanding officers to be independent. It was hard for King to change his ways. "Sometimes I got a kind of obsession of interfering with admirals who had to do the job," he later wrote, "although sometimes I believed I could have done a better job myself. But I got myself in hand enough not to interfere unless it seemed that it really had to be done."

The upshot was that a month after taking command King issued another fleet order entitled "Exercise of Command — Excess of Detail in Orders and Instructions." Commanders were assumed to be competent until proven otherwise. "Train them — by guidance and supervision — to exercise foresight, to think, to decide and to act for themselves," wrote King in his order. "Stop 'nursing' them. Finally, train ourselves to be satisfied with 'acceptable solutions' even though they are not 'staff solutions' or other particular solutions that we ourselves prefer." *

King preached with the zeal of a convert. He issued another order in late April, "Exercise of Command — Correct Use of Initiative," which reinforced his earlier pronouncements.† Still King was dissatisfied. In late November 1941, he wrote an admonitory letter to Rear Admiral Francis L. Reichmuth, commanding the Atlantic Fleet destroyers, who had just issued detailed instructions on avoiding collisions. "I note," wrote King, "that you *require* all commanding officers to do what they are supposed to be competent to do without being *required* to do it. I feel I should also say to you that this is not the first time that I have noted a tendency on your part to overdo your supervision of subordinates under your jurisdiction. I am fully aware of your zeal for the service and of your endeavor to conduct your affairs to the advantage of the service, but I think you should take more fully into account the policy [of initiative]. I am also fully aware that the said Fleet policy has caused in some instances — and is likely to continue to cause in other instances — difficulties, and even hazards, by reason of the lack of seasoned capacity on the part of some commanding officers. None the less, I am convinced that *in the long run* the said Fleet policy will produce greater 'dividends' in efficiency than if we keep on trying to prescribe too much in detail just *how* each and every occurrence shall be dealt with."

While en route to the Caribbean in early January, King received a portentous message disseminated Navy-wide by the Secretary of the Navy. The position of Commander in Chief, U.S. Fleet (Admiral J. O. Richardson), was abolished. The "U.S. Fleet" would be divided into three separate fleets: Atlantic, Pacific, and Asiatic. There were few details. King could only speculate how he personally would be affected.

When King arrived in Guantánamo Bay, two welcome letters amplified the message. One was from Nimitz, who reported that, to everyone's surprise, Roosevelt had decided on 6 January that King's force was to be designated the Atlantic Fleet. King would receive a commensurate promotion to full admiral in the near future. In the interim King's appointment to vice admiral was in the mail. The fourth star came sooner than expected. A senior flag officer decided to retire rather than to serve under Kimmel, who suddenly outranked him. The Navy Department promptly assigned the four-star vacancy to King.

The other letter was from Knox, congratulating King on his new

* For the complete text see Appendix I.
† For the complete text see Appendix II.

The Commander in Chief, Atlantic Fleet, and Secretary of the Navy Frank Knox (U.S. Navy photograph)

status as Commander in Chief, Atlantic Fleet, and inviting King to correspond with him "to maintain the closest possible relationship . . . which will promote the freest possible exchange of ideas. I am still a great deal of a novice in this Navy business, and I am depending upon you men to help me along in my education."

Meanwhile there were momentous changes in the Pacific. Roosevelt fired Richardson over a dispute on keeping the fleet in Pearl Harbor and replaced him with Husband E. Kimmel, who was designated Commander in Chief, Pacific Fleet. Admiral Thomas C. Hart became Commander in Chief, Asiatic Fleet. Kimmel would assume the role of Commander in Chief, U.S. Fleet, if two or more of the fleets were to operate together.

The USS *Texas*, at anchor in the Caribbean, bustled to prepare for King's ceremonial assumption to fleet command on 1 February 1941. Sailors holystoned her teak decks and polished her brightwork. Barges and gigs drew smartly alongside, discharging senior officers gathering to witness the ritual. As each officer ascended the accommodation ladder the boatswain's pipe wailed, while the loudspeaker announced arrivals. Visitors and crew assembled aft, the senior officers in dress whites with swords, the Marine honor guard in khakis, and the sailors in whites.

With everyone in place, King appeared. After the appropriate honors he walked to the microphone and read his orders. His four-star flag was broken at the main. King spoke briefly and returned to his cabin, which was near the forward accommodation ladder tended by the *Texas* gunnery officer, Charles W. Moses.

"May I congratulate you, sir?" he said.

King stopped but did not reply. Instead he looked at his flag, flying high above.

"Now we can get started," said King. Then he entered his cabin.

King's most immediate concern was Fleet Landing Exercise Seven (Flex 7), an annual winter event to train the Navy and Marine Corps in amphibious warfare. Equipment and doctrine were still largely experimental, yet each practice developed and refined the tactics successfully used in the Second World War. King was such a neophyte in the business that he underestimated the problems of getting troops ashore. In his judgment the Marines were loafing by using the same broad, sandy, hospitable landing beaches on the Vieques and Culebra Islands of Puerto Rico, year after year. King decided to make things tougher by ordering the Marines to land on St. John's Island. It had narrow muddy beaches, rugged terrain, and unfamiliar features. In short, it was entirely unsuitable for an amphibious assault.

The Marine commander, Brigadier General Holland M. Smith, was stunned at King's change of plans. Irascible and sensitive to any criticism of his beloved Marine Corps, Smith had everything set for Culebra. King was being unreasonable — probably out of ignorance, Smith surmised. Beach selection was crucial: in time of war it would be murderous to assault an ill-suited beach on short notice. But King, who rarely changed his decisions, was adamant. Accustomed to ordering surprise exercises with the fleet, he demanded the same of the Marines. Smith protested so vehemently, however, that King finally canceled St. John.

Forced to work together, King and Smith had to tolerate each other, but there were still petty disagreements. At breakfast both men squabbled over the sole copy of the radio press. "It was quite a scene," recalled the communication officer, Thomas S. Webb. He solved the dispute by sending each a personal copy of the news.

The Marines meanwhile were experimenting with a device that could both swim in water and crawl over land, designated a landing vehicle, tracked (LVT). An enthusiastic Marine junior officer, Victor H. Krulak, briefed King on its capabilities. "Admiral," he said, "would you like to ride in one?"

"Oh," said King, "there's one hereabouts?"

"There is indeed," said Krulak.

"I really haven't much time," said King. "I have just a few minutes, and I've got to go somewhere else."

"It won't take long," urged Krulak, "and I think you'll really be illuminated."

King reluctantly agreed. Glancing at his watch, he went down the accommodation ladder and entered the LVT. After circling near *Texas* for several minutes, King was ready to return. Krulak pressed King to stay long enough to see how the LVT could cross the coral reef. "It will only take a minute," said Krulak reassuringly, and they turned toward the beach. The LVT clambered impressively upon an offshore reef—and then threw a track.

"And there he was," Krulak later said. "Mad at me, in his whites, anxious to go somewhere for an appointment. No boat could reach us because we were on the reef. He had to crawl over the side of that damned machine and wade in his white uniform, water up to his waist, to the beach and then he was picked up by a truck and taken away."

But King was forgiving. King's Marine staff officer during the Second World War, Oman T. Pfeiffer, later commented: "Admiral King was very partial towards Marines, and I thought and still think that this came from his previous experience with Marines on maneuvers under the command of General Holland M. Smith. This was the beginning of Admiral King's education in amphibious warfare and the capabilities of the Marines."

While the Americans practiced war in the Caribbean, Great Britain was fighting alone against Germany and Italy. Roosevelt was committed to aiding Great Britain, however possibly, by all measures short of war. Stark's concern was the need to develop joint plans with the British. In the First World War he had been an aide to Sims during the chaotic efforts of the United States Navy to fight alongside the Royal Navy. Stark was determined not to allow a recurrence; he wanted plans made *before* the United States entered the Second World War as a British ally.

King's Atlantic Fleet was the principal force available to help Great Britain, either in peace or in war. King knew it was not ready. He had two main concerns: the lack of ships, exacerbated by delays in overhauls, and peacetime habits despite the imminence of war. "There is still too much 'business as usual,'" he wrote Knox from the Caribbean, "whereas we are now in an emergency (duly declared by the President) which bids fair to become intensified at short notice."

That was what Knox wanted to hear. "I am not at all surprised," he replied in late January, "but I am gratified to know that the Commander-in-Chief of the Atlantic Fleet recognizes the existence of an emergency and is taking proper measures to meet it. I knew you would!"

King's letters to the Navy Department warned that most of his ships needed repairs, overhauls, and alterations to improve their combat readiness. Stark acted by bringing King to Washington from the Caribbean to ask when the work should be done. "If you're going to do it," said King, "do it now." Knox and Stark agreed. The fleet would be temporarily immobilized in the shipyards to be ready for a long war. Soon afterward both Stark and Knox visited King in the Caribbean. King later remarked that, as a result of that visit, Knox "began to understand that [I] might be useful."

Shortages in men, ships, and materiel handicapped the Atlantic Fleet for months to come. King fatalistically accepted them. His letters to Stark and other flag officers ended with the phrase, "Remain cheerful!" which Sims had used when the unprepared American Navy had lurched into the First World War. King also assured Nimitz that the Atlantic Fleet would accept without complaint whatever officers the Bureau of Navigation provided. "I take this attitude," wrote King, "because I recognize the demands the Bureau has to meet just now — and — in the belief that this Fleet will be given every proper consideration in the assignment of personnel even if it is relatively small and has some older ships in it."

King would not allow shorthandedness to become an excuse for pessimism or apathy. As emphasis King issued yet another of his famous fleet orders, "Making the Best of What We Have," on 24 March 1941. "I expect the officers of the Atlantic Fleet," King wrote, "to be the leaders in what may be called the 'pioneering spirit' — to lead in the determination that the difficulties and discomforts — personnel, material, operations, waiting — shall be dealt with as 'enemies' to be overcome — by our own efforts. . . . We must all do all we can with what we have."

"He would listen to no excuse," recalled staff officer Madeira, "that a directive could not be carried out because the commander didn't think he had the requisite wherewithal. . . . For this he would saw you off at the knees."

A copy of King's fleet order came to Knox's desk, and the Secretary dashed off an appreciative note. "I cannot refrain from expressing to you my delight over the spirit of it and its manner of expression," wrote Knox on 3 April 1941. "To make the best of what we have in the face of grave danger is, of course, the only philosophy for us to pursue."

Knox was not exaggerating. U-boats were devastating British shipping, surface raiders were a constant threat, and Churchill had warned Roosevelt that the Vichy government might deliver the French fleet at Oran to the Germans. German air and ground forces were pouring into the eastern Mediterranean, challenging Britain's control of the Suez Canal. The Royal Navy was extended to the limit, and it needed immediate help.

British and American planners in late March had concluded the so-called ABC-1 Staff Agreement (later the genesis for Anglo-American wartime cooperation), obligating King to help the Royal Navy to escort trans-Atlantic convoys. A special force under Rear Admiral Arthur L. Bristol had been created in early January, but it would not be ready for escort duty until summer regardless of the Agreement. That might be too late. "The situation is obviously critical in the Atlantic," Stark wrote King on 4 April. "In my opinion, it is hopeless except as we take strong measures to save it." Several days later Stark transferred three battleships, a carrier, four cruisers, and two destroyer squadrons from the Pacific to the Atlantic Fleet.

Ironically, King did not know the details of the ABC-1 Agreement. When he asked Stark for information, Stark sent him to Rear Admiral Robert L. Ghormley, an American representative during the negotiations. Ghormley refused to show the plans to King. King insisted he had Stark's permission. "Are you *sure* Stark said that?" asked Ghormley.

King stormed back to Stark. Stark tried to soothe King's feelings, but the upshot was that King was not allowed to see the plans that he was supposed to implement.

King's responsibilities expanded as 1941 wore on. As a fleet commander he was no longer a tactician, maneuvering ships with surprise signals on the flaghoist. Now his ships were spread across the Atlantic Ocean on dangerous assignments. It was time for King to get organized.

He needed, first of all, a proper flagship; ancient *Texas* would not do. He had been promised the USS *Augusta*, a fast, long-range heavy cruiser designed as a flagship. *Augusta*, however, was in overhaul at Mare Island Naval Shipyard, California, following a seven-year deploy-

King's first flagship, USS *Texas* (Courtesy Walter Muir Whitehill)

King's second flagship, USS *Augusta* (Courtesy Walter Muir Whitehill)

ment to the Far East. King prodded, Mare Island finished a month early, and King broke his flag in *Augusta* in late April.

King had to be near enough to Washington to get there on short notice; consultations with Stark and Knox had become so frequent that King had a permanent office in the Navy Department. He also wanted to be centrally located for operations at sea. King decided upon Newport, Rhode Island.

Augusta entered her new home port in the spring of 1941 and moored within sight of the Naval War College. The college president was King's old friend Ned Kalbfus, who had reverted to a rear admiral following his temporary four-star assignment as King's boss three years before. As he was now the junior, Kalbfus sent a message to the flagship: "At what time may Rear Admiral Kalbfus call upon Admiral King?" King responded with the nicest sense of grace and diplomacy. "Admiral King will call upon the President of the Naval War College at whatever time it is convenient for the president to receive him."

Augusta moored to a large buoy off Jamestown Island. A single telephone line was King's only direct contact with the mainland, and it frequently broke as the buoy twisted in the tidal current. King summoned the commanding officer of the naval station. "You will keep that line in service," said King, "if you have to keep a boatload of repairmen at the buoy twenty-four hours a day."

King was handicapped by vague instructions from Washington. The only certainty was that Roosevelt wanted King's fleet to protect British ships and possessions from the Germans. There were sure to be confrontations between American and German forces, and commanding officers needed some rules of engagement. But Roosevelt was ambivalent, and Stark became progressively more frustrated and upset in dealing with the President. "To some of my very pointed questions," Stark wrote to a friend in late July, "which all of us would like to have answered, I get a smile or a 'Betty, please don't ask me that!' Policy seems something never fixed, always fluid and changing."

In the absence of definitive guidance, King developed a simple plan for deploying his fleet. He would station a force of battleships, cruisers, and destroyers off Maine and Canada to escort North Atlantic convoys against the threat of U-boats and surface raiders. A small group of old cruisers and destroyers would go to the South Atlantic; King was forever worried about a German invasion threat from Senegal to Brazil. Finally, he would maintain a reserve force off the Atlantic coast for deployment anywhere in the Atlantic.

In mid-May King inspected the American naval facilities under construction in Bermuda. When he arrived he was welcomed by two young naval aviators and a civil engineer officer. King asked whether the American seaplane patrol squadron at Bermuda had honored a recent British request to help search for a French warship in the Caribbean. One of the aviators, Philip A. Tague, told King he had been ordered not to fly more than fifty miles from Bermuda. The other aviator, who commanded the squadron, confirmed that the orders had been in writing.

"Get them," said King.

The squadron commander hurried away.

King turned to the engineer and asked for plans for the base. They were in the office. "They are not doing a hell of a lot of good there," said King. The engineer quickly left. King resumed walking with only Tague remaining.

"Admiral," said Tague, "we actually flew two patrol planes out to two hundred miles to support the British."

King seemed pleased. "His warmth and openness with me, a very junior officer in my first personal meeting with him," Tague later said, "seemed to reveal his true personality . . . as we reached the dock and his barge, he astonished me with the statement that he felt that we were really in the war in the Atlantic."

King was serious about being at war. When *Augusta* was returning to Newport on 24 May, King received the electrifying news that the German battleship *Bismarck* was loose in the North Atlantic convoy lanes, pursued by the Royal Navy. King ordered his long-range naval patrol planes in Newfoundland to search for the German.* The aircraft flew through North Atlantic fog and weather, many nearly crashed, and none found *Bismarck*. King, meanwhile, told his staff aviation officer not to allow the aircraft to land in Narragansett Bay, perhaps to avoid publicity. Nevertheless, one plane diverted to Newport from Argentia. As it taxied past *Augusta*, the aviation officer groped for an explanation.

"Admiral," he said, "there must be a Narragansett Bay in Newfoundland."

"There had better be," King replied.

Bismarck's escapade humiliated the Royal Navy and Churchill's government. Crete was about to fall under German air power, and with it would fall Great Britain's control of the eastern Mediterranean. Roosevelt decided he had to arouse more public support for the British. On the pretext that German naval power was endangering American security, Roosevelt proclaimed an unlimited national emergency on 27 May

* This may have been in response to a plea from Churchill to Roosevelt to help find the *Bismarck*.

1941 (ironically, the day that *Bismarck* was destroyed). The Navy (that is, King's Atlantic Fleet) would take such steps as necessary to combat the German threat.

Three weeks after Roosevelt's proclamation, Stark ordered King to take United States troops to relieve the British garrison in Iceland. King organized a task force of twenty-five ships under the command of Rear Admiral David M. LeBreton, which landed a brigade of Marines in Iceland on 8 July 1941. British soldiers were free to fight elsewhere. The island would remain secure, and it would be used as an American aircraft and escort base as well. King also established naval anchorages in Casco Bay, Maine, and at Argentia, allowing warships of the Atlantic Fleet to be closer to the North Atlantic convoy lanes.

On 19 July 1941 King issued his Operation Plan Number 6. The Atlantic Fleet, said King, would escort and protect all shipping between North America and Iceland. (Roosevelt changed his mind a few days later and told Stark to exclude British shipping — more presidential ambivalence.) Rear Admiral Jonas H. Ingram would patrol with four obsolescent cruisers and five destroyers in the Trinidad–Cape Verde Islands–Natal triangle, operating from the Brazilian ports of Recife and Bahia. Small detachments of destroyers and patrol aircraft would cover the Caribbean and Gulf of Mexico.

And what were their orders? Roosevelt still was ambiguous, so King arbitrarily ordered his fleet to track any German warships they discovered and to report their positions to the British. If the Germans attacked any ships or territory under American protection, they were to be captured or destroyed. It was an "anomalous situation, neither peace nor war," wrote historian Samuel Eliot Morison. "Although this service was essentially a belligerent one, Admiral King's operation plans of July had to be so cautiously worded that commanders of the United States ships and planes were not sure what they were expected to do if a German raider, submarine or aircraft was encountered. Were they to shoot first and let the Navy explain, or only fire if fired upon? Was it to be Concord Bridge or Lexington Green?"

12

The Atlantic Conference

Augusta's commanding officer puzzled over an order he had just received from King. Without explanation or amplification, King had suddenly directed *Augusta* to leave Newport on 2 August 1941 and to proceed to New York City via Long Island Sound. The skipper knew there was no point in asking questions from King. One simply obeyed.

As *Augusta* entered the open sea, the cruiser *Tuscaloosa* fell in astern, while four destroyers screened ahead. That afternoon *Augusta* anchored near the East River. A barge delivered workmen from Brooklyn Navy Yard to install special ramps and other devices that could only be for the President.

The next day was Sunday. The church pennant flew above the national ensign as the chaplain conducted services. After the final "amen" the crew went to lunch, speculating excitedly. Their commanding officer knew little more than the mess cooks. Late in the afternoon a destroyer came alongside and disembarked Admiral Stark and General George C. Marshall, Chief of Staff of the United States Army. Then she went alongside *Tuscaloosa* to disembark other army and naval officers.

The ships next went to an anchorage off Martha's Vineyard, arriving in midafternoon of the fourth. Late that evening a flashing light broke the darkness. *Augusta* signalmen clattered a signal lamp in return. "Tell the Admiral," said the signalman, "that the *Potomac* has just entered the anchorage with President Roosevelt aboard." Another exchange of signals. "*Potomac* will come alongside at first light."

Some months before — in the middle of April — King had been summoned to Hyde Park to confer with the President. The two men spoke alone in a secluded cottage on the President's estate. Roosevelt disclosed that he was anxious to meet with Churchill because only so much could be accomplished by letter, telegram, and envoy. For political and security reasons Roosevelt favored a clandestine rendezvous at sea.

Roosevelt was a geography buff, and he produced maps and charts, which he obviously had been studying. After a long discussion it was decided that the meeting should be in Argentia, Newfoundland, following Roosevelt's visit to Prime Minister Mackenzie King of Canada. Roosevelt pledged the Admiral to secrecy — he was not even to tell Knox and Stark — and they arranged a code word that Roosevelt later would use over the phone if the trip was on. King was mildly amused by Roosevelt's air of conspiracy. For a number of reasons, Roosevelt postponed his plans. Then, on 25 July, Roosevelt once again summoned King to Hyde Park. This time the decision was firm. The President and the Prime Minister would meet in Argentia. It would have to be done secretly, largely because of the U-boat threat. To maintain security King had issued only the minimum orders necessary. Not even the *Augusta* captain had known. Nor had *Tuscaloosa*'s skipper known that he was a backup ship in the event of a casualty to *Augusta*.

Now with Roosevelt and his party aboard, King ordered a series of courses and speeds that directed the force northeasterly. Fog reduced the visibility, but King drove on at 22 knots, trusting *Augusta*'s radar to detect ships and avoid collision. It was a serious misjudgment. The radar was primitive and unreliable. (Modern radars still fail to detect ships under certain conditions.) There was no need to hurry to Argentia. King had forty-eight hours to spare and could have slowed without being late. As it was, King's force pushed through dense fog in some of the most heavily traveled fishing grounds and shipping lanes in the North Atlantic. He was lucky that there were no collisions.

Augusta and her escorts arrived at Argentia on 7 August on an unexpectedly clear morning. Passing through the submarine nets and by the patrolling destroyers, the force anchored in Ship Harbor, Placentia Bay. There they joined other ships of the Atlantic Fleet, including several old battleships on call to the British should German raiders again break into the Atlantic.

They waited. King and Stark went sightseeing by air, and the President fished. Foul weather came and stayed for the next two days, to everyone's annoyance and discomfort.

On the morning of 9 August word was passed that *Prince of Wales* was arriving. The battleship's bulk loomed through the fog; then she broke into the sunshine. She was magnificent: crew manning the rail, guard paraded, the Prime Minister on the bridge. *Prince of Wales* passed close aboard, appropriate honors were exchanged, then she anchored astern of *Augusta*. Churchill and his party came aboard with the usual flourish of boatswain's pipe and sideboys.

It was the first time King had ever seen the Prime Minister in person. He was startled to discover that Churchill in real life was short and stout with a florid complexion, and that he wore quixotic clothing * in lieu of suit and tie. Following the introductions, Roosevelt and Churchill dined alone, while the British and American representatives gathered for lunch with King as host.† It was a time for getting to know one's future allies. "The first evening was spent in a family dinner," wrote the President's physician, Rear Admiral Ross McIntire. "It was a gay gathering; I have never seen a happier group meeting on such a serious subject."

The spirit of comradeship flourished the next day. The Americans visited *Prince of Wales* for an Anglo-American corporate worship—liturgy from the Book of Common Prayer, hymns selected by Churchill for their grandeur and majesty, the spectacular scene of warships of two great nations gathered together in the barren, remote, windswept anchorage. Socializing resumed that afternoon and into the evening. Through it all, King noted, Churchill seemed to be talking, talking, talking, and Roosevelt listening.

Formal work began on Monday. Roosevelt wanted an agreed-upon statement of Anglo-American foreign policy to justify—publicly—this unprecedented meeting with Churchill. As this was a political matter, the naval and military leaders met separately to discuss their own specialized interests. The British had brought an agenda which allowed them to control the discussion. The Americans, who had not prepared for Argentia, had no choice but to follow the British initiatives. As will be seen in later chapters, it would become a familiar problem for the American negotiators in future conferences. "Although I was supposed to be in the official party," King later wrote, "I didn't say very much. But I was doing a deal of thinking and listening."

The remarkable aspect of the meetings that King attended was the implied attitude that the United States and Great Britain were allied against Germany, when ostensibly the two countries were respectively neutral and belligerent. Discussions dealt primarily with allocating American-produced war materiel among the United States, Great Britain, and the

* On this occasion, a Brother of Trinity House uniform.

† The American delegates to the military staff talks were Stark, King, Marshall, Rear Admiral R. K. Turner, Major General Henry H. Arnold, Colonel Charles W. Bundy, and Commander Forrest P. Sherman. The British party included General Sir John Dill, Admiral Sir Dudley Pound, and Air Chief Marshal Sir Wilfrid Freeman.

King and Stark standing behind Roosevelt and Churchill following the worship service on *Prince of Wales* (U.S. Navy photograph)

Soviet Union.* But King was most interested in the decision that the Atlantic Fleet would escort British shipping, as well as neutral shipping, between the United States and Iceland.

King's impressions of the British were mixed. He got along so well with the First Sea Lord, Admiral Sir Dudley Pound, that they became close friends. King was willing to assist the Royal Navy in the Atlantic during the remainder of 1941; he was, for instance, ready to put his large warships under British control in the event a German raider escaped into the Atlantic.

But in his earlier years, at least, King had mistrusted Britain's motives. In his 1933 Naval War College thesis, King adopted Mahan's view that Great Britain historically suppressed maritime competition. Regardless of alliances, the British would oppose any American challenge to British supremacy. King even predicted that Great Britain was a potential enemy. "In the future," wrote King nine years before Argentia, "the

* At war with Germany since June.

questions of trade, of shipping, and of naval strength may lead to war."

King received an education at Argentia in the British skill at negotiating. The British had perfected the technique of a united front that never admitted to internal dissension. King was a novice by comparison. He embarrassed Marshall — in front of the British — by asking whether and when the Army would relieve the Marines in Iceland. (Marshall had been unable to provide soldiers for Iceland and resented King's implied criticism.) To all appearances King and Marshall had revealed differences that weakened American unity. It was the first of many instances when American interests would suffer because of their unresolved disputes.

Roosevelt and Churchill had agreed upon the text for the Atlantic Charter when the conference adjourned. As King had been committed to escorting British merchantmen, it was inevitable that Americans and Germans soon would be shooting at one another. The time was not long in coming. On 4 September the destroyer USS *Greer*, en route to Iceland, discovered a U-boat while assisting a British aircraft. While *Greer* tracked the U-boat on sonar, British aircraft attacked with depth charges. The German captain had to rid himself of the hound that was attracting the hunters.

The U-boat fired a torpedo at *Greer*, which the destroyer evaded. The *Greer*'s embarked division commander, Commander George W. Johnson, ordered counterattacks with depth charges. The fight lasted for several hours, finally ending in the evening with neither ship damaged. Although Roosevelt had ordered the U-boat destroyed, the local commander at Iceland did not renew the search. After reading the report, King angrily wrote upon it, "?!!?!? K."

Roosevelt seized the *Greer* incident to justify what he intended to do anyway: that is, to escort British shipping. Warlike pronouncements began thundering from Washington. Some doubters, however, wondered aloud whether Johnson had unnecessarily provoked the U-boat. King summoned Johnson to reassure him. "As long as I command the Atlantic Fleet," said King, "no one is going to nail your tail to the mast because you defended yourself."

King drove his Atlantic Fleet hard during the fall and early winter of 1941. The cruel North Atlantic weather pounded King's ships and crews whether at sea or in port at Iceland and Argentia. Some people cracked. The commanding officer of a battleship in Iceland complained "that he was having a hard time and would like to come home," recalled

King. "I sent him home all right. His wife had cancer, and that was too bad, but he should not have done what he did."

In an effort to get younger, tougher commanders at sea, the Navy Department decreed that the average ages of destroyer squadron commanders had to be lowered to forty-five or less; destroyer division commanders to forty-three or less; and destroyer commanding officers to less than forty-one. Captain Morton L. Deyo (who had praised King's virtues to two Secretaries of the Navy), commanding Destroyer Squadron Eleven, suddenly found himself overage and transferred on short notice to command of a heavy cruiser. King felt he owed Deyo an explanation, so he wrote that he could not intercede because of "policy." It was a ploy that King often used: blaming the monolithic Navy Department even though King may have approved or initiated the objectionable policy. Although Deyo became a flag officer, the irony of being transferred by the Admiral he had helped and the Secretary he had served must not have escaped him.

King mauled any task force commander who seemed to be flagging. He wanted fighters, and his favorites were Rear Admirals Jonas C. Ingram and Robert C. ("Ike") Giffen. The indomitable Ingram had the lonely task of patrolling the distant South Atlantic with an antiquated force. Despite his wife's serious illness, he still wrote to King with a cheerful confidence. "Your thin blue line in the South Atlantic is doing its stuff and is constantly on the job," Ingram had written in late July. "Jean continues to be in critical condition in Indiana with her men folk scattered from Iceland to Pearl Harbor, but I hope for the best."

When a cruiser of Ingram's force seized the German raider *Odenwald* that fall, King was delighted. "Nice work by the *Omaha*," King wrote to Ingram, "and tonight comes the word that they are bringing her in! By the way, this one capture seems to justify all the cruising that has been done towards the Cape Verdes."

The pressure affected everyone. Giffen once entered Newport in his flagship and came aboard *Augusta* to call upon King. King met him at the quarterdeck.

"What the hell are you doing in port?" said King.

Giffen turned to the OOD and asked for his barge.

"Why do you want your barge alongside?" asked King. "Didn't you come to see me?"

"I'm going to sea," said Giffen.

"Come on, Ike, cool down," said King. "Come in."

By mid-October the Atlantic Fleet suffered its first casualties in its undeclared war with Germany. The destroyer *Kearny* was damaged by a German torpedo, losing eleven men. King's frame of mind was fatalistic. "I am sure you realize," King wrote to a friend," that the *Kearny* incident is but the first of many that, in the nature of things, are bound to occur. It is likely that repetition will lead to open assumption of a war status — and what then? The Navy cannot do much more than is now being done — we are still more than a year away from any marked accession of any ships of the '2-ocean Navy.' . . . So — if a war status comes about — what to do?!? I'm afraid the citizenry will have to learn the bitter truth that war is not waged with words or promises or vituperation but with the realities of peril, hardships, and killing — vide Winston Churchill's 'blood, sweat and tears.' . . . I know you will not think me 'down-hearted' — I am only exercising my 'talents' for facing the facts — and there are grim facts to be faced — the sooner the better!"

Interference from Washington, insatiable demands for information, and frequent trips to the Navy Department and the White House compounded King's worries. "Not even my developed (and boasted!) capacity for decentralization," King complained to a friend," has sufficed to deal with matters that have come to hand these past few weeks." To Stark he protested, "Apropos of this 'curiosity' — this urge to 'brag' — this idea that 'we must do something — no matter what' — I am convinced that we . . . must bear down on it by 'educating' people to curb their 'curiosity,' to take for granted that the people-on-the-spot are doing their utmost, and to understand that being badgered by questions and suggestions does not help but rather hinders!"

In the last days of October King received word that two more of his ships had been torpedoed, the oiler *Salinas* and the destroyer *Reuben James.* The latter had sunk with great loss of life. "It shook him up," recalled his flag secretary, George L. Russell. "I know he didn't drink after that, unless a glass of wine would count, and that only occasionally."

Russell's comment bears further explanation. King had been a heavy drinker. Whether he had been an alcoholic depends upon one's definition. Regardless, it took willpower to quit. In addition to sherry, King would occasionally drink beer. Either drink was moderate compared to his earlier habits. Having changed his own ways, King became intolerant of problem drinkers. A troubled Marine officer who once served with King on *Lexington* asked for special treatment in the fall of 1942. "It has been clearly indicated to me," King replied, "that your trouble is that intoxicating liquor and business do not mix, and you have had considerable difficulty in learning this fact . . . while I have seen fit to be blunt — even brutal, it may be of interest to you to know that I, myself, went on the wagon in regard to 'hard liquor' as long ago as March, 1941 — for the duration and, very likely, after."

Because of public apathy and naval secrecy, Americans remained ignorant of the sacrifices by the men of the Atlantic Fleet. The Navy Department, hoping to compensate them with medals and commendations, asked King for his comments in early November. He replied to Stark, "I suggest that we 'go slow' in this matter of making heroes out of these people who have, after all, done the jobs they are trained to do. The earlier incidents [*Kearny*, *Salinas*, and *Reuben James*] loom large by contrast with peacetime conditions — but can be expected to become commonplace incidents as we get further along."

And to Nimitz he wrote, "Personally, I do not favor such awards unless the incidents indicate clearly deeds which are 'above and beyond the call of duty.' I sincerely hope that there will be no repetition of certain awards made during the last war where people were, in effect, decorated when they lost their ships. This is not to say that they were to blame for losing their ships, but certainly there was no cause whatever for commendation. . . . I do not consider my opinion as being 'hard-boiled' — naturally! — merely 'realistic.' "

King, however, soon gained public recognition of his own. An editor from *Life* magazine, Joseph J. Thorndike, Jr., interviewed King in late October for a featured article. Thorndike's first draft went to King and met heavy going. "I might as well say — as might be expected — that I do not care for this writeup," wrote King. "I find it a singular combination of fact, fiction, and fancy." King then offered a number of suggestions, which Thorndike incorporated into his article. King was delighted with the result.

King appeared on the cover of *Life* in its 24 November 1941 issue. Entitled "King of the Atlantic: America's Triple-Threat Admiral is the Stern, Daring Model of a War Commander," the article projected King as a tough, aggressive, confident seagoing flag officer. The public was assured that the Atlantic Fleet was well led. Little was said about the undeclared war and the American casualties.

King passed his sixty-third birthday on 23 November 1941. One year remained until retirement, a depressing thought for King. The Navy was his entire life, and he could not conceive of leaving it. The fatigue of eighteen-hour workdays added to his despair for the future. "It was the only time I ever sensed that he felt completely down and out," a close friend recalled. "King wrote a number of letters to us saying that he was sure his career would be ended after his tour with the Atlantic Fleet; he was sure that there was nothing more ahead for him."

On Saturday, 6 December, *Augusta* swung at her buoy in Narragansett Bay. King was aboard signing an unusually large number of letters. Some were official. Still he took time to write to friends in Lorain, or to Academy classmates urging them to come to Annapolis for their fortieth anniversary.

The Admiral was tired. The biweekly trips to Washington had been ordeals. The staff knew he disliked going there. "Well, I've got to go down to Washington again," he would say, "to straighten out those dumb bastards once more."

In the afternoon King went ashore to walk and to visit the Newport Reading Room, then returned to his flagship. At sunset the ship's bugler sounded colors, and the watch lowered the colors on the forecastle and fantail. The quarterdeck watch shivered in the winter wind.

After dinner King watched the ship's movie, then returned to his cabin. He read for a short while, selecting a book from his collection of biographies and histories. His mind relaxed. A steward brought him his customary glass of orange juice just before bedtime. King turned off his light and went to sleep.

13

Taking Command

SUNDAY, 7 December 1941, was a normal workday for King. His steward wakened him at 0700, and King exercised for his customary ten minutes before shaving and dressing. Narciso Arce, his Filipino cook, prepared breakfast in the flag pantry. After he had eaten, King worked at his desk until lunch, where he was joined by his new chief of staff, Rear Admiral Olaf M. Hustvedt. When lunch was over, King retired for his ritual nap.

A Marine orderly brought a message to Hustvedt. The Japanese had attacked Pearl Harbor. Hustvedt entered King's cabin and handed the message to the Admiral. King read it without comment. The staff routine the remainder of the day was unchanged.

Abby Dunlap, one of King's "adopted daughters," was aboard *Augusta* visiting her husband, Stan. King told her about the attack and allowed her to use the single phone line to call her sister, Betsy Matter, another of King's favorites, then living in Norfolk with her husband, Dick. Betsy thought that Abby was joking. King took the phone.

"Where is Dick?" asked King.

"He's sleeping," said Betsy.

"Tell Dick to get up and go to his base," said King. "The Japanese are attacking Pearl Harbor." Betsy was incredulous.

"We are dead serious," said King. "Tell Dick to go to the base immediately."

Betsy believed him. Then she exclaimed that if King had been in command in the Pacific there would have been no surprise attack.

"There are some that don't think so," replied King.

The next morning King informed his aide, Harry Sanders, to be prepared to leave by train for Washington that afternoon. Sanders did not ask about the uniform; King always traveled in civilian clothes when he went to Washington. Later in the morning a message arrived saying that New York City was under attack. King did not take the report seriously. He still intended to go to Washington.

After lunch, the Admiral's black barge came alongside for King and Sanders. King's sedan and Marine driver were waiting at the landing. They drove past the farms and woods surrounding Narragansett Bay to the picturesque train station at Kingston, Rhode Island. The two officers boarded the train and found their seats, which the staff had managed to reserve in the parlor car. King went home when he arrived in Washington that evening. Earlier in the day Roosevelt had gone before Congress and asked for a declaration of war against Japan. Congress complied, and the war was official.

Next morning, 9 December, King went to the White House and Sanders went to the Navy Department. It was like an "ant hill with the top kicked off," recalled Sanders. When King returned from the White House, Sanders told him he had a complete report on the losses at Pearl Harbor. King had only one comment. "We're living in a fool's paradise," he said.

King remained in Washington for the next four days, but no one, not even King, remembers what was said or done. Everyone seemed stunned by the cascading catastrophes. Japanese aircraft bombed Guam, Wake, Hong Kong, Singapore, and the Philippines. Japanese soldiers simultaneously landed north of Luzon and on the east coast of the Malay Peninsula. By Wednesday, the ninth, Guam had fallen, *Prince of Wales* and *Repulse* were sunk off Malaya, and Wake Island was under amphibious attack. On Thursday Germany and Italy declared war on the United States. It was time for King to return to Newport and take charge of his fleet.

His stay was brief. On the fifteenth King traveled back to Washington by overnight train. After arriving next morning he met with Secretary Knox, who had just returned from a flying trip to Pearl Harbor to assess the damage. Knox told King that he and Roosevelt had conferred the night before and had made two crucial decisions. First, Nimitz would relieve Kimmel as Commander in Chief, Pacific Fleet. Kimmel would be brought home for the inevitable investigations. Second, King would become Commander in Chief, U.S. Fleet (CINCUS), resurrecting the position that Roosevelt had abolished in January.

King was not sure he wanted the job. Stark seemed a more logical choice, said King. After all, Stark was the CNO, and he was the senior admiral in the Navy — he should command the fleet. Knox insisted that he wanted King. In that case, said King, there was much to resolve. Before the war CINCUS was at sea in a battleship. Now everything had changed. King obviously would have to command the fleet from Washington. His frequent trips from Newport had convinced him that his headquarters had to be in the capitol to be near the White House and Navy Department. "Where the power is," King once explained, "that is where the headquarters have to be."

What, then, of his relationship with Stark? The CNO's duties included war plans and the strategic direction of the Navy. Furthermore, he was the principal naval advisor to the President. Yet the scope of the CNO's authority had never been altogether clear. With both Stark and King physically present in the Navy Department, there inevitably would be problems of jurisdiction and responsibility. Knox agreed that King's position had to be defined. The upshot was that Knox directed two members of the General Board, Walton R. Sexton and J. O. Richardson, to draft an appropriate executive order for the President's signature.

That afternoon King, Knox, and Stark called on the President. There were several prerequisites that King wanted Roosevelt to accept before King took the job. The acronym "CINCUS" sounded too much like "sink us," an unpleasant reminder of Pearl Harbor. King wanted to substitute COMINCH. Roosevelt agreed.

Next, said King, he wanted to avoid press conferences and appearances before Congress except under extraordinary circumstances. Roosevelt again was agreeable, except that he stipulated that someone would have to be a spokesman for the Navy Department.

And finally King made his most audacious demand: command authority over the bureaus in the Navy Department. (The bureaus had retained their independence for over a century, and neither Roosevelt nor the Congress wanted to change the system.) That would require a change in federal law, replied the President. The best that he could promise was to replace any bureau chief who did not cooperate with King.

The following day, 17 December, King read the Sexton-Richardson executive order draft. He made several editorial changes but accepted the gist of the document. The next day Roosevelt's signature made it official as Executive Order 8984, "Prescribing the Duties of the Commander in Chief of the United States Fleet and the Cooperative Duties of the Chief of Naval Operations." *

It was one of the most remarkable documents of the Second World War. Years of political opposition and controversy had stymied any

* See Appendix III for the full text of the order.

federal law that conveyed the authority that Roosevelt had given King in a matter of forty-eight hours. King had suddenly assumed powers that had been denied to the Chief of Naval Operations ever since that office had been established in 1915.

There were two key elements in the executive order. The first was that King would have "supreme command of the operating forces comprising the several fleets of the United States Navy and the operating forces of the Naval Coastal Frontier Command. . . ." The other was that King would be directly responsible to the President. His status with the Secretary of the Navy was vague. According to the order, COMINCH would be under the Secretary's "general direction." A vague phrase, indeed.

The order also defined the COMINCH-CNO association. The CNO would develop long-range war plans, COMINCH the current war plans. That delineation would never be clear, to the confusion of Navy Department planners. Left unsaid were such crucial matters as who would advise the President, and who would represent the Navy during conferences with the British. Presumably it would be Stark as before, but King certainly had to be included.

King moved quickly to consolidate his authority by telling his aide, Harry Sanders, to draft a "polite" note to Stark. When signed by King it read, "I would appreciate your preparing a memorandum stating what functions and responsibilities the CNO should turn over to COMINCH."

King left Newport for the final time that year on 20 December. A utility aircraft met him at the Naval Air Station, Quonset Point, Rhode Island, for the flight to Washington. The pilot, Frank A. Brandley, had tried to get a new Lockheed Lodestar executive aircraft at the Naval Air Station, Anacostia, Washington, but the operations officer had given him the older plane instead. "Ernie did not seem to mind," Brandley later said. "As a matter of fact he seemed to be relaxed and appeared to enjoy the ride down."

King went to his office at the Navy Department to start fighting the war. "Nothing was ready," King later said. "I had to start with nothing."

First he needed a staff. Several came directly from his Atlantic Fleet staff: aides Ruthven E. Libby and Charles B. Lanman, and Frog Low as operations officer. George Russell would come later as flag secretary once the paperwork was squared away in Newport. King avoided taking everyone in consideration of his successor. Others came from Stark's CNO organization: brilliant, irascible Richmond K. ("Kelly") Turner from war plans; solid, dependable Willis A. Lee from fleet training; and

Roland M. Brainard from ship movements. All found themselves working for King before the end of December.

King's selection of his chief of staff evolved from the need to designate his replacement in the Atlantic. Stark had always planned that in the event of war his principal assistant, Rear Admiral Royal E. Ingersoll, would take command of the Pacific Fleet; that Nimitz would take command of the Asiatic Fleet; and that King would remain in the Atlantic. (Just what Stark expected to do with Kimmel and Hart is not known.) Stark's scheme had been overtaken by events. Knox had decided that Nimitz would command the Pacific Fleet, and there was no need to replace Hart because his diminutive Asiatic Fleet was not expected to survive the Japanese drive in the Southwest Pacific. King reasoned by process of elimination that Ingersoll should take command of the Atlantic Fleet.

Stark objected. Ingersoll, he said, had become irreplaceable.

"You cannot keep him," said King. "He is needed at sea." King next suggested Rear Admirals Frederick J. Horne, then awaiting retirement on the General Board, and Russell Willson, the Superintendent of the Naval Academy. "Take the one you want to replace Ingersoll," said King, "and I will take the other as my chief of staff. Sleep on it and tell me tomorrow."

Stark agreed to give up Ingersoll and chose Horne to replace him. King, who had been shipmates with Willson on Mayo's staff, phoned Willson late Christmas night to tell him he was to become King's chief of staff.

Willson had gone to bed earlier that evening a happy man. Nimitz had asked him to serve in the Pacific, and Willson had been overjoyed to accept. Willson's daughter, Eunice, answered the phone. "The caller didn't identify himself," she later said, "but somehow I knew — Admiral King had a very distinctive way of speaking. I had to wake my father, which was probably just as well, since it gave him a chance to brace himself; we both knew what must be coming. It was heartbreaking for me to watch him as he replied, 'Yes sir; it's a great honor, sir,' while his face turned pale and he almost wept with disappointment and frustration."

Another important selection was a Deputy Chief of Staff for Operations. Rear Admiral Richard S. Edwards, the commander of the Atlantic submarine force, had impressed King. They had met at Casco Bay, and King was struck by Edwards's "horse sense." He was the man that King wanted.

"Upon my arrival in Washington on 29 December," Edwards later wrote, "I found Admiral King enthroned in the most disreputable office

I have ever seen. Someone had moved out in a hurry, taking the furniture with him, but not the dirt. The Admiral had liberated a flat top desk from somewhere and a couple of chairs. He sat on one side of the desk; opposite him sat Russell Willson. I and my assistant [Low] borrowed a broken down table from a friend who was out to lunch and set up shop in a corner of the Admiral's office. . . . That was all there was. I recall thinking that as the headquarters of the greatest navy in the world it fell somewhat short of being impressive."

Most officers were reluctant to go to the COMINCH staff in those early months, wanting sea duty to fight the war. A phone call from COMINCH to the Bureau of Naval Personnel, however, took precedence over personal wishes. Those at sea tried to stay there. Captain Charles M. ("Savvy") Cooke, Jr., commanding the battleship *Pennsylvania,* resisted orders to serve as King's chief planning officer in early 1942. King replied, "I am fully in sympathy with your wish to stay at sea — but — have also to remark that you must expect to be placed where others consider that you can do the most good to the general cause — in which I am sure you will agree."

Cooke still protested, so King wrote again. "I think it trite to say that we all must serve where we can do the most for the Navy," said King, "and that that has to be judged by other people than ourselves. It is my considered judgment that you are needed here — not only because of your talents but because you will be fresh from direct contact with the sea-going forces which will do us all here much good."

This was King's earliest policy statement of rotating staff officers between sea duty and COMINCH. There were two exceptions, two officers whom King regarded as indispensable and who remained with King throughout the war. One was Dick Edwards. The other was Savvy Cooke.

Congress had limited the numbers of enlisted men authorized for Washington duty, forcing the use of civilians in Stark's CNO organization. Many were transferred to COMINCH. At the usual quitting time they went home, war or no war. This was intolerable to King. His working hours were around the clock, seven days a week. He directed that senior enlisted men * replace the civilians, and by early March they were gone.

Although the staff enlisted men were among the best, many could not do the work; COMINCH routine was shockingly different from a ship's office. In due time officer and enlisted women — WAVES — replaced most of the men. "Business began to hum," recalled a COMINCH staff

* Mostly chief yeomen, who were clerical and administrative specialists.

officer. Eventually more than 300 women, specially selected for their brains, motivation, and skills, handled a variety of administrative tasks. They were magnificent.

King did retain a male enlisted man — later promoted to ensign — as his personal secretary (known as an "admiral's writer"). "He was the best security risk in the world," Russell later said, "because he couldn't remember anything for more than two hours."

King also wanted (in addition to a staff) an airplane, an automobile, and a flagship. Even before taking office King asked Stark for a "twin-engine plane of appropriate characteristics." A day later the Chief of the Bureau of Aeronautics found that his Lockheed Lodestar belonged to King. King's car came from Arthur C. Hoffman, a vice president of A & P, who gave King a Cadillac which he used throughout the war.

But most important, King wanted a proper flagship. Although he would be stationed in Washington, King insisted that he had to be able to go to sea at any time. He knew what ship he wanted, William K. Vanderbilt's magnificent motor yacht, *Alva*, now renamed USS *Plymouth* for naval service. King soon changed his mind and selected instead the former Dodge family yacht, *Delphine*, a 1,200-ton, 257-foot luxury ship built in 1921. He personally selected as her commanding officer Commander Charles F. Grisham, a former enlisted man who had proved his worth to King at New London. Grisham went to a Detroit shipyard to supervise *Delphine*'s conversion, and in the interim King used another former yacht, the USS *Vixen*, which had been Edwards's flagship when he had commanded the Atlantic submarine force. *Vixen* later became Ingersoll's Atlantic Fleet flagship.

King wanted a suitable name for his flagship and circulated a memorandum among his staff for comment and discussion. Among the names under consideration were *Unity*, *Wolverine*, *Excelsior*, *Defiance*, *Revenge*, *Vengeance*, *Undaunted*, and *Nemesis*. King finally selected *Dauntless*. In early summer of 1942 she moored at the Washington Navy Yard, where she was to remain, except for brief interludes, for the war. Certain members of King's staff were ostensibly assigned to the flagship, although they neither lived nor messed aboard ship unless they were watch officers. This "sea duty" drew sea pay, which was technically legal but much resented by others of the staff. The only staff officer living aboard for any period of time would be Savvy Cooke, who could not afford to bring his family to Washington.*

King lived in seclusion aboard *Dauntless*. The only exceptions were

* Edwards and Willson lived aboard briefly.

Frederick J. Horne (National Archives 80-G-302279)

Russell Willson (National Archives 80-G-302374)

Charles M. Cooke, Jr. (National Archives 80-G-302333)

Richard S. Edwards (National Archives 80-G-302294)

USS *Dauntless*, King's flagship and home (U.S. Navy photograph)

King's official residence, the Naval Observatory, where Mattie lived (Courtesy Ernest J. King, Jr.)

Sunday afternoons with his family at his official residence, the Naval Observatory in northwest Washington. The flagship provided a quiet place to think and rest without disruptions. Life at home had always swirled with noise and people. And there were other prerogatives and amenities that only *Dauntless* could provide. At least one congressman questioned the justification for an expensive ship to provide King with a private bedroom, but the subject was dropped.

King wanted to take command as COMINCH on 1 January 1942, hoping that history would disassociate him with the disastrous events of 1941. When pushed by Knox to fix a date in late December, King stalled with the excuse that he was still getting organized. "Well," Knox finally asked, "what are you waiting for?" In the end, King took command as COMINCH on 30 December 1941.

14

Opening Moves

THE UNITED STATES and Great Britain were finally allies in war. Roosevelt and Churchill arranged to meet in Washington just before Christmas. The Prime Minister and his advisors arrived on 22 December prepared to discuss grand strategy and combined operations. They came as seasoned warriors, ready to counsel and advise the inexperienced Americans, whom they expected to find in shock and disarray after Pearl Harbor. The British too were worried about the rapid Japanese conquests; as Japan seemed to be the most immediate enemy, the Americans might reverse the ABC-1 Staff Agreement of March 1941 that the defeat of Germany was first priority.

The U.S. team had had little time to prepare for the First Washington Conference (ARCADIA). The exigencies of daily crises took priority over long-range strategic planning. Information from the Far East was sporadic, and all of it was bad. Marshall was preoccupied with MacArthur's losing battle in the Philippines, Stark was trying to salvage the shattered Pacific and Asiatic fleets, and King was simply trying to find office space and a staff.

The first plenary meeting began in the late afternoon of 23 December at the White House. The British delegation was relatively small: Churchill; Lord Beaverbrook, chief of war production; Admiral of the Fleet Sir Dudley Pound, the First Sea Lord; Field Marshal Sir John Dill, who recently had resigned as Chief of the Imperial General Staff because of ill health and incompatibility with Churchill; and Air Chief Marshal Sir Charles Portal, Chief of the Air Staff. They were a tightly knit group, accustomed to working together, with two years of strategic planning experience in the war against Germany.

The American recorder, Captain John L. McCrea, was impressed with the British as the conference went along. "They knew their stuff," McCrea remembered. "They all talked exceedingly well and made much sense. The staff organization was superb, as well. Three brigadiers did the bulk of the work, and their reports of the meetings were masterpieces."

The Americans, in contrast, were an ad hoc committee headed by the President. His civilian advisors were the indispensable Harry Hopkins, Secretary of War Henry Stimson, and Frank Knox. Marshall, of course, represented the Army, which included the Army Air Forces. Lieutenant General Henry H. Arnold sat in as an opposite number to Portal. Although "Hap" Arnold was subordinate to Marshall, Portal was his own man. Pound may have wondered whether Stark or King represented the United States Navy. Both were present.

Roosevelt and Churchill opened the meeting. The President spoke cautiously of containing enemy aggression, of holding key areas and maintaining lines of communications, and of mobilizing resources for the future. Churchill wanted to inject a spirit of confidence and optimism that the Americans presumably needed at the moment. He was more aggressive and spoke of invading French North Africa. Singapore, he stressed, would be held, and the Royal Navy was ready to help in the Pacific.

King listened, and he said little. When the meeting ended, the President spoke briefly with his military advisors before going to dinner with Churchill. (Their conversation was unrecorded.) That evening King attended a dinner party of American and British military leaders at the Carlton Hotel. The predominant mood was one of harmony and goodwill.

Marshall would become the chief American spokesman during ARCADIA. While the Allies affirmed the Germany-First concept, long-range plans were difficult because the future was so unpredictable. The immediate crises in the Pacific demanded attention. While the Allied leaders talked in Washington, the Japanese seized Wake Island, Hong Kong, and Manila, and Japanese forces landed in Borneo, Mindanao, Luzon, and the Netherlands East Indies. The Philippines were doomed, but Churchill kept insisting that Singapore was an impregnable "fortress."

The Japanese had to be stopped somewhere; everyone agreed it had to be Australia and its sea lines of communication to Hawaii. The loss of Australia and the remainder of the Western Pacific might trigger a Pan-Asiatic movement of all the brown and yellow races. "That might complicate our situation there," said the Prime Minister, thinking of the millions in India seeking independence from Great Britain.

The Allies faced two immediate problems trying to contain the Japanese. One was that forces from five different countries — the United States, Great Britain, the Netherlands, Australia, and New Zealand — were fighting haphazardly for want of a common commander. The other problem (a handicap throughout the war) was a shortage of shipping needed to move forces and supplies to the war zones. Marshall attempted to solve the first problem with a surprise appeal to his colleagues on Christmas Day. "I am convinced that there must be one man in command of the entire theater — air, ground, and ships," said Marshall. "We can not manage by cooperation. Human frailties are such that there would be emphatic unwillingness to place portions of troops under another service. If we make a plan for unified command now, it will solve nine-tenths of our troubles."

Marshall had overstated his case. Unity of command alone would not stop the Japanese. And then there were the historical objections. The British balked at having their national forces under a foreigner. Portal wanted first to decide what forces should go to the Far East before discussing who would command them, and King agreed. King's own initial feelings about Marshall's proposal are uncertain. Marshall had not discussed it with him beforehand, so King characteristically would want time to think about it. Nevertheless, King was the only one of the five American flag officers present who even responded to Marshall. (Brigadier General Dwight D. Eisenhower, Marshall's war plans officer, was encouraged.) "It would certainly be better," said King, "to decide at home the general line of action to be followed in the Southwest Pacific area than to have it discussed by a committee on the spot." King then raised an issue that had wrecked coalitions in the past, an issue that everyone knew had somehow to be resolved. "If there is to be a single commander," said King, "it will be very difficult for him to reconcile the various national interests."

The question of unity of command was referred to a joint study group.

A plenary meeting convened the next day. The President himself put the unity-of-command issue on the table. He was for it. Churchill was against it. Knox supported the President, but an Army general at the meeting thought that King was only "lukewarm." On the twenty-seventh Marshall continued to seek support both from the President and the Navy. Encouraged by the President's enthusiastic approval in a morning meeting, Marshall met with Knox, Stark, King, and a number of other flag officers in Stark's office at noon.

Stimson, and perhaps Marshall, felt that Knox and King were on their side. The other flag officers seemed either opposed or indifferent. In King's opinion his naval colleagues were still too "stunned" by events to grasp Marshall's proposals. King was clearheaded enough to see that a unified command in the Southwest Pacific was a "natural" under the circumstances. Marshall then suggested that the Americans nominate British General Sir Archibald Wavell as supreme commander. He was experienced, he was available from his command in India, the Americans had no one readily available, and a British nominee might get Churchill's approval. Again some of the admirals objected, but again King supported Marshall. "When King said this," an Army officer recorded; "all the other Navy people smiled and concurred in their own way. . . . Admiral Stark finally gave his blessing. . . ."

The Americans at last had achieved a united front, albeit belatedly. They would nominate Wavell when the time seemed right. First they had to resolve the scope of the supreme commander's duties — whoever he might be. That afternoon the Allied naval and military leaders again met to discuss how to limit the hypothetical supreme commander so as to protect national interests. The Dutch were most concerned with the Netherlands East Indies, the British with Malaya, the Americans with the Philippines, and the Australians and New Zealanders with their home territory. But on the whole the British seemed amenable to some kind of unified command. (The Australians, Dutch, and New Zealanders were neither asked nor represented.) A quick decision was imperative, and the staff planners began drafting an appropriate charter for submission to Roosevelt and Churchill.

Only Churchill remained unconvinced. His American allies were about to test his attitude toward coalition warfare and his willingness to compromise. Would Churchill subordinate the interests of Great Britain to the interests of the alliance? It had already become clear that there was a divergence of basic thinking between the Americans and the British. "In the military as in the commercial or production spheres," Churchill later wrote, "the American mind runs naturally to broad, sweeping, logical conclusions on the largest scale. It is on these that they build their practical thought and action. They feel that once the foundation has been planned on true and comprehensive lines all other stages will follow naturally and almost inevitably. The British mind does not work quite in this way. We do not think that logic and clearcut principles are necessarily the sole keys to what ought to be done in swiftly changing and indefinable situations. In war particularly we assign a larger importance to opportunism and improvisation, seeking rather to live and conquer in accordance with the unfolding event than to aspire to dominate it often by fundamental decisions. There is room for much argument about both views. The difference is one of emphasis, but it is deep-seated."

Churchill finally came around. By the time he left late on the twenty-eighth for a short visit to Canada, the combined efforts of Roosevelt, Hopkins, and Marshall had persuaded the Prime Minister to agree to appointing Wavell supreme commander in the Southwest Pacific theater. Churchill drafted a telegram to his war cabinet for approval, nominating Wavell and specifying his duties and authority. Yet Churchill still had reservations. He mistakenly believed that King and Stark still opposed the unification concept, reinforcing his personal feelings that the Royal Navy should never be subordinate to an army officer, even if he were British. Consequently he proposed in his telegram that an American admiral command the combined naval forces and merely "conform to [rather than obey] the plans and policies of the supreme commander."

The American leaders met with the President at noon on the twenty-eighth to consider Churchill's telegram, which he had left with Hopkins to show the President. Marshall argued that "conform" was ambiguous and removed the combined naval forces from Wavell's command. Roosevelt agreed. The telegram had to be changed. King, Hopkins, and Marshall stepped into an adjacent room to change its wording. King's pen first slashed through the offensive statement about conforming. King then changed the telegram to read that all naval forces — American, British, Dutch, and Australian — would be under Wavell's command. King also deleted Churchill's presumptuous statement in the same telegram that the British would "assume responsibility for the security of the Atlantic Ocean in the existing close collaboration with United States naval forces there assigned." That matter had not even been discussed. In the end, Churchill accepted the American editing and sent off the telegram, urging his government's approval.

While King backed a unified command in this instance, his support was qualified. "I have no intention whatever," he wrote to a colleague during ARCADIA, "of acceding to any unity of command proposals that are not premised on a particular situation in a particular area at a particular time for a more or less particular period. During the brief time that I have been on my current job, I have found it necessary to find time to point out to some 'amateur strategists' in high places that unity of command is not a panacea for all military difficulties — and I shall continue to do so."

There were other pressing matters during that noon meeting on the twenty-eighth — the succession of disasters in the Pacific, for instance. The President rebuked the Navy for its bungling during the previous several days, particularly the withdrawal of the Wake Island relief force. (Knox earlier had discussed Wake Island with Churchill. "We ordered our fleet to fight a battle with the Japanese to relieve Wake Island, and now within a few hours of steaming the admiral [Pye] has decided to turn back. What would you do with your admiral in a case like this?" Churchill replied, "It is dangerous to meddle with admirals when they say they can't do things. They have always got the weather or fuel or something to argue about.")

Roosevelt wanted action. A force of cruisers and destroyers, he suggested, could sweep those areas where small Japanese task groups presumably were located. If they contacted a superior force, their high speed would enable them to escape. The President did not grasp the dangers of operating without air cover. The 10 December loss of *Repulse* and *Prince of Wales* to Japanese aircraft off Malaya was the most recent example. Fast surface ships could not outrun aircraft. The President's suggestions were tactically impractical, but his will to hit back — somehow — at the Japanese Navy was apparent. His own navy seemed cautious and hesitant. "The Japanese are getting awfully close to home," said Roosevelt.

Roosevelt obviously wanted assurance that the Navy intended to do something, that it would act rather than react, and that it had some kind of plan for carrying the war to the Japanese. Stark offered little encouragement. King had answers. His first priority was to hold the sea line of communication between Hawaii and Midway, the second to reinforce and hold the line from Hawaii to Samoa. "All other projects must give way to this," said King, by inference including the President's scheme. As to the withdrawal from Wake, Pye "was undoubtedly taking the broad viewpoint."

Roosevelt stubbornly responded that he wanted some kind of contact with the Japanese Navy. The conference then turned to other matters.

Wavell's proposed command still bedeviled Roosevelt. There were too many loose ends, too many ambiguities. Roosevelt invited King to lunch on 29 December to get the Admiral's opinion. Who, asked the President, would give Wavell (or any other Allied supreme commander) his orders? This was a hoary problem with coalition warfare that defied solution. Each country providing forces would want a vote. Yet the frictions and delays in consulting everyone had destroyed coalitions and would be intolerable in the war against the Axis. The President and the

Admiral deliberated as they ate, and when lunch was over, King left with instructions to think things over and return with an answer.

Roosevelt had, in his own way, made King his surrogate. Through King he had given an ultimatum to the chiefs of staff. The President wanted no further delay; there was no more time for debate. King had to get an agreement that afternoon and report back to the President.

King hurriedly drafted a plan for consideration. When the chiefs of staff assembled, however, Admiral Pound beat him to the punch. The British had a solution, he announced, which they hoped the Americans would accept. The gist of their plan was to "utilize existing machinery" to get rapid decisions, in lieu of creating a special body to supervise Wavell. Other governments would be excluded from what they now called the Chief of Staff Committee: the British and American chiefs of staff. This committee alone, argued the British, with final approval from the President and Prime Minister, would determine Allied strategy and direct the Allied supreme commanders.

So that was it. The American and British chiefs of staff would run the war and the lesser countries would follow orders. Now King had his say. He had just seen the President, said King, and the President wanted a quick answer. Then King read his own proposal, claiming it too would achieve rapid decisions through existing machinery. Yet what King proposed was entirely the opposite, for he suggested creating a new body, which he called the Southwestern Pacific Council, separate and distinct from the Chiefs of Staff Committee, and which would include representatives from the Netherlands and Australia. Whether King's proposal was his idea or whether he was speaking for Roosevelt is not certain, but in any event King did not support it with any vigor.

Sensing a possible delay in accepting the principle of unity of command, Marshall tried to defer the entire question of organization, regarding it as an impediment to negotiations. King disagreed. Establishing the machinery, he argued, was an indispensable part of creating a unified command. In that case, responded Marshall, he was prepared to accept the British proposal. King was so uncommitted to his own proposal that without hesitation he too agreed to the British plan. Stark quickly followed suit, and the chiefs of staff immediately forwarded the British plan to Roosevelt and Churchill for final approval.

Churchill promptly approved, having known about the plan beforehand. Once again the British had acted in unison. The Americans still floundered. The President held out for a separate body, along the lines King had proposed and then abandoned, with Australian, New Zealand,

and Dutch representation. But his chiefs of staff were adamant, insisting that the President accept the British plan.

Once again Roosevelt called upon King for advice over lunch in the President's office on the thirty-first of December. Their discussion is unrecorded, but the gist of King's arguments can be inferred by his remarks to an intimate group of war correspondents some months later. "It was obvious," King explained, "that with so many participants in the war, decisions could not be made by a show of hands. Nothing could be accomplished by such means. As the United States and Great Britain were financing the war and doing most of the fighting, they should therefore run the war, make the final decisions, and control the military machine. This is a hard-boiled method bound to cause friction and unhappiness among the smaller nations who thought that they should have a voice in the military decisions, but it is the only way to function effectively."

After lunch King arrived late at the chiefs of staff conference, but he brought good news. He reported that he "had reason to believe" that the President would approve the British plan which the chiefs of staff had endorsed.

King's statement marked the genesis of the Combined Chiefs of Staff (CCS) organization and the procedures by which they controlled the strategic direction of the Second World War. Other details had to be resolved, but by the end of ARCADIA it had been agreed that the Allied headquarters would be in Washington. King, Marshall, Stark, and Arnold would be designated the Joint Chiefs of Staff (JCS), the equivalent to the British Chiefs of Staff of Field Marshal Alan Brooke (who replaced Dill as Chief of the Imperial General Staff), Pound, and Portal. The British would maintain a liaison group (the British Joint Staff Mission) in Washington, headed by Dill, who would work directly with the Joint Chiefs of Staff on day-to-day matters. Periodically the JCS and the British Chiefs of Staff, together with Roosevelt and Churchill, would meet to decide upon grand strategy and other crucial matters affecting the war. It would be the most successful coalition in the history of warfare.

Churchill went to Florida for a short vacation on 6 January, accompanied by Marshall at the Prime Minister's request, and for several days there were no further meetings. While relaxing and organizing his thoughts, Churchill concluded that Hitler would attempt to defeat Great Britain in 1942 before the United States could mobilize. The war against

Japan would, for a number of reasons, have to be secondary. He did not, however, believe in an entirely passive defense in the Pacific. Rather—in true British fashion—Churchill wishfully envisioned amphibious raids to create "a reign of terror among the enemy's detached garrisons. . . ." These views were relayed to both the President and Marshall. While Churchill ruminated about grand strategy in the Florida sun, the Japanese continued to rampage in the Southwest Pacific. The British had steered the discussions toward Germany before Churchill went on vacation, but by Churchill's return Japan was uppermost in the minds of King and Stark.

The CCS meetings resumed on 10 January. By the next afternoon Stark forced the British to consider whether the Allies should reinforce the Pacific at the expense of the European theater, which for the moment was stable. The discussions were indecisive, any ultimate decisions depending upon whether adequate shipping was available to meet the needs of both theaters.

The talks then turned to a subject which King regarded as vital: the defense of island bases between Hawaii and Australia. As the CCS were unanimous that Australia had to be held, the sea lines of communications leading to Australia from the east obviously had to be safeguarded. Such key bases as New Caledonia, Fiji, and American Samoa had to be reinforced, and air and naval forces would be needed to protect convoys all the way to Australia. King had already instructed Nimitz to hold the line from Hawaii to Samoa, and American Marines would land in Samoa by late January. But the Pacific Fleet was unable to protect communications between Samoa and Australia; that responsibility, argued King, belonged to Britain, Australia, and New Zealand. (Disregarding Churchill's earlier offers to help in the Pacific, the British planners claimed that they and their Dominions had neither troops nor ships to spare.) King was particularly concerned with the vulnerability of New Caledonia, 900 miles due east of Australia. As it dominated the eastern approaches to Australia and had valuable nickel resources, it was probably a prime Japanese objective. King wanted troops and aircraft sent there immediately, arguing that it was vital to the entire security of the ABDA * command.

None of the other Americans present seconded King, and some even spoke against him. Arnold declared that he did not want to send air reinforcements to New Caledonia. His heavy bombers on the way to Australia, said Arnold, could simply fly over New Caledonia if it was

* *A*merican-*B*ritish-*D*utch-*A*ustralia, the acronym for Wavell's Southwest Pacific unified command.

occupied by the Japanese. But ships cannot fly, King retorted, and Australia's safety depended upon ships carrying supplies and troops. If New Caledonia fell, convoys would have to detour far to the south, causing intolerable delays in reinforcing Australia. On that sour note of American discord, the meeting ended.

While the CCS haggled on Sunday, 11 January, Japan declared war against the Dutch and invaded the Netherlands East Indies. King became even more convinced that Japan had to take first priority. He envisioned the Japanese seizing Hawaii, the Aleutians, and even Alaska if no one opposed them, and he desperately wanted to stop them before they got to Australia. Yet to King the British were unwilling to shift their emphasis from the European theater. Portal, for example, objected to any suggestion to divert replacement aircraft from the Middle East.

The next afternoon, 12 January, the CCS assembled for their tenth ARCADIA meeting. Marshall finally came to King's side and proposed sending 10,000 American troops to New Caledonia out of some 21,800 destined for the Far East. Marshall also proposed to send aircraft, gasoline, and war materiel, as well. But the shipping would have to come from the Atlantic; the numbers of American garrison troops sent to Iceland and Northern Ireland (to relieve British troops) would have to be reduced. The British accepted the reduction, but even with that compensation there still would not be enough ships. The only alternative was to diminish Russian Lend-Lease deliveries by 30 percent to release ships for the Pacific. And that, declared the CCS, was a political matter for Roosevelt and Churchill to decide at the plenary meeting scheduled for later in the afternoon.

The subsequent meeting soon focused upon the lack of shipping to satisfy both the Australian requirements and Lend-Lease commitments to Russia. Both Roosevelt and Marshall were willing to sacrifice New Caledonia if additional ships could not be found. King continued to argue for New Caledonia. Russia could do with less. Archangel was probably closed for the winter, said the Admiral, and he wondered whether the Russians could even absorb their quota of supplies because of limited port facilities. The President replied that the Russians claimed Archangel was open, and that Russia could handle everything the United States was supposed to send.

"How important is the occupation of New Caledonia?" the President asked King. King repeated his earlier arguments.

"Would it be easy to reconquer?" asked Roosevelt.

"None will be easy to reconquer once they are occupied," said King.

Hopkins interjected with a fresh perspective. Only seven ships were needed, he said, to make up the 30 percent reduction to Russia. Certainly, said Hopkins, those seven ships could be found somewhere. Roosevelt agreed. Ships would be found. New Caledonia would be reinforced; Marshall's convoy would be sent.

Hopkins had been the key. "Lord Root of the Matter," Churchill had called him, half jokingly, half seriously. "Hopkins did a grand job," King later said. "He did a lot to keep the President on the beam and even more to keep Churchill on the beam. . . . I've seldom seen a man whose head was screwed on so tight." King time and again found himself agreeing with Hopkins's reasoning, but he preferred to let Hopkins do the talking.

King's own influence at the Allied conferences frequently was unrecorded in the official minutes, but he could advise Roosevelt without saying a word. "I can remember many times in his study at the White House, especially when Churchill was there," King later explained. "I would not say anything, but when the President would look at me I would shake my head no. He would not always agree with me, but I would shake my head very slightly so that other people would not see it."

ARCADIA adjourned on 14 January. The British went home. King could now devote his full efforts to directing the Navy at war.

When King took command as COMINCH on 30 December 1941, his first act was to send marching orders to Nimitz, about to take command of the Pacific Fleet. King identified the boundaries for containing the Japanese. Nimitz's first priority was to safeguard the sea lines of communication from the United States to Hawaii and thence to Midway. The second priority was to maintain communications with Australia, chiefly by safeguarding the Hawaii-Samoa line of communication. King urged Nimitz to extend that line westward to Fiji at the earliest possible date.

King's next concern was to reinforce Samoa, the linchpin in the Hawaii-Australia line of communication. Nimitz used almost the entire Pacific Fleet to escort the Marine forces there in mid-January. Once the Marines were ashore, the next question was how to use the American carriers. *Saratoga* was out of action following a submarine attack, and only *Lexington*, *Enterprise*, and *Yorktown* were available.* King and Nimitz decided upon nuisance raids in the Gilberts and Marshalls, which raised American morale, partially satisfied Roosevelt's demand for ac-

* USS *Ranger* was in the Atlantic.

tion, but did nothing to slow the Japanese advance toward Australia.

The ABDA command, so laboriously fashioned by the CCS, rapidly disintegrated from a combination of Japanese pressure and Allied weaknesses. Both the Dutch and British criticized Admiral Thomas C. Hart, the combined naval commander under Wavell. He was, they charged, too sick to continue in command, and their complaints reached Roosevelt. As the ABDA area was doomed in any event, Roosevelt decided to bring Hart home despite King's objections that Hart and the Navy would be humiliated. King was furious at the Dutch for what he considered their mistreatment of Hart, and he never forgave them. It is true that Hart was not a well man. The Dutch were about to lose everything, and in such a crisis they overlooked American feelings.

While the Japanese southward advance enveloped the Netherlands East Indies and threatened northern Australia, other Japanese forces seized Rabaul in the Bismarck Archipelago in late January. Clearly the Japanese were now headed eastward down the Solomon Islands, threatening the eastern approaches to Australia. King's reaction was immediate. He proposed as an expedient yet another unified command in Australian and New Zealand waters — ANZAC — under an American flag officer, Rear Admiral H. Fairfax Leary. It was done. There was no squabble this time about who would give orders. Leary would report to one man alone: Ernest J. King. King also advised Nimitz that the Pacific Fleet, still tied down in defense of Hawaii, would be expected to go to the South Pacific to help protect Australia.

Air power had been thus far the key to Japan's victories. ABDA naval forces, devoid of aircraft carriers or effective land-based air coverage, lay naked to enemy aircraft operating from carriers, seaplane tenders, and airfields. Although Arnold was rushing Army aircraft to the Pacific, their immediate effect was negligible. If King expected to stop the Japanese he would have to use his three remaining carriers, but Nimitz and his staff were reluctant to risk them unnecessarily. If the carriers were lost or damaged, the entire Pacific would be defenseless. The thinking in Pearl Harbor was to hold them there to await developments.

King earlier had decided to place Leary and his ANZAC command under COMINCH rather than CINCPAC * control because King regarded Nimitz as an unproven fleet commander, not yet ready to be trusted unreservedly. It would become an awkward situation. King and Leary were half a world apart, and communicating would be laborious. Although King did solicit Nimitz's opinion on how best to employ the

* Acronym for Commander in Chief, Pacific Fleet.

carriers, King precipitately transferred one carrier task group to Leary before Nimitz could even reply. When Nimitz belatedly recommended holding the other two carriers in reserve, King disagreed and ordered them to attack Japanese ships and bases.

Such efforts were futile. Even before they began, Singapore fell on 15 February, and Java would not hold out much longer. The *Lexington* task group under Vice Admiral Wilson Brown in the ANZAC area was unable to launch a planned attack against Rabaul. Vice Admiral William F. Halsey in *Enterprise* belabored Wake Island, a useless attack based upon wishful thinking that it would somehow intimidate the Japanese. King meanwhile ordered Rear Admiral Frank Jack Fletcher in *Yorktown* to patrol near the Phoenix Islands as a central reserve. In retrospect King's strategy is susceptible to criticism.

King's naval forces were numerically inferior to Japanese naval forces. The Japanese had ten carriers, the Americans three. All the American battleships were either sunk, damaged, or otherwise unavailable; the Japanese had twelve. Some twenty-five Japanese cruisers outnumbered the fifteen remaining cruisers of the Pacific Fleet. There were similar disparities in destroyers and submarines. Conventional naval strategy would have massed the Pacific Fleet at vital points to hit the Japanese where the Americans could enjoy local superiority. Yet King ordered piecemeal raids, scattering his few carriers beyond mutually supporting distance. A three-carrier strike at Rabaul, for example, could have impeded the Japanese movement toward the Solomons. King's desire to hit offensively at the Japanese was sound, as was his strategy to protect his lines of communication between Hawaii and Australia. Yet random carrier raids did little to implement that strategy, even though such raids were less risky to the irreplaceable carriers.

Still, in other circumstances outnumbered fleets often withdrew and avoided battle. But King insisted that his carriers remain at sea, hitting the enemy at every opportunity, and using their mobility to counteract Japanese moves. After Brown had been continuously at sea with the *Lexington* for almost two months, he asked permission from Nimitz to retire from the combat zone for fresh provisions. Nimitz passed the message on to King, who responded to the effect, "Carry on as long as you have hardtack, beans, and corn willy. What the hell are you worrying about?"

Knox saw the message. "My God!" he said to King. "Did you send that message?"

"I did," said King.

"Thank God for that," said Knox.

King meanwhile continued to organize his headquarters. Among his chief concerns was the matter of intelligence. His temporary flag secretary, Commander George C. Dyer, still was considered the staff intelligence officer, the normal collateral duty for an afloat staff. In mid-January King summoned Dyer into his office. "This Pearl Harbor disaster has a terrible smell," said King. "Something went completely wrong with our intelligence activities." King told Dyer to investigate and report back in a week.

The Office of Naval Intelligence (ONI) under Rear Admiral Alan G. Kirk presumably was responsible for gathering and disseminating wartime intelligence within the Navy Department, but it functioned under handicaps. Rear Admiral Kelly Turner, as Director of War Plans, felt that ONI should restrict itself to providing raw data, which War Plans would assess and evaluate. Turner, supported by Stark and Ingersoll, generally ignored ONI as a consequence, creating animosity between the operational planners and the intelligence specialists. The implication grew that these conflicts had contributed to the Navy's unpreparedness at Pearl Harbor.

In early 1941 Stark had established a Combined Operations and Intelligence Center (COIC), following a British example of a map room purporting to show the position of all American, Allied, and enemy ships. Stark appointed Rear Admiral Frank T. Leighton as the COIC director. "I don't think he wanted the job particularly," intelligence staff officer Arthur H. McCollum later said, "and he was very much in a fog as to what was required." COIC became "a chartroom with buttons to move around for ships and locations, but they got so bemused with different shapes of buttons that they couldn't see the woods for the trees."

While commanding the Atlantic Fleet in 1941, King resented Leighton's incessant requests for information on the locations of Atlantic Fleet ships. "Leighton is keeping a score board and card index on the whereabouts of each and every ship at all hours of the day and night," King wrote to Jonas Ingram in the fall of 1941. "He is the one who is continually 'pestering' you and Cook and me about these matters, so that he can keep his little toys and other play things in order."

So Leighton was already in jeopardy when King became COMINCH. His fall from grace was inevitable. After several months had passed King called Commander Dyer into his office. "You relieve Admiral Leighton," said King. "I want him out of the Navy Department before four-thirty this afternoon."

Leighton left two captains behind who presumably would resent being subordinate to Dyer. Deputy Chief of Staff Dick Edwards solved the problem by immediately transferring them so that everyone who remained under Dyer was junior in rank. Dyer thus became King's de facto intelligence officer, but he still needed seniority in order to deal with his Army colonel counterpart. King made Dyer a captain on the spot.

Despite such expedients King's intelligence organization was still ambiguous, having no place within the three COMINCH divisions of plans, operations, and readiness. King's old friend and classmate Vice Admiral William Pye (who had returned from the Pacific to head the Naval War College) recommended a fourth division for intelligence. King readily agreed, and for the remainder of the war a rear admiral served concurrently as Assistant Chief of Staff for Combat Intelligence and Director of ONI. Dyer — and his successors — continued as King's personal intelligence officer, however.

The COIC became King's private war room, available to only a select few. King immediately canceled the requirement for ship movements reports that had so irritated him as CINCLANT * in 1941, so COMINCH staff officers frequently had to guess at ship locations. The reduced message traffic was worth it as far as King was concerned.

King fought paper work incessantly, even ordering the Navy to turn in half of its typewriters and mimeograph machines. The order was frivolous and impossible to enforce, but its intent was clear. In early 1943 King sent a memorandum — on his instantly recognizable 2″ x 3″ yellow sheet — to Rear Admiral John S. McCain, the Chief of the Bureau of Aeronautics.

"I observed yesterday," wrote King, "that the door of room 1909 bore the label 'Duplicating Section, Bureau of Aeronautics' and beside the door the names of two (2) lieuts.(j.g.). I will be interested to know what important factors of duplication require the services of two (2) officers. E.J.K."

McCain replied that the office was the principal center for issuing directives and instructions to the fleet (as King suspected). "The officer in charge of this section was in the printing business prior to entering the Navy," McCain concluded. King let the matter drop, but he had made his point.

As the COMINCH staff continued to shake down it became apparent that King and Russell Willson, his chief of staff, were incompatible. Willson wanted to deliberate on problems for which King wanted quick answers. It was particularly discouraging when King, using what seemed

* Acronym for Commander in Chief, Atlantic Fleet.

COMINCH, FILE

UNITED STATES FLEET
HEADQUARTERS OF THE COMMANDER IN CHIEF
NAVY DEPARTMENT, WASHINGTON, D. C.

3 July 1944

From: Commander in Chief, United States Fleet and Chief of Naval Operations.
To : Chief of Staff, U.S. Fleet.
Vice Chief of Naval Operations.

1. For appropriate circulation.

E J King

King's view on paperwork (Courtesy Walter Muir Whitehill)

to be snap judgment, summarily rejected Willson's well-reasoned recommendations. It seemed wasted effort, and the strain began to affect Willson's health.

Living with King aboard *Dauntless* was awkward. Occasionally Willson got home and confided his problems to his daughter. "You will *never* guess what Rey looks at first in the morning newspaper . . . the comic page! He positively *roars* over 'Dagwood and Blondie' and then passes it over to me. I think it's childish and not even mildly amusing. Is there something wrong with me?"

King admitted to himself he had been wrong in asking Willson to work for him. He decided to send Willson to the Pacific, which would have removed him without embarrassment. That plan failed. A physical examination in September 1942 revealed that Willson had a bad heart, and doctors told King that he had to be relieved from strenuous duty. His health broken, Willson went on to serve as naval member of the Joint Strategic Survey Committee, an advisory group of senior officers unburdened with other duties.

That news allowed King in good conscience to seek a new chief of staff. He briefly considered Vice Admiral Pye, but Knox disliked Pye for having recalled the Wake Island relief expedition. Another drawback was Pye's indecisiveness; King once remarked that Pye "lives in an ivory tower."

In the end King selected Dick Edwards, who tried at first to decline, hoping to return to sea. "How the hell could I have managed things if I had not had Edwards with me?" King later said, again and again. "He never promoted his own interests, and he was always working for me." Edwards remained with King throughout the war, an exception to King's policy of frequent rotation between COMINCH staff and sea duty.

One final organizational problem remained, and it was the most serious of all. King was finding it impossible to function as COMINCH so long as Stark remained in Washington as CNO. Despite the good intentions of both admirals, their responsibilities and authority frequently overlapped. When Knox and King conferred with the President, King insisted that the command relationship had to be clarified, one way or the other. "Don't worry," said Roosevelt. "We'll take care of that."

The President's solution came in early March. King would be both COMINCH *and* CNO. Stark went to London to an expediently created post, Commander in Chief, U.S. Naval Forces, Europe. As the offices of COMINCH and CNO had never before been combined, King consulted the General Board and asked Sexton and Richardson to draft an appropriate presidential executive order defining King's new duties. Sexton suggested that Richardson start that evening, and together the two would polish it over the weekend. The next morning, however, King hurried in and told Richardson that the President intended to announce his decision at a cabinet meeting about to convene. King wanted the draft just as it was, and the two men hastily reviewed what Richardson had written. At the last moment Richardson suggested inserting two words, "and direction," and King agreed. It was a portentous phrase, for it gave King the authority over the bureaus of the Navy Department that had been denied the CNO ever since the office had been created in 1915.

Roosevelt accepted and promptly signed the draft as Executive Order 9096 of 12 March 1942.* It made King the most powerful naval officer in the history of the United States. As COMINCH, King was directly responsible to the President and was the principal naval advisor to the President on the conduct of the war. King's duties as CNO would be the preparation, readiness, and logistical support of the operating forces, as well as the coordination *and direction* of the bureaus and offices of the Navy Department. But his status with the Secretary of the Navy was as ambiguous as before. The executive order said that King, in general, would work under the "direction" of the Secretary. That phrase could be interpreted in many ways, and it led to a continuing series of conflicts between King and Knox, and then Knox's successor in May 1944, James V. Forrestal. But there was no doubt that King now had complete military control of the Navy. With Stark in London, King's authority was absolute and uncontested by any other naval officer. Never before had an American naval officer exercised the authority and responsibility delegated to King by the President of the United States, and never again would one do so.

The next day King received a letter from Hopkins. "I can't tell you how pleased I was," he wrote, "when the President told me of the action he was going to take about you. I think it is perfectly grand and I have a feeling it is going to be one of the most important things the President has done during the war. Great luck to you."

* See Appendix IV for the full text.

15

Organizing for War

After Arcadia had adjourned and Churchill and his entourage had departed, the American leadership was still far from organized to fight the war. King, Stark, Marshall, and Arnold had seemed the logical American representatives to confer with the British Chiefs of Staff, but the four Americans as a body were without a collective identity.

The British Chiefs of Staff had left representatives in Washington, known as the British Joint Staff Mission: Field Marshal Sir John Dill, Admiral Sir Charles Little, Lieutenant General Sir Colville Wemyss, and Air Marshal A. T. Harris. The Americans were expected to deal with the Mission on a day-to-day basis for the direction of the Allied war effort. Their first Washington meeting was convened on 23 January 1942, nine days after the last Arcadia meeting. King, Stark, Marshall, and Arnold simply showed up to represent the United States, establishing a precedent that would never be questioned.

"It is not certain, however," JCS historian Vernon E. Davis has written, "whether this membership was simply recognized as inherently correct, whatever its formal justification, or the officers were at some time directly appointed by the President. At any rate, as soon as their status became clear it was possible to refer to them more conveniently as the 'United States Chiefs of Staff,' or, as the logic of the agreed definition of terms suggested, as the 'Joint Chiefs of Staff.' "

The title itself of Joint Chiefs of Staff (JCS) was a misnomer from the standpoint of its four members, since Marshall was the only officer whose literal title was chief of staff. Be that as it may, the JCS, together with the British Joint Staff Mission, comprised the full-time Combined Chiefs of Staff (CCS) organization in Washington. But when the CCS finally had time to think things over, they were beset with organizational misgivings. King observed that they were without legal status at their very first meeting on 23 January 1942. The paper on post-ARCADIA collaboration — which was in fact the CCS charter — had not been approved by either Roosevelt or Churchill. Furthermore, said King, the paper (which had been drafted during ARCADIA) needed revision in order to strengthen CCS authority. As one example, King argued that the CCS should have jurisdiction over all areas of the world, rather than solely in the ABDA theater. The CCS agreed with King, and they directed their Combined Staff Planners to rewrite the charter, which the CCS approved on 10 February.*

The next step in the quest for legal recognition of the CCS was to get Roosevelt and Churchill to approve the revised charter. As Roosevelt was closest, it was sent to the White House. But there it became sidetracked, as did so many papers passing between the President and the JCS in those early months before systematic procedures were established. Roosevelt finally approved the charter on 21 April 1942 with the airy notation, "OK FDR." That hurdle cleared, Churchill was next. But for whatever reasons, Churchill neither approved nor disapproved the charter. He simply ignored it throughout the war.

The charter, whatever its formal legal status, was limited to the organization of the CCS alone, that is, the Americans and British collectively. But what of the JCS? It was authorized by implication only, and at best on the tenuous rationale that it was part of the CCS organization, which Roosevelt had approved. But the President never would specifically authorize the JCS as a separate entity. Thus the JCS functioned in limbo, doing whatever its members thought best with due regard for any guidance they could get from the President.

King would be forever disturbed by the hazy legal status of the JCS, and he constantly sought solutions. As there was an existing authorized organization called the Joint Board, King hoped that it perhaps could share its legitimacy with the JCS if the two could somehow be merged. Headed by the Chief of Staff of the Army and the CNO, the board had been established before the Second World War for cooperative planning between the Army and Navy. When war began it had been the only American interservice planning body, so by necessity its activities had increased since 7 December, especially during ARCADIA. King as COMINCH alone was not officially a member, but he attended its meetings nevertheless.

* The revised charter's formal designation was CCS 9/1, "War Collaboration between United Nations."

King barraged his colleagues with remedies. At a 28 January JCS meeting, he recommended that the Joint Board and the JCS establish a joint secretariat because both agencies had so much in common. Three days later King urged Marshall and Stark to revise the memberships of the two agencies to make them identical. Although he supported having Arnold as a member, King opposed any naval air representative. Arnold commanded forces and was needed as an opposite number to Portal; the Chief of the Bureau of Aeronautics commanded nothing. Thus King saw no reason to include the bureau chief on either the JCS or the Joint Board, even if Arnold gave the Army an extra vote.

If the memberships were identical, Marshall responded, why continue the Joint Board? Another aspect was that King's proposed merger would retain many of the undesirable characteristics of the Joint Board. The board was subordinate to the Secretaries of the Navy and War, for example, and there were restrictions to the broad authority desired by the service chiefs. In other words, the JCS wanted the benefits of the board's legality without its legal limitations.

In the end the JCS emerged by reason of semantics. The Joint Board was never officially disestablished. Instead it atrophied, because its members ceased to convene meetings in the name of the board. Whenever the service chiefs met, they simply called themselves the JCS.

Given the obscure status of the JCS, the public wondered who was running the war in the early months of 1942. Disaster after disaster stirred public accusations that Army-Navy disunity was to blame. A clamor arose, both in the press and in the Congress, for a department of national defense under a civilian secretary, or, as an alternative, a Joint General Staff superior to the JCS with a single chief reporting directly to the President.

King loudly opposed both ideas and wrote hot, scolding letters defending the JCS system. There was, for example, a letter to Congressman J. G. Scrugham on 11 February 1942, who had complained to King in an earlier letter.

"I am sure," wrote King, "that you yourself appreciate the fact that 'unity of command' is not the panacea for all military difficulties. It is, in fact, not easy to attain correctly nor to implement effectively — much depends upon the selection of the right man to exercise 'unity of command.'

"I think that all the proponents of a single department of national defense, or of its equivalent, do not think the matter through — for instance, practically all of the schemes of that character overlook the basic fact that the President of the United States is, by the Constitution, Commander in Chief of the Army and Navy, so that his views should be determining as to the means he employs to exercise his supreme command. . . .

"The 'U.S. Chiefs of Staff' are the military advisors of . . . the President. Considering whether a 'super-general staff' should be set up, headed by a 'super-chief of staff,' consideration must be given to the fact that we have *now* very few officers who know anything but their own service. . . . Further, it has to be recognized that such a super-body would have to *act* through the 'U.S. Chiefs of Staff,' either severally or collectively, and would thus introduce into the 'machinery' another step in the procedure, which of itself would almost surely involve delay in getting things done."

King then closed his letter with an expression of his cavalier attitude toward the Congress in the early war years. "Needless to say," concluded King, "I would be glad to discuss this matter with you at some time when I am not as busy as I am at present."

As King had used the phrase "U.S. Chiefs of Staff" rather than "Joint Chiefs of Staff," it is not surprising that even his letters failed to clarify the issue. Eventually the "JCS" title caught on, but few people still knew what it did or what it was for. Eventually King appealed to Hopkins in a memorandum dated 17 September 1942: "The press continues to 'howl' about the lack of unity in 'high command.' I have met with at least one member of the Cabinet who was 'enlightened and encouraged' to learn of the functions and duties of the Joint U.S. Chiefs of Staff and of the Combined Chiefs of Staff.

"Would it not be well to make up a press release which embodied all the main features of the JCoS-CCoS set-up so that the 'man in the street' could have assurance that the war is being conducted other than 'by guess and by God.' . . .

"As to such a release giving aid and comfort to the enemy, it would seem that it would have an opposite effect, especially as regards appreciation of the factual unity of effort among our own people."

Roosevelt and Hopkins must have agreed. In early October King wrote columnist David Lawrence that the JCS intended to issue a press release later that month dealing with unity of command. The press release never materialized. Instead it became a segment of the text of the President's radio address to the nation on the evening of 12 October 1942. In a most general way the President explained the functions of the JCS and CCS, although he substituted the vague and misleading term "joint staff." Roosevelt did identify the JCS members by name and insisted — contrary to charges — that they were in harmony concerning the plans and strategy for the American war effort. "As Commander in Chief," Roosevelt concluded, "I have at all times also been in substantial agreement." This passage in Roosevelt's speech may have been intended to alleviate criticism, but it probably contributed little to the public's understanding of the JCS. *Time* magazine did not even mention that portion of the President's address. Even the terms "Combined Chiefs of Staff" and "Joint Chiefs of Staff" rarely were used by the press during the early years of the war. Ignorance and misunderstanding would not go away.

The public was not alone in demanding a reorganization of the high command. Even before King became COMINCH, Marshall and his Army planners had advocated a Joint General Staff, although they realized that the Navy (especially Turner and Ingersoll) opposed the idea. In late January 1942 Marshall revived the issue, urging "a single head for the Army and the Navy, with a Joint Staff, responsible solely to the Commander in Chief." The JCS referred the proposal to its planners* for resolution, but instead of a compromise the differences were exacerbated by a clash between the Army and Navy representatives. It seemed to a suspicious King that Marshall wanted to be that "single head." Said King after the war, "I feel quite sure that Marshall, right from the beginning, thought he was going to manage everything. If he had had his way there would have been no Joint Chiefs of Staff."

King continued to fight Marshall's ideas on staff organization. The JCS lost a member when Stark left in March, and Roosevelt had signed an executive order making both King and Marshall directly responsible to him as Commander in Chief. He also had given both men unprecedented command authority over their respective services. King now argued that under the circumstances the appointment of a Chief of the Joint General Staff, with supreme authority over the Army and Navy, would prevent King and Marshall from seeing the President whenever they felt it necessary. Marshall, now reversing himself, concurred that a Chief of the Joint General Staff was a bad idea. With that said, there was an implied agreement to accept the status quo.

There still existed, however, the problem of liaison between the White House and the JCS. Papers were actually being delayed, even lost, before they reached the President. Marshall argued that the President needed an officer serving him directly, who could present the views

* Known as the Joint Staff Planners (JPS). The abbreviation "JSP" was not used, to avoid confusion with a similar acronym.

of the JCS, expedite presidential decisions when necessary, and serve as the JCS spokesman. This officer could also serve as a conduit for the President to communicate with the JCS, for the President met with them infrequently as a body. As it was, no one could predict whom Roosevelt would contact for business that affected the JCS as a whole.

Neither the President nor King wanted such a liaison officer. Marshall persisted. In the early summer of 1942 he nominated Admiral Leahy, who was returning to the United States having served as Ambassador to Vichy. He seemed perfect: a close and trusted friend of the President, experienced both as an officer and diplomat, and able to get along with people. Smart too, not an intellectual, but he had common sense and a steady temperament to conciliate disputes within the JCS. As a naval officer he presumably would be acceptable to King — except that King still opposed the creation of the post on principle.

Roosevelt became convinced and overruled King's objections. In early July 1942 the President announced that Leahy would be recalled to active duty in order to serve as his personal chief of staff, emphasizing that Leahy would be solely a presidential aide for liaison with the Army and Navy. But Leahy did join the JCS and through seniority became its chairman. Presumably he would be neutral and not a naval partisan. Although he voted in all JCS decisions and participated in JCS deliberations, Leahy was an equal among equals and had no command authority. King and Marshall could still see the President whenever they pleased.

By the summer of 1942 the JCS had settled the organization that would remain throughout the war: King, Leahy, Marshall, and Arnold. Still they were unhappy with their quasilegal status. In June 1943 they again appealed to the President through the Director of the Budget, Harold D. Smith. "The Joint Chiefs of Staff," wrote Leahy, "consider it advisable to have their organization and a definition of their functions made a matter of record in order that their status may be clarified in the eyes of the various government agencies with which they must deal."

Smith talked with the members of the JCS to discover their motive. He learned that they were frustrated in persuading civilian agencies to deliver war materiel the JCS wanted. "From our discussions," Smith explained to the President, "it appears that Admiral King more than any of the members feels the need for an Executive order. He desires a definite written statement of authority, particularly in respect to the authority of the Joint Chiefs over the war supply programs. He does

The JCS at lunch. L. to r., Leahy, Arnold, Marshall, and King (U.S. Navy photograph)

not believe that these programs should be questioned by such civilian agencies as the WPB." *

Smith was not convinced. Everything was running smoothly, argued Smith, and an executive order would be superfluous. Roosevelt agreed. "It seems to me that such an order," Roosevelt replied to Leahy, "would provide no benefits and might in some way impair flexibility of operations."

So in the strange world of Washington a civilian budget director had thwarted the quest for legal recognition by the highest military officers of the land. King and the JCS continued to serve solely at the pleasure of the President, whose approval and confidence were the only authority they would ever need or ever get.

And how did Roosevelt feel about the men of the JCS? Hopkins knew, because he and Roosevelt talked about them. "He is going to

* The War Production Board, under Donald M. Nelson, with whom the JCS clashed throughout the war. See Chapters 19 and 31 for a discussion of logistics.

have many of the same problems," wrote Hopkins in his diary in late January 1942, "that Lincoln had with generals and admirals whose records look awfully good but who well may turn out to be the McClellans of this war. The only difference between Lincoln and Roosevelt is that I think Roosevelt will act much faster in replacing those fellows.

"This war can't be won with . . . men who are thinking only about retiring to farms somewhere and who won't take great and bold risks and Roosevelt has a whole hatful of them in the Army and Navy that will have to be liquidated before we really get on with our fighting.

"Fortunately he has got in King, Marshall, and Arnold three people who really like to fight."

Whether Roosevelt liked him or not, King still dreaded the approach of 23 November 1942, his sixty-fourth birthday and mandatory retirement. In early August King passed a rigorous physical examination, which helped his spirits, but he still worried whether Roosevelt would allow him to remain on active duty. In October King forced the issue. In a short letter to Roosevelt, he wrote, "It appears proper that I should bring to your notice the fact that the record shows that I shall attain the age of 64 years on November 23rd next — one month from today.

"I am, as always, at your service."

The letter came back from the White House with the President's handwriting on the bottom.

> E.J.K.
> So what, old top?
> I may send you a Birthday present!
> FDR

King was elated, so much so that he called in his flag secretary to share in his rejoicing that the President wanted him to continue fighting the war.

By the end of February 1942 Allied forces in the ABDA theater were nearly beaten. Wavell relinquished his command to the Dutch and returned to India, whence he had come. "This was the end of the first attempt at unified command in the Pacific," wrote JCS historian Grace Hayes. "ABDA had existed in a period of crisis and uncertainty, when the JCS and CCS organizations were just being developed and when they were confronted with numerous problems for whose solution there was no precedent. ABDA and its detailed problems occupied the chiefs' attention to an extent that commands established later in the war did not, but those commands would profit from this first experience. While ABDA had not succeeded in holding against the determined Japanese advance, by the time of its dissolution that advance had been slowed to a considerable extent, and ABDA's successors in the Pacific could stabilize a line of defense and shortly take the first steps of the offensive that finally led to the defeat of Japan."

With ABDA about to go under, King knew it was time to reorganize areas of responsibility in the Pacific. The loss of Sumatra was about to split the ABDA area down the center, so on 17 February King recommended that Great Britain take responsibility for everything to the west and call it the China-Burma-India theater. Given his concern about the Hawaii-Australia lines of communication, King argued that the ANZAC area should go directly under Nimitz. Others too could see the need for such redefinitions.

Boundary lines became immaterial when it became evident that the Philippines were doomed. On a late Sunday afternoon, February twenty-second, Roosevelt summoned King, Hopkins, and Marshall for a conference to decide the fate of MacArthur, who had moved his headquarters to Corregidor. When the conference ended, Roosevelt had decided to order MacArthur to Australia. The next day Wavell received orders to dissolve ABDA. Allied forces and plans in the Pacific were in shambles.

Despite the despair and confusion, King clung to one strategic view: safeguarding the Hawaii-Australia lines of communication. Time and again he forced JCS attention toward that area of the Pacific. But even under pressure the JCS characteristically did not cope with crises through dramatic meetings. Instead they exchanged memoranda, as if time were still available and the War and Navy Departments somehow so separated that face-to-face meetings were impractical.

For example, on 24 February Marshall wrote King for details on protecting the lines of communication to Australia. Administrative snarls delayed Marshall's memorandum from reaching King's desk until 2 March, the day that the JCS would meet for only the third time as a body since ARCADIA had adjourned six weeks earlier. Pressed for time, King quickly drafted his reply. It was typed, and King then proceeded to the meeting, where he handed his memorandum to his colleagues. "The general scheme or concept of operations," King had written, "is not only to protect the lines of communications with Australia but, in so doing, to set up 'strong points' from which a step-by-step general advance can be made through the New Hebrides, Solomons, and the Bismarck Archipelago."

Advance? King was talking about an advance when Allied forces were being demolished by the Japanese? The chiefs read on. King intended to employ his Marines "to seize and occupy" strong points in an advance to the northwest from bases in the South Pacific, to be relieved by Army garrison troops so that the Marines could continue their assaults against the Japanese. And where did the Army fit in? Well, said King, provide two, perhaps three Army divisions as garrison troops, eight groups of assorted Army aircraft, and King's offense could begin. His colleagues listened to King expand upon that memorandum, but the meeting ended without a decision.

One aspect was clear, however. King had challenged the Germany-First strategy agreed upon during ARCADIA (and even earlier in the ABC-1 Staff Agreement and at Argentia). As will be seen, the Germany-First strategy was open to interpretation, but in essence the Allies considered Germany a more dangerous enemy than Japan. Therefore Allied resources would mass and attack Germany first, while far smaller numbers of Allied forces would go to the Pacific solely to contain further Japanese aggression. Not until Germany was defeated would the Allies mount an offensive in the Pacific to defeat Japan. Yet King had proposed an immediate offensive, certainly not one in the future after Germany had been beaten. Although it was not at once apparent (perhaps not even to King), King had embarked upon the most important contribution he would make to victory in the Second World War.

As so often happened in the early war years, strategic plans were overtaken by events. Several days after the March second JCS meeting, Roosevelt received an uncharacteristically gloomy message from Churchill. "We have suffered the greatest disaster in our history at Singapore," * said the Prime Minister, "and other misfortunes will come thick and fast upon us. . . . It is not easy to assign limits to the Japanese aggression." Disturbed by Churchill's pessimism, Roosevelt conferred with the JCS to find a way to respond to the Prime Minister. With the Pacific war failing and Churchill faltering, the President was grasping for straws. King offered something much more substantial; a plan that put the entire war into perspective and showed how the Japanese could be beaten.†

Great Britain and Russia, wrote King in his plan, were committed to

* Singapore had surrendered to the Japanese on 15 February.

† See Appendix V for the entire text.

fighting Germany in the Middle East and Eastern Front respectively. The United States' major contribution to those two countries should be munitions, food, and raw material. Turning to the Pacific, King identified Australia and New Zealand as "white man's countries" that had to be held "because of the repercussions among the non-white races of the world." King then repeated an argument he had presented earlier to the JCS: reinforce bases on the Hawaii-Australia line of communication for an eventual American assault into the Solomon Islands, New Guinea, and the Bismarck Archipelago.

King's plan looked so good to Roosevelt that he passed it on to Churchill. While the Prime Minister had despaired over the Japanese victories, he still hoped that Japan could be contained "without prejudice to the plans against Hitler across the Atlantic we have talked of together." The President dispelled that kind of wishful thinking. Something would have to give from Europe in order to stop the Japanese. "American contribution to an air offensive against Germany in 1942 would be somewhat curtailed," said the President's reply, "and any American contribution to land operations on the Continent of Europe in 1942 will be materially reduced. . . ."

By this series of events, culminating in the need to reassure Churchill following the fall of Singapore, Roosevelt had tacitly approved King's Pacific strategy.

The next step was to decide upon the areas of responsibility in the Pacific. The British had conceded the entire Pacific Ocean to the United States, but there still remained the definition of boundaries and commanders among the United States armed forces. As usual, there were many ideas. Marshall, always a strong advocate of unified command, wanted MacArthur in charge of the entire Pacific theater. Strong public sentiment favored MacArthur, as well.

King had no intention of allowing MacArthur any such authority. For twenty years the Navy had been preparing to fight a naval war against Japan. Now that the war had begun, it would have been heresy for the Navy to be subordinate to the Army and MacArthur. The Pacific Fleet would never be under the General's operational control, King vowed, if for no other reason than that King believed that MacArthur knew nothing about sea power.

On the other hand, MacArthur would never subordinate himself to Nimitz or to any other admiral. Nor could the problem be solved by returning MacArthur to the United States. No one wanted him there. To Roosevelt he was a future political rival. To the JCS he threatened to become a single head of the armed services, a proposal with strong congressional support. As MacArthur had to remain overseas, he and Nimitz would have to share the Pacific theater. It would be up to King and Marshall to decide upon the boundaries.

It would require hard bargaining. Marshall got things started when he learned that Australia and New Zealand would seek representation on the CCS. They also wanted an "ANZAC Council," which would be supreme to the CCS in determining grand strategy in the Pacific. With Marshall's encouragement, the dominions on 7 March submitted their proposals to the JCS via the British Chiefs of Staff. Marshall and the Army planners, headed by Eisenhower, supported the ANZAC proposal, even though it would have wrecked the earlier agreement that the American-British CCS would direct the Pacific war effort.*

The Army endorsement was astonishing. In retrospect, perhaps Marshall was taking an extreme bargaining position in his impending negotiations with King. To supplement the ANZAC proposal, Eisenhower and his Army planners drafted their own plan for dividing the Pacific between the Army and the Navy. The plan included a proposed Southwest Pacific area bounded by the line Philippines-Samoa and thence south along the meridian 170 west. This area would be under MacArthur's command, while everything to the northeast would be commanded by an American naval officer. In essence MacArthur — not the Navy — would carry out the strategy proposed by King and approved by the President several days earlier: to strike northwesterly into the Solomons. Eisenhower's Army plan also implied that MacArthur would command the considerable naval and Marine forces that King intended to commit to that area in support of his strategy.

King was astounded by such audacity. When the JCS met on 9 March, King vehemently opposed both the "ANZAC Council" plan and the Army boundary plan. The former, King said, would have "cut across the whole system of command and operations of the United States Pacific Fleet." Marshall quickly dropped that idea. Then turning to the Army's plan, King argued that it was illogical to combine Australia and New Zealand in the same strategic area, as Eisenhower and his planners had proposed. New Zealand, as well as the South Pacific islands of New Caledonia, Fiji, and Samoa, were strong points on the sea line of communication between Australia and Hawaii. Defending this line was primarily a naval matter, the responsibility of Nimitz and the Pacific Fleet. Australia, on the other hand, together with the adjacent Netherlands East Indies and New Guinea, were closer together and

* CCS 9/1, "War Collaboration between United Nations," above.

more suitable for combined land-air operations. They logically belonged in a separate strategic area, presumably under MacArthur's command.

King buttressed his arguments with his own written plan, developed by Turner and the naval planners. The Army area (according to the plan) would encompass Australia and the approaches to it through New Guinea and the Netherlands East Indies. Its eastern boundary would lie between the Solomon Islands and the New Hebrides. The Navy would cover the remaining areas of the Pacific. Unity of command would be disregarded because there would be two area commanders, presumably Nimitz and MacArthur. And to whom would they report? To the JCS, said King. The JCS — not a single person — would exercise supreme command in the Pacific.

So King wanted a war run by a committee, contrary to Marshall's cherished ideal of a single supreme commander in each major theater. Now Marshall had to decide. Would it be King's plan or Eisenhower's plan? The General voted for King. He did ask for one concession. Could not the Philippines be included in MacArthur's area for "psychological reasons"? King acquiesced. Thus almost by afterthought the JCS sanctioned MacArthur's dream of returning to the Philippines.

The next step was to write the appropriate directives, or charters, to MacArthur and Nimitz. Once again the Navy planners under Turner took the initiative, and Marshall accepted the Navy-originated directives at a JCS meeting on 30 March 1942. The directives defined the authority and responsibilities of both MacArthur and Nimitz, specifying that both would be responsible to the JCS. Each would receive his orders from his own head of service — that is, Marshall and King — who in turn would represent the JCS. On 31 March 1942 the directives were approved by the President.

In a period of one month — March 1942 — King had inspired and advocated the plans and strategy that would govern the entire course of the war in the Pacific.

King was still bothered by public demands to give first priority to defending the continental United States. Realizing that Roosevelt and the Congress might yield to such pressure, King drafted a memorandum to Roosevelt reflecting King's philosophy on carrying the war to the enemy despite the instinctive tendency to think defensively. Written for the entire JCS to endorse, we do not know if it was ever seen by Roosevelt. Nevertheless, as it so vividly reflects King's way of thinking during the worst months of the war, I quote it in its entirety.

We have become greatly concerned [wrote King] over the views of the American people — as reflected in the press and correspondence and conversations within our knowledge — in regard to the demands for local defense of communities, localities, war production plants, etc.

These views are quite without regard for the realities involved in the conduct of this war, especially at this time and for some months to come, while production is going from low gear to second gear and gathering speed to go into high gear.

Not only is what we are *now* producing obligated in part to Russia, to Britain and to others of the United Nations — to enable them to put all possible effort into the war — but what is available to *us* is better employed in war areas where we are actively engaged, rather than being kept here at home in the continental U.S. to meet in part the manifold demands for local defense.

It seems not to be apparent to the public, as indicated in the opening paragraph, that the best defense is offense — offense in those war areas where the enemy actually is, remote though they are from the continental U.S. — offense which will keep the enemy engaged and occupied to such an extent that he cannot gather the means to make any serious threat to the continental U.S.

Granted that enemy submarines may occasionally shell our shores, even that enemy aircraft may sporadically rouse our people to demand even more local defense, the best method is to fight him where he is to be found, to seek him out rather than to husband our fighting strength at home and await his coming.

No fighter ever won his fight by covering up — by merely fending off the other fellow's blows. The winner hits and keeps on hitting even though he has to take some stiff blows in order to be able to keep on hitting.

It is our request that — in your own time and in your own way — you bring these fundamental premises for the conduct of this war to the serious attention of the public and the press.

16

Stopping the Japanese: Coral Sea and Midway

THE KING-INSPIRED JCS directive dividing the Pacific between Nimitz and MacArthur was signed by the President on 31 March 1942. It created two specific command positions for Nimitz. The first was Commander in Chief, Pacific Ocean Areas (CINCPOA), which gave Nimitz unified command over all Navy, Marine Corps, and Army ground and air forces assigned to his area. His second position, Commander in Chief, Pacific Fleet (CINCPAC), gave Nimitz operational control of all naval forces in the Pacific Ocean, except those temporarily assigned to MacArthur's Southwest Pacific Area. In practice, these latter forces were restricted to submarines, amphibious assault, and amphibious support ships. These included cruisers, destroyers, and occasionally battleships on loan for specific operations. King and Nimitz would never give control of the carrier strike forces to MacArthur.

The directive also told Nimitz what King expected him to do. Nimitz's primary missions were to protect and hold what he had and to prepare for major amphibious assaults in the Solomons, New Guinea, and the Bismarck Archipelago. In the meantime, King expected Nimitz to hit the Japanese at every opportunity. His messages to Nimitz continually urged aggressiveness, including an extraordinary message on 30 March. "You are requested," wired King, "to read the article, 'There Is Only One Mistake: To Do Nothing,' by Charles F. Kettering in the March 29th issue of *Saturday Evening Post* and to see to it that it is brought to the attention of all your principal subordinates and other key officers."

King may have had in mind Rear Admiral Frank Jack Fletcher, flying his flag from the carrier *Yorktown* operating in the Coral Sea. King mistakenly assumed that Fletcher was near some Japanese transports at Rabaul, which were perhaps preparing for another southward Japanese

King and Nimitz at Pearl Harbor, 1944 (U.S. Navy photograph)

advance. Fletcher was actually en route to Noumea, New Caledonia, to refuel. If the transports began heading south, Fletcher advised, he would defer fueling, take station off northeastern Australia, and await further orders.

King was furious. Now that he knew where Fletcher was, it seemed to him that Fletcher had been retreating before an advancing enemy. Fletcher compounded that sin by waiting for someone to tell him what to do next. Thus on the same day that King sent his *Saturday Evening Post* message to Nimitz, he also blasted Fletcher: "Your 292346 * not understood, if it means you are retiring from enemy vicinity in order to refuel." King then reminded Fletcher of his mission: "The situation in the area [Coral Sea] where you are now operating requires constant activity of a task force like yours to keep enemy occupied." King concluded that he expected Fletcher to pressure the Japanese until relieved.

* Numbers used to identify a message by day of the month and hour of the day.

From that day onward King mistrusted Fletcher, but he decided to talk with Nimitz before taking action.

King's thirst for blood was infectious. Two members of his planning staff, Frog Low and Donald Duncan, developed a scheme to raise morale and avenge the attack on Pearl Harbor: an aircraft carrier would launch Army B-25 medium bombers against Tokyo. After bombing the Japanese capital, the planes would land in China. King embraced the idea and got the approval of Arnold, Marshall, and the President. King was so concerned with secrecy that he withheld the details of the raid from Roosevelt until the task force was on the way toward Japan. Only seven people knew the full plan: King, Low, Duncan, Nimitz, and Arnold; Halsey, who commanded the carrier task force; and Marc Mitscher, who commanded the carrier *Hornet*, which had embarked the Army bombers.

On 18 April Lieutenant Colonel James H. Doolittle and his courageous airmen attacked Japan with sixteen bombers. American morale was considerably brightened when the jubilant President later announced the raid. Nevertheless, King's advocacy of the plan was not sound military judgment, because it was inconsistent with his strategy of confronting the Japanese south of the equator. Two of the Navy's precious carriers, *Enterprise* and *Hornet*, had been dispersed to the North Pacific Ocean in order to support the raid. The risk was unnecessary, and they were unavailable when they were needed to fight the Japanese Navy in the Coral Sea. The raid was, in reality, a diversion to make the public think that American forces were on the offensive.

Americans on the offensive? Nothing could have been further from the truth. Even while the Tokyo raiders were steaming toward their target, intelligence analysts predicted a major Japanese offensive in the Southwest Pacific for some time in late April. Although there was some wishful thinking that the Japanese might delay their plans to chase Halsey, King's intelligence staff was more realistic. They were certain of an amphibious attack on Port Moresby, on the southeastern coast of New Guinea, during the first week of May. Port Moresby was crucial, the only useful Allied base left in New Guinea. In Japanese hands it would threaten King's precious sea lines of communication to eastern Australia. King warned Nimitz to prepare accordingly.

By then King must have realized that he had miscalculated. He had deprived Nimitz of two carriers (*Enterprise* and *Hornet*) that were needed to defend Port Moresby. King also had to depend upon the one admiral he had come to mistrust, Frank Jack Fletcher, for he would command the only two carriers available in the South Pacific, *Yorktown* and *Lexington*. His best carrier admiral, Halsey, was thousands of miles to the north, returning from Japan. There was no way for King to redeem his error. He had to hope for the best.

Although Port Moresby was in MacArthur's area, he would be ignored by the Navy. King intended to stop the Japanese amphibious assault at sea, not on land. MacArthur's forces would not be involved. Still, MacArthur technically should have controlled the carrier task forces in the Southwest Pacific; King had stipulated in the JCS directive to MacArthur that he was to take on all Japanese forces in his area, including the Japanese Navy. Yet the ink was hardly dry on the document when King revealed that, in practice, only he and Nimitz would fight the war at sea, regardless in whose area it evolved.

King and Nimitz arranged to meet in San Francisco on 25 April to resolve the worsening situation in the Pacific. (It would be the first of their eighteen wartime conferences held either in San Francisco, Pearl Harbor, or Washington.) Nimitz brought his plan to defend Port Moresby. He would stop the Japanese invasion force in the Coral Sea and intended to engage all four of his carriers — if the Japanese waited long enough for Halsey to get there. Otherwise Fletcher's two carriers would have to do.

King was pleased with Nimitz's plan because it got the carriers into the South Pacific, where King wanted them. Hitherto the CINCPAC staff had tried to retain some of the carriers in Pearl Harbor in reserve for a possible attack on Hawaii. King had suspected for some time that cautious members of the CINCPAC staff had been giving bad advice, so much so that King suggested that Nimitz rid Pearl Harbor of "pessimists and defeatists."

The discussion then turned to flag officer assignments in the Pacific theater, a topic whenever King and Nimitz met. Having been the Chief of Naval Personnel before the war, Nimitz knew both the merits and the faults of the Navy's senior officers. Thus King respected Nimitz's judgment and solicited his advice. But Nimitz had also been tainted by the bureau; King distrusted him as a "fixer." Nimitz was too lenient with his subordinates, at least in King's judgment, and he charged Nimitz to deal more decisively with those that erred. "I could never understand," King would say, "why people in command were so touchy about kicking people out." In retrospect, the Navy benefited by the compromises between King's ruthlessness and Nimitz's accommodation.

Choosing a flag officer who would satisfy both King and Nimitz was complicated. A candidate first had to be available by virtue of nearing the end of his current assignment. Availability was, in fact, the most important criterion, because good men normally were not precipitously reassigned in midterm. Such considerations as seniority, qualifications, experience, and professional reputation narrowed the range of choices even further. Added to this, Secretary Knox wanted younger flag officers in responsible positions and older admirals forced into retirement. Although Knox rarely interfered with combat assignments, he still could veto a flag officer whom he disliked.

Another complication was that Nimitz, on principle, did not like to ask for key subordinates by name. If a personal choice failed to perform it was hard to get rid of him, either because of friendship or the embarrassing admission of having made a poor selection. Instead, Nimitz maintained, it was proper for the Chief of Naval Personnel, Rear Admiral Randall R. Jacobs, to decide upon important assignments, because Jacobs was presumably better informed. And, pragmatically, if a bureau-appointed officer was a flop, Nimitz would be justified to ask for a relief. In order to avoid unpleasantness, therefore, at times he preferred to let King and Jacobs do the hiring and firing.*

Given these complexities, flag officer assignments were normally the result of a number of interactions rather than arbitrary decisions by King alone. The most pressing need in April 1942 was to select a commander for the newly created South Pacific Area, that part of Nimitz's Pacific Ocean Areas domain located south of the equator and east of the 159th parallel. Vice Admiral Robert E. Ghormley, the senior American naval officer in London, would soon be available when he was relieved by Stark. Ghormley was generally regarded as a skillful planner and strategist and had the reputation, in King's words, of being a "very able man." Nimitz nominated Ghormley and King approved. It was a choice they would regret.

The two admirals next turned to the use of aircraft carriers, which had replaced the battleship as the foundation of the fleet. Young, aggressive aviation flag officers were needed to command the carrier task groups, but they were too few and too junior. Thus nonaviators Wilson Brown and Frank Jack Fletcher were two of the three carrier group commanders in the early months of the war. The third was Halsey; only he possessed the ideal combination of seniority, aviation experience, and fighting spirit. Nimitz himself was a surface officer. Clearly, there was a need to reorganize naval aviation, and King and Nimitz debated the ways and means. But everything would have to wait until the current South Pacific crises were over.

* King often suspected that Nimitz and Jacobs, as incorrigible "fixers," claimed they were firing people on King's orders.

Another topic was radio intelligence. The Americans' ability to break the Japanese code was a priceless asset, but it had to be a well-kept secret. Otherwise the Japanese might be alerted to change their code. Both Nimitz and King trusted that their own codes were secure from Japanese cryptanalysis.

The first wartime meeting between King and Nimitz adjourned on 27 April after three days of discussions. Nimitz returned to Pearl Harbor and King to Washington. The Battle of the Coral Sea began a week later.

Even before the battle began, King read about it in the newspaper, which quoted MacArthur's headquarters that a major Japanese naval offensive was imminent. King was appalled. If the Japanese read the newspaper reports, they could surmise that the Americans were breaking their code. King complained vehemently about MacArthur's breach of security to Marshall, who in turn warned MacArthur.

As was so often the case when a major naval battle was being fought, King frequently had to do without information on its progress. The Battle of the Coral Sea first established this pattern. The American naval forces usually maintained radio silence before contacting the enemy; the first sign that the fighting had begun was often an intercepted Japanese message. Situation reports from the American naval commanders were either sporadic and late or incomplete and inaccurate. It usually took days for King to learn what had happened.

King disciplined himself not to press his combat commanders for information while a battle was being fought. King's "rule," as he called it, was to "let them go on" rather than to signal "How are you doing?" As he once explained at a press conference, he would not interfere by sending messages "because they need all the communications they can use in order to coordinate their work effectively."

The Battle of the Coral Sea began in early May. Halsey never made it. There were confused engagements between Fletcher's forces and a Japanese covering force which lasted for several days. Consquently the Japanese canceled their assault on Port Moresby. The first of Fletcher's reports indicated one Japanese carrier sunk, another badly damaged. Although *Lexington* and *Yorktown* had both been hit and damaged, neither apparently had been badly hurt.

Nimitz sent a message of effusive praise to Fletcher, with a copy to King: "Congratulations on your glorious accomplishment of the last two days. Your aggressive actions have the admiration of the entire Pacific Fleet. Well done to you, your officers, and men. You have filled our hearts with pride and have maintained the highest traditions of the Navy."

Nimitz's message was premature. *Lexington* later sank from her wounds. Still Nimitz recommended to King that Fletcher be promoted to vice admiral and awarded the Distinguished Service Medal, on the premise that Fletcher had "utilized with consummate skill the information supplied him, and by these engagements . . . won a victory with decisive and far-reaching consequences for the Allied cause." King said no. Losing *Lexington* — King's former command and a ship he loved — was neither a victory nor reason to reward Fletcher. Nimitz must have forgotten the letter that King had written to him in 1941: King would not give medals to commanders who lost their ships.

King treated sinkings with great secrecy. So concerned was King with concealing the loss of *Lexington* that he avoided telling Admiral Sir Dudley Pound three weeks after she had gone down. Instead he told the First Sea Lord only that she had been damaged. During the Guadalcanal campaign King would withhold losses even from Marshall's immediate planning staff, who he felt could not keep secrets. He trusted Knox least of all. As a former newspaper publisher, Knox instinctively liked to publicize naval activities. King had a simple solution — he did not tell Knox anything.

Intercepted Japanese messages hinted at offenses other than Coral Sea, but the times and places remained uncertain. Nimitz suspected that Midway was next, perhaps in late May, and he sought to concentrate his three remaining carriers west of Hawaii. King recognized that the Japanese could strike anywhere in the Pacific, but unlike Nimitz he still believed that their next move would be in the South Pacific against the Hawaii-Australia line of communication.

King's way of thinking changed dramatically after the Coral Sea battle. He no longer was so willing to risk his precious carriers. Now cautious and defensive, he even suggested to Nimitz that carrier aircraft be flown ashore to augment land-based aircraft "in order to preserve our carriers. . . ." Furthermore, said King, he did not want Halsey to operate beyond range of Allied land-based air. Perhaps his attitude had changed by the chilling loss of *Lexington*, which he remembered so well as a huge, powerful, seemingly invulnerable warship. *Enterprise*, *Hornet*, and *Yorktown* could be sunk just as quickly.

Nimitz was less pessimistic. The carriers should retain their aircraft, he advised King, so that they could act as a mobile reserve. Nimitz's intelligence analysts were intercepting the same Japanese messages that were available to King's staff, but their conclusions were different. From Pearl Harbor it seemed that the Central Pacific was the Japanese target. In any event, Nimitz wanted the freedom to move his carriers as he thought best, but a month earlier King had ordered him to keep at least two carriers in the South Pacific. So there Halsey's *Enterprise-Hornet* group had to remain, while *Yorktown* returned to Pearl Harbor to repair damage received in the Coral Sea. *Saratoga* and *Wasp* on the West Coast were unavailable. There was nothing left to defend the Central Pacific.

Nimitz pressed King to reconsider keeping Halsey down south. "Time and distance involved require a definite decision in the near future," warned Nimitz on 14 May. King procrastinated. The next day he replied that he still believed that the Japanese would attack in the South Pacific. Nimitz stubbornly responded that *he* still believed they would hit Midway Island.

Nimitz decided to break the impasse. Without waiting for King's permission, Nimitz ordered Halsey to leave the South Pacific and so informed King. If King disagreed, he could cancel the order. On the other hand, if King remained silent he would implicitly condone Nimitz's initiative, even though it contravened King's April directive. It was a common tactic to force a reluctant senior into a decision.

Yet it could also backfire. Nimitz decided he needed more than King's implied assent. On 16 May, in a message tactfully phrased to make his point without provoking King's temper, Nimitz repeated that he thought that the major attack would be against Midway. Perhaps, he suggested, if King's intelligence analysts would reassess their data they might agree. Nimitz reassured his volatile boss that Halsey would return to the South Pacific if new information revealed that area as the Japanese objective.

King could see that Nimitz was uneasy at having disobeyed him and wanted a vote of confidence. Still King temporized. It was his nature to ponder complex problems and to weigh all relevant information. With a life-and-death matter at stake, King avoided premature decisions. Consequently he withheld action as long as possible, much to Nimitz's annoyance when Nimitz needed answers.

After further discussions with his intelligence analysts, King concluded — finally — that Nimitz was probably correct. On 17 May he sent Nimitz the welcome news that he agreed with the decision to return Halsey to the Central Pacific.

These message exchanges between King and Nimitz established their liaison procedures before and during major battles and campaigns. King tried to avoid direct orders, preferring a consensus with Nimitz after exchanging views. Each was sensitive to the prerogatives of the other, each respected the other's judgment, and neither unnecessarily opposed the wishes of the other. Their dialogue often became a cautious verbal sparring, with messages characterized by restraint, circumlocution, and caveats. King, for example, would use such phrases as "suggest you consider," or he would observe that a course of action "now appears questionable." If King wanted to be more emphatic: "I consider these operations inadvisable." But if necessary, King could still be direct, emphatic, and unambiguous. Before the Battle of Midway, still concerned about conserving his carriers, King ordered Nimitz "to employ strong attrition tactics and not — repeat — not allow our forces to accept such decisive action as would be likely to incur heavy losses in our carriers and cruisers."

Above all, the King-Nimitz messages manifested their realization that their decisions would affect the course of the war and American lives. Thus their decisions were preceded by the most careful and deliberate thinking of which they were capable.

Nimitz had guessed right. The mammoth Japanese fleet converged in the Central Pacific west of Hawaii. The Battle of Midway was fought and won on the fourth of June, 1942. When it was over the Americans had sunk four Japanese carriers and lost *Yorktown*. The Japanese offensive momentum in the Pacific had been stopped.

There was an aftermath of the battle that precipitated one of King's most violent reactions during the entire war. Code breaking allowed the Americans to win at Midway, and King was fanatically determined to prevent the Japanese from learning that the Americans were reading their messages. That could best be achieved by saying nothing about American naval actions (even victories) in order to deny the enemy any useful information. If that meant forfeiting the public's "right to know" about wartime operations, said King, that's the way it would have to be.

But a victory of the magnitude of Midway was news that could not be suppressed. King had to say *something* to the press to explain how his carriers just happened to be at the right place at the right time to surprise and sink four Japanese carriers. He could not, of course, tell the truth and reveal his code breaking. After conferring with Marshall, King fabricated a story that the Navy had expected "energetic measures" from the Japanese following the Tokyo raid and the Battle of the Coral Sea. Given that strategic situation, it was not unexpected that the Japanese would attack Midway. On Sunday afternoon, June seventh, King held a press conference in order to issue his contrived report of the battle. The United States Navy, King explained, had taken a calculated risk in guessing the Japanese intentions and had been lucky enough to have guessed right. His answers to specific questions were ambiguous enough to conceal anything substantial.

A reporter asked whether King would be holding regular press conferences in the future.

"No, indeed," replied the Admiral. He had agreed to this conference only because of the special circumstances of the Battle of Midway.

Then King spoke off the record. His voice hardened. The Washington *Times-Herald*, said King, had published an article that morning claiming that the Americans had known *in advance* that the Japanese would attack Midway. "This information came unmistakably from a leak that may involve very serious consequences," said King. "It compromises a vital and secret source of information which will henceforth be closed to us. The military consequences are so obvious that I do not need to dwell on them, nor to request you to be on your guard against, even inadvertently, being a party to any disclosure which will give aid and comfort to the enemy."

A short time later King learned that the Chicago *Tribune* had a similar story on its front page. The headline said it all: "Navy Had Word of Jap Plan to Strike at Sea." Nimitz's secret message to the fleet on Japanese intentions and the Japanese order of battle had been reproduced verbatim for millions of Americans (and presumably Japanese agents) to read. The Japanese were bound to conclude that the Americans had broken their code, and they would then so radically change their encryption procedures that an invaluable source of intelligence would disappear forever.

King was in a white fury at his headquarters while his staff frantically tried to discover the source of the leak. An investigation revealed that Commander Morton T. Seligman, until recently the executive officer of *Lexington*, had shown Nimitz's dispatch to *Tribune* war correspondent Stanley Johnston, who had subsequently filed his story with his newspaper.

Frank Knox and the Navy Department squared off against Colonel Robert R. McCormick, publisher of the *Tribune*. Chief planner Savvy Cooke called him "a goddam traitor," reflecting the indignation in COMINCH headquarters. McCormick protested that his paper had compromised nothing of value to the enemy, a claim which King rebuked in a personal letter to the publisher.

McCormick and the *Tribune* had enemies in Washington for reasons beyond the Midway revelation. The *Tribune* and the Roosevelt Administration despised each other. Frank Knox's *Daily News* was a Chicago competitor, as well. The depth of the antipathy is reflected in an October 1942 letter from Secretary of Commerce Harold L. Ickes to the President. The Secretary also bitterly hated McCormick.

"Once I suggested," wrote Ickes, "that the fine large steamers that carry news-print from the CHICAGO TRIBUNE's paper mills in Canada to its place of defilement on the Chicago River, be requisitioned by the Army or the Navy. I still think that my idea was a bright one.

"Now I pass on another suggestion. I understand that certain Canadian papers are taking vigorous exception to the CHICAGO TRIBUNE's attitude in the war. Why could not the Canadian government be encouraged to shut off this news-print at the source, on the ground that when it gets to this country it is put to a use that is of aid and comfort to the enemy?

"I make no charge for these bright little thoughts."

Roosevelt may have taken the letter seriously. He sent it on to Knox with the notation, "Please speak to me and no one else about this!"

Neither McCormick nor Johnston came to trial because the Navy refused, for obvious reasons, to produce the relevant evidence. As for Seligman, King cast about for an appropriate punishment. With the concurrence of Roosevelt and Knox, King arranged that Seligman would never be promoted to captain, and he retired from active duty in 1944.

The Japanese apparently did not read the American newspapers. Their code remained unchanged.

17

Eyes Toward Germany: Operation Torch

WHILE KING'S ATTENTION was primarily focused on Japan, Marshall, in contrast, had his eyes on Germany. The Germany-First decision, confirmed at the First Washington Conference in January 1942, was overtaken by crises in the Pacific. Marshall fretted at the piecemeal employment of Allied forces in the absence of a long-range plan against Germany. And that plan, in Marshall's mind, should be an early invasion of the European continent.

Marshall saw that somehow he would have to shift attention from the Pacific to Europe. He began with Roosevelt. By late March the President agreed with Marshall's concept of an invasion in Europe at the earliest possible moment. The British were next. Accompanied by Hopkins, Marshall flew to Great Britain in early April. He returned triumphant. Churchill and his chiefs of staff had agreed to a cross-Channel invasion perhaps as early as 1942 (SLEDGEHAMMER) and certainly no later than 1943 (ROUNDUP). But British reversals in the Middle East made Churchill regret his promises. In June the Prime Minister came to Washington on short notice to reassess the war in Europe.*

King had had mixed feelings toward European strategy in the early months of 1942. He had supported Germany-First in principle, but he resented using the European theater as an excuse to withhold reinforcements for the Pacific. King could retaliate by threatening to withdraw naval resources from the Atlantic, but that kind of intimidation could backfire. During an early June meeting with Marshall and Vice Admiral Louis Mountbatten, the Prime Minister's personal representative, King balked when asked to find and train the crews necessary for the thou-

* The subsequent series of meetings became known as the Second Washington Conference,

sands of landing craft needed for a cross-Channel invasion. Marshall replied that the Army would train its own crews if necessary.

Afterward Mountbatten, as one sailor to another, counseled King not to let the Army do the Navy's job. Regardless of what King did or said, the invasion of Europe was inevitable. King listened without comment, then asked for Mountbatten's recommendation. Mountbatten advised King to assign a top flag officer to work with the British in developing the plans necessary for providing landing craft and crews. The next day King ordered Rear Admiral H. Kent Hewitt to London. (He would become the Navy's top amphibious commander in the Mediterranean.) When Mountbatten told Marshall, the General was jubilant. It seemed that King had finally committed himself to supporting the Army in the war against Germany.

Secretary of War Henry Stimson saw King a different way. He and King disliked each other intensely, and Stimson's antipathy is evident in his diary. During a White House meeting on 17 June, just before the Second Washington Conference, Marshall vigorously argued his cross-Channel case before a vacillating President. "King wobbled around in a way that made me rather sick with him," Stimson wrote in his diary. "He is firm and brave outside of the White House, but as soon as he gets in the presence of the President he crumbles up. But a few words of cross examination on my part put him in a rather indefensible position."

The Second Washington Conference began on 19 June and ended on 25 June. King was usually absent from the CCS meetings and sent either Horne or Willson as his representative. King was also absent from most of the ad hoc meetings in Hyde Park and Washington. Indeed, in the seven days of continuous gatherings, King was present only three times. In addition to one CCS meeting, King went to the White House on the evening of 21 June to help Roosevelt comfort Churchill, who had just learned of the fall of Tobruk. King's only other meeting was at the White House on 23 June to discuss shipping losses in the Battle of the Atlantic.

The reason for his absences is not recorded, but he was probably preoccupied with planning for Guadalcanal. As a result, King was a faint voice in Marshall's fight to save SLEDGEHAMMER and ROUNDUP. King's only help came during the CCS conference on 20 June, a "stinking, hot day" according to the new Chief of the Imperial General Staff, General Sir Alan Brooke. The British were reeling from endless disasters in the Mediterranean and Middle East. Thinking more about saving Egypt than invading Europe, Brooke incessantly urged that the Allies invade North Africa instead of France.

King objected. A North Africa invasion,* he said, would require shipping that the Americans did not have. He was desperately scrounging ships for the Guadalcanal campaign only weeks away, and the Battle of the Atlantic was creating terrible shipping losses, as well. As the Allies did not have control of the sea in the Atlantic, convoys going to North Africa would be vulnerable. Thus, said King, he was "entirely opposed to any idea of carrying out GYMNAST in 1942."

But King would not go the whole way by advocating SLEDGEHAMMER and ROUNDUP as alternatives — perhaps for the obvious fact that if he could not provide naval support for North Africa, neither could he support an invasion of Western Europe. Marshall had to carry on alone in arguing for a cross-Channel invasion.

Marshall neither won nor lost. The conference ended inconclusively and Allied strategy went into limbo. But after Churchill returned to Great Britain the War Cabinet forced the issue by resolutely opposing SLEDGEHAMMER and advocating GYMNAST. Churchill cabled their decision to Roosevelt on 8 July 1942. The War Cabinet hoped, said Churchill, that the Americans would agree to invade North Africa.

King met with the JCS on 10 July to hear Marshall read the bad news contained in Churchill's message. When he finished, Marshall was obviously in a pique: he wanted nothing to do with GYMNAST. If the British would not support a cross-Channel invasion, to hell with them. In an about-face, Marshall proposed to throw everything against Japan. King promptly (gleefully?) cosigned a memorandum prepared by Marshall for the President. If the British persisted in advocating North Africa rather than Europe, said the memorandum, "we are definitely of the opinion that we should turn to the Pacific and strike decisively against Japan."

Marshall asserted after the war that his memorandum — actually an ultimatum — was a bluff. Perhaps so. The Pacific theater would be a naval war; the huge army that Marshall was creating belonged on the continent of Europe. Yet King had nothing to lose by supporting Marshall's turnabout. King would take anything he could get while the American and British army leaders squabbled over European strategy. When in due time they finally did agree, King once again would see the Pacific relegated to a secondary theater.

Roosevelt called Marshall's bluff by demanding an immediate detailed strategic plan for the Pacific. It was a Sunday morning. No such plan existed, and the President knew it. King hastily gathered with the JCS, and, together with their staffs, they contrived a plan within several

* Code-named GYMNAST.

hours. After it had been signed jointly by King, Arnold, and Marshall, an officer messenger went by air to deliver it to the President at Hyde Park.

Roosevelt read the plan in his study. His naval aide, John McCrea, could tell that the President was "much annoyed." The President laid the JCS paper aside, then without hesitation scrawled a memorandum in reply to King and the other members of the JCS. "I have carefully read your estimate of Sunday," wrote Roosevelt.

> My first impression is that it is exactly what Germany hoped the United States would do following Pearl Harbor. Secondly it does not in fact provide use of American Troops in fighting except in a lot of islands whose occupation will not affect the world situation this year or next. Third: it does not help Russia or The Near East.
>
> Therefore it is disapproved as of the present.
>
> Roosevelt C in C

King and Marshall had blundered owing to their political naïveté. Roosevelt was under intense pressure to establish a second front to divert German troops from Russia. King and Marshall even acknowledged that their preposterous plan would worsen the military situation on the Eastern Front, but they lamely rationalized that concentrating on Japan would help Russia in the event that Japan and the USSR went to war. It was equally absurd for King and Marshall to imagine that Roosevelt would abandon the British after years of active alliance, especially as Churchill was fighting for his political survival following the Middle East debacles. Again, they rationalized that by attacking Japan it would help the British in the Middle East by diverting Japanese attention away from India.

Still another political factor that King and Marshall overlooked was the looming off-year congressional elections in November. Roosevelt feared he would lose the Democratic majority in both houses as a reaction to public disapproval of his Administration's direction of the war. He wanted American troops fighting German soldiers by the early fall of 1942, preferably before the elections, in order to win votes. If North Africa was the only choice of battlefields, the President felt that there it must be.

Although the JCS were not politically ignorant, they still planned unrealistically on purely military terms. Politics were disregarded, Marshall admitted after the war, because the military were aliens to the political processes. When the JCS could no longer ignore the intrusion of politics, they would finally acknowledge its impact.

The events related above are a vivid example. The JCS received the President's veto from Hyde Park on 14 July and learned that Roosevelt intended to send King, Hopkins, and Marshall to London after he had spoken with them in Washington on the fifteenth. King, Marshall, and Arnold assembled with their advisors to divine Roosevelt's intentions. One participant later wrote, ". . . it was indicated that unquestionably the President would require military operations in Africa. The relative merits of operations in Africa, in Northwest Africa, and in the Middle East were discussed. All agreed to the many arguments previously advanced among military men in the Army and Navy that operations in the Pacific would be the alternative if SLEDGEHAMMER and BOLERO were not accepted wholeheartedly by the British. However, there was an acceptance that our political system would require major operations this year in Africa."

Years after the war Marshall admitted to his want of political perceptiveness. "We failed to see that the leader in a democracy has to keep the people entertained," said Marshall. "The people demand action. We couldn't wait to be completely ready."

Perhaps Leahy best emphasized the reasons why senior army and naval officers were politically unsophisticated. "As a high-ranking member of the armed services," he wrote after the war, "it had been my fixed policy not to participate in domestic partisan politics. This personal attitude was in no sense a disparagement of American politics but was one generally followed by the professional leadership of the armed services, which must work in harmony with both Republican and Democratic administrations to protect at all times the security that makes our democracy possible." Leahy was so bewildered by watching Roosevelt during the 1944 presidential elections that the President joked that, when it came to politics, the Admiral belonged in the Middle Ages. Leahy thought that the Dark Ages would have been a more appropriate description.

King himself rarely discussed politics. The only indication of his political beliefs was contained in his Naval War College thesis of 1932, which expressed contempt both for politicians and for American political processes.* There is no reason to believe that his attitude had changed during the Second World War.

King flew with Marshall to London on 16 July taking a single aide, Commander Ruthven E. Libby. As he and Marshall, together with Hopkins, were about to reconcile the course of the entire Second World

* See Chapter 9.

War, it is remarkable that King went without a staff. Logistics, for example, were the sine qua non of any plan under consideration, yet King's logistical planners remained in Washington. King apparently intended to rely upon his own wits and whatever assistance he could obtain from Stark and Stark's London staff.

The Americans arrived in England on Friday, 17 July, and immediately received an invitation from Churchill to join him at Chequers. King and Marshall declined, citing the press of business. Before tackling the British they were anxious to confer with Eisenhower, who had arrived in London several weeks earlier to take command of the U.S. forces in Europe. Eisenhower's staff had reserved rooms at Claridge's and had transformed the fourth floor into a military headquarters. American soldiers guarded the doors — with one exception. A Marine stood watch at the entrance to King's suite.

Furious at the apparent snub, Churchill phoned Hopkins. The Americans had even asked to see the British Chiefs of Staff, complained Churchill, before seeing him first. Churchill had to be placated.

"Hell, I'll have to go to Chequers," said Hopkins. "Churchill is raising the devil."

"Why you?" asked King.

"My job, damn it," said Hopkins.

"Of course," said King, "you might like to go down there anyway."

"You get the hell out of here," said Hopkins.

King, Marshall, and their advisors worked over the weekend, examining strategic alternatives and trying to reach a consensus before confronting the British on Monday. They were under terrible strain. Their President and Commander in Chief had charged them to find an agreement with the British that would bring American soldiers into battle with German soldiers in 1942. Yet there were hosts of crises to consider. Russia might collapse. The Japanese were still on the move in the South Pacific. Rommel was threatening Egypt. The Allies had lost control of the sea in the Battle of the Atlantic, so that it was questionable whether Great Britain could survive economically, much less mount an offensive. Malta was being held only by enormous sacrifices of British naval resources. The central Mediterranean was dominated by the Axis; British control of either end of the Mediterranean was tenuous.

Thus the Allies were entangled in a global war against two ruthless nations with huge, powerful, battle-experienced armed forces. The American armed forces were green and untested. The task before them was staggering. Although King and Marshall had been preparing for high command for their entire professional lives, they now found themselves groping. The Second World War had so expanded in magnitude and complexity that it had surpassed anything they could have imagined. At stake was the future of the free world and millions of lives.

Their inexperience was most glaring in amphibious warfare. A successful amphibious assault requires control of the sea and the air, overwhelming combat power, and secure lines of communication to the objective. There were none of these advantages in 1942, but that did not matter because the Army planners had a blinding loyalty to Marshall. Marshall was fixed on the idea of attacking Germany on the continent; his planners, only deceiving themselves, said it could be done — it had to be done, because that was what Marshall wanted. The Army's most vociferous proponent, Brigadier General Albert C. Wedemeyer, argued that superior Army leadership, fortified with will and desire, would compensate for deficiencies in men and equipment. As Wedemeyer was a Marshall protégé and an influential strategic planner, no other Army planner dared disagree.

Some senior naval planners were more pragmatic. Kelly Turner, for example, had opposed the idea before he had left for Guadalcanal in early June. Stark too doubted the wisdom of SLEDGEHAMMER, but he was a minority of one. He could not stop the Army planners from concocting a scheme to establish a beachhead on the Cherbourg peninsula in late 1942, followed by a full-scale invasion in the spring of 1943. Never mind that the Allies had only six divisions, which would be massacred by the twenty-five German divisions in France — or that the Channel weather in the fall and winter would wreck the sea lines of communication to France and frustrate Allied air support.

A cross-Channel invasion in 1942 would have been suicidal. Yet King, who should have known better, supported the plan. He had his reasons. Although King was in London, his mind undoubtedly was in the Pacific, for the Guadalcanal assault in early August was imminent. King had needed Marshall's concessions and cooperation to get final JCS approval of King's Guadalcanal plan, and he also knew that he would need Marshall's goodwill when King would ask for the inevitable reinforcements for the South Pacific in the fall. Perhaps King now felt obligated to support Marshall as a quid pro quo in the General's crusade for SLEDGEHAMMER, tacitly acknowledging Marshall's predominance in European matters. For whatever reasons, King agreed to support Marshall when they met with the British on the Monday morning following the frenzied weekend at Claridge's.

The British correctly perceived the fatuousness of Marshall's plan and refused to accept it. Roosevelt finally cabled Marshall to forget

SLEDGEHAMMER and to get a British agreement to *something* in 1942, preferably a joint British-American invasion of French North Africa. Marshall, under duress, dejectedly sat in his room at Claridge's and began writing a new plan to conform with Roosevelt's ultimatum. "Just as I was finishing," Marshall later said, "King came in. It is remarkable, but he accepted [North Africa] without a quibble. Usually he argued over all our plans."

Was it really so remarkable? Perhaps King knew that an invasion of North Africa was inevitable under the circumstances, and that Marshall's continental plan had never had a chance.

The British Chiefs of Staff readily agreed to Marshall's new proposal, but not Churchill. The Prime Minister complicated matters several days later by suggesting to Roosevelt that Marshall — not Eisenhower — take the supreme command in Europe (and thus North Africa). Roosevelt delayed designating anyone for weeks. Although Marshall refused to discuss the subject with the President or to press for a decision, King and Arnold must have urged the President to keep Marshall in Washington. Finally, the President agreed. But it would not be the last time that there would be intense pressure for Marshall to become the supreme commander in Europe.

Before returning to the United States, King met with two other world figures. One was Charles de Gaulle, who pressed for a meeting with King and Marshall. The Frenchman wanted the Americans to come to him as political recognition that he was a de facto head of state. The State Department squelched that idea. The proud, haughty de Gaulle had to call on the Americans because he was junior in military rank. "How he hated it," King later said. As the United States was the only country that could help de Gaulle's aspirations, King expected that he would try to be pleasant. But de Gaulle was a "cold fish," King later said. King and Marshall responded in kind. The awkward meeting was mercifully short.

King's call on King George VI was agreeable. The monarch wore a uniform of an admiral of the fleet, and the two men sipped tea and swapped sea stories. The war was scarcely mentioned.

The main social event was a formal dinner arranged by the Royal Navy in King's honor, held at the Royal Naval College at Greenwich. Although Churchill had not been invited, he came anyway. It was a grand affair. After a brief welcoming speech, King rose to reply and told them what they wanted to hear. He recalled with pleasure his past association with the Royal Navy, pledged his cooperation in the present war, and predicted an inevitable Allied victory.

Afterward, King's aide, Ruthven Libby, remarked, "The British will think you are going to do everything for them."

"I had to say something to make them happy," King replied.

Mission accomplished, King and Marshall flew back to the United States, stopping briefly at the Naval Air Station, Presque Isle, Maine, in the early morning. The famished travelers went into the mess hall for breakfast. King was accustomed to eating well and had suffered from the austere British meals, so he ordered everything on the menu. The astonished waiter went to the galley and returned with a plate overflowing with pancakes and eggs.

"How did you get that?" asked Marshall.

"I asked for it," replied King, tearing into his meal. Libby watched in amazement. "If I can't get out of the mess hall," said King to his aide, "roll me up in a corner of the plane. But I think I'll make it."

Afterward King and Marshall visited the galley so that King could thank the cooks. Almost as an afterthought, Marshall followed suit. "In the Navy it is proper to say some nice things to the cook," King later remarked, "but apparently that was not the way of the Army."

The details of the North African invasion (Operation Torch) were left hanging after the London agreement. Months of confusion and irresolution preceded the landing on 8 November 1942, in large measure owing to Marshall's dislike for Torch and King's preoccupation with the Pacific. Torch's ultimate success was the culmination of improvisation by both the Navy and the Army. Despite King's apprehensions about sufficient shipping, his staff somehow found enough combatants and amphibious ships. Perhaps the most important thing that King did was to appoint Rear Admiral Kent Hewitt as the naval amphibious commander. Hewitt was magnificent. Through his leadership and organizational genius the United States Navy was ready for its first major amphibious assault of the Second World War.

As Torch eliminated any cross-Channel assault in 1943, Allied grand strategy needed a new definition as 1942 drew to a close. Decisions had to be made about future operations in the Mediterranean, military assistance to Russia and China, the Battle of the Atlantic, and the war in the Pacific. These questions would be addressed when the Allies met in Casablanca in early January 1943.

18

Striking Back: Guadalcanal

AMERICAN LONG-RANGE strategic planning was erratic throughout the spring and early summer of 1942. There were many reasons, starting with logistics. The shortages of men and materiel would not be alleviated until the United States was fully mobilized. That would take months. The machinations preceding the July decision to invade North Africa had also disrupted orderly planning. The battles of Coral Sea and Midway were similarly distracting.

Despite Marshall's temporary aberration in July to favor the war against Japan, his planners consistently gave the European theater top priority in troops, aircraft, and materiel. The Pacific, in the Army view, rated only enough for a passive defense. Naval planners, reflecting King's way of thinking, demanded adequate numbers of combat forces in the Pacific for a limited offensive. A passive defense would permit the Japanese to consolidate their gains by default and to exploit and develop their conquests of raw materials and natural resources. If the Allies left the Japanese alone until they had defeated Germany, the eventual counteroffensive in the Pacific would become more costly as time went on. As the Battle of the Coral Sea had grown near, King had begun to fear that the Japanese spring offensive would be too strong for him to handle. His concern had shifted from mounting a limited offensive to avoiding further losses.

On 4 May the JCS had met, hoping to find a way to distribute their inadequate forces between the two theaters. King had assured Marshall that he supported BOLERO,* but not at the expense of dangerously reducing American Pacific forces. First priority should go to holding

* Code name for the accumulation of forces in England for an eventual cross-Channel invasion.

what the United States had in the Pacific, argued King, rather than diverting resources to BOLERO for an indeterminate offensive in the future. Marshall disagreed. BOLERO had to come first. Apparently he was willing to concede additional territory to the Japanese if that was what it took to keep resources flowing to England. Given their all-or-nothing attitude, there did not seem to be any middle ground for King and Marshall. For one of the few times during the war they bucked their dispute to the President for resolution.

Roosevelt decided in favor of Marshall and BOLERO.

King had been too preoccupied with Coral Sea and Midway to brood over Roosevelt's rejection of his Pacific strategy. Once those battles were over, King had a breathing spell, and his thoughts again turned to the offense. When he realized how badly the Japanese had been beaten at Midway, King's instinctive response was to hit back while the Japanese were momentarily stunned. The American victory had to be exploited immediately, King insisted, before the Japanese recovered their offensive momentum.

Plans once dormant were revived, both in Washington and in the Pacific. MacArthur was the first to be heard. On 8 June he proposed a grandiose offensive to seize Rabaul with himself in command (as he had been assured by Marshall). King studied MacArthur's proposal and warned Marshall that any amphibious assault in the South Pacific would have to be a naval operation under naval command — not under MacArthur. But Marshall was not listening. On 12 June he endorsed MacArthur's Rabaul plan on the mistaken assumption that King would provide whatever ships and Marines MacArthur needed. Mesmerized by MacArthur's optimism, Marshall was edging away from his concept of a passive defense in the Pacific.

Some two weeks were frittered away in mid-June while Navy planners studied the MacArthur-Marshall proposal and made plans of their own. Finally, on 23 June, King and Cooke rebutted MacArthur's scheme as too ambitious because Rabaul was too heavily defended. The Navy's alternative was an indirect approach through the eastern Solomons, where the Japanese were weaker. In any event, said King, he would never allow MacArthur to command any major naval forces. A naval officer under Nimitz would have to command whatever amphibious assault was finally agreed upon.

Impatient with further delay, King brazenly forced the issue. Not even allowing Marshall time to reply, King ordered Nimitz to prepare to seize Tulagi in the Solomons by amphibious assault, using naval and

Marine forces. King's audacity was astounding. He intended that Nimitz intrude into MacArthur's Southwest Pacific Area with a major offensive with the approval of neither the President nor the JCS. King's order also defied the President's decision not to increase American strength in the Pacific. Once American forces had been committed under Nimitz, a call for reinforcements was inevitable.

King was too shrewd a sea lawyer to have acted without some semblance of legal justification, and he used to his advantage Roosevelt's ambiguity in dealing with the JCS. In early March Roosevelt had approved King's memorandum for a limited offensive into the Solomons, and it had never been canceled. Nimitz's CINCPOA charter (drafted by the Navy and approved by the JCS and the President) could be interpreted as authorizing Nimitz to conduct amphibious assaults in MacArthur's area. Finally, the President had not specifically forbidden King to attack in the Pacific when he had adjudicated the King-Marshall dispute over theater priorities. Indeed, King very carefully had not ordered Nimitz in the strict sense to carry out the assault, but rather to *prepare* for such an assault in contemplation of eventual JCS approval. In any event, the President's executive order had authorized King to command the Navy and Marine Corps, and, by God, King was doing just that.

On 25 June King presented the JCS with the fait accompli, then boldly asked for concurrence that Nimitz should attack Tulagi. Having promised the command to MacArthur, Marshall was in a bind. MacArthur added to the confusion by scrubbing his earlier plan of a bold, direct assault against Rabaul, now concurring with King's plan for an indirect approach via Tulagi and the Solomons. Whatever the objective, Marshall still wanted MacArthur in command.

King was unsympathetic with Marshall's dilemma in dealing with the imperious MacArthur, who had been a prewar Chief of Staff of the Army when Marshall had still been a colonel. Marshall, he believed, "would do anything rather than disagree with MacArthur." (Nimitz was unquestionably an obedient subordinate to King, but MacArthur's association with Marshall would be tenuous and tempestuous throughout the war.) King also suspected that Stimson uncritically supported MacArthur and pressured Marshall to appease the Southwest Pacific commander. This made King dislike Stimson even more.

Marshall left his element and began foundering in uncharted waters when he argued that MacArthur should control fleet movements in his own area. His ignorance of naval communication procedures, for example, was glaringly exposed in a memorandum to King. "His basic trouble," King later said, "was that like all Army officers he knew nothing about sea power and very little about air power."

The squabble over who was to command what in the Pacific went on. King argued that speed was essential; further delay would allow the Japanese to recover from their Midway defeat and to resume their offensive in the Solomons. Reminding Marshall of their earlier agreement that the Army would exercise supreme command in Europe, King expected a quid pro quo in the Pacific. But with or without Army support, King intended to invade the Solomons. He instructed Nimitz to proceed with his invasion plans even though "there would probably be some delay in reaching a decision on the extent of the Army's participation."

Marshall pondered King's ultimatum for three days. His mood worsened when he received an agitated dispatch from MacArthur, who was furious, almost paranoid, at King's presumptuousness in ordering Nimitz into MacArthur's area. The Navy, said MacArthur, was conspiring to reduce the Army in the Pacific to no more than an occupation force.

Marshall finally suggested on 29 June that he and King talk about who would command the operation. (Incredibly, the two men up to this point had only exchanged memoranda.) King readily agreed. By 30 June they had fashioned a clever compromise. MacArthur's insistence that he command all operations in his area became irrelevant by the simple expedient of moving Nimitz's western boundary line into MacArthur's territory. The result was that Nimitz's South Pacific Area was enlarged to include the eastern Solomons, including Tulagi. Vice Admiral Robert L. Ghormley would command the eastern Solomons assault, identified as Task I. Subsequent assaults, referred to as Tasks II and III, would follow in the western Solomons, eastern New Guinea, and the Bismarck Archipelago. As these latter areas were still in MacArthur's domain, the General would be in command. After nearly a month of haggling, King and Marshall were finally able to agree on their Pacific strategy on 2 July. The eastern Solomons landings would begin on 1 August 1942. The American counteroffensive in the Pacific was almost underway.

Nimitz had flown to San Francisco on 30 June in response to a summons from King. During the landing his amphibious plane hit a log and capsized, and Nimitz was nearly killed. Badly battered, he was happy to hear that the meeting was delayed while King concluded his negotiations with Marshall to get JCS approval for the eastern Solomons invasion.

On the fourth of July King and Nimitz met at the Twelfth Naval District Headquarters. King explained that the eastern Solomons were only the start. King was thinking ahead. After the Solomons and New Guinea were seized and secured, said King, the next objectives would be Truk, Saipan, and Guam. These were King's ideas alone. It was immaterial to King that they did not include MacArthur and his cherished return to the Philippines, or that the JCS had not agreed to any plans beyond the Solomons and New Guinea.

Kelly Turner also attended the meeting, although he no longer was King's war plans officer. In early spring King had told Turner to expect an assignment to the Pacific. Turner had been surprised. (King suspected Turner thought he was indispensable.) Who, he had been asked, would take his place? "Cooke will," replied King. Later King had told Turner he would command the South Pacific amphibious forces. Turner had protested: he knew too little about amphibious warfare.

"You will learn," said King.

Turner's attitude was typical. Few senior naval officers understood amphibious warfare, a subject largely ignored by the Navy before the Second World War. King's reasoning for assigning Turner was simple. First, Nimitz wanted Turner in the job. Second, Turner had planned the operation, so it was logical for him to participate in it. Finally, Turner resembled King — brilliant, caustic, arrogant, and tactless. If anyone could succeed with Operation WATCHTOWER (the code name for the eastern Solomons assault), it would be Turner.

Now at San Francisco Turner presented King and Nimitz with his concept of operations in the eastern Solomons (Task I). He intended to occupy the Santa Cruz Islands; to seize Tulagi, Florida, and the Guadalcanal Islands in the eastern Solomons; to occupy Funafuti in the Ellice Islands; and to reinforce the Army garrison on Espíritu Santo Island in the New Hebrides. After a general discussion, King and Nimitz approved Turner's objectives. Turner excused himself and left for the South Pacific.

Operation WATCHTOWER discussion ended with Turner's departure. The conference went on to other topics, personnel assignments and policies, for example, as King, Nimitz, and Jacobs sought the best men for the most important jobs. It seemed as if WATCHTOWER had been removed from their minds. The decision had been made, commanders and forces assigned, and there was nothing more to say. It was King's nature not to discuss his decisions, for he regarded them as finished business. Everyone had had his say, especially in Washington, and King was weary from weeks of debate. If anyone had second thoughts about WATCHTOWER, he knew better than to voice them to King.

In retrospect, King's advocacy of WATCHTOWER could have been a disaster. What we have noted about the planning for a cross-Channel attack was equally true in considering WATCHTOWER. An amphibious assault is the most dangerous of all major military operations. The risks of failure are so great that the attacker needs every possible advantage in his favor: control of the sea and the air, superior combat power to overwhelm the defending enemy, and secure lines of communication. The understrength and inexperienced forces King intended to employ enjoyed none of these advantages. Everything was done in haste. Kelly Turner, for example, was unable to take command of the assault forces until less than three weeks before they landed on Tulagi and Guadalcanal. Undeterred, King demanded that the operations carry on, regardless of the confusion and cries of alarm from the local commanders.

Vice Admiral Ghormley had gone from London to the South Pacific to act as the supreme commander of all forces (including Turner's) engaged in WATCHTOWER. After talking to a pessimistic MacArthur on 8 July, Ghormley doubted the wisdom of carrying out WATCHTOWER in early August. Enemy activity in the Solomons and New Guinea was increasing, and MacArthur and Ghormley felt — rightly so — that their forces were inadequate for Tasks I, II, and III. Together they urged the JCS to delay the South Pacific offensive until they got reinforcements. Ghormley's ready acceptance of MacArthur's views would be the first of many times that senior naval officers would succumb to the General's power of persuasion.

When their joint message hit Washington, King was furious. MacArthur, he said, was vacillating and fainthearted. "Three weeks ago MacArthur stated that, if he could be furnished amphibious forces and two carriers, he could push right through to Rabaul," King told Marshall. "He now feels that he not only cannot undertake this extended operation but not even the Tulagi operation." Privately, King suspected that MacArthur was sulking because he had been denied supreme command in the South Pacific. "He could not understand that he was not to manage everything," King later said. "He couldn't believe that. Of course he was absolutely against going into Guadalcanal, and he said so."

Yet King could not summarily dismiss their warnings. MacArthur and Ghormley were the commanders responsible for the operation's success, and it was their prerogative to express a legitimate concern. A classic military problem was facing them: an enemy force was growing progressively stronger, and the longer the American attack was delayed, the more formidable the enemy would become. On the other hand, a delay would also strengthen the American forces. Should the Americans attack at once, or later? Might it not be better to wait and take time to prepare properly? The latter, said King, was MacArthur's philosophy, "to have everything ready before advancing." * As a student of military history, King knew that many commanders of the past had lost opportunities for victory by waiting. (McClellan at Richmond in 1862 is a classic example.) Although one's own forces may not be entirely ready, the enemy may be even less ready. King believed he still had an edge on the Japanese in the eastern Solomons, but the advantage could turn in favor of the Japanese if the Americans did not attack immediately.

King also had other crucial reason for urging an immediate attack. He could not count on help from Marshall, so there was no reason to wait for Army reinforcements which might never appear. On the other hand, once the Americans were ashore and fighting in the eastern Solomons, Marshall might be persuaded to support the operation to avoid a potential American defeat.

The objections of Ghormley and MacArthur notwithstanding, King told Marshall that the assault was more urgent than ever. Marshall, too, wanted to move along. On 10 July they jointly ordered Ghormley and MacArthur to press on. They were not to worry about Tasks II and III, said King and Marshall, but rather they were to do what was "absolutely essential" for Operation WATCHTOWER alone. Ghormley, perhaps realizing that his hesitancy was unwelcome in Washington, replied the following day that he had sufficient forces for Task I if he could count upon air support from MacArthur.†

King's mood began to change by mid-July. He finally began to worry openly about the perils of WATCHTOWER. Ghormley probably had enough forces to get ashore, King reasoned, but could he withstand counterattacks? And what about plans to drive westward after WATCHTOWER was completed? Where were these forces to come from? Although King once had told Marshall that he was ready to go it alone in the South Pacific, King now had second thoughts. He began to

* It was not MacArthur's philosophy later in the war. Realizing that he would never get the forces he wanted, he became a master of improvisation and expediency.

† It was wishful thinking. MacArthur subsequently did not provide air support to Ghormley.

besiege Marshall and Arnold for men, guns, and aircraft to support Ghormley.

King's pleas were futile. After King, Hopkins, and Marshall had returned from their mid-July trip to Great Britain to nail down European strategy, Marshall had lost interest in a speck of an island in the far Pacific called Guadalcanal. His attention had become focused on the North African landing scheduled for that fall. Marshall naturally wanted all his available strength for that theater alone. Arnold had always been reluctant to send his aircraft to the Pacific; now more than ever he was determined to concentrate his air power in the European and Mediterranean theaters. MacArthur would become entangled in the Papua peninsula in eastern New Guinea and would have nothing to spare for WATCHTOWER. King's Navy and Marine Corps would be very much alone.

"At last we have started," Nimitz reported to King on 7 August 1942. The attack on Guadalcanal and Tulagi was underway. The Japanese had been caught by surprise.

Several hours passed. "No report yet from Ghormley," wired Nimitz. The only indication of activity was through intercepted Japanese radio messages. "No direct report from the south," wired Nimitz again, twenty-four hours after the attack had begun. A frustrating pattern had been set. For the next several days the reports from the South Pacific were garbled and confusing, because of what Nimitz reported as "extreme communication difficulties."

King's duty officer, George Russell, entered King's bedroom on the *Dauntless* in the early morning hours of 12 August. Something was up. One rarely disturbed King after he had turned in. It would be a long war, King needed his sleep, and there was nothing he could do in the middle of the night that would have any immediate effect on a distant battle. Bad news normally waited until morning.

But this time Russell woke King and turned on the light. "Admiral, you've got to see this," said Russell. "It isn't good."

It was a long-delayed report from Turner. A Japanese naval force at Savo Island near Guadalcanal had sunk four cruisers, damaged another, and had damaged two destroyers. "Heavy casualties, majority saved," reported Turner. The transports supporting the Marines ashore were not attacked, but they were retiring from Guadalcanal because of "impending heavy attacks." None of the Japanese ships had apparently been sunk or damaged.

King read the message in disbelief several times before returning it to Russell. "I can't thank you for bringing me this one," said King. His mind raced for some explanation of what might have happened. "They must have decoded the dispatch wrong," King finally said. "Tell them to decode it again."

King was crushed. "That, as far as I am concerned, was the blackest day of the war," he later said. "The whole future then became unpredictable."

King slumped back into bed after Russell left the room. He knew he had suffered a terrible setback to his policy of attack, attack, attack. Savo Island had matured him at age sixty-four.

The next morning King released a message asking for a confirmation of the naval losses and an explanation of what had happened. Ghormley finally gave a detailed report a day later. It sounded horrible. The Japanese had surprised the American surface force patrolling near Savo Island on the approaches to the Guadalcanal landing site. In a savage night encounter, the Japanese had demolished the American warships but by the grace of God had not fallen upon the unprotected amphibious shipping.

King next made two key decisions. He sent a team of investigators, retired Admiral Arthur J. Hepburn and Captain DeWitt C. Ramsey (whom King called his "fox terrier"), to the South Pacific. His other decision was to suppress the news of the sinking; disclosure would reveal to the Japanese the extent of the American disaster, even though they already might have had a fairly accurate assessment. But King also feared repercussions in Washington, for the Guadalcanal invasion had been his personal project. His first try at an offensive against the Japanese had begun with a debacle.

On the very day that King was trying to cope with the Savo Island news, he received a letter from the President that was unintentionally ironic.

> Dear Ernie: —
>
> You will remember "the sweet young thing" whom I told about Douglas MacArthur rowing his family from Corregidor to Australia — and later told about Shangri-La as the take-off place for the Tokio bombers.
>
> Well, she came in to dinner last night and this time *she* told *me* something.
>
> She said "We are going to win this war. The Navy is tough.

And the toughest man in the Navy — Admiral King — proves it. He shaves every morning with a blowtorch."

Glad to know you!

As ever yours,
/s/ F.D.R.

P.S. I am trying to verify another rumor — that you cut your toenails with a torpedo net cutter.

By the date of the letter — 12 August — and its contents, King obviously had not told the President about Savo Island, for King had only learned of it early that morning. Presumably King informed the President once he had confirmation, and he likewise told Marshall and Knox before the end of August. The news also was common knowledge among King's operational planners. "We had all known about it," a senior planner later said, "but we were very close-mouthed. We didn't discuss things that we weren't supposed to discuss. Secrecy was very important. . . ."

But others did not know. Several weeks after the Battle of Savo Island, New York *Times* war correspondent Hanson Baldwin appeared before the Joint Staff Planners (JPS), the thirty or so senior officers from all three services responsible directly to the JCS for all strategic planning. The JPS had invited Baldwin, who was respected by all the services, to tell about his impressions of the South Pacific during his recent visit there.

In the course of his briefing Baldwin named the cruisers that had been sunk at Savo Island. To his astonishment, Captain Charles R. Brown, one of King's naval planners, leaped to his feet and started yelling. "I object to that. I object to that," Brown hotly protested. "This is top secret information. Admiral King has given the strictest orders that no one is to know about this." Baldwin was flabbergasted. He had told no one, he responded, including his own newspaper, but he had assumed that the JPS had asked him to the meeting to find out what was happening in the South Pacific.

Brown, known for his volatility, again protested. Finally the JPS chairman, Major General Wedemeyer, asked Baldwin to confine his remarks to the importance of air power in the South Pacific. Visibly angry, Brown sat down and the meeting continued.

Baldwin was convinced that King had withheld news of American naval losses from most of the Army and Air Corps officers on the JPS. "They had no idea of what had happened at Guadalcanal or Savo, no idea at all," Baldwin later said. "And these same officers were supposed to be planning! That, I think, is a hell of a way to run a war."

However extreme King's other motives may appear, he did have good reason to suspect that Army planners talked too much. During the supposedly secret planning for the early November invasion of North Africa, King had begun to hear its code name, TORCH, mentioned casually in public. King's security officer discovered that sixty-one naval officers in Washington had knowledge of TORCH. That was too many, said King, and he gave hell to the security officer. King later apologized when he learned that 1,324 Army officers in Washington knew about TORCH.

The JCS had subsequently ordered increased security, but King obviously did not trust the Army. His suspicions were confirmed when Drew Pearson publicized the Baldwin-Brown fracas several days later. Brown accused Baldwin as the source of the leak, but the newspaperman despised Pearson and angrily wrote Brown that someone else at the meeting must have talked afterward. One suspects a disgruntled Army officer. The naval members of the JPS would hardly complain to Pearson that King had been withholding information from the Army.

The campaign for Guadalcanal became a six-month battle of attrition. Neither side would quit, yet neither side could muster the strength for a decisive victory. King never had enough ships because of losses, the demands of the Battle of the Atlantic, and the invasion of North Africa. The Pacific Fleet suffered grievously, twenty-four ships lost, including two carriers and eight cruisers, as well as many others damaged. At one time in the fall of 1942 King had but one operational aircraft carrier in the Pacific. Nor were there ever enough combat troops or aircraft on Guadalcanal during the desperate months of the fall of 1942. North Africa still came first.

Thus the greatest defect of the Guadalcanal campaign was that there were neither plans nor forces available for an extended struggle. King knew this, knew that his burning desire to become involved on Guadalcanal was a calculated risk. Perhaps he thought he could get away with it if Marshall and Arnold would send reinforcements to avoid defeat. Yet both were ready to sacrifice Guadalcanal rather than to divert forces from TORCH, even though Roosevelt in late October had ordered Guadalcanal held at all costs.

King was undeservedly lucky when Rear Admiral Mikawa decided to retire from Guadalcanal after winning the Battle of Savo Island. The Japanese admiral could have destroyed every American transport at Guadalcanal, still filled with food, ammunition, and supplies for the

Marines ashore. Had they been sunk, King's hopes for Guadalcanal would have been doomed.

Critics have charged that King had used poor judgment in choosing Ghormley to command the South Pacific Area, but that is hindsight. Nimitz had agreed on Ghormley's assignment, and there was no reason in the beginning to suspect that Ghormley would falter. Performance in war is unpredictable when it is based solely upon peacetime reputation. There were both happy surprises and shocking disappointments. Some excelled, others failed. King later believed that Ghormley's problem was his bad teeth which caused him intense pain and discomfort, an ailment King had been unaware of until Ghormley returned to Washington from the Pacific. Perhaps this experience influenced King to insist upon regular physical examinations for all his flag officers.

In the end, the Americans won because of their own tenacity as well as the Japanese tactics of committing their forces piecemeal rather than massing for a coordinated attack. King and Nimitz were committed irrevocably to winning Guadalcanal. When Ghormley became defeatist, they fired him. Substituting Halsey for Ghormley invigorated the Americans on Guadalcanal and led ultimately to the American victory. It was Halsey's finest hour.

19

Wars on the Home Front

BY LATE 1942 King's COMINCH headquarters was well established for fighting a war, both abroad and at home. Walter Muir Whitehill, in civilian life a historian, had been commissioned as a reserve naval officer for service in the Office of Naval Records and Library. His first impressions vividly describe King's Washington domain.

"The Navy Department on Constitution Avenue," wrote Whitehill, "was an immense building * in which unadorned offices of standard size stretched interminably along dreary corridors. When built as a temporary structure in 1918 it had seemed a model of efficient use of space, but the additions and alterations of a quarter of a century — coupled with wartime crowding — had turned it into a curiously chaotic rabbit warren. In few places short of the palace of Versailles before 1789 could such widely divergent characters have jostled elbows in corridors. In most parts of the building, flag officers en route to vital conferences collided with whistling messengers delivering mail by tricycle, ensigns' wives bringing babies to the dispensary, plumbers with tools, civil servants in search of a cup of coffee, and laborers engaged in the perennial pastime of shifting somebody's desk and filing case from one place to another.

"But on the front corridor of the third deck, between the fifth and eighth wings, there was a subtle difference in the atmosphere. Civil servants rarely emerged from doorways; there was a brisk sea-going air to the officers and enlisted men who were to be seen, and even the irrepressible tricyclists delivered their mail with less danger to life and limb than elsewhere. No sign or barrier marked the boundaries of

* Known as Main Navy.

COMINCH Headquarters, yet they were plainly discernible. It was evident that this region was unlike others, and that in some inexplicable manner it suggested being afloat rather than ashore.

"Being without previous naval experience, I was unaware of the changes in naval administration that had taken place since Pearl Harbor, but as I went my way and kept my ears open it became abundantly clear that COMINCH, who inhabited these Headquarters, was indeed bull of the woods. Whoever and whatever he might be, there could be no doubt of the extent to which he had impressed an austere personality upon the scene."

The scene that Whitehill saw and described was King's primary headquarters, where as COMINCH he commanded the Navy worldwide. Of his two hats as COMINCH and CNO, King considered that the former occupied 98 percent of his time. He relied upon Vice Admiral Horne as surrogate CNO to handle all congressional liaison, procurement, logistics, and administration.

As befitted the central headquarters of the operational Navy, the COMINCH staff comprised the finest professional naval officers obtainable, proven combat veterans who knew the needs of the fleet and the realities of war. After a year or so in Washington they returned to the fleet, often to serve in a campaign they had helped to plan, to be replaced by a fresh infusion of seasoned warriors. King's staff was not, however, predominantly Regular Navy; reservists, both men and women, occupied specialized restricted billets. But the key jobs went to the elite of the naval officers' corps, many of whom later became admirals. Arleigh A. Burke and George W. Anderson, Jr., for example, were future CNOs, and future four-star admirals included Richard L. Conolly, H. Page Smith, Donald B. Duncan, Charles D. Griffin, Robert L. Dennison, Charles R. Brown, and Waldemar F. Wendt. All three of King's flag secretaries—George L. Russell, Howard E. Orem, and Neil K. Dietrich—became flag officers, as well.

The COMINCH organization had to adapt to the expanding demands of a burgeoning navy fighting a global war. King wanted a small staff for reasons of efficiency; any request for increased numbers required ample justification and King's grudging approval. The staff nevertheless grew to over six hundred officers and enlisted personnel. It concurrently became less efficient. "I found out early in the game," recalled staff officer Robert B. Pirie, "that, working on a big staff like that, to try to get action taken on dispatches or papers that I was trying to move in a hurry . . . would just take days, literally, to go around and get initials from half a dozen people between my level and Admiral King. So I finally just took the things up and got him to release them direct. . . . Admiral King was very good about that."

Nevertheless, the staff officers regarded themselves as a small, overworked group compared to the traditionally larger Army staffs. "I was puzzled," staff officer Gordon A. McLean later said, "by the contrast between Admiral King's minute planning section and those of Generals Marshall and Arnold. Evidently Admiral King believed that 'too many cooks spoil the broth.' He was the most efficient person that I have ever known. Consistent therewith, we in Future Plans worked fourteen hours, seven days a week during the eighteen months that I was part of the organization."

The strain on King's staff produced heart attacks and eventually a suicide. This tragedy so disturbed King that he got a full-time doctor to keep everyone healthy. "A schedule was announced monthly," recalled staff officer Oman T. Pfeiffer, "with the date and hour for each officer's physical examination, and it was considered almost a crime to miss that appointment." The doctor installed a gymnasium, and King encouraged his staff to exercise, to shower, and to return to work refreshed. King's own routine was a rubdown in the dispensary several times a week.

King worked in isolation from most of his staff, allowing only Edwards and Cooke unlimited access. Business was conducted in writing, with King's rules for brevity unchanged from his prewar standards. "He didn't want any memoranda of more than one page," recalled Pirie. "He wouldn't have anything to do with them. If you sent him a memorandum that didn't have your signature at the bottom of the page, he'd throw it in the wastebasket, and you'd wonder where it was."

"His desk was something of a rat's nest," recalled Russell. "He wasn't a so-called clean-desk man. He was a miserable housekeeper; the papers were six inches deep on his desk. His incoming basket was always overflowing, although he always knew where everything was." At the end of the day King left his papers adrift. When charwomen cleaned King's office in the early evening, the COMINCH duty officer routinely took station in King's chair as a security precaution until they departed. Much of the material was so sensitive that King's staff thought it should be concealed from even the duty officer. Would King cover his desk with a sheet? King indignantly refused. The desk remained uncovered.

There were no regular conferences. If King wanted to discuss a problem, he simply summoned the appropriate staff officer. Thus most people saw the Admiral only in passing. The younger officers regarded King with awe. "We all on the staff respected and admired him tremendously, with an occasional twinge of fear and trepidation," remembered one staff officer.

"I never knew of King being unkind to a subordinate," recalled another staff officer, H. Page Smith. "He was always correct in his relationships. . . . His personality — to a junior — was one of great reserve, quiet dignity, and enormous and tangible force. It was very easy to accord him respect and accept his leadership. . . . As far as his staff could see he had all the best military characteristics to a superlative degree. When my wife first saw him, she asked, 'Who is that handsome man?' He looked and acted the part of a Fleet Admiral."

Some who worked more intimately with King often saw him differently. Captain Allan E. Smith received a terse note from King (written on King's instantly recognizable tiny sheet of yellow memo paper) to prepare a map of the Pacific showing potential lines of advance against the Japanese, for use during a JCS meeting.

Smith hastily fashioned a chart, and he included several arrows as highlights. Just before the meeting King questioned the arrows.

"I thought you wanted them," Smith lamely explained.

"Get them off," snapped King. Smith erased frantically, leaving an embarrassing smear when the JCS meeting convened.

Another yellow memo from King said simply, "Write a United States Fleet Operating Plan." Smith toiled for a week to produce a plan to govern standing operating procedures for every ship in the huge wartime Navy. Cooke and Edwards endorsed the plan and sent it to King for approval. Weeks passed. The plan gathered dust, a victim of King's procrastination.

Smith finally wrote asking that King either approve the plan or tell Smith what was wrong with it. The summons to King's office came the next day. Smith entered, then stood at attention before King seated at his desk. For several minutes King ignored him. Finally King looked up and held out Smith's memorandum.

"Did you write that?" asked King.

"Yes, sir."

"Don't ever tell me anything like that again," said King, "until you are sitting in this chair."

"Aye, aye, sir."

Smith fled. Two months later he left to command a battleship, neither knowing nor caring about the fate of his operation plan. Before war's end he was a flag officer, an example of the individualists on the staff who fared well despite King's ire.

But King could be ruthless in replacing a staff officer who failed to

Main Navy (U.S. Navy photograph)

King's office (Courtesy Walter Muir Whitehill)

perform in a critical assignment. The intelligence staff seemed particularly vulnerable. It will be recalled that King had banished Rear Admiral Leighton as his combat intelligence officer in early 1942. He struck again in the late summer of 1944. Commander William R. Smedberg III was serving in the Southwest Pacific as chief of staff to a bombardment task force commander preparing to support MacArthur's invasion of Leyte. Early one morning in August 1944, a breathless messenger delivered a dispatch from COMINCH. Smedberg read it in stunned disbelief.

COMMANDER SMEDBERG HEREBY DETACHED CS CTF 39 X REPORT SOONEST COMINCH WASHINGTON X PRIORITY ONE

Detaching so important an officer without warning was unprecedented, especially just before a major naval battle. But the message was imperative, straight from King and not the Bureau of Naval Personnel. Smedberg went packing for Washington half a world away. Three days later he presented himself before a dumfounded George Russell. "The old man must have written the dispatch himself," said Russell, and he ushered Smedberg into King's office.

"What took you so long to get here?" said King. Smedberg responded that he thought he had broken all travel records.

King then explained why he was there. Given his combat experience, Smedberg presumably knew the value of intelligence to the operating forces. But they weren't getting it, said King, because his intelligence specialists were protecting their sources. King intended to solve the problem. "Go down the corridor," said King, "and relieve Captain Jones * as head of my combat intelligence division."

Smedberg was staggered. "I have no experience in intelligence work," he protested.

"You've used plenty of it," King replied. "You know what is needed. Now get to work. See to it that those who need it get it, and those who do not need it do *not* get it."

Russell took Smedberg into Jones's office, introduced Smedberg, and then announced that Smedberg was his relief. Jones, four years senior to Smedberg and renowned as an intelligence expert, stared in disbelief. "What experience have you had?" he asked.

"None," replied Smedberg.

Jones was crushed.

"It made no difference to King that I was very junior to a number of the section heads in my newly acquired division," Smedberg later said. "Admiral King completely disregarded normal procedures when he wanted some drastic changes made."

* Name fictitious.

Smedberg sensed that King's staff was uneasy. "During the day," recalled Smedberg, "there would normally be from three to perhaps ten or twelve officers in the War Room at any one time. Within a few minutes of Admiral King's entrance into the room, everyone seemed to have evaporated into thin air, disappeared, flag officers as well as captains and the few commanders who were authorized. No one seemed to want to be where King was."

Dick Edwards, whose husky physique and bluff personality disguised a bad heart, provided the lubricant that kept the staff machinery functioning, especially during King's long absences for conferences. Calm, efficient, and intelligent, Edwards was the perfect chief of staff, freeing King from details. The staff worshiped him. He was their father confessor, ever available, ever willing to take their troubles upon himself.

King thought that Edwards was too available. "For God's sakes, close your door," King would urge.

"Oh, no," Edwards invariably replied. "I might miss something." This so exasperated King that he once responded that he "would lock the damned door for him" so that Edwards could work without distractions.

King eventually ordered Edwards to take ten days' leave, but after three days Edwards appeared for lunch. "I told you to get the hell out of here and stay out," said King.

"I just came to get something to eat," said Edwards. "I've paid for my lunch."

Despite King's dependence upon Edwards, King could still be a bastard. After weeks of work Edwards once submitted a plan to King for approval. King returned it with a red-penciled notation, "Take this to the head with you."

Savvy Cooke was King's physically frail but intellectually powerful chief planner, for whom King had great expectations. Although Cooke was almost indispensable, King wanted Cooke to get combat experience to help his career. Edwards, however, told King that Cooke wanted to remain in COMINCH headquarters. "Cooke was apparently afraid everything would fall apart if he was not there," King later commented.

King confronted Cooke directly. "You've done a damned good job," said King. "I want you to be COMINCH in due time. I want you to go to sea now."

"If you don't mind," Cooke replied, "I'd like to carry on with my job with you." King reluctantly agreed.

Secretary of the Navy Frank Knox rarely ascended into King's inner sanctum on the third deck of Main Navy. King, however, descended each morning to the Secretary's office on the second deck for a 0830 conference attended by the bureau chiefs and the COMINCH department heads. It was King's outward and visible sign of subordination to civilian control of the Navy.

Roosevelt's executive order designating King as both COMINCH and CNO had in many ways made King independent of Knox. When it came to strategy and fleet operations Knox was excluded. Yet the Navy also included a bureaucratic shore establishment that grew in size and complexity; bases, schools, training centers, and shipyards proliferated. As their sole purpose was to support the fleet, they belonged to Knox as far as King was concerned.

Although careful not to transgress upon King's prerogatives, Knox was accustomed to exercising authority and could not be intimidated in matters of principle. Before the regular conference convened one morning in mid-1942, King and Knox were speaking in low voices. The only other officer in the room was the President's naval aide, John McCrea. Suddenly Knox's voice rose angrily.

"Admiral King, that matter has been settled; I don't want you to raise it again. I trust you understand that the final word has been said."

His face flushed, Knox turned to his papers. The silence was finally relieved by the arrival of the other regular conference participants. Afterward, King summoned McCrea to his office.

"Did you hear what passed between me and the Secretary?" asked King. McCrea said he had.

"I want to inform you that I am going to make an issue of this," said King. "I have never been so spoken to since I can remember. I just want to make sure that you heard what was said."

McCrea reminded King that Knox had been within bounds as King's boss. More important, said McCrea, the President had enough problems. A fight between Knox and King would be an added and unwelcome burden. Reddening with anger, King wheeled about and faced his office window. McCrea was appalled at his presumptuousness in lecturing King and stared at the Admiral's back fearing the worst. King turned to glare at McCrea.

"Good day," said King.

McCrea fled. King said nothing more about Knox.

Usually the relations between King and Knox were quiescent. Both men undoubtedly tried to control their tempers, Knox probably more so, as his memoranda to King were mostly deferential. King, on the other hand, could be rude whenever he felt that Knox had intruded into King's affairs. In early 1943, for example, Knox told Carl Vinson that the Navy intended to build an airfield at the Naval Academy. Knox had not consulted with King beforehand, and King sent him a stinging rebuke. "As the matter now stands," wrote King, "no steps are being taken to implement the acquisition of an airfield nor to include flight training in the curriculum of the Naval Academy."

Another episode, perhaps apocryphal but nevertheless "common knowledge" in the Navy Department, related that Knox had ordered Nimitz to send a battleship to a West Coast port for a public relations event. King purportedly flew into a rage and confronted Knox in the Secretary's office. "Don't you ever again issue a movement order to one of my ships," King allegedly said before he stormed out. Whether true or not, this was the perception that others had of King and Knox.

On matters of serious policy their differences could become brutal. Knox sponsored the idea of providing rest and rehabilitation centers for sailors returning to the States, exhausted from war. The facilities, however, went largely unused. Physical fitness drills directed by gym instructors had little appeal to veterans long deprived of domestic amenities. Knox was so miffed that he ordered the fleet commanders to send men to the centers forthwith, evoking an immediate protest from Ingersoll in the Atlantic. King told Russell to draft a memorandum to Knox, arguing that it was not the duty of the fleet to support the shore establishment. With memorandum in hand, King stormed below to have it out with Knox, accompanied by Edwards.

"How did it go?" Russell asked Edwards when it was over.

"The gutters ran with blood," Edwards replied, "but King won his point."

Such episodes characterized King's hostility toward civilian authority. "One explanation of King's resentment," wrote naval historian Robert Albion, "might have been that even with the greatest concentration of power ever bestowed upon an American naval officer, he still had to defer to his civilian superiors." King's deference was grudgingly given and marked by strife. The Admiral constantly sought to consolidate his power within the Navy Department and to exclude Knox and his principal assistants (particularly Under Secretary James V. Forrestal). Knox and Forrestal had no quarrel with King's operational control of the Navy. But they did consider those operational duties, together with King's CCS-JCS strategic planning responsibilities, as enough for one man. Their own role—as they saw it—was to manage the Navy's logistical support, particularly the production and procurement of war materiel, a field in which they were more competent than King.

King, however, wanted logistical support entirely under his control, subjugating the civilians to no more than complaisant providers of what he needed to fight the war. If the civilians controlled production schedules, King would argue, they could obstruct his war plans by telling him what he could or could not have. King failed to comprehend that wartime logistical support was incredibly complex, demanding the finest civilian industrial and managerial minds to make things work among conflicting priorities and shortages of resources. King simply wanted to order what he needed. With the nation at war, King would maintain, the civilians were obliged to support the professional warriors without question. His JCS colleagues shared this belief.

King's ire frequently centered on the Bureaus of Ships, Aeronautics, and Ordnance — traditionally autonomous, independent of the CNO, and responsible solely to Congress and the Secretary of the Navy. Reflecting the antipathy of most seagoing officers, King regarded the bureaus as inefficient and unresponsive to the needs of the fleet. Knox and Forrestal, he believed, were too naïve and inexperienced to master the vagaries of the bureau system. Lacking a firm hand, the bureaus would perpetuate their old ways, hurting the war effort. King's remedy was to make the bureau chiefs directly responsible to him. He would make them produce. Conveniently for King, that was the way that Admirals Sexton and Richardson had drafted the momentous 12 March 1942 executive order.*

Knox must not have realized, until it was too late, that the wording of that order imperiled his own authority. The expediency of war and a stroke of the President's pen had eliminated four decades of political opposition to CNO control of the bureaus. "When I came in," King later explained, "I was able to say that as Chief of Naval Operations I would tell people what was to be done in a general way and direct them to build this or that so that the war would carry on."

When Roosevelt had signed the executive order he had unthinkingly incited King by a casual suggestion to "streamline" the Navy Department. King moved swiftly. Five days later he announced his intentions. "It is apparent that I have to undertake this work personally," he wrote to his key subordinates, "and I must have help and advice. As I see it, the new organization will cut across existing lines of law and regulations, necessarily, if it is to be the effective machine that we need."

King's call for "help and advice" was, as usual, perfunctory. He already had decided what he wanted: four "grand divisions," Material, Personnel, Readiness, and Operations, all under his personal control.

* See Appendix IV.

Primary authority would reside in the Operations Division: that is, COMINCH headquarters. The other three divisions would exist solely to support Operations. "The be-all and end-all of the projected military organization is the conduct of active operations by the active seagoing forces," King emphasized. "The key idea, therefore, is that the entire military set up is premised on operating requirements, initially and continuously." His memorandum ended with unjustified optimism: "It should not be too difficult to create and implement the four grand divisions."

By the end of May 1942 King had completed his plan to emasculate civilian authority. Roosevelt was appalled. It was a reorganization, not a streamlining, said the President, and he did not want the administrative structure of the Navy changed in the middle of the war. Looking at King's proposed organization chart, Roosevelt protested that ". . . it would take the Navy Department at least one year just to learn what is meant by it. . . ."

King ignored the President's objections by boldly invoking his Navy Department reorganization on 28 May, informing neither Roosevelt nor Knox. "The need for it was so obvious," King later said, "that I simply directed that it be put into effect. But I stumbled on one little pebble. I neglected to consult the President or the Secretary first."

The repercussions — many initiated by the bureau chiefs, fearing the loss of their autonomy — soon reached the White House. By now alarmed, Roosevelt summoned Knox and King on 9 June. King quibbled and stalled: he was only obeying the President's orders and did not understand the President's objections. After all, King argued in his best sea-lawyer style, Roosevelt had allowed Marshall drastically to reorganize the Department of the Army, and King assumed that the President had wanted King to follow suit. Realizing how he had given King license to kill, Roosevelt finally announced that *he* would reorganize the Navy Department. King's plan was left in abeyance. After the meeting Knox suggested that King cancel or suspend his directive until the President had developed his own plan. But King was still optimistic. Roosevelt, he said, would probably accept the gist of King's plan.

King was wrong. After three days of stewing, Roosevelt decided not to tinker with the Navy Department. On 12 June he ordered Knox to cancel everything that King had issued for the past thirty days dealing with reorganizations. "There may be more of them which neither you nor I have seen," said Roosevelt, adding that he wanted a copy of the cancellation order as reassurance. "The more I think of [King's] orders which you and I saw, the more outrageous I think it is that [King] went ahead to do, without your approval or mine, what I had already disapproved when I turned down the general plan of reorganization. I am very much inclined to send for the Officers down the line and give them a good dressing down. They are old enough to know better — and old enough to know that you are the Secretary of the Navy and that I am Commander-in-Chief of the Navy."

Even though Knox had brought King to Washington in December 1941, he now felt threatened by King's pursuit of power. In self-defense Knox tried to get King out of Washington on the pretext that he should take command of the Pacific Fleet. Shortly before the Battle of Midway, for example, Knox urged King "to go to sea and manage that battle."

King was astounded. "Isn't Nimitz doing all right?" he asked.

"Yes," said Knox, "but the top man should be there," and he continued to insist forevermore that King go to the Pacific. "That was the craziest idea," King later said. "To have sent me over there to take command in the field was absolutely wrong in every way." King later admitted that as COMINCH he might have been justified in going to sea, but as a member of the JCS he had to remain in Washington. "The President's job was in the White House," said King. "If he moved out at any time, then the Joint Chiefs of Staff would go with him. The headquarters had to be where the President himself was."

Knox's next scheme was to dilute King's authority by making Horne the CNO. The Secretary first broached the subject following the Quebec Conference of August 1943. Should not King concentrate solely on his responsibilities as COMINCH? asked Knox. "He surprised and amazed me," King later said. "I never knew exactly what troubled him."

(The thing troubling Knox was King's resumption of his reorganization efforts. The command structure of naval shipyards had to be changed, King maintained, to make them respond to the needs of the fleet. Repairs were taking too long and ships were being delayed. But Roosevelt by then was opposed to any scheme originated by King. Just before the conference he had written to Knox: "F.K. Tell Ernie *once more:* No reorganizing of the Navy Dept. set-up during the war. Let's win it first. F.D.R.") *

In point of fact, Horne was CNO in every way save title alone. He was, for example, the principal uniformed naval spokesman before

* King had told Nimitz several months before that to say "no change should be made because we are at war" was a poor argument, and he was "sick of hearing it."

Congress, and budgets and financial management were almost entirely under his purview. As a Christian Scientist he neither smoked nor drank, and at their home he and his wife entertained many young couples who regarded the Hornes with great affection. A staff officer regarded Horne as "the greatest listener I ever knew." Nevertheless, Horne could be ruthless. Early in the war he fired the Director of Naval Communications, a rear admiral, for refusing to adopt communication decryption procedures that Horne felt were essential.

King himself respected Horne's brains and managerial ability. The two had served together on the General Board, and Horne remarked to a friend that one of the things he could do for the Navy was to keep King under control. The two admirals had an informal agreement that King would manage the war and Horne would manage the logistical matters. "Horne was a yes man," King later said, "but a very able man all the same. . . . I have never liked him and never knew why."

King's dislike perhaps stemmed from Knox's unwelcome suggestion at Quebec that King relinquish his CNO title to Horne. When King returned to Washington he sent for Horne. "Where in hell did this idea come from?" King demanded. "How did you manage it?"

"I had nothing to do with it," Horne protested. "The Secretary asked me about it, and I said that the present setup was O.K."

"I don't believe it," said King. Too many things had happened to indicate that Horne wanted his job. King later commented, "Of course Horne would have liked to have been Chief of Naval Operations. Who wouldn't? But I am afraid he was not quite frank with me. . . . The trouble was that he wanted to run with the hares and the hounds too."

By early January 1944 the anti-King forces gathered momentum. Forrestal got Leahy's concurrence that the COMINCH-CNO positions should be separated, and that the CNO should be directly under the Secretary of the Navy. As Leahy was so close to the President, his opinion carried weight. At about the same time the President and Knox cornered Carl Vinson, who seemed swayed by Knox's arguments to shear King of his CNO authority.

Such intrigues got King's attention, and he suspected Forrestal as the principal instigator. "Forrestal believed, but never said to me, that I had too much power myself," King later said. "He hated like hell that I had both jobs. But I was too strong for him to make any change. I asked Edwards what he knew about it, and he said not to worry because Forrestal always wanted to manage this and change that."

As the power struggle intensified, King decided to counterattack. He reckoned that the President would be reluctant to fire him as CNO because Roosevelt would have to change his 13 March 1942 executive order. "If he did that," King later said, "it would seem to the country that he had made a mistake. That's politics for you." King also felt that Roosevelt distrusted Forrestal's motives. "I think FDR knew what Forrestal really was and thought it was better for me to carry on with both jobs, because Forrestal would have tried to manage the whole thing. FDR always had two strings in his bow."

King's most telling blow, however, was in winning over Vinson. On 11 February 1944 Vinson sent letters to both the President and to Knox retracting his earlier support of Knox's proposal and affirming — emphatically — that he wanted King to retain both positions. Knox knew that King was behind it. "When I was away sick," he wrote to the President, "the attached letter came to my office from Carl Vinson. It bears internal evidence of having been prepared, I think, in the Navy Department. . . . You will not fail to observe in the language employed in the letter . . . that there is the same old effort to consolidate all authority in one person, and that not the Secretary of the Navy."

His position secure, King resumed his campaign through the first months of 1944 to reorganize the Navy Department. The battle went into the summer as the bureau chiefs and the civilian executives fought back. When the smoke cleared in late September, Horne was the most visible casualty. King had persuaded Roosevelt to elevate Edwards to a newly created position of "Deputy COMINCH–Deputy CNO," inserting Edwards in the chain of command between King and Horne. Cooke meanwhile relieved Edwards as chief of staff to COMINCH.

The reassignments evoked charges from the press and radio that Horne had been demoted. To still such criticism, King released a press statement on 4 October 1944 justifying the moves as consistent with the "well-known principle of division of labor." Instead of two men as his top assistants, said King, he now had three. "It should therefore be clearly understood," said King's press release, "that the duties now assigned to Vice Admiral Edwards do *not* constitute a demotion of Vice Admiral Horne or anyone else."

After the war King was much more candid on what he had done to Horne. "I eased him out," said King, "finally."

20

Roosevelt, Congress, and the Press

THE PRESIDENT'S MEDDLING in naval affairs had not abated once the United States had entered the Second World War. Roosevelt did abstain from tinkering with promotions and assignments as a concession to Frank Knox, but otherwise the Navy remained the President's favorite pastime.

King knew it. In January 1942 he carefully selected a new presidential naval aide, Captain John L. McCrea, who was about to command a cruiser after a year as special aide to Stark. McCrea was unhappy. Not only would he lose his cruiser, but aide duty cost money — McCrea's money. King brushed the complaints aside. "This country is at war," said King, "and you can afford anything your assignment may require."

After Roosevelt had approved McCrea's nomination, King summoned McCrea to his office. "I need hardly tell you, Captain," said King, "that you have achieved a minor degree of notoriety by being assigned to duty as the Naval Aide to the President of the United States. Experience has led me to the conviction that if anyone succeeds by hard work or rare good fortune, or both, to raise his head this far above the herd [King held his forefinger a half inch above his thumb], there are untold numbers of sons-of-bitches standing by ready and willing to knock him down. Another thing you will no doubt be amazed at are the number of people your senior, who heretofore have never given you a tumble, who will now address you as 'John, old boy.' Don't be flattered by it. It is just part of the pattern I have outlined."

King then explained that McCrea would be King's messenger with Roosevelt. McCrea would attend Knox's morning conferences and would have access to all dispatches. "I wish you well," King concluded. "You can see me at any time."

As King knew he would, Roosevelt told McCrea to tell him everything that was happening in the Navy Department. Sunday mornings in the President's bedroom became a quiet time to brief the President and for the President to reminisce "when I was in the Navy." As McCrea was serving two masters, he knew the pitfalls. Early on he told King, Knox, and Stark: "If there are things going on you don't want the President to know about, just don't tell me." There were three understanding smiles in response.

King realized, of course, that McCrea's intimacy with the President could work both ways. It could hurt King, for McCrea undoubtedly had given the President a copy of King's order to reorganize the Navy Department in the spring of 1942, which alerted Roosevelt to kill it.* On the other hand, McCrea could help King. A memorandum on 10 February 1942 from McCrea to King is an example.

> Last night I showed the attached despatch to the President. When he came to the last sentence he remarked substantially as follows —
>
> Certainly I'll be glad to do it. See that this despatch is brought to my attention in a few days when I start work on the speech.
>
> The President did not ask for it, but I respectfully suggest that a brief memorandum giving the facts which in your judgment *can* be disclosed would be of assistance to the President in drafting his speech.†

Roosevelt ordered McCrea to fashion a war room in the White House, an idea he got from Churchill during the ARCADIA Conference in December 1941. Directly across from the war room was the "doctor's office," where Roosevelt would go in the late afternoon for relief from his sinus trouble, which he blamed on the White House air conditioning. It was a time for Roosevelt to relax, to feed Fala, and to shed his fatigue. The President would recline in a dentist's chair, Ross McIntire would pack his sinuses, and Navy doctor George A. Fox would massage his legs. Afterward Roosevelt would enter the war room for McCrea to brief him on developments. It was Roosevelt's way of knowing what King and his Navy were doing.

Roosevelt fancied himself as a geography expert because of his stamp

* See Chapter 19.

† The dispatch is not recorded; Roosevelt's speech was a radio address on the war delivered on Monday evening, 23 February 1942.

collecting, and he owned several globes and a portfolio of National Geographic maps. Sometimes he would show off. As Stimson so often disparaged the war in the Pacific, Roosevelt decided that his Secretary of War "needed a lesson in geography." Stimson sat glumly in the war room one Sunday evening as Roosevelt lectured. The Pacific Ocean, said the President, was a hell of a lot bigger than the Atlantic, and he hoped that Stimson could see the difference.

In the early years of the war Roosevelt frequently summoned King to the White House, either alone or with others. He did not need an invitation; King could see the President whenever he pleased, a privilege he used but did not abuse. King always assumed that he had earned Roosevelt's confidence by being blunt and forthright. "Leahy had the basic idea that anything the President wanted must be done at once," King later said. "I had other ideas. I would at least argue with him, which I think Roosevelt rather liked."

King's biggest gripe was the President's double-talk. "Roosevelt was a little tricky," King later said, "and in some ways the truth was not always in him." King also worried about Churchill's powers of persuasion with Roosevelt. King respected and admired Churchill, but he also prided himself in bucking the Prime Minister if they disagreed. In contrast, King thought that Churchill had gotten his way with Roosevelt far too often. (And in King's opinion, Marshall was even more a pushover to Churchill's persuasiveness.)

Meetings between Roosevelt and the JCS were impromptu and usually convened to deal with a specific problem. The President would decide who would attend, presumably those whom he wanted for advice. The record shows that King was in the White House some thirty-two times during 1942, although there may have been other meetings that were not on the President's appointment calendar. The scheduled appointments then diminished for the remainder of the war: eight in 1943, nine in 1944, and one in 1945. In contrast, Churchill met with the British Chiefs of Staff almost daily.

Roosevelt's dabbling with the Navy intruded into wartime operations, much to King's annoyance. Bypassing King entirely, Roosevelt sent dispatches to Admiral Hart in the Southwest Pacific in early 1942, telling him how to set up surveillance patrols against the onrushing Japanese. This may explain why King personally took operational control of naval forces in the South Pacific in the early months of the war.* It is not likely that Nimitz could have withstood Roosevelt's interference.

The President tried to avoid face-to-face showdowns with King. If

* See Chapter 14.

he had something to say that would rile King, he would use Leahy, Knox, or his naval aides as reluctant surrogates. After the Savo Island debacle, Roosevelt suggested to Knox that carrier task groups employ fewer cruisers and more destroyers. (FDR presumably felt that cruisers could be more profitably used in defending beachheads.) As Knox was the least qualified official in the Navy Department to discuss tactics, King presumably drafted the reply for Knox's signature: the Navy knew best (it said) and would keep the status quo. Roosevelt was smart enough not to overrule King's professional judgment, but he still wanted the last word. Thus Leahy found himself dragged into the discussion when he received word from Roosevelt that the Navy Department memorandum should "receive further study." It did not, of course.

Leahy had another unpleasant chore when he entered King's office in mid-1944. King was surprised because Leahy rarely came to see him. Leahy explained that Roosevelt, obviously jealous of his own "commander in chief" title, wanted King, Nimitz, and Ingersoll to change their titles as fleet "commanders in chief."

"Is that an order?" asked King.

"No," said Leahy, "but he'd like to have it done."

"When I get the orders," said King, "I will do exactly that. Otherwise not." The subject was dropped.

Roosevelt's interference in naval matters could become capricious. An exchange of correspondence between Knox and Roosevelt in January 1943 is illustrative. "My dear Mr. President," Knox began. "Recently when I had my last talk with you, you gave me the names of a group of young officers who are serving in the Navy, with the request that I discover just what their duties were and why they were retained in Washington. I have just received the enclosed comments on all of them and I pass this report along for your information.

"On the whole, I do not think that much criticism can be appropriately directed at any of these men. They all seem to be doing a pretty good job and several of them have already been ordered to sea."

The list included Clarence Douglas Dillon, Ernest Dupont, Jr., Leonard K. Firestone, Henry S. Morgan, and Robert W. Sarnoff. "I have yours of January fourth in regard to a group of young officers in the Navy Department," Roosevelt replied. "Why not order them all to sea?"

Roosevelt insisted on having his way in naming ships, a prerogative ever since his Navy Department days. The carrier *Shangri-La*, for example, was a carryover from Roosevelt's mythical base for Doolittle's Tokyo bombers. On the other hand, Roosevelt time and again refused to allow any ship to be named after the late Admiral Robert E. Coontz, a former CNO whom Roosevelt had disliked.*

All in all, Roosevelt lost more than he won. King continued to perpetuate what Roosevelt had known for years: the Navy could and would resist domination. "The admirals are really something to cope with—and I should know," he once told a colleague. "To change anything in the Na-a-vy is like punching a feather bed. You punch it with your right and you punch it with your left until you are finally exhausted, and then you find the damn bed just as it was before you started punching."

There was at least one naval organization that the President could boss without irking King. In late August 1942 McCrea received the following memorandum.

> Will you tell the Navy Band
> that I don't like the way they
> play the Star Spangled Banner—
> it should not have a lot of
> frills in it?
>
> F.D.R.

As a condition to King accepting the job as COMINCH, Roosevelt had promised that the Admiral would not have to appear before Congress. There were several reasons. First, King did not have the time. Second, he disliked politicians, although he did have friends in Congress. Third, as Chief of the Bureau of Aeronautics he had been uncomfortable before congressional committees. Although he always was well informed, it was a strain to speak extemporaneously in public.

George Russell served as King's political advisor, because of his experience as a legislative liaison officer with Congress. "I have come to the conclusion that good witnesses on the Hill are probably born," Russell told the author. "Admiral King was not born to be a good one, and I used what influence I had to keep him from appearing side by side with General Marshall, who was a superior witness. The Admiral got along just fine with Mr. Vinson in the privacy of the chairman's office, but he did not react well to the questions asked on committee hearings."

King was entirely aware of his speaking problem. "Marshall would sound off without any notes," King once explained, "and he spoke very well indeed. I had trouble in that way, for I at least had to have notes and usually had to have my remarks written out. My education was defective . . . it is a great help if you have been trained as a speaker."

Knox, Forrestal, Horne, the bureau chiefs, and Rear Admiral Ezra G.

* The USS *Coontz,* a guided-missile destroyer, was commissioned in 1960.

Allen, the Navy's Budget Officer, were the Navy's principal spokesmen. The Navy's most influential congressional allies were Carl Vinson and his colleagues of the House Naval Affairs Committee. As they were the Navy's most zealous advocates in Congress, King was properly deferential to Vinson both privately and publicly. In a 1944 ceremony recognizing Vinson's thirtieth year in the House, King extolled his benefactor. "Chairman Vinson has the confidence and esteem of the entire naval service," said King. "He seems imbued with a sixth sense which tells him when to support the legislation we present, and when to give us a sound spanking and send us back to the Navy Department. I think that sixth sense is common sense."

Other committee chairmen assumed King was too busy to come to the Hill, and they were too intimidated to ask for more than a few moments of his time. King limited himself to token appearances to coincide with the introduction of legislation. His routine was first to summarize the progress of the war, then to praise the Congress for its most recent support and cooperation, and finally to ask that Congress continue to finance the Navy's war effort.

King could barely conceal both his scorn for Congress as an institution and his resentment that congressional neglect had emasculated the Navy before the war. Handicapped at first with a shattered, outnumbered Navy, King was short-tempered with the legislators whom he blamed for his predicament. In February 1942 he appeared before the House Appropriations Committee, whose members seemed awed by his presence and apprehensive of the war suddenly thrust upon them. Chief among their concerns was a way to mobilize America's war production while avoiding the industrial chaos of the First World War.

King was in no mood to reassure them. "We need everything we can get," he said, adding emphatically that the military should determine production priorities of war materiel, a theme he was to repeat again and again. The committee asked King for advice on organizing and controlling America's war industry. "Now you are out of my sphere," said King, "and in one in which I do not consider myself competent to talk." Given King's later efforts to wrest procurement control from civilian managers, it was a revealing and contradictory admission.

It took money to fight the war, but King disdained any discussion of how much he needed. In March 1943 Knox was about to submit the Navy's fiscal 1944 budget, which would be the largest in history. Knox sent the budget request to King for his comments; King tossed it to George Russell for review. Russell then drafted a memorandum consisting of three short paragraphs dealing with minor editorial changes.

King signed it and returned it to Knox. And that was the extent of King's concern for how much money the Navy Department wanted or how it would be used.

How things had changed! In the lean prewar years King's predecessors had labored, pleaded, and cajoled for congressional approval of the Navy's modest budget requests. With a war on, King simply expected a submissive Congress to appropriate unlimited funds, without question. It took a plea from the Chairman of the House Naval Appropriations Subcommittee to induce King even to speak in support of the 1944 budget request. I quote Congressman Harry R. Sheppard's personal letter to King in its entirety, because it manifests so perfectly the association between King and the Congress.

"Shortly after the 1st of April," wrote Sheppard, "we shall begin the hearings on the Department's 1944 budget, which, I understand, will far exceed any that has gone before.

"I do not wish to trespass a moment upon your time, but I do believe it would have a most salutary effect if you could arrange to appear for about five minutes and make a statement to the effect, if you feel that you can do so, that you wish to indicate your satisfaction with the support the Navy has had from the Congress, that such support has had much to do with the successes that have attended the service since the declaration of war, and that you feel, with the continually expanding organization the country has every reason to expect results that will measure up, at least, to the best traditions of our naval arm. A statement somewhat along these lines, coming from you, would be most inspiring and helpful.

"Of course," Sheppard concluded, "by suggesting the foregoing, I do not mean to preclude you from making any suggestions or submitting any recommendations which you feel would be in the interest of aiding you in the discharge of the tremendous responsibility which you are carrying. We should welcome any word from you about ways in which we may be of help."

King simply passed the letter to Russell with the notation:

Expedite {
Take to Budg. Off
for comment
Draft reply
do "remarks"
}
K

Several weeks later King condescendingly went before Sheppard's committee and read a brief statement. Its gist was that King needed the money to fight the war, and he expected Congress to give it to him. His remarks included a warning not to quibble with the Navy's budget request. "War inevitably results in waste," said King, "waste of men and materials and money — that is one reason for our hatred of war. It is the waste of men that hurts most, but we dislike the waste of material and of money, too. We cannot afford to pussyfoot when it comes to appropriating money to carry on. Every dollar that appears in the budget estimates is needed, to the best of our knowledge and belief, to prosecute the war successfully. We invite Congressional scrutiny of the figures submitted, but it is our belief that if the matter of appropriations is approached from the peacetime point of view, instead of from the war or realistic point of view, we shall be unable to prosecute the war effectively. In other words, the Congress automatically shares the responsibility for the conduct of the war in respect to the funds appropriated."

Then, to mollify any congressmen offended by King's threat, King offered a sop. "To date," King concluded, "the Congress had understood our requirements, or, if it did not fully understand, has accepted our statements with respect to them, and has appropriated the necessary funds. Without these funds and without the cooperation of the Congress, the naval establishment could not have functioned as effectively as it has. It is gratifying to the Navy to know that you have confidence in us, and to be met everywhere by an attitude indicating the desire to be helpful.

"I take this opportunity to assure the House of Representatives through your Committee, that we appreciate their support and that the confidence is mutual."

On Wednesday, 19 May 1943, a month after King's abbreviated appearance, Sheppard introduced the $28.5 billion naval appropriation bill. It was calculated timing. The House had been packed at noon to hear Winston Churchill, but that afternoon the floor was nearly empty. Only twenty Republicans and seven Democrats were on hand to discuss the bill. "Is it not necessary," asked Representative Claire E. Hoffman, "to have at least one member on the floor for each billion dollars contained in an appropriation bill?" Hoffman's sarcasm had no effect, of course. The bill passed.

So money was never a problem. Congress readily deferred to professional judgment and willingly appropriated what the Navy said it needed to fight the war. The harmony between the Navy and Congress was, in large measure, based upon political logic: the Navy tacitly forced Congress to provide what was asked on the unassailable argument that the war would thereby be shortened and lives saved. But it was one thing to appropriate money, and quite a different matter to use it wisely and efficiently, as the voters demanded. Charges of waste and corruption were frequent, and Congress conducted extensive investigations into how well the billions were being spent (the Truman Committee being the most visible). King remained aloof and let Knox, Forrestal, and the logistical experts of the Navy Department answer to Congress.

Now and then a member of Congress would try to draw King into a controversy. In April 1943 Senator Joseph C. O'Mahoney sent King a letter expressing the Senator's views on grand strategy. King gave the puzzling letter to Russell for comment.

"He is probably above average in intelligence and in influence in the Senate," wrote Russell in response. "He knows perfectly well that he has no business to ask you to commit yourself on the subjects raised by him in his letter, and for that reason (I assume) refrains from asking you to do so. He tells you what he thinks and lets it go at that, hoping, probably, that you will say something to give him ammunition.

"In its rabble-rousing style, his letter is full of exaggerations and meaningless unsupported conclusions, but he is by no means unique in feeling that the war with Germany is Britain's war and the war with Japan is our war, and that we ought to fight our own war first. Mr. Vinson, you will recall, reached a similar but slightly different conclusion by dissimilar reasoning.

"I see no reason to tell him anything," Russell concluded.

King followed Russell's advice.

The only serious squabble between King and Congress occurred in the summer of 1944. King had issued his annual "Report of Progress" in the spring, a public pronouncement of the Navy's wartime accomplishments. Buried within its pages was the statement, "After we were no longer bound by the (1922) treaty, the proposal was made to proceed with the fortification of Guam, but after considerable debate in Congress, it was rejected." As 1944 was an election year, Congress overreacted to any suggestion that its prewar acts had unduly harmed America's readiness for war. Politicians looking for issues stirred up such a rumpus that senators up for reelection publicly demanded that King explain "his castigation of Congress for failure to fortify Guam." Other senators labeled King's statement as an "unjustified charge" and a "false accusation."

The most influential legislator agitating for an apology was Senator David I. Walsh, chairman of the Senate Naval Affairs Committee. Forrestal answered him with a restrained yet factual statement by King, substantiating that the senators were shouting about a technicality and that King had been right. The tempest soon subsided.

Freedom of the press was a sore issue during the Second World War, for it raised an irresolvable conflict between military secrecy and the public's right to know. It was especially hard with King, for he was the despair of the press. A more uncooperative celebrity could not be imagined. His public-be-damned attitude was demonstrated time and again throughout the war, as, for example, in his letter to Pathé News during the Battle of Midway.

"I am fully aware," wrote King, "of the desires of the newsreel companies and other purveyors of information to acquaint the public in detail with news of action with the enemy at the earliest practicable date.

"I am also fully aware that all too often, even inadvertently, the purveyors of information to the public are not prone to exercise any discrimination in regard to giving 'aid and comfort' to the enemy. In this respect, I feel very strongly that military considerations outweigh the satisfying of a very natural and proper curiosity.

"I assume," King continued, "that you and your colleagues know that the piecing of information together — after the manner of a jig saw puzzle — is common military practice, which we ourselves carry out to the best of our ability. It is not necessary to complete the 'jig saw puzzle' in order to gain vital information but only to fit together a key part or parts thereof, in order to become possessed of important military information.

"In closing, I wish to add to what I have previously said that I am in full sympathy with education and information of the public on military matters and events — always provided that it is done without giving 'aid and comfort' to the enemy."

At issue was the need of a wartime government for popular support. In a democracy, that support is largely influenced by what the public reads and hears about events on the battlefield. For a number of reasons Marshall consistently tried to rally the American people. But King was indifferent, so totally absorbed was he in the military aspects of fighting a war. Someone else — preferably the politicians — would have to take charge of public morale. Still, he grudgingly acknowledged that from time to time the public had to be told something, and often he personally drafted or heavily edited the Navy's press releases.

The Roosevelt Administration recognized the need to keep the public informed and the value of propaganda. In June 1942 Roosevelt established the Office of War Information (OWI) and appointed Elmer Davis as its director. Davis, a veteran newspaperman and radio newscaster, was known for his integrity and his belief in the freedom of the press. Davis's mandate was to coordinate the dissemination of war information by all federal agencies and to develop propaganda programs at home and abroad. It was a thankless task. Roosevelt ignored him, the armed services thought he gave away classified information, and powerful special-interest groups considered him a press agent for the Administration.

For all that, Davis was indomitable. After receiving his appointment, Davis called on King and said that he wanted to be told everything about naval operations. King refused. Davis persisted, insisting that the President had told him that he should have access to all information. King responded that Roosevelt would have to put it in writing; otherwise he would tell Davis nothing. From then on there was only animosity between them. Those within OWI felt that if King had his way he would issue but one statement — an announcement that the war was over.

Davis once protested to King about a March 1943 story on the JCS that OWI had released and had then been forced to retract after King had objected. "I should like to point out, however, that this is being done solely as a matter of courtesy and comity," wrote Davis. "This Office recognizes the right of the Navy High Command and the Army High Command to revise our proposed publications in the interest of security as well as of factual accuracy, and I think you will acknowledge that the Navy's wishes on these points have been scrupulously respected. We do not, however, recognize any right on your part to make revisions merely affecting the language or presentation of a news story or its content, except insofar as security and factual accuracy are concerned. Writing a news story is a matter which requires some experience and technical skill. If those who lack this experience and skill undertake it, the result is apt to be very much as if I should make suggestions on naval strategy.

"The version which you approved has been stripped of virtually all material which could make it of interest to the public. With certain excisions it might be suitable for publication in a government manual, but it is the opinion of our editorial staff that very few newspapers would be interested in it. Besides, it contains certain eulogistic phrases, such as 'the best military brains in the country,' which, while undoubtedly true, represent editorial opinion such as is not ordinarily introduced into a news story and such as this Office could not issue without indicat-

Despite King's indifference to public morale, in this instance he contributed to wartime propaganda. (Courtesy Naval Historical Center)

ing the source. Accordingly, we feel it best to drop the whole matter of any endeavor to present the work of the Joint Chiefs of Staff to the public — an endeavor which, you will recall, was undertaken upon your suggestion."

King read the letter, wrote "Tut-tut!" in the margin, and chucked it into his outgoing basket.

In early September 1943, Davis got Roosevelt to write a letter to the Secretaries of War, State, and the Navy, telling them to cooperate with OWI. Roosevelt was preaching to the choir. Knox wanted to publicize the Navy's achievements, and when he first had become Secretary of the Navy he had been frustrated by the Navy's reticence. Finally Knox asked who was number one on the Navy's lineal list. The answer was Arthur J. Hepburn, the Navy's most senior flag officer by date of rank but at that time a permanent rear admiral awaiting retirement while serving on the General Board. Knox directed that Hepburn be made director of public relations. "Knox assured me," a friend later said, "that if Hepburn issued an order it would be obeyed because it came from 'number one.' "

But Roosevelt's letter to Knox, inspired by Davis, made no impression on King. He had decided shortly after the war began that Knox talked too much. Their mutual friend Rawleigh Warner came to see King in early 1942 and complained that King would not tell Knox anything.

"Why should I?" said King. "The first thing he does is to tell the reporters everything he knows." The Washington journalists were well aware of this. Lyle Wilson, for example, remembered that King regarded Knox "with an amused, respectful distaste that was something to see. I know that King sometimes short-circuited information from Knox on the theory that he couldn't keep a secret."

King also deliberately withheld operational information from the civilian assistant secretaries by simply ignoring them. Assistant Secretary for Air Artemus L. Gates asked questions that King disparaged as so naïve that they were not worth answering. Under Secretary Ralph A. Bard tried for months to invite King to lunch, invitations that King politely but consistently refused, until Bard finally gave up.

"I didn't have time to educate those people," King later said.

Midway through the war King discovered that Marshall intended to issue a report extolling the Army's recent achievements. Encouraged by David Lawrence, publisher of the *U.S. News and World Report,* King decided he needed something of his own to insure that the Navy got its share of credit. King summoned his newly arrived flag secretary, Howard E. Orem, into his office. "Write a report on the progress of the war," ordered King.

Orem staggered from King's office. "I was the world's worst writer," said Orem afterward, and he tried to foist the job on someone else. There were no volunteers. Orem finally appealed to Edwards, who gave the job to Russell. Until then Russell had assumed he was returning to sea, but instead he was given a huge stack of battle narratives. Six months later he had finished writing King's first report of the war. King was so proud of it that *U.S. News and World Report* published it in March 1944. Lawrence gave tens of thousands of free copies to King, and they were widely distributed throughout the Navy.

But King's report was an exception to his philosophy of "deeds, not words." Staff officer William Smedberg saw this first hand. "Admiral King's views were that the Navy's performance would speak for itself," said Smedberg years later, "and that we did not have to sing our praises or blow our own horn. On another occasion, the services were discussing, among themselves, about going to Congress for a much needed pay raise. King vetoed the idea, saying that when we have won the war a grateful nation will give us the increase we had earned. I can almost hear him saying those words. How little he knew about a nation's gratitude to its military people, once the threat to their lives and enterprises had been removed. I guess he never read Kipling's 'Tommy Atkins.' "

Meanwhile, Forrestal was becoming progressively more worried by talk of service unification in Congress. Despite King's report, Forrestal believed that the Navy was being undersold. In contrast, the Army and its Air Force were exploiting public relations to promote a unification plan inimical to the Navy. By then Secretary of the Navy in September 1944, Forrestal wrote to a friend, "I have been telling King, Nimitz and Company it is my judgment that as of today the Navy has lost its case and that, either in Congress or in a public poll, the Army's point of view would prevail." Forrestal decided that the Navy had to get into the publicity business, and that meant dealing with King first.

As King's combat intelligence officer, Smedberg had briefed Forrestal on several occasions. The Secretary had been so impressed with his poise that he decided that Smedberg was the man to meet the press. He went to King's office, the two men spoke, and then King sent for Smedberg.

Smedberg entered King's office. The Admiral's face was flushed, while Forrestal was unperturbed.

"Smedberg," said King, "Mr. Forrestal wants you to brief the press and radio and news media at least once a week on our operations."

Smedberg was aghast. He was the one man at COMINCH headquarters, he protested, who should *not* have the job. As he was privy to the most sensitive intelligence about the war, he might inadvertently reveal secret information.

King turned to Forrestal. "You see," said King, "that's exactly why I said he could not do it."

"Admiral King," said Forrestal, "I have told you that I want Captain Smedberg to brief the press. The Japs haven't been able to sink our fleet, but if you had your way, you would sink the United States Navy. You refuse to permit publicity about our Navy. Pretty soon the whole country is going to think this war is being won by the Army and Air Force and that the Navy has nothing to do because you won't permit anything to be written about the Navy. I want Captain Smedberg once a week at least and before every impending operation to give the press the background of the operation coming up."

King glared at Forrestal. "Aye, aye, sir," King finally said. "He will do it."

After Forrestal had left, King again called in Smedberg. "You know and I know," said King, "that you're the last person in the world who should do this. I have my orders. You're to do it, but God help you if you ever tell them a damned thing about what we're going to do." Despite the perils, Smedberg performed admirably as a "high naval spokesman." "Not once was my name mentioned or a confidence violated by that splendid group of patriotic American newspeople," Smedberg later said.

Forrestal's desire for publicity rippled throughout the fleet, requiring commanding officers to provide grist for the mill. In November 1944 Nimitz sent a copy of the following letter to King, which he had received from the commanding officer of the USS *Capricornus*, a prosaic amphibious cargo ship.

"A canvass of Officer personnel at present attached to this vessel," wrote the captain, "shows none qualified to prepare a readable narrative of the ship's operations. The fact that no report or memorandum ever reaches the Commanding Officer that is not a mass of grammatical and orthographic errors is a sad commentary on modern schools and colleges.

"The part so far played by Capricornus in the Pacific has been inconspicuous. The only newsworthy item occurring during the recent Leyte Operation happened during a nuisance raid by the enemy, when one of the ship's Boat Group was sitting on the gunwale of his LCM and received a charge of friendly shrapnel in an unmentionable portion of his anatomy which protruded over the side.

"The Commanding Officer, whose education is a product of the horse and buggy or early General Grant era, will endeavor to fulfill the requirements of reference (a) whenever the opportunity presents itself."

Or, as King once wrote in August 1942, "Naval Officers prefer to make history rather than to write it — because of which preference they probably do a better job of the former."

Still, King was not totally insensitive to public relations. Thousands of letters from private citizens came to his office, and he and his staff tried to answer as many as possible. They addressed every imaginable subject, including requests for written articles, statements, endorsements, and forewords. King was so conscientious that he expected his flag secretary to evaluate each letter and to draft an "appropriate" reply. If the letter was one of hundreds containing bizarre or impractical schemes for winning the war, a form letter would suffice, assuring the writer that "the ideas which you set forth are being given appropriate consideration by the proper authorities." If King was requested to make a statement for charitable or patriotic motives — war bonds or the Red Cross, for example — he usually complied. The Navy Relief Society was King's favorite charity, as it served the best interests of the sailor who needed help. King even aided a "Second Front" lobbying organization, the Committee of Russian War Relief, by sending a message that was read at a Madison Square Garden rally.

Other requests required a more ingenious response. The president of the Planned Parenthood Federation of America, apparently unaware that King had seven children, solicited King's views on the development of a postwar population policy. King hustled the letter to Russell with the notation, "?K." Russell wrote a diplomatic response: "It would not be correct to state that the Admiral is not interested in postwar problems. He is, however, too busily engaged in current war problems to undertake a study [of population control] and has asked me to advise you to that effect."

Some of King's letters were written — and not too well — outside his staff. On the twenty-fifth anniversary of the Soviet Union, the Navy's public relations office drafted a florid letter of congratulations to the Chief of Staff of the Soviet Navy, which was grandiloquent to the point of absurdity. "Tone this down," wrote King on the margin. "I don't talk like this!!" A revised letter, reduced by half and restrained in tone, was substituted.

King relied upon the same public relations staff for the innocuous canned speeches he used for his infrequent public appearances. He occasionally addressed FBI graduating classes and so admired J. Edgar

Making himself seen. King inspects the cruiser USS *Boise.* (National Archives 80-G-40066)

Hoover's leather-bound speech notebook that Hoover sent him one as a gift. As King was a 32nd Degree Mason he was receptive to invitations to large Masonic gatherings, and as the Navy's top leader he felt obliged to make himself seen at Navy bases, ship launchings, and commissionings.

The thousands of requests for his autographed photo were always honored. A Navy photographer, Captain Robert S. Quackenbush, remembered the day he took one of King's official pictures. Knowing King's impatience, he had his equipment ready well in advance.

"What do I do?" asked King when he arrived.

"Place your feet on those chalk marks on the floor, face the camera, and look pleasant," replied Quackenbush. King followed orders, and in a few minutes the operation was completed. "I compliment you and your crew," said King as he left. "That is the way I like to do business."

Another photographer was horrified when the lights failed and the studio went black as King was posing. When lighting was restored, King had neither moved nor spoken. In time the picture was taken, and King left without comment.

Whether King liked it or not, he was a celebrity. To an officer at the Naval Aircraft Factory who wanted to manufacture and sell miniature busts of King, King wrote, "I do not wish any such action taken — if you please — as I am not in favor of undue publicity of any kind. Again, changes in 'high command' can and often do take place."

Lorain's pride — in their hometown boy made good — both pleased and embarrassed King. King's roots had always remained in his childhood home, and he never stopped writing letters to old friends there. He mourned their deaths and sent flowers for their funerals. For those still living King retained happy memories. "I hope you will remember me to Mrs. Eddy when next you see her," wrote King to a Lorain friend, Edward A. Braun, in February 1942. "I wish particularly that you would give Mrs. Whitehouse my love when you next see her — she has always been a devoted friend and well-wisher."

Very early in the war the people of Lorain wanted to honor their hero. Among the suggestions was a proposal to hang his portrait in the high school. "I hardly know what to say about your project for the high school," King wrote to Braun, "but I do recognize that the turn of fortune's wheel has brought me to a degree of prominence which involves, perhaps, recognition of it in some permanent form in my home town. I leave it to your good judgment as to what is to be done about it — perhaps it will be well to await further developments, if any."

By midsummer 1942 the mayor proclaimed that "Ernest J. King Day" would be celebrated in Lorain, and he asked King to be there. "I am quite overwhelmed at the honor that my native city has in mind for me," wrote King in reply, "and am of the opinion that it would be much better for me to 'wait and see' what the future has in store. However, if it is the case that the matter is already underway, I feel that I should accept the proposal in the spirit in which it is made, which I appreciate more than I know how to say. I will do my best to come 'home' on August 30, 1942."

King went home. It was a patriotic, emotional, fraternal celebration, with speeches and a parade attended by the governor of Ohio. Some weeks later, when the battle for Guadalcanal was going badly, King heard rumors that Lorain wanted to name a park after him. "I am fully conscious of the good motives behind this project," he wrote the mayor, "and greatly appreciate the implied honor — but I am reluctant to have such an honor premised on what I have been able to do to date. At some later time if and when, by the grace of God, I shall have done much that is worth-while in the service of our country, I will be happy if my fellow-citizens of Lorain shall wish to do something of this kind — but not now, please."

In October 1961 Lorain dedicated a high school to Ernest J. King. In recent years travelers on the city's outskirts might read a roadside sign that King was born there. Otherwise there are no visible memorials.

Both during and after the war King received many offers for his memoirs, all of which he declined.* Neither would King grant interviews for magazine articles. Forrest Davis, a writer for the *Saturday Evening Post* and a friend of Howard Orem, reminded Orem how Marshall and other military leaders had been publicized in the *Post.* It was only fair, argued Davis, that King should receive equal exposure. Despite his misgivings, Orem said he would try to convince King, and after weeks of Orem's wheedling the Admiral gave in. Davis had a way with King, for after several interviews King invited Davis to dinner on the *Dauntless*, one of the few civilians ever allowed within the inner sanctum.

In early October 1944, Davis submitted the manuscript (entitled "King's Way to Tokyo") to Orem for King's approval. As Davis had a deadline, Orem sent the manuscript to King without first reviewing it. It came back with King's notation, "I don't like this! K."

King characteristically refused to say what he disliked. Orem and Davis tried to read King's mind and worked on the article until King finally seemed satisfied. The publishers then asked for permission to take King's picture for illustrations. Wrote King in response: "There are *enough* photos available now! K." Despite King's obstinacy, a reasonably good article finally appeared in the *Saturday Evening Post* on 9 December 1944.

Until then King had been so inaccessible that journalists had resorted to conjecture and hearsay when describing or quoting him. This invariably infuriated King, especially if the material seemed to be propaganda for a separate air force. In February 1943, William B. Huie sent King his book entitled *The Fight for Air Power* and asked for King's reaction. "It is obvious," King responded, "that you are ill-informed—or have been ill-advised (by your sponsors?)—as to my aviation experience. Further, you have attributed to me remarks which I can assure you I have never made, no matter from what source you may have taken them. These are matters which it was within your discretion to verify."

Drew Pearson surpassed all others in his ability to anger King. After Pearson had written one such article impugning the Admiral's name, King prepared a letter back to Pearson to the effect that he couldn't compete with a skunk, then asked Russell to read it.

"You can't mail the letter," said Russell.

"Why not?" asked King.

"Because I won't let you," said Russell.

* Until, of course, he decided to team up with Walter Muir Whitehill.

King tore up the letter, stormed into his outer office, and announced to everyone that his staff would not let him do what he wanted.

It is understandable, then, why King and the press regarded each other with suspicion and hostility, especially in the early years of the war. The press charged the Navy with suppressing bad news about its losses and giving the public a false impression; King charged the press with trying to discredit the Navy and with jeopardizing security. A vicious circle developed. King and his staff withheld information, forcing journalists to publish stories based on rumor and speculation. The stories infuriated King and his staff, reinforcing their determination not to speak to the press. Controversy over the battles at Guadalcanal created bitterness and antagonism that seemed to destroy the last hopes of any understanding or cooperation.

King's attorney, Cornelius H. ("Nelie") Bull, agonized about the newspaper attacks against King and King's deepening mistrust — almost hatred — of the press. The two had been friends and confidants for years, the lawyer familiarly addressing King as "skipper." As a former newspaperman, Bull had many friends in the press. One of his closest was Glen C. H. Perry, the assistant chief of the Washington bureau of the New York *Sun*, and when they took lunch at the Press Club round table they talked about King.

Bull was convinced that King had enemies in the armed services who were discrediting King to the press. Over drinks one October afternoon, Bull shared his forebodings with Perry. Things were so bad in the South Pacific that he feared King might get fired. That would be a tragedy, said Bull. The country needed King to win the war. Perry suggested that if King met privately with selected members of the press, he might win some much-needed support. Bull agreed to ask and reported back that King had accepted the idea, but with grave reservations. Everything that King said would have to be off the record. If anything leaked, the deal was off. Given his opinion of the press, King did not think there would be more than one meeting.

Bull and Perry knew it was common practice for government and military leaders to hold off-the-record sessions. Marshall did it, but his method had flaws. The General met in his office during working hours with from twenty-five to thirty newsmen invited by the Army. Those who were left out had hurt feelings. Those who did attend were too many for an informal give-and-take, and Marshall's office was inhibiting in itself.

To avoid these problems Bull and Perry decided that the first meeting would be at Bull's Alexandria home. Perry and Roscoe Drummond of the *Christian Science Monitor* would select and invite the participants. They telephoned invitations to six of their closest colleagues, who immediately accepted,* and the eight newsmen gathered at Bull's home on the evening of Sunday, 6 November 1942.

King arrived at eight o'clock, and Bull made the introductions. The Admiral then sat in an easy chair, sipped on a glass of beer, and began to talk about the war. "He spoke with great frankness for about an hour," Perry recalled, "and then answered questions for another two hours. It was a memorable experience, and King had completely charmed and won the newspaper group."

The gatherings (Bull called them "seminars") continued for the remainder of the war, sixteen in all. The group expanded to twenty-six members (although the number at any one gathering remained small), and later they proudly referred to themselves as "The Surviving Veterans of the Battle of Virginia." They should have called themselves the Disciples of King.

When Nelie Bull died of a heart attack in early 1944, the newsmen feared the meetings would end. But one day Phelps H. Adams of the New York *Sun* received a call from King saying that both he and Forrestal would like the meetings to continue. Adams was delighted, and they agreed to meet next at Adams's home.

Adams later described King's first visit in a letter to the author. "My wife, Ruth, had put a washtub full of cracked ice and bottled beer in front of the fireplace, had arranged all the chairs we possessed around it, and had then retired to her room upstairs to be sequestered there for the duration so that no errant secret spoken below should reach her ears. In fact, she never saw nor met the Admiral until after the war was over.

"He, however, did not overlook her presence. With true Navy courtesy, he arrived at the first meeting with a large bottle of Macadamia nuts — in those days almost impossible to get at any price — and asked me to present them to her with his compliments. Then he greeted the assembled correspondents, took his place in an overstuffed arm chair we had reserved for him, thanked me for the glass of beer I placed on the end table beside him . . . and began to review the entire war for us, on a global scale, as he always did on these occasions.

"He told us what had happened, what was happening, and, often, what was likely to happen next," Adams continued. "He reported the

* Ray Henle, Pittsburgh *Post-Dispatch;* Bert Andrews, New York *Herald-Tribune;* Barnet Nover, Washington *Post;* Raymond Clapper, Scripps-Howard newspapers; Ernest Lindley, *Newsweek;* Marquis Childs, St. Louis *Post-Dispatch.*

bad news as fully as the good news, and in many cases, explained what went wrong on the one hand, and what strategy, weapon, or combination of both, had brought success on the other.

"Throughout, he was completely at ease and always patient, welcoming the questions that frequently interrupted his narrative, and answering them frankly and easily. It was, in short, a conversational evening with group participation — not a monologue by a guest speaker. He was a friend among friends.

"The thing that never failed to astonish me — and, I think, the others of our group — was the uninhibited disclosure of highly sensitive information which, if published by any one of us, might have seriously embarrassed the war effort and would certainly have ended King's naval career. There was never a moment's doubt that his words were gospel; nor was there the slightest suspicion that his statements might be shaded with bias in an attempt to place the Navy or the total war effort in a more favorable light than was justified by the events of the moment.

"There were, of course," Adams went on to explain, "top secret matters of which he did not speak to us — and of which, in fact, he could not have spoken to his colleagues in the aforementioned map room. For example, he never mentioned the atomic bomb or gave the slightest hint — so far as I know — of its existence or impending existence until after Hiroshima.

"And so it went — usually for three to four hours. During the first three or so hours King would finish five glasses of beer. Then he would rise, go upstairs to the 'head,' and return for one final glass before leaving. This gave us a chance to clear up the loose ends of the session. During the evening he would light an occasional cigarette, consuming six to eight, I would guess, all told. He smoked neither excessively nor compulsively.

"He seemed to enjoy himself at these meetings. Perhaps they provided a release for him by giving him the opportunity to talk freely about these hush-hush things. And perhaps as he discussed with us the pros and cons of future plans of action that had not yet been resolved, it helped to clear his own thinking and to sharpen his perspective. In any event, he always seemed genuinely pleased, and we who had shared the evening with him were completely fascinated.

"As these conferences continued," Adams then said, "it became apparent to us that Ernie King was — above all — a realist; that he did not indulge in wishful thinking or close his eyes to unpleasant problems in the hope that they would go away. It was probably this characteristic above all others which gave him the reputation of being an 'old curmudgeon' with whom it was difficult to 'get along.' When it came to decisions regarding the conduct of the war, or anything else affecting the armed forces in general and the Navy in particular, he spoke his mind forthrightly and argued unswervingly, whether his adversary at the moment was the President of the United States, the Secretary of the Navy, or the Prime Minister of England. The language of diplomacy was a tongue utterly foreign to him in disagreements of this nature, and he spoke to us frankly about some of them."

The motives of King and his inner circle of newsmen deserve analysis. Historian Forrest Pogue was speaking for most public figures when he wrote that Marshall "had learned that the best way to keep a secret out of the newspapers was to reveal it to responsible newsmen and then explain why it could not be printed." Those who met with King did so with an implied vow of silence. Having been told everything, they would print nothing. Undoubtedly flattered to be included in the group, and awed by King's stature and personality despite their familiarity with men in high places, they were reluctant to publish anything that King could regard as a betrayal of trust. That would have ended the meetings.

Had King subtly muzzled the press? As the "press" embraces thousands of people, the twenty-six members of King's group were a very small part of it. While influential, they certainly did not control the free press of America. As King's belligerence toward the press as a whole remained unaltered, the impact of King's meetings is difficult to judge. They kept a bad situation from getting worse but in the long run probably did not improve the Navy's reputation with the public.

King's group certainly believed in the worth of the meetings. "What others did with the information they got from Admiral King, I don't know," Adams later said, "but Glen [Perry] and I sent complete memoranda to the *Sun*'s New York office for the information of the executive editor. This information was of great value to him in evaluating the importance and significance of the fragmentary news despatches as they filtered through censorship from the various fronts; and it enabled them to detect and reject rumors and scare stories spread innocently or by enemy propaganda machines. It was helpful in preventing the accidental and premature publication of information or speculation that might have aided the enemy; and above all, it closed completely and irreversibly the 'credibility gap' that was rapidly widening between the military and the press at the time Admiral King was first persuaded to meet eight gentlemen of the press at Cornelius Bull's house that fateful night in the fall of 1942.

"Thanks to Admiral King — and to the other leaders who took us into their confidence — we *did* know what the score was; and we could cover the news intelligently as it developed.

"Without their confidence the nation's press could not have functioned as well and as informatively as it did; and the nation, of course, would have been the poorer."

Glen Perry felt that there was another dividend for the correspondents. "As King came to know us and trust us," Perry later said, "we felt free to get him on the phone or even to drop in at his office if we had something we felt was important enough to justify disturbing him. We were, needless to say, careful not to abuse the privilege. . . . A lot of firm friendships grew out of the correspondents' discovery that King was not only a great officer but a great guy, and King's discovery that the correspondents were smart, close-mouthed when it counted, and also nice guys."

21

Casablanca

DURING THE FALL and early winter of 1942 the Americans devoted their energy and attention to North Africa and Guadalcanal. The Americans and British had landed in North Africa on 8 November 1942, starting a campaign that would continue until the following May. Guadalcanal would not be secured until early February 1943. Both campaigns were touch-and-go; JCS staff officers worrying about immediate crises had scant time to think about long-range strategic plans. This uncertainty perplexed the logistical planners. Lacking guidance about future strategy, they could not intelligently decide on what materiel to procure. Nevertheless, American war production gained momentum, even though much of what was being produced might never be used, and, conversely, unforeseen shortages might arise once future strategy had been developed.

King and his JCS colleagues were handicapped in many ways when they tried to plan ahead in late 1942. Unpredictable variables affected scheduling. Operations after TORCH would depend upon when North Africa was finally cleared of Germans, while future plans in the Pacific were contingent upon when Guadalcanal was ultimately won. And "when" those campaigns would end was anyone's guess.

Enemy intentions were another variable. Code breaking did not always reveal how the enemy was thinking or the reasons for enemy decisions. King confessed that he could not understand Japanese psychology: Japan's violent reaction at Guadalcanal was both unexpected and, from a Western viewpoint, irrational. King was also puzzled why Japanese submarines did not attack his exposed sea lines of communication in the Pacific. "In fact, the Japs are not doing a lot of things they could do to annoy us," King remarked to the Alexandria reporters on the evening of 30 November 1942.

King went on to explain that evening that the war would go through four phases, and he used boxing tactics as an analogy.

(1) Defensive phase . . . a boxer covering up.
(2) Defensive-offensive phase . . . a boxer covering up while seeking an opening to counterpunch.
(3) Offensive-defensive phase . . . blocking punches with one hand while hitting with the other.
(4) Offensive phase . . . hitting with both hands.

King considered that he was in Phase 3 against Japan. What about Germany? he was asked. Well, that was not so clear, King replied. Germany had to be defeated first, he said, and he would support that decision with whatever naval resources were necessary. But at the moment King had an open mind on what to do next against Germany. If the Allies could control the Mediterranean, he explained, it would be a form of blockade against Germany. And without question, a seizure of Sicily would restore the Mediterranean to the Allies. Furthermore, he agreed with the British that a secure sea line of communication from Gibraltar to the Suez Canal was essential. But he was dubious about assaulting the Italian mainland, even though doing so might force Italy to surrender. He predicted that the Germans would fight there in any event, and the Alps barricaded Allied entry into Austria and southern Germany. The cross-Channel invasion, King believed, was inevitable, but he had no preference as to the best time to do it.

As King explained it to his rapt audience, Russia was the key to European strategy. She had the manpower. She had the best geographical position to cross Germany's borders. Thus King wanted to keep sending Lend-Lease materiel to keep her in the war. "In the last analysis," King predicted, "Russia will do nine-tenths of the job of defeating Germany."

Turning to the Pacific, King told the reporters he wanted to prevent the Japanese from digging in and consolidating their conquests. If left undisturbed while the Allies fought Germany, argued King, the Japanese defenses would become increasingly formidable, ultimately prolonging the war and increasing American casualties. King was convinced that American industry could produce enough materiel for simultaneous offensives against both Germany and Japan. The question was how to divide it between the two theaters. In late 1942 King reckoned that the Pacific theater's share was only 15 percent. He wanted at least twice that amount going to the Pacific. This would allow forces under Nimitz, striking northward from the Solomons and westward from Hawaii, to drive across the Central Pacific toward the Philippines. Once they had been seized, the Japanese would be isolated from their raw materials in the Southwest Pacific and could be starved into submission through blockade. (Later King would change his objective from the Philippines to Formosa.)

China was critical in King's thinking. She, like Russia, was a primitive industrial nation with reservoirs of manpower, while Great Britain would soon run out of men. The industries of the United States and Great Britain would equip the Chinese and Russian armies. King's idea was to save American lives by getting China and Russia to fight the bulk of the Japanese and German armies. To keep China in the war, King meant to open a road through Burma to provide a flow of materiel to the Chinese armies. Both Roosevelt and Marshall agreed with him, King told the reporters.

King mistrusted the optimistic theories of air-power advocates. Using the phrase "RAF psychology," King thought their concepts of winning the war by air power alone was "dangerous thinking." Aircraft were fine, he thought, as long as they were airborne, but they could not stay there indefinitely. "They must come to earth sometime," said King.

The fall of 1942 turned into winter. Still there was no decision what to do after North Africa and Guadalcanal. To get things moving, Roosevelt and Churchill began to discuss a meeting to decide upon future strategy. Just before Thanksgiving Roosevelt summoned the JCS to solicit their ideas, but they had little to offer. On 10 December he again summoned the JCS; King was in California with Nimitz, so Edwards attended. Again the JCS had nothing to say. Roosevelt seemed unconcerned. There was no need for a decision for several months, he said, and meanwhile the buildup of American forces could continue both in Great Britain and North Africa. After an inconclusive discussion, the meeting adjourned.

Roosevelt and Churchill finally agreed to meet in Casablanca in mid-January 1943. On 7 January Roosevelt met with the JCS to try to define the American position on future strategy, reminding them that the British at Casablanca would have a plan and would stick to it. For the third time he discovered that King and his JCS colleagues were in disarray and disunited. Reasoning that eventually King and Marshall would resolve their differences, he told them to do as they thought best. It was a shaky way to plan a war.

Although Roosevelt never asked why, King and the JCS would not produce their own strategic proposal for the Casablanca Conference because the job was too much for them. King, Marshall, Arnold, and their staffs had neither the training nor experience for the demands of joint and combined planning. They were accustomed from prewar habits to developing plans for their service alone. With the exceptions of the venerable Joint Board and the prewar ABC conferences, the Army and Navy planners had shown little inclination for coordination with their sister service or Great Britain. Chapter 17 addressed the JCS neglect of the political factors that were so important to Roosevelt and Churchill. Yet foreign policy guidance was rarely offered by Roosevelt, and the State Department was never consulted. The JCS planners labored in a vacuum.

King's chief planner was Rear Admiral Savvy Cooke. The two admirals were so close intellectually and philosophically that Cooke functioned as King's alter ego in all matters dealing with strategy. Cooke's staff was deliberately small. A rear admiral and four captains served as his immediate assistants, and four other senior officers worked on future plans. During most of 1942 Cooke's overworked staff got so involved in immediate crises and in coordinating naval forces assigned to North Africa, Guadalcanal, and the Battle of the Atlantic that there were neither time nor people to think about long-range grand strategy.

Cooke also served as the senior naval member of the Joint Staff Planners (JPS), a committee of representatives from the Navy, Army, and Army Air Force. Their workload was enormous. Whenever King and the other JCS members disagreed or were unprepared to decide upon a problem, they automatically passed the buck to the JPS for resolution. But resolutions were usually wishful thinking. Cooke and the other planners regarded themselves as service advocates rather than as conciliators. More often than not they repeated and sharpened the same arguments heard at the JCS level. Thus, when the JPS got done with a problem they often had made things worse by reinforcing the opposing views of each service.

Administrative inertia compounded the conflicts. The JPS met weekly. Unresolved disputes were tabled until the next meeting a week later (and sometimes ad infinitum), regardless of urgency. Such delays allowed months to pass without action on important questions. Absenteeism slowed things even more, and Cooke was the greatest offender. During the last seven months of 1942 he attended only twelve of thirty-five JPS meetings. This apparently did not worry him — the next senior naval representative simply echoed Cooke's well-known positions. If Cooke did not like a decision made in his absence, he could simply veto it after reading the minutes.

Time and again the JPS went full circle and returned the deadlocked issues to the JCS. The JCS went by the rule that all decisions needed a unanimous vote. As there frequently were one or more dissenters, the JCS would simply put off deciding anything. As a last resort they could refer an irreconcilable matter to the President, an extreme procedure rarely used. No one wanted FDR to get involved in JCS business any more than necessary.

These self-imposed delays frustrated the theater commanders, who needed timely decisions to facilitate their own planning. Nimitz was particularly impatient, especially in late 1944 when he knew the Japanese were reinforcing Iwo Jima and Okinawa while the JCS wrangled over whether and when they should be assaulted. King, however, accepted the delays as the price he had to pay to preserve the principle of the unanimous vote. If the majority could overrule the minority (usually King), the JCS might make a hasty decision they would later regret. In other words, no decision at all was better than the possibility of making a bad decision. So King was never in a hurry when making grand strategy; a unanimous decision, he believed, would always be the best decision. Whatever the delay, it was worth waiting for. "I firmly believed," King said after the war, "that all matters had to be looked over thoroughly and completely (if it took days or weeks or months) until 'all hands' had the time to think over the gist of the problem from every angle."

Another advantage of a unanimous vote, from King's view, was that it was the only way that many of his pet projects got approved. If the JCS had operated by majority rule, King later said, the Guadalcanal and Central Pacific campaigns would never have been authorized because he would have been outvoted. So yes indeed, there were delays while the JCS deliberated, admitted King, but never beyond the time it was *essential* for the operating forces to have the decision. "I am not aware," wrote King to Nimitz in late 1945, "that the interval between concept . . . and decision cost us military success or put us at a sensible disadvantage with the enemy." King's apologia is open to dispute, as will be seen in later chapters.

When King and the JCS finally recognized that immediate crises distracted the JPS from long-range strategic planning, they belatedly established two other committees that they thought would have the time: the Joint U.S. Strategic Committee (JUSSC) and the Joint Strategic Survey Committee (JSSC). At first neither was very effective. The former got bogged down with other tasks, while the latter came too late to contribute much to the Casablanca preparations.

King usually ignored planning committees in any event. In his mind they generated many staff studies that were neither presented to nor approved by the JCS or CCS. Those papers that did come before the JCS rarely were approved in toto. "When the JCS came to act on any one of these documents," JCS planner Robert L. Dennison later said, "they never approved a paper because they couldn't agree on the reasons that led to these various conclusions. They might agree with the conclusion, but for different reasons, so all they ever approved was the recommendation, which was a simple one- or two-paragraph thing." After the war King chided historians for devoting undue attention to the committee papers. The major decisions were made by King and his colleagues behind closed doors, he said, and staff studies had little influence.

As the Casablanca Conference approached the JCS could dawdle no longer. In late December they met to try to resolve their bargaining position before facing the British. They finally agreed upon a three-page position paper, reflecting the individual special interests of King, Marshall, and Arnold, which had nothing in common.

- An offensive in the Pacific
- A cross-Channel invasion in 1943
- A strategic air offensive against Germany.

Given their lack of resources, the Americans were daydreaming. Their paper could not be taken seriously. The British, having the JCS paper in advance, replied with two memoranda of their own, which manifested their superb staff work and thorough preparation. In fifteen well-reasoned pages the British countered that they wanted to continue offensive operations in the Mediterranean, to delay a cross-Channel invasion, and to minimize the war in the Pacific.

Their conflicting positions having been stated, the Americans and British got underway for Casablanca.

On 9 January 1943 King and the Joint Chiefs left Washington by air for Casablanca. The first leg of the trip was marred by sharp words between King and Marshall. Marshall, Arnold, and Dill flew in one plane, while King flew in another. Their first stop was Puerto Rico. King was the first to arrive, but a message from Marshall directed King to remain airborne so Marshall could land first. As Marshall was the senior, King had to circle the airfield. King later complained to Marshall about wasting gas, but his real gripe was Marshall's pettiness in pulling rank. To avoid recurrences, it was arranged that Marshall's plane would always leave in time to arrive first.

On 13 January King arrived in Casablanca and went to the conference headquarters at the Anfa Hotel. Located on the outskirts of the city, the hotel surmounted a hill overlooking the ocean, and the clear, comfortable weather was a welcome change from Washington and London. Villas for the VIPs were located on the hotel grounds, landscaped with palm trees, bougainvillea, and orange groves. Sentries and barricades were everywhere, and fighter aircraft circled protectively overhead.

King, Marshall, and Arnold had preceded the President by several days to allow time to meet with the British Chiefs of Staff beforehand. Leahy had taken ill and had remained behind. On the afternoon of their arrival the three service chiefs gathered with their staffs to review their positions for the following day. King spoke first. Grand strategy should receive top priority, he insisted, and it was most important that the CCS revise the ratio of men and materiel between the European and Pacific theaters. The 15 percent ratio apportioned against Japan was not enough. (Although the ratio was largely King's intuitive estimate, it was never questioned by the CCS.) The British would try to discuss the details of individual operations, warned King. Grand strategy had to come first. Marshall and Arnold were swept up by King's pep talk. Yes, by God, they would negotiate with a united front.

The first CCS meeting was scheduled for 1030 the following morning, January fourteenth, a Thursday. The JCS met two hours earlier for a final review. King again stressed the importance of seizing the initiative and persuading the British to resolve the basic issues before going into details. After all, said King, the United States had become the stronger power of the two. It was incumbent on the JCS to show the way in determining the strategy of the war. Motivated and spiritually invigorated, King and the JCS went briskly forth for their first official meeting with Brooke, Pound, and Portal.

The British once again were better prepared. They had done their homework and had position papers on virtually any topic that might arise. Knowing what they wanted, they knew how to get it. The British had brought their usual large staff of expert planners, while the Americans had but a few. King's only assistants were Cooke and King's aide for JCS matters, Ruthven Libby.

The American-British staffs together were known as the Combined Staff Planners (CPS). They would soon become inundated with work flowing from the formal CCS meetings. In some cases the CCS would not always be sure exactly what they had agreed upon or had resolved.

Consequently they would expect the CPS to reduce their hours of wandering oral exchanges into terse written summaries. Another staff chore would be to draft revised position papers for their chiefs to use as a focus of discussion for subsequent meetings. Thus, the planners would be forced to labor while their chiefs slept or socialized between meetings. The undermanned American staff would soon become so overworked that local American staff officers would be brought in to help.

The British also knew in advance what the Americans wanted, for Field Marshal Sir John Dill had kept London well informed from his position as the senior British liaison officer in Washington. While the JCS had been holding their own last-minute sessions on the thirteenth, Dill had simultaneously been briefing the British Chiefs of Staff. Dill reported that the Americans (especially King) suspected that the British had little interest in or understanding of the war in the Pacific. Once Germany was defeated there was a feeling (again principally King's) that the British would not fight Japan with any great enthusiasm.

Dill emphasized that King's attitude was crucial. King controlled most of the scarce Allied landing craft, without which no operation could succeed. If King felt that they were critically needed in the Pacific, he might not send them to Europe. And he would never allow landing craft to remain idle in Europe if they were being detained for indefinite future operations. King had even more clout in the eyes of the British when they heard that King had persuaded Marshall to send more to the Pacific. It was obvious, said Dill, that the British would have to respect King's views.

Dill also recognized the same trend as did King: the Americans produced and controlled an ever larger share of the resources, so the Americans would demand a proportionately greater voice in Allied strategy. Churchill, too, understood this, and he instructed the British chiefs not to hurry and try to force an agreement. Let the Americans have their say, cautioned the Prime Minister.

King's worrisome influence on the British was expressed in a diary of Sir Ian Jacob, secretary to the British Chiefs of Staff. "Our Chiefs," wrote Jacob on 14 January, "felt that they knew so little of what was really going on in the Pacific, of what the U.S. Navy planned to do, and of the amount of resources that these plans would absorb, that some enlightenment would be valuable. They also felt that 'Uncle Ernie' would take a less jaundiced view of the rest of the world if he had been able to shoot his line about the Pacific and really get it off his chest."

When the first CCS meeting began midmorning on the fourteenth, the Americans jumped off just as they had planned. Marshall began by declaring that the first order of business should be the allocation of resources between the two theaters, which in his mind should be 70:30. (So King *had* gotten to Marshall! thought the British.) After King seconded Marshall's proposal, the British immediately changed the subject. For the remainder of the morning they dominated the discussion with their appraisals of the conduct of the war. King was silent — until Portal roused him by stating that the defeat of the German submarine menace should receive first priority from Allied air power. King retorted that in his judgment the Royal Air Force was doing very little toward bombing submarine construction yards and installations. On that sour note the meeting adjourned for lunch.

Perhaps realizing that by having monopolized the morning's meeting the British might have alienated King, Brooke that afternoon invited King to enlighten the British on the Pacific war. King did. After summarizing the previous year's operations, King hammered home his by now familiar arguments for increasing the pressure against Japan, emphasizing the importance of seizing the Marianas because of their central position astride Japanese sea lines of communication. King took no pride of authorship in the strategy that he was advocating. It had been developed at the Naval War College, King explained, and it was understood and accepted by nearly all naval officers. To show their unanimity Marshall and Arnold reinforced King's arguments, especially with respect to aiding China by opening the Burma Road.

The British predictably countered with their obdurate objections, including their doubts about enough resources for simultaneous offenses in both theaters. As the British talked, it seemed more and more to King that they had no interest in the war with Japan, not then, perhaps never. King finally lost patience, and he interjected a question that was on everyone's mind on the JCS. Who, he asked, would have the principal burden of defeating Japan once Germany had been knocked out of the war?

In his own blunt way, King had confronted the British with the historical suspicion that had wrecked past wartime coalitions, the suspicion by one ally that another was shirking. And King did mistrust the British. When he had met with his inner circle of newsmen at Alexandria six weeks earlier, King had said then that Churchill's main interest was to preserve the British Empire, and that cooperating with the United States to win the war took lower priority. In King's mind, winning the war as soon as possible had to be first priority.

Brooke instantly recognized the dangerous implications of King's

The Americans at Casablanca. King and Marshall sit with Roosevelt. Back row, l. to r.: Hopkins, Arnold, Lieutenant General B. B. Somerville, and Averill Harriman. (U.S. Navy photograph)

question. Both he and Portal tried to assure King of Britain's commitment to defeat Japan as well as Germany. King had so disturbed the British, however, that Churchill himself dramatically reassured the Americans several days later. "I wish to make it clear," said Churchill, "that if and when Hitler breaks down, all of the British resources and effort will be turned toward the defeat of Japan. Not only are British interests involved, but her honor as well." Churchill even offered to enter into a formal treaty if Roosevelt thought it necessary. The President declined. The point had been made.

When the afternoon meeting had adjourned, the question of Pacific strategy remained unresolved, but King was making progress. Before the Casablanca Conference King had been unable to persuade either Marshall or Arnold to accept King's concept of a Central Pacific drive toward the Philippines. Now their attitudes had changed. Although King had been speaking for himself during the first CCS meeting at Casablanca, Marshall and Arnold had to agree with him in front of the British. By imposition, then, King's views had become JCS policy. In time, King's views would become sanctioned by the CCS, as well, for the strategy for the Pacific that King advocated that afternoon in Casablanca would become reality ten months later.

The British had begun to take full measure of King. Sir Ian Jacob wrote his impressions following the first day's meetings on the fourteenth. "King is well over sixty," wrote Jacob, "but active, tall and spare, with an alert and self-confident bearing. He seems to wear a protective covering of horn which it is hard to penetrate. He gives the impression of being exceedingly narrow-minded and to be always on the lookout for slights or attempts to put something over on him. . . . His manners are good as a rule, but he is angular and stiff and finds it difficult, if not impossible, really to unbend. I am convinced, however, that there is much more to him than appears on the surface, and that if one could get beneath the horn shell that one would be surprised at what one would find beneath."

Lieutenant General Sir Hastings Ismay, Churchill's personal chief of staff, was less charitable. "He was as tough as nails and carried himself as stiffly as a poker," wrote Ismay in his memoirs. "He was blunt and stand-offish, almost to the point of rudeness. At the start, he was intolerant and suspicious of all things British, especially the Royal Navy; but he was almost equally intolerant and suspicious of the American Army. War against Japan was the problem to which he had devoted the study of a lifetime, and he resented the idea of American resources being used for any other purpose than to destroy Japanese. He mistrusted Churchill's powers of advocacy, and was apprehensive that he would wheedle President Roosevelt into neglecting the war in the Pacific."

King himself had begun to size up the British chiefs. He respected them individually and as a group. He considered Air Chief Marshal Sir John Portal by far the most able and intelligent, whose understanding of strategy and tactics transcended his air warfare specialty. Arnold was no match in terms of intellect.

Admiral of the Fleet Sir Dudley Pound, whom King considered a good friend (perhaps because they both enjoyed parties), usually confined his attention to naval affairs. Pound was slowly dying from a brain tumor that made him groggy during the CCS meetings. Yet he always wakened when the navies were mentioned, and his views (to King at least) were always sound.

King's great adversary would be General Sir Alan Brooke, Chief of the Imperial General Staff, the top military man in England.* Brooke's ideas seemed to King inflexible. There were personal irritations too. "He talked so damned fast," King later said, "that it was hard to understand what he was saying."

Dill was the great conciliator, unable to get along with Churchill as Brooke's predecessor but perfect in Washington. King very much liked him, and he credited Dill with alleviating many potential clashes between the JCS and the British Chiefs of Staff. Indeed, all the Americans liked Dill, and they mourned his death later in the war.

Despite the British show of unanimity, King was well aware of their internal conflicts that they tried to conceal. "They had plenty of fights with Churchill," King said after the war. "We knew that. In comparison we had very little trouble with Roosevelt."

It was customary for the Americans and British to socialize between meetings. The conferees dined together in a rooftop restaurant at the Anfa Hotel, and King noted how the British relished their oranges after doing without in Great Britain. These informal gatherings resolved many problems that were never officially recorded. Roosevelt did his share of promoting harmony by inviting everyone to dinner after the first day's conferences had ended. It was such a pleasant evening that most everyone remained up past midnight.

"King became nicely lit towards the end of the evening," wrote Brooke in his diary when the party was over. "As a result he got more and more pompous and, with a thick voice and many gesticulations, he explained to the President the best way to set up the political French organisation for control of North Africa. This led to many arguments with P.M. [Prime Minister] who failed to appreciate fully the condition King was in. Most amusing to watch."

Brooke was correct that King had ideas on the politics of North Africa. King wanted to trust the French, to arm them, and to give them something to do to help the war effort against Germany, a view not shared by Churchill and the British chiefs. But Brooke's assertion that King was drunk may have been a mistaken perception. Perhaps it was the first time that Brooke had ever seen King relax at a party. King could still enjoy himself even though he was off hard liquor for the duration. But knowing Roosevelt and Churchill there were probably many toasts, and King may have had one glass of wine too many.

* After a subsequent promotion he would become simply Field Marshal Alanbrooke.

The Combined Chiefs of Staff and their advisors fall in behind Roosevelt and Churchill. L. to r., Arnold, King, Marshall, Pound, Portal, Brooke, Dill, and Mountbatten. (National Archives 80-G-35135)

Amidst the mixture of camaraderie and suspicion the Allied leaders finally drifted off to bed. The first day of the Casablanca Conference was officially over.

Progress came slowly during the next three days. Everyone agreed that the Battle of the Atlantic took first priority. As for the war in Europe, the JCS agreed among themselves to go along with the British. They were ready to accept the invasion of Sicily (Operation HUSKY) and to abandon a 1943 cross-Channel invasion. But the British in exchange would have to agree to an intensified war in the Pacific. They would find on that issue the British would not compromise. Nor would King.

The British by now regarded King as their most formidable obstacle, so Churchill characteristically invited the Admiral to luncheon. "When I arrived at his villa," King later wrote, "I became interested because

I was the only guest. He did most of the talking, and what a smooth talker he was. I had something to say, but I was on guard because I was sure that he wanted something. Apparently, however, he was just looking me over because I had not had, before this, the chance to chat with him except for five minutes. So he talked about the Levant and how he could get the Nazis out of Africa and then hit them in Italy, since he was still thinking about the 'under-belly' of Europe. Of course, he wanted first to clean up North Africa so that shipping would not have to go around the Cape of Good Hope, and in this all hands agreed. . . ."

The luncheon failed to break the impasse, so Roosevelt decided to help by inviting the Prime Minister to a small dinner party at his villa on Sunday evening, 17 January. King was the only member of the CCS who attended.

This time King did the talking. Throughout the dinner and afterward King pounded on Churchill, trying to get him to accept, or at least to understand better, the American views on Pacific strategy. It was not solely an American show, said King. The British had to get themselves involved too. With that King brought up Operation ANAKIM, the British reentry into Burma that would open a supply route via the Burma Road to the Chinese Army. Roosevelt, King, and Marshall were committed to keeping China in the war so that the Chinese Army could pin the Japanese Army on the Asian mainland, keeping it away from the American forces in the Pacific.

Roosevelt also advocated ANAKIM for political reasons, as a show of good faith to Chiang Kai-shek. Slowly, ever so slowly, Roosevelt and King shifted Churchill's focus from Britain's imperial interests in the Mediterranean to American interests in the Far East. Churchill simply did not trust Chiang, even if Roosevelt did. Yet as much as Churchill hated to send British soldiers into Asian jungles to hack a road to China, Roosevelt and King had him cornered. In the end he agreed to ANAKIM. Churchill's concession was a triumph for King, although it would be short-lived.

It was a stormy evening. Churchill remained adamant against King's plans for the Pacific. He even accused King in front of Roosevelt of withholding information about the landing-craft program and the disposition of American forces in the Pacific. (It was, in fact, an admission of Britain's dependence upon King's ships in order to carry on the war.) When the evening ended it was clear to Churchill that King was unyielding about carrying on in the Pacific. Moreover, there was very little that the British could do to stop him. Eventually they would have to give in.

The next morning the CCS convened for their most decisive meeting. Whether the British Chiefs of Staff felt betrayed by Churchill's unilateral acceptance on ANAKIM the night before is unrecorded, but at least it had been a switch from the British tactic of isolating Roosevelt from the JCS. In submitting to King's fait accompli, Brooke could only ask if there would be enough landing craft both for ANAKIM and for all other contemplated operations.* King expansively promised to provide whatever landing craft were required. With that, the matter was settled. ANAKIM was on. Or so it seemed.

From there, however, the conference again degenerated into wrangling about the apportionment of resources between Europe and the Pacific. Tempers began to flare when the British began to pry into the reasons *why* King needed more men and materiel. Whatever was done in the Pacific (said Brooke again and again) could not be allowed to prejudice the earliest possible defeat of Germany. King finally became exasperated. "That expression," he said, "might be read as meaning that *anything* which is done in the Pacific would interfere with the earliest possible defeat of Germany and that the Pacific theater should therefore remain totally inactive." Portal quickly tried to mollify King (that was not the British attitude, he said), but by now King was really mad.

"We have on many occasions been close to disaster in the Pacific," said King, his way of reminding the British that shortages had caused those near-disasters. The sole role of the CCS, King insisted, was to determine how much should be sent to each theater. The British had no business getting into the details of the Pacific war. That theater belonged to the Americans, and they alone would decide what was to be done there. The Americans had not been consulted before the British had undertaken operations in Madagascar and Somaliland, nor did they expect to be. The same rules applied to American operations in the Pacific.

Brooke despaired. "We seemed to be making no progress," he wrote in his diary. "King still evidently wrapped up in the war in the Pacific at the expense of everything else." The meeting adjourned for lunch at one o'clock in the afternoon.

The British huddled during the luncheon break and quickly drafted a paper that they hoped would satisfy King. When the meeting reconvened two hours later they gave the paper to King and the JCS.† King's eyes quickly swept to the paragraph headed "Operations in the Pacific and Far East." There were three major statements.

(1) "Operations in these theaters shall continue with the forces allo-

* Whatever those might be! Many were "contemplated," but few were approved.
† Identified as C.C.S. 155.

cated, with the object of maintaining pressure on Japan, retaining the initiative and attaining a position of readiness for the full scale offensive against Japan by the United Nations as soon as Germany is defeated.

(2) "These operations must be kept within such limits as will not, in the opinion of the Combined Chiefs of Staff, jeopardize the capacity of the United Nations to take advantage of any favorable opportunity that may present itself for the decisive defeat of Germany in 1943.

(3) "Subject to the above reservation, plans and preparations shall be made for:

a. The recapture of Burma (Anakim) beginning in 1943.

b. Operations, after the capture of Rabaul, against the Marshalls and Carolines if time and resources allow without prejudice to Anakim."

King had gotten what he wanted. Although the statement contained several escape clauses, it was nevertheless an unequivocal commitment by the CCS to intensify the war against Japan. Furthermore, it authorized a Central Pacific offensive, which obviously would be under Nimitz.

What the paper did not do was to specify the ratio of forces between the two theaters as King had urged. An amendment (undoubtedly at King's insistence) corrected the omission and strengthened King's hand still further: "In order that these European operations and preparations are not prejudiced by the necessity to divert forces to retrieve an adverse situation elsewhere, adequate forces shall be allocated to the Pacific and Far Eastern Theaters." *

At first glance the phrase "adequate forces" might seem ambiguous, but King could make it work for him. King now had a CCS blessing to send Nimitz what he needed in the Central Pacific while preempting any British complaints that King was willfully withholding shipping from the European theater. The phrase also gave King a wedge to pry troops and aircraft from Marshall and Arnold, for both had supported his arguments for the war against Japan. Having gotten his way in the Pacific, King could be magnanimous in return. A hopeful Winston Churchill later wired the British War Cabinet, "Admiral King even went so far as to say that if it was decided to do Sicily he would find the necessary escorts."

The British compromise proposal had also included the invasion of Sicily, the commitment to win the Battle of the Atlantic, an intensified

* The wording of the CCS documents can be fascinating. In this example it implies that the war in Europe would benefit by sending more arms and men to the Pacific. This is a clever circumlocution to make the statement more palatable to the British, because it still implies that Europe is the more important of the two theaters as a matter of principle.

bomber offensive against Germany, and all possible aid to the Soviet Union. There was something to please everybody, except Marshall. His cherished 1943 cross-Channel invasion was officially dead.

In the late afternoon the CCS met with Roosevelt and Churchill to announce their general agreement. After Brooke had summarized the coalition strategy for 1943, a discussion followed.

Then King spoke, the only time he would speak during the meeting. It had taken some days for the chiefs of staff to express themselves, said King, but in principle they were all agreed. Their agreement would go a long way toward establishing a policy of how the Allies were to win the war. He personally would have desired a complete concept for concluding the war, but he nevertheless was well pleased with it as it was.

The feeling of relief from the British side must have been almost audible.

The Casablanca Conference still had work to do even though the basic strategy had been resolved. For five days the Allied leaders developed those details necessary to implement their strategic decisions. The CCS met for the last time on the evening of 23 January. It was largely a ceremonial exchange of compliments and good wishes. King had the final word. "I fully agree with Sir Alan Brooke," said King, "as to the great value of the basic strategic plan which has been worked out at this conference. In my view this has been the biggest step forward to the winning of the war."

Historians have since criticized the results, or the lack of results, at Casablanca. The decisions, it has been written, were too broad and general, making them susceptible to different interpretations and leading inevitably to future arguments and disagreements. There was no grand strategic plan beyond 1943, and there was no clear ratio of the apportionment of resources between the Pacific and European theaters. Inevitably, these historians conclude, the logisticians still lacked the guidance they needed for long-range procurement.

Their criticisms overlook the pragmatic aspects of strategic planning. Given the unpredictable variables of a world war, especially the plans and reactions of the enemy, the Allies could not have committed themselves to an irrevocable grand strategy several years in advance, even if it would have simplified matters for the logisticians. Sometimes the CCS simply had to await developments before planning their next move.

Even those commitments and decisions that were firmly agreed upon were susceptible to change. Operation ANAKIM is the best example. At Casablanca everyone agreed it would be done in late 1943, but in the end it was canceled. Rabaul is another example, approved for invasion but ultimately bypassed. Strategic planners are not omniscient, and strategy must be flexible to adapt to changing circumstances. As coalition warfare by its nature was dependent upon a willingness to compromise between the Allies, the wording of their agreements necessarily was expressed in general terms. There is much in favor of the British theory of opportunism, but it was tempered by the American insistence that decisions and commitments could not be postponed indefinitely. So if historians and logisticians complain about the lack of long-range strategic planning by the CCS during the Second World War, their arguments can be answered only by the fact that total war is complex, wasteful, imprecise, and unpredictable.

In any event, the American-British alliance in the Second World War was the most successful in history and infinitely superior to that of the Axis Powers whom they were fighting. This is one point we must never forget.

22

The Battle of the Atlantic

The United States Navy was not ready for the Battle of the Atlantic when King became COMINCH in December 1941. Owing to prewar naval disarmament treaties, isolationism, the Depression, and a variety of other causes, the Navy had neither the resources nor the tactical doctrine for fighting submarines. Even though King's Atlantic Fleet had escorted convoys during much of 1941, its readiness had deteriorated from wear and tear and lack of training.

Germany too had been unprepared for submarine warfare, for Hitler had expected that his army and air force alone would win Europe by force of arms. The German Navy did not seem important to him. Yet by December 1941 events had so changed that the German submarine force had expanded enormously and had nearly severed Britain's sea lines of communications.

Admiral Karl Dönitz, the German Navy's U-boat commander, capitalized on America's vulnerability once his country had declared war against the United States. He knew that as an industrialized nation the United States required raw materials for her factories. When America mobilized and also became the principal supplier of arms and munitions for her allies, her need for raw materials intensified enormously. Many of them were imported by sea from South and Central America. Oil, for example, came from wells in the Netherlands West Indies and from Venezuela. Bauxite (the basic ingredient for aluminum aircraft fuselages) was mined in the Guianas and Brazil for oceanic shipment to America. Such basic foodstuffs as coffee and sugar were also imported by sea.

Moreover, raw materials and bulk commodities produced in the United States often were transported via coastal sea lanes to industrial centers on the East Coast. Texas oil was loaded into tankers in ports in the Gulf of Mexico for shipment north. The great eastern cities depended upon coastal shipping for coal, iron, concrete, and lumber. If anything were to happen to these ships, the nation's railroads and highways did not have the capacity to take their place.

Dönitz correctly assumed that the United States lacked escorts and aircraft to protect this vital inter-America shipping, and, furthermore, that the United States would be shocked, confused, and distracted by the recent attack against Pearl Harbor. Under these circumstances, merchantmen off the East Coast would be easy picking. Dönitz asked Hitler for permission to attack immediately, calling his plan Operation *Paukenschlag* ("Drumroll"). Hitler approved it on 12 December 1941.

Sending U-boats across the Atlantic to American shores was a bold scheme. At first none were in the western Atlantic in obedience to Hitler's prewar orders to stand clear. Owing to other commitments Dönitz could order only five U-boats to the United States. When they arrived, their commanding officers were astounded. America was acting as if there were no war. Coastal shipping steamed independently with lights showing at night. There were neither convoys nor organized ASW * forces. The U-boats fell upon the merchant shipping like wolves upon sheep.

Paukenschlag was a massacre. Merchantmen were torpedoed within sight of spectators ashore, and resort beaches were covered with oil, debris, and occasionally bodies of seamen. Pillars of smoke from burning ships became common off the coast. Yet Americans refused to darken their cities at night, allowing U-boats to see and sink merchantmen silhouetted against the lights ashore. Eventually the Germans remained surfaced even by day and used their deck guns to conserve torpedoes. During the first four months of 1942 the Germans sank 87 ships totaling 515,000 tons in coastal waters. During March alone, 28 ships of some 160,000 tons were sunk off America's Atlantic shores.

As bad as it was, there were greater disasters in the rest of the world that took King's attention. As we have seen, King's immediate priorities once war began were to stop Japan and, together with Marshall, to work with the British Chiefs of Staff to develop a unified Allied strategy. As King could give only a portion of his time to the Battle of the Atlantic, he delegated the immediate responsibility for coastal waters to Vice Admiral Adolphus Andrews, his Annapolis classmate commanding the Eastern Sea Frontier with headquarters in New York City. The actual ships and planes that would have to fight the U-boats, however, were

* Anti-Submarine Warfare.

commanded by Admiral Royal R. Ingersoll, who had relieved King as Commander in Chief, Atlantic Fleet.

It was an unwieldy and cumbersome arrangement. Andrews's organization was intended to administer the Third Naval District's mundane shore establishments. Suddenly his staff had to fight a war at sea. The headquarters in downtown Manhattan were without facilities necessary to control the polyglot air and surface ASW forces scattered from Maine to Florida. Ingersoll could never provide Andrews the numbers of forces the latter requested because of fleet commitments to escort trans-Atlantic convoys and, later, to support amphibious operations in North Africa. Conversely, Andrews was reluctant to return ships to Ingersoll without an order from King. Ingersoll, meanwhile, following Navy tradition, had established his headquarters on a small flagship that was frequently underway, complicating communications with Washington and New York. And, much like Andrews's New York headquarters, Ingersoll's flagship was not equipped to coordinate the American ASW effort. Still, King thought he had done the right thing with Andrews and Ingersoll. "You will have noted," he wrote to a flag officer in late February, "how far we have gone in our endeavors to clear the way toward unity of command by putting our own house in order in regard to the sea frontier, wherein unity of command of sea frontier forces and local defense forces is attained by putting them under one officer — the sea frontier commander [Andrews]."

But the sinkings continued, and Andrews's forces could not kill a single U-boat. When King questioned Andrews's delay in organizing coastal convoys, Andrews retorted that without escorts there was no point in using convoys. In the meantime, said Andrews, the merchantmen might just as well steam independently. King apologized and promised additional ships and planes when they became available.

But King was not always so charitable. Early in the war Andrews sent a lengthy dispatch to a naval district commandant, prescribing precisely how he was to employ his handful of patrol craft. "When Admiral King read the long message from Andrews," staff officer Alan R. McFarland recalled, "he practically hit the ceiling." King immediately drafted a message canceling Andrews's directive. "Do not presume you are on the bridge of every ship under your command," said King.

Dönitz's strategy centered about his so-called "tonnage theory," by which he intended to sink merchantmen more rapidly than they could be replaced. Theoretically the Allied merchant fleet would inexorably dwindle. His strategy seemed to be working in early 1942, because losses far exceeded new construction. As American shipyards had a limited capacity, a priority had to be established between building merchantmen or building destroyer escorts to protect convoys. King tackled the question in an extraordinary memorandum dated 4 May 1942, addressed to all bureaus and offices of the Navy Department.

> Subject: Combatting the Submarine Menace — Building Merchant Ships vs Building Anti-Submarine Craft.
>
> 1. It is desired that "all hands" take note of the alternatives posed in the following questions:
>
> "Shall we continue to try to build merchant ships faster than enemy submarines can sink them?
>
> or,
>
> Shall we build anti-submarine craft of such character and in such numbers that we can sink submarines faster than the enemy can build them!"
>
> 2. The answer appears obvious.* It shall be made the premise for seeking priorities in the building program — and for "educating" all who have to do with the means for getting on with the war.
>
> 3. The foregoing premise has an obvious extension which embraces the general construction of combatant ships wherewith to overcome enemy means for the destruction of merchant shipping unless duly opposed by combatant ships of appropriate characteristics in adequate numbers in integrated combinations.
>
> E. J. KING

The question of building priorities was a major issue when Churchill and his advisors arrived in mid-June 1942 for the Second Washington Conference. On 23 June Roosevelt, Churchill, and King met in the White House with shipping advisors from both nations. King opened the discussion with a platitude that one ship saved was worth two ships sunk. The only way to save them was to provide adequate escorts — therefore the destroyer escort (DE) building program should receive high priority. Churchill agreed, but Emory S. Land, who headed the War Shipping Administration, countered that King's proposed DE program would prevent the building of from 100 to 150 merchantmen. Lewis W. Douglas, Land's deputy administrator, reinforced the argument that merchantmen should be given first priority, as they were in short supply.

Churchill had second thoughts. "One ship saved may be better than

* But perhaps not to the reader. King favored the latter alternative.

two ships sunk," he said, "but it is also far better that one ship deliver munitions to the fighting front than no ships at all."

Nothing was resolved. Despite blizzards of memoranda among Roosevelt, Hopkins, the JCS, and the War Production Board, DE construction lagged throughout the remainder of 1942. Roosevelt's decision to invade North Africa in November 1942 further disrupted the DE program as shipyards switched to emergency production of amphibious assault shipping. By 30 June 1943, twenty months after the United States had been at war with Germany, only 25 DEs had been commissioned. By war's end, however, some 498 had finally been built.

American ASW aircraft were as scarce as escort ships in early 1942, and the story behind this grievous shortage was complex and longstanding. Before the Second World War there had been a prolonged series of disputes over the organization, command, and control of naval and military aircraft. In the early 1920s Brigadier General Billy Mitchell and his followers had argued that all aircraft belonged in a separate service independent of the Army and the Navy. Congress rejected Mitchell's ideas and authorized each service to have its own integral air arm.

Questions arose as to the missions of each service's air forces. Navy aircraft would fly from carriers and Army aircraft would fly from airfields, but whose aircraft would be responsible for coastal defense and surveillance? In that case the Navy wanted to come ashore, insisting upon its own land-based, long-range aircraft for patrolling United States coastal waters. The Army objected, contending that any combat aircraft operating from an airfield had to be their own. If the Navy wanted long-range patrol aircraft, the Army said, let the Navy use seaplanes. The Army won its case in Congress, forcing the Navy to build seaplanes. But by January 1942 these were too few to protect the thousands of miles of threatened sea lanes in the Western Hemisphere. King quickly realized that he needed the Army Air Force and asked Marshall for help. The Army lent 84 medium bombers to assist the Navy and eventually provided over 300 aircraft to find U-boats on the East Coast, the Gulf of Mexico, and in the Caribbean.

It was not a harmonious arrangement. The Army pilots were trained neither for ASW nor for open-water navigation, and the patrols were usually long and boring. They would have much preferred the excitement of bombing Germany, the mission for which their aircraft and their training had been intended.

There were frequent disagreements on tactics and command-and-control procedures, as well. King, Arnold, and Stimson had bitter arguments. Thus both the Army and the Navy were eager to get the Army out of the ASW business. Eventually Arnold agreed to transfer a portion of his bombers to the Navy to be flown by Navy pilots. Both services undoubtedly were relieved once they could pursue what they considered to be their primary missions against Germany.

"The submarine situation on the east coast approaches the 'desperate,' " King wrote to a flag officer in March 1942. "All in all, we have to do the best we can with what we've got." Later in the month he was even more emphatic. In a memorandum to several other flag officers, King referred to the Battle of the Atlantic as the "desperate submarine attack situation along the Atlantic Coast."

King was inundated with complaints and advice from all quarters, including one such letter from Vinson. "The facts of the matter are," replied King, "that we have not yet got the 'tools' that are necessary to protect shipping in the Eastern Sea Frontier (Florida to Maine) — or anywhere else. Production is months upon months behind schedule.

"We have been — and are — taking over, manning and equipping every vessel of every kind that has any worthwhile characteristics for operations off shore and along shore. Included in these is a growing number of small craft which have no real military value but are being used solely as 'rescue vessels' whose primary mission is the rescue of survivors."

By the end of February 1942, Dönitz's small U-boat force had sunk some 31 ships off the East Coast. The frustrated, flailing ASW forces — such as they were — had not sunk a single submarine, because of their haphazard employment by Andrews. As tankers were frequent victims, worried oil company representatives asked to meet with the War and Navy Departments. The meeting convened on 4 March 1942.

The civilians were skeptical of ASW efforts thus far and suspected that the services still did not comprehend what was happening. Their tankers, they said, were being sunk faster than they could be replaced, and there were sailing delays because crews feared going to sea. Sooner or later, they insisted, there would be a "real shortage" of oil on the East Coast. Only so much could be delivered by means other than tankers. Could not more protection be provided?

The service representatives recited their standard excuses. Adequate ASW escorts and aircraft were unavailable. Forces were needed elsewhere for other high-priority commitments. Everything possible was being done.

But was it? The representatives of the oil companies suggested several elementary measures that would protect the tankers without additional ships and planes. For example, the coastal cities were still illuminated at night. Could not the government order them to turn off their lights? The service spokesmen hemmed and hawed: there was no federal law to make the cities do it, and so far they would not voluntarily cooperate. Miami Beach, for example, did not want to inconvenience its visitors during the tourist season.

The civilians persisted. If the services could not protect the merchantmen, could not the Navy at least route them closer to the coast and allow them to enter protected harbors at night? The Navy responded that it "would look into it." Finally, another civilian announced that he was forming a volunteer corps of civilian fliers to "combat the submarine menace." Although they would be unarmed, they could at least report any submarines they saw as well as increase the morale of tanker crews, "who now complain that they seldom see any protecting aircraft." The Army responded that it had no objection.

It is worth emphasizing that these initiatives came from laymen — oil company executives — rather than from professional naval and army officers. The most immediate benefit was the Army's offer to lend aircraft to the Navy. By mid-May the government was able to enforce coastal blackouts, and by early April the Navy established a partial convoy system whereby merchantmen were escorted by small craft by day and remained overnight in protected anchorages.

Soon after this meeting with the oil companies (and perhaps prodded by their suggestions), King appointed an informal board consisting of representatives from his own staff and from major commands involved with ASW. Find a way, he said, to organize escorted convoys in the Western Hemisphere. "Escort is not just one way of handling the submarine menace," he maintained, "it is the only way that gives any promise of success. The so-called hunting and patrol operations have time and again proved futile."

In late March King approved the board's plan, known as the Interlocking Convoy System, which matched available protection with what had to be protected. Convoys were routed and controlled by a schedule that resembled the one used by railroads. It probably was the best possible plan under the circumstances, yet it still could not compensate for lack of escorts and aircraft. They could not be everywhere. If they concentrated in one area, Dönitz would send his U-boats elsewhere. When East Coast defenses became stronger and better organized, Dönitz was forced to back off from the coastal convoys. But U-boats soon were operating in the Gulf of Mexico and the Caribbean, so that Allied shipping losses throughout 1942 continued to be astronomical.

King may have accepted the suggestions of the oil company representatives in March, but usually such advice — which he considered gratuitous — was unwelcome. In mid-April a U-boat shelled a refinery at Curaçao, Netherlands West Indies, a major source of petroleum. King received the news at lunch from an aide, who also reported that Under Secretary of State Sumner Welles was on the phone demanding to know how the Navy intended to prevent the same thing from recurring at nearby Aruba. (A U-boat had shelled Aruba two months earlier.) Russell Willson arose to take the phone.

"Let me handle this," said King. He went to the phone. "Welles, I hear you want to know what the Navy is going to do about Aruba. I don't know what Admiral Hoover * is going to do. If you'll take care of the diplomats, I'll take care of the Navy."

The President could not be treated so brusquely. In early July FDR urged King by memo to expedite organizing convoys, citing statistics that convoys dramatically reduced shipping losses. "I still do not understand the long delay in making all ships sail under escort," Roosevelt concluded. "I realize the problem of making up escorts for convoys but about three months have elapsed since we undertook it. I also realize that strict observance of convoy rules will slow up voyages of many ships but, frankly, I think it has taken an unconscionable time to get things going, and further I do not think that we are utilizing a large number of escort vessels which could be used, especially in the Summer time. We must speed things up and we must use the available tools even though they are not just what we would like to have."

King responded two days later. "I am in entire accord with your view as to the advantages of escorted convoys," King replied. "I have established convoy systems, beginning with the most dangerous areas, as acquisition of escort vessels permitted. I have used vessels of every type and size that can keep up with the ships they guard. I have accepted the smallest escorts that give promise of a reasonable degree of protection. . . ."

King went on to explain why convoy protection was still slow in coming, then concluded, "My goal — and I believe yours also — is to get every ship under escort. For this purpose we (the United States and Great Britain) need a very large number — roughly 1000 — of sea-going escort vessels of DE or corvette type. I am doing my best to get them quickly."

The public and press, too, demanded explanations. King did not want to be bothered. In mid-1942 he finally released an imperious statement

* Rear Admiral John H. Hoover, Commandant Caribbean Sea Frontier.

that began, "I have been urged to make some reply — or at least some acknowledgement — regarding the volume of criticism of the conduct of the anti-submarine campaign in those Atlantic waters where the U.S. has responsibility.

"It must be obvious that we of the Navy are even more concerned than are any of the critics or any of the other citizens of the U.S. because we have the responsibility and the critics have not."

King then quoted an article by Charles F. Kettering in the 28 March issue of the *Saturday Evening Post.* Kettering's theme was that undue criticism of the country's leaders would harm America's war efforts. "I heartily subscribe to Mr. Kettering's views," King then concluded, "and wish now to assure everyone concerned that the Navy will follow the rule 'Do the best you can with what you've got.' The submarine menace will, in time, be brought under control. I say 'in time' because only time will bring into service the adequate numbers of sea-going escort vessels which are essential to the extension of the use of convoys. It is obvious that escorted convoys are a major factor in the protection of shipping in that they enable enemy submarines to be met with and to be attacked and, when escort vessels are adequate in numbers, to be tracked down and destroyed."

Among the greatest demands on Allied shipping were convoys carrying Lend-Lease materiel to Russia. German aircraft and U-boats devastated convoys struggling through the Arctic Ocean to the ports of Murmansk and Archangel. Although the convoys were the Royal Navy's responsibility, the diversion of shipping to Russia affected the Battle of the Atlantic everywhere. Admiral Pound expressed the dilemma in an 18 May letter to King. "These Russian Convoys are becoming a regular millstone round our necks," Pound wrote, "and cause a steady attrition in both cruisers and destroyers. . . . The whole thing is a most unsound operation with the dice loaded against us in every direction, but at the same time I do, of course, recognize the necessity of doing all we can to help the Russians at the present time. What we do not know is how much what we are sending them really means to them. If the armaments we are sending them are absolutely vital to them at the present moment then of course we must continue to send them, but if it would do almost equally well if they arrived in July instead of during May and June then there is an unanswerable case for ceasing to endeavour to run these convoys whilst we are hemmed in by the ice."

King replied several days later. "I am very much in sympathy with your views," he wrote, "about the difficulties of running the Russian convoys for the next few weeks, but feel bound to say that we can only expect loud violent repercussions on the political level originating, of course, in Russia itself. However, I am prepared to support your views whenever you may decide to propose the change."

Both Roosevelt and Churchill were determined not to renege on their commitment to Stalin unless there was no alternative. The moment of truth came in July 1942. Shipping losses that month were so terribly appalling that nothing seemed left for a convoy to Russia. Groping for some way to provide better protection, King had even proposed stationing Allied aircraft near Murmansk. Eisenhower, then in London, warned that such a plan would not work, and it was dropped. After conferring with King, Roosevelt agreed with Churchill that the Prime Minister should advise Stalin that the next promised convoy would not be coming. Stalin received the news by commenting that his "naval experts" found the British arguments for canceling the convoy "untenable." The problem of convoys for Russia would continue to bedevil King and Pound for months to come.

Dönitz was winning the 1942 Battle of the Atlantic, at least statistically. In the Atlantic and Arctic Oceans U-boats had sunk over 1,000 merchantmen while losing only 106 German and Italian submarines worldwide. Allied shipping losses worldwide from all causes were 8.33 million tons, some 5.7 millions of this from U-boats in the Atlantic. Merchantmen construction lagged behind destruction, as Dönitz had hoped. Yet Dönitz was building U-boats at the rate of one per day by July 1942, and during a nine-month period in mid-1942 he averaged 75 submarines on station in the Atlantic. During all of 1942 American efforts to sink U-boats had been futile, only sixteen destroyed in twelve months. The Allies had to find a way to sink U-boats faster than the Germans could build replacements.

The Battle of the Atlantic was first priority when Roosevelt, Churchill, and the CCS met at Casablanca in January 1943. The British and Canadians thus far had been fighting most of the battle. A major problem was that American, British, and Canadian ASW forces each went their own way, failing to confer on common strategy or to exchange intelligence information and technical data. A team effort was imperative.

The crux of the problem was whether to combine for joint operations or whether to assign each country a zone of responsibility. King supported the latter alternative. He did not want to mix ships of different nationalities because of their inherent differences in doctrine and procedure. Let's work together, King advocated, but each in his own part of the ocean.

King then offered some more immediate suggestions. Could not the Royal Air Force hit the U-boats before they went to sea? The Bomber Command's notoriously inaccurate nighttime raids against German cities were to King a wasted effort. He urged instead that British bombers attack U-boat factories, shipyards, and bases. Under the circumstances, the Royal Air Force reluctantly agreed to shift some of their attacks to submarine-related targets. (A few weeks later Pound wrote King about the initial results. British bombers had attacked the German U-boat base at Lorient. There was much superficial damage, to be sure, but the U-boats themselves were unscathed because they were protected by concrete shelters. "I hope very much that we shall now go on to other ports," warned Pound, "but there is a very strong party here who want to get the whole bombing effort back again on to Germany.") *

A way to win the Battle of the Atlantic was not going to be found at Casablanca. There was not enough time, and the CCS agreed that a solution needed additional study and effort. Acting on the suggestion of Vice Admiral Nelles of the Royal Navy, King arranged another conference after Casablanca, solely to settle ASW matters. Thus the so-called Washington Convoy Conference secretly convened in Washington on 1 March 1943. There were about a hundred participants, including a score of flag and general officers, all representing the navies and air forces of the United States, Great Britain, and Canada. They comprised their countries' finest ASW talent, and thanks to King they had gathered together to find a way to win the Battle of the Atlantic.

King opened the conference with a keynote address, stressing to the conferees the scope of the task before them. "I take upon myself," said King, "the privilege of offering some advice as to how you should go about the matter at hand. You cannot consider anti-submarine warfare as divorced from the rest of the war effort. You must keep in mind the broad military decisions that have been approved by the Prime Minister and the President, upon which every phase of warfare must be based. . . ."

King reminded the British that they had to keep supplies flowing to Russia. "North Russian convoys must be provided for in any plan that the United States may be expected to accept," he said to his audience, but he also recognized the importance of Great Britain. "The United Kingdom," he said, "must be kept supplied as the citadel of war effort against Germany." King knew that the conference would generate bold schemes for finding and killing U-boats, but he was thinking con-

* Strategic bombing on the whole proved to be ineffective. The Germans protected their shipyards, and Allied airmen preferred other targets.

servatively. He charged the audience with but a single essentially defensive task: find a way to escort convoys and get them safely to their destinations.

Other senior service representatives spoke. King then withdrew. When the conference ended twelve days later, the three countries had agreed with King's concept of dividing the oceans into zones of responsibility. The British and Canadians retained control of North Atlantic convoys, while the United States became responsible for the Central Atlantic and the Interlocking Convoy system. Other procedures for Allied cooperation were also agreed upon.

King still had to get his own house in order. The sea war had become too vast and complex to be directed from the cramped facilities of Ingersoll's diminutive flagship. American ASW was handicapped in other ways, as well. King finally decided that one central authority was needed to organize, route, and protect the convoys; to direct and coordinate ASW ships and aircraft; to gather and collate operational intelligence; to sponsor the research and development of advanced ASW weapons and technology; and to administer the ASW training programs.

In early 1943 King established such an organization — in his own headquarters. King called it the Tenth Fleet, although it was without a ship to call its own. The ASW operating forces would remain under Ingersoll's nominal command. But King was stymied in his effort to find someone to command Tenth Fleet. He considered three rear admirals who were available, but none was suitable.

Selecting the Tenth Fleet chief of staff was easier. King chose Francis S. Low, newly promoted to rear admiral. (The reader will recall that "Frog" Low was a submarine officer who served under King on the General Board secretariat, on the Atlantic Fleet staff, and finally on King's COMINCH staff. In March 1942 Low had left to command a Pacific cruiser.) "Frog Low probably knew as much about King's way of thinking as anybody on the staff," Howard Orem later said. "He did not have the brilliant mind that King had, but he was a terrific worker, very logical and very loyal. He would get things done. If you had a tough job, you would give it to Frog Low."

Low fretted at King's delay in naming a Tenth Fleet commander. Finally in desperation he confronted the Admiral. "The Tenth Fleet commander should be a naval aviator," said Low.

King seemed slightly desperate himself. He hesitated for a moment, then replied, "He is."

"Who?" asked Low.

"Me," said King.

And so it was settled. King later explained his decision. "There were not the proper people available," he said, "so I wanted to keep it under myself." In reality, however, Low ran Tenth Fleet operations, with King exercising only general supervision. Command relations with Ingersoll were understandably sensitive. Low would tactfully recommend that Ingersoll take some appropriate action, rather than issuing orders directly to a ship of the Atlantic Fleet. King's authority to bypass Ingersoll was considered only once, when Ingersoll — in King's mind — had used poor judgment in a developing situation.

"I am going to take operational control," said King.

"You cannot do it," said Low.

"Who says I can't?" said King.

Low qualified his impetuous remark by explaining that matters were being worked out, making it unnecessary for King to interfere. This seemed to mollify King, and nothing more was said.

The Tenth Fleet staff comprised a specialized group of about fifty men and women, officers and enlisted persons, stationed in a control room near King's office. Every ship, every plane, and every merchantman that moved in the areas under American responsibility was monitored and controlled by Low and his staff. The Battle of the Atlantic had become a nautical chess game between Dönitz and Low.

King was obsessed with security. The fact that the Americans and British were decrypting many of the coded messages between Dönitz and his U-boats was the most closely guarded secret of all. King severely limited the number of those who knew about it, whereas the British gave the information a wider distribution. On the other hand, the British were more reluctant to act on decrypted information for fear of alerting the Germans that the Allies were reading their messages. King was more daring and ambushed U-boats at the risk of making the Germans wonder how the Allies knew where their U-boats would be.

King was so zealous about security that he even kept things from Low. Low confronted William R. Smedberg, King's combat intelligence officer, with his suspicions. Smedberg confirmed that indeed there was intelligence about enemy submarines that Low was not receiving. Low demanded to know everything.

"Sir," replied Smedberg, "my orders from Admiral King are that you are to know about any submarine in the Atlantic. If I know of a Japanese submarine coming from the Pacific into the Atlantic, you will know about that well ahead of time. But my orders are that you are not to know anything about enemy submarine activity in the Pacific."

Low was furious, but he was unable to persuade King to change his

Rear Admiral Francis S. ("Frog") Low, who directed the Battle of the Atlantic through the Tenth Fleet (National Archives 80-G-302311)

orders. But King was true to his word. Smedberg told Low about a huge Japanese submarine carrying important scientists to Germany to gather information on German weapon technology. When the submarine reached the Atlantic it began transmitting messages that betrayed its location. Low stationed three carrier ASW groups across the submarine's path, and the submarine was discovered and destroyed. "The kill was shortly confirmed by frantic Japanese signals asking the Germans for information on their submarine," Low later said. "Neither nation ever learned anything from anyone."

When the Allies seemed to be winning the Battle of the Atlantic by mid-1943, King worried that people would be tempted to reveal how and why the Allies were succeeding. King cautioned those involved in the battle not to divulge any information on new ASW developments. "Since any leakage of information," King reminded Emory Land, "would enable the Japanese to increase the efficiency of their anti-submarine measures, I am most anxious that every effort be made to maintain security. . . .

"I am particularly concerned that the optimistic attitude that now exists as to the war against U-boats may result in misguided enthusiasm in the course of which those who know our secrets may be inclined to tell all they know under the impression that, once the U-boats are overcome, it will make no difference who knows how we did it."

By mid-1944 Churchill was among those eager to tell all, for on August eighth he proposed to Roosevelt that the Allies publicize their success in the Battle of the Atlantic. King was appalled and urged Roosevelt to say no. Disclosing the tactics and equipment used to defeat the U-boats, King argued, might permit the Japanese to adopt the same means against American submarines in the Pacific. The President later sent a note of caution to Churchill in November 1944, after reading a news report by a Royal Air Force officer about such U-boat developments as the snorkel.* King worried that the Japanese might incorporate these improvements in their own submarines, perhaps on the assumption that the Germans were not sharing information with their Japanese allies.

One of the Navy's greatest intelligence successes was the capture of the German submarine *U-505* by Captain Daniel V. Gallery's carrier ASW group in June 1944. The German Navy assumed that *U-505* had been sunk and did not know that the U-boat had been captured. Gallery later gave King a German propaganda book from *U-505* entitled *Roosevelt's Kampf*. Roosevelt, it said, intended to rule the world. King gave

* An air breathing device allowing a U-boat to use its diesel engines while submerged near the surface.

the souvenir to Roosevelt, who wrote a thank-you note to Gallery. The President's good manners effectively compromised the secret about the U-boat's capture. Somehow Low read the President's letter and became enraged at Gallery, for now too many people in the White House knew too much. Gallery, of course, explained that it was King who had given Roosevelt the book. "They dropped the idea of teaching anybody anything about security," Gallery later recalled.

One of the most bizarre episodes in the Battle of the Atlantic was King's fascination with a convicted forger and former sailor named Cooper Beale Wysong. An inmate of the Michigan state prison in mid-1942, Wysong sent an unsolicited set of detailed plans to King which he termed a "Continental Shore Sub Patrol." The drawings and charts were so beautifully executed that King sent a complimentary letter to the convict. This encouraged Wysong to submit other plans and suggestions, all with the same superb workmanship. Whatever else he may have been, King reasoned, Wysong certainly was an artist with a flair for organization work.

After a year of such activity, Wysong asked King to request a parole so that he could do more for the Navy. King's staff had been concerned before at King's interest in Wysong. Now they were horrified. "I appreciate the favorable impression Wysong has made," wrote Russell. "He may not be such a bad character, and then again, he may be worse. Whatever he is, I can not advocate your being a party to getting him out of prison — for all I know, he has been working up to this for the past year. If you are nevertheless disposed to help him, on the gamble that he is too able to stay where he is, the only thing to do is find out the other side of the story from the State of Michigan."

"Draft letter," wrote King, and the next day he signed it, addressed to Governor Harry Kelly. A month later King looked ridiculous. "Jackson Convict Denied Freedom to Perfect Sub," headlined the Detroit *Times* on 27 August 1943. "Cooper Beale Wysong, Jackson prison inmate whose plans for an anti-submarine patrol have been hailed by Admiral Ernest J. King, commander in chief of the U.S. fleet, is not going to exchange his prison garb for navy blue.

"Despite Admiral King's request to Gov. Kelly that Wysong be paroled to give his amazing genius to the navy, the state parole board has ruled that it can give no more paroles to the smooth-tongued prisoner who graduated from the University of Indiana at 19, but has been behind prison bars since 1921 because of get-rich-quick schemes."

The article then quoted the parole board: "This man has had all the chances of parole that any man is entitled to. Each time on parole he has been involved in get-rich-quick schemes and has inveigled and embarrassed highly respected citizens of various communities. On many occasions he has saved himself from jail and prison sentences through his powers of persuasion and glib talk. We consider him incorrigible and an extremely poor risk for parole. Our board will no longer assume responsibility for his conduct in community life." In a similar article the Detroit *News* reported that King had praised Wysong's "deep knowledge of naval strategy." Said the *News*, "Wysong has been convicted four times in Michigan and twice in other states on bad check charges and has violated his parole three times in Michigan."

King had made a damned fool of himself.

Allied technology and industry finally provided the numbers of sophisticated ships and aircraft needed to overwhelm Dönitz. The North Atlantic convoys eventually received nearly continuous land-based air protection. In those areas beyond range of airfields, convoy escorts fitted with radar and improved weapons rammed through the wolf packs. The big break came during May 1943. Dönitz lost 41 U-boats, and he withdrew his dwindling fleet into the relative safety of the central Atlantic. It was the final repudiation of his tonnage theory. By July merchantman production exceeded losses and would continue at that rate for the remainder of the war. During the twelve months preceding the invasion of Normandy, convoys bearing arms and men to the British Isles passed unopposed.

Dönitz continued to shift his forces from one area of the ocean to another, searching for weaknesses in the convoys. None could be found. Escort ships and aircraft seemed everywhere. Beginning in mid-1943 escort carriers could provide air cover to convoys anywhere on the oceans. The carriers also operated as "hunter-killer" groups by attacking U-boats that had betrayed their positions by radio transmissions. Low's successor, Rear Admiral Alan R. McCann, later recalled, "I had a particularly outstanding lieutenant commander who would brief King every morning at 0900. He emphasized the locations of the various German submarines as if he knew exactly where they were, as I think he usually did. At least we made believe that he knew their locations."

King was forever worried that Japanese submarines would attack America's vulnerable shipping in the Pacific. But they never did. Instead their submarines supported their battle fleet, went on reconnaissance, or carried cargo to isloated garrisons. Although they did sink several valuable warships, the misuse of Japanese submarines was a godsend, for it allowed King to concentrate his limited ASW resources in the Atlantic.

"If the Japanese had done what they could have done," King said after the war, "they might have raised hell with the West Coast–Hawaii convoys. Thank the Lord they did not understand or learn much about managing U-boats from the Nazis."

By June 1943 King became cautiously optimistic. In a letter to Vice Admiral Andrews he wrote, "The U-boat situation looks very encouraging *for the time being*. In these matters I am afraid I am a hard-boiled skeptic — but I am always glad to be disappointed in my pessimism!"

On Navy Day, 25 October 1943, King decided he could publicly announce good news about the Battle of the Atlantic. Speaking in Indianapolis, King said, "The success of the Nazi U-boats against our shipping has been radically diminished." Citing statistics that he said were "convincing proof that our convoy system has been successful," King concluded, "Submarines have not been driven from the seas, but they have changed status from menace to problem."

King's speech was reported inconspicuously in the back pages of the New York *Times*, apparently having been regarded as Navy Day rhetoric. *Time* magazine mentioned it not at all. The public remained largely unaware that the Battle of the Atlantic had been won.

23

After Casablanca: Ships

King and his colleagues returned one by one to the United States in late January 1943, ready to implement the decisions made at Casablanca. Plans for the European theater were fairly clear: a midsummer invasion of Sicily, a strategic bombing offensive against Germany, an affirmation of continued aid to Russia, and, most important, the defeat of the U-boat threat.

But the Pacific was another matter. The CCS had authorized the seizure of the Marshalls and Carolines, and King was anxious to get started. But Nimitz was pessimistic. Before he began any new offensive he wanted more ships and men. When the two admirals met in San Francisco in February, King reluctantly agreed to wait until Nimitz's forces were substantially stronger. That would take months, as America's war production was just approaching full capacity.

The protracted war in the South Pacific was no less perplexing. The CCS had authorized the seizure of Rabaul, the huge Japanese base dominating the western Solomons and the Bismarck Archipelago. The JCS had to decide what forces would be assigned and who would command them. Although Rabaul was within MacArthur's area of responsibility, King continued to insist that Nimitz, through his subordinate Halsey, carry out the operation. Only the Navy, argued King, should command amphibious assaults, regardless of where they were. Marshall felt the Army could do it just as well and insisted upon MacArthur.

The matter of jurisdiction remained stalled until the JCS convened the so-called Pacific Military Conference in Washington on 12 March 1943. Staff officers represented Nimitz, MacArthur, and Halsey, while King represented the JCS. After briefing the visitors on the results of the Casablanca Conference, King invited Major General Richard K. Sutherland, chief of staff to MacArthur, to present his plan for taking Rabaul. Sutherland did, including MacArthur's shopping list of the forces he needed to do the job.

Sutherland effectively forced the Washington planners to interpret a key yet ambiguous phrase of the Casablanca agreement, which read, ". . . adequate forces shall be allocated to the Pacific and Far Eastern Theaters." The War Department reported the following day that it could provide MacArthur the troops but not the aircraft. The bulk of their aircraft had to go to Europe for strategic bombing, leaving very little for MacArthur.

The allocation of forces had become so critical that Anglo-American statements born of compromise only confused and angered the JPS. Definite ratios between competing theaters had to be established, but the ambiguous agreements at Casablanca were often so vague as to be meaningless. Just what did constitute "adequate numbers"? That very question sparked a savage debate between Cooke and Brigadier General Orval A. Anderson, the Army Air Force JPS planner. The Pacific representatives sat in awed silence as (to quote Mahan) "the admiral and the general quarrelled, as was not uncommon in days when neither had an intelligent comprehension of the other's business." Their disagreement on who would get what aircraft was bucked up to the JCS.

On 16 March the JCS met with the JPS and the Pacific representatives to try to resolve the issue. Despite Cooke's repeated pleas for specific guidance, it was soon apparent that King and his JCS colleagues could not interpret what they had agreed upon at Casablanca. Leahy finally injected the most compelling argument. "Whether Germany is bombed or not," said Leahy, "the American forces in Africa and the South Pacific must be adequately protected. If those troops are neglected, the Joint Chiefs of Staff could not face the people of the United States."

It was that sobering thought that forced the JCS to lower their expectations. MacArthur would go only part of the way to Rabaul in 1943, and the JCS would give him enough forces for at least that limited objective. Their belated reassessment was symptomatic of the Joint Chiefs' leisurely way of doing business, for it came almost two months after the initial decision at Casablanca that the Americans would go all the way to Rabaul.

Meanwhile, King's plans for the Central Pacific were being stymied, although there was one consolation. When the JCS decided to hold MacArthur back in the South Pacific, King suggested to Marshall that they get on with the recapture of Attu, which had fallen in the Battle of

Midway. Marshall agreed, and the JCS approved King's proposal. It was far, far short of the Pacific offensive King had envisioned earlier.

There was one more vexing problem to be resolved, that of command for the now limited Rabaul offensive. Would it be MacArthur or Nimitz? King finally yielded to Marshall in the interests of harmony. MacArthur would command, Halsey would "cooperate," and Nimitz could withdraw ships from the Solomons if danger threatened elsewhere.

The Casablanca Conference and the press of business when King returned had exhausted him. "I had about 3 weeks away from Washington — but — I didn't have 3 minutes away from 'the job,'" he wrote a friend. Weariness and pessimism could not be shed, even in the seclusion of his quarters aboard *Dauntless*. In a moment of melancholia King wrote to a classmate, John T. Burwell, who had retired from the Navy years before and was living in Millwood, Virginia. "I think it likely that it will surprise you to get a letter from me — but it will be no surprise to find that I have a favor to ask," wrote King.

"It is this — do you know of any small place (say, 5-30 acres) in your part of the country that is for sale — preferably one that one man can take care of and that has a 'modest' house and outbuildings?

"My objective is to acquire such a place — not too far from Washington — in readiness for the time when I give up hard work (this kind, at any rate) — and also, perhaps, to have in hand a place that I can live off, in case 'hard times should come knocking at the door.'

"I know this is a good deal to ask of you but I do feel that you will do what you can to meet my request.

"Life here is strenuous, of course, but so far I have managed to keep well and, on the whole, to remain as cheerful as circumstances allow — that is to say, I am not down-hearted in any way."

King's letter was an extreme example of his need to escape from the burdens of war. King's aides had become accustomed to his disappearing at about four o'clock each afternoon and not returning until time for supper on *Dauntless*. No one knew where he went. Once an unexpected summons came from the White House, and the frantic staff had no way to find him. Sometimes King would be away for as long as two or three days with no explanation other than "relaxation."

Most of King's afternoons and weekends were spent with women.

Two of them were Abby Dunlap and Betsy Matter, the two sisters (and Navy wives) whom King had first known in Coronado during the late nineteen thirties. King had kept in touch ever since, especially when

Stan Dunlap had served on King's Atlantic Fleet staff in 1941. When war came Dunlap went to sea, so Abby and her mother moved to a farm in Cockeysville, Maryland, just outside Washington. Betsy was often there, as well. Another frequent visitor was Mrs. Edward R. Stettinius. The farm became one of King's havens.

King had such an extraordinary friendship with the Dunlaps that he even became godfather to one of their children. "Abby was a very special person," Betsy once explained, "and she made people happy when they were around her. When 'A.K.' [Admiral King] was with Abby he could be amused and relaxed. He would return to work refreshed and ready for anything. He was crazy about both of them, both Abby and Stan."

Betsy resembled her sister. Both were warm, cheerful, beautiful young women who loved King and pampered him. "We were trying desperately to protect him," Betsy later recalled. "We wanted to give him a place where he could relax. Sometimes before he arrived we would cook chicken and corn. Then we would all sit out on the terrace and eat. Everyone would put their feet up and be completely relaxed."

King usually first had to unwind. "There would be times," Betsy later said, "when he would come in and sit in the tiny drawing room, stay in there for perhaps a half hour, and never say a word to anyone. We would leave him alone, and he would just sit there on the Victorian sofa with his feet stretched out and his head back. After a while he would come out and talk to people."

Sometimes the talk would be glib and lighthearted. The odor of ducks drifted into the living room one afternoon, and Betsy wondered why King seemed to ignore it. "Don't you smell it?" she asked.

"Of course I do," said King, "but I'm too much of a gentleman to say so." They both laughed. Abby and Betsy were pleased when the Admiral would laugh — Abby told him he should do it more often. King sent Abby the famous picture of him laughing during a wartime class reunion. King had inscribed the photograph, "Abby, you see it can be done."

It was a freewheeling atmosphere of give-and-take where few subjects were taboo. Abby and Betsy had husbands, brothers, and brothers-in-law in the armed forces, so the war was much on their minds. Often King would talk about his family, especially his daughters, or about current events and people in high places. If the women were facetious and irreverent King would be amused, and he was particularly tolerant with Betsy's ingenuousness. "He would reprimand me very gently," Betsy re-

King laughing at his class reunion. *Abby, you see it can be done.* (U.S. Navy photograph)

called. "I think he was trying to put some sense into my head. But he did it in a very gentle and subtle way." *

King's letters to Betsy when she was living in Norfolk reveal how he missed her company. "Do hope that you will be coming up this way," he wrote, still feeling the strain of Casablanca in February 1943. "I'd like so much to see you — and I don't seem to be able to come down your way. Yes — please — when you come up, do drop me a note giving your address and phone number. . . . Please take care of your sweet self. . . ."

Even when she was away, Betsy knew how to cheer him up. "All during the war I would send cartoons and jokes to him," Betsy later said. "He had a marvelous sense of humor, and very few people realized it." Afterward Betsy wondered if she had not perhaps been impertinent and presumptuous, but King always asked for more. "Please continue to send me the clippings," he wrote in the same post-Casablanca letter. "I get a lot of fun out of them!"

In the summer of 1944 Betsy moved to Patuxent Naval Air Station in Maryland to be with her husband, and there she had a premature baby. "At about four o'clock in the morning the doctor came in and said he had just received the strangest call," Betsy vividly remembered. "It seems that Admiral King had just called and asked the hospital if it wanted an incubator."

A letter, together with a book, arrived a few days later. "Dear Betsy," it began. "I have heard — from Abby — that you are in the hospital — and the reason why. I am sorry!

"I hope that this volume may serve to lighten your days — while you are speeding to entire convalescence.

"With love, I am

Ernest King"

King had another hideaway for weekend retreats. It was the northern Virginia farm of Paul and Charlotte Pihl, whom King had known since the early nineteen thirties. Paul Pihl was a senior naval officer and aeronautical engineering specialist who had served on King's staffs before the war. He was once again with King in Washington as a logistical planner. Hard working and innovative, Pihl was devoted to King. His wife Charlotte was a sister of Wendell Willkie. Coming from a political family, she was intellectually sophisticated and astute in the ways of Washington.

* "Stop being a Martha and be a Mary," King once told her, for Martha had busied herself around the house while Mary sat at Christ's feet and listened. "He knew the Bible backwards and forwards and could use it to make his point," recalled Betsy.

Their friendship had begun when they both had attended the same parties. King frequently came alone (Mattie disliked parties) and gravitated toward the Pihls. King discovered that Charlotte was interested in him, in his career, and in his ideas. She was someone he could talk to — about anything and everything that was on his mind. In time Charlotte became King's confidante.

The Pihls' farm overlooked the Shenandoah Valley. King usually arrived alone and went to the guest house, a stone building converted to a library. Inside were bedrooms and a huge living room with a large fireplace and book-lined walls. It was his haven — his Shangri-La, King called it — and there he remained, often missing meals and asking only for a sandwich. He sometimes brought papers, but more often not. The house was quiet and comfortable. King could think. No one disturbed him.

"The farm was such a great relaxation for him from the tensions of his work," Charlotte told the author. "He certainly loved it. When we first bought the farm Ernest was always talking about wanting to make an investment to make some money. He talked about possibly buying a share of our farm, perhaps by buying some cattle. We were against it, for if anything happened to him and our relationship became known, we could get into trouble. But we did let him buy several pigs and cows and then they were his, and he enjoyed going out to see *his* animals. He would be interested in how they were being cared for, and so on.

"He was always interested in what was happening on the farm, and what kind of crops we were planting and growing. Paul was working in Washington, so I ran the farm. That made it possible for Ernest to stick his nose in. He had to do a little bossing and arguing here and there."

Paul Pihl went to the West Coast in 1944, and Charlotte lived alone on the farm. King continued his weekend visits, and the two would talk for hours. Predictably, rumors began, given King's reputation with women. King did not help things. "He used to embarrass me," Charlotte recalled. "People would be standing around, and he would lean out the window and holler, 'Charlotte! Why did you have to leave so early?' "

Charlotte was aware of the talk. Some called her King's Lady Hamilton. "As far as I am concerned," said Charlotte years later, "my being the sister of Wendell Willkie caused great rumor and gossiping in Washington. A friend once told me that she had been with a group of people who were speculating on my relationship with the Admiral. Finally she spoke out and said that if you knew Paul Pihl, if anything was going on between his wife and any man, King included, that Paul would of course kick him out of the house immediately."

On vacation in Louisiana with classmate John M. Caffery (Courtesy Naval Historical Center)

Mattie began to resent the fact that King had time for Charlotte but not for her. Often she called to ask if her husband was at the farm. Charlotte would offer to have him come to the phone, but Mattie would ask Charlotte not to tell King she had called. Several times Charlotte invited Mattie to the farm, but Mattie refused. "Ernest doesn't want me to come up there," she explained.

King tried unsuccessfully to arrange longer vacations. Over coffee aboard *Dauntless* he reminisced happily about his duck-hunting expedition before the war, and he planned with George Russell to do it again in late 1942. As shotgun shells were scarce, Russell spoke to a contact in the Bureau of Ordnance. Four cases of shotgun shells quickly materialized. "But the Old Man never had a chance to go hunting," Russell later said. "He had to go to the Casablanca Conference."

King managed his only legitimate vacation in the early spring of 1944, spending eight days with his Academy roommate, John M. Caffery. No one recognized the Admiral, either on Caffery's sugar plantation or in the nearby town of Franklin, Louisiana. "I found it a different world—and restful," wrote King to Betsy, "so I almost literally 'did nothing—and did it slow.' "

King had made many promises during the Casablanca Conference in order to get British cooperation, promises that he could deliver the ships needed for the Battle of the Atlantic, the invasions of Sicily and Burma, and an offensive in the Pacific. Yet getting those ships was usually more than King could handle. Much of the procurement program (the so-called Two-Ocean Navy Act, for example) had been established before King became COMINCH and CNO, and the shipbuilding industry was committed to programs that had acquired a momentum of their own.

In theory, King (as the Navy's operational commander) would determine what he needed, Congress would authorize the procurement and appropriate the funds, and logisticians Horne, Knox, and Forrestal would deliver the ships. So much for the theory. Shortages of raw materials, of manufacturing facilities, and of industrial manpower made shipbuilding but one competitor among many wartime programs. Conflicting priorities were tough to resolve. King exacerbated these problems by not telling his logisticians enough about what he wanted. Future plans were so secret that those who had to deliver the ships might not even know the ships were needed. But the fault did not always lie wholly within King and his staff. In many cases the logisticians did not try very hard to talk to the planners.

Another problem was rearranged priorities, resulting from ship losses and changing strategic plans. The decision to invade North Africa, for example, gave priority to landing craft over destroyer escorts during mid-1942. "These changes in emphasis were one of the severest strains on the whole procurement system," wrote historians Robert G. Albion and Robert H. Connery in their book *Forrestal and the Navy*. "The building of a major warship, for example, required a myriad of different parts from hundreds, if not thousands, of contractors and subcontractors, and all had to be scheduled to reach the shipyard at the exact time to be fitted into construction. Such items loomed large in the estimate of materials and facilities which Forrestal was trying to make more systematic; but all such planning went out the window when battleships, for instance, were sidetracked for small landing craft."

In line with his theory that all he needed was a shopping list, King sent Secretary Knox a one-page memorandum on 15 May 1942 asking for 1.67 billion tons of warships for the two years 1942 and 1943.* These ships, said King in so many words, were what he needed to fight the war. Whether the United States had the resources to build them was not one of King's concerns. The only obstacle that mattered to him was the President. "It is considered advisable," King concluded, "that Presidential authority be obtained for initiating legislation for this combatant ship building program." Roosevelt obviously would have the final word, and Knox was no more than King's courier.

War or no war, King's requisition was not holy writ as far as Roosevelt was concerned. The President had longstanding ideas of his own about ship design and construction, as King probably had anticipated. "I wish you and Admiral King would talk with me about this proposed new building program," Roosevelt wrote to Knox a week later. "I should like especially to talk over the desirability of building 45,000 ton aircraft carriers, and the possibility of cutting the size of 27,000 ton aircraft carriers by four or five thousand tons and putting the saved tonnage into aircraft carriers of approximately twelve to fourteen thousand tons.

"Also, I should like to discuss the relative advantages of 13,600 ton heavy cruisers vs. the 11,000 ton heavy cruisers. I am inclined to go along without further ado with the program for the small light cruisers, the destroyers, and the escort vessels."

Roosevelt moderated over ship construction throughout the war, even to such details as canceling contracts for patrol craft and disposing of

* The simplicity of King's way of doing business is astounding when compared to the hundreds of pounds of paper generated today to justify shipbuilding programs. King did it with a one-page memorandum!

excess boats requisitioned early in the war. The President's dominance over King in these matters can best be illustrated by two controversial issues: escort aircraft carriers (CVE) and landing craft.

The President's memorandum above reflected his early interest in building small, cheap aircraft carriers, both to fight U-boats in the Battle of the Atlantic and to provide additional air support in the Pacific. Although a small number of escort carriers were by then being converted from merchant hulls, King had not proposed any additional CVEs in his 15 May memorandum. The Bureau of Ships was developing a standard design for possible future construction, but King's memorandum implied that he saw no immediate need for them.

About two weeks after King had signed his memorandum, industrialist Henry J. Kaiser approached the Bureau of Ships and proposed building some thirty or more CVEs of his own design within six months, providing the Navy did not interfere. Kaiser, who was almost without experience in ship construction, was figuratively thrown out on his ear, for the Bureau of Ships zealously guarded its prerogative as the sole designer of naval ships. Kaiser appealed to the President. In questions of emergency production of war materiel Roosevelt believed that energy was more important than efficiency, speed was often as important as quality, and costs mattered less than results. Roosevelt felt he recognized these qualities in Kaiser and ordered King to accept Kaiser's offer.

"Kaiser had the craziest ideas about machinery," King later said. "I didn't agree with the damned things, but FDR decided." After the CVEs began entering the fleet in quantity, King changed his mind. "When the Kaiser carriers really got started," said King after the war, "they did quite well."

The CVE program was placid compared to the landing-craft donnybrook with Andrew J. Higgins. Higgins was a flamboyant mass-production expert from Louisiana who denounced eastern financiers and Washington bureaucrats. Whether you liked him or not, he had designed a landing craft that would work, and he could produce it in great quantity. As might be imagined, the Bureau of Ships clung to its own inferior design, which was even unseaworthy under some conditions. The bureau's intransigence provoked Higgins to use his political connections. He appealed to Senator Harry Truman's Senate Investigations Committee, and Truman sent a scathing letter to Knox in the summer of 1942. The Secretary became appalled when he discovered the bureau's obduracy, and while he promised to start using Higgins's boats, he pleaded with Truman not to publicize the case. Nevertheless Drew Pearson published the story in September 1942, prolonging the ill will despite Higgins's real service to the Navy.

King hated Higgins, regardless of the merits of Higgins's design and his indispensable role as King's chief supplier of landing craft. A July 1943 letter that King personally wrote to Higgins illustrates their mutual antipathy. "Yesterday one of my aides said you were on the telephone," wrote King, "whereupon, being busy and about to leave the office for luncheon, I asked him to find out what your business with me might be.

"The word brought to me was to the effect that you were available if I wished to see you — my reply was to the effect that unless *you* wished to see me, I did not wish to see you.

"Some time later the same aide told me that you had called again on the telephone and asked him to repeat what I had said. When he had done so, you made a remark to the effect that you wanted to get the facts straight for the record, in case of a post-mortem.

"I have now to request that you inform me — in writing — as to the significance of the remarks made by you in your second telephone call, the substance of which is indicated in the last sentence of the preceding paragraph."

Higgins's reply, if any, is not recorded.

The need for merchant shipping grew throughout the war, and the very lack of it was the greatest impediment to Allied strategic designs. King and the President, together with Emory Land, searched for means to build more merchant ships and to use more efficiently those already available. It was the kind of problem that stimulated Roosevelt's ingenuity, and his fertile mind concocted a number of imaginative schemes that King tried to suppress as impractical. One Roosevelt brainstorm was a small, gasoline-driven merchantman dubbed "Sea Otter," which he directed King to develop. A prominent naval designer, Joseph W. Powell, was soon hired as a special assistant to Knox, with the task of finding reasons why Roosevelt's ideas would not work. One of his first assignments was to arrange the demise of Sea Otter.

By early 1945 the end of the war was in sight. Questions were being asked in Washington to justify continuing the Navy's wartime shipbuilding program. Harold D. Smith, the Director of the Budget, sent the President a two-page memorandum in January 1945, urging disapproval of the Navy's request for 84 new warships costing $1.8 billion.* Below his signature Smith wrote a postscript: "I sometimes ask myself — what

* That sum today might buy one aircraft carrier.

kind of insurance does the Navy want? Must it have several times the fleet of the enemy to establish self-confidence? I cannot believe it. It may be time to call a halt."

Smith's memorandum challenged the Navy's rationale for its future shipbuilding program. King was the logical spokesman to defend the Navy's request. The size and composition of the fleet should have been foremost among King's concerns, yet it was a responsibility that he inexplicably shunned. The question of whether to continue a huge shipbuilding program had already been addressed by a COMINCH staff committee headed by Rear Admiral Walter S. DeLany, King's Assistant Chief of Staff for Readiness. DeLany concluded that the war against Japan could extend well into 1948, and that there should be no reduction in shipbuilding.

DeLany had written the study solely for King on the assumption that the document would stop in King's office. To DeLany's chagrin, however, King forwarded the study to Forrestal with a perfunctory endorsement. Forrestal did not like DeLany's conclusions. The Secretary favored reducing shipbuilding expenditures, so he admonished DeLany for contradicting the Secretary's way of thinking. DeLany, already miffed at King for passing the buck, told Forrestal that he resented the implication that he was disloyal and that he intended to speak frankly when asked his opinion. His opinion was unchanged — the Navy should continue to build. The discussion ended.

In the tangled politics of Washington it made little difference what Forrestal or DeLany — or for that matter, King — thought about the size of the fleet. For it was Carl Vinson who had decided that the Navy needed 84 ships in the 1945 budget. Both King and Forrestal supported Vinson for the record. Indeed, Vinson even insisted that the Navy Department officially ask for the ships that Vinson had decided the Navy needed. Faced with a fait accompli, Roosevelt felt he owed his conscientious budget director at least the courtesy of a reply, and he asked Forrestal to write it for him. Forrestal passed the writing task on to King. King prepared (or had prepared for him) a convincing justification, which Roosevelt signed and sent back to Smith. It concluded, "I am inclined to support the proposal of the Secretary of the Navy."

Six weeks later Roosevelt changed his mind. Japanese sea power no longer existed as a threat, the Philippines and Iwo Jima had fallen, and the war's end could be more reliably predicted. It would certainly be over before the 1945-program ships could be delivered. So Roosevelt ordered the entire 1945 program canceled, and Vinson concurred. King tried to salvage something and asked for twelve CVEs, the very ships he had spurned in the beginning of the war. Roosevelt agreed, but in the end they too were canceled. The Navy's wartime shipbuilding program was finally over.

In retrospect, there had never been enough ships to fight the war. King was forced to juggle ships from one ocean to the other and, in the European theater, from one front to another. King allowed Nimitz a relatively free hand in moving ships within the Pacific, but the Atlantic was a different matter. King bypassed Ingersoll and communicated directly with his two principal European commanders, Admirals Stark and Hewitt, and through them controlled the allocation and distribution of ships overseas. Although Hewitt was ostensibly subordinate first to Eisenhower and later to Field Marshal Sir Harold L. Alexander,* King often bypassed the entire chain of command to deal directly with Hewitt. When King wanted ships moved into or out of the Mediterranean he simply told Hewitt to do it, leaving Hewitt with the embarrassing task of explaining to the theater commander why he was suddenly without ships he had been counting upon.

It was for these kinds of reasons that the British never trusted King and suspected that he often withheld shipping to thwart British aspirations. Sometimes they were right. On the other hand, King kept his word when he finally promised ships for an operation. Small wonder King was sensitive to all matters dealing with the assignment of American ships to the British, and he alone released all messages addressed to the Admiralty or to a Royal Navy command.

The COMINCH staff was taxed to account for King's thousands of ships. His war room showed only where ships had been, where they were going, and when they were scheduled to arrive. King was not interested in their daily locations en route. King's operations division — the "ship counters," as they called themselves — had other handicaps besides a shortage of information about the active fleet. Ships entered service daily, some so new that King's staff were often unsure what they were for. Still they had to be brought aboard and administratively assigned. To their credit, a captain and two lieutenant commanders kept the huge fleet organized and could usually tell King what ships were available for an impending operation.

King's staff shifted ships from one place to another by issuing a standard movement order. One such order got a newly commissioned submarine underway for the Pacific via the Panama Canal. En route it saw a periscope, made a laconic sighting report, and without pausing

* Successive Commanders in Chief, Mediterranean Theater.

continued its transit toward the Canal. When King saw the message, he asked the submarine what it had done about the periscope. "Nothing," came the reply; there was no certainty it even was a periscope, and in any event the submarine's mission was to proceed to the Panama Canal. The fact that it might have been a U-boat periscope seems not to have registered in the mind of the submarine skipper.

"King hit the ceiling," recalled COMINCH staff officer Charles M. Keyes, "and he asked the submarine what in the world could be more important than sinking an enemy submarine. As a result, every movement order after that time always included the sentence that the ship in transit, regardless of the circumstances, was to attack and destroy whatever enemy forces it might discover. This, of course, got rather ridiculous at times. For example, a small landing craft might have been built in Baltimore, after which it would proceed down Chesapeake Bay to Norfolk. Yet the movement order would still say it was to attack and destroy any enemy forces it might find."

However many ships King might have gotten to bring against the Axis, by themselves they were still inanimate steel vessels. It took men to bring a ship alive so it could fight. And getting those men was another of King's greatest challenges of the war.

24

After Casablanca: Men

As ships were built and entered the fleet, men had to be found and trained to command and operate them. That task belonged to Vice Admiral Randall R. Jacobs, the Chief of Naval Personnel, who had been a prewar assistant to Nimitz in the bureau. When Nimitz went to Pearl Harbor after the attack on Pearl Harbor, he convinced Knox to appoint Jacobs as his relief. Jacobs was a Pennsylvania Dutchman known for his stern and stubborn character, although at home, with friends and family, he could be friendly and amiable. Jacobs remained as head of the bureau throughout the war and was regarded throughout the Navy Department as "King's man."

Contrary to that reputation, Jacobs did not enjoy King's absolute confidence. "I knew there was something he was doing that was wrong," * King said after the war, "but I had to trust somebody." King regarded Jacobs as a fixer, who, like his predecessors Leahy and Nimitz, was given to compromise and equivocation. "The people I dislike," King once said, "are those who agree and say 'I think I can work that out.' For example, when Admiral Nimitz got together with General MacArthur and the President [in July 1944], the President wished to go into the Philippine Islands. Admiral Nimitz made some such remark as, 'Mr. President, if you want to go to the Philippines rather than Formosa, we can work that out.' You have to have that kind of mind to manage personnel. Promise anything. The question of putting it over is something else."

Jacobs's responsibilities were enormous. The Navy started the war with 325,000 people and ended it with 3,400,000. This figure was attained despite Roosevelt's persistent opposition, for the President maintained that the Navy always asked for more men than it really needed.

* King never said what it was.

Randall R. Jacobs, wartime Chief of Naval Personnel (National Archives 80-G-302278)

Less than a year before the war began, for example, Knox forwarded a request to the President to authorize an increase in naval manpower.

Roosevelt replied, "The dear, delightful officers of the regular Navy are doing to you today just what other officers were trying to do to me a quarter of a century ago. If you and I were regular officers of the Navy, you and I would do the same thing!"

Roosevelt held the view that it only took one year to train a crew for a new ship. "I don't believe in more Congressional authorizations. What I want for the 1942 Budget is the total number of men needed to man our ships during the fiscal year 1942 — not the total number of men needed to man battleships, cruisers, destroyers, etc., which will be completed in 1945.

"I think you will see my point.

"There is one other factor which the Bureau of Navigation * is wrong about. They are now asking for 115% of a fully manned ship under war conditions. In time of peace — or war — this unduly crowds the ship, makes for poorer morale, makes for epidemics, and is destructive of the idea of a 'happy ship.' Take the case of some of our ships today. There are too many men on board, either from the point of view of health or happiness.

"100% means 100% of perfection from the fighting point of view. 115% means a headache from every point of view. . . .

"This is a period of flux. I want no authorizations for what may happen beyond July 1, 1942.

"All of us may be dead when that time comes!"

As war approached, Roosevelt's refusal to plan more than a year ahead was the despair of the Navy. When war came, the Navy was undermanned as a result. Men had to be gotten in a hurry. The ensuing wartime mobilization was marked by chaos and confusion despite the best efforts of Jacobs and his bureau.

King's solution for conserving manpower was to reduce the shore establishment and send its men to sea. It was a natural attitude. Fleet-oriented officers traditionally believed that the shore establishment was bloated, and that it hindered rather than helped the ships at sea. Having achieved a position to do something about it, King attacked his shore bases with a vengeance. One of his favorite inquisition bodies was the Navy Manpower Survey Board, which was extraordinarily successful in finding men ashore and impressing them for sea duty.

Each in his own way, King and Roosevelt sought to limit the numbers of men and women in uniform. But despite good intentions, King's

* Later, the Bureau of Naval Personnel.

inability to predict the Navy's manpower needs was exceeded only by that of Roosevelt. A September 1943 memorandum that King drafted and sent to Knox shows King's simplistic philosophy of manpower economy and his weakness in logistical planning. "Consideration of the manpower problem in this country," wrote King, "has already led to some minor recommendations regarding the 'freezing' of certain categories of naval personnel.

"Further extended consideration of this issue now leads me to recommend that the Navy, the Marine Corps, and the Coast Guard be called upon to show cause why the manpower strength of all three services should not be 'frozen' at the figure approved by the President for attainment as of 31 December 1943." *

The President's 1943 manpower ceilings that King hoped to "freeze" had been won from Roosevelt only through the combined efforts of Budget Director Harold Smith and Admirals Leahy and Jacobs. By late 1943 even those figures were unrealistic. The JCS had just returned from the Teheran Conference and was committed to a cross-Channel invasion in the spring of 1944. Now King's logistical planners told him the Navy needed more men — many more. King began to realize that he would have to retreat from his position that the December 1943 levels could be frozen. King submitted his increased estimates to the President through Knox in February 1944, and again the President predictably balked.

"You would have difficulty in procuring personnel as fast as you suggest," he wrote Knox, "and I do not want any more training facilities built. I think you can make some improvements in the use of personnel, so as to keep within the figures I have already approved."

It took a threat from Knox (obviously initiated by King) to change Roosevelt's mind: the Navy would have to cease recruiting, and it would have to "drastically curtail presently scheduled operations." More simply stated, the Navy would have to stop fighting. This was an argument that the President could not resist, and with his approval the Navy's manpower began its climb beyond the three-million mark.

But even with the new ceiling, recruits were scarce. By March 1944 the Selective Service was barely providing its quota, and the Bureau of Naval Personnel searched for ways and means to economize with those already in uniform. Taking the larger view, King recognized that the entire country was short of manpower, both for the armed services and for the defense industries producing materiel for war. He would not ask Roosevelt for more men (he told Nimitz in May 1944) until he was

* Approximately two million men for the Navy.

convinced there were no other alternatives. Indeed, King had optimistically predicted several weeks before that the personnel on board by that September would be enough to finish the war.

Again he was wrong. By July 1944 King once again had to ask for more men, this time some additional 390,000. He still preached efficiency and as one expedient proposed removing older ships from service. When Nimitz argued that older ships could still support amphibious operations, King agreed but then reiterated that "he was faced with a serious manpower problem." It was a problem that would bedevil King until the end of the war.

Although King could not get involved in most of the details of managing people, King had exclusive jurisdiction over flag officers. With few exceptions, King exercised absolute control over their careers through his power to assign them at his discretion. Jacobs kept a large book containing the names and records of virtually every flag officer and senior captain in the Navy, and he would help King to decide how to get the right man in the right place at the right time. (We have seen in Chapter 16 how King also conferred with Nimitz before deciding upon flag assignments to the Pacific.)

A flag officer had to be qualified by experience as a captain before King would send him into combat. Line captains who aspired to flag rank got their mandatory experience by commanding a large warship overseas for at least six months. Another requisite for promotion was to be less than fifty-five years old. The turnover of commanding officers was correspondingly brisk. Although sailors might remain on the same ship throughout the war, captains, executive officers, and department heads changed with unsettling frequency. Flag officers and senior captains about to take command in a combat theater still needed "seasoning," which they got through temporary duty on a combatant staff or ship beforehand.

Granted, there were other considerations involved in flag assignments. For instance, King sent Rear Admiral Harry W. Hill to command the Tarawa assault because he had shown voluntary interest in amphibious preparations for Operation Torch while waiting in Washington for orders. As another example, MacArthur's chief of staff, Major General Sutherland, told King in Washington in March 1943 that he did not like Vice Admirals Herbert F. Leary and Arthur S. Carpender, both of whom had served as the senior naval officer in MacArthur's Southwest Pacific Area. "Carpender was too damn easy and didn't understand very well," said King afterward. "MacArthur didn't want him so I sent [Rear

Admiral Thomas C.] Kinkaid. I didn't think he had very many brains either, but he carried on with MacArthur through the war and did very well. He got tough with MacArthur on many things, especially when they got into the Philippines."

Perhaps King chose Kinkaid because he had saved the Navy's reputation earlier from an imbroglio in Alaska. From time to time flag officers in visible positions embarrassed the Navy and King. King's old shipmate, Rear Admiral Robert A. Theobald, the senior naval officer in Alaska, was one of them. Despite his reputation as a thinker, he had failed through poor tactics to prevent the Japanese from seizing Attu and Kiska during the Battle of Midway. Once the Japanese had dug in Theobald could not stop their reinforcements and resupply. Resenting his thankless assignment to Alaska and being of a quarrelsome disposition, Theobald alienated himself from both Nimitz and the Army forces in Alaska. He had to go. Kinkaid relieved him in early 1943.

When Theobald returned to Washington he demanded an explanation from King. Remembering Theobald's mercurial temper from earlier years, King tried to be tactful. But Theobald could not be pacified and demanded to know exactly what he had done wrong. King got mad and told him, making Theobald sorry that he had asked. He finished his career as a district commandant, another example of a peacetime reputation ruined by the war.

Theobald was one of several flag officers who had returned to Washington in disgrace. Admiral Thomas C. Hart commanded the ABDA naval forces in the Far East in early 1942. Hart lost his vigor and was increasingly criticized by the Dutch as being too ill and disspirited to carry on.* In order to placate the Dutch (and also the British), Roosevelt ordered Hart to relinquish his command to a Dutch admiral and to come home. Under ordinary circumstances Hart would have reverted to his permanent rank of rear admiral, and Knox told Hart that he wanted him to retire.

King felt that the Dutch had been unfair. Reverting Hart to rear admiral, although standard practice, could be interpreted as an admission that the Dutch had been right. "I was not going to allow the Dutch," King later said, "to think that he was coming down." Hart first knew of King's support when he visited King in his office. Not knowing King personally, Hart feared the worst. Instead he was gladdened. "He let me know," Hart later recalled, "that he had been sure that I was not sick or too decrepit for my job in ABDA and expressed regret that he had to act as he did in my removal."

* See Chapter 14.

King allowed Hart to retain his four stars and his title of Commander in Chief, Asiatic Fleet, even though the fleet no longer existed. King also went to Roosevelt and Knox and proposed a law that would allow a flag officer to retire as either a three- or a four-star admiral if he had held that rank for a year or more. Knox opposed the idea, but Roosevelt favored it. So did Carl Vinson. The law was passed, and Hart was allowed to retire honorably as a full admiral on 30 June 1942. He then served on the General Board and later was appointed as an interim senator from Connecticut. King had saved Hart's self-respect and his reputation.

Knox (and later Forrestal) influenced flag assignments to some extent. Knox had veto power over those tainted by Pearl Harbor and could also overrule King on flag assignments to the Navy Department. When the job as Chief of the Bureau of Ordnance became vacant in late 1943, the contenders had narrowed to Rear Admirals Carleton H. Wright and George F. Hussey, Jr. King favored Wright because he had just been in the war zone and (in King's words) had "a fresh view of matters in the Bureau of Ordnance, rather than a view predicated on recent and lengthy close association." Knox favored Hussey, among other reasons because he was younger by two years. Hussey got the job.

As the more junior flag officers moved into active fleet commands, King and Jacobs had to find jobs ashore for the vice admirals — and other flag officers as well — who were finished at sea but unwilling to retire before the legal retirement age of sixty-four. Many stayed beyond that age because no one wanted to quit with a war on, a war for which they had trained for a lifetime but which was about to pass them by.

King decided to make room ashore by enforcing retirements at sixty-four, a policy causing no end of anguish. King received poignant letters, many from friends or classmates, pleading to remain on active duty. "There surely must be some place in the Naval organization where I can do my bit," wrote a Navy Yard commandant in June 1942, "as I certainly do not want to sit on the side-lines during this war. Will you please give this your most earnest consideration?"

King wrote a sympathetic reply that offered a glimmer of hope, for during the first year and a half of the war he and Jacobs tried to employ retired officers in capacities other than command. But by mid-1943 even that expedient had to go. "Jacobs and I are already experiencing some difficulties because of the employment of retired officers on active duty," King wrote to another supplicant, "and we foresee that we may have to adopt the current Army plan of taking retired officers off active duty, which would be an extension of the existing policy in regard to retired officers in command status."

Trying as always to soften the blow, King concluded, "I am sorry to have to confirm what you have previously been told. You may be sure that there is no question whatever as to the good job you are doing—nor any dissatisfaction of any kind or degree." But some still hung on. As late as July 1945 some fifty-seven retired flag officers and several hundred retired captains remained on active duty.

Some were ingenious in avoiding retirement, including one Captain Walter G. Roper, who had been anchor man in the Naval Academy Class of 1898. Roper had persuaded Vice Admiral Jonas Ingram, King's representative in South America, to give him a job in Brazil. "What a hell of a time Ingram had with Roper," King recalled. "Ingram finally arranged for Roper to manage a rest camp in Recife, which I had to inspect. Hell, I got tired of inspecting, but it was part of my job."

Roper had assembled and trained a dozen ponies, and he arranged a race in King's honor. The race degenerated into a tangled mass of frightened horses and cursing men. Ingram was mortified. "Why the hell don't you get rid of him," said Ingram, "and send him somewhere else?"

"If Roper had worked half as hard at the Naval Academy as he did with his pony race," King replied, "he would have been at the head of his class rather than the bottom."

Another senior officer who came out of retirement was Rear Admiral Richard E. Byrd. Forced to leave the Navy as a junior officer on a medical disability, Byrd earned fame and further promotion as a polar explorer. He returned to active duty through political connections when war began and became King's self-appointed aviation advisor. One day a COMINCH staff officer who had just reported for duty received a memorandum from King: "Keep Dickie Byrd out of my office, EJK."

"It was a little obscure to me how I was going to keep Byrd out of his office," the staff officer recalled, "because I wasn't the guardian of his front office. But Byrd was becoming a damned nuisance with his Antarctic ideas, and he was bothering Admiral King." The staff officer decided there was nothing he could do. "That's the last I ever heard of it," said the staff officer. "I never saw him."

But Byrd was not easily dismissed, and Roosevelt insisted that he be assigned to a "suitable" aviation billet. King finally decided upon a long inspection trip to the Pacific. As Byrd was about to leave in April 1945 he sent a remarkable memorandum to King: "While I am away in the Pacific my brother Harry wants you to feel absolutely free to come to him, without any formality, about anything at any time. He has many friends in the Senate, and is close to President Truman since he controlled the 88 votes in the Chicago Convention that were finally turned over to nominate Truman for the vice presidency. So you must not hesitate to call on Harry. Anything you say to him will be treated entirely confidential. I believe Harry is going to write you himself.

"And further, don't forget that Jimmy Byrnes wants you to come to him at any time that he can help you. He is a close friend of my brother's and also of President Truman."

Most naval officers gauge the success or failure of their careers by whether or not they are promoted. Their morale, incentive, and performance depend upon whether they accept and understand the basis for promotion and consider it to be fair and impartial. Before the war, promotions were orderly and tightly managed, using selection boards of senior naval officers. But after war began, officers could not be spared from the fleet to convene selection boards, and the rapidly expanding officers' corps would make the peacetime system too slow and cumbersome. A new promotion system had to be devised as a wartime expedient.

On 30 June 1942 Congress suspended selection boards for the duration. In their place the Navy substituted a "panel" of officers who would recommend other officers for selection up to the rank of captain. The panel's recommendations were forwarded to the Secretary of the Navy, who convened a board of review comprised of King, Horne, Jacobs, Edwards, and a handful of other flag officers as appropriate. They made the final decisions. The list was not made public.

The promotions to rear admiral were handled somewhat differently. From time to time the Bureau of Naval Personnel sent lists of eligible captains to a number of flag officers in the fleet and asked for their recommendations. This system was admittedly imperfect and often unfair, because a flag officer might not know all the captains on the list and might thereby fail to vote for an otherwise well qualified captain. These votes were then tabulated in Washington, whereupon the Secretary of the Navy convened a board of King, Edwards, Horne, Jacobs, and usually the Chief of the Bureau of Aeronautics, as there was a great need for aviation flag officers. At least four votes were needed for selection.

King saw the dangers of mobilization and tried mightily to limit the number of line admirals in the Regular Navy. What King feared was that when the war was over the Navy would contract and become stuck with too many tenured peacetime flag officers. Promotions to admiral would be stifled. With no room at the top, promotions in the lower ranks would also slow, even cease. The naval officer corps would stagnate.

King succeeded. There were perhaps a hundred flag officers when war began, and about 225 when it ended. As the Navy's total manpower was ten times greater at war's end than in December 1941, King had kept his admirals from increasing geometrically. Although staff corps, reservists, and retirees on active duty brought the overall flag strength to about three hundred, many of these latter officers could be immediately released at war's end.

King was frequently embarrassed by the imperfections of the wartime selection system, especially when a newly promoted flag officer failed to achieve King's expectations. Promotions to any rank required Senate confirmation. King wanted to circumvent the system during the war, however, by making all promotions probationary and not subject to Senate approval. If a newly promoted officer failed to perform under King's plan, the Navy Department could revert the officer to his original rank. Roosevelt accepted the idea, but the Senate did not, jealously preserving its confirmation prerogative.

The Army's solution was literally to rip the stars from a general's shoulders and to replace them with a colonel's eagles. But the Navy—for reasons imposed by Congress—gave immediate tenure to its flag officers, regardless of subsequent performance. King's solution was to bounce a poor performer into an inconsequential shore-duty job. King recalled after the war that less than a dozen had been so transferred, although the number was probably higher.

King tried to overcome the tenure problem by resurrecting the grade of commodore, an ambiguous one-star rank ostensibly equivalent to brigadier general. The Navy had abolished the rank years before, presumably because a commodore was not a "flag" officer, although a brigadier general was a "general" officer.* King's idea was to promote captains to commodore, evaluate them for six months, then promote the best ones to rear admiral (not unlike the trial of a deacon before he is ordained priest). Roosevelt agreed, but as features of this plan again conflicted with the Senate's confirmation prerogative, King did not get his way.

* The matter of equivalent ranks is complicated. A rear admiral has two stars, so a newly promoted rear admiral immediately becomes senior to a one-star brigadier general who may have held that rank for several years. Navy rear admirals are also divided into two categories, upper-half and lower-half, thereby indicating seniority and pay classification, although all wear two stars. Together with the naval practice of spot promotions (explained later), temporary promotions, and "frocking" (wearing the insignia but not receiving the equivalent pay), the insignia worn by a naval officer is frequently misleading.

King soon found another use for commodores. There was intense pressure to promote reserve captains and retired captains on active duty in order to recognize those with important wartime jobs. Such officers were "spot" promoted, an expedient of advancing to higher rank by administrative fiat. King wanted to restrict the numbers of spot promotions to rear admiral and convinced Knox and Roosevelt to substitute the lesser rank of commodore, which was reestablished in April 1943.

The President's approval was contingent upon the rank being given solely to "fighting men," a restriction that the Navy Department frequently ignored. But perhaps because of the President's policy, the commodore's role was expanded beyond King's original concept to include regular line captains who had group commands or chief of staff assignments in the fleet. Many senior flag officers — Halsey, for one — did not like the commodore rank because few went on to become flag officers. (Arleigh Burke, chief of staff to Marc Mitscher, was one of the conspicuous exceptions.) Whatever the pros and cons, by mid-1945 there were over one hundred commodores on the active list of the Regular Navy. After the war the rank was again eliminated.

The law that allowed Hart to retire as a four-star admiral gave wartime tenure to all other three- and four-star flag officers as well. Once a flag officer had been promoted to vice admiral he stayed a vice admiral, even though he may have been a bust. And unless a senior flag officer had reached mandatory retirement age, he could continue on active duty for the duration. Some became an "embarrassment" to King, but, as he told Nimitz in December 1942, he was "stuck with them."

But King had no one to blame but himself. Nearly every vice admiral who had been promoted during the war had been recommended by King to the Secretary of the Navy. There were no selection boards for promotion above rear admiral, unless King could be considered a board of one. If the Secretary approved King's recommendation the nomination went to the White House, probably with Vinson's concurrence. In some cases King had to argue at length with the Secretary over a nominee's merits. Other nominations were swiftly approved, especially if they coincided with a battle in which the nominees were involved — and winning.

King revealed the complexities of wartime promotions in a July 1943 letter to Adolphus Andrews. "The old question of promotion of senior officers has been difficult — and even vexing," wrote King, "and continues to require a great deal of consideration by both Jacobs and myself. . . . Jacobs and I will continue to feel our way along in this matter because we have reason to know that, unless we go slow, we shall find ourselves under great pressure to recommend promotions on the basis of 'long and faithful service' — which is not enough!

"It would take too much of my time and yours to write all the factors that enter into the question of promotion to commodore and the 'spot' promotions to rear admiral. It is understandable, of course, that the 'wholesale' promotions in the Army have led many people to the snap opinion that the Navy should do likewise. So far, however, I think it can be said that the Navy has justified every one of the promotions made, even if it seemed to have been slow about it. The situation is complicated, naturally, by the 'special privileges' accorded to the staff corps, but I hardly need to tell you that this is none of my doing." *

Promotions sometimes became ludicrous. When retired Admiral William H. Standley was appointed as Ambassador to the Soviet Union in the middle of the war, he asked for a junior captain from King's staff as his naval attaché. King was willing, but Standley insisted that the captain be promoted to have seniority equivalent to the other naval attachés in Moscow. As the captain had been in his present rank little more than a year, King nominated him for commodore. Roosevelt, however, refused to approve because of his policy that the rank was for "fighting men" only. Standley finally persuaded King to recommend the captain for a spot promotion to rear admiral. Roosevelt immediately approved. Standley left for Moscow with the youngest rear admiral in the United States Navy, who had just passed his forty-fourth birthday.

War traditionally means faster promotions for more officers, but in King's navy many career officers still failed selection. Hurt and resentful, those who had been passed over often blamed the wartime promotion system. And in peace or war there would always be jealousy and envy and the question, "Why him and not me?" Horne passed the gist of these grievances to King in a February 1943 memorandum. "Throughout the past six months," wrote Horne, "I have had come to my ears a number of complaints regarding the selection of officers to flag rank with particular stress laid upon the lack of knowledge as to how selections are made, with the direct inference that this uncertainty is having an adverse effect on morale." King was unconcerned. "Of course," he replied to Horne, "we all realize the complaints do not come from the 'haves' but from the 'have nots' and that it will probably always be that way!"

King was in a position to know. Scores of letters crossed King's desk

* King was referring to the decades of controversy between the line and the staff (Supply Corps and Medical Corps, for example) over equitable promotion policies.

from special pleaders, officers and enlisted persons alike, who had been passed over, were seeking better assignments, or were asking favors or special consideration. King miraculously found time to answer them all. Many replies he wrote himself, while others were written by his personal staff with King's guidance to use "appropriate phraseology." Usually, before answering, the staff would get information from the Bureau of Naval Personnel on the supplicant's service background and current status, and in most cases the recommendations of the bureau were incorporated in King's reply.

In some cases King would be able to help. He was, for example, willing to write letters of recommendation for those seeking commissions, appointments, or civilian employment, yet he would never go beyond his own personal knowledge of the individual.

Many people had served with King during his forty-plus years of naval service, and many tried to capitalize on those past associations. King was invariably kind to old shipmates, yet if they were in trouble through their own misconduct, he made them accept the consequences. To a Marine lieutenant colonel, he wrote, "It seems that your professional reputation is high — just as it was when we served together in the Lexington. It has been very clearly indicated to me that your trouble is one which is expressed as follows — intoxicating liquor and business do not mix and you have had considerable difficulty in learning this fact. The particular incident made known to me is one which occurred in April, 1941, in Guantanamo, when the maximum disciplinary action, short of general court martial, was taken in your case. . . ." King admitted that he was being "blunt — even brutal," and he counseled the officer to go on the wagon as King already had done. The officer could still redeem himself, said King, if he would take King's advice.

A commander wrote to King in 1944, "Just learned that the last selection board gave me a down chit for Captain. Will you please get out Captain Gallery's last fitness report on me and have them reconsider and promote me to Captain."

King immediately replied, "I have your letter of May 14th which — to put it mildly — amazes me.

"You should know that promotion is still governed by application of the selection principle in the form of a panel of at least 9 senior officers. Consequently, I would not think of taking steps to 'have them reconsider and promote me to captain.'

"The thing for you to do is to address a letter to the selection panel via the Chief of Naval Personnel, in which you brief the 'high points' of your record and explain the 'low points' (if any)."

King's response showed his reverence toward selection boards. Their decisions were inviolable, and he would not interfere. He sympathized with those who had been passed over, yet if they asked King why they had failed selection, he rarely would speculate. Instead he would answer simply, "Lack of votes." To a disappointed captain and friend who had been passed over for flag selection, King wrote, "Personally, I have been careful to refrain from participation in the selection process except in so far as my services have been 'requisitioned' by the Secretary, just as the services of other flag officers have been 'requisitioned.' . . . I do not know that this response to your letter will be satisfactory to you — however, it is the best that I can do in the circumstances."

In retrospect, there has been considerable speculation about King's influence in wartime promotions. He did, of course, to a large degree establish promotion policy, but that was within the prerogative of his office. Promotions to vice admiral and admiral, as well, were almost entirely dependent upon King's approval, yet those too had always been the CNO's prerogative. Given King's long-held respect for the Navy's selection board system, there is every reason to conclude that he did abide by the decisions on promotions to rear admiral and below. To date no one has proved that King used his authority and prestige unfairly to influence the promotion of those he favored or disfavored,* the sole exception being the unfortunate Commander Seligman, who had compromised security during the Battle of Midway.

Promotions aside, there nevertheless was a feeling on King's staff that he sometimes did grant special favors to special friends. "He was always a sucker for old shipmates," George Russell later said, "some of whom I thought were on the worthless side, trying to work him for something." For example, a senior naval officer and friend of King who had been executive officer of a ship sunk early in the war had obviously become mentally disturbed by the experience. It was not his first disaster; he also had survived a dirigible crash in the 1930s. Disregarding the advice of his staff, King ordered the Bureau of Naval Personnel to give the officer a command ashore. He lasted only a few weeks and then returned to the hospital. King still continued to try to salvage the officer's career until he finally retired. It was such episodes that caused the COMINCH staff to conclude that, if King did have a "blind spot," it was his indiscriminate solicitude toward shipmates of ages past.

Without question King was loyal to those who had served him well, and his memory was long. In July 1942, as King was inspecting a naval air station in Texas, he recognized a chief boatswain's mate, Clifford F.

* See the author's additional comments on this subject in the bibliography.

Jones, who had been a star first baseman on the championship baseball team that King had organized on USS *Wright* fifteen years earlier. The sailor told King that he intended to christen his infant son Ernest Joseph King several days later. King was so moved that he afterward wrote to Jones, "Naming your new-born son for me was an honor and a tribute that I deeply appreciate and shall never forget.

"However, this young namesake of mine doesn't know what is going on, at this time. When he is old enough to understand, I wish him to have something he can grasp, physically as well as mentally — so I am sending, under separate cover, a silver cup duly inscribed."

25

Trident

As winter waned and spring approached in early 1943, the war in Africa was nearly over and the Solomons were almost secured. The eternal question of What next? again faced the Allies. The invasion of Sicily was already confirmed, for it had been authorized at the Casablanca Conference in January. But the Allies still had to resolve whether to invade the Italian mainland. And the greatest issue of all was when and under what circumstances to invade France.

In the Far East the British had failed to take the Burmese coastal city of Akyab, which the Casablanca Conference had envisioned as a preliminary to Operation Anakim (the seizure of Burma). Dismayed by operations in southeastern Asian jungles, the British were ready to abandon Anakim. China, meanwhile, was demanding help that Anakim was supposed to provide. The two principal American general officers in China, Joseph W. Stilwell and Claire Chennault, could not even agree what that help should be Stilwell wanted support for his ground forces, while Chennault advocated air power.

Finally, there was the question of the war in the Pacific. Although the CCS had approved King's concept of offensive operations there, the allocation of resources between the European and Pacific theaters was unresolved.

Given these issues, another CCS conference was inevitable. And when the CCS did meet, the Americans were determined to be better prepared. Recalling the Casablanca Conference, King remarked to his JCS colleagues that every time the British had brought up a subject, they always had a paper ready to support it. The unity and staff work of the British had so galled the Americans that they finally had resolved to beat the British at their own game. Next time they would overwhelm the British with a blizzard of position papers.

Good position papers depend on efficient staffs, which had not been a distinguishing feature of the JCS during 1942 and early 1943. During the first months of 1943 the JCS struggled to reorganize itself into more efficient planning committees, and by early May King and Marshall were generally satisfied. It was almost too late. Roosevelt and Churchill had arranged on short notice to meet in Washington on 12 May for what became known as the TRIDENT Conference. Caught by surprise once again, the JCS ordered their newly formed Joint War Plans Committee (JWPC) to produce position papers — and fast.

Captain Charles J. Moore was the senior naval member of the JWPC, and he later related the reaction when they heard that the British were coming. "The Joint War Plans Committee was established on Saturday the first of May," Moore recalled, "and on Sunday the second of May we learned that Mr. Churchill and the British Chiefs of Staff, with all their planners, were coming to Washington the following week for a conference. We had no knowledge of the agenda or what the British aims were or why they were coming, and we had to make a conjecture of what we should do first."

The JWPC, together with the Joint Strategic Survey Committee,* produced a profusion of papers by laboring day and night against the deadline of the British arrival. King scarcely had time to read them, much less change anything, so he and Marshall were forced to accept what their planners had written and to hope for the best.

The British meanwhile traveled to the United States on the *Queen Mary* with a staff of more than a hundred, who generated position papers as relentlessly as their American counterparts. Brooke was pessimistic. "I do not look forward to these meetings," he wrote in his diary during the voyage, "in fact I hate the thought of them. They will entail hours of argument and hard work trying to convince [the Americans] that Germany must be defeated first. . . . It is all so maddening, as it is not difficult in this case to see that, unless our united efforts are directed to defeat Germany and hold Japan, the war may go on indefinitely." King was the obstacle that Brooke dreaded. "The American departure from our basic strategy was mainly due to Admiral King," Brooke wrote in his memoirs.

Brooke believed to the very end that King sent ships and materiel to the Pacific to the detriment of the war against Germany. It is true that King never let Brooke forget that he controlled most of the shipping.

* See Chapter 21.

It was a bargaining technique that King had used before, and not always subtly. When the British later hedged during TRIDENT on establishing a date for the cross-Channel invasion, King reminded them of the "dangers of tying down forces and equipment to await eventualities." Without a firm date, said King ominously, landing craft and other valuable equipment that were urgently required in the Pacific would be lying idle in England. King's message was unmistakable.

Brooke's pessimism was made worse because he had reason to believe that American public opinion favored intensifying the war against Japan. "This was the emotional background against which Brooke and his colleagues had to contend," wrote Brooke's biographer, Arthur Bryant. "Its spokesman was the tough and stubborn King — the old crustacean, as one of his countrymen called him — the ablest strategist on the American Chiefs of Staff, though overshadowed in statesmanship and grandeur of character by the great Virginian, Marshall. It was supported by the prestige, the immense manpower — three times larger than that of Britain — and the productive capacity of the most vigorous and self-confident nation on earth."

It would be the first CCS conference attended by Leahy, who by his seniority became chairman during the TRIDENT meetings. Leahy was accustomed to the role, as he was also the chairman ex officio of the JCS. Given the frequent division between his JCS colleagues, Leahy's greatest contribution was to arbitrate behind closed doors by asking the right questions.

One of Leahy's keenest observers was Captain Robert L. Dennison, a JCS staff officer.* "Leahy was the one that could bring this group together," Dennison later said. "He didn't really use any pressure, but his technique was most interesting. . . . Marshall, for example, would start discussing some plan of his, something he thought we ought to be doing next, and Leahy would say: 'Well George, I'm just a simple sailor. Would you please back up and start from the beginning and make it simple, just tell me step one, two, and three, and so on.'

"Well, Marshall or Arnold, or whoever it was, kept falling for this thing, and they would back up and explain to this 'simple old sailor.' And as they did it — which is what Leahy knew damned well would happen — and went through these various steps, they themselves would find out the weakness or misconception or that there was something wrong with it. So he didn't have to start out by saying: 'This is a stupid idea and it won't work.' "

* Later he served as naval aide to President Truman, then went on to become Commander in Chief, Atlantic Fleet.

King, however, often saw through Leahy, having known him for forty years. During a discussion of current Japanese operations, Leahy chided King for his caution. "When I was a boy," said Leahy, "I was brought up with the idea that the U.S. Navy was invincible."

"Admiral," responded King, "when you were a boy, who would have believed that the Japanese would have taken over the Philippines and Southeast Asia?"

The first plenary meetings, on 12 May, opened with long soliloquies by Roosevelt and Churchill. The CCS got down to business on the thirteenth. By now the conflicting views of the two countries had become so well known that each could have recited the other's arguments by heart. The CCS knew they would eventually have to compromise, but they were constrained because their staff officers were in the same room. As the staff had written the position papers they had a proprietary interest in the proceedings, intimidating their chiefs by their presence alone not to deviate from the party line.

Leahy immediately got to the point as he opened the first meeting. He intended to read, said Leahy, the JCS strategic concept for defeating the Axis. The British listened, asked for time to study the one-page paper, and said they would respond to it the next day. The meeting then went on to discuss other business.

Next day the British identified their first major disagreement with the JCS paper, the so-called "paragraph 2.b" statement dealing with the war against Japan. "Simultaneously, in cooperation with our allies," it read, "to maintain and extend unremitting pressure against Japan in the Pacific and from China." That kind of pressure, said Brooke, could well cause a vacuum that would suck forces away from Europe and jeopardize the war against Germany.

Leahy responded with an even more emphatic statement of Pacific strategy. Reading from a JCS paper entitled "Conduct of the War in 1943–1944," Leahy intoned: "Simultaneously, in cooperation with other Pacific Powers concerned, to maintain and extend unremitting pressure against Japan with the purpose of continually reducing her military power and attaining positions from which her ultimate unconditional surrender can be forced."

The King-Brooke struggle was underway.

Two days later the CCS had not yet even agreed upon an agenda. They had listened the day before to opinions on the war in China, which had only added to the already overwhelming complexity and scope of the worldwide problems facing the CCS. Where were they to begin?

King was waiting for just such a moment. One of his primary objectives at the TRIDENT Conference was to develop a "master plan" for the conduct of the war. The American chiefs had tried for this at Casablanca but had failed. Undeterred, King and the JCS wanted to try again to get British agreement on a long-range plan. (And they wanted it in writing. King once confided to friends that the British "were apt to forget what they had promised.") Such a plan would be difficult, because the British still preferred a policy of opportunism and avoided long-term commitments.

King now spoke. "The first step," he said, "should be to set out agreed basic fundamentals." It was a theme which King repeated again and again: the need to address strategy as a whole from the broadest possible view; the need to agree upon a framework of what was essential to win the war; and then — and only then — to develop plans to implement the broad strategy. This time Brooke agreed. The planners tried to articulate those basic fundamentals overnight, but they only confirmed what was already apparent. The Americans and British could not agree on the broad strategy for the defeat of Japan. The best they could do was to define their differences in writing.

The impasse over Japan strained everyone's nerves. The questions of the cross-Channel invasion, future operations in the Mediterranean, and aid to Russia and China — all seemed capable of compromise. But Japan was different. King had Marshall and Leahy on his side and would not back down. Nor would Brooke. Marshall arranged for the CCS to spend the weekend relaxing at Williamsburg to ease the tension.

On Monday, 17 May, the CCS resumed their morning meetings. Still feeling hindered by the presence of their subordinates, they finally cleared the room so they could speak freely and off the record. All recognized their mandate to negotiate an agreement on future grand strategy — Roosevelt and Churchill expected it of them. King, for one, vividly remembered that at Casablanca the two political leaders had refused to accept what the CCS had first proposed. "They told us we would have to do *much* better," King later said. "We sharpened our pencils and worked like beavers. Then in the final session Roosevelt and Churchill patted each other on the back and congratulated each other on what expert needlers they were."

Now the issues at TRIDENT were on the table, and the bargaining could begin. The British wanted to invade Italy and continue operations in the Mediterranean. Knock Italy out of the war, they maintained, and Japan and Germany would be demoralized. Nonsense, King retorted.

The CCS at TRIDENT. The staff officers inhibited compromise until they were cleared out. (U.S. Navy photograph)

Italy strained and drained Germany's resources. Let Hitler keep it. Italy's only benefit to the Allies would be airfields for attacking southern Germany. But it would be more of a liability. If the Italians became wards of the Allies, it would require scarce shipping to provide them with food, coal, and other supplies. And what about the British idea of attacking the continent through Italy? "Hannibal and Napoleon crossed the Alps," said King, "but times are different now."

The British zeal for the Mediterranean was a contrast to their aversion to opening the Burma Road to China. Jungle warfare produced few benefits from the British view. The Japanese had whipped the British when they had tried to seize a foothold in Burma's northwest coast. Roosevelt and the JCS desperately wanted to keep China in the war and had summoned both Stilwell and Chennault to Washington to plead their special cases. If China fell, King visualized prolonging the war by ten to fifteen years. King wondered why Japan did not finish the job: China was for the taking. Somchow the Allies had to provide moral and logistical support to Chiang's shaky government. But everything depended on the British, and Field Marshal Wavell, the British theater commander, seemed to King a defeatist who missed opportunities.

If China seemed insoluble, European strategy seemed to King "simple and entirely obvious." The Soviet Union would hammer Germany while the Allies supported the Russians with supplies and with diversionary attacks to divert German manpower. Marshall probably did not like to think of his cross-Channel invasion plan as a "diversion" but rather as a decisive supporting attack. Whatever its definition, King and Marshall wanted the British to agree that the spring of 1944 would see a landing on the continent.

In the give-and-take of their closed sessions, the Americans and British made a deal. The British could continue limited operations in Italy and could defer their offensive in Burma. In return, the British committed themselves to a May first date for the invasion of France. Most important to King, the British were almost ready to agree to an intensified offensive in the Pacific.

The breakthrough came on Friday, 21 May, a regular morning meeting of the CCS. It convened first in closed session, disposed of several topics, and then the chiefs turned to agenda item number four, "Operations in the Pacific and Far East." Eleven members of the British planning staff, headed by Dill and Ismay, entered the room. King was about to educate the British on strategy in the Pacific.

King began by explaining that the United States Navy had been studying the strategy for a war against Japan for the past thirty to forty years. Thus his own ideas were neither original nor novel but had evolved from the best minds at the Naval War College and the Navy Department. As the Philippines had become an American possession following the Spanish-American War, they had dominated American strategic thinking ever since. Given their wealth of natural resources and their proximity to the raw materials of the so-called "Southern Resources Area," they had always been considered a prime target for Japanese aggression. The United States Navy had been expected to defend the Philippines, or if they had been lost, to recapture them.

There were three possible avenues of approach to recover the Philippines, King said. One was a straight line from Hawaii through the Central Pacific. The other two routes were to the north or the south of that line. For a number of reasons the Central Pacific approach was best. In any case, the Japanese fleet had to be defeated and the Mariana Islands assaulted and taken.

The Mariana Islands? His listeners must have been puzzled. There was no mention of the Marianas in any of the American position papers.

Indeed, one of the authors (Captain Moore) had intentionally avoided mentioning the Marianas because he did not feel they were necessary to recapture the Philippines. King as usual had paid scant attention to many of the papers developed by the Joint War Plans Committee. He knew what he wanted. The planners be damned.

King paused to review developments in the Pacific to date and explained why the Americans had done as they had thus far. Then he addressed the future.

All operations in the Pacific, said King, should be directed toward severing the Japanese lines of communication and recapturing the Philippines. *The Marianas were the key*. With the Marianas in American hands, the enemy sea lines of communications to the Carolines would be severed, and the Americans would be in a central position to strike westward toward the Philippines or China, or northwestward toward Japan. Furthermore, given the strategic importance of the Marianas to the Japanese, the Japanese fleet would have to come out and fight. When the Pacific Fleet had finished it off, the Pacific Ocean would belong to the Allies. Japan would be helpless.

If King sounded pedagogical, it was not surprising. He had had lots of practice trying to enlighten the United States Army on the principles of Pacific strategy. "It took me three months to educate Marshall about the importance of the Marianas," King said after the war, "but any educated naval officer would have understood it."

King then went on to explain that Japan would ultimately be defeated by attrition. The Americans would converge to "positions of readiness" from which they would attack Japan with a combination of blockade, bombing, and amphibious assault. While trying to protect the remnants of their empire, the Japanese would lose increasing numbers of ships, planes, and men.

But King warned that Japan was still dangerous and unpredictable. In fact, King admitted, they were an enigma to him, because he could not understand their way of thinking. For example, the Russian Maritime Provinces were adjacent to the Japanese home islands and a threat to Japanese security. Russia would surely turn against Japan, King believed, either sooner or later. As Russia at the moment was entirely absorbed with Germany, Japan could take Russia's Pacific coast whenever it pleased. So it seemed inexplicable to King that Japan refrained from attacking Russia preemptively to help her German ally and to protect her own security. King was also puzzled about why the Japanese did not finish their conquest of China, or why they so misused their submarines by not attacking unescorted American shipping in the Pacific.

"Japan is not doing a lot of things," King remarked shortly after TRIDENT, "they might otherwise do to embarrass us." The Japanese having finally been ejected from Guadalcanal and the Solomons, it seemed to King "incredible that they would accept the loss of face. I expect a real blow-off."

King concluded his presentation with a final plea to accelerate the war in the Pacific. The British were impressed. Brooke later wrote about the meeting in his diary: "The work was easier and there was less controversy. We dealt with the Pacific and accepted what was put forward."

With agreement almost in sight, the British continued to balk over the wording on the JCS statement of Pacific strategy — the so-called paragraph 2.b., which the JCS had slightly revised.* To the British the statement seemed open-ended and liable to be construed as carte blanche for King to concentrate resources in the Pacific at the expense of the European theater. To protect their own interests, the British wanted to modify the statement with a clause that King regarded as too restricting.

As mentioned before, King and the JCS were determined to get the British to commit themselves in writing. Not only would such written agreements prevent misunderstandings, but they would also force the chiefs to clarify their thinking. Consequently many of the arguments within the CCS were over semantics, for the papers that they finally agreed upon were in effect binding contracts between the two parties, contracts that defined how the war would be fought and what each country would contribute to the total war effort. Such papers had to be precise and unambiguous. A word or a phrase could dramatically alter the course of the war. Fortunately for the Allied war effort, the Americans and British spoke the same language. In a way, then, the CCS resembled a group of lawyers negotiating a contract, but the contract was deadly serious. It affected the lives of millions of men.

The JCS met early on the morning of Monday, 24 May, to discuss their stand on CCS 242/2 before the later CCS meeting, when they would resume the battle of semantics. Studying the paper in detail, the Americans agreed to recommend a large number of changes in the wording of the text. But on paragraph 2.b there was no agreement. Leahy and Marshall urged King to accept the British amendment,

* "Simultaneously with forcing an unconditional surrender of the Axis in Europe, in cooperation with other Pacific powers concerned, to maintain and extend unremitting pressure against Japan with the purpose of continually reducing her military power and attaining positions from which her ultimate surrender can be forced." This crucial paragraph was contained in a draft paper entitled "CCS 242/2, Report to the President and Prime Minister on the Final Agreed Summary of Conclusions Reached by the Combined Chiefs of Staff," dated 23 May 1943.

which would have allowed an intensified effort against Japan only if that effort were "consistent" with bringing about the unconditional surrender of the Axis in Europe at the earliest possible date.

King refused to yield to his colleagues. "The British amendment," said King, "is, in effect, a lever which could be used to stress European action at the expense of our Pacific effort." The words that subsequently passed between him and the other members of the JCS were unrecorded by the JCS secretary, who wrote only that there was "a prolonged discussion," a euphemism for angry arguments.

King prevailed. The JCS could not be disunited against the British, and they agreed that they would insist that the American version be accepted. If necessary they would appeal to Roosevelt. King had achieved the first step in ratifying his war plan against Japan.

United in purpose the Americans then moved to another room to meet with the British. Paragraph 2.b immediately came before the floor. Leahy and Marshall took up the cudgels while King remained silent. Neither side would give in. "Our difficulties still depended on our different outlook as regards the Pacific," Brooke wrote in his diary. In the end, Pound offered a compromise solution, an amendment whereby the CCS would give "consideration" to any major Pacific offensive before it was actually begun. That satisfied King. Pound's proposed amendment seemed innocuous enough. It was agreed upon by the CCS, undoubtedly with a profound sense of relief. They went on with their work of editing and refining the remainder of CCS 242/2.

King had achieved the second step in ratifying his war plan against Japan.

The third and last step of ratification came the following day when Roosevelt and Churchill approved the final version of the CCS master plan for the war against the Axis. King now had written authority to press on in the Pacific.

King was delighted with the final results of TRIDENT. As Mountbatten had been absent because of illness, King wrote him an assessment: "The Trident Conference was eminently worthwhile, and you will see in the final 'overall' paper that we have a document which is complete in itself as to the conduct of the war, being up-to-date as to concept, standing commitments, and projected operations — together with a 'balance sheet' as to ways and means."

The British went home. King began his next task of transforming the TRIDENT agreements into detailed plans for the war in the Pacific.

26

Accountability

FOR ALL HIS INTEREST in Navy men and women, it was not King's job to involve himself in the daily concerns of naval personnel management. There would undoubtedly be cases of misuse of manpower, but King accepted them as inevitable in wartime mobilization. Occasionally, though, he did try to correct specific instances of poor management. For example, in September 1942 he wrote to Jacobs and the Commandants of the Marine Corps and Coast Guard, "It is noticeable that there are on duty in Washington — and at headquarters elsewhere in the several districts, etc. — a very considerable number of young able-bodied men doing ordinary sentry duty, messenger service, etc." King suggested that they be released to go to war. Those unfit for combat could replace them.

This elementary policy was applied in his own office. One of King's enlisted Marine orderlies, named "Speed" Weidner, had been beseeching Marine Corps headquarters for a transfer to a war zone. But Weidner had been performing so well that the Marine Corps wanted him to stay put. When King asked Weidner how he liked his job, the Marine told him the truth. King rang for an aide.

"Speed does not like his duty here in Washington and wants to fight the Japanese," said King. "See that he gets what he wants."

That night Speed Weidner boarded a plane for San Diego and within days was fighting on Guam.

The Navy Department continued inexorably to grow throughout the war, especially in Washington. King did not like it, but the forces of expansion were too much for him to handle, given the other demands on his time and energy. He would lash out now and then, more to vent his frustration than from any real hope of reversing the trend. In March 1943 he wrote to Knox that Naval Intelligence, Public Relations, and Naval Photography had all the people they needed. The Secretary, he suggested, should instruct the Chief of Naval Personnel to stop their further enlargement. But nothing could stem the swelling numbers. A year later the Navy and other federal agencies were running out of room in Washington, and Roosevelt refused to authorize any new office buildings. If any more people were assigned to the Navy Department, Knox told King, they would have to be jammed into whatever space was already available.

It was such memoranda that provoked King into periodic outbursts. In this case King ordered his inspector general to investigate ways and means to eliminate "unnecessary" personnel. "I express my personal conviction," wrote King, "that there is at least 10 percent — in some cases 20 percent — more personnel than are actually required for effective war effort." But King was shouting in the wind.

Another way to get men into combat was to replace them with women. Some had served in the Navy before. Joy Hancock had been a "yeomanette" during the First World War and had served in public relations under King when he was Chief of the Bureau of Aeronautics during the nineteen thirties. When war came again Joy Hancock returned to the Navy. To her surprise, a King aide said that the Admiral wanted to see her. Remembering how she had once come scrambling with steno pad and pencil whenever King had called, she entered his office. King greeted her.

"Weren't you in World War One?" asked King.

"Yes, Admiral, I was."

"Then why aren't you wearing your World War One ribbon?" asked King.

"I thought of it, Admiral," she replied, "but there's no precedent. I think I'm the only woman in the Navy now who served in World War One."

"You should wear it," said King. "I have one for you." King picked up a ribbon from his desk. "Come here," he said.

Joy Hancock stepped forward, and King lifted the flap on her pocket. "I think that's as good a place as any."

King pinned on the ribbon, kissed her on both cheeks, and they shook hands. Joy Hancock practically wept.

"You're doing a good job now," said King. "Go ahead." She left in a euphoric daze.

King congratulating Mildred McAfee, the Navy's senior woman officer (Courtesy U.S. Naval Institute)

By Christmas 1942 the five hundred WAVES on duty in Washington invited their commanding officers to a brunch at the Statler Hotel. Most accepted. The newly commissioned women were bright, well educated, conscientious — but ingenuous. The seating was arranged by protocol, and a young woman officer recently graduated from Northampton was detailed to greet and seat the VIPs. A tall, lean admiral, his sleeves ablaze with gold, entered the dining room.

"Good morning, sir," said the sprightly ensign. "If you'll tell me your name, I'll tell you where to sit."

"The name is King," said the admiral.

Mildred McAfee, the Navy's senior woman officer at the time, recalled the scene. "I think he might have chewed out a boy who did this," she said, "but Betty was so nice and so innocent and so polite. They always forgive us for little mistakes."

In contrast to the Navy's acceptance of women, it restricted black Americans to duty as stewards and laborers, and most of the latter served ashore in the United States. The other services had similar policies, generally reflecting America's practice of racial discrimination.

King's attitude toward blacks was one of benevolent ignorance. As he had had little personal contact with black Americans, his conception of them and their culture was influenced largely by what he read. His favorite author was Octavus Roy Cohen, a prolific writer whose stories in the *Saturday Evening Post* were immensely popular in the twenties and thirties. King "loved" Cohen's stories, which purported to portray the southern blacks' way of living. In reality they were cruel distortions. Cohen, in a 1925 newspaper interview, explained his style of writing, and from that interview one can infer how Cohen's stories conditioned King's thinking. "What some Negroes in the North who are cultured do not understand," said Cohen, "is that I am writing about only one type of the race. My tales are concerned with the African Negroes of the South, who are the descendants of slaves. They are the happiest people on the face of the globe, and their lives, far from being filled with sorrow, are extremely happy throughout unless they have sickness or death with which to contend."

King also liked Negro spiritual singing and so enjoyed *Green Pastures*, a popular Negro fantasy play, that he saw it several times while a student at the Naval War College. He liked to collect and repeat ethnic "jokes" that portrayed blacks as lackadaisical and subservient; older black men were referred to as "darkies"; if servants they were "boys"; and occasionally they were "niggers." Although not a racist in the pejorative sense, King reflected the prevailing racial prejudices of his generation.

So King saw no reason to interfere with the Navy's policy of restricting blacks to menial tasks. It was not until James Forrestal became Secretary of the Navy that the status of blacks was seriously challenged. Less than two weeks after his appointment in May 1944, Forrestal wrote to Roosevelt, "From a morale standpoint, the Negroes resent the fact that they are not assigned to general service billets at sea, and white personnel resent the fact that Negroes have been given less hazardous assignments ashore." Forrestal considered the Navy's policy of discrimination a waste of valuable manpower, and he asked Roosevelt to approve sending black sailors to sea. The reply was a laconic, "J.F. O.K. F.D.R."

For the remainder of the war King supported the concept of allowing black sailors to serve on warships. He may have been spurred by Forrestal; he also was faced with a white manpower shortage and came to regard blacks as a limited substitute. King made mild suggestions to this effect during his periodic conferences with Nimitz, but no one wanted to discuss the subject, and King did not persist.

But there was at least a measure of limited progress. Black stewards had already been manning guns at sea, and as the war ended blacks were allowed into the deck and artificer ratings. Eventually a destroyer escort was manned and officered by blacks. The first hesitant steps had been made to integrate the Navy. It would take years to complete.

Such token measures were not enough. Several months after Forrestal's memorandum a racial rebellion hit the Navy full force. Several hundred black enlisted stevedores refused to load an ammunition ship at the naval ammunition depot in Port Chicago, California. There were a number of contributing causes stemming from the Navy's segregation policies, and in their ignorance local Navy officials failed to realize how these policies had angered and frustrated the blacks. Searching for reasons, these officials blamed "agitators" and the psychological effects of an explosion of an ammunition ship at a depot from which the black sailors had just been transferred.

The Navy's action was to prosecute fifty blacks by general court-martial on the charge of mutiny, while more than two hundred others were charged with disobeying orders and were tried by summary court-martial. When the President received the report he wrote to Forrestal, "It seems to me we should remember in the summary court martials of these 208 men that they were activated by mass fear and that this was understandable. Their punishment should be nominal." *

King's Navy had suffered a mutiny (so it said) and no one in authority understood why it had happened. King's opinion was neither solicited nor offered.

Blacks were not the only minority race in the Navy who suffered from official discrimination. Filipinos had served for decades as stewards and were prized for their loyalty, cheerfulness, and diligence. They could never aspire beyond being officers' servants, however, and their distinctive uniforms manifested their subservient status.

Early in the war the Filipinos were authorized to be promoted to a rate equivalent to chief petty officer, but their uniforms remained unchanged. In January 1943 King received an anguished letter from a Filipino who once had served for him. Although the writing was labored, its message was clear. "Admiral," it began, "I hope you will ex-

* The fifty tried by general court-martial were found guilty and sentenced to a dishonorable discharge and fifteen years of confinement at hard labor. The Secretary of the Navy in an act of clemency remitted the sentences.

couse me for addressing this few line to you I hope that you will extend your great help which the only I know will give a good result. In vew Admiral not much but it mean a lot of me & others that will concern, because we have been dreaming for years & years & wishing that some day we will have a chief rating & thank Lord our wish been granted we ar proud & we try with our heart the best our ability to keep & perform our duty."

The Filipino went on to explain that he recently had been promoted to chief officers' steward, had bought the traditional chief petty officer's insignia and cap device, but had then been told he could not wear them.

"No I often wonder Admiral," he continued, "if we the mess-branch mean anything or will harm any one if we wear the same uniform of the other chief of other branches. I mean the same uniform that they taking away from us now. . . .

"So Admiral will you please help us so we can wear uniform like chief even only for duration? I guess Admiral you will like to see us be proud once. I have wrote you this Admiral because I don't no one to help us & fight our right but you. . . . I hope Admiral you will give us your kindly help."

King passed the letter to Jacobs at the Bureau of Naval Personnel with the notation, "Please read —." The gist of Jacobs's response can be inferred. White chief petty officers were intensely jealous of their uniform, and a sailor worked years for the right to wear it. They would resent the Filipinos, whom they scorned as servants and foreigners. It would be unwise during wartime to tamper with the chiefs' morale as they were the "backbone of the Navy," and so the argument went.

King's reply to the Filipino steward was a disgrace. "It is considered," wrote King, "that military requirements make it necessary to distinguish between Officer's Chief Stewards and Chief Petty Officers who are required to perform certain military duties not required of Officer's Chief Stewards. I do not consider this need lessen your pride in the Naval uniform which you wear."

It was harder to refuse another Filipino's request — that of the exiled President of the Philippines, Manuel L. Quezon, who asked King to allow a young Filipino to train for a commission in the Naval Reserve. The man's father was a Philippine Army officer who had fought heroically on Corregidor and had escaped with Quezon to serve in his cabinet in exile. Jacobs advised King that although it would be lawful to grant the commission, it would be contrary to Bureau of Naval Personnel policy.

Once again King acted shamefully when confronted with a moral crisis. His compromise solution was to allow the Filipino patriot's son to enter the Coast Guard's reserve officers' training program.

Although King's behavior towards blacks and Filipinos was inexcusably racist and unjust by today's standards, King must be understood in the context of the times. The social attitudes of the armed forces reflect those of the American people as a whole. The evils of racial discrimination in the United States during the 1930s and 1940s are well known and need not be repeated here. Not until 1947 did a courageous President, Harry Truman, officially prohibit segregation in the armed forces. But human rights and equal opportunity came as slowly to the Navy as it did to the rest of our nation. It took a courageous CNO, Admiral Elmo R. Zumwalt, to abolish the last of the Navy's institutional racism in the early 1970s. Even so, some injustices may still remain.

King could have been a leader in bringing racial equality to the Navy. But like most officers of that era, he was too much a creature of his environment. He did not aggressively enforce racial discrimination; he passively allowed it to persist. Perhaps he saw the unfairness of it all, but he still lacked the will to risk the internal turmoil of social reform in time of war. Justice would have to wait.

As the Navy grew and became dominated by civilians temporarily in uniform, the traditional methods of naval discipline were taxed and strained. Civilians regarded "Rocks and Shoals," the Navy's code of conduct, as harsh and oppressing, and the Navy's peacetime judicial system was frequently too cumbersome and inefficient to handle the increased numbers of cases. Yet it was imperative that discipline be enforced—especially in war.

Problems came from many sources. During the Guadalcanal crises in the fall of 1942, King heard that merchant seamen manning supply ships in the war zone often refused to work. Disregarding such legal matters as union contracts and overtime wage scales, King brusquely ordered his task force and task group commanders to exert their "authority" to make the civilians work or to punish them accordingly. It was a typical King solution: simple, direct, and often impossible to implement. The obvious problem was to define the authority of naval commanders over civilians in a war zone, and that King failed to do.

Disciplining those in uniform was a matter that King understood more clearly. He wanted Rocks and Shoals enforced both in letter and in spirit. When standards seemed lax, he reacted strongly and not always wisely. When he reviewed the lenient sentences of four Marines who had pleaded guilty to a serious crime, he was outraged. "The sentences awarded in these cases are grossly inadequate to the crime committed," he wrote Knox in April 1944.* As the reviewing authorities — including King — could not increase the punishment, King resorted to asking Knox "to advise the court and Judge Advocate of the Navy Department's displeasure." What King had done was to exert improper command pressure on the Navy's justice system. Such methods inevitably discredit the Navy and invite congressional reform. Rocks and Shoals was abolished in 1951 and replaced with the Uniform Code of Military Justice.

King could influence naval discipline in many ways. After the carrier USS *Franklin* miraculously survived a bombing attack off Japan in 1945, her commanding officer asked for a general court-martial for seven of his officers on charges of cowardice. Nimitz doubted that the charges were justified, so King ordered his inspector general to investigate. Another factor was that the *Franklin*'s survival and escape had been publicized as the finest example of naval heroism, so any charges of cowardice would have harmed that image. Several weeks later King advised Nimitz that the *Franklin*'s commanding officer had dropped the charges.

King's most direct involvement in shipboard discipline came in the case of an American submarine, USS *Queenfish*, and a Japanese merchantman, the *Awa Maru*. Through an agreement between the Japanese and United States governments in early April 1945, *Awa Maru* was allowed to carry American relief supplies from Siberia to American prisoners in the Netherlands East Indies. The United States, in return, guaranteed safe passage to the *Awa Maru* and ordered American naval forces not to attack her. Through a series of bizarre circumstances, however, the *Queenfish* mistakenly sank the Japanese ship in a dense fog.

The Americans feared that the Japanese might retaliate against the POWs. (Over two thousand Japanese crewmen and passengers had perished.) If the Japanese did protest, said Nimitz in his initial report to King, the United States should consider a cover story that the *Awa Maru* hit a Japanese mine.

When King received the news from Nimitz he became distraught. Edwards pleaded with him to calm down and not to act precipitately before the facts were known, but King would not listen. He immediately ordered that *Queenfish* return to port, that her captain be relieved, and that he be tried by court-martial. Five days passed before King asked Nimitz for additional information.

Vice Admiral Charles A. Lockwood, the Pacific Fleet submarine com-

* The record does not show what the crimes were, but they were probably a criminal offense. Murder, rape, larceny, and assault were not uncommon in the services.

mander, felt that *Awa Maru* had gotten what she deserved. The Japanese had illegally exploited her safe-passage guarantee because most of her cargo had been war materiel and not relief supplies.* Lockwood came to Washington and pleaded with King and Forrestal that the fault was as much his as that of the *Queenfish*'s captain, Commander Charles E. Loughlin. His warning message to Loughlin had been ambiguous, said Lockwood, and Loughlin was a superb officer who deserved every possible consideration and clemency.

Neither King nor Forrestal was moved. The general court-martial convened, found Loughlin guilty of a minor charge of negligence in obeying orders, and awarded a letter of admonition as punishment. Nimitz was furious with the court's leniency and issued letters of reprimand to its members, a harsher punishment than they had awarded Loughlin. (King was not the only admiral who tried to coerce the courts.) King himself issued an edict that Loughlin was not to have another command. His career was apparently ruined. After the war, however, he was promoted to rear admiral. Loughlin, in fact, believed that the *Awa Maru* episode benefited his career because it made him a cause célèbre among sympathetic fellow submariners.

King insisted in nearly every instance that someone had to be accountable when something went seriously wrong. His was an extreme view: major accidents and unnecessary losses were not an act of God but someone's act of negligence. Yet accountability is often difficult to ascertain, and it can become blurred by circumstances. The sinking of cruiser *Indianapolis* stands as an example. A Japanese submarine torpedoed the American warship in the final days of the war, and hundreds of her crewmen died of exposure afterward because no one knew she was missing. Public indignation forced the Navy to act. Someone had to take the blame.

No one knew the *Indianapolis* had sunk because the Navy did not have a system for reporting the movement of its ships and for alerting appropriate authorities if a ship did not arrive on schedule. Such a reporting procedure did not exist because King did not want one; he felt it created red tape and unnecessary paperwork. King was culpable to the extent that he created the system. But the origin of the system did not become an issue.

In order to appease the public outcry, the Navy Department ordered a general court-martial of the *Indianapolis* commanding officer, Captain Charles B. McVay III, on charges of inefficiency and negligence. The court-martial itself, in December 1945, was scandalous. (King retired

* Confirmed by debris.

shortly after it began.) Many captains had lost their ships during the war, but McVay was the only one to be court-martialed. The prosecution even used the captain of the Japanese submarine as a witness, which provoked furious editorials and was denounced by a congressional resolution.

In February 1946 McVay was found guilty of having hazarded his ship's safety by having failed to steer an evasive course, the usual practice of avoiding submarine attack. McVay's punishment was to lose 100 numbers in seniority, which would be a typical sentence for commanding officers who damaged or grounded their ships through negligence. The loss of seniority was not the gist of the punishment. What did matter was that McVay was publicly disgraced and lost any chance of further promotion. Upon recommendation of the court, McVay's sentence was remitted and he returned to duty. He retired as a captain in 1949 after thirty years of commissioned service.

The *Indianapolis* tragedy was not King's finest hour. Not only was he responsible for creating the system that allowed her loss to go unnoticed, but he also must share responsibility with Forrestal for allowing McVay's humiliating court-martial.

Sometimes senior admirals were held accountable. Throughout the war there were series of investigations concerning American unpreparedness for the Japanese attack on Pearl Harbor. King, of course, was uninvolved, as he had been in the Atlantic before and during the attack, but wartime investigative reports and recommendations required his endorsement. His actions and statements throughout those years of inquiries were vacillating and inconsistent.

Shortly after Kimmel was fired as CINCPAC, King sent him several sympathetic letters. Kimmel was grateful. "Many thanks for your note and the sentiment you express therein," he wrote to King on 24 December 1941. "It gives me a great deal of comfort. Whatever the findings of the board may be, you may rest assured I used my own best judgment and gave all my time to my job."

King thought of Kimmel as "a damned stubborn fellow, with the funniest ideas." It seemed to King that Kimmel had tried to do too much himself and had become too involved in details. Furthermore, according to King, Kimmel should have delegated more responsibility to Rear Admiral Claude C. Bloch, who as Commandant of the Fourth Naval District should properly have handled the defenses of Hawaii while Kimmel looked after the fleet.

Roosevelt established the first Pearl Harbor investigation committee in early 1942, under former Supreme Court Justice Owen Roberts. King was disturbed by what he considered the injustice of the committee's findings. "It seems to me that this committee did not get into the real meat of the matter," King later wrote, "but merely selected a 'scapegoat' to satisfy the popular demand for fixing the responsibility for the Pearl Harbor debacle. For instance, Admiral Kimmel was not asked the important questions nor was he given the proper chance to speak for himself. In fact, he and General Short were 'sold down the river' as a political expedient!"

King wrote yet another letter of consolation to Kimmel in March 1942, which Kimmel once again appreciated. "You know, of course, that my services are available," wrote Kimmel. "If the department does not employ me I want to find some other useful work to do." It would turn out, however, that Kimmel would spend the remainder of the war defending himself before successive boards of investigation.

As the Army had been responsible for defending Pearl Harbor from air attack, King afterward resented what he considered the Army's reticence in acknowledging any fault. "That's why I didn't like Stimson," he once remarked. When Roosevelt sent Stark to London in early 1942, King regarded the move as an exile for Stark's part in the Pearl Harbor disaster. Marshall, King believed, should have gotten the same treatment. "I have never been able to understand," wrote King after the war, "how or why FDR could fire Admiral Stark without doing the same to General Marshall. In my opinion one could not possibly be more suspect than the other."

The Roberts report satisfied no one. Congress wanted Kimmel and Short tried by general court-martial, while Republicans charged that the Roosevelt Administration was suppressing evidence of its own culpability. As a compromise, Congress enacted a law in the summer of 1944 directing the War and Navy Departments to conduct their own investigations. Forrestal appointed a three-officer Pearl Harbor Court of Inquiry, and its report reached King's desk in October 1944.* It was probably the first time that King had most of the facts before him. The report practically burned a hole in his desk — everyone wanted to see it. Roosevelt was running for his fourth term, the national elections were only weeks away, and the Republicans were sure that the report contained material that could be used against the President.

Under these circumstances King had to decide whether to make the report public. He probably did not give a damn whether Roosevelt or anyone else would be politically embarrassed. What did concern him was that much of it revealed the Navy's ability to break the Japanese

* Coinciding with the Battle of Leyte Gulf. King led a complicated life.

code. If those portions of the report were deleted, King wrote to Forrestal, "the picture would be disjointed and full of unexplained gaps. I think this would lead to a demand of Congress and by the Press for more information, on the ground that the part made public was incomplete, and that withholding of any information is indicative of a desire on the part of the Navy to 'whitewash' high naval officers. A situation such as this might well lead to discussions that would inadvertently disclose just the information that we feel is vital to keep secret."

One such "discussion" could well have involved Kimmel, who had been demanding a public court-martial to vindicate himself. "The potentialities are particularly dangerous," warned King, "because Admiral Kimmel's civilian lawyers have now been informed, so I understand, of the existence and content of the many Japanese messages in question. I know of no means of keeping these lawyers from talking in public, except such ethical views as they may have concerning their responsibility for not doing anything that would jeopardize war operations. It is a question just how far they could be restrained by ethical considerations, if the Navy Department were to make public the part of the record which is unfavorable to Admiral Kimmel, while suppressing that part which he regards as a main element of his defense."

King's conclusion was simple: "I recommend that there be no public release whatsoever." Then he added the caveat that ". . . something should be done to suppress the rumors and irresponsible accusations that are now current." But that "something" was not to include "publicizing all or any part of the record."

Having said that, King addressed the accountability of Kimmel and Stark for what had happened at Pearl Harbor. "Despite the evidence that no naval officer was at fault to a degree likely to result in conviction if brought to trial," wrote King, "nevertheless the Navy cannot evade a share of responsibility for the Pearl Harbor incident. That disaster cannot be regarded as an act of God, beyond human power to prevent or mitigate. It is true that the country as a whole is basically responsible in that the people were unwilling to support an adequate army and navy until it was too late to repair the consequences of past neglect in time to deal effectively with the attack that ushered in the war. It is true that the Army was responsible for local defense at Pearl Harbor. Nevertheless, some things could have been done by the Navy to lessen the success of the initial Japanese blow. Admiral Stark and Admiral Kimmel were the responsible officers. . . .

"The derelictions on the part of Admiral Stark and Admiral Kimmel were faults of omission rather than faults of commission. In the case in question they indicate lack of the superior judgment necessary for exercising command commensurate with their rank and their assigned duties, rather than culpable inefficiency. Since trial by general court martial is not warranted by the evidence adduced, appropriate administrative action would appear to be the relegation of both of these officers to positions in which lack of superior judgment may not result in future errors."

Given King's incontrovertible arguments for protecting national security in war, neither the board's report nor King's endorsement was published. When Forrestal confirmed the delay by appointing Admiral H. Kent Hewitt to continue the investigation, Congress and the press became resigned to waiting until the war was over before all the reports would be made public.

By the summer of 1945 it was apparent that the war was nearing its end. Forrestal wanted the full Pearl Harbor story ready for press release, and he pressured King to repeat his censure of Stark and Kimmel in his endorsement to Hewitt's report. King by then had second thoughts. His earlier indictments of Stark and Kimmel now seemed to be too harsh, and he stalled for time.

But Forrestal was adamant. Stark and Kimmel had to be penalized. Kimmel had retired, but Stark was still in London. Forrestal ordered him relieved. King wrote the bad news to Stark in early June 1945. "It is the decision of the secretary," wrote King, "that . . . you shall come home — and go to inactive duty." King added that he had told Forrestal that he wanted Stark to stay on until August in order to reorganize the naval forces in Europe, and there he remained until the war was over.

After Hiroshima and Nagasaki had been destroyed by the atomic bomb, it was apparent that the war could end at any time. King tried to concentrate on those cataclysmic events, but Forrestal, fiercely committed to releasing the Pearl Harbor reports the moment the war was over, kept hammering on King. Edwards, too, urged King to sign the Hewitt report endorsement (which Edwards had drafted). King first rewrote it, then finally signed it. "I was too damned busy," he rationalized after the war.

King's endorsement, dated 13 August 1945, essentially repeated his November 1944 endorsement to the Pearl Harbor Court of Inquiry report. "Admiral Stark and Admiral Kimmel," wrote King, "though not culpable to a degree warranting formal disciplinary action, were nevertheless inadequate in emergency, due to the lack of the superior judgment necessary for exercising command commensurate with their duties. Appropriate action appears to me to be the relegation of both of these officers to positions in which their lack of superior strategic judgment may not result in future errors."

Two days later Stark was relieved and came home.

When King finally reflected how Stark had served his nation as the senior naval officer in Europe, he became conscience-stricken. Belatedly trying to make amends, King wrote a memorandum to Forrestal on 16 August 1945, lavishly praising Stark and recommending that he receive the Distinguished Service Medal for his duty in London. "His performance of his manifold duties," wrote King, "was distinguished by such exceptional tact, intelligence, judgment, devotion to duty and professional skill as to reflect great credit upon himself, the naval service and his country."

Forrestal, of course, ignored King's recommendation, but his successor, John L. Sullivan, awarded the decoration to Stark three years later. Still troubled, King recanted entirely in April 1948. Writing to the Navy Department that he had been in "error," he asked that his endorsement of Hewitt's report be expunged and the two admirals vindicated. Even that was not enough. He had to let the public know of his repentance. That November a newspaper article carried the headlines: "Admiral King Would Clear Stark, Kimmel: Withdraws Condemnation of Two Officers Made in Report on Pearl Harbor."

It was the only time that King ever admitted he had been wrong.

27

Getting Ready—1943

One of King's most prized prerogatives was his well-appointed personal aircraft, which he used for trips within the continental United States. A small, all-weather, two-engined transport called the Lockheed Lodestar, it cruised at 200 knots and had all the latest communication and navigational equipment. It was much sought after by Navy Department dignitaries, but King would lend it to others only under extraordinary circumstances.

King's pilot during much of 1943, Lieutenant Commander John J. Hyland, had apprehensions about the assignment.* "It seemed to me that there were a few pilots senior to me who were better qualified," he later said, "but they had either been ashore too long or maneuvered themselves out of the way. Nobody really wanted the job, including myself. In fact, it was the best thing that could have happened to me, but I was too stupid to realize it then."

Early on, Hyland received a phone call from an aide to one of the Assistant Secretaries of the Navy, asking if the Lodestar would be available at a certain date. Hyland innocently replied that it was not scheduled for King's use at that time. The Assistant Secretary then asked King for the plane with the understanding that King would not be needing it. King was livid but had to accede. Afterward King issued an order that only his aide could give information on the status of his aircraft.

The trips to San Francisco to meet with Nimitz were long overnight flights. King either slept on a couch or sat at a desk equipped with earphones and aeronautical charts so he could navigate. The cross-country

* Hyland rose to the rank of admiral and became Commander in Chief, U.S. Pacific Fleet.

trips frazzled the other passengers, especially Cooke, who suffered from a frail constitution. King always seemed refreshed and ready to work.

King regarded weather more as a nuisance than a hazard. He wanted to stick to his schedule and hated staying on the ground when he was ready to go. If the weather reports were threatening, King would still take off rather than wait, hoping to find a break in the weather. When he heard en route on a trip to San Francisco that the airfields were closed because of fog, King pressed on. Hyland groped through the darkness and terrified King's aides by descending upon a highway he had misidentified as a lighted runway. King was simply irked that Hyland took so long to land.

Given King's determination to keep moving regardless of weather, Hyland frequently was forced to make unscheduled fueling stops at various military airfields across the country. Although Hyland tried to alert the base commander in advance, on several occasions he was unable to make radio contact and landed unannounced. When King was recognized there would be panic at the airfield. King's reaction was unpredictable. Usually he was courteous to the surprised base commander or duty officer.

There were also unpleasant incidents. "On just a couple of occasions," Hyland recalled, "I and the whole party would be terribly embarrassed by Admiral King's rudeness to the base commander when he would come tearing up ten minutes later to greet King. King would literally eat the poor guy up despite the fact there was no reasonable way he could have been on hand. So King had an unpredictable side to his nature which none of us ever understood. When he was bad he was *really* bad; but considering his responsibility I don't feel I should criticize him too harshly. Actually such incidents were rare, but when they occurred they were remarkable. I'm sure anyone on the receiving end never forgot it and probably never forgave it either."

The beginning of the TRIDENT conference on 12 May 1943 had coincided with the long-delayed American assault on Attu in the Aleutian Islands, which had been occupied by the Japanese almost a year earlier during the Battle of Midway. Alaskan operations since then had been confused and frustrating. The Attu assault under the command of Rear Admiral Kinkaid was no exception. The Americans still were amateurs in amphibious warfare. King received little information as to progress, but when Kinkaid on the fourth day fired the Army major general commanding the landing force, it was obvious that all was not well.

The slow-moving battle was still in progress when King met with

Nimitz in San Francisco on 28 May. King was understandably anxious to learn what had happened on Attu, for it had been only the third American amphibious assault of the war (the others being Guadalcanal and North Africa). King's Central Pacific offensive depended entirely upon whether American amphibious forces could seize islands, and Attu was an early test. King hoped to learn something from the commanding general of the Western Defense Command, Lieutenant General J. L. DeWitt, who had come to San Francisco to brief King on the battle.

The general knew little more than King. He could neither report how many Japanese had been killed after seventeen days of fighting nor how many remained. The situation in Alaska remained a mystery.

King and Nimitz turned to the future. The TRIDENT Conference had given Nimitz authority to begin his drive through the Central Pacific. The Marshalls, explained King, were the first objective. But the CCS had not established a timetable, had not specified which of the Marshall Islands were to be seized, and had not identified which forces were to be used. It was up to King and Nimitz and their staffs to work out the details.

Such details would be based more on speculation than on experience. The Central Pacific campaign would be a violent confrontation between the two great sea powers, with an intensity and complexity without precedent. Carrier warfare, amphibious warfare, and mobile logistical support would predominate. Hundreds of ships, thousands of planes, and hundreds of thousands of men would be swept into the greatest war at sea in history. Yet in mid-1943 such concepts were still largely unproven theories.

With so much at stake and with so many uncertainties, it would require an extraordinarily able officer to command the Central Pacific forces. Nimitz nominated Rear Admiral Raymond A. Spruance, who had proven himself in combat at the Battle of Midway as well as intellectually as Nimitz's chief of staff for the past year. King agreed. Spruance was the only naval officer, King conceded, who was smarter than he. "As to brains," King once said, "Spruance is the best flag officer in the Navy." In recognition of Spruance's new assignment, King arranged for his immediate promotion to vice admiral. It came so suddenly that Spruance could not even be told why he had received his third star until several days later.

The next most important assignment would be Spruance's amphibious force commander. Nimitz already knew that Spruance would want Rear Admiral Richmond Kelly Turner. He was perfect for the job. Kelly Turner's brain power was legendary, and he had proven at

Guadalcanal he could fight. Having known Turner ever since they had been classmates at Pensacola in 1927, King knew that Turner had the will and the energy to mobilize the Pacific's amphibious forces. Turner got the command with King's blessing.

King and Nimitz also had to select a landing force commander, who obviously would be a Marine general. Again Nimitz knew that Spruance would want Major General Holland M. Smith, whom Spruance regarded as the premier expert in amphibious warfare. King remembered Smith from their tempestuous partnership during the amphibious exercises in Puerto Rico in early 1941. He was willing to accept him now, but Nimitz wanted to think about it, perhaps because of Smith's contentiousness. King agreed to leave the decision to Nimitz. (Smith got the job.)

Three more days of meetings followed with the usual free-wheeling discussion over a wide range of agenda topics. One moment King and Nimitz might discuss the availability of Marine and Army divisions, then suddenly shift to the question of insignia and badges for PT boat crews. King and Nimitz were so well informed and had so much in common that their minds could shift easily from strategy to tactics, logistics to administration, or from people to weapons. They spoke with an economy of words, for time was short, and there was much to talk about. The air fairly crackled. Policy decisions with momentous consequences were frequently made in moments.

From San Francisco King and Nimitz flew to San Diego on 1 June for a current report from Rear Admiral Francis W. Rockwell, the naval assault force commander at Attu. The Japanese had made a last banzai charge on 29 May, said Rockwell, and the island was finally secured. Although the invasion had succeeded, he continued, there had been many mistakes. It was apparent that all the services had more to learn about amphibious warfare before the Central Pacific offensive began.

One conclusion was starkly evident: it would be a brutal war. "All agree that the only way to beat the Japs is to kill t[illegible] all," said the conference minutes. "They will not surrender and our troops are taking no chances and are killing them anyway."

By the time that King returned to Washington the Joint Staff Planners, prodded by Cooke, had already begun to study how to invade the Marshalls. But the planners were not moving fast enough. It was essential to King that the Americans become irrevocably committed to Central Pacific operations at the earliest possible moment, before the British would hedge on their agreements and commitments made at TRIDENT.

They might, for example, renege on their implied assent to shift shipping from the Atlantic to the Pacific. Once the Central Pacific operations were underway, King reasoned, the British would be less likely to change their minds.

In order to accelerate these plans and preparations, King submitted a proposal to the JCS on 11 June that was a kick in the head to the Army. It contained three separate recommendations.

(1) Invade the Marshalls by 1 November and establish dates for subsequent assaults.

(2) Force MacArthur to specify his future operations, including "firm dates," so the JCS could allocate forces between Nimitz and MacArthur.

(3) Authorize Nimitz to coordinate and schedule all offensive operations in the Pacific.

The third proposal once again had resurrected the divisive and emotional issue of a supreme commander for the entire Pacific theater. King knew full well that neither Marshall nor MacArthur would agree to it, so he must have had other motives. Perhaps King remembered how Marshall and Arnold had withheld troops and aircraft from the battle for Guadalcanal. This time King wanted assurances that his plans for the Pacific would not be shortchanged. So undoubtedly those startling June eleventh proposals were actually bargaining devices to jolt the JCS into giving Nimitz adequate resources and a firm date. When the smoke cleared, King's plans for the Marshalls had tentative JCS approval. The third proposal for Nimitz as supreme commander was tabled.

But MacArthur had not yet been heard. As King had prodded him for his plans in the Southwest Pacific, MacArthur replied in full measure. He objected strenuously to releasing any of his forces to Nimitz—including his two Marine divisions—and he denounced the entire concept of a Central Pacific offensive. All American resources, he demanded, should be sent to his theater so that he could capture Rabaul, "the great strategic prize." The other members of the JCS began to vacillate, so King was once again alone in supporting Nimitz over MacArthur.

The Joint Staff Planners sought a compromise and found one: MacArthur would bypass Rabaul, continue his advance along the northern coast of New Guinea, and release one Marine division, the 2nd, to Nimitz. Marshall would assign the 27th Infantry Division to Nimitz, allowing MacArthur to retain the 1st Marine Division. Arnold would provide additional aircraft to the Central Pacific. Nimitz would first seize the Gilbert Islands on 1 November for tactical reasons before moving on to the Marshalls. The end result was that *both* Nimitz and MacArthur could go to the offensive because American industry, now becoming prodigious, was able to provide enough for everyone. Each offensive would support the other, pounding the Japanese on two fronts.

The JCS approved their planners' recommendations on 20 July 1943. King further suggested slipping the Gilberts target date to 15 November to coincide with MacArthur's assault. His colleagues agreed. That afternoon the JCS sent Nimitz a formal directive to open the Central Pacific offensive.

King's cherished plans for the Pacific were approaching reality.

Although the general strategy for the Pacific had been settled, the organization for the Pacific forces had not. The role of the Marine Corps to some extent was still undefined. King would have preferred to use Marines exclusively as amphibious assault troops and to use the Army for garrison duty only. The 7th Infantry Division's performance on Attu could have reinforced this feeling. The Army was accustomed to deliberate attacks supported by artillery and armor, while the Marines employed shock and speed. The Army claimed that its tactics resulted in fewer casualties, but the Marines' way was quicker. As it took the Army longer to capture an island, the fleet was exposed to more danger because it was forced to remain in restricted waters while supporting the troops ashore. From the Navy's view the Marines' way was best. But King knew that there would never be enough Marines available for the entire Pacific offensive, so Army troops would have to be trained for amphibious warfare as well. He made this emphatically clear to the Marine Corps and the Navy, Holland Smith's opinions notwithstanding.*

King also wanted the Marine Corps under his personal control. They were part of the Department of the Navy, but the Commandant of the Marine Corps reported to the Secretary of the Navy. As the Commandant's status with King was hazy, King decided to clarify it. In the summer of 1943, after TRIDENT, King summoned Lieutenant General Thomas Holcomb, the Commandant of the Marine Corps, to tell him bluntly that the Marines had to come under COMINCH and become an integral part of the Navy. Otherwise, he warned, they might be absorbed into the Army.

King had been alerted to this threat by his senior Marine advisor, Colonel Oman T. Pfeiffer, a member of a JCS committee studying how to avoid "duplication and waste." The Army Air Force representatives were manipulating the committee to justify establishing a separate air

* Smith had belabored the Army's performance on Attu.

force, which would swallow up naval air; and, as Pfeiffer later said, "another very apparent aim was to eliminate or reduce the Marine Corps to impotence."

Pfeiffer was not an alarmist. The Army planned to expand to more than 200 divisions, and the Marine Corps was a competitor for scarce manpower. George Marshall himself had remarked in Pfeiffer's presence, "I am going to see that the Marines never win another war." (King would not have been shocked. Marshall had often told King that he did not like the Marine Corps and wanted it kept small — very small.)

The Marines, of course, needed men for the war in the Pacific. Four divisions had been authorized, but they would not be enough. There was considerable opposition. In the summer of 1943 Colonel Ray T. Maddocks (an Army representative on the JCS committee) denounced a fifth Marine division as a wasteful and unnecessary duplication of the Army. Pfeiffer and Maddocks had hot words, and afterward Pfeiffer went to General Holcomb. Time was short. If Holcomb wanted that additional division, advised Pfeiffer, he had better ask for it immediately.

"That afternoon a three-page recommendation from General Holcomb came to my desk for Admiral King," Pfeiffer later recalled. "I had learned early in my association with Admiral King that he was a man who thought that if you couldn't put everything you had to say on one sheet of paper, you didn't know what you were talking about. I reworked the Commandant's letter and got it on one page, called General Holcomb, and told him what I had done. General Holcomb both approved and signed it the next morning. I added a short covering memo, and by that evening Admiral King had put his OK on it. And that is the way that the Marine Corps got its fifth division." *

Having promised Army forces to King for the Central Pacific, Marshall had second thoughts about (1) their being under Nimitz's command and (2) whether Nimitz should retain his dual role as Commander in Chief, Pacific Ocean Areas, and Commander in Chief, Pacific Fleet. In the first role he controlled all the forces — Navy, Marine, and Army — in his theater. In his second role he commanded only the fleet. In effect, he was his own commanding officer.

Marshall felt that Nimitz should act solely as a theater commander now that the 27th Infantry Division and Army aircraft would be in the Gilberts assault. Neither MacArthur nor Eisenhower exercised direct command of Army troops in their theaters, argued Marshall; ipso facto, Nimitz should not exercise direct command of the Pacific Fleet in his

* The 5th Marine Division later fought on Iwo Jima.

theater. Marshall's real worry was that Nimitz's staff were predominantly naval officers, preoccupied with the fleet and inexperienced with Army requirements. The solution, in Marshall's mind, was to remove Nimitz from active fleet operations and to assign him a more balanced joint staff that represented all the services in his theater.

King would not listen. The present arrangement had worked well for the past eighteen months, he asserted. The JCS charter of March 1942 had specifically authorized Nimitz to wear both hats, and King did not want it changed now.

But King had a more compelling motive for retaining the status quo. So long as Nimitz commanded the Pacific Fleet, King was his boss. Through Nimitz he could control fleet operations and administration without consulting the JCS. If Nimitz were to lose his fleet command, his relationship with King would be drastically changed. As a theater commander he would report directly to the JCS, and the Chiefs would then control Pacific Fleet movements rather than King.

All this was very much on King's mind when he and Cooke next met with Nimitz in San Francisco on 30 July 1943. Cooke reported that the Army felt that Nimitz was too involved with the fleet and did not consult the Army during planning. Nimitz admitted to nothing and insisted that he was cooperating. King seemed satisfied with Nimitz's explanation. "The Army is too academic on this subject," said King.

Cooke persisted. "The Army will keep pushing on this project," he said.

All right, said King, let's do something to keep the Army quiet. He turned to Nimitz. "Get some officers on your staff thinking exclusively of theater planning."

But King had an even deeper concern with Nimitz: he never entirely trusted Nimitz's judgment. In King's mind, Nimitz took bad advice and was too willing to compromise with the Army in the interests of harmony. "If only I could keep him tight on what he's supposed to do," King once said to Charlotte Pihl. "Somebody gets ahold of him and I have to straighten him out."

King's frequent trips to see Nimitz indicate the extent of King's anxiety to keep Nimitz under his thumb. In contrast, Marshall saw Eisenhower hardly at all and MacArthur but once.

Why, then, did King retain Nimitz in the Pacific? The answer is obvious. There was no other place for Nimitz to go, given his seniority and prestige, so he had to remain in the Pacific. And as long as he was there, King would never allow anything or anyone to come between him and Nimitz.

King's most emphatic instruction to Nimitz at the San Francisco meeting was "to keep pressure on the Japs." Both Marshall and Arnold were behind him, said King. If possible, King wanted to start new operations before the others ended, in order to keep rolling and to keep the Japanese off balance. Satisfied that the preparations for the Gilberts assault in November were on track, King returned to Washington.

28

Aviation

AIR POWER, whether naval or military, was one of the most emotional issues of the Second World War. It aroused passions either for or against, and as a new and untested form of warfare struggling for status it was subject both to extravagant claims and to violent denunciations. The wartime efforts of Army Air Force extremists to unify all of the nation's air forces into one service exacerbated suspicions and hostilities even more.

In the last months of peace in 1941, Rear Admiral John H. Towers, Chief of the Bureau of Aeronautics, had scheduled a press conference in his conference room. It would be an ordeal, for Towers was inherently shy. It was a hidden facet of his personality. People thought of him as a strident advocate of naval aviation, notorious for his feuds with senior surface officers. But Towers had something to say to the press that day that overcame his shyness.

"The aircraft carrier will spearhead the next war," said Towers. It was a daring statement. The surface officers who ran the Navy Department had always said that the battleship was the Navy's principal warship.

The reporters at first were silent. Finally one spoke: "Will you repeat that, Admiral?"

"It's the aircraft carrier that will spearhead the action in the next war," said Towers.

The publicity given such statements put Towers on the cover of *Time* magazine in June 1941. Once war began he would help make his prediction come true.

Towers was dismayed and apprehensive when King became

COMINCH in December 1941. Over the years he had become almost paranoid and saw enemies everywhere — enemies both to him and to naval aviation. Towers regarded King as one of the greatest enemies of all. King had snared the job as Chief of the Bureau of Aeronautics in 1933 when Towers had thought it had been his. Later King had flown his flag on *Saratoga* when Towers had been her skipper, and Towers had bad memories from that experience. The final split (at least in Towers's mind) had come at the Coronado Hotel in San Diego one evening during the 1930s. King's behavior had been so objectionable that Towers had accosted King in the lavatory, calling him, among other things, a "penny-whistle." "King never forgave me," Towers would tell his friends. "That was the one great mistake of my career."

Events in early 1942 seemed to confirm Towers's fears that King still held a grudge from that night at the hotel. Marshall invited Towers to join the JCS to represent naval aviation, but King would not give his consent. King antagonized Towers even more by attempting to reorganize the Navy Department so as to bring the bureau chiefs directly under his control. Finally, in October 1942, King dispatched Towers to Pearl Harbor as Commander, Naval Air Forces, Pacific. It was commonly understood that King simply wanted Towers out of Washington. Nimitz took him reluctantly. Towers would be responsible for the administration and readiness of the carrier forces, but he would never be allowed to take them into battle.

Towers never knew King's true feelings toward him and toward naval aviation. He did not know, for example, that King was accustomed to insults at parties and shrugged them off. King had even saved his career. When King had been Chief of the Bureau of Aeronautics, a medical board had tried to force Towers into retirement because of defective vision. King interceded with Leahy, then Chief of the Bureau of Navigation. Towers was needed for naval aviation, argued King, and the Navy could not afford to lose him. Towers remained in the Navy. "Towers was a very able naval officer and aviator," King later wrote. "However, he was a man who was not easy to get to know well; I was never against him nor for him."

War came and King had to decide how best to use Towers — and naval aviation. King believed in its value from long association. But too many aviators, King believed, both Army and Navy, were given to rash, enthusiastic predictions of victory through air power alone, creating intense political pressure to create a separate air force that included both land-based and sea-based aircraft.

An early 1941 paper by Commander Forrest P. Sherman,* entitled "The Case Against the United Air Force," reflected the opposition to such ideas within the Department of the Navy. "It is, of course, not necessary for me to tell you with which side my own sentiments lie," King wrote Sherman. "I sincerely hope that this matter of the separate air force will not break out into the open, although I feel confident that while it would prove troublesome for a time, ultimately we would be able to have others see it our way."

It was wishful thinking. Once the war was underway, demands for a separate air force intensified. The Army Air Force boasted (incorrectly) that B-17 bombers won the Battle of Midway and with similar claims otherwise strengthened their case for an independent service. King would have to fight to keep naval aviation intact.

King was handicapped because his own service was in disarray. On 7 December 1941 Towers's prediction had come true. Japanese aircraft carriers turned the world upside down, and for the first few months they were indomitable. American aircraft carriers — not battleships — finally stopped the Japanese fleet at Coral Sea and Midway. But instead of the elation of winning, naval aviators suffered from bitter discontent. In those stunning events at sea their carriers had replaced the battleships. Surely, they thought, victory over Japan would depend largely upon them. But they were still a minority without voice in the naval hierarchy. Conservative surface officers would not relinquish their power to the brash and assertive fliers who were years their juniors. Old prejudices and hard feelings from prewar days would not go away. Given the lack of senior aviators, the early carrier task forces were often commanded by surface flag officers whose inexperienced judgment often hazarded the aviators' lives. The aviators more and more mistrusted those in authority who did not wear wings on their breasts.

Such grievances were dynamite. Naval aviators were indispensable to victory. Unless their problems were solved, those advocating a separate air arm might actually take over the carriers. King's solution was to give his aviators a greater say in fighting the war.

King had to start in Pearl Harbor. Neither Nimitz nor his chief of staff, Spruance, was an aviator. There were few aviators on the CINCPAC staff. Flag aviators were also scarce. Bill Halsey, Aubrey W. Fitch, and John S. McCain were needed in the South Pacific and could not be spared for duty in Pearl Harbor. Someone with the commensurate prestige, reputation, and seniority was needed to represent naval avia-

* A brilliant strategist and planner who later became a CNO.

tion in the Pacific. Jack Towers was the natural, indeed the only, man for the job. In October 1942 Towers left Washington and went to Pearl Harbor. Before leaving he demanded and got a promotion to vice admiral.

Towers fulfilled King's expectations in full measure. Although Nimitz came to hate Towers, he could not ignore him. Towers did so well that, in the latter part of the war, King time and again approached Nimitz and suggested that Towers be given command at sea. Nimitz would never allow it. Contrary to popular belief, it was Nimitz and not King who prevented Towers from flying his flag at sea during the Second World War.

Shortly after the war began, King received a gratuitous letter from retired Admiral Harry E. Yarnell that contained an eight-page estimate of the situation. Yarnell had "ability and brains," according to King, so he was worth listening to. King was "impressed" with the assessment, he told Yarnell, but he was too busy to assimilate it. Nothing more passed between them for over a year.

As King began to search for ways to pacify his naval aviators and to establish sound aviation policies, he remembered Yarnell as an expert in such matters. (Yarnell had commissioned the *Saratoga* as her commanding officer and later had served as Commander, Aircraft, Battle Force, from 1931 to 1933. His last duty before retirement in 1939 had been as Commander in Chief of the Asiatic Fleet, so he was well informed on Pacific strategy as well.) On 16 June 1943 King wrote to Yarnell and asked him to return to active duty as an aviation adviser.

Yarnell did, and in the next few months he created a furor by his notorious "aviation survey," a questionnaire sent directly to fleet aviators soliciting their opinions. He got them. The response was explosive. Naval aviation was being misused and poorly managed, they charged, and they called for immediate reforms. While many of the recommendations were radical, the inference was clear. The aviators were hurt, angry, and frustrated.

Yarnell's opinion poll had also agitated Nimitz, because (among other reasons) Yarnell had bypassed him to stir up trouble with his subordinates. When the rumbles reached Nimitz, he belatedly took his own survey. He was shocked by the responses. Rear Admiral Frederick C. Sherman wanted to replace King, Nimitz, and Spruance — and all other commanders of mixed forces that included air — with active aviators. Towers said the same thing. Either he or Fitch should replace Spruance as commander of the Central Pacific forces, or else Spruance's chief of staff should be an aviator. He also urged that naval aviators receive more important commands.

King had sown a hurricane with Yarnell. In early November 1943, about two weeks before the landings on Tarawa, Yarnell submitted his recommendations to the Secretary of the Navy and to Horne (Horne ostensibly had authorized the survey.) They were drastic: a four-star aviator as the JCS equivalent to Arnold with authority to command naval aviation as a separate force, and a naval aviator to replace Nimitz.

Yarnell also wanted King out of Washington. That was nothing new. The month before he had urged King to lead the fleet against Japan. "You should get away from Washington with its politics, petty squabbles, speech writing, and all the distractions that take time and energy," wrote Yarnell, "all of which should be concentrated on how we can lick the Jap. That is the one big job for the Navy."

Despite all this, King was probably pleased with the results. Nimitz had been forced to include Towers in operational planning, and senior aviation officers came to Nimitz's staff. The aviators now knew they had been heard and that their importance had become recognized.

King, in fact, had deliberately strengthened naval aviation even before Yarnell's survey began. The day after asking Yarnell to return to active duty, King asked Knox to get the President's approval for a Deputy Chief of Naval Operations for Air (DCNO[AIR]). Although the President had rejected a similar proposition the year before, King wanted to try again in order to placate the aviators clamoring for status. The DCNO(AIR) would also assume many of the tasks — planning, personnel, and training, for example — that had formerly belonged to the Bureau of Aeronautics. It was a clever way for King to weaken the bureau system he so disliked while increasing the power of his own office. (The DCNO would report directly to him.) Towers yelped from distant Pearl Harbor. The new office, he wrote, was "unsound, probably is illegal, and is confusing and overlapping." But Knox did as King had asked and got Roosevelt's approval. The final flourish was to make the new DCNO(AIR) a vice admiral's billet to give it more prestige.

The first incumbent was quickly selected. It would be John S. McCain, the Chief of the Bureau of Aeronautics, a wizened extrovert who rolled his own cigarettes and littered the floors with tobacco. He was a character. Unlike his predecessors, he locked open the swinging doors of his office so he could call his secretary, an elderly spinster accustomed to the intercom. It had been a shock at first to hear him shout, "Hey, woman. Get in here!" When inspecting aircraft factories his attention was as much on the woman employees as it was on the assembly lines.*

Why, then, did King choose McCain? "He was not very much in the way of brains," King later said, "but he was a fighter." Another plus was his loyalty to King. He was also available and in Washington. The handful of other senior aviators were needed elsewhere.

King announced McCain's ascension with a carefully prepared press release on 16 July 1943, most of which he wrote himself. Naval aviation had suddenly gained visibility in the Department of the Navy.

After McCain became DCNO(AIR) he began his own survey concurrently with Yarnell's. By early October McCain privately submitted his report to King. It contained some of the best advice that King would ever receive. Unlike Yarnell's report, it was both sound and realistic.

"I have investigated with some thoroughness," wrote McCain, "the condition of Aviation as within the Navy. . . . Without exception, the older Naval aviators can not be separated from the Navy or made disloyal thereto with a hammer and a chisel. They feel, as a whole, that the Naval aviator, treated with consideration as a specialist, does not receive the consideration he should have as a Naval officer better rounded, they think, than most others, in planning and in intermediate commands. They seem to feel that the Naval aviator as a well-rounded Naval officer is qualified to, and should, in due order, speak for the Navy as a whole on various planning committees and planning subcommittees; that is, they feel that Aviation in the Navy has become of age, that the airplane is the hardest hitting unit, and that, as such aviators should no longer be advisers but should, in due order, be the advised.

"Take the organization of most committees and sub-committees as between the Army and the Navy. They have, with almost uniformity, consisted of an Army ground officer, an Army air officer, and a Navy non-aviator. The non-aviator has, in general, ably represented the entire Navy, frequently calling on available aviation advice. The aviators think that they could as well or better represent the entire Navy, calling, when necessary, on non-aviator advice."

"All of them feel strongly," McCain continued, "that in task forces where the major purpose is air, such task force should be commanded by an aviator. When mixed forces are involved, the commander, if a non-aviator, should have an aviator as chief of staff, and vice versa. The commander should be dependent upon the mission, — if mainly air, then an air man. If landing operations are involved, then the commander should be a non-aviator. There are numberless operations that could be

* At sea his personal trademark was a disreputable cap with the grommet removed.

correctly decided either way, and fair allocations should be made by the Commanders in Chief.

"The above referred to expressions of opinion all come from regulars, some of them well down the list in rank and service. Like all good Naval officers, these believe in settling all Naval differences within the Navy and are tight-lipped to all the outside world."

Having made his point that aviators wanted more command and staff assignments, McCain mentioned the uneasiness of reserve aviators about postwar careers and recommended publishing a policy statement. Then he passed on to what he considered one of the greatest problems: publicity. "Most widely criticized by all hands within or without the Navy, in the newspaper world and elsewhere, is the Navy publicity policy with respect to air. Mr. Hanson Baldwin, Spig Wead, and other qualified publicists, all state that all the Navy has to do in order firmly to intrench its case against any united or combined air force is a simple recital of facts.

"All newspaper correspondents state that when aboard ship or in the field with the Navy they receive magnificent treatment. All, with uniformity, state that at Nimitz headquarters they are treated with hostility and suspicion. A representative of a national magazine, who wished to return home from the Pacific in a great hurry after covering many operations out there, applied to Admiral Nimitz staff for transportation by aircraft, and was told the best they could do would entail about a week's delay. He then went to General Richardson * and was on his way from Honolulu within a few hours.

"It is the considered opinion of several correspondents of the highest character," McCain concluded, "that such policy pursued by the Navy in comparison with the Army, steadily loses friends both in war and prospective peace, and literally throws them into the arms of a separate air force."

McCain next recommended early promotions of the younger aviators to give them seniority for task group commands and important staff assignments. "The promotion nerve is the most sensitive nerve of all in any military establishment," wrote McCain. "It is wrong to promote one man because another man is promoted; it is wrong not to promote a man when there is a military need for him in his new rank. Of the two wrongs, the first is the lesser, and the second is the greater military crime. Every element of human nature enters into this matter of promotion. Pressures are recurring from all angles. All kinds of motivations and all kinds of influences inherent in human nature are unceasingly at

* The senior Army officer in Hawaii.

work. In a matter so damnably involved as this one is, where expediency is quickly uncovered and is harmful rather than helpful, the only course is to go Presbyterian and do what the job demands." McCain then concluded, "There is a positive need of large increases in flag ranks in the Aeronautical Organization."

Respecting King's strong feelings, McCain carefully addressed the matter of publicity. "I believe there is only one fault in releases by the Navy Department — one and one only. That is, that your subordinates are afraid to release and afraid to speak to you, and, hence, kill."

McCain ended his report with some philosophical observations. "Steam marked the passing of the profession of sail, and wiped out a profession. I do NOT share your apprehension that air marks the passing of the trained and experienced non-aviator, nor does it deny him adequate command outlets for his professional qualifications." McCain felt that surface fleets would continue to be needed, but their status would change. "They are now," McCain asserted, "except the submarine, the auxiliaries of air. This is a patent fact, and like all facts, should be freely acknowledged."

McCain had given King much to think about. King quickly agreed that more aviators belonged in staff assignments and took immediate action. But McCain's call for more aviation flag officers was old business. A few weeks earlier McCain had asked for fifty-seven. As there were only thirty-eight in the fleet, McCain had argued that nineteen more aviators should be promoted to rear admiral.

King thought it an extravagant request, determined as he was to limit the number of admirals regardless of their specialty. Furthermore, the general contention that aviators did not receive their fair share of flag promotions was not true. Ever since the war began King had been perceptive enough to realize that many more flying admirals would be needed to command the Navy's air forces. Naval aviators had since dominated the flag promotion lists throughout 1942 and 1943. From November 1942 to August 1943 twenty-six of forty new rear admirals were aviators; from January through August 1943, nineteen of twenty-seven.

Now, in September 1943, McCain was asking for even more. King felt that he had nearly all that were necessary to fight the rest of the war. With an arbitrary stroke of his pen he approved only nine of the nineteen that McCain had recommended. But the need for more air admirals did not abate. Between October 1943 (the date of McCain's status report) to the end of the war, thirty more captains were promoted to rear admiral. Nineteen were aviators. Even so, naval aviation had expanded so dramatically that there were never enough senior aviators to command at sea.

King must be given credit for his foresight in promoting most of the key flag aviators *before* he had heard from McCain and Yarnell. Some of his finest carrier task force admirals had been promoted in 1942. DeWitt C. Ramsey, Alfred E. Montgomery, Ralph E. Davison, Gerald W. Bogan, and Arthur W. Radford are striking examples. Others followed in 1943, including Jocko Clark and Thomas L. Sprague. And still other superb flag aviators occupied key planning positions well before the fall of 1943. Forrest Sherman became Nimitz's war plans officer; Arthur C. Davis and Donald B. Duncan served both on King's staff and in the Pacific. King would have been justified if he had felt that McCain and Yarnell were being unduly critical about command and promotion. But it is perceptions that count, and the aviators still perceived that they were being slighted.

There were vexing issues besides promotions. A problem that often arose was seniority among admirals when carriers and their screening surface ships merged into a task group. The surface screen commander frequently was a salty battleship or cruiser division commander, considerably senior to the youthful carrier division commander. For centuries, tradition had accorded tactical command to the senior admiral regardless of his qualifications. The old seadog might know nothing about airplanes, but he was still entitled to run the show. King's solution broke hallowed precedent. The carrier admiral would be in tactical command, regardless of seniority, while the task group was underway.

A McCain recommendation that King did implement (in January 1944) was to pair aviators and surface officers as commanders and chiefs of staff. If a fleet or task force commander was an aviator, his chief of staff would be a surface officer, and vice versa. The intent was to placate those aviators who resented such officers as Spruance and Kinkaid, both nonaviators who commanded entire fleets containing naval air forces. Still, no one liked the new arrangement even though the policy went both ways. The most outspoken was carrier commander Marc Mitscher, who ostracized Arleigh Burke when the famed destroyerman became Mitscher's chief of staff. (Burke soon got accepted, however.) Spruance tried to retain Captain Charles J. ("Carl") Moore, a surface officer, as his Fifth Fleet chief of staff, but King's policy prevailed when Arthur Davis eventually relieved Moore in the late summer of 1944.

These policies still did not go far enough in the opinion of many aviators. They were still excluded from the naval hierarchy. By the summer of 1945 there were fourteen fleet admirals and admirals. Among them

Halsey alone was considered by the aviation community as one of their own. King, Horne, and Turner wore wings, but they were not regarded as "active" aviators.* Of thirty-five vice admirals in July 1945, only seven were aviators.

Why did the active aviators fail during the war to dominate the uppermost echelons of naval command? King was largely responsible. Naval warfare had become so vast and complicated that aviation was but one part of the whole. King needed senior flag officers who were generalists rather than specialists, and who understood grand strategy, logistics, and joint operations. Intelligence, judgment, and maturity counted the most. Naval aviators concerned solely with acting as aviation advocates had no place at this level of command.

King had more faith in surface officers than did the aviation zealots. He resented the pejorative phrase "battleship admiral" because it implied that a flag officer without wings was not qualified to command a force that included carriers. Naval aviation had remained so integral with fleet operations, King would say, that most flag officers were "air-conscious" even though they may never have flown an aircraft or commanded a carrier. King also believed that the surface admirals' skepticism was a healthy balance to the aviators' exuberance about the virtues of air power.

Another consideration was King's policy to limit the numbers of senior flag officers. There were few openings for younger aviators because many senior surface officers remained on active duty until forced into retirement. The aviators would have to wait their turn. Many truly superior aviators had only recently become rear admirals and could not attain enough seniority to be considered for three and four stars during the war.

Finally, there were only three flag aviators whom King and Nimitz trusted to handle large carrier task forces at sea: Halsey, Mitscher, and McCain. Of the three, only Mitscher has escaped criticism from historians evaluating their combat records during 1944 and 1945. Many of Halsey's and McCain's shortcomings are attributable to fatigue; all three were physically and mentally exhausted by war's end. (McCain died of heart failure shortly after V-J Day.) King and Nimitz thought that they were attuned to their health (it was a subject frequently discussed), but King never appreciated how tired they really were.

There were other aviators who perhaps could have spelled the trio. John Hoover, Frederick Sherman, and Patrick Bellinger come immedi-

* Horne was an aviation observer.

KING TAKES MARSHALL TO SEA TO LEARN ABOUT NAVAL AIR POWER

The *Lexington* skipper, Captain Felix B. Stump, greets King and Marshall at the quarterdeck (National Archives 80-G-73268)

Watching flight operations from the bridge (U.S. Navy photograph)

Inspecting a carrier aircraft at close range (National Archives 80-G-73278)

ately to mind. The most obvious choice was Towers. But, of course, Nimitz would not allow Towers to go to sea, while King at first felt that Towers could best serve ashore as the chief aviation spokesman in Pearl Harbor. In early 1944 King elevated Towers to the position of Deputy Commander in Chief, Pacific Fleet and Pacific Ocean Areas. Some historians consider this move as a concession to Forrestal's insistence that aviators be given more prominence and prestige. Perhaps. It is just as logical to conclude that the initiative came from King. So long as Towers was in Pearl Harbor, King knew that naval aviation was in good hands.

What, then, was King's role in developing and supporting naval aviation during the Second World War? Clearly, he was the prime mover. He foresaw the naval air forces that would be needed to defeat Japan in the Pacific. He provided the flag officers that would be needed to command the carrier task groups. When he recognized the increasing animosity between surface officers and aviators, he provided an outlet for the aviators' legitimate complaints through the Yarnell and McCain surveys in 1943.

Yet King recognized the need to balance the fleet between air, surface combatant, amphibious, and submarine forces. Aviation had its place in the fleet, and its importance was growing, but King would not subordinate the entire Navy solely to the aircraft carrier and its more enthusiastic proponents. King could not and would not neglect the remainder of the Navy. Each combat arm had its own vital role, and together their roles were orchestrated by King. Furthermore, he had to be sensitive to the personalities involved. The aviators had to be reassured, but not at the price of antagonizing the rest of the Navy.

King kept informed about all aspects of naval aviation. At first he distrusted the escort carriers and opposed their construction. Yet he solicited letters from their first commanding officers to discover how well the ships were operating. Eventually he recognized that their value far outweighed their inherent defects and limitations. When a new patrol plane experienced technical defects as it entered the fleet in early 1943, King became directly involved. In a letter to Rear Admiral Pat Bellinger, King wrote, "I have just seen a copy of your letter No. 18L-43 and wish to congratulate you on the forceful statements and 'horse sense' it contains. It should do a lot of good in your outfit—or any other outfit!

"I am as deeply concerned as you and McCain are about the Martin Patrol Planes. McCain tells me that you understand the *necessity* to make these planes over into useful planes if it can possibly be done. However, I have the feeling that your people concerned with these planes have adopted what may be called a 'defeatist' attitude. If I am right in this feeling, such an attitude must be eradicated—and it is up to you to do it! I don't need to tell you that we cannot tolerate in the Naval service people who think that they are entitled to pick and choose what they will do or what they will work with. They should be made to see that the defects of the Martin Patrol Planes comprise what we may call 'enemies' which we must lick. I know that you will do your utmost in this matter."

The pressure for a separate, independent American air force would not go away. The Royal Air Force, King believed, was constantly urging Arnold to model his service after the British. And yet, King argued, the RAF had been less than successful against German industry and U-boat facilities, or in cooperating with the assault troops at Sicily.

RAF claims to the contrary, King would maintain, the RAF would not win the war by itself. It had to be a part of the armed forces team.

He heard the same argument for a separate air force from Marshall. To straighten him out, King took Marshall to sea aboard the new USS *Lexington* in July 1943. Marshall roamed the carrier for two days, then left, presumably better informed than before — or so King hoped. Marshall, however, persisted in nagging King and later Leahy. When King refused to listen and Leahy was noncommittal, Marshall had his deputy chief of staff, Lieutenant General Joseph T. McNarney (an Army aviator), work on Horne. In time Horne agreed to a joint Army-Navy committee to study the feasibility of an independent air force. King was furious. In his last years he wrote bitterly, "I sent for Admiral Horne and asked him why in the hell he agreed to even start such a set-up to which his answer was that he thought the idea was rather good. By that time the 'fat was in the fire' indeed!!! They started at once to work up their *propaganda* which finally became the program of the so-called *unification* which was finally voted in Congress. Now look at the damn thing!!!"

King did not profess that naval aviation should supplant land-based air, nor did he seek public debate. To his chagrin the Washington *Post* ran a front-page article on 13 August 1943 entitled "Air Power: Key to Modern Strategy." It quoted King that Army aviation should end at the shoreline and suggested that he was a reactionary opponent of nonnaval aviation. "I am sure you would wish," King wrote to the author of the article, "in the interests of truth and fairness, to know that no matter how many times this statement has been, or will be, repeated it remains what it was when it was first printed — a distortion of the facts for propaganda purposes — in short, a lie."

King failed to win the battle for popular support. His disdain for publicity continued throughout the war despite McCain's October 1943 plea, despite Forrestal's efforts to publicize the Navy's accomplishments, and despite King's private meetings with journalists and correspondents. King had his own way to fight the proponents of a separate air force: he lashed out against them — but only in sporadic outbursts. He had neither the time nor the will for a permanent, sustained propaganda campaign to champion the United States Navy before the American people, or to tangle with the Army Air Force publicists. King's sole, single-minded objective was to win the war as soon as possible. Nothing else could compete for his attention so long as the war still had to be won. When it was over he would retire. His job would be done. Someone else would have to take the burden of the postwar political battles.

In the five years following V-J Day the Navy became embroiled in an internecine struggle with the newly independent United States Air Force. At issue were the merits of the aircraft carrier versus the B-36 intercontinental bomber. The Navy lost the fight, a new aircraft carrier was canceled, and only the Korean War rescued the carrier from oblivion.

29

The Fleet Admiral

THE NAVY by custom and tradition likes to keep its uniforms. The officer's blue service and white service uniforms worn today have remained the same for over a half-century. When a recent CNO abolished the sailor's familiar white hat and bell-bottom uniform, its replacement was so unpopular that the next CNO restored the original uniform. Changes have not come easily, but changes were an obsession with King.

He tinkered with uniforms in the early months of the war, primarily to reduce the size of an officer's wardrobe. By the time the American and British convened for the TRIDENT Conference in May 1943, King modeled a new look. In lieu of the familiar double-breasted blue uniform, King wore a single-breasted gray uniform with black buttons and black insignia. It would become his most notorious contribution to the Second World War.

The prewar Navy had worn blues in cool weather and whites when it was warm. These were gradually supplemented with wartime khakis, which became popular as a practical working uniform, especially in the Pacific. King hated them because they looked like the Army uniform. "I repeat what I have said many times before," he wrote in an official letter in June 1942. "In my view, khaki is not to be considered as other than a stopgap." By the summer of 1942 King started to fashion a permanent "naval working uniform." He liked the Marine Corps herringbone cloth, but, as he told his bureau chiefs, "consideration may well cause the arrival at a decision to develop a tough cloth which is dark gray in color."

By early April 1943 King had decided that his new working uniform would be colored gray for a number of reasons. White uniforms at sea were visible to enemy scouts and made attractive targets for strafing aircraft, while gray would blend with the color of the ships. Another virtue of a gray uniform would be its "simplicity and utility." Dress uniforms adorned with swords and gold ornamentation, King believed, were ostentatious; they reflected an elitism that offended civilians and enlisted men. The austere gray uniform, King informed the Navy Department, would "make officers' uniforms more nearly consonant with democratic principles."

Secretary Knox approved King's gray uniform in April 1943. Everyone loathed it. Those outside Washington refused to wear it, and Nimitz even banned it. King could hardly ignore such intransigence and sent a message in early 1944 asking Nimitz whether it was true that officers in the Pacific were forbidden to wear grays. Nimitz's response was a masterpiece of equivocation: "Inquiry discloses some local commands while not prohibiting gray have expressed preference for khaki. Am fully aware gray is authorized and will issue appropriate clarifying directive." Nevertheless, the gray uniform remained forever taboo in the Pacific.

Things were different in Washington, where King could enforce his regulations. William Smedberg remembered the transition after he had arrived at COMINCH headquarters from sea duty in the Pacific. "I was immediately included in the daily morning meeting with the Admiral and principal members of his staff," said Smedberg after the war. "The first time I noted that I was the only one present in khaki. All the others were in the 'King Gray' which I detested. After about three mornings, even I began to feel uncomfortable about being the only one in khaki. . . . Savvy Cooke took me aside after the meeting and said, 'Smeddy, have you noted the Admiral's look when he sees your khaki? It won't be long before he explodes.' I bought a gray uniform that afternoon, off the rack, and never wore khaki again while on his staff." Although Leahy occasionally wore grays (perhaps to support King), khakis persevered even in Washington, and no one was consistent. During the First Quebec Conference in August 1943 Leahy wore grays, the JCS secretary, Captain Forrest B. Royal, wore khakis, and King wore blues.

King remodeled his own uniforms so often that he seemed to disregard any regulations whatsoever. When inspecting troops he frequently wore a tarnished, battered admiral's cap. (In this respect he was not unlike many naval officers who love to affect a salty air by keeping their old, seagoing caps.) Another ugly combination that King sponsored was a blue uniform with gray shirt and collar insignia. King also designed his own white dress uniform with a white shirt and black tie that replaced the traditional high-necked collar. The variety was endless. King was elegant in his regulation blue service uniform, glittering with gold braid and ribbons — and a white handkerchief in his breast pocket. "Many officers thought this to be a breach of the uniform regulations," recalled a King staff officer. "King was aware of this. He liked a bit of white."

King was persistent. In early 1945 he even proposed a heavier gray uniform to replace the blue service. Randall Jacobs refused even to consider it because — he said — of material procurement problems. King dropped that plan but continued to fiddle with other modifications for the remainder of the war. Before he retired King made one final plea to Forrestal to keep the grays and to eliminate the blues and the whites. It was wrong, King argued, for the United States Navy to copy its uniforms after an international style inspired by the Royal Navy. The Americans should be unique. King even wanted to eliminate the officer's dress sword. "It is an open question," he wrote to Forrestal, "whether swords should be prescribed for 'full dress' — blue or white. They are an item of expense — worn only on special occasions. Personally, I prefer the 'dirk' rather than the sword, especially for naval personnel as it is an encumbrance in getting about aboard ship."

When King retired, the gray uniform went with him. Khakis had come to stay, and blues and whites remained.

At the beginning of the war the Navy had no coherent policy for awards and decorations. In December 1941 there were only four authorized decorations: the Medal of Honor, the Navy Cross, the Distinguished Service Medal, and the Distinguished Flying Cross. These could be awarded only by the Secretary of the Navy upon the recommendation of an ad hoc board. Anticipating increased numbers of recommendations for awards, the Navy Department established a permanent Board of Decorations and Medals in early 1942. But the board lacked guidance. The Navy's few decorations were freely distributed in the absence of rules and regulations and became cheapened. As a Navy historian later commented, "There persisted a notable tendency by some commanding officers to confuse an assigned mission well done with heroism or performance above and beyond the call of duty." The Navy's answer was to establish medals of lesser degree, but still without policy guidance.

The problem was almost entirely attributable to King's idealism. "Every naval officer has a job to do," King once told Betsy Matter during the war. "He should do that job out of a sense of duty and should not get recognition for having done what he has been trained to do. His only reward should be the satisfaction of knowing that he has done the job well and to the best of his ability." When King visited Hawaii in 1944, Nimitz proudly showed off his communicators who kept him in touch with his fleet. "These men are doing one of the best jobs in the world," said Nimitz. King was unmoved. "That's what they are being paid to do," he replied.

Halsey once learned a lesson in King's conservatism when he wrote King in the summer of 1943 asking for special treatment for a subordinate. "You raise the question of ——— with regard to his being placed in command of a combatant ship," King replied, "which will involve an additional spot promotion. There is no use blinking the fact that ———'s record throughout the years is not a creditable one. However, so far as I am concerned, I take the view that any officer can 'redeem' himself by outstanding and *long-continued* demonstration of professional capacity in combat work. Along with this view goes the realization, on my part, that the service in general will not understand such promotions unless the case is so clear-cut and exceptional as to enable the service to appreciate that special outstanding and *repeated* performances have been the cause of the 'unusual' promotion.

"Your letter to me affords the opportunity of making mention of something else that has bothered me for some time. It is the award of decorations on such a scale as to diminish the value of the decoration. The number of Navy Crosses awarded has been out of proportion to what would appear the realities of the case, viewed in perspective. It is true that a large number of Navy Crosses were issued before the Silver Star Medal — and the Navy and Marine Corps Medal — became available for award. I know you will not misunderstand me when I say that I think that too many Navy Crosses have been awarded for acts which are *not* in the category of being 'next door' to the requirements for the award of the Medal of Honor. Again, they seem to have been issued to some individuals, in some cases at least, because they would be 'dissatisfied' if their services were not considered of equal merit with those people who have already received the award. In the beginning of hostilities, the contrast between peace and war quite naturally led to the doing of anything of a combat nature being considered outstanding, but we have now been engaged in combat operations for a year and a half and should be able to make awards on the basis of exceptional merit as viewed in perspective. I repeat, I think that the 'me too' expectations of personnel have been satisfied to a greater extent than is warranted by the facts. I am reminded of the old saying of a Superintendent of the Naval

Academy to the effect that if everybody dishes out 4.0's * with both hands, how are the really exceptional performances to be recognized?"

King may have distrusted Halsey's motives. "Halsey had a Marine officer in the South Pacific," King said after the war, "who was a big, fat man and a drinker — although I didn't mind that. But he was not able. Halsey would give him 4.0 fitness reports but then would ask the Commandant of the Marine Corps to have this officer sent home.

"A lot of people would give 4.0 to everyone — good, bad, or indifferent. I had one admiral reporting on me who put 4.0 right through. I never gave any 4.0 — only 3.9."

King's attitude was a paradox. He griped about too many people getting decorations, but he refused to establish a policy that would end the confusion. Nimitz was his voice of conscience, besieging King to approve the Purple Heart or to define different grades for the Legion of Merit. But it was futile. King did nothing. Nimitz tried to force the issue at their January 1944 meeting in San Francisco by demanding a formal board to standardize the awarding of decorations. All the services had different rules, argued Nimitz, and the Army Air Force was notably generous. If the services could not agree on a common policy, then the President should act. King stalled with a promise to study the problem.

King's thinking began to change in June 1944. Just before King had left to watch the Normandy landings, Abby Dunlap had warned him that when the war was over the Army Air Force would get all the credit and the Navy would be forgotten. King thought she was too pessimistic. But when he next saw Abby and Betsy Matter following the invasion, he told Abby she had been right.

King's new attitude became evident when his principal naval commander at Normandy, Rear Admiral Alan G. Kirk, returned to Washington several months later. As the two admirals passed in a corridor of the Navy Department, King stopped and stared intently at Kirk's chest.

"I don't see any decoration on your bosom for this operation," said King.

"No one has ever given me one," replied Kirk.

King was astounded. "Weren't you recommended?" he asked.

"Yes, I was, by General Eisenhower for the Army Distinguished Service Medal," said Kirk.

King could not conceal his dismay. Wheels turned. Several weeks later Secretary of War Stimson awarded Kirk the DSM in an elaborate ceremony in the War Department offices of the Pentagon.

* A 4.0 is traditionally the Navy's highest numerical grade.

When the war was over, so much criticism arose about the way in which awards had been made that the Secretary of the Navy appointed a Board of Review for Decorations and Medals. It convened on 22 December 1945 with Admiral Horne as chairman. The board's report was released in April 1947. One of the major criticisms it had investigated was "inconsistency among the various delegated authorities in awarding medals." The board agreed with that charge with little comment. King had utterly failed to establish a coherent awards policy during his tenure.

In the years just before the Second World War, four officers had been entitled to the four-star rank of admiral. The CNO had always been one of the four. Another had been the Commander in Chief, U.S. Fleet (CINCUS at the time), whose title was changed to Commander in Chief, Pacific Fleet, when Kimmel took command in early 1941. When King became Commander in Chief, Atlantic Fleet, he inherited the four stars that had been worn until then by Commander, Battle Force. The fourth set of stars had been worn by Admiral Hart, the Commander in Chief, Asiatic Fleet.

There had been even fewer vice admirals, only three as late as June 1941. These two highest ranks went with the job with no increase in salary. When a flag officer no longer occupied a three- or four-star billet, he reverted to rear admiral, the highest permanent flag rank by law.

Only four admirals were authorized in the early months of the war: King, Nimitz, Ingersoll in the Atlantic, and Stark in London. Halsey was the first to break precedent. Owing to his publicized carrier raids, and upon assumption of the South Pacific Theater command, he received a fourth star in November 1942.

Congress, of course, had to confirm Halsey's promotion. Historically wary of high rank, Congress had always thought that four admirals had been enough. But Carl Vinson liked and admired Halsey and was willing to make him the Navy's fifth admiral. Through his good offices Congress approved Halsey's nomination. (Eisenhower received his fourth star at about the same time, to give him seniority as supreme commander for the invasion of North Africa.)

It was obvious to King that the expansion of the armed forces would require even more four-star flag and general officers. Ad hoc promotions would not do, King argued to his colleagues. A formal policy was needed, acceptable to Congress, Roosevelt, and the JCS. In a 17 November 1942 memorandum to Marshall and Leahy, King wrote, "I therefore suggest that we consider the matter and make appropriate recommendations to the President." Then King raised a related subject. "We should also recognize the fact that there is a need to prepare for ranks *higher* than that of Admiral or General. As to such ranks, I suggest Arch-Admiral and Arch-General, rather than Admiral of the Fleet and Field Marshal."

"The time had come to establish a five-star rank," said King after the war, adding, "Marshall said he was against it." (Although Marshall would not admit it, King suspected that while General of the Armies John J. Pershing was still alive Marshall would not ask for an equivalent rank.) Another obstacle — an awkward obstacle — was trying to find an appropriate way to ask Congress to create such an exalted rank for themselves.

The only hope for approval was for King and Marshall to unite, as King knew from events of the First World War. "After that war," wrote King to a colleague in January 1944, "there would have been higher promotions in the Navy if Sims and others hadn't raised hell with themselves. Sims and [Henry B.] Wilson couldn't agree on anything, so Mayo lost out. There was great trouble between Sims and Wilson in Brest. They always hated each other. If they could have agreed they would have been promoted."

King had sent Knox a copy of his memorandum to Marshall. "I completely agree with the idea of an increase of rank for you and Marshall," responded Knox, "but I confess I do not like the suggestion of Arch Admiral. It sounds too much like a church designation, although the use of the word 'arch' in that connection does indicate the highest, which is the proper designation for this rank. However, I still think I like Admiral of the Fleet a darn sight better than I do Arch Admiral, and I like Field Marshal much better than Arch General."

The question of titles was difficult to resolve. King's dislike of "Admiral of the Fleet" may have stemmed from a similar title in the Royal Navy which he did not want to imitate. The problems with "Field Marshal Marshall" were obvious. But King's "arch" titles encountered heavy weather. "In fact," King complained to a friend, "when the matter was being discussed, I found that the proposal was viewed facetiously!"

Titles continued to be bandied by others. Roosevelt favored "Chief Admiral" and "Chief General." King at one point even suggested "Captain Admiral" and "Colonel General." Knox in exasperation wrote to King, "Personally I don't care very much how the title is fixed so long as recognition is given to the pre-eminence of the command you both exercise." In early January 1944 King proposed "Fleet Admiral," the title that was ultimately adopted.

King's campaign for five stars, which had begun in November 1942, became quiescent until the First Quebec Conference in August 1943. The conference became a showdown with the British on such matters as a cross-Channel invasion and the Pacific offensive. The United States had become the senior partner in terms of combat power and economic strength, yet the American leaders were still junior in rank. "Admiral King came back in an absolute rage," remembered Betsy Matter. "He was furious because we were making the major contribution to the war effort, and yet the British were still acting as if they were the country which had the greatest say in running the war."

King now wanted his five stars more than ever. Following his return from the Cairo-Teheran Conference in December 1943, King had gotten Leahy's concurrence, but Marshall was still noncommittal. King continued to agitate. In early January 1944 he received a letter from retired Admiral William V. Pratt, the CNO in the early 1930s. Pratt was worried that when Pershing died Marshall would inherit his title and five stars. The former CNO wanted the Navy — and King — to have equal recognition and status, and he recalled how personal jealousies had prevented the Navy from getting a five-star officer after the First World War. "Neither one of them was big enough to see," wrote Pratt, "that in this struggle for personal recognition the Navy as a whole suffered."

King exploited Pratt's letter as a fresh opportunity to buttress his own proposal. "I am personally indifferent to what may happen to me," he replied to Pratt. "However, it has long been my view — which coincides with yours — that the high command positions in the Navy and the Army should be duly recognized by the provision of higher rank. Certainly, the echelons of high command appropriate to our current military setup are not properly recognized nor emphasized when the highest ranks are general and admiral."

King sent Knox both Pratt's letter and his own reply. "I have had several talks with the President," Knox responded, "on increased rank for you and Marshall — the last one only the other day. At that time I was directed to talk the matter over with Chairman Vinson and then both Vinson and I were to see the President. I have talked with Vinson and arrangements have been made at the White House for the final conference with F.D.R. as soon as his health permitted."

Roosevelt's support had meanwhile become apparent when he told Leahy to expect a promotion. Leahy diplomatically feigned surprise. "The other members of the Joint Chiefs of Staff," he told Roosevelt, "are entitled to the same reward as you propose to give me." Later

Vinson raised the question with Leahy, who repeated what he had told the President. Now everyone was in line, overcoming Marshall's objections. The long legislative process began.

But complications persisted. Vinson wanted King and Marshall to have six-star ranks. "What I am seriously concerned about," wrote King to Marshall on 21 January 1944, "is that there are in prospect many promotions *in Washington* which will have serious repercussions in the Forces overseas unless provision is made for proportional promotion in the operating forces. . . . Mr. Vinson has been advised of the foregoing views and appears to be agreeable to inclusion of a '5-star rank' but insistent on a '6-star rank.' I have got word to him that, personally, I have no desire whatever for the '6-star rank' unless and until a '5-star-rank' is provided for — and further, that I think it advisable that any promotion in prospect in connection with Cominch-CNO should *first* be to '5-star rank.' "

The "tortuous legislative journey" (in Leahy's words) became stalled in early April 1944 by a New York *Herald Tribune* article headlined, "Marshall Asks That New Rank Bill Be Shelved." The article quoted War Department and congressional spokesmen who asserted that Marshall had a number of objections to the bill, which had been introduced in January. The article ended with the statement, "Friends of Admiral King were quick to point out that, like General Marshall, he too, was not in the least interested in 'gathering a new title.' "

King hit the roof. The Navy's Director of Public Relations scurried over to the War Department to find out who had talked. He reported his findings in a memorandum for King: "General Marshall conveys his respects to the Commander in Chief, U.S. Fleet and wishes to state that no member of his staff or Department transmitted information contained in the attached article to the press."

Passage of the bill required ten months. The Senate on 11 December 1944 approved a House bill that authorized Roosevelt to appoint four fleet admirals and four generals of the army. On 15 December the Senate confirmed Leahy, King, and Nimitz for the Navy and Marshall, MacArthur, Eisenhower, and Arnold for the Army. A nomination for the fourth fleet admiral was not submitted, as the Navy could not decide whom to nominate.

King was in a dilemma. Forrestal — by then Secretary of the Navy — told King to decide upon a nominee. Vinson publicly supported Halsey. King favored Spruance, but he was understandably reluctant to oppose Vinson. Another factor was Halsey's public popularity. Spruance consistently avoided publicity. After stalling for months "to think the thing

King's notorious gray uniform (Courtesy Walter Muir Whitehill)

King and Marshall self-consciously display their new five-star uniforms for the press (National Archives 80-G-47659)

over," King passed the buck back to Forrestal by writing a memorandum containing the pros and cons of six possible candidates: Spruance, Halsey, Ingersoll, Ingram, Kinkaid, and Hewitt. (King was silent about Halsey's problems with typhoons or his close call at Leyte Gulf.) "I think Forrestal took it to the White House and put it up to Truman," King later said, "although I am not sure how the decision was finally made." Halsey eventually got the five stars. Congress compensated Spruance by authorizing full pay as an admiral for life.

And so, thanks to King, the five-star rank was established for a select group of America's naval and military leaders. By law they remained on active duty until death, together with privileges including an aide and an office. But Congress was penurious with the salary that went with the new rank. Until 1955 the pay of all flag officers, from rear admiral to fleet admiral, was the same. In 1955 Congress enacted legislation that gave a higher salary to vice admirals and admirals. But the Navy's fleet admirals — and the generals of the army — did not get a pay raise. Their salary was limited to the two-star rank level, which amounted to $1,076 per month. Congress authorized further pay increases in 1958, 1963, and 1965 but specifically prohibited pay increases for the remaining living five-star officers. Nimitz continued to receive only $1,076 per month until he died in 1966, while an admiral on active duty received twice that amount. Furthermore, the legislation was such that a widow of a five-star officer received a lesser pension than the widow of a lower-ranking flag officer.

Fleet admiral was a rank that served its purpose during the war and afterward. It distinguished King and his colleagues in a way that was both fitting and appropriate. The very title conveyed a sense of grandeur and majesty that seemed to characterize those who wore the uniform. When Nimitz died the rank passed out of existence, probably forever.

30

Quadrant: The First Quebec Conference

THE THIRD WASHINGTON CONFERENCE (TRIDENT) in May 1943 had left unfinished business. After Sicily was seized in August there remained the question of whether to continue advancing in the Mediterranean or to mass forces in Great Britain for a cross-Channel assault. In the China-Burma-India (CBI) theater the Americans feared that the British were stalling on opening the Burma Road to China. A third problem was to define long-range strategy in the Pacific beyond the Marshalls and the Carolines. It was imperative for the British and Americans to have another planning conference. It convened in Quebec in August 1943 under the code name QUADRANT.

Decisions had to be made about what operations would follow the invasion of Sicily in July 1943. When he reviewed the results, King had been disappointed. He had hoped to trap from sixty to seventy thousand German troops on the island, on the mistaken assumption that the Allied navy controlled the Straits of Messina. The ease with which the Germans escaped from Sicily surprised King and revealed his unfamiliarity with the details of major operations after they had been authorized by the CCS.

Italy was central to British strategic thinking as the next target for invasion following Sicily. King still viewed it as a liability to whichever power controlled it, whether Germany or the Allies. It was, in fact, such a liability that King would not have been surprised if Germany voluntarily withdrew from the Italian peninsula. With Sicily about to fall, King expected the Italian government to collapse momentarily. And when Italy did quit fighting, King believed, the Allies would have to reconsider their unconditional surrender policy. He never had taken that policy seriously; it was "just another phrase." "We cannot utterly destroy any country," King maintained. At least some Fascist officials would have to be retained to govern Italy under Allied occupation. King knew Marshal Pietro Badoglio personally and considered him the only real soldier in Italy.* Badoglio was the kind of former enemy, King believed, who could be trusted in a future Italian government.

But King's main concern was, as always, the war against Japan. By the summer of 1943 MacArthur and Halsey were moving ahead in New Guinea and the Solomons, and American submarines were bleeding Japan's merchant marine. King reckoned that the Japanese had started the war with six million tons of shipping and had acquired another one million tons by seizure and new construction in 1942. (Both estimates were remarkably accurate.) Initial assessments of Japanese losses were "illusory," King believed, and he and Nimitz had developed a "hard-boiled" system of computing enemy losses.† By the most conservative figures Japan had lost one-and-a-half million tons since the war began. (It was a good estimate. The actual figures were 1,780,000 tons.) The Japanese could not build more than a million tons per year of combined warships and merchantmen, so their losses would increase as American submarines entered the fleet. Consequently, reasoned King, the Japanese would become hard pressed to support their outlying bases which he intended to attack. One indication of Japan's shortages was their use of wooden barges for inter-island shipping in the Central Pacific.

Despite the CCS commitment to a Pacific offensive, it was six months behind King's personal schedule. He was still dissatisfied with the allocation of resources between theaters. The Pacific still was receiving but 15 percent of the total, and King wanted twice that amount. The Japanese were "digging in" and exploiting their new wealth of tin, rubber, and oil. Seething with impatience, King regarded the looming QUADRANT Conference as a time to get moving in the Pacific.

We know now that King's assessment of Japan's economy was in error. Japan had gone to war to get raw materials, but she could never get enough of them to her factories. Her merchant marine became weakened by attrition and her shipyards were inadequate. Most of Japan's limited shipping directly supported her armed forces, leaving few ships available for industrial imports. But these facts were not discovered until after the war. In July 1943 King believed that Japan was using "captured rubber, tin, and oil to a fare-thee-well." Even then his reasoning

* How well King knew Badoglio is not certain.

† King never described the system, but it was probably the decryption of enemy messages.

was inconsistent, given his knowledge of Japanese shipping losses. Yet King maintained — at least for the record — that the Japanese were still able to import at a high level.

Concurrent with the American effort in the Pacific was the need to keep China in the war. King never changed his conviction: if China's huge army could be supported logistically via the Burma Road, it would occupy most of the Japanese Army on the Asian mainland, keeping enemy soldiers out of the Pacific and away from American forces. King insisted that the British honor their TRIDENT commitment to open the Burma Road, a commitment he perceived to be waning throughout the summer of 1943 owing to British apathy toward the entire CBI theater.

As a sign of good faith, King wanted the British to designate a supreme commander for Burma. The British had nominated Air Chief Marshal Sir Sholto Douglas in June, but Marshall thought he was anti-American. The JCS counterproposed Admiral Sir Andrew B. Cunningham or Air Marshal Sir Arthur Tedder. Both were first-rate officers who could give the Burma offensive a chance of success. But the British insisted on Douglas. The argument became an impasse. During the July JCS meetings King insisted that the matter be taken immediately before the President or the British Chiefs of Staff, but Marshall deferred action because "negotiations were in progress."

The confused command structure in the CBI theater complicated everything. Chiang was, of course, the supreme commander in China. Stilwell and Chennault served respectively as his ground and air commanders and as his advisors. King liked them both and thought that Chennault was a "genius." Nevertheless King did worry that Chennault's air attacks would provoke the Japanese to overrun his unprotected airfields.* King also felt that Chennault was unrealistic in demanding that his forces receive all the tonnage flown into China. King wanted Stilwell to get his share.

Concerned that Stilwell had been "pushed around." especially by the Army Air Force, both King and Marshall hoped to prevent recurrences. King regarded Stilwell as a "great soldier who speaks Chinese, thinks in Chinese, and who knows the situation in China." King would have preferred Stilwell as the CBI supreme commander, but the theater belonged to Britain, and a British officer would have to be in command. It did not disturb King that Stilwell and Chennault were obvious rivals. Their differences would never become serious, King reasoned, because both were exceptional soldiers working toward a common objective.

Chiang was a different matter. The Generalissimo was too set in his

* Which is exactly what happened.

ways, King would say, and he ridiculed Chiang's pretentious advice for employing the Allied fleet to support CBI operations.

Everything seemed to depend upon the British opening the Burmese supply route to China. Developments in early August reinforced King's suspicions that the British were flagging. A report on the progress of their plans was generally negative and revealed that certain amphibious assault ships would arrive late from the Mediterranean. King's annoyance mounted when he received two letters from Admiral Sir Percy Noble of the British mission in Washington. In the first, Noble asked that American naval liaison officers be assigned to the British fleet in the Indian Ocean. King refused because Noble's letter implied that the British expected American warships to help attack Burma. In the second, Noble asked King for extra landing craft for the CBI theater. Again King refused. Such a transfer would sacrifice landing craft needed for the eventual cross-Channel invasion, said King. The British had an obligation to provide their share of landing craft in the CBI theater. King was emphatic. He would not substitute any of his own shipping.

One late July evening, several weeks before the conference, King sat in Nelie Bull's Alexandria home for one of his regular seminars with selected war correspondents. The conversation drifted toward American-British interplay on the CCS.

"What happens," asked a journalist, "when the Combined Chiefs disagree?"

"The decision is up to the President and Churchill," King replied.

"Who usually wins in such cases?"

King paused. "Mr. Churchill is a *very* persuasive talker, you know." King credited Hopkins with keeping the President "straight" when the Prime Minister was trying to sway FDR. "I like Churchill very much," continued King. "But it must never be forgotten that Churchill is first, last, and all the time for the British. That is as it should be, but one should never forget it when talking to him."

King laughed. "I always keep my hand on my watch whenever Churchill is talking and trying to sell a point." Then King compared the minds of Churchill and Roosevelt. "Churchill has read all the books on strategy," King remarked. "Roosevelt has them read to him."

With the QUADRANT Conference scheduled for 14 August, the JCS met with Roosevelt on the tenth to confirm the American positions. Following a wide-ranging discussion, the President agreed to insist upon a cross-Channel operation — Operation OVERLORD — and to resist any British arguments for further delay. The chiefs also urged Roosevelt to prod the British into action in the CBI theater. When the meeting ended, Marshall emphasized to FDR that decisions once made should not be changed. It was the General's way of reminding Roosevelt to back his JCS and not to acquiesce to Churchill's eloquent appeals.

On the morning of Friday, the thirteenth of August, King's Lodestar lifted from the Anacostia Naval Air Station and turned north for the six-hour flight to Quebec. The other members of the JCS went by separate planes. Over Montreal the pilot, Lieutenant Commander Hyland, received a report that the airport at Quebec was closed to weather. "As usual, Admiral King wasn't impressed with this news," Hyland later recalled, "and since it is only about 160 miles from Montreal to Quebec we could press on and give it a go. If we couldn't get in we could always return to Montreal; if that got socked in in the meantime we could go back to New York. My biggest concern was really that the field was too small and not equipped with a standard radio range. I had to fly lower and lower as we went on, but I had a good map and had marked it up quite carefully, so we knew where we were. Well, we got in under a ceiling of less than three hundred feet by flying visually and *low*. We don't do that sort of thing anymore. All the other pilots elected to land at Montreal and wait until the next day, so that night in the old Château Frontenac the Navy group was the only one present. The next day at lunch Admiral King made a point of taking me around and introducing me to all the high rank who had spent the night in Montreal, and all of whom were pleasantly informed that we had gotten in the day before with no difficulty."

Château Frontenac is a stately old hotel adorned with spires and towers, overlooking the Saint Lawrence River. The Canadian government had given the entire hotel to the CCS and their staffs. Everything was under one roof: lodging, meals, offices, conference rooms, radio communication centers—even movies for those who had time. Royal Canadian Mounted Police in red tunics provided security. The setting proved to be ideal. Before lunch the chiefs often strolled on a boardwalk high above the Saint Lawrence between the hotel and river. On free afternoons there were drives in the countryside or visits to historical monuments. On one weekend there was a trip down the Saint Lawrence on a steamer. Quebec allowed everyone to relax, to escape from the heat and distractions of Washington, and once again to compromise their differences on the conduct of the war.

The quieting atmosphere of Quebec would be needed. Marshall spoke of QUADRANT in terms of "the spirit of winning" and "fighting it out." And to King it would be a "showdown" on Europe and Burma. The

British had traveled to Quebec on the *Queen Mary*, and in their preconference discussions afloat they were troubled with King. A report from the British Joint Staff Mission in Washington had warned that "serious difficulties may lie ahead in 'Quadrant.' . . . We think it fair to say that for some time past it has been Admiral King's determination to effect such progress before 'Quadrant' regarding operations in Pacific that his position will be impregnable." They also reported that King's staff had unilaterally developed the plans for the war against Japan while ignoring the British planners. (King had ordered Smedberg, his combat intelligence officer, not to tell the British Joint Staff Mission "anything about our future operations.") The mission report next summarized King's displeasure with Britain's progress in Burma, then concluded, "Today we have had confirmation from Embassy source that strong efforts are being made to convince everyone from President downwards that his [King's] free hand in the Pacific must be assured, that the British must play all out in Burma, and that Mediterranean must temper accordingly. . . ."

The report had its effect on Brooke. "As far as I can gather," he wrote in his diary on 11 August, "King is at the back of most of the trouble and with his Pacific outlook is always opposed to most operations in Europe."

The first meeting on the morning of 14 August was largely a British review of the European war. With Sicily nearly secure and the Italian government disintegrating, the British were naturally eager to press on into Italy. It would give the Allies a foothold on the continent and an avenue of approach into central Europe. Hitler would have to send more troops to defend Italy, weakening the German army in France and helping OVERLORD. Churchill even thought an Allied presence in Italy would encourage partisans in the Balkans to revolt against Hitler's armies of occupation. And although the British might not admit it, Churchill wanted to get to central Europe ahead of the Russians.

The Americans wanted nothing to do with Italy. Leahy's diary recorded the American response (which was not evident in the minutes). "A difference of opinion was apparent from the onset," wrote Leahy, "as to the value of the Italian campaign toward our common war effort against Germany. General Marshall was very positive in his attitude against a Mediterranean commitment. Admiral King was determined not to have a single American warship, so badly needed in the Pacific operations, diverted to any extra operations in that area so favored by our British allies. British insistence on expanding the Italian operations provoked King to very undiplomatic language, to use a mild term."

Following lunch the CCS convened to hear the American view of the war in the Pacific. King began with his familiar assertion that he was being deprived of adequate means to fight Japan, illustrating by numerical ratios how a slight decrease of European forces would greatly increase the relative power of the Pacific forces. King's JCS colleagues chimed in, forcing the British to agree that, yes indeed, a master plan was needed for the defeat of Japan. The Americans, of course, intended to do all of the planning and all of the fighting in the Pacific itself, but they also bluntly told the British what was expected of them: "In the Asiatic Theater . . . the British will begin the ejection of the Japanese from Burma. This will constitute a further pressure against the Japanese and will increase the attrition of their military power. The early increase in assistance to China is of the utmost importance in keeping her in the war."

By now the British were on the defensive. There were immense difficulties in the CBI theater, they said, and they stalled for time until the meeting ended.

The following day the CCS returned to European strategy, the one area that Brooke hoped the American and British thought alike. OVERLORD should be the principal offensive operation in 1944, said Brooke, with supporting attacks in Italy to weaken Germany before OVERLORD began. But as always, the Americans and British continued to disagree on the conditions necessary for OVERLORD to succeed.

King could no longer contain himself. "As I understand it," he said, "the British Chiefs of Staff have serious doubts as to the possibility of accomplishing OVERLORD." Brooke repeated the British arguments that German strength had to be reduced through operations in Italy to give OVERLORD a good chance of success. Otherwise the British did not want to land in France. (Brooke had commanded a division in France in 1940 and had learned to respect the German Army.)

There were other ways besides Italy, King responded. Marshall picked up the argument. The wrangling continued.

The next day, Monday, 16 August, the chiefs met in closed session. A second day of closed-door bargaining finally produced a unified statement. It was, as with most CCS documents, a compromise. And as with most CCS compromises, it was so ambiguous that either side could interpret it differently, but in general the American view prevailed. The target date for OVERLORD became 1 May 1944, and OVERLORD would have priority for resources over the Mediterranean theater.

The British position on Italy had become analogous to King's position on Japan. Both theaters had been or were about to become secondary, yet each proponent did not want his special theater to be unduly ne-

The CCS in Quebec. Note the three different naval uniforms worn by Leahy, King, and Captain Royal. Pound and Mountbatten are in whites. (U.S. Army photograph)

glected. The British cleverly stole a phrase that King had successfully used earlier in defining Pacific strategy: the CCS agreed that the Allies would maintain "unremitting pressure" on the Germans in northern Italy.

With European strategy settled for the moment, the CCS turned again to the Pacific and the Far East. The initial discussions were exploratory. King dismissed the occasional British suggestions on Pacific strategy. He would inform the British of his intentions. He did not want their advice.

When the turn came for the British to discuss their intentions in the CBI theater, they spoke of "long-range penetration groups," a concept of using skirmishers to prepare for the main advance in Burma. This scheme was the only source of optimism. Otherwise the deliberations became mired in the mud of Burma. Even when the conference room was cleared for an executive session, the chiefs for all their skill at compromise could not untangle the problems of monsoon floods, impassable terrain, Chinese intransigence, American impatience, British pessimism, and Japanese tenacity.

Tempers were unraveling by the time Mountbatten offered a change of subject. With the grudging consent of Brooke, Mountbatten delivered a zealous sales talk on the virtues of the "Habbakuk," a floating seadrome made of Pykrete—a frozen mixture of pulp and water. King listened wonderingly. He liked Mountbatten and respected his brains, but now the young admiral seemed wrapped in fantasy. He spoke of constructing airfields at sea of unlimited size, suitable for even the largest aircraft, and maintained by means of a simple refrigeration plant. The scheme was an outgrowth of an earlier British idea of using icebergs, but, as Mountbatten enthusiastically explained, Pykrete was in every way superior to ice.

To prove his case Mountbatten had arranged a demonstration. Two large blocks were wheeled into the conference room, one ice and the other Pykrete, accompanied by a Professor Bernal, one of the Habbakuk technical specialists. An ax was produced, and the chiefs chose Arnold to test the toughness of the new material. Arnold easily split the ice, but when he swung at the Pykrete the ax rebounded with such shock that Arnold was momentarily stunned.

Mountbatten dramatically removed a pistol from his pocket and announced that he would next demonstrate Pykrete's resistance to gunfire. King and the other chiefs discretely withdrew behind the firing line as Mountbatten raised his weapon, aimed, and fired. The ice shattered. Mountbatten fired next at the Pykrete. It remained intact, and King felt the wind of the ricocheting bullet as it whipped past his leg. "The damn fool," King snorted years later. Confusion erupted both inside and outside the conference room, and someone was heard to cry, perhaps allegorically, "My God! Now they're shooting at each other!"

Afterward the staff secretary wondered how the fiasco should be described in the official minutes. After some thought, he wrote, "Professor Bernal demonstrated with the aid of samples of pykrete the various qualities of this material."

Despite Mountbatten's temporay aberration, King and his American colleagues immediately accepted the British nomination of Mountbatten to command the CBI. Mountbatten needed encouragement for his hopeless task, and King privately conveyed his complete support. As a gesture of friendship King gave Mountbatten a U.S. Navy uniform button. Mountbatten was delighted and later wrote, "I have obtained the King's permission to wear your button on my khaki uniform and shall be very proud and honored to do so." When the carrier *Saratoga* visited Mountbatten's command in April 1944, Mountbatten inspected the ship and announced he was wearing King's button. In a letter to King describing the visit, Mountbatten thought King would be "amused" to know that "they all stood on tip-toe in their anxiety to see the famous button." *

* General Albert C. Wedemeyer recently told the author that Mountbatten had an entire collection of buttons.

As the war went on, King would grow increasingly bitter about the British failure to support Mountbatten's operations in Southeast Asia. He considered it a deliberate neglect. King could never forgive the British for it.

The British had their Pykrete, but the Americans suffered embarrassment of their own doing, as well. During the second day of the conference (14 August), King announced that the invasion of Kiska was scheduled for the following day. The invasion was important for a number of reasons. It was the final stage in driving the Japanese from American territory in Alaska, and it was also a test of American amphibious assault techniques, a precursor of the kind of offensive operation that King claimed would win the war in the Pacific. There were indications, King explained to the chiefs, that the Japanese might have partially evacuated the island, but the assault would continue as planned on the assumption that the Japanese were defending with a large force.

The Americans went ashore following a prolonged naval and air bombardment. Not a single Japanese was found. All had escaped undetected under cover of weather. Although it was a relief that there was no fighting and were no casualties, the British at Quebec must have wondered at the American system of intelligence gathering. Was it a bad omen for the future?

Whatever the tensions during their official deliberations, the chiefs remained amiable during social hours. Given their familiarity with military history, they shared a common interest in the battlefields of Quebec. One day the chiefs toured the Plains of Abraham, the site of a French and British battle in 1759. The guide was flustered by the questions of the greatest assembled body of military experts in the world, and the disgruntled chiefs wandered about the battlefield looking for explanatory markers. By chance an old French priest passed by, a conversation began, and Brooke, acting as interpreter, discovered an authority on the battle. Dressed in cassock and shovel hat, the priest took center stage. "He really knew what he was talking about," King later remembered. The attentive chiefs listened respectfully as the old man instructed them in the art of wars past.

It took time, but the CCS produced an agreement that satisfied Roosevelt and Churchill. The CCS oral deliberations were long and tedious. Afterward the laboring Combined Staff Planners strove to interpret what their bosses had said in the afternoons and to reduce it to writing.*

* There were twelve principal American planners, six each representing the Navy and the Army respectively. Russell Willson, Savvy Cooke, and Rear Admiral

After all-night sessions they produced papers that the chiefs read and digested the following morning and were prepared to approve when they convened in the afternoons. Often the differences between the Americans and British chiefs were more imagined than real, and the planners were experts at fashioning a consensus that everyone could accept.

King never got his master plan. There were too many unpredictable variables. On the other hand, King and his JCS colleagues moved the British away from their strategy of opportunism and toward commitments to carry out specific operations at specific dates. Of greatest importance to the Americans were:

• OVERLORD, scheduled for 1 May 1944. It would receive first priority in the European theater, and further operations in the Mediterranean would be limited by whatever resources were already there. The Mediterranean had become a secondary theater.

• An invasion of southern France concurrent with OVERLORD.

• Intensified operations to force the defeat of Japan within twelve months of the defeat of Germany. The Pacific was now so important that King could expect a change in the 85:15 resources ratio. In particular, the CCS approved the seizure of the Gilberts, Marshalls, Carolines, Palaus, and the Marianas.

• MacArthur would bypass Rabaul and press on to northwest New Guinea.

• Mountbatten would open the Burma Road. (The British Chiefs of Staff would later void this agreement, to King's disgust.) There was an irony about the geographical boundaries of Mountbatten's command: namely, Burma, Ceylon, Thailand, the Malay Peninsula, and Sumatra. Only Ceylon was under Allied control. The Japanese held everything else.

King's own post-conference assessment was out of focus. He claimed that there was now an "exact blueprint" for the defeat of both Germany and Japan. That was not so. Meeting with his circle of journalists in Alexandria, King reported, "Provided we have no serious setbacks or upsets, we know where we are headed and what we shall need to win." On the basis of the QUADRANT plans, King concluded it would take another year to defeat Germany and another three years to defeat Japan.

QUADRANT marked the beginning of a trend toward political consid-

Oscar C. Badger were the three senior naval representatives. The influence of these planners has never been fully appreciated. By late 1943 the Americans had become every bit as skillful as the British in developing the papers, studies, and analyses that were essential to the CCS conferences.

erations. The forces that the service chiefs commanded were everywhere on the offensive. Salerno was about to be invaded, MacArthur was advancing in New Guinea, the Battle of the Atlantic was going well. Allied bombers were hitting Germany, and Nimitz was preparing to invade Tarawa. The Russians were mauling the German Army on the Eastern Front and gaining offensive momentum. The military course of the war was becoming apparent, which perhaps explains why the CCS were able to agree on strategy and policy in such a relatively short time at Quebec. Significantly, political considerations had begun more and more to absorb the attention of Roosevelt and Churchill. Victory was certain. The civilian leaders had to begin thinking about the postwar world.

31

Planning and Logistics

King returned to Washington from Quebec and resumed his fixed daily routine. Reveille was at 0700, followed by limbering-up exercises and a shower. He ate a solitary breakfast at 0730, then went to the fantail just before 0800. At eight o'clock a bugle sounded attention. King faced aft and saluted the colors. After carry-on King entered his waiting car at the foot of the brow.

King left the car near the Mall and walked the remaining distance to Main Navy, entering his office on the third floor at 0821. The rest of the morning was unstructured, save for a mandatory daily conference with the Secretary of the Navy. When he returned he read correspondence and reports and met with members of his staff who needed to see him.

Lunch was at 1245 in a small mess adjacent to his office. His dozen or so messmates were his personal staff, Edwards and Cooke being the senior and the flag lieutenant the junior. The staff was always on time and waited for King if he was delayed. "What are you waiting for?" King would ask, but they still would not start before he arrived.

"This mess was noticeable for a fixed custom," a junior member, Malcolm F. Schoeffel, later recalled. "When King was present he, Edwards, and Cooke carried on an animated and informative conversation. In general, the rest of us confined ourselves to 'please pass the butter' or answering when spoken to. This was no matter of an order. It was just that King's personality so dominated us and the discussions of the First Ward were so interesting that the rest of us had little reason to break in. The quiet of the Fourth Ward was noted and reported by Britishers who lunched with us.

"When King was away and Edwards was in the chair, the difference was stupefying, for we all chattered like magpies. Edwards was a lot of fun. Once there was a question King was very anxious to see settled, but the State Department delayed taking a position because Secretary Byrnes was on a foreign trip. As Edwards explained to King, 'The State Department fiddles while Byrnes roams.' When Edwards was made Deputy COMINCH he was moved into a different office. He had always said his job was to handle the things King left in the lower left-hand drawer. So now he asked that his new office be equipped with furniture that was 'nothing but lower left-hand drawers.' "

The interactions between an admiral and his staff vary with the individuals involved. The staff recommends; the admiral decides. King and Edwards understood each other and did not mince words. Once they discussed the numbers of officers required on a submarine squadron staff. King wanted to minimize the number, while Edwards — himself a veteran submariner — wanted three staff officers senior to the squadron's commanding officers. King wrote his reaction:

Why??? if this idea
were followed, Nimitz would require at least
3 V. Adms on his STAFF!!!
K

"I had occasion to change his mind more than once," recalled George Russell, "but it was always by the written memo. I could not, or did not, see fit to do much arguing with him orally. Donald Duncan was one of the few who could do that — he just wouldn't leave until he had made his point."

Howard Orem's experience was that King was willing to listen to sensible arguments if they were brief and well thought out. "It didn't take him long to get the gist," said Orem years later. "Once King had made up his mind on something there was no use pursuing it any further that day, because you couldn't change it. The best thing was to approach him a day or so later and try again from a different angle."

King's flag lieutenants were adept at humoring the Admiral and were generally relaxed in his company. If, for example, King growled for his morning paper, aide Charles C. Kirkpatrick would produce it with a flourish. "Kirkpatrick was a Texan," observed another staff officer, "and he had enough of the extrovert about him that he was good tonic for the Old Man. So the two of them got along very well together."

There were times that King was the soul of consideration. He would not, for example, order anyone to do anything that was not an official duty. "I went with King to the Army-Navy football game in 1945," recalled Neil Dietrich. "He called me and asked me if I would like to go with him. That was typical of King, because he would never demand that you go with him, and he would let you say no. He would never be upset if you declined an invitation. There were other people who believed that their aides should never have any life of their own but should be one-hundred percent at the beck and call of the boss. That was not the way it was with Admiral King."

Leo H. Thebaud, a staff officer who had known King for years, once accepted King's invitation to serve as his temporary aide at an Argentine Embassy ceremony. King was to receive a decoration and felt he might need an interpreter; Thebaud was multilingual and experienced in embassy functions. "I was alongside his parked car in ample time," Thebaud later said, "and I got in on his left, his flag flying in the bow. He was utterly delightful. All small talk about life in Washington. . . . Everybody at the embassy was fluent in English so that my presence merely added a touch to the scenery. On our way back to the Navy Department he asked where I lived and ordered the driver to stop there. I was indeed touched!"

In September 1945 Thebaud was ordered to the American Embassy in Paris, without his family. He protested to King that he had seen his family only six months during the war and that another prolonged separation was unfair. "Take your family along," said King.

"I was the first Navy wife in Europe," Laurie Thebaud recalled. "I think he let me go because he knew I had lived in Paris before the war when my husband had been assistant naval attaché, and that I was from a service family and 'knew the ropes' of living in France and being attached to the embassy."

Another Navy family benefited from King's kindness in a far more poignant and dramatic way. King's assistant flag secretary, Lawrence B. Cook, was struck with polio in September 1945 and went to the new Bethesda Naval Hospital. His condition worsened over worry about his pregnant wife, who was unable to reserve a bed in the crowded Washington hospitals. Bethesda did not provide maternity services. Neil Dietrich spoke to the Admiral. King phoned Bethesda's commanding officer and ordered him to admit Cook's wife. "It was the first dependent's delivery there," Cook wrote to the author years later, "and set the stage for thousands to follow during the years. It was a miracle for me, giving me so much comfort and encouragement that I was able to return to limited duty in sixteen months and full duty in three years. Ernest King did this."

But one could never tell with King. Rear Admiral Bernhard H. Bieri served on King's staff through much of the war as a planner, an assistant chief of staff, and as a special projects officer. When the day finally came for him to leave for a new assignment he entered King's office to say goodbye. There was some small talk, and then King asked Bieri if he was married. Bieri replied that he had a wife as well as five sons who were in the armed services.

"I never knew that," said King.

Once a week King would lunch with Leahy, Marshall, and Arnold. King and Marshall had established a working partnership whenever they met with the British, but they were never friends and were frequently adversaries. With others present King and Marshall would address each other as "Admiral" and "General." In private they undoubtedly used last names, a common practice among senior officers. King had mixed feelings about Marshall. Sometimes he spoke of Marshall as an "able man" who could be "very good." Yet King regarded himself as intellectually superior to his colleagues. Marshall could be "stupid"; Arnold "didn't know what he was talking about" and was a "yes man for Marshall"; and Leahy was a "fixer" who had "things about him" that King "did not greatly like." Their feelings toward King were undoubtedly much the same.

The JCS had shaken down into a reasonably efficient organization by late 1943. It still had problems. King's major complaint was that the JCS went outside its jurisdiction. A self-styled "great dissenter," King also objected when his colleagues tried to resolve issues by a vote. "I could not and did not agree with this procedure," King later recorded, "because I firmly believed that all matters, large or small, should be looked over thoroughly and completely (if it took days or weeks or months) until 'all hands' had the time to think over the gist of the problem from every angle. Then, if we couldn't agree, the decision should be left to the President himself. . . . I contended that the *voting* procedure was in most instances unnecessary!"

Things brought before the JCS indeed were often trivial. In September 1944, with the Axis powers in retreat, Leahy, tongue in cheek, signed the following memorandum to the President: "You have requested an expression of opinion from the Joint Chiefs of Staff as to the danger of loss or damage from enemy action that is likely to result from returning the originals of the Constitution and the Declaration of Independence to their peace-time depository in the Library of Congress.

"The Joint Chiefs of Staff believe the danger of loss or damage to these documents from enemy action would be negligible if they were returned."

In May 1944 King received a facetious letter from a Navy captain on the feasibility of using Texas jack rabbits to clear German minefields. King replied to the captain that he had forwarded the letter to the JCS "classified as SECRET so that the relative merits of Texas grown jack rabbits may remain unknown to our enemies."

The Washington planners gradually changed their attention from detailed plans to long-range strategy. In mid-1942 these planners had developed almost every aspect of the Guadalcanal assault. The emphasis changed as the overseas staffs became larger and more proficient. By late 1943 the detailed plans were developed by the people who had to execute them. The Washington planners could concentrate upon logistical support and providing preliminary studies to assist the operational staffs. As one example, King allowed Nimitz to decide which atolls were to be seized in the Marshalls, while King provided Nimitz with the necessary ships, troops, and aircraft.

The COMINCH planners maintained a single chart showing the status of planning, logistical support, troops, ships, and aircraft for the next four major operations. But the chart was deceptive because it could be so wrong. As we shall see, King and his staff grossly miscalculated the requirements for amphibious assault shipping, creating shortages that hampered Allied operations worldwide. These shortages already were apparent in the summer of 1943. Marshall had warned about them at Quebec. Where had King gone wrong?

The problem began in mid-1942. The Navy was forced into an emergency building program for landing ships and craft for the North African landing in November 1942 and the anticipated 1943 invasion of France. But by September 1942 it was obvious that there would not be any cross-Channel invasion the following year. King convinced the JCS that the construction of assault shipping could be substantially reduced, and he reoriented the shipyards to building desperately needed destroyer escorts (for the Battle of the Atlantic) and other warships. Thus by mid-1943 amphibious shipping had lost first priority.

It was hard to decide how many amphibious ships to build because future operations were so uncertain. The shipyards could produce only so many ships each year, and someone had to decide how many of each kind they should build. King did not give very good answers. On the one hand he advocated a master war plan that would clarify future ship requirements. King never fully achieved such a plan, and the CCS compromises often were so vaguely worded that no one could tell how many ships would be needed. On the other hand, King would defer long-range plans "to think things over" while the shipbuilders waited impatiently for answers. There was yet another problem. Influenced by King's penchant for secrecy, his COMINCH operational planners were reluctant to disclose future plans to Horne's procurement planners. The civilians were even less informed, even though Knox, Forrestal, and their principal assistants had to buy what King would need.

The shortages of amphibious shipping manifested an unfamiliarity with logistics within the Navy Department. As King was preoccupied with grand strategy, it will be remembered that he left logistical planning to others, principally Horne and his top assistant, Rear Admiral Lynde D. McCormick. But it seemed to Captain Paul Pihl, an aircraft procurement officer on Horne's staff, that logistics was a mess.* An aeronautical engineering specialist, Pihl understood the principles of logistical support for the fleet from years of experience. But he was one of few. Most aspiring officers had spurned logistical assignments before the war.

By early 1943 Pihl wondered if those in higher authority knew how to provide the fleet with the materiel it needed. One of his greatest concerns was with Horne. "It was his job," Pihl told the author, "and he didn't have the faintest idea what the hell he was going to do with it. Horne had had no previous experience with logistics, and he tended to go by the old Navy tradition that you didn't get involved in what was happening in the engine room unless something went wrong, and then you brought a person up and bawled him out for it. In other words, Horne did not really get involved in what his subordinates were doing and thus was not informed as to whether or not they were actually doing their jobs with respect to logistical planning. Horne thought of himself as a kind of 'broad aspect guy' and did not like to get himself involved in details."

Pihl felt that King too was unaware of the Navy's logistical needs. Having known King for years, he felt free to enter King's office one day in early 1943 to express his misgivings. King was so impressed that he brought Pihl to the COMINCH staff to establish a logistics study group. "I pulled in people from the CNO's production division as well as from the Bureau of Ordnance and Bureau of Ships," Pihl later said. "As we were working directly for King we rated top priority and soon found ourselves being briefed or reading top secret plans. Our group

* The reader will recall Paul and Charlotte Pihl from earlier chapters.

then provided a summary of the total logistical effort that would be required to support the strategic plans in the Pacific.

"In the spring of 1943 I had this all put together in a big presentation for Admiral King. King, Horne, Forrestal, and the bureau chiefs were there, so I was pretty well scared. Professional briefers did the talking, and we had some extraordinary charts including one that showed how the logistical support would have to originate from the West Coast and then be distributed throughout the reaches of the Pacific. It looked like a tree trunk with branches. I called it a ventilation chart. It was a complete surprise to Horne, who I think initially opposed my working on King's personal staff. But after he saw the presentation he agreed that the coherent way we had presented the whole logistic picture was certainly something which he could find very useful."

One of the most immediate results of Pihl's presentation was the realization that small escort carriers (first conceived to fight U-boats in the Atlantic) would be needed in the Pacific to augment the fast attack carriers. "Up to that time," Pihl later said, "there had been no realization how we were going to get the aircraft and ordnance out to where they were needed in the Pacific. . . . That's the sort of thing King liked. It was the first time he had seen the big picture."

Thanks to Pihl, King finally began to think more about logistics. But once King gripped a problem he often developed a sweeping, all-encompassing solution that was absolutely impractical. Several of Pihl's staff went to the West Coast in April 1943 to investigate indications that overseas shipments were being delayed. Upon their return they confirmed that the shore establishment, especially on the West Coast, was clogging the pipeline to Nimitz. King felt he knew what was wrong: excess warehouses and stateside sailors had made the shore establishment too large and unwieldy. In a 1 May 1943 memo to Knox, King had his own solution. "I have to recommend," he wrote, "that the construction of storehouses cease forthwith throughout the Naval services. There should be enough storehouses now constructed to meet all reasonable needs. . . . What inevitably happens is that the agency for whom storehouses are built then wish to fill them; consequently, the material stored therein becomes for the most part inactive, which results in virtual 'hoarding' because the material involved does not keep on the move." King also thought that there were more than enough "personnel facilities" within the United States.

King's solution (if you can call it that) was extreme. Reflecting the seagoing officers' distrust of everything ashore, King recommended "that all construction in all shore establishments of the Navy be stopped, because I am of the opinion that expansion which has already taken place will suffice, when judiciously allocated and used, to meet all reasonable needs of the Naval service.

"The foregoing recommendations derive not only from my conviction that we are already overexpanded in facilities in many respects, but also because, in order to make the war effort effective, the manpower and material situations in this country do not allow the use of labor and material in any further expansion of the Naval shore establishment within the continental limits of the United States."

King had followed his own rule of compressing every problem and its solution into a one-page memorandum. With a figurative wave of his hand he had asked Knox to stop building anything more. But Knox had been burned once before. In November 1942 he had stopped work on "facilities ashore designed for the convenience and comfort of personnel. . . ." These included family quarters, chapels, auditoriums, greenhouses, swimming pools, hostess houses, and solariums. The bureau chiefs protested that Knox's order would only result in confusion and false economy, so Knox gave in. He was unreceptive when King asked for the same thing the following spring.

Pihl, meanwhile, had established a Logistical Organization Planning Unit (LOPU) in April 1944 to review logistics procedures and to recommend improvements. When he went to the West Coast he found waste and confusion worse than ever. Vital materiel was being lost, delayed, misplaced, or missent. Pihl reported the details to King. "There is no overall coordinated supervision of the operation of logistic activities on the Pacific Coast," he wrote. "Coordination is sporadic and extracurricular . . . there is no individual or agency in the CNO organization who is solely responsible for the operation of the logistic agencies supporting the Fleets in the Pacific." And so went the damning report.

Horne did not take kindly to Phil's criticism. As he stated rather huffily in his forwarding endorsement to King. "The Vice Chief of Naval Operations [Horne] is responsible for the logistics support of the entire Navy.

"It must be recognized," Horne continued, "that the present working organization, despite certain deficiencies of logistic organization and control, has supported the war in the Pacific effectively and, except for some minor delays imposed by shipping and production difficulties, the requirements of our forces have been adequately met. It is a matter of fact and record that the degree of efficiency and comfort our advance forces enjoy is beyond anything previously experienced in warfare." Horne concluded that he would carefully study Pihl's report and correct what he could, but not with any urgency. "Any action taken," he warned King, "should be done with caution."

But King had lost patience. In an earlier effort to solve the West Coast problems he had combined the coastal naval districts into the Western Sea Frontier under a vice admiral. The first commander, King later said, was "a nice man with no force at all." The second incumbent, said King, was "a nice fellow who didn't know what the hell it was all about." By the fall of 1944 King brought in Ingersoll from the Atlantic Fleet. With the Battle of the Atlantic won, Ingersoll's job had diminished in importance. King called Ingersoll to Washington to tell him he would be the logistics czar of the West Coast. "It's a hard job you've got," King told the taciturn Ingersoll. Knowing just how hard and unglamorous it would be, King gave Ingersoll two other hats — Deputy COMINCH and Deputy CNO — in addition to the sea frontier command. Ingersoll would have plenty of authority plus prestige for his ego. "I was like Pooh Bah in *The Mikado*," Ingersoll later said. "If I couldn't accomplish what I wanted under one hat, I could accomplish it under another."

Seeing Ingersoll's lack of enthusiasm for his dreary reassignment, King made a confidential promise. "If anything happens to Nimitz," said King, "you will be in line for that command." Ingersoll did not perceptibly brighten, because Nimitz's health was known to be excellent. But, good and loyal naval officer that he was, Ingersoll packed his bags and went west. Pihl went with him. Things improved considerably.

Pihl's emphasis on logistical planning had centered on the Pacific. The European theater, particularly its needs for amphibious shipping, did not receive equivalent attention. Shipping requirements were seen only dimly. The British reluctance in 1943 to embrace wholeheartedly a cross-Channel invasion created doubt in King's mind that the invasion ever would materialize. Moreover, as 1943 moved into fall, the OVERLORD planning staff had no supreme commander. OVERLORD planning had no sense of urgency, and King would not build excess landing craft solely on the expectation that the OVERLORD planners might later decide they needed more. King's staff, preoccupied with the Pacific, did not press for commitments in the European Theater. Later shortages were almost inevitable.

If the lack of a supreme commander handicapped serious planning for OVERLORD, it would have seemed incumbent for Roosevelt and Churchill to name someone. The subject first came to King's attention during the QUADRANT Conference. Frank Knox had invited himself to

Quebec, as Stimson was already there at the President's invitation. When Knox and King met, Knox reported that it appeared that Marshall would receive the supreme command in Europe.

"Marshall cannot be spared from his present job," said King emphatically.

"Why not?" asked Knox.

King explained that Marshall was so indispensable to the JCS that his leaving would disrupt the Washington high command. Marshall was needed more as Chief of Staff of the Army.

"Who will remember Marshall after the war if he remains in Washington?" asked Knox. "Everyone remembers Pershing from the first war, but who remembers the Chief of Staff?"

King argued that this war was different. It was worldwide, whereas the first war had centered upon the Atlantic and Europe. King had his differences with Marshall, but the four members of the JCS were a team that King wanted intact.

During the conference Marshall confirmed to his colleagues that Roosevelt wanted him for the job. As Marshall had become an interested party, he would have nothing more to say. King later spoke with Leahy and Arnold. They too agreed that Marshall should not change jobs, and each spoke alone to the President. Perhaps sensing the opposition of Marshall's colleagues, Roosevelt deferred a decision.

Other important people, including Churchill, Hopkins, and Stimson, urged Roosevelt to appoint Marshall. The General kept discretely quiet, although King assumed he wanted the job. "And why not?" King later remarked. "It would have been the best job that any military man could get during the war." Newspaper articles began to appear, making Marshall's future a matter of public debate. With newspapers against the move, Roosevelt continued to stall.

King may well have caused many of these articles to be written. Journalist Glen Perry of the New York *Sun* had helped organize King's inner circle of newspapermen and war correspondents who met periodically with King at Nelie Bull's Alexandria home. King invited Perry to his office one day in the early fall of 1943. King explained that Churchill was exerting enormous pressure on Roosevelt to send Marshall to Europe, but that the other chiefs wanted Marshall to remain in Washington. "I would appreciate it," said King, "if you and your colleagues would help us out with articles and editorials saying how much Marshall is needed right here, and emphasizing what a good job he is doing."

Perry agreed to speak to others and filed his own story.* Whatever

* Marquis Childs complied with a similar request from King.

the effects of King's initiative, the press did intensify its attention on Marshall. Leahy later wrote in his diary, "The public assumed that Roosevelt would name Marshall as Supreme Commander. There was vehement objection to such a move in the press. . . . Roosevelt did not talk about the problem very much. I had a feeling that . . . he was stalling for time. I definitely had the impression that he was being influenced more by the adverse public reaction than by anything that took place within the military groups."

The decision on who would command OVERLORD would have to wait.

While OVERLORD planning sputtered, the Central Pacific offensive was about to begin. On 25 September 1943 King met with Nimitz for the first time in Pearl Harbor. The meeting began with a discussion of Operation GALVANIC, the seizure of the Gilbert Islands. The general plan was simultaneous assaults of Tarawa Atoll and Nauru Island, separated over 400 miles from each other. To King's surprise, Spruance read a paper initiated by Holland Smith arguing against Nauru. It was too heavily defended, it was too close to the main Japanese naval base at Truk, and it would divide Spruance's naval forces beyond mutual supporting distance.

Makin was a better alternative, Spruance explained. It was closer to the Marshalls (the next objective), it was large enough for an airfield, and it was close enough to Tarawa so that Spruance's fleet could mass yet cover both assaults. King was at first reluctant to delete Nauru, explaining that he wanted the proposed front to have "suitable breadth." Why he wanted a 400-mile front is not clear, but apparently both he and Cooke regarded Nauru as a potential flanking threat to the north-south lines of communication through the Gilberts. It was also possible that King and Cooke favored a two-axis approach in order to confuse and divide the Japanese air and naval forces defending the Gilberts. The concept of a two-front approach obviously appealed to King; he wanted to do the same thing on a larger scale through New Guinea and the Central Pacific.*

Spruance's arguments prevailed. Having striven for a Central Pacific offensive for a year and a half, King was reluctant to overrule the combat leaders who were responsible for its success. With so much at stake, it had to succeed. He sent a message to the JCS recommending Makin. The next day he received JCS concurrence.

* A little-known fact, for King always has been considered a proponent of the single-front thrust through the Central Pacific. Yet during QUADRANT he was very much in favor of going through New Guinea at the same time.

The usual array of other topics came before King and Nimitz as the conference progressed. On the second day Nimitz reported that the submariners still were complaining about dud torpedoes. Ever since the war began the torpedoes had run too deeply and magnetic exploders had failed to work; now even the contact exploders were suspect. It was a problem that King should have tackled earlier. Instead he was more interested in increasing the submarines' antiaircraft armament, on the impractical theory that the submarines should fight back when under air attack. Submariners preferred to dive to escape enemy aircraft, but King was insistent. Eventually he directed that a system be developed to operate antiaircraft guns from the conning tower, using the periscope. Nothing ever came of it.

Rear Admiral Charles A. Lockwood, Commander Submarines, Pacific, was headquartered at Pearl Harbor. Getting King's ear, he reported that after extensive testing his men had discovered that the contact exploders were too flimsy. The sailors themselves could modify the exploders to make them reliable. Lockwood wanted to do it immediately, without waiting for official approval from the Bureau of Ordnance, which could take months. King gave his permission. The torpedoes would finally function reliably. It was about time.

The submarine force — the Silent Service — was deliberately shielded from any publicity (whether good or bad) as a matter of policy. Its success depended upon anonymity. Code breakers reading Japanese messages directed submarines to perhaps half of the more than one thousand merchantmen sunk during the war, a tactic never publicly revealed for obvious reasons. The very security of the submarines depended upon stealth and surprise. The less the Japanese knew about their equipment and doctrine, the better. King realized how intelligence on U-boat capabilities and employment had helped him win the Battle of the Atlantic. He would not allow the Japanese a similar advantage against his own submarines. Silence paid off. Although the Americans would lose some 52 submarines during the war, the Germans lost 41 in May 1943 alone and 781 total.

Despite bad torpedoes and other problems, Lockwood's submarines had begun to hurt the Japanese merchant marine by the fall of 1943. Before the war was over they would isolate Japan from the sea and contribute mightily to victory in the Pacific. Given the importance of the submarine command, King wanted Lockwood to receive appropriate recognition. During the first day's meeting (25 September), King introduced the possibility of promoting Lockwood to vice admiral. Nothing was decided at the time. By the second day King pressed the issue by suggesting that Lockwood receive a spot promotion. King kept insisting (why Nimitz did not immediately agree is puzzling), and when King returned to Washington, Lockwood became a vice admiral.

Other action items that King brought back from Pearl Harbor reveal the diversity of subjects that he customarily discussed with Nimitz. For example:

• "Investigate the entire subject of RI [radio intercept] information of Japanese Army movements and intentions." (Nimitz had complained that, despite the wonders of ULTRA, he was not receiving intelligence on intercepted Japanese Army messages. King was astounded. He was receiving it. Why wasn't Nimitz? The COMINCH combat intelligence officer would eventually be fired.)

• "Take necessary action to comply with instructions relative to control of merchant ships and their rerouting." (King was upset that Nimitz's staff was telling merchantmen skippers the location of Japanese submarines. That compromised the fact that the Americans were locating the enemy submarines by radio direction fixes. "Just reroute the merchantmen as necessary," King had ordered. "They don't have to know why.")

• "Take up with the Surgeon General the matter of appropriate instructions for thorough physical examinations for all officers over 54." (King was constantly concerned about the health of his senior officers. If they were not fit for strenuous duty, he wanted to know about it.)

• "Chief of Naval Personnel to investigate training of colored base companies." (Jacobs suggested that black sailors in forward base areas receive small-arms training so that they could see some action against Japanese stragglers. Halsey asserted that black Marines in his area had done very well. All troops should be trained to fight, said Halsey.)

• "Look into the discharging of Navy Nurses when married." (The minutes are mute as to who brought this up. It probably was Nimitz, who did not want uniformed women in Pearl Harbor. Halsey, on the other hand, loved nurses. They improved his morale.)

Dauntless was a godsend to King when he returned to Washington and resumed his routine. He went to his flagship at day's end and rarely missed supper. His only table companion was the staff duty officer. Afterward King sometimes watched a movie with the crew before retiring to his cabin, which had retained its luxurious furnishings from its days as a millionaire's yacht. There he could be alone with his papers and his books. It was a time for him to think.

King often reflected on the killing of the war. Neil Dietrich later recalled, "I don't think King took any pleasure in the thought of combat itself; rather I think he wanted the responsibility of command. Generally he regarded the enemy in the abstract. I never heard him refer to the enemy in derogatory terms like 'nips' or those 'yellow bastards.' He would not use such phrases as 'we'll mow them down' or 'we'll slaughter them.' Rather, they were the enemy. It was his job to beat them."

Deaths brought sorrow, especially if it was in a family he knew. King often wrote personal letters of sympathy. Other times he would make phone calls or send messages. "He took a great interest in casualty figures and loss of life," said Dietrich. "He was always interested in comparing actual casualties with the estimated losses beforehand. There is no question that he was very much aware of the loss of human life."

King also visited the wounded in naval hospitals. In July 1944 he stopped in Pearl Harbor. "I tried to speak to every man who had been wounded in the Central Pacific fighting," King later wrote, "which for me was a hard thing to do. But I must say that most of them seemed to be quite cheerful."

In the summer of 1944 King received word that Admiral Kimmel's son was presumed lost when the submarine he commanded had failed to return from a war patrol. As Kimmel was in Washington suffering through the interminable Pearl Harbor investigations, King sent a staff flag officer to deliver the tragic news, together with a message of King's sympathy.

King also arranged for an airplane to fly Kimmel to New York City to be with his wife. Kimmel, however, told King's emissary that he could not go to New York because the court of inquiry wanted him in Washington the next morning. No matter, King replied. He was to go to his wife and remain with her as long as necessary. King would see that the court would stand adjourned until Kimmel was ready to return. Kimmel went to New York.

Kimmel had one other son serving in submarines. King ordered him to shore duty so that Kimmel would not lose another son to the war.

32
Cairo-Teheran

As the summer of 1943 turned into fall it was time to think about Russia. The Red Army was driving westward while the Americans and British were planning an eastward offensive. It was increasingly evident that the Americans and British had to coordinate their efforts against Germany with Russian strategy.

King held strong views on the Russians that summer and discussed them during his private sessions with the journalists in Alexandria. He believed that Stalin was "playing a lone hand" and supported neither Roosevelt's unconditional surrender policy nor the postwar concept of a United Nations. There were those statesmen who worried that Stalin and the communist movement intended to occupy Europe after the war. King did not think so — Stalin was "too damn smart" to do that because it would provoke western Europeans into rebellion and another war. Stalin probably would limit himself, King believed, to the Baltic States and eastern Poland, content to remain east of a line through Poland to the Black Sea.

Historically, Russia had always sought a warm-water outlet to the sea, hence the centuries of wars and disputes over the Bosporus. Giving Russia what she always had wanted would ensure permanent peace, or so King reasoned. One way was to make the Bosporus an international waterway like the Suez Canal. King would also guarantee Russia access to the Atlantic both in the Baltic and in the Black Sea. He was willing to concede Estonia, Latvia, and Lithuania to Russia to provide Baltic ports, and he suggested making the Kattegat and Skagerrak international waterways to assure Russia of an exit from the Baltic into the Atlantic.

King still held to his basic European strategy: let Russia do most of the fighting, given her manpower and advantageous geographical position. King admitted that the true military situation in Russia was rather a mystery. The Russians were "very closed-mouthed" about their combat power, their reserves, or how well they were equipped to carry on the war against Germany. "Our observers are still not being permitted to observe anything," said King. Nevertheless it was in the best interests of the United States to maintain the flow of Lend-Lease materiel.

While the Murmansk convoys were the most publicized means of shipping materiel to Russia, the Russians were also using about a hundred merchantmen between Vladivostok and American northwestern ports. About half were Liberty ships manned by Russian crews. King was amazed that the Japanese allowed them to pass under a technicality of international law. Their cargoes, King acknowledged, could be classified as unfinished munitions "only by the greatest stretch of the imagination." They were obviously intended for use against Germany (which, after all, was Japan's ally), or else they were being stockpiled for a war against Japan.

King worried that the Japanese might swoop upon the Russian merchantmen when they were congregated in the Sea of Japan. The Japanese were desperate for shipping and had to be tempted by the ships jammed into Vladivostok Harbor because of dockside congestion. They already had seized three Liberties, claiming they were enemy-owned. But they had not confiscated their cargoes, and Japan finally released the ships under diplomatic pressure from Stalin.

King could only speculate what Stalin would do in the event of a wholesale seizure. Surely he would demand their return, but whether it would mean war was anyone's guess. King did not even know whether Stalin had anything to fight the Japanese with.

King explained his views on the prospects of a war between Russia and Japan during one of his clandestine meetings with war correspondents in July 1943. "We have told the Russians," said King, "that if Japan attacked them it would take a minimum of three months for us to get real aid to them in Siberia, so they had better tell us about what they have and what they would need. No dice! Then we tried to bait them with a promise of a hundred heavy bombers, which we would agree to hold in readiness should Japan attack. Stalin said, 'Never mind holding them. Give them to us now. We can use them.' So that did not work. The Russians take possession of the Lend-Lease planes at Fairbanks, Alaska, and their own pilots fly them home. We never get into Russia by air."

While King may have wanted information from the Russians, he deliberately withheld information from them, even after Russia went to war against Japan in 1945. William Smedberg, King's combat intelligence officer, understood at first that he would be expected to exchange information of mutual value with a Russian naval captain. Then King clarified things. "Under no circumstances," warned King, "are you to tell that Russian anything important about our forces." The Russian cooperated with information about Japanese defenses gathered by Soviet spies in Japan. Smedberg, following King's orders, did not reciprocate. "I would tell him a few things that were common knowledge," Smedberg later said. "I had some things I could tell him that sounded important, but we weren't telling him anything that he could not have dug out some other way."

Following QUADRANT, King thought that the Russians might negotiate a separate peace with Germany once they had advanced to their original borders. In such an event King doubted whether the United States and Great Britain alone could defeat Germany, who could then send all her forces west as she had done after Russia's collapse in the First World War. To forestall such a calamity, King wanted to be in France by the following spring to give the Allies a foothold should Russia cease fighting.

So the Americans and the British had a lot to talk about with the Russians. After long discussions it was agreed that they would meet in December 1943, probably in Teheran. As Roosevelt's health did not permit a trans-Atlantic air crossing, he would have to travel by sea. King chose the recently commissioned battleship USS *Iowa*. The threat of U-boats had confined her shakedown cruise to Chesapeake Bay, and King wanted her at sea to stretch her legs. Furthermore, *Iowa*'s commanding officer was John McCrea, once Roosevelt's naval aide. As King knew and trusted McCrea, he felt it would be a safe and comfortable voyage.

King ordered *Iowa* from Argentia to Norfolk, and when McCrea arrived he flew to Washington to see King. After explaining why Roosevelt had to go overseas, King emphasized the need for secrecy in order to avoid U-boats. *Iowa* would have to accommodate a forty-man party, including the President and the JCS. Her destination would be a port in the Mediterranean. The President would cover the remainder of his trip by air.

King wondered aloud what to do with *Iowa* while awaiting the President's return. McCrea mentioned a suggestion by Edwards: release *Iowa* and use a heavy cruiser for the return trip. After a prolonged silence King spoke with cold finality: "I shall not subject the President to a westward December crossing of the Atlantic in a heavy cruiser. *Iowa* will remain available for that duty." (When McCrea relayed King's remarks, Edwards gently laughed.)

King and McCrea then discussed the details of the President's itinerary. "It was always a pleasure to deal with Admiral King," McCrea later said. "He was strictly business. He was a man of few words, and there was never any doubt as to what he said or what he wanted." King ended the briefing by telling McCrea that the President wanted to see him. McCrea found Roosevelt in a good mood and looking forward to the trip.

After returning to the *Iowa*, McCrea devised an alternate plan for getting Roosevelt aboard. He first cleared it with Ingersoll, then returned to Washington to present it to King. "I approve of your proposal," said King. "It contributes substantially to secrecy and provides for less wear and tear on the President." King then dispatched McCrea to the White House. "Tell Ernie I approve the proposed change," said Roosevelt.

On 11 November 1943 there was an unaccustomed early morning bustle aboard *Dauntless* at the Washington Navy Yard. Sailors checked the watch, quarter, and station bills to verify their sea detail stations, and the deck force removed rat guards and struck down the quarterdeck awnings. A puff of smoke from the stack revealed that fires had been lighted in the boilers, and below decks the engineers tested the ship's two engines.

Dauntless was about to get underway.

Even though she sported a pretentious coat of camouflage paint and a deck gun on her forecastle, it had been difficult to think of *Dauntless* as a flagship ready for war at sea. Her commanding officer, Commander Charles F. Grisham, had striven to make her useful as a training facility for her eight officers and one hundred sailors, most of whom would later go to sea. Nevertheless she served mostly as King's sanctuary, made fast to the pier at a cost of $250,000 a year.

Marshall and Arnold came aboard accompanied by their immediate staffs, and Rear Admirals Cooke, Bieri, and Badger embarked as King's principal planning assistants. *Dauntless* backed into the Potomac River, pointed her bow downstream, and got underway. That afternoon her lookouts sighted the imposing silhouette of the *Iowa* at anchor off Point Lookout, where the Potomac River enters the Chesapeake Bay. *Dauntless* came alongside the battleship, a brow was rigged, and the passengers came aboard. King's Marine orderly and personal steward brought up the rear.

King asked McCrea about preparations for receiving the President. McCrea said he was ready. A former executive officer of USS *Pennsylvania* when she had been a fleet flagship, McCrea was accustomed to VIPs and had arranged for such amenities as escort officers and guidebooks. McCrea did have to apologize for the modest quarters. Roosevelt would live in McCrea's in-port cabin. Leahy and Marshall (both senior to King) would berth in the flag and chief of staff cabins respectively. King rated an austere officer's stateroom. McCrea offered King one of his two sea cabins if he preferred. King declined. McCrea might need them. King seemed satisfied that *Iowa* was ready and went off to look around the battleship.

The next morning, 12 November, the presidential yacht *Potomac* came alongside and Roosevelt came aboard, accompanied by Leahy, Hopkins, Ross McIntire, Wilson Brown, and Pa Watson.* On the forecastle the deck force hosed the mud from the anchor chain as the windlass groaned to break the anchor from the bottom. Less than an hour after Roosevelt's arrival, *Iowa* was steaming down the Chesapeake Bay for Hampton Roads.

McCrea had discharged most of *Iowa*'s fuel to reduce her draft for the trip to Point Lookout. Now she reclaimed it in Hampton Roads from two oilers, which came alongside in the early evening. The battleship was topped off by late evening. Roosevelt had a sailor's superstition that it was unlucky to get underway for sea on a Friday, so *Iowa* waited to weigh anchor unil just past midnight. Standing out to sea she was met by a three-destroyer escort and increased speed to 25 knots.

Iowa and her precious cargo were entering a war zone where U-boats still lurked. Everyone hoped that the Germans did not know that Roosevelt was at sea. Not even the escorting destroyers knew. The huge warship had to depend upon her speed for protection. The destroyer screen was along for the ride because heavy seas blanked their sonars. While they pitched and rolled, *Iowa* plowed steadily on.

The weather cleared the second day at sea, a Sunday. In the afternoon *Iowa* went to general quarters for a firing demonstration to impress the President and his party, who were on deck to watch the show. *Iowa*'s antiaircraft guns banged away at makeshift targets. Suddenly *Iowa* lurched and changed course. An alarm rang, followed by an excited voice over the public address system screaming, "Torpedo defense! This is not a drill!" A muffled explosion aft sent tremors through the battleship.

King bolted for the bridge, found McCrea amid a babble of confu-

* Vice Admiral Brown was FDR's naval aide, and Major General P. A. ("Pa") Watson his military aide.

sion, and spoke softly into his ear. "Captain McCrea," purred King, "what is this interlude?" McCrea explained that one of the destroyers, USS *W. D. Porter,* had accidently fired a torpedo at the *Iowa.* King listened and went below.*

Trying to restrain his fury, King explained things to Roosevelt. King wanted to relieve the commanding officer immediately, but Roosevelt — to King's astonishment — wanted nothing done, to avoid publicity. Afterward, McCrea (being a prudent officer and taking nothing for granted) sent a message to the screening destroyers: "*Iowa* henceforth will not be used as a point of aim in drills."

The voyage quieted down. With free time and confined quarters, King usually joined Roosevelt for an evening movie. Otherwise he prowled the ship. The second night out he summoned McCrea to McCrea's sea cabin. "Why is *Iowa* zigzagging after dark?" he asked.

McCrea explained that while he was in Washington, King's staff had told him that U-boats might have radars and had advised zigzagging even at night.

"Thank you," said King.

One evening King and McCrea again found themselves in McCrea's sea cabin. King sat in the only chair while McCrea perched on his bunk. King was well read on Mahan, especially his *Types of Naval Officers*, a series of short biographies of heroes from the age of sail. The conversation turned from Mahan's ideas to King's own views of the many American naval officers whom King had known, including Hugh Rodman, a colorful flag officer with whom King had often clashed in earlier years.

"Rodman was lacking in many respects which I consider essential in a flag officer," said King. It was King's way of needling McCrea, who respected Rodman, having served under him three times. "My defense of Rodman was accepted grudgingly," he later remarked. King also spoke of his admiration for Mayo. Then, unexpectedly, he began to appraise contemporary naval officers "on the way up." To McCrea's surprise, King suddenly began talking about McCrea himself.

"You know, McCrea," said King, "I regard you as a good officer, but you could be a lot better. The trouble is, you have one outstanding weakness."

McCrea asked what it was.

* An investigation later revealed that the destroyer had been using *Iowa* as a target for torpedo firing practice, and that the torpedomen had not removed a firing primer.

"Your big weakness, McCrea, is that you are not a son of a bitch. And a good naval officer has to be a son of a bitch."

McCrea thought fast. "Well, Admiral King, you may be right," he replied, "but I feel that I know when to be a son of a bitch, and I would, I think, rather have it that way, rather than feel that every time I walked down the deck the universal under-the-breath remark would be 'there goes a son of a bitch.' And besides, Admiral King, you are a good naval officer and universally regarded as such."

McCrea looked King squarely in the eye. "I must say, I have never heard anyone refer to you as a son of a bitch."

King returned the look and arose from his chair. "He stomped out of my cabin," McCrea later said, "knowing full well that I was lying."

The evening's discussion had ended.

On 15 November, the third day at sea, King and the JCS gathered with Roosevelt and Hopkins for a planning session. The President had rested the first two days underway and was ready to resume work. He began by announcing that they would meet Stalin in Teheran. (Roosevelt had received this news four days before, but apparently this was the first time that King had heard it confirmed.) There would also be a preliminary meeting in Cairo for the British and Americans to resolve their differences before going on to Teheran. Churchill had insisted on it, said Roosevelt, and the Prime Minister did not want any Russian representatives to attend.

Curiously, Russia was hardly mentioned, even though the Russians were the whole point of the trip. Instead they spoke briefly about meeting the British in Cairo: Roosevelt still wanted Marshall to be the supreme commander in Europe; Roosevelt would insist that the British limit their aspirations in the Balkans and eastern Mediterranean. But most of the meeting covered miscellaneous topics, even the question of the future of the Galápagos Islands, a million miles away from the war.

Iowa continued to race eastward across the Atlantic, meeting relays of escorts which stayed with her until their fuel was nearly exhausted and then were relieved by other escort groups. *Iowa* was scheduled to pass through Gibraltar the evening of Friday, 19 November, and to arrive at Oran the next morning. King, Hopkins, and the Joint Chiefs gathered with the President that Friday afternoon for a final meeting that would last over three hours.

The question of command in the European theater led the agenda. The JCS, after several meetings among themselves, had suggested two alternatives to Roosevelt. Option "A" was to appoint one supreme commander over Europe, the Mediterranean, and the Allies' strategic air forces. The other, option "B," would appoint a separate commander for each area, each responsible to the CCS. King opened the debate by telling Roosevelt that he favored the first option because it was logical. OVERLORD was only a part of the whole, said King. There had been many difficulties in the Mediterranean owing to a lack of unified command, and the British for some time had wanted one man in charge. Using British reasoning, argued King, there should be one man in command of everything. Thus, King maintained, option "A" should appeal to the British.

Leahy interjected that while option "A" might be logical, it was not necessarily acceptable. Not said, but certainly implied, was the assumption that the supreme commander would be an American. The British war cabinet might not want to relinquish their control over the British armed forces, especially those defending the home islands. King responded that it was time for the British to discard their defensive thinking. "The best defense is a vigorous offense," said King, asserting that option "A" made for the best offensive command organization.

Roosevelt too favored option "A," although he recognized the potential war cabinet objections and the likelihood of an eventual compromise. Then Roosevelt asked for a prediction of relative American-British strength as of the first of January, 1944. The consensus was that American forces would be by far the more powerful, inferring that an American should be the supreme commander. And yet the JCS so favored option "A" that they were willing to accept Sir John Dill as the supreme commander in order to get British agreement.

The discussion continued for some time, especially on the matter of command in the Mediterranean. But nothing could be decided until Roosevelt could talk with Churchill at Cairo. Left unsaid was the name of the American nominee for the supreme command under option "A," but everyone knew that Marshall was the President's choice.

The talk then shifted to Germany's political future. It was a topic seldom heard when the JCS met. Despite the need to coordinate military operations with political goals, as a matter of practice the JCS had refused to become involved in politics and foreign policy.* Yet there were so many political questions that the JCS finally had to ask for guidance. The JCS assumed that Germany would be divided into zones

* See Chapter 17.

of occupation, and they wanted the Allied armies to end up where they belonged. There was also the question of how many American occupation troops would remain in Europe.

The political nature of the forthcoming Cairo-Teheran conferences (code-named SEXTANT and EUREKA respectively) was self-evident by the unusually large State Department contingent, including W. Averell Harriman, Ambassador in the Soviet Union; Charles E. Bohlen, First Secretary in the American Embassy at Moscow; and John G. Winant, Ambassador in the United Kingdom. Hopkins was, of course, Roosevelt's principal political adviser. Interestingly enough, Secretary of State Cordell Hull and Under Secretary of State Edward R. Stettinius remained behind, although Anthony Eden, British Secretary of State for Foreign Affairs, accompanied Churchill.

When the Second Cairo Conference later drew to a close during the first week in December, Stettinius wrote a letter to King from his office in Washington. The letter suggests the remoteness between State and the JCS and clarifies why the JCS had to ask Roosevelt for political guidance at the last moment.

"The Liaison Committee," wrote the Under Secretary, "constituted of you, General Marshall and myself has been inactive since I have been in the State Department. Recently I have considered whether it is worthwhile for the Committee to continue. You will recall it was established several years ago by Presidential directive in order to assist in bringing about closer operating relationships between the War, Navy and State Departments.

"After a careful study of the matter, my own tentative conclusion is to maintain the Committee on an inactive basis. This conclusion was reached because the meetings which are now held by our three Secretaries provide a channel through which the most important problems of the three Departments can be discussed. Also, based on our experience thus far, I find that we can always get together personally or by means of telephone on short notice to discuss important matters without waiting for a meeting."

Stettinius's contention that the three Secretaries routinely discussed "the most important problems" was fallacious. Knox never became involved in strategy, nor did Stimson to any great degree. No one (other than perhaps the President) coordinated foreign policy with military strategy, despite Stettinius's suggestion that he was only a telephone call away.

"Subject to your concurrence," Stettinius concluded, "it is my suggestion that, while we keep the Committee in existence, we do not plan to meet regularly. If at any time one of the three of us wish to have a meeting of the group, it could easily be arranged. I might add that I have discussed this matter with Secretary Hull and he is in agreement with this proposal. I should greatly appreciate your reaction to this suggestion."

"Draft concurrence," wrote King on the letter's margin.

Although *Iowa* was approaching her destination of Oran, King had not yet told McCrea what *Iowa* should do during the conference. Even Cooke did not know. As time grew short, King became increasingly reticent. Orders, he said, would be forthcoming in "due course." McCrea stopped asking.

Iowa entered port in the early dawn, passing the upper works of sunken French ships nearby. The crew assembled on deck to watch the President lowered in a breeches buoy to a boat alongside. An *Iowa* observer later recalled, "It was a very dramatic sight to see this single, lonely figure lowered precariously into this 'rowboat.' "

McCrea — still without orders — prepared to stop King before the Admiral disembarked. At the last moment King handed him a scrap of paper. McCrea unfolded it and began reading: "*Iowa* and escorts depart Oran no later than 1800. Proceed to Bahia, Brazil and await orders from the Commander in Chief."

McCrea showed the extraordinary operation order to Cooke. They both smiled.

Cars were waiting pierside to drive the President and his party to La Sevia airfield, some fifty miles inland from Oran. The steep, winding, twisting road passed through native villages and terminated at the airfield where several Douglas C-54 transports waited. On the theory that too many eggs should not be in one basket, the President, Leahy, and Hopkins flew in one plane, accompanied by Eisenhower, who had met the President in Oran. King and Arnold flew in a second plane, and Marshall went in a third.

King's aircraft thundered aloft and headed eastward toward Tunis, 650 miles away and the first stop on the way to Cairo. Turbulent air buffeted the transport as it paralleled the North African coast. In time an escort of fighter aircraft joined to protect the caravan in the event of a surprise German air attack. Everyone hoped, of course, that the stringent security precautions would prevent the Germans from knowing that Roosevelt and the JCS were traveling in the Mediterranean theater of war.

In the early afternoon King's aircraft began to descend as it approached the El Aouina military airfield outside Tunis. Only seven months before, it had been a German airbase, and wrecked aircraft still littered the perimeter of the field. (Tunis had been the scene of Germany's final stand in North Africa.) When King disembarked, the President was about to be whisked away, accompanied by two of his sons, Franklin and Elliott, and by Eisenhower. King and the remaining members of the party, having been met by a large contingent of Americans, British, and French, followed by car to Eisenhower's headquarters.

After lunch, King and Marshall walked across the barren ground where Carthage had stood two thousand years before. The Romans had so obliterated Carthage during the Third Punic War that archaeologists since have never found more than traces of the once splendid city. The two most recent conquerors of Carthage nevertheless tried to find something — anything. They found nothing. King and Marshall concluded that the Romans had been thorough indeed.

Both men were by then fatigued. When Eisenhower offered his cottage for the night, it was gratefully accepted. Eisenhower had been invited to dinner with Roosevelt, while King and Marshall, to their delight, had a free evening. Before Eisenhower left he sat with them in the living room.

Abruptly, King started talking about the OVERLORD command. Early in the war, King explained, Churchill and Roosevelt apparently had agreed that Alanbrooke (a conjunction of Alan Brooke) should be in command. Later, as the American strength became preponderant, Roosevelt changed his mind because he believed that public opinion would demand an American commander. Churchill had to concur and had the unhappy task of telling Alanbrooke. King, too, believed that the supreme commander should be an American general, and that his deputy should be British.

From time to time King and Eisenhower paused to debate some theoretical aspects of the OVERLORD and the Mediterranean supreme commands. It seemed logical, for instance, that if an American got the former, a British general should get the latter. "The time has come," asserted King, "for the President and Churchill to decide who the OVERLORD commander should be." Marshall said nothing.

King next explained that Roosevelt wanted the supreme command for Marshall, then bluntly enumerated the reasons why he and the remainder of the JCS wanted Marshall to remain in Washington. "Even then," King later recalled, "Marshall said *nothing*." Eisenhower too remembered that, during King's explanation, "General Marshall remained completely silent; he seemed embarrassed."

King kept on talking. "You, Eisenhower, are the proper man to become the supreme commander for the Allies in Europe."

Eisenhower finally rose to leave for his dinner with Roosevelt. King walked him to the door. "I hate to lose General Marshall as Chief of Staff," said King, "but my loss is consoled by the knowledge that I will have you to work with in his job."

Eisenhower's naval aide, Captain Harry C. Butcher, had listened to the dialogue between King and Eisenhower. "General Marshall had not mentioned or indicated anything about Ike's probable assignment," wrote Butcher in his diary, "and Ike was embarrassed, not only by the warmth of the Admiral's statement, but by the spontaneity of his comment in General Marshall's silent presence."

King never revealed his motives for his extraordinary conversation with Eisenhower that evening. Perhaps King simply wanted to brief Eisenhower on developments, as Roosevelt was sure to discuss the supreme command with Eisenhower, probably that very evening at dinner. The conversation also reminded Marshall how strongly his colleagues wanted him to remain on the JCS.

Next morning King flew to Cairo, sightseeing over the great desert battlefields still littered with wrecked tanks and vehicles. After a nine-hour flight he arrived in Cairo, then motored to Mena House, a hotel on the city's outskirts near the great pyramids. Here the Americans and British would try to agree upon a united front before meeting the Russians in Teheran. King and his staff were billeted in two nearby villas staffed with native cooks, American soldiers, and a uniformed British woman in charge. The entire area was surrounded with barricades and sentries.

Ten days of conferences followed.

Dudley Pound no longer sat with the British Chiefs of Staff. King had known that Pound had been sick, for Churchill had privately told King about Pound's brain tumor earlier in the fall. Despite his will to live, Pound finally succumbed. King had lost a good friend.

Admiral of the Fleet Sir Andrew B. Cunningham replaced Pound as the First Sea Lord. Cairo would be his first experience as the senior British naval representative on the CCS. It was an onerous duty he would have preferred to avoid, for Cunningham was happiest when fighting at sea. He and King had met many times before. In 1942, as the senior British naval representative in Washington, Cunningham had often called on King. Their meetings had frequently been tempestuous, as Cunningham later recalled in his memoirs. "A man of immense capacity and ability," wrote Cunningham, "quite ruthless in his methods,

[King] was not an easy person to get on with. He was tough and liked to be considered tough, and at times became rude and overbearing. It was not many weeks before we had some straight speaking over the trifling matter of lending four or five American submarines for work on our side of the Atlantic. He was offensive, and I told him what I thought of his method of advancing allied unity and amity."

King's attitude toward Cunningham undoubtedly had stemmed from an earlier press conference, during which the British admiral had charged that the American contribution to the Battle of the Atlantic was wholly inadequate. King was still smarting when Cunningham had asked for the American submarines. "I therefore interpreted Cunningham's inquiry as a 'needle' directed at me," King later said, "and I was indeed very abrupt and rude with him — and purposefully so. . . . I was very rough with him."

George Russell remembered the encounter. "Apparently there had been an agreement," he recalled, "that the British would provide the submarines for the Mediterranean, and they wanted to go back on that agreement and have the United States Navy provide the submarines. King refused to do it, and Cunningham got insistent and started pounding on the table. King stood up and said, 'Britannia may have ruled the waves for three hundred years, but she doesn't anymore. There's the door.' "

The two men were so alike that such conflicts were inevitable. Yet Cunningham recorded that he and King "parted friends. . . . On the whole I think Ernest King was the right man in the right place, though one could hardly call him a good co-operator." King himself was happy to see Cunningham on the CCS in late 1943. "Then they got a *man*," said King. "A fighter. He would fight like hell. When I had something to say against the British he would stand up and say, 'I don't like that.' "

The Cairo meetings tackled two principal problems, European operations and the Far East. Generalissimo Chiang Kai-shek, accompanied by Madame Chiang and a large Chinese contingent, were at Cairo for the latter discussions. Despite King's desire to aid China, by his own admission he had little official contact with them. When the Chinese military leaders talked before the CCS, King simply listened. Toward the end of the first week King was a luncheon guest of the "Missimo" and "Madame." It must not have made much of an impression. "I don't recall exactly what we talked about," King later said, "but I'm sure that Madame was making every effort to get help for the Chinese."

King, meanwhile, had passed his sixty-fifth birthday on 23 November, the day after the First Cairo Conference had begun. It had been, recalled Alanbrooke after the war, a "very Chinese day." It had begun in the President's villa with a plenary meeting at eleven in the morning. The Generalissimo and Madame made their first official appearance before the combined American and British dignitaries, and everyone had been dazzled by Madame's charms.

That afternoon the differences in the American and British concepts of strategy were laid raw. Alanbrooke provoked a storm when he advocated canceling amphibious operations in Burma in order to provide additional landing craft for operations in the Mediterranean. King became enraged at Alanbrooke's repeated attempts to void Britain's Southeast Asian commitments. The official minutes are, as usual, mute on what was said in anger, but some participants remembered the heat and the fire. "Brooke got nasty and King got good and sore," recorded Stilwell in his diary. "King almost climbed over the table at Brooke. God, he was mad. I wish he had socked him."

That evening the British invited the Americans to dinner. Marshall could not come, as Churchill had snared him into a separate dinner engagement, but King, Leahy, and Arnold accepted. Passions by then had subsided, and the amazing ability of the chiefs to leave their differences on the doorstep was again apparent. King's colleagues observed King's birthday, and the evening passed pleasantly in good food, good conversation, and good fellowship. "King was as nice as could be," recorded Alanbrooke, "and quite transformed from his morning's attitude."

Despite such interludes the fundamental issues separating the Americans and British on the Far East could not be resolved. It was evident that Mountbatten and the Chinese had many differences. And there were Chinese demands for additional materiel that the Allies either could not or would not provide. Planning got nowhere.

Nor was there significant progress on planning for OVERLORD or Mediterranean operations. The same arguments pro and con were resurrected time and again. During the final Cairo meeting on 26 November, the British (whose antipathy toward the Chinese had grown after talking to them at Cairo) once again suggested canceling amphibious operations in Burma to provide more landing craft in Europe. King would not hear of it. The land campaign in Burma would fail without the supporting amphibious assault, argued King. "Our object is to make use of China and her manpower," he insisted. Any delay in opening the Burma Road would delay the end of the war. As indifferent as he may have been to the intransigent Chinese generals, King still wanted the men they commanded to get on with the war against Japan. Marshall and Leahy supported King.

With this the CCS went into executive session. Still they could not agree. The British accepted OVERLORD, but only in principle.* The Americans did not want further involvement in the Mediterranean. The First Cairo Conference ended with the Allies in disarray. Each would make a separate appeal to Stalin. Whatever the Russian wanted — whether an irrevocable commitment to OVERLORD or an intensified Mediterranean offensive — would determine American and British strategy for the remainder of the war.

Ironically, Ambassador Harriman earlier in the week had warned the JCS not to affront the Russians at Teheran with an American-British grand strategy as a fait accompli. Harriman had no cause to worry.

King flew from Cairo to Teheran on 27 November with Arnold on a five-hour flight. King, as usual, was keenly interested in the geography below. Most of the American staff officers had remained in Cairo. Those who did accompany the JCS, together with King, Marshall, and Arnold, were billeted at a U.S. Army base outside Teheran. The accommodations were comfortable but austere, and everyone — including King — ate in a central mess hall.

The day after he arrived, King joined his colleagues for a late Sunday morning conference with the President and Hopkins. Roosevelt was billeted in the Soviet compound within the city walls. The American compound outside the city, Stalin had said, was unsafe, and he felt that Roosevelt would be better off under Russian care. King would have had to agree. The Russians required a United States Army colonel to vouch for King before he could pass through the main gate. (King was privately miffed that his uniform alone was not sufficient identification.) Once inside, King had an uneasy feeling that the Soviet security forces would leap from the woodwork at the slightest excuse.

The Roosevelt-JCS meeting reviewed the American and British positions and speculated what the Russians would want of the Allies. Neither King nor anyone else could predict what Stalin would do or say. Everyone was apprehensive that Stalin would want a second front at once. In that case OVERLORD would be dead, as it was at least a half year away. The British would then get their way in the Mediterranean, because it would divert German troops immediately.

* The QUADRANT agreement for a 1 May 1944 invasion date seems to have been disregarded.

Following lunch at the Army base, Marshall and Arnold left for a drive in the country. (Roosevelt had told them there would be no further meetings that day.) King declined an invitation to join them in order to do some paperwork. To King's surprise, the President unexpectedly summoned the JCS to the Soviet compound later in the afternoon. With Marshall and Arnold off in the wilderness, King and Leahy alone showed up to represent the JCS.

The two admirals found they would only be spectators at the first meeting among the three political giants. Roosevelt, Churchill, and Stalin did all the talking. Everyone else listened. King was destined to remain silent at all three plenary meetings, except when asked an occasional question by the President. Later he told his inner circle of Alexandria reporters about his first impression.

"Roosevelt made quite a speech," King related to his fascinated audience, "how fine it was for everybody to be gathered into this historic meeting. When he had finished his oration, he passed the ball to Churchill who, in his best manner, made another oration. After these two had finished, it was the turn of Stalin to speak. 'The sentiments expressed appear to be appropriate to the occasion, and I subscribe to them,' said Stalin. When he spoke again his interpreter became uncomfortable. After a pause the interpreter spoke. 'Marshal Stalin says now let's get down to business.' "

Roosevelt launched into a long review of the war. As King had heard it all before, his mind wandered. Stalin fascinated him, so King studied him intently. He seemed enigmatic. Two aides spoke to him frequently, but Stalin rarely responded. As Roosevelt droned on, interspersed with the voice of Stalin's interpreter, King became mesmerized by Stalin's doodling. Finally Roosevelt got to the point. How, he asked Stalin, could the Allies best assist the Soviet Union?

To King's surprise, Stalin began talking about the war against Japan. It was a subject considered too sensitive to raise unless the Russians brought it up. (In fact, the CCS did not even have an agenda for Teheran, deferring to the Russians on the topics for discussion.) He regretted, Stalin said, that the war against Germany had taken all his resources. But when Germany had been defeated, Russia would then join the Allies against Japan. In a matter of minutes Stalin had settled a year and a half of speculation by King and his JCS colleagues.

Stalin next turned to the war against Germany. He first reviewed the military situation on the Eastern Front. Everyone listened as he led up to his expectations for a second front. Then it came. *Stalin wanted an amphibious assault in northern France, and perhaps even in southern*

France. Further operations in Italy or the eastern Mediterranean, said Stalin, would be indecisive. So OVERLORD was on! And Marshall was not even present for the realization of his dream. King would tell him about it later.

Churchill tried desperately to salvage the British position, but Stalin was unmoved. He wanted OVERLORD. Churchill also tried to convince Stalin to get Turkey into the war, but Stalin felt that Turkey would remain neutral.

"In my opinion," said a disgruntled Churchill, "the Turks are crazy."

"There are some people," replied Stalin, "who apparently prefer to remain crazy."

The first plenary meeting came to a close. King was impressed. "Stalin knew just what it was he wanted when he came to Teheran," King said to the Alexandria reporters afterward, "and he got it. Stalin is a stark realist, and there is no foolishness about him. He speaks briefly and directly to the point — not a wasted word."

King was again a passive spectator during the second plenary meeting in the late afternoon of the twenty-ninth. As King could have predicted, Stalin wanted to know who would command OVERLORD. Roosevelt and Churchill said that it had not been decided. "Then nothing will come of these operations," said Stalin.

Roosevelt promised a quick answer. During the remainder of the meeting Churchill tried to revive his Mediterranean plans, but Stalin refused to consider any alternatives to OVERLORD.

King meanwhile continued to study the Russian. Stalin's physique seemed quite ordinary. His uniform was unusual, almost iridescent in the sunlight. King had heard that the material was exclusively for Stalin, and he mused whether anyone else would even want to wear it. King had also heard that Stalin's left hand was abnormally small and partially paralyzed, but he saw no evidence of it. By the end of the second plenary meeting King noticed that Stalin used the phrases "Russia" and "Russian" rather than "Soviet," apparently as a way to inspire Russian nationalism. King even deceived himself that Stalin had lost interest in proselytizing for communism. And one evening King saw a more animated Stalin, drinking vodka and getting tight at Churchill's sixty-ninth birthday celebration.

On the morning of the third plenary session the CCS met beforehand to decide — on Stalin's insistence — upon dates for OVERLORD and Operation ANVIL, the landing in southern France. It soon developed that the availability of the always scarce landing craft would control the schedule. Although Stalin thought that ANVIL should precede OVERLORD,

Marshall felt they should be simultaneous. King supported Marshall, and the others agreed.

King then expanded upon the question of landing craft. Although he never disputed that there were chronic shortages in Europe, he also had never offered to divert any from the Pacific, nor did anyone ever dare ask him to. And King would never allow another emergency building program like the one in 1942.

But there were other ways to alleviate the shortages. King pledged his landing-craft repair facilities as first priority to OVERLORD to get damaged craft back into action. He also advocated more stringent control over those landing craft already in Europe because local commanders hoarded them for "other uses of convenience." Some "uses" were humanitarian, for instance, delivering food and supplies for civilian relief in occupied territory. King believed that the Italians were better fed than ever before, in peace or war, owing to American generosity. Such programs, said King, were wasting scarce American shipping. Italy had become a "pain in the neck," but, King believed, the Allies had taken the job and had to go through with it. "It will be necessary to be hardhearted," King concluded. "We must cut out anything that is being taken across the beaches which is not absolutely necessary." No one disagreed.

When King had finished talking, the CCS continued to search for a common agreement on a date for OVERLORD. They had to have an answer for Stalin. At issue was the persistent British reluctance to pick a date and stick to it. Unless conditions on the continent were just right, they seemed prepared to postpone OVERLORD indefinitely. Although the CCS once had thought that 1 May 1944 was a feasible date, the British now wanted to wait until the middle of July.

"Damn," said King. "Your Prime Minister wants to keep all Allied forces actively engaged, and yet the two-and-a-half-month delay you propose would immobilize thirty-five divisions waiting in the United Kingdom for OVERLORD. I have always felt that OVERLORD is the way to break Germany's back."

Cunningham spoke up. "What two-and-a-half-month delay? The earliest possible date for OVERLORD is 1 June."

King and Leahy were bewildered. Was not the first of May the date that had been agreed upon earlier? Even the imperturbable Leahy finally lost patience. Did Alanbrooke believe, asked Leahy, that Germany would have to collapse before it was safe to land in France? Alanbrooke testily replied he felt the conditions for an invasion would be met in

1944, "provided the enemy were met on other fronts, i.e., the Mediterranean as well."

After more of the same the CCS agreed that the Allied advance in Italy should proceed to the Pisa-Rimini line, which would detain 68 LSTs * needed for OVERLORD until the last moment. Second, OVERLORD and ANVIL would be simultaneous, the size of ANVIL being contingent upon the availability of landing craft. Third, OVERLORD would be launched "during May." Armed with these recommendations, Roosevelt and Churchill met with Stalin for lunch in the early afternoon. The President read the CCS recommendations. The official minutes recorded that Stalin "expressed great satisfaction with this decision."

The third and final plenary meeting that afternoon was pro forma. Stalin confirmed his approval of the CCS proposals and pledged a massive offensive the following spring to support the landings in France. On that auspicious note the meeting ended. A sumptuous dinner party that evening, replete with oratorical toasts and expressions of unity and friendship, climaxed the Teheran Conference.

Next day King returned to Cairo. His schedule had prevented any sightseeing of Teheran during his three-and-a-half-day stay. "But there were available in the officers' mess," King later wrote, "some good things that were sent from India by the Army. They were rather cheap, so I bought some small things to recall that I had been there."

There was unfinished business in Cairo before the Americans could return home. Along the way the CCS stopped at Jerusalem, so that the British chiefs could entertain their American colleagues at the King David Hotel in return for the American hospitality in Washington. King was delighted with the opportunity to explore the ancient city. Although King did not go to church, he knew the Bible, so he was eager to see the places he had read about.

In the evening King called upon the British governor. His British hosts seemed particularly keen to tell him about the status of the Jews in Palestine. "The governor had been a good friend of Dill," King later wrote in his memoirs, "and he told us that the Jews were always trying to make trouble in or out of Palestine. The Jews had been training under arms for years, and the British wanted them to serve in the British Army. Of course, what the Jews really wanted was to be able to get a separate state for themselves, which they were calling 'Israel.' "

There is no evidence that King ever wrote about or even thought

* Landing Ship, Tank, a particularly valuable amphibious assault ship.

about European Jews other than in his brief written recollections of his visit to Jerusalem in December 1943. The Holocaust never appeared in his papers or his memoirs.

Before leaving Jerusalem for Cairo, King was driven to a fortress church, on the outskirts of Jerusalem, which dated from the Crusades. Monks took King inside and showed him the well that had sustained the inhabitants during sieges. As King ate their cakes and drank their wine, the monks enthralled the Admiral with stories about the church's history. King finally left, reluctantly, for his plane was waiting. "We gave them a little money for the church," wrote King. Then he returned to the business of war.

The CCS began the Second Cairo Conference on the afternoon of Friday, 3 December. At issue was the size and scope of Operation ANVIL. The British insisted that a two-division assault was necessary for success. The CCS would somehow have to find the necessary landing craft. On the contrary, said King, the Teheran agreements limited ANVIL to the availability of landing craft. There had been no decision on the strength of the assault force. These two arguments established the theme for the next five days of intensive debate.

Portal resurrected the persistent British solution for finding additional landing craft: abandon BUCCANEER,* abandon all plans for amphibious operations in Burma, abandon the Allied commitment to support China by opening the Burma Road. The British intensified their arguments as the days passed in Cairo, for they had never shared America's belief in the need to support China. ANVIL now provided another rationale: Churchill advocated ANVIL so fervently that it led one to believe it had been his idea and not Stalin's. The British Chiefs of Staff provided an "anvil chorus" of assent for their Prime Minister.

Roosevelt and Churchill were anxious to return home, perhaps for domestic reasons, and probably to force the CCS into early agreements. The CCS resisted, predicting days, even weeks, to settle matters. Would it not be possible then, asked Churchill, for the CCS to remain at Cairo after he and Roosevelt had left in order to "work out their problems together"? King replied that there were too many problems that could only be resolved by Roosevelt and Churchill. Clearly, King and the CCS wanted them to stay in Cairo as long as necessary. But the pressure from the civilian leaders began to have its effect.

King tried to save BUCCANEER by making concessions. He could provide, he said, additional landing craft from new construction, originally

* Code name for the amphibious phase of ANAKIM.

King striding through Recife, Brazil, in company with Vice Admiral Jones Ingram. King was returning from Teheran and stopped to see his commander of the South Atlantic forces. (National Archives 80-G-44061)

planned for the Pacific, to support a two-division assault in ANVIL without having to use BUCCANEER resources.

"A fruitful contribution," Churchill interjected.

King tried other ways to salvage BUCCANEER. The United States Navy was converting passenger liners into troop carriers, he said, to lessen the shipping shortage. He refuted British arguments that Japanese air power had grown so powerful that it threatened BUCCANEER. (If more air support was needed, King later said, then he would lend four to six escort carriers to augment Mountbatten's air forces.)

Churchill could not be swayed, so King used what he considered his most telling argument. "We made a definite commitment to the Generalissimo," said King, "that there would be an amphibious operation in

Burma in the spring." Churchill replied that he, personally, had never made such a commitment. It would be a mistake for the Generalissimo to assume otherwise.

Further debate resolved nothing, and so the first plenary meeting ended, as the minutes have recorded, "with an injunction from the President and Prime Minister to their respective staffs to meet together and try to reach agreement on the points at issue in the light of the discussion which had taken place."

But there would be no agreement. On the afternoon of the third day of the conference, Roosevelt summoned the JCS to his villa. He had decided, said the President, to stop fighting the British about BUCCANEER. It was their operation. He could not force them to do it against their will. King later asserted in his memoirs that Roosevelt had finally given in from fatigue and Churchill's incessant "hammering" on the President. King also faulted his JCS colleagues for finally agreeing with Roosevelt to abandon BUCCANEER. "But *I*, myself," wrote King, "wouldn't give even an inch." Not that it mattered. As Leahy wrote in his diary, Roosevelt "was the Commander in Chief and that ended the argument."

When the CCS met the following day, 6 December, BUCCANEER was officially canceled without comment. The landing craft that had been assigned to Southeast Asia were to return for OVERLORD and ANVIL.

The final meeting was held on 7 December, two years after the American entry into the Second World War. The grand strategy for the remainder of the war had now been determined. Germany would be crushed between the Allied army in France and the Red Army in the east.

After months of delay, Roosevelt the day before had decided that Eisenhower would command OVERLORD. Marshall would remain in Washington.

King's apprehensions about China never materialized. The Chinese army kept fighting. The Japanese retained most of their army on the mainland, where it remained largely inactive. As a result, Japanese defensive measures in the Marshalls and the Marianas would be incomplete and undermanned when assaulted by American forces in 1944. Nor would Japanese troops oppose MacArthur in any strength in the Southwest Pacific. Not until the invasions of the Philippines, Iwo Jima, and Okinawa would the Japanese army employ a significant number of troops against the American amphibious forces, but even then they were far fewer than the total number of troops still on the China mainland. But King, of course, had no way of predicting the failure of the Japanese army to make better use of its potential.

King returned to the United States on 12 December. He had been gone a month and a day. Years later King finished writing his memoirs for 1943 and concluded, "It was altogether a very interesting year for me."

33

Onward in the Pacific

As the Second World War entered the year 1944, United Nations forces were preparing for major offensives both in Europe and in the Pacific. American factories were producing an abundance of materiel, not only for American forces but for Great Britain, Russia, and lesser allies as well. The invasion of France would begin in the spring supported by a massive Russian offensive. Amphibious assault forces would attack Anzio in order to outflank German forces on the Italian peninsula and to hasten the capture of Rome. The Allies had won the Battle of the Atlantic, while American and British bombers continued to destroy German cities and industries.

American forces in the Pacific had seized Tarawa and would soon assault the Marshalls. MacArthur, meanwhile, was beginning his final offensive to smash through the Bismarck Archipelago. American submarines in the Pacific were strangling the Japanese merchant marine. Only in Southeast Asia were Allied offensive plans in a quandary, owing to the decision at Cairo to cancel Buccaneer.

The Cairo-Teheran conferences had focused upon the war in Europe. Relatively little time had been devoted to the Pacific, for it was, after all, an all-American venture. Without much debate the CCS had scheduled a two-front advance, by Nimitz in the Central Pacific and MacArthur in the Southwest Pacific, reaffirming the basic strategic plan agreed upon earlier at Quadrant.

The schedules were deliberately tentative. "We are convinced that the sequence of operations must be flexible," the CCS had agreed, "and we must be prepared to take all manner of short cuts made possible by developments in the situation." An early defeat of the Japanese fleet or unexpected Japanese withdrawals would dramatically alter plans. Given such uncertainties, the JCS did not plan too far into the future. Pacific strategy was opportunistic in the traditional British manner, even though the Americans had advocated inviolate dates and long-range planning in Europe.

It would take months for the JCS to decide what to do after the fall of the Marshalls in February 1944. Such protracted deliberations seemed necessary to King to get a sound decision that the JCS would accept. To Nimitz, however, they were maddening, frustrating delays that jeopardized orderly planning for future offensives.

King had an open mind about the Pacific immediately following the Cairo-Teheran conferences. His views had not changed substantially since his War College student days: as the Americans advanced westward their lines of communication would lengthen while the Japanese lines shortened. "From the Japanese viewpoint," he mused with his circle of Alexandria journalists one evening, "is it better strategy for them to let us come to the very end of our long lines of communications and then attack us? Why should they come to meet us on some middle ground and away from their bases? We have to come to them, and they know it. Therefore they will make it as difficult as possible. Because we would *like* them to come out is no military reason why they should do as we wish. Also — and maybe more important — the Japs have had a taste of what a wallop the American Navy packs and does not like the taste."

The island of Truk in the Caroline Islands was very much on King's mind. The CCS had approved its seizure following the fall of the Marshalls, in line with years of traditional naval thinking. Its magnificent harbor and adjacent airfields made it Japan's major Central Pacific base and a threat to any westward advance. But its terrain was formidable. An amphibious assault would be so costly that many on the JCS staff wanted to bypass it. But, wondered King, where "does one light" if it is bypassed? A heavy carrier raid was being planned in the near future that would test Truk's defenses, so in the interim King deferred a decision.

King met with Nimitz and Halsey in San Francisco on 3 and 4 January 1944 to talk about the implications of the Cairo-Teheran conferences. The Mariana Islands, said King, were the key to the Pacific. In American hands they could block Japanese lines of communication to the Carolines, and their central position made them an ideal base for a further advance westward to the China coast. For that matter, stressed King, all operations were to be aimed at getting to China in order to exploit Chinese manpower and to establish bases for the final assault against the Japanese mainland.

Forrest Sherman, Nimitz's war plans officer, noted that by going directly to the Marianas that Truk might well be bypassed. After further discussion some short-term decisions were made, but long-range plans remained undecided. Still, King left San Francisco with the impression that Nimitz and his staff had generally agreed on the importance of the Marianas.

He was wrong. Representatives of Nimitz, Halsey, and MacArthur met in Pearl Harbor on 27 and 28 January to coordinate their immediate operations. Inevitably, they also talked of the future. Lieutenant General Sutherland, MacArthur's chief of staff, argued that pooling all the Pacific resources in the Southwest Pacific Area was the quickest way to seize the Philippines and to move on to China. Nimitz, Sherman, and the CINCPAC staff seemed sympathetic to Sutherland's proposal, which had been so long advocated by MacArthur. Furthermore, it was obvious that no one at Pearl Harbor shared King's enthusiasm for the Marianas. A delighted Sutherland wired MacArthur that he had won Nimitz's support.

When King read the minutes of the Pearl Harbor conference, he became enraged at Nimitz's defection. In a scathing letter to Nimitz, he wrote, "I have read your conference notes with much interest and I must add with indignant dismay. Apparently, neither those who advocated the concentration of effort in the Southwest Pacific, nor those who admitted the possibility of such a procedure, gave thought nor undertook to state when and if the Japanese occupation and use of the Marianas and Carolines was to be terminated. I assume that even the Southwest Pacific advocates will admit that sometime or other this thorn in the side of our communications to the western Pacific must be removed. In other words, at some time or other we must take out time and forces to carry out this job. . . .

"A number of conferees, particularly Towers, stated, and his statements were allowed to go unrefuted, that the object of taking the Marianas was to provide for B-29 bombing attack against the Japanese Empire. Of course, that was never the object. That was merely one of the results that would ensue from this operation, which was to be taken to dry up the Carolines, facilitating the capture or neutralization of the Carolines, and to speed up the clearing of the line of communications to the northern Philippine area. . . .

"The idea of rolling up the Japanese along the New Guinea coast, throughout Halmahera and Mindanao, and up through the Philippines to Luzon, as our major strategic concept, to the exclusion of clearing our Central Pacific line of communications to the Philippines, is to me absurd. Further, it is not in accordance with the decisions of the Joint Chiefs of Staff."

King assumed, his letter continued, that Nimitz agreed with King's strategic views of the Pacific, and he recapitulated them for Nimitz's benefit. Emphasizing again the importance of the Marianas and the Carolines, King then outlined his own strategic concept for the defeat of Japan.

(1) — Japan will ultimately be forced to her "inner ring" of defense — Japan, Korea, Manchuria, Shantung, etc.
(2) — Everything that we do must be related to (1).
(3) — (1) requires use of China as a base — and of Chinese manpower to secure and maintain the base.
(4) — (3) requires availability of ports in China — none of which are accessible north of Formosa.
(5) — Luzon is the key point for opening up sea routes to Ports in China.
(6) — Central Pacific general objective is Luzon.
(7) — (6) requires clearing Japs out of Carolines, Marianas, Pelews — and holding them.
(8) — (7) cuts Jap lines of communications to Netherlands East Indies east of Philippine Islands — also protects flank of advance from S.W. Pacific to Mindanao.
(9) — (7) has priority over advance from S.W. Pacific to Mindanao.
(10) — Occupation and use of Mindanao will not open communications with ports in China — Mindoro Strait is controlled from Luzon — Balabac Strait is too far to southward.
(11) — Occupation and use of Mindanao is primarily to effect reoccupation of Philippine Islands which will roll-up against tremendous difficulties.
(12) — (10) and (11) emphasize (5), (6), (7), (8).

Such was King's master plan to defeat Japan, but he would have a hard time selling it to the JCS. Following up on the encouraging news (to him) from Sutherland at Pearl Harbor, MacArthur sent Marshall a message on 2 February that flew in the face of King's ideas. Based upon Sutherland's proposal to Nimitz, MacArthur advocated a single Southwest Pacific drive. A dual drive, even though authorized by the CCS, would be "two weak thrusts" which would delay victory over Japan by six months. King's concept of seizing or neutralizing the Marianas and the Carolines, MacArthur continued, would "not attain a major strategic objective," nor would those islands provide adequate harbors or airfields to support an eventual assault against the Philippines. MacArthur ended his dispatch with a plea that "all available ground, air and assault forces in the Pacific" be sent to him as the only sure way to defeat Japan in the shortest possible time.

King, already fuming over Nimitz's inconstancy at the Pearl Harbor conference, reacted as one would expect to MacArthur's proposal. Apparently, wrote King to Marshall, General MacArthur had not accepted the CCS decisions at Cairo that there would be a dual drive across the Pacific and that the Central Pacific took priority in scheduling and resources. Now was not the time to change those decisions. King ended by recommending that Marshall tell MacArthur to obey orders.

But MacArthur's influence was irrepressible. On the same day that King sent his scolding letter to Nimitz, Sutherland and Sherman arrived in Washington to discuss future operations with the JCS. Marshall despaired at the welter of conflicting proposals, observed that it was up to the JCS to decide about the future, and with King's concurrence the entire matter was referred to the JCS planners.

King, meanwhile, continued to be unhappy with Nimitz. By mid-February King wanted to bypass Truk, but Nimitz still wanted to capture it. Nor could King detect any substantial support from Nimitz on the Marianas. Finally, it seemed to King that Nimitz was endangering security by talking to the press about future operations. Consequently he wrote again to Nimitz, revealing his misgiving and advising Nimitz to be ready to come to Washington for consultations. Timing would be critical. Towers recently had become Nimitz's deputy, and King did not entirely trust Towers to run the war in the Pacific while Nimitz was away.

The struggle in Washington to articulate Pacific strategy continued through February and into early March. The JCS planners clearly favored a dual thrust with primary emphasis in the Central Pacific, but MacArthur from afar harangued Marshall for the major share of the action. Under the circumstances, King might have been justifiably hostile and antagonistic toward the General. The opposite was true. "King played ball with him all the time," recalled Bernhard Bieri, who was King's war plans officer in early 1944. "As far as I could see, he was very respectful and considerate of everything that MacArthur asked, except he wouldn't let him command the fleet."

Bieri recalled how King had hastily assembled a ragtag group of ships early in the war to provide MacArthur a rudimentary amphibious capability. "Then MacArthur ran into the question of manning these ships and said he needed five thousand men. King said, 'Give him five thousand Coast Guard men.' So we did."

Army landing force commanders normally shared a common command ship with the naval officer amphibious force commander. But MacArthur insisted that his Army commanders have their own command ships during amphibious assaults. "We young fellows," Bieri later said, "didn't see any reason why we should change the rules for MacArthur, but when we took it up with King, he said, 'Give him the ships.' So we did."

King's attitude toward MacArthur was consistent with his attitude toward his JCS colleagues or the British. He would disagree with them during deliberations, but once strategy was decided, King would honor the Navy's commitments.

But the decisions for the Pacific were slow in coming. Even after the Marshalls had fallen in February, the JCS had not given Nimitz his next assignment. By early March King was pressing his colleagues for action. In a memo to Marshall, King wrote, "I am as anxious as you are to have a comprehensive plan for operations against the Japanese, but I feel that we should not put off a decision as to what is to be done in the immediate future, at this time when our tremendously powerful forces can be thrown against an enemy who is obviously bewildered by recent events."

But Marshall had MacArthur on his mind and was not ready to agree upon anything — at least not until he had heard from Nimitz, who was coming to Washington. Marshall was uncomfortable when discussing the pros and cons of amphibious warfare, and he wanted time to ponder such an unfamiliar subject. During the Teheran Conference he had admitted to Alanbrooke and to Russian Marshal Voroshiloff that his military education had been based on roads, rivers, and railroads. Since the beginning of the Second World War, said Marshall, he had been acquiring an education based on oceans, and he had had to learn all over again.

One of King's most exasperating problems was that many of his own naval officers disagreed with him about the Marianas. Its harbors were not well suited for large fleet anchorages, nor was it on the most direct route to the Philippines, Formosa, and the China coast. Senior naval officers in the Pacific assumed that it would be used chiefly as a B-29 bomber base and did not want to expend Navy blood and treasure to help the Army Air Force. Vice Admiral Kinkaid, Commander Seventh Fleet, remarked in late January that "any talk of the Marianas for a base leaves me entirely cold."

When Nimitz arrived in Washington in early March, the JCS and its planners hoped finally to resolve Pacific strategy. MacArthur had been invited; characteristically he had declined with the usual explanation that he could not leave his headquarters while his forces were in action. Sutherland, his surrogate, found himself outnumbered. Had MacArthur come to Washington, his ideas might have been adopted. But he did not come, and King dominated. When the Joint War Plans Committee on March eighth recommended bypassing the Marianas, Bieri and his colleagues on the Joint Staff Planners told them to include the Marianas. Even Nimitz fell in line.

By 12 March the time had come for final decisions. The JCS went into closed session to consider King's proposed directives to Nimitz and MacArthur. King by now had Arnold's support, for Arnold urgently needed a base within range of Japan for his new B-29 bombers. The Marianas were ideal. Although he and King wanted the Marianas for different reasons, together they undoubtedly influenced Marshall and Leahy. When the JCS emerged from seclusion they announced that:

- MacArthur would complete the isolation of Rabaul.
- MacArthur would proceed westward along the northern coast of New Guinea, followed by the seizure of Mindanao on 15 November 1944.
- Nimitz would bypass Truk, seize the southern Marianas on 15 June and isolate the Carolines, and then seize the Palaus on 15 September in order to provide a base from which the Pacific Fleet could support MacArthur's attack against Mindanao.
- Nimitz would seize Formosa on 15 February 1945, or, if first necessary to support an attack on Formosa, MacArthur would seize Luzon on 15 February.

Following the fall of Formosa, the next objective would be the China coast.

Nimitz and MacArthur finally had their marching orders.

The Japanese fleet was on King's mind in the spring of 1944. Its warships had not been in battle for over a year, and in that interval King reckoned it certainly must have been refitted and strengthened. It had abandoned Truk following Spruance's attack with Task Force 58 in mid-February. Presumably the fleet was now divided between Southeast Asia and the home islands.

Would the fleet oppose Spruance at the Marianas in June? No one could know, of course, but King hoped that it would. Until it was destroyed, the Imperial Japanese Navy would remain a threat. A fleet action required a willingness on both sides to fight. The United States Navy was willing, King remarked to his Alexandria journalists one April evening, but the Japanese were unpredictable. They could not be expected to "cooperate" in the destruction of their fleet, but the Marianas might be important enough for them to risk a fight. "If the Jap fleet does not come out when we hit the Marianas," said King, "we shall have to dig it out of waters right around home."

The guessing game went on. When King met with Nimitz in early May for one of their periodic conferences in San Francisco, King announced that a fleet action in the Marianas was unlikely. But, said King, the Japanese fleet certainly would react when the Americans invaded Formosa in early 1945.

Following the conference, King had second thoughts after reading messages from Nimitz that the Japanese fleet was concentrating in the Philippines, about four days' steaming time from the southern Marianas. Nimitz seemed unworried—which worried King. On 18 May Nimitz informed MacArthur that "enemy is now basing important fleet units in southern Philippines," and he asked MacArthur to send his submarines to intercept the Japanese warships. It would take far more than MacArthur's few submarines to stop them. King began reading Spruance's operations order to discover what the Fifth Fleet intended to do if the Japanese fleet came to Saipan. He was not reassured. Neither Spruance nor Mitscher had a comprehensive plan for a fleet action, both preferring to wait until the situation developed.

Nimitz had no end of schemes for diverting the Japanese fleet. Halsey had worked himself out of a job as Commander, South Pacific, by evicting the Japanese into MacArthur's Southwest Pacific Area. King and Nimitz had discussed his reassignment during their early May meeting in San Francisco, but nothing had been decided.

Following the meeting the papers publicized the fact that King, Nimitz, and Halsey had met in San Francisco. At first Nimitz worried that the Japanese would infer that a new offensive was imminent. Then Nimitz had a brainstorm: start a rumor that Halsey would command a northern operation, which would deceive the Japanese about American intentions in the Marianas and New Guinea.* "Such belief might have salutary effects on enemy strategic redisposition of fleet units," wired Nimitz on 20 May.

* A scheme similar to the Allied deception plan that Patton would land an army at Pas-de-Calais in June 1944.

King did not think much of Nimitz's deception plan, which, he told Nimitz, was "not considered advisable because of practical difficulties involved in prevention of leakage of facts."

King's greatest worry was whether Spruance's Fifth Fleet would be prepared for a decisive fleet action. It was King's understanding that all the battleships would operate together, and he fretted that the ponderous prewar battleships would impede the newer, faster ones should they have to maneuver to form a battle line. King was particularly apprehensive about the lack of training, for many of the ships and men of the Fifth Fleet were new and untried.

Nimitz soothingly replied that he shared King's concern, but he assured King that Mitscher's carrier Task Force 58 could handle the Japanese fleet and that the Fifth Fleet would rehearse for a possible surface engagement. The next day, 24 May, Nimitz advised King that he believed that much of the Japanese fleet had left Singapore and had moved to the Philippines. As a precaution, Nimitz suggested that the British fleet in the eastern Indian Ocean conduct a diversionary attack in Southeast Asia to distract the Japanese from the looming Marianas assault. "Do this. K," wrote King on Nimitz's message, but the British could not act on such short notice. Nimitz was thinking impulsively by asking MacArthur or the British for help, or by spreading rumors about Halsey.

The Fifth Fleet would have to stop the Japanese, and King became even more worried that the Fifth Fleet was not ready. King could smell trouble if the Japanese acted aggressively. Spruance planned to detach fully half of his attack carriers two days before the Saipan landings for attacks against airdromes in the Bonins far to the north. They would be far away from Saipan during the initial landings when the amphibious forces were particularly vulnerable. If the Japanese fleet were to appear, said King, it would be as strong as the remaining half of Task Force 58.

On 28 May Nimitz again reassured King that Spruance would make every provision for a fleet action. "Destruction of the enemy fleet is always the prime objective of our naval forces," wired Nimitz. "Attempts by enemy fleet units to interfere with amphibious operations are both hoped for and provided against. . . ."

Nimitz's message was totally misleading. Spruance did not expect the Japanese fleet to interfere with the Saipan landings. And Spruance most certainly did not hope that the Japanese would interfere with the landings. When the Japanese did come forth for what became known as the Battle of the Philippine Sea, the destruction of the Japanese fleet was not Spruance's prime objective. Spruance considered the protection of the landing forces on Saipan as his first priority. As a result, most of the Japanese fleet escaped despite heavy losses.

The Battle of the Philippine Sea will always be controversial, perhaps even more so now that we know that Nimitz and Spruance had such different intentions. Nimitz's assurances to King, whether deliberate or not, were fallacious. King's premonitions had indeed been justified. He had tried to warn Nimitz that he was headed for trouble, but he could not fight Nimitz's war for him. Having said all there was to say, King turned his attention to the Atlantic, where Operation OVERLORD was about to begin.

34

Overlord and Anvil

With Eisenhower now in command of Overlord, plans and preparations gained momentum in early 1944. But Anvil was in trouble. Soon after Eisenhower arrived in England, he warned the JCS that the British felt that Anvil's resources could be better used to reinforce Overlord. By February, however, the British changed their reasoning. Operations in Italy were going so badly that the British now wanted to retain Anvil's troops and amphibious shipping.

On 21 February the JCS met with the President to advise him of British pressure to cancel Anvil, a measure which the JCS vehemently opposed. Roosevelt agreed with the JCS. He had promised Stalin to land in southern France, and the Russians had been "tickled to death." Roosevelt did not want to break that promise. "The Russians would not be happy," said Roosevelt, "even if we told them it would mean two or more divisions for Overlord."

King remarked that even now Overlord had so many troops that the English Channel would already be congested. Two more divisions would clog it even more. This reminded Roosevelt to ask King what he had done about Roosevelt's earlier suggestion of sending small boats to England. (Roosevelt had suggested using large numbers of ships' lifeboats, then lying idle on the East Coast, during the invasion "as rescue craft or other possible useful employment.")

It was a subject King had hoped the President had forgotten. "There are so many craft involved now," said King, "that one could almost walk dry-shod from one side of the channel to the other." Roosevelt persisted. King replied that "the matter was being examined," his usual method of circumventing a Roosevelt suggestion he did not like and hoped that the President would not pursue. Afterward King sent a memo, citing the lifeboats' unseaworthiness in the Channel, the lack of trained crews, and the logistical burden of getting them to England. His advice once again rejected, Roosevelt complained to Leahy, "I rather expected that Admiral King would answer as he did . . . in regard to the use of small craft. . . . I should hate to be accused of not doing all we can in case a lot of drowning people are floating around in the Channel."

The discussion in the White House returned to other matters. Roosevelt declared that he would not send troops to the Balkans as Churchill had requested, nor would the United States get involved in European political problems. Having been illuminated on Roosevelt's most current foreign policy, the JCS took their leave.

The debate over ANVIL would not subside. The British got their way, and by April it was indefinitely postponed.

Frank Knox died of a heart attack on 28 April 1944. Roosevelt nominated James V. Forrestal, then serving as Under Secretary of the Navy, as his successor. Having served in the Navy Department since the summer of 1940, Forrestal had established an excellent record as an executive and as a manager of the Navy's materiel procurement program. His nomination was popularly received, and Senate confirmation was unanimous. King had a new civilian boss.

King and Forrestal had had little previous contact. Their responsibilities rarely overlapped, although they had tussled when King had tried to reorganize the Navy Department — and when Forrestal had attempted to remove King's CNO hat. Forrestal had intruded into King's operational domain but once, in February 1942. Forrestal had sent a memorandum to King that read, "Since the 7th of December, numerous meetings of committees and planning bodies have been held to determine broad plans for the prosecution of the war. I should like to have one page of specific plans that have been evolved and the manner in which they are being prosecuted." King probably chucked the memorandum into his wastepaper basket.

King had secretly hoped that he would be asked to recommend Knox's successor, but, as he wrote Rawleigh Warner, an old Knox associate, "Despite your expectations, I was *not* consulted as to the filling of the big vacancy." When it became apparent that Forrestal would be confirmed, King decided to see Forrestal. Describing the meeting in the same letter to Warner, King wrote, "I am sure it will be of interest to you that, after due reflection, I went yesterday afternoon to the new incumbent and laid the situation on the line, as I saw it, about my feel-

King watches Forrestal taking the oath of office as the new Secretary of the Navy (National Archives 80-G-45571)

ing as to the agencies and activities of the Navy in general and the Navy Department in particular. It was an unpalatable job for me but I am bound to say that it was, all things considered, received amiably enough. Anyway, I have done what I thought I had to do. Among other things that I took up was the matter of what I have called the 'cleavage' organization of the Navy Department, on which point it was said that my judgment in the matter was accepted, so I hope there will be no more of that.

"Mrs. Knox left for Manchester at midday on Monday. I went with my aide to see her off, and she then appeared as cheerful as anyone had any right to expect."

When Forrestal first entered the Navy Department, he had scorned flag officers because they were willing to work for "chickenfeed." But as he came to know them his respect grew. Forrestal regarded King as a brilliant strategist but a poor administrator, and it was in administration that their differences became most apparent. He seemed to respect

King and to bear him no animosity. King, on the other hand, more and more disliked Forrestal with the passing of time. Forrestal, he said, deliberately "needled" him.

Robert G. Albion and Robert H. Connery summed up the two conflicting personalities in their book, *Forrestal and the Navy:* "More fundamental doubtless was the interaction from their very different personalities and their opposite approach to problems. Forrestal's temperament seemed to have been more annoying to King than the admiral's mannerisms were to Forrestal. The patterns of their thinking were not all alike. Forrestal's approach was more intellectual and less direct. Interested in ideas for their own value, he liked to speculate and discuss at length. One of his favorite expressions was 'That seems like a good idea, what do you think of it?' All this was apparently intensely irritating to King, who was entirely down-to-earth and practical in dealing with a situation. Blunt almost to the point of rudeness, he wasted no time on nonsense, but to get on with the war. Firm in his convictions—and generally conservative in outlook—he either accepted or rejected a proposition and for him that ended the matter. He apparently did not appreciate that Forrestal's method was a definite means of getting to the heart of a problem by sorting out the issues, and not just idle conversation."

There were also other reasons for their antipathy. Some of King's closest friends hated Forrestal for his ambition, attitudes that may have affected King. Later, near the end of the war, King would argue bitterly with Forrestal over a flag selection list. King also resented civilian authority, which he obeyed—coldly, correctly, but certainly not willingly. And King in his own way could needle Forrestal, as well. A COMINCH staff officer, Richard D. Shepard, remembered one such episode. "One morning I was invited to appear in Secretary Forrestal's office at 1000," Shepard recalled, "with two other Naval Academy classmates to stand with a classmate's recent widow for presentation of a posthumous medal. We filed in, stood where we were told, and Mr. Forrestal soon came in with medal box in hand, fidgeting, at 0958 or so. Precisely on the stroke of 1000, in slowly strode the tall Ernie King, nodded briefly to Mr. Secretary and the short ceremony went on. Forrestal appeared to me to be noticeably annoyed. Why . . . because of King's cool manner, because of his promptness to a fault, because of Forrestal's having to wait in embarrassment for the on-the-second appearance of his subordinate? I never knew."

Whereas Stimson and Marshall had an open door between their offices, the one deck between the offices of King and Forrestal was an almost insurmountable barrier. Forrestal did try to communicate by convening a regular Monday morning meeting, which included the principal civilian Secretaries, together with King and about five principal Navy Department flag officers. Forrestal invited others only if the agenda warranted. Such meetings discussed only logistical and administrative matters, so Forrestal still remained uninformed about strategic decisions and fleet employment. On 25 September 1944 he tried again to get King to tell him what was happening in the world of operations. "I should like to be currently informed," wrote Forrestal, "on matters considered by the Joint Chiefs of Staff organization which have a bearing on political decisions. I sometimes find that when such matters come up for discussion I am unaware that careful study has already been given thereto by the Joint Chiefs of Staff.

"It would be of assistance to me, in this connection, if you would arrange to have sent to me, when issued, copies of all studies, documents and recommendations furnished to the Secretary of State by the Joint Chiefs of Staff or its committees."

King agreed to cooperate, and many papers did get to Forrestal. During the Potsdam Conference in 1945 King even sent several letters to Forrestal, perhaps because Stimson had been invited and Forrestal had not. Forrestal in return tried to inform King about political developments at the cabinet level. But something went wrong. When Forrestal's initial memorandum was relegated to the files, Edwards appended a melancholy note: "Herewith the ashes of a once good idea."

When OVERLORD was a month and a half away King met with his Alexandria journalists. Glen Perry afterward sent a memorandum about the meeting to his New York editor. "As the day of invasion draws near," he wrote, "the actual news budget of these conferences grows smaller and smaller. What interested me most was the almost complete change in the general atmosphere since the last conference with this speaker [King]. At that time, you will recall, I reported a distinct note of pessimism that pervaded the entire evening. Last night, no vestige of that note remained. Our guest contemplated the future with apparent equanimity, and not even a discussion of the situation in Burma quenched his enthusiasm for the general prospect. From all of which, I am led to the conclusion that the British haven't been annoying him much recently. Also, he has just returned from a ten day rest."

Although King lived in solitude aboard *Dauntless*, he still saw his family. Sunday afternoons at the Observatory were a time for his daughters, grandchildren, relatives, and family friends. Mildred, the youngest daughter and the family favorite, was married at the Observatory in September 1942 in a colorful wedding. A beaming King in dress whites escorted Mildred to the altar, as he had his other daughters.

In November 1943 Mattie suffered a heart attack. Her physicians persuaded her to stop smoking, but she was still overweight. King convened a family council, and a family friend, John J. Ballentine, Jr., watched and listened. "It was awesome to see King's mind work," he later said. "He identified all the possible solutions, discussed each thoroughly, and then decided what was best for Mattie. I could easily imagine his using the same kind of incisive reasoning when he was planning the war."

In the days just before the invasion of Normandy, King's family made King a troubled man. One daughter had become an alcoholic, and her marriage was a disaster. Another son-in-law stationed overseas came home on emergency leave to be with his sick child. King told his distraught daughter that her husband could stay no more than one or two nights because he was needed elsewhere. The daughter begged King to intercede, to do something to allow her husband to remain at home during the family crisis. When King told her that her husband had to go, his daughter threatened never again to speak to him. King was crushed and despondent, but he did not change the orders.

To add to his worries, another daughter was hospitalized with appendicitis. Worse yet, Mattie had broken her hip and her physicians were reluctant to perform surgery because of her heart condition. "The poor man was beside himself," said Betsy Matter, recalling the afternoon just before OVERLORD when King had visited her and Abby at the farm. "All of us were terribly upset as a consequence."

There was trouble of another kind concerning Rear Admiral Alan Kirk, the senior American naval officer in OVERLORD. He had seemed a logical choice, having served as Commander, Amphibious Forces, Atlantic Fleet, and later having commanded an amphibious assault force at Sicily. As a former naval attaché in London and then as chief of staff to Stark in 1942, Kirk seemed familiar both with amphibious warfare and with the British. Unfortunately, Kirk did not like the British, particularly Admiral Sir Bertram Ramsey, the senior naval commander for OVERLORD.

Several weeks before the Normandy landing King received a disturbing letter from Stark in London, which implied that there were bad feelings between Ramsey and Kirk. But Stark was so circumspect that King could not be sure, so he asked Edwards for his opinion. Edwards returned later in the day. "If I can read anything," said Edwards, "what Stark really says is that Kirk won't do."

King agreed. "But this is no time to change him," said King. He left Kirk where he was and hoped for the best.

During the first days of June, King's attention was divided between the Marianas and OVERLORD. King had given the commanders the naval resources that they needed and whatever advice he thought would help. Then he had become a spectator to the inexorable events preceding the opening salvos at Saipan and Normandy. That two such mammoth amphibious assaults, a half-world apart, could be launched simultaneously in mid-1944 was a triumph of America's industrial capacity to produce the materiel of war.

It was also a triumph for King. Two years before, few Allied planners would have predicted that even a limited offensive would have been possible against the Japanese until Germany was first defeated. June 1944 was a culmination of hopes and dreams for King — and for Marshall. Each had gotten what he wanted.

The Channel weather deteriorated as the fourth of June approached, and Eisenhower decided to delay the landings until June sixth. When assured of OVERLORD's initial success, King, Marshall, and Arnold flew to England on June eighth. Their ostensible reason was to be there if things went wrong and quick decisions by the CCS were needed. They probably went more to do some sightseeing at the Normandy beaches.

After delays caused by fog, the travel-weary JCS arrived in London on June ninth, where they were warmly greeted under sunny skies by the British Chiefs of Staff. After resting at Stanwell Place (an estate outside London serving as their temporary headquarters), the JCS went to the War Cabinet offices the next day for an informal CCS meeting. The JCS had informed the British that they were not bringing a large staff and would not be prepared for a full-dress conference. After a general review of the war on all fronts, King briefed the others on the imminent Marianas assault and other developments in the Pacific.

The next day the British lunched with the JCS at Stanwell Place, followed by another meeting. Encouraging reports from the beachhead engendered a good mood that was made even better when the British agreed to limit their operations in Italy and to consider a new date for ANVIL. Important stuff, certainly, but they could hardly conceal their impatience to see what was happening at Normandy.

That evening the chiefs boarded an overnight train to Portsmouth. With Churchill acting as host, everyone was exuberant. Tension dissipated, the tension of years of debate and planning and of the threat of unexpected disasters. Churchill was at his loquacious best, and his gaiety was infectious. There was a feeling of excitement and enthusiasm for what they had achieved and what they would see in the morning.

There was good reason for their abrupt change of mood. When they had faced each other across conference tables to decide upon grand strategy, King and his CCS colleagues had been isolated from the battlefronts. Their deliberations had seemed academic, almost hypothetical. Divisions, corps, armies, ships, fleets, airplanes, and men could become abstract statistics. In one figurative breath the four American and three British officers could decide to move a division from here to there or to change a date for a major offensive. Their decisions initiated events that affected millions of men and billions of dollars worth of the materiel of war. Although the CCS were professional officers with years of service, they had never before experienced an amphibious assault on the scale of the Normandy invasion. Its impact and magnitude had therefore been conceived in faith and envisioned in their imaginations. Their sense of relief that it seemed to be working must have been overwhelming.

The next morning a happy Eisenhower met the train in Portsmouth. The British went their way on a Royal Navy destroyer, while the Americans boarded an American destroyer. Then they were underway to see what they had wrought. King had not been far wrong when he had talked about walking dry-shod across the Channel. The destroyer dodged about the hundreds of ships, lighters, and barges ferrying supplies and reinforcements to the beachhead. Arnold glanced skyward. Not one enemy aircraft was in sight. Allied control of the air was absolute.

Sounds of naval gunfire and artillery became audible as the destroyer approached the Normandy beaches. Rear Admirals Kirk and James L. Hall met the JCS in a subchaser for a tour from seaward. Warships belched their heavy projectiles inland; massive amphibious ships unloaded their cargoes into small craft nestling alongside. Huge portable breakwaters (Mulberrys) protected the landing craft — the scarce, precious landing craft — jammed against the shoreline disgorging cargo that collected in great piles on the beach. Long columns of soldiers and vehicles snaked toward the front lines.

The JCS next clambered into a wheeled amphibian (DUKW), which slammed through the waves and headed ashore. They landed at Omaha Beach. Battle debris was everywhere, attesting to the ferocity of the fighting a few days earlier. As King walked inland the pastoral countryside created a startling contrast. "We are surrounded by fat cattle lying in luscious pastures with their paws crossed," Churchill reportedly said as he toured the same area.

Lieutenant General Omar N. Bradley guided the visitors the few miles inland that safety would permit, for German forces still surrounded the beachhead. There was lunch with Bradley's field commanders, then more sightseeing. By afternoon, however, King was anxious to return to Portsmouth for a dinner engagement with Churchill aboard his train.

King and Marshall returned on time but discovered that Churchill would be late. The Prime Minister wanted his destroyer to fire at the enemy for the vicarious satisfaction of having engaged the Germans in combat. While Churchill dallied, King sipped sherry in Churchill's railroad car. Time dragged. King drank one glass, then several more. When Churchill arrived it was obvious that he had been drinking en route, and he insisted that it continue. Champagne appeared. Churchill exhorted everyone to join him in celebration. "I managed it," King later said, "but it was too much for me." It was the only time we know of that King broke his vow of sobriety during the war.

Three days of CCS meetings resumed in London. King prematurely reported an early success in the Marianas, and the CCS discussed alternatives for future operations in the Pacific. Then other facets of the war were examined, including the current British crises in the CBI. The Japanese were besieging British-Indian forces at Imphal, and the issue was in doubt. King was dismayed by what he considered the "defeatist" attitudes of Field Marshals Wavell and Claude Auchinleck, the British army commanders who, King believed, were undercutting Mountbatten. Miraculously, China was not collapsing, much to King's surprise. "Chiang is holding his country together by pure skill," King had said in April, when he despaired of the British ever opening the Burma Road. As usual the CBI theater heated emotions on both sides, and, as usual, nothing conclusive was changed or decided. The only way to get supplies to China, King concluded, was for the Americans to seize a port on the China coast.

The CCS did agree in principle to a secondary amphibious assault of the ANVIL type, somewhere in Europe later that summer, probably in southern France, but perhaps elsewhere. They withheld a final decision until the situation developed in Normandy and on the Eastern Front. As a preliminary move, King precipitately decided to detach Rear Admiral Don P. Moon from OVERLORD and to send him to the Mediterranean to assist Vice Admiral Kent Hewitt, who would com-

King, Marshall, Arnold, and Eisenhower approaching the Normandy beaches (U.S. Army photograph)

Going ashore in a DUKW (U.S. Army photograph)

mand the naval forces whenever Anvil was finally confirmed. Having talked with Moon several days before, King had been impressed with his amphibious expertise. Disregarding objections that Moon was needed at Normandy, King made his decision without fully considering the consequences.

The result was a tragedy. Moon was a perfectionist who worried too much and failed to delegate authority. He arrived in the Mediterranean in the midst of hasty planning and preparations and succumbed to strain and overwork. Just before the landings in southern France, Moon killed himself.

Although they supported Anvil "in principle," Churchill and the British Chiefs of Staff insisted until the last moment that Allied resources could be better used in Italy. Strategic considerations aside, it was a matter of British pride. Great Britain hated to see their Italian theater relegated to a secondary priority. This, along with Britain's lackluster performance in Burma, meant that British armed forces no longer were predominant in any major theater of the war.*

No matter what the British said, King became even more disillusioned with the Italian campaign during the first months of 1944. Anzio had been a debacle. The January 1944 amphibious assault had been intended to seize Rome and to isolate German armies to the south. But Major General John P. Lucas, the Anzio commander, had stayed put and had not driven inland in spite of light resistance, allowing the Germans time to regroup. Then the Germans nearly threw the American forces back into the Tyrrhenian Sea. King faulted Lucas for his conservative interpretation of his orders and for not using his initiative to exploit the situation. King was also mystified about why neither General Alexander nor Lieutenant General Mark W. Clark had compelled Lucas to advance. Both were his immediate superiors and had been on the scene. It was King's opinion that Anzio had "been bungled from the beginning."

King saw no reason to defer Anvil by sending anything more to Italy. The Allies had promised Russia to invade southern France. To King, Roosevelt, and the JCS, that promise was irrevocable. Churchill finally, reluctantly, grudgingly assented. Anvil was scheduled for 15 August.

While in London, King provoked the already touchy British by shifting naval forces between theaters. After King had returned to the United States, Churchill sent a protesting message to Roosevelt. "We

* The British performance in Burma would improve spectacularly under General W. J. Slim.

are much concerned," wired Churchill, "at the consequences of the directions which have been given by Admiral King to Admiral Stark about transferring the great mass of American ships from the Overlord battle to the Mediterranean. This is surely not the time to withdraw such a great American naval component without consultation with the Admiralty and the Supreme Commanders concerned, or the specific approval of the Combined Chiefs of Staff.

"Very important strategic decisions have to be taken by the Combined Chiefs of Staff and by you and me about the form of diversion from the forces against Overlord to be effected from the Mediterranean. These grave matters are now under close and urgent consideration by General Wilson * and General Eisenhower, following the lead given to them by the Combined Chiefs of Staff, and arising from the discussions which they had so recently here in London together. No decisions can be taken until we have had the considered view of the two Supreme Commanders concerned."

But the British had overreacted. It was King's intention to expedite ANVIL by withdrawing amphibious forces from Normandy at the earliest moment. Knowing that local commanders hoarded such shipping even after it was no longer essential, King had specified to Stark on 15 June which ships to transfer. But not one ship would move until the CCS approved. Nor was King bypassing Eisenhower. King calmly wired Stark to show Churchill the directive which would explain everything.

But Churchill had raised a larger issue: the control of national forces within a coalition. It was a classic dilemma of coalition warfare. Could King withdraw American naval forces from a combined operation without consulting the British, the supreme commander, or, for that matter, the JCS? In this instance, he had not. But that did not stop the British from perceiving that King manipulated the American naval forces to suit his own purposes or to blackmail the British. His directive to Stark seemed to confirm their suspicions, and the British hastily made the wrong conclusion.

But the controversy about moving shipping from OVERLORD to ANVIL was a mere flurry compared to the violent storm surrounding Greece in December 1944. The British, while trying to land troops following Germany's evacuation in late 1944, were confronted by communist Greek guerrillas who wanted to seize political control. This Churchill would not allow. Shooting began, and Churchill decided to occupy

* General Sir Henry M. "Jumbo" Wilson, Supreme Allied Commander, Mediterranean.

"I wanted to show myself": King visits Vice Adm. H. Kent Hewitt, his man on the spot in the Mediterranean.

Athens by force of arms. The press began to report that British soldiers, using Lend-Lease weapons, were killing Greek "patriots." Outraged protests erupted in the United States and Great Britain. Undaunted and convinced of the righteousness of his cause, Churchill sent reinforcements to Greece, passionately committing himself to pacifying Greece regardless of the political risks to himself and his government. It was a time when Churchill desperately needed the support and sympathy of his American ally.

On December eighth King received a disturbing message from Hewitt in the Mediterranean. "In view Greek situation and reported attitude State Department," wired Hewitt, "attention invited fact U.S. LSTs currently employed ferrying troops and materials Taranto to Piraeus."

Hewitt later explained why he had sent the message. "Stettinius made a speech," said Hewitt, "in which he said that the matter of the government of Greece was something for the Greek people themselves to decide, and that we would take no part in it, one side or the other. Well, when I read that news, my amphibious forces — LSTs and various things — were moving British troops, transports, supplies, and everything else into Greece, and in view of the Secretary of State's statement, I thought I'd better remind the Navy Department what we were doing, which I did."

Despite the obvious political implications, and although Stettinius a year before had reminded King that he was but a phone call away, King apparently consulted no one outside his immediate staff. Acting unilaterally, King immediately replied to Hewitt, "U.S. LSTs are not to be used for ferrying troops and military equipment to Greece."

Hewitt promptly ordered the American ships to stand fast and so advised his British colleagues. They were appalled. As Hewitt presumably worked for Wilson and not King, the British considered ordering him to disregard King's directive. "I'm very sorry," Hewitt told them. "You can give me any orders you like, but not one of my ships will move until Admiral King changes his orders." Hewitt apprised King of the initial British reaction: "Position . . . is that withdrawal of resources thought to be available during progress of war operation is unfortunate."

Replied King, "The 'war' referred to does not appear to be a war in which the United States is participating."

Unexpectedly unable to reinforce Greece, the British commanders appealed to Churchill. Already under strain, Churchill became frenzied when he learned what King had done. On the evening of Saturday, December ninth, Churchill phoned Hopkins on the trans-Atlantic line. The connection was so bad that all Hopkins could understand was that it was about Greece. In the morning he went to the White House Map Room and learned for the first time about King's directive. Now Hopkins knew why Churchill had phoned, and he immediately went to Leahy. Whatever the merits of King's order, said Hopkins, King had intruded into politics and had bypassed the chain of command. Such a matter was the sole prerogative of Roosevelt. King should withdraw his order, said Hopkins, until and unless the President approved.

Leahy agreed and told Hopkins that he had phoned King when he had first seen the message and had told King that he had made a mistake. But Leahy had no authority to compel King to countermand the order. With Hopkins standing by, Leahy phoned King to ask him again to release the LSTs. No one, apparently, wanted to tell Roosevelt, least of all his two principal advisors.

King believed — perhaps self-righteously — that he had been enforcing policy, as he understood it, of the President and the JCS. "The President did not want U.S. troops in Greece any more than the JCS did," King later explained. "The British were, of course, trying to get into Greece and were trying to edge us in also. You could see at once what they were trying to do." At Leahy's urging ("A fixer again," King later growled), King agreed to change his order to Hewitt. A much-relieved Hopkins then turned to the task of trying to calm his infuriated British allies.

King was willing to go along with Leahy and Hopkins on the tenth because the crisis had been overtaken by events. In fact, King already had modified his order the day before, following a meeting with the British Joint Staff Mission in Washington. The decision was to transfer ten LSTs to the British under Lend-Lease, the very ships that even then were loaded for Greece. "This transfer can be effected immediately," King wired Hewitt. "Unloading of U.S. LSTs now in progress can be completed. LSTs loading are not to move forward to Greek ports under U.S. flag." Presumably the American crews would remain aboard under British flag until the British could provide replacement crews.

It was a clever compromise. King and the United States avoided direct involvement in Greece while still helping Great Britain. Although shock waves would still reverberate for several days from London, the problem had been neatly solved by a transparent expedient.

35

Strategic Decisions in the Pacific

If the Japanese in the summer of 1944 had tried to base their defensive plans upon American intentions, they would have been without any useful information. Although MacArthur would soon complete the seizure of New Guinea and Nimitz the seizure of the Marianas, plans for subsequent operations were vague. The CCS had authorized the invasions of the Philippines, Formosa, and the intermediate Palau Islands, all leading toward a beachhead in China. But such plans were only a concept. Months of debate and indecision would follow before the JCS would issue new directions to the Pacific commanders.

The principal problem involved Luzon and Formosa. Either island in American hands would sever Japanese lines of communication to Southeast Asia, the source of vital Japanese raw materials and Japan's reason for war. Either would also serve as a base for an assault against the Chinese mainland. Thus each had its merits as the next major American objective. Given the limitations in available forces, however, the Americans could not attack the two islands simultaneously. One would have to be attacked first, the other later. And once either had been occupied, the question arose whether it would ever be necessary to seize the other.

King was the greatest advocate (and some thought the sole advocate) for Formosa. It was closer to Japan and China and astride Japanese lines of communication to the south. Its seizure, King maintained, would eliminate the need even to invade the Philippines, for the Japanese forces there would be isolated and impotent. As Formosa was in Nimitz's area of operations, it would be the Navy's responsibility.

MacArthur, of course, opposed any such proposal. If the Philippines were bypassed, his theater would become secondary. In addition to his military justification for seizing the Philippines, MacArthur argued that

King and Nimitz arrive to inspect Ebeye Island in the Marshalls, July 1944 (Courtesy J. H. Hentz and Naval Historical Center)

Surveying Ebeye (Courtesy J. H. Hentz and Naval Historical Center)

Preparing to tour Saipan despite Holland Smith's misgivings. John Hoover stands on the left. (U.S. Navy photograph)

Aboard USS *Indianapolis* with Nimitz and Spruance (National Archives 80-G-287121)

an invasion of Formosa needed land-based air support from the Philippines. Finally, and most emphatically, MacArthur stressed America's moral obligation to liberate the Filipinos and restore their freedom.

Given the irreconcilable views of King and MacArthur, no compromise seemed possible. One or the other would have to yield.

In mid-July King flew to Pearl Harbor for another of his periodic conferences with Nimitz. After preliminary discussions on 13 and 14 July dealing primarily with flag officer assignments and administration, King and Nimitz flew to Saipan. "I wanted to show myself," King later explained, "as I had had very little opportunity to be in the Pacific."

Spruance met King and Nimitz when they landed at Saipan on the seventeenth. Following the Battle of the Philippine Sea, Spruance had been criticized even though Mitscher's carrier planes had destroyed the Japanese air forces.* Contrary to Nimitz's earlier assurances to King that the Japanese fleet would have first priority, Spruance had decided that his primary mission had been to cover the amphibious forces at Saipan. The Japanese fleet had escaped. "Spruance, you did a damn good job there," said King immediately upon leaving the plane. "No matter what other people tell you, your decision was correct."

King wanted to tour the island. Holland Smith thought it would be too hazardous, even though Saipan was secured. King insisted, so the expedition got underway by jeep with a conspicuous escort of Marines. "Our cavalcade came dangerously near sniper haunts several times," Smith later wrote, "but the two visitors were too absorbed in the general picture of the battle to worry about the personal equation, and nobody has ever accused Ernie King or Chester Nimitz of lack of guts or equilibrium."

Smith characteristically bragged about his troops. "Give me three Marine divisions," he told King, "and I'll take Luzon."

King glared at Smith. "What kind of meat have you been eating?"

"The same kind you've been eating for the last forty years," Smith replied.

Afterward King conferred about future strategy aboard Spruance's flagship, *Indianapolis*. Spruance and Turner did not favor Formosa at the exclusion of the Philippines. If Formosa had to be taken, then Luzon should be seized first for a fleet anchorage in Manila Bay. The Marianas, they argued, could not provide adequate harbors and base facilities to support an assault against Formosa.

* The so-called Marianas Turkey Shoot.

As Spruance was against Formosa, King asked what he recommended after the Marianas.

"Okinawa," said Spruance.

"Can you take it?" asked King.

"I think so," said Spruance, "if we can find a way to transfer heavy ammunition at sea." (Until then, ammunition replenishment had been by lighter in protected anchorages. But off Okinawa Spruance could not afford to send his ships 1,400 miles to the nearest American anchorage at Saipan. Some method had to be devised to replenish ammunition to warships underway in the combat area.)

Spruance also saw a need to seize Iwo Jima first, as an air base to support fleet operations against Okinawa and the Ryukyu Islands. Okinawa itself would serve as an air base to interdict Japanese shipping in the East China Sea and to sever Japanese lines to the south, completing the blockade against Japan. The war could be won without invading the Japanese mainland.

These were compelling arguments. King respected Spruance's brains and strategic wisdom, and he recognized the merits of Spruance's ideas. But King would not change his mind about Formosa.

On their return to Pearl Harbor King and Nimitz first learned that Roosevelt was en route to Hawaii by warship to see Nimitz and MacArthur. Leahy was with the President, but the other members of the JCS were not invited. Ostensibly Roosevelt did not need their advice because he already knew they were split between the Philippines and Formosa. He would decide for them, with a grand entrance into Pearl Harbor and a publicized conference with his two theater commanders. King deprecated Roosevelt's foray as a political stunt to help his reelection campaign. "He had to show the voters that he was commander in chief," King later said.

With Nimitz as the naval spokesman, King could arbitrarily have ordered him to advocate Formosa. Instead he let Nimitz decide for himself. Nimitz could argue persuasively for Formosa only if he believed in it. Otherwise Roosevelt would sense that Nimitz was an unwilling surrogate and MacArthur would have the advantage.

King intensified his effort on 20 and 21 July to persuade Nimitz and his skeptical staff of the merits of Formosa. King first reminded them that the JCS already had approved Formosa, so the question was not whether but when and how. Spruance's reservations to the contrary, King insisted that an assault on Formosa could be staged from the Marianas—if only Nimitz and his pessimistic subordinates would gird themselves to develop the Marianas harbors, ports, and airfields.

And there's the catch, Towers interjected. The B-29s assigned to the Marianas would divert logistical support from fleet base development. Which took priority?

King answered that fleet bases came first. The JCS had approved four B-29 groups. Additional bombers would take lower priority until the JCS decided otherwise. King promised to confer with the JCS to ensure a complete understanding. It seemed to King that Nimitz's staff was looking for excuses. "Getting on with the war," stressed King, "is more important than worrying about logistical support for additional B-29 groups arriving in the Marianas."

Spurred by Spruance's suggestion, King demanded a study of ways and means to reprovision and to replenish ammunition at sea. If something could be done, the Formosa assault could be better supported (even though Spruance had been thinking about Okinawa). Nimitz responded that he was dubious about handling battleship projectiles and heavy bombs, but King would not tolerate such pessimism. "*Admiral Nimitz will thoroughly investigate this idea,*" the minutes record. He did. In time, American warships were able to remain at sea to rearm and replenish.

The debate continued through the following day. Nimitz's staff was still unconvinced, particularly Towers, who enumerated the logistical difficulties of attacking Formosa from the Marianas. King answered that such difficulties could be mastered through proper planning and timing. The discussion then turned to the carriers. They certainly could not remain idle while waiting for the JCS to decide upon future objectives. For the first time the concept of carrier strikes on Japan was explored. The consensus was that they could be feasible in late January 1945.

Too late, King snapped. Why not hit Japan by the end of 1944? "Draw up plans," he ordered Nimitz, "for the bombing of the Japanese homeland." With those words King initiated, perhaps unintentionally, the competition for the strategic bombing mission between carriers and heavy Air Force bombers that would persist long after the war itself was over.

Towers elaborated on the subject of bombing Japan. As the United States had expended such effort to secure the Marianas as a B-29 base, the Navy should move quickly to make the bombers even more effective. Iwo Jima, said Towers, would be invaluable as an intermediate air base on the B-29 route between Japan and the Marianas. The consensus was to defer Iwo Jima until the Philippines and Formosa had been seized. Nevertheless King instructed Nimitz to prepare invasion plans for a later date.

King left for the mainland before Roosevelt arrived. After meetings with MacArthur and Nimitz, Roosevelt declared that he favored the Philippines. Thanks to Nimitz's pro forma arguments in King's behalf, Roosevelt did not entirely rule out Formosa. King had hoped for a great deal more. "Nimitz let me down," King later said, blaming Nimitz's tendency to be a "trimmer": that is, a compromiser in the fashion of officers from the Bureau of Naval Personnel. "Why the hell do they have to trim all the time?"

The President's visit to Pearl Harbor had not resolved anything, although it had gotten the JCS off dead center. Knowing Roosevelt's preference, King was willing to acquiesce to an invasion of the Philippines. Neither Marshall nor MacArthur, however, would support an invasion of Formosa as a quid pro quo. As the Army would provide most of the troops, Marshall had begun to wonder whether Formosa was even necessary. As a compromise, the Navy suggested occupying only a part of Formosa to save manpower. It was a dumb idea. The Army doubted that the Japanese would cooperate by allowing the Americans to establish uncontested boundary lines. As usual the JCS decided nothing, and desultory planning discussions extended into early fall.

Nimitz fumed at Washington's indecision, and rightly so. One way or the other, Nimitz was determined to move west. In mid-August King learned that Nimitz intended to transfer his headquarters from Pearl Harbor to recently occupied Guam. "I have not approved any such move," wired King. Nimitz apologized for not having consulted King, then belatedly asked for King's approval. After Nimitz sent additional justification, King gave his assent.

The JCS continued to stall and wrangle well into September, allowing the Japanese a respite to strengthen their defenses. Then, finally, a tentative agreement emerged. MacArthur would assault Leyte in late December in order to provide a base for a further advance against either Formosa or Luzon in early 1945. That having been decided, the JCS departed for another conference with the British.

The Second Quebec Conference (Octagon) had been Churchill's idea. The JCS considered such a conference unnecessary because the Allies by then were victorious nearly everywhere. The American and British armies in France had reached the German border, and the Red Army was advancing from the east. Germany's defeat seemed imminent. In the Pacific, Japan was steadily weakening. Having occupied New Guinea, MacArthur was preparing to return to the Philippines. Nimitz shortly would assault the Palau Islands. The Japanese navy, air forces, and merchant marine had been mangled; only the Japanese army remained largely unchallenged. Pacific strategy was still unsettled, but that problem belonged solely to the JCS, and they had no desire to consult the British on that issue.

Churchill's problems were more political than strategic. With Germany in full retreat there were many unresolved postwar considerations. What, for example, would be the boundaries for the Allied occupation armies? Churchill also intended to get Britain into the war against Japan. Until then the British contribution had been insignificant. "The time had now come for the liberation of Asia," Churchill wrote in his memoirs, "and I was determined that we should play our full and equal part in it. What I feared most at this stage of the war was that the United States would say in after-years, 'We came to your help in Europe and you left us alone to finish off Japan.' We had to regain on the field of battle our rightful possessions in the Far East, and not have them handed back to us at the peace table."

In King's opinion, Britain already had had her chance in Burma and had botched it. He was also aware that the Royal Navy was largely unemployed and wanted to enter the Pacific war, an idea that King absolutely opposed. Unaccustomed to remaining at sea for long durations, the British had not developed the mobile logistical support perfected by the Pacific Fleet. It seemed to King that the additional combat power of the Royal Navy would not compensate for the added logistical burden it would impose on American resources.

Churchill forced the issue at the first plenary meeting on 13 September. After reviewing British interests in the Far East and Pacific, Churchill expounded the ways in which the British armed forces might actively assist their American allies. Then Churchill dramatically offered the British battle fleet to join the main operations against Japan under an American supreme commander. Roosevelt accepted the offer while King glowered. Churchill resumed his oration, and the President responded with his own summation of the state of the war as he saw it.

Then Churchill returned to the subject of the Royal Navy in the Pacific. How would it be used? Roosevelt answered noncommittally, then King added that he was preparing a paper for study by the CCS. Sensing King's evasion, Churchill persisted. Could not the newer British warships replace those older American warships suffering from age and wear? King refused to commit himself. The matter, he said, was under examination.

"The offer has been made," said Churchill. "Is it accepted?"

"It is," said the President.

The subject was dropped for the moment, then raised again at a CCS meeting the following day. It was one of their most emotional and acrimonious confrontations during the war. "Admiral King, adamant as ever," wrote Cunningham in his memoirs, "hotly refused to have anything to do with it, and tried to persuade us that the President's acceptance of the offer did not mean what had been said. King, having turned his guns on General Marshall, was finally called to order by Admiral Leahy, the President's Chief of Staff, with the remark: 'I don't think we should wash our linen in public.' "

The pride and prestige of the Royal Navy and of Great Britain were at stake. No longer the greatest sea power, the British faced an intractable American admiral whose navy had become the most powerful in the world. King was humiliating them by insisting that he could win the Pacific war without their help. Not only was King unwilling to share in the glory, but, most galling of all, he called the Royal Navy a liability.*

As with most imbroglios between the Americans and the British, the differences were resolved by compromise. "King with the other American Chiefs of Staff against him," wrote Cunningham, "eventually gave way; but with very bad grace." The British fleet would participate in the main operations against Japan, but only if it could become balanced and self-supporting. Under no circumstances would King's Navy provide the Royal Navy's logistical support. "The atmosphere was less stormy when we met King next afternoon," wrote Cunningham. "He was resigned to the use of our fleet in the Pacific; but made it quite clear that it must expect no assistance from the Americans. From this rather unhelpful attitude he never budged."

The British eventually moved heaven and earth to become self-sufficient. King's misgivings never materialized, and the Royal Navy made a splendid contribution in the Pacific during 1945. Task Force 57 (the British carriers with Vice Admiral Sir H. B. Rawlings) justified themselves by neutralizing Japanese airfields in the Sakishima Gunto islands, 250 miles southwest of Okinawa, and by frequently hitting Formosa as well.

While the CCS met in Quebec, Nimitz's forces prepared to invade Yap and the Palau Islands. Halsey's Third Fleet in support had been

* The minutes of this conference are unusually revealing, for normally they are discreet summaries that too often obscure what really passed between the chiefs. The minutes of the 14 September 1944 conference, however, reflect not only the substance of the debate but also the heat and fire. Because of their uniqueness, they are reproduced in Appendix VI.

pounding the central Philippines. On 13 September Halsey advised Nimitz that Japanese defenses were so weak that he recommended bypassing the Palaus and immediately invading the Philippines.

The JCS had been receiving copies of the messages from the Pacific throughout the thirteenth. That evening King was in his dressing gown preparing for dinner when his aide, Alexander S. McDill, entered King's suite and handed him a message from Nimitz to MacArthur. The message said that Nimitz still wanted to seize the Palaus but was willing to bypass Yap. This would release the XXIV Army Corps and its associated amphibious assault shipping. Nimitz offered these forces, then loading in Pearl Harbor, for an early assault against Leyte. Normally King would write marginal notes for action on a message and return it to his aide. This time, however, he stuffed it in his pocket and went to dinner.

That evening King and the JCS conferred on the implications of Nimitz's offer to MacArthur. Their months of indecision were being overtaken by events forced by Nimitz and Halsey. King and his colleagues decided to urge MacArthur to accept Nimitz's offer of additional troops, saying it was "highly to be desired and would advance the progress of the war in your [MacArthur's] theater by many months as well as simplifying the arrangements for future operations."

The next evening, 14 September, King and his colleagues were dining with their Canadian hosts. A staff officer appeared, and the JCS excused themselves. MacArthur's message had been received. The General proposed to accept the XXIV Corps, and, given the apparent weakness of Japanese defenses in the Philippines, to advance the invasion date on Leyte from 20 December to 20 October. The JCS planners already had drafted a message of approval. Now the JCS thought fast. In less than an hour they ended their discussion and ordered MacArthur and Nimitz to attack Leyte forthwith and to bypass Yap. The JCS agreed with Nimitz to follow plans against the Palau Islands, an unfortunate decision as the value of the islands did not compensate for the subsequent heavy American casualties.

The following morning King apprised the British Chiefs of Staff of the JCS directive to MacArthur and Nimitz. Once again the Americans had not consulted their British colleagues, substantiating that the Pacific was an exclusive American domain. The official minutes recorded simply, "The Combined Chiefs of Staff took note with interest of Admiral King's remarks on the progress of the campaign in the Pacific."

Octagon adjourned on 16 September without deciding upon operations following the invasion of Leyte. King began the last step in that direction when he began writing to Edwards and Horne upon his diminutive yellow memo pad on the eighteenth.

> CoS
> VCNO
> Prepare agenda—and appropriate memos—for discussion with Cincpac-CincPoa at end of September. Have ready not later than 26 September.
>
> K

While King's staff prepared accordingly, King and the JCS resumed their wrangling. Although there was still general agreement that Formosa was a legitimate objective, King and Marshall differed on timing and who should command the invasion. There the matter stood when King once again left for San Francisco and a meeting with Nimitz on 29 September.

Nimitz and Sherman finally convinced King that the Americans could not and should not invade Formosa. Their reasoning was incontrovertible: the Army could not provide enough soldiers. Marshall's earlier decision to limit the Army to ninety divisions had indirectly deprived King of the troops needed to seize and occupy a heavily defended land mass as large as Formosa. MacArthur had first call on Army forces in the Pacific. Meanwhile it had become obvious that Germany would continue fighting into 1945, so that Army troops would not be released from the European theater for months to come.

Then the good news. The Army could provide enough troops to assault Okinawa, and Nimitz had enough Marines for Iwo Jima. Nimitz and Sherman recommended seizing both in early 1945.

"Why Iwo Jima?" asked King. In his mind it was now a liability. Sherman responded that the Army Air Force wanted Iwo Jima as a fighter base to provide escorts for the B-29s attacking Japan. The discussion went on and on. King still battled to salvage Formosa, with the help of Cooke. Then he would assail the wisdom of assaulting Iwo Jima and Okinawa. Spruance was amazed at King's stubbornness against the force of logic.

"Why are you so quiet?" King suddenly asked Spruance. "I thought you wanted Okinawa instead of Formosa."

"Nimitz and Sherman are doing very well," replied Spruance. "I have nothing to add."

King finally capitulated.

On 3 October the JCS ordered MacArthur to seize and occupy Luzon and Nimitz to seize Iwo Jima and Okinawa. The only strategic question remaining was whether to invade Japan.

MacArthur's return to the Philippines began on schedule as his soldiers went ashore at Leyte on 20 October 1944. It was a stupendous operation. Halsey's Third Fleet, covering the amphibious assault from a distance, was to prevent Japanese air and naval interference. Two Army corps comprising four divisions landed in two different sectors, transported and closely supported by Kinkaid's Seventh Fleet. Kinkaid reported to MacArthur, but Halsey was virtually independent, reporting nominally to Nimitz in remote Guam. King's long-standing refusal to allow MacArthur operational control of fast carrier task forces had divided the command at Leyte.

The Japanese air forces and battle fleet came out to fight. The shooting started. Kinkaid's old battleships under Rear Admiral Jesse B. Oldendorf smashed a Japanese surface force at the Battle of Surigao Strait, while Halsey's carrier aircraft swarmed upon another surface force in San Bernardino Strait. With no one coordinating Kinkaid and Halsey, it was inevitable that misunderstandings would develop. Unreliable communications further disrupted attempts at cooperation between the two fleet commanders.

The Battle of Leyte Gulf degenerated into a bewildering melee off Samar with American escort carriers and destroyers fighting Japanese battleships and cruisers, while Halsey was decoyed to the north by Japanese carriers devoid of aircraft. King confined himself to reading dispatches from his combat commanders. Halsey, in particular, flooded the airwaves with reports of his intentions and actions. King initialed the messages without comment.

On 25 October the battle had reached its crescendo, but King was unsure what had happened because of incomplete and garbled reports. Public attention, for the moment, was focused upon the Navy in the Philippines rather than the Army or the Army Air Force. Hoping for good publicity, Forrestal scheduled a press conference that afternoon to exploit the clamor for information. It turned out to be a public relations extravaganza. A cluster of flag officers under Forrestal's watchful eye dutifully presented themselves before the press and extolled the Navy's distinctive role in defeating the Axis.

King had little to say until the press asked for details on Leyte Gulf. Even then King was noncommittal, because, he explained, he did not pester his commanders for information during a battle. Someone asked why the Japanese had split into three forces. King laughed. "Well," he said, "one of the rules of General Jackson was 'mislead, mystify, and confuse the enemy.' If that's their strategy, why that's what they may have been doing."

When he was not meeting the press, King had been trying to explain to the JCS and the British Joint Staff Mission what was happening in Leyte Gulf. To assist King, William Smedberg appeared on short notice with charts and diagrams. In the course of his briefing Smedberg reported that the Japanese northern decoy group included two old battleships, *Ise* and *Hyuga.*

King interrupted. "Gentlemen, Captain Smedberg has only been here a short time, and he's made a mistake. *Ise* and *Hyuga* are two of the newest Japanese battleships."

Smedberg knew the ships of the Japanese fleet as well as those of his own navy, and he knew King was wrong. "I beg your pardon, Admiral King," said Smedberg, "but *Ise* and *Hyuga* are old battleships, about the *New Mexico* or *Idaho* class. They have been converted so they have flight decks in the after part of the ship. They're not carriers. They can fly planes off, but they can't get them back."

King glared. "Proceed, Captain Smedberg."

After the briefing Smedberg was summoned to King's office. "Smedberg," said King, "if you ever correct me again in front of my peers, you'd better be damned sure you're right. I found out you were correct in this instance. You be damned sure you're correct the next time you ever do a thing like that. I'll crucify you if you're wrong. That's all."

"I left shaking like an aspen leaf," Smedberg later said, "but King never held it against me. The fitness reports he gave me were among the best I've ever had in my career."

The greatest controversy over the Battle of Leyte Gulf was whether Halsey had been correct to leave San Bernadino Strait unguarded to attack Ozawa's decoy force with Task Force 38. At issue was Halsey's message designating his fast battleships as Task Force 34, to be detached upon his order to guard San Bernadino Strait. Halsey never issued the detachment order and took the battleships with him. Nimitz and Kinkaid mistakenly assumed that they had remained behind. Therein the controversy lies.

Although some of King's staff were as confused as Nimitz and Kinkaid, King says that he never assumed that Task Force 34 was guarding the strait. King instead has blamed Kinkaid for failing to patrol the strait with aircraft that could have discovered and warned of Kurita's warships approaching Leyte Gulf. Less than two weeks after the battle, King sent Kinkaid a message asking him to justify his actions during the battle. The message had a clear implication that Kinkaid and not Halsey had been responsible for the near disaster. There was no answer. King sent another — again no response. An aide finally reminded King that no reply had been received. King shrugged. "There is no possible answer," he said.*

Halsey did not suffer from reticence. When the fighting had barely subsided on 25 October, he broadcast a message defending his movements and decisions, beginning with a preamble "that there be no misunderstanding concerning recent operations of the 3rd Fleet." Halsey concluded, "The back of the Jap navy has been broken in the course of supporting our landings in Leyte." King initialed Halsey's apologia without comment. Next day Halsey even named the battle for the benefit of historians. "The pursuit phase of the Battle of the Western Pacific is now in progress," Halsey jubilantly declared. "And those that escape the surface and air forces are committed to the tender mercies of the implacable submarines."

But Halsey's bravado suddenly changed several hours later on the twenty-sixth, when he warned MacArthur of Third Fleet ammunition shortages and pilot fatigue. "I am unable to provide any extended direct air support," Halsey said. "When will your shore based air take over air defense at the objective?" King waited for a response, not from MacArthur but from Nimitz. It was not long in coming. "Cover and support forces of the Southwest Pacific until otherwise directed by me," Nimitz ordered. King's policy of supporting MacArthur once the commitment had been made was being vigorously enforced by Nimitz, who then proceeded to castigate Halsey for his logistical shortages.

The recriminations and second-guessing would persist for years, and King must be held accountable for his own responsibility for events at Leyte Gulf. First, there is the matter of divided responsibilities. Halsey worked for Nimitz rather than MacArthur, because of King. Next, there is the question of Halsey's mission. King knew that Halsey's orders from Nimitz specified, "In case opportunity for destruction of major portion of the enemy fleet is offered or can be created, such destruction becomes the primary task." It is likely that King directed Nimitz (if not in writing, then at least orally) to give such an order

* Kinkaid said after the war that he had sent an answer to King's message, and he assumed it had been misplaced before it got to King. Historian Gerald E. Wheeler told the author that Kinkaid gave King a copy of his response in 1951. Apparently it was not in time for King to change his criticism of Kinkaid on page 580 of his memoirs, *Fleet Admiral King: A Naval Record*.

King and Bill Halsey (National Archives 80-G-43467)

to Halsey. The order also was exactly what Nimitz and Halsey wanted. In any event, King knew that Halsey would attack the Japanese fleet if it came near the Philippines, unlike Spruance at Saipan. Halsey was known for being headstrong and impetuous. Yet King by default gave Halsey carte blanche to abandon the beachhead in an operation that demanded the very closest cooperation between the amphibious forces and the covering forces.

For King to have criticized Halsey would by implication have been to criticize the decisions and policies that had established Halsey's responsibilities and course of action: King's own. Furthermore, Halsey was far too outspoken and far too popular with the press for King to have risked provoking Halsey to defend himself. In a moment of indiscretion the voluble Halsey might have said something to the press that the Navy would regret. To criticize Halsey would also have implied that the Battle of Leyte Gulf had been other than a glorious victory for the United States Navy. Such a suggestion could have brought the Pacific Fleet under MacArthur's operational control, on the theory that unity of command would prevent future mistakes — mistakes caused by King's insistence on a divided command when the Navy worked with MacArthur.

Leyte Gulf was one of many instances when Halsey caused King anxiety and embarrassment. One problem was that he talked too much and not always wisely, proclaiming his hatred for the Japanese and his overoptimism for early victory. King and Nimitz were forever cautioning restraint.

Halsey had become a public hero when his audacious carrier raids in early 1942 had thrilled the American people at a time when most of the news was bad. When the Americans were losing Guadalcanal in the fall of 1942, Halsey relieved Ghormley and came as a godsend to the South Pacific forces. Halsey saved Guadalcanal for King.

By early 1943 Halsey began to make mistakes and errors in judgment in the South Pacific, much of which King excused as sloppy staff work. Although Halsey was a fighter and a leader, he hated administration and paperwork. He needed a good chief of staff, King decided, and the incumbent, Captain Miles R. Browning, was erratic and unreliable. "Browning was no damn good at all," King later said. "He had no brains and no understanding."

Halsey liked Browning and wanted to keep him, crediting him for many of Halsey's successes in early 1942; he had gotten Browning a spot promotion to captain as a reward. Despite King's self-proclaimed ruthlessness, Halsey's influence was such that King had to bribe him into giving up Browning. The price was a new *Essex*-class carrier for Browning, the USS *Hornet*, even though the aviation community as a whole resented Browning's getting such a choice command. But, as King later temporized, the "idea was to get rid of him at once," and if it took a new carrier, so be it. Browning predictably flopped as a commanding officer. Marc Mitscher fired him, and he spent the remainder of the war in exile on the faculty of an Army staff college.

Halsey's new chief of staff was Robert B. Carney, who later became a CNO. Halsey still made mistakes that distressed King, and King frequently considered removing Halsey from the Pacific. But he never did. "He is the greatest leader of men that we have," King would say. "The men are crazy about him, and they will follow him anywhere." One of King's staff officers, a close observer of King's despair with Halsey's ups and downs, later remarked, "I suppose King's reaction was rather like Lincoln's over Grant's drinking: 'I'll keep him. He fights.' "

36
Climax

FRANKLIN D. ROOSEVELT was inaugurated for his fourth term on 20 January 1945. The restrained ceremony near the south portico of the White House (rather than the Capitol) reflected Roosevelt's poor health. The JCS were there, although King apparently would have preferred to miss it. "We were told to attend the inauguration," King later wrote.

Within a few days Roosevelt, his political advisors, and the JCS were underway for Yalta. As victory in Europe was inevitable within weeks — a few months at most — there were profound postwar political questions that had to be resolved among Roosevelt, Churchill, and Stalin. The JCS would have little to contribute, except about the question of when and under what circumstances the Russians would go to war against Japan.

The President was too ill to fly across the Atlantic, so he traveled on the cruiser *Quincy*. He was accompanied by Leahy, James Byrnes, various advisors, and his daughter. King and Marshall flew in separate planes so that a single accident would not kill them both. Major General Laurence S. Kuter represented the Army Air Force because Arnold was recuperating from a heart attack.

King flew in luxurious style. His aircraft, a four-engined C-54, had been equipped with a plush interior, comfortable chairs and bunks, an efficient and well-stocked galley, and an expert naval flight crew. King's aviation plans officer, Captain Paul D. Stroop, had made all the necessary arrangements (including lifeguard destroyers across the Atlantic) and came along as third pilot.

After stopovers in Bermuda and Casablanca, King arrived in Malta on 29 January. The JCS and their staffs were billeted in Tigne House,

Royal Artillery Barracks, constructed of the porous yellow limestone indigenous to Malta. The interior was so cold and damp from heavy rain that the heaters in each room were useless. That night King burrowed into bed beneath a mound of blankets reinforced with his overcoat, raincoat, and dressing gown. It was not enough. At three in the morning King scampered out of bed and piled more coal on the diminutive fire so he could survive until breakfast. "Lots of people," King later wryly remarked, "would have liked to see a five-star admiral stoking those small coal grates in the middle of the night."

The preliminary meetings began next day. Compared with that of earlier conferences, the agenda was limited. The one military item of significance in Europe was the question of when and how Eisenhower's forces would cross the Rhine to enter Germany. Eisenhower wanted a primary attack in the north, supported by a secondary attack to the south to divide the defending German force. Eisenhower had also implied that he intended to close the Rhine on a broad front and to destroy the Germans west of the Rhine before crossing the river.

The British believed that Eisenhower was too hesitant, that he had not been bold and aggressive in the latter months of 1944, and that his plan to cross the Rhine was too cautious and too conservative. The British favored Montgomery's concept of a single, powerful thrust carrying through to Berlin. Montgomery had been outspoken both in supporting his idea and in criticizing Eisenhower's restraint. Furthermore, Churchill wanted to occupy as much of Germany as soon as possible, in order to prevent Stalin from swallowing Germany whole with his Red Army.

Marshall naturally supported Eisenhower. Allied field commanders, said Marshall, deserved latitude in running the war in their own theaters. The question became not so much one of Eisenhower's strategy, but rather one of Eisenhower's leadership. The British literally gave Eisenhower a vote of no-confidence, infuriating King and Marshall. As was customary when tempers flared, the CCS went into closed session. Everyone was angry, Marshall perhaps more so than the others. "We were in a situation," King later wrote, "where neither would give an inch, so the matter had to be carried over until FDR arrived in Malta."

Roosevelt arrived in Valetta Harbor the following morning, February second. It was a warm, sunny day, and crowds of Maltese lined the quay to watch and to cheer. It was a moving spectacle to Churchill. "I watched the scene from the deck of the *Orion*," he later wrote. "As the American cruiser steamed slowly past us towards her berth alongside the quay wall I could see the figure of the President seated on the bridge, and we waved to each other. With the escort of Spitfires overhead, the salutes, and the bands of the ships' companies in the harbour playing 'The Star-spangled Banner' it was a splendid scene."

King and his colleagues joined the visitors swarming aboard *Quincy*. The President (sitting in his "pet" chair, King noted) received them on deck in the warmth of the sun. The President's health was on everyone's mind. King had assumed that the sea voyage would have helped, but he could see that Roosevelt "was a very sick man." When Leahy joined them the JCS went inside with Roosevelt. The haggard President was attentive during the half-hour briefing. When he heard about the dispute about crossing the Rhine, Roosevelt perked up. Asking for a map of the region, he commented that he once had "biked" where Eisenhower wanted his supporting attack. On that whimsical premise the President promptly approved Eisenhower's offensive plans. King and Marshall, buoyed by the President's support, took their leave. When they entered the barge waiting alongside they did not want to talk in the presence of the crew. "Both of us looked at each other and just nodded," King later said.

In less than a half-hour King and Marshall met with the British Chiefs of Staff to prepare their combined report to be delivered to the President and Prime Minister later in the day. At six o'clock that evening everyone gathered aboard *Quincy*. King regarded such conferences as the formal mechanism by which Roosevelt and Churchill decided upon grand strategy. In reality, the two political leaders usually ratified most of what the CCS already had agreed should be done. The normal procedure was to address each topic individually as it appeared on the CCS report. Some passed without comment, while others might be discussed and sometimes amended on the basis of the comments of Roosevelt and Churchill. Often there were prolonged discussions on vocabulary and terminology. The ultimate approval of each topic was frequently implied rather than explicitly stated. As we have seen, the final result was a document which King considered as a binding contract between the Americans and the British specifying how each side would contribute and cooperate in fighting the Axis.

"Churchill did most of the talking that night," King later said. "Roosevelt seemed to understand what was said, but he didn't say much, using nods rather than speaking." Finally the CCS report came to Eisenhower's plans for crossing the Rhine. "The President and the Prime Minister," the official minutes duly recorded, "were informed that complete agreement had been reached on the question." King and

Marshall obviously had forced the British chiefs to acquiesce to Roosevelt and the JCS. With the United States providing most of the combat power, the British had little choice. It was galling to the British. "I noted that Brooke was rather glum," King later said, "after Roosevelt and Churchill agreed to what Eisenhower wanted done. . . ."

The heated closed session the day before marked the last time that the JCS and the British Chiefs of Staff would have any major disagreements for the remainder of the war. The usual social warmth and Anglican comradeship would prevail thereafter.

Following the plenary meeting on February second, King met his son, Joe, who was an ensign aboard the cruiser USS *Savannah*. He took Joe to dinner and proudly introduced him around. His colleagues, King recalled, were "very nice to us." Next day Joe had lunch with his father, then joined King and his colleagues for sightseeing in the afternoon. That evening King explained that he was expected at a formal dinner, and Joe had not been invited. They said good-bye.

King saw another familiar face in Malta, his protégé Charles Grisham, whom King had chosen to command *Dauntless* when the war began. Once an enlisted coal passer and now a captain, Grisham commanded the cruiser *Memphis*, Hewitt's Mediterranean flagship. He seemed to be a very happy man," King recalled, "to be able to hoist my five-star flag when I came on board."

The Americans and British flew to Yalta, apprehensive from earlier reports from Churchill that it was inaccessible, uninhabitable, and unhealthy. "If we had spent ten years on research," Churchill reportedly had said, "we could not have found a worse place in the world than Yalta." After a seven-hour flight King landed at Saki airfield on the Crimean peninsula, rejoining the others who had flown in separate aircraft. The area swarmed with dignitaries, many waiting for Roosevelt's arrival later in the day. King was greeted by Fleet Admiral Nikolay G. Kuznetsov, the People's Commissar of the Soviet Navy.

The Russians had erected a large tent. Inside was a long table covered with silver, crystal, linen, and great quantities of elaborate food, vodka, and wine. After recovering from their surprise most of the Americans dug in. King took only coffee, having eaten on his plane. He would have taken sherry, but there was none.

Following the meal, the visitors entered cars and drove eighty miles over a mountain. "The road was very rough indeed," King later observed, "because the Nazis made sure that the Russians couldn't repair

King with his son, Joe, a midshipman in September 1942 (Courtesy Ernest J. King, Jr.)

them in a long time." The countryside and towns had been devastated. Russian troops, some of them women, patrolled the entire route, their numbers increasing near the end of the trip.

Before the war Yalta had been a small health resort on the southern coast of the Crimean peninsula, picturesquely situated in a coastal valley protected from harsh weather by mountains. The Americans were to be billeted in Livadia Palace, on the outskirts of Yalta, once the czar's summer palace. Although German occupation forces had stripped and vandalized the once-magnificent buildings, the Russians had scoured eastern Europe for chefs, servants, and furnishings to rehabilitate the palace and to restore a measure of its former grandeur in time for the conference. American military and naval personnel had helped by disinfecting the rooms. As a precaution, the flagship USS *Catoctin* had steamed through the Dardanelles and into Sevastopol, some fifty miles away, in order to provide administrative and logistical support.

The palace was not without hardships. Bathrooms were scarce. Even King had to wait in line. Most of the staff were crammed into dormitory-style bedrooms. King lived alone in the czarina's boudoir, a source of many jokes throughout the conference. Platoons of armed soldiers provided security. "The afternoon that I arrived," King later wrote, "I thought I would take a walk through the grounds. But I found out that the Russian guards seemed to be everywhere, asking me to show my special pass. At least one guard was under each tree or shrub, so I gave up and didn't try to take a stroll."

Things still happened to bring smiles. Roosevelt's staff needed oranges for the President's Old-Fashion cocktails. The next day a Red Army truck arrived to deliver an orange tree for the President's quarters.

It is a principle of coalition warfare that political interests predominate when the common enemy is nearly beaten. That principle held firm at Yalta. Germany's defeat was inevitable. From the military view there remained only the need to prevent collisions between the Allied and Russian armies converging upon Germany. As Marshall and Kuter were responsible for such coordination, King had little to say to the Soviet military staff on European matters. King did review Allied plans in the Pacific, but neither he nor the Russians were willing to exchange detailed information. "I didn't tell anything that was really important," King later said, and he knew the Russians were reciprocating.

Paul Stroop reflected the common feeling of the JCS during the meetings. "The military staff conferences at Yalta, were, to my mind, not very important," he later said. "Certainly, I could tell from the attitude of the people who attended that they felt they were accomplishing nothing and that the conference should be adjourned, simply because the war was going favorably for the Allies, the strategy had been established, General Bedell Smith [Eisenhower's chief of staff] brought down the latest reports of operations, and it was obvious that the business at hand could only be in the area of political decisions."

Political decisions did predominate, and the JCS were rarely consulted or otherwise involved, particularly King. They neither volunteered political advice, nor were they asked. Having remained deliberately aloof from political questions throughout the war, the JCS remained isolated from politics at Yalta.

King's primary interest in Russia was the extent and the timing of Stalin's voluntary commitment to declare war on Japan. The CCS at the time of Yalta had estimated that the war would last at least eighteen months after the defeat of Germany, so King and the JCS wanted Russia's help. Later, there were sensational congressional investigations of the Yalta agreements amid charges of treason and betrayal. Senator William F. Knowland asked King in June 1951 why Russia had been brought into the war. "It was the belief of the Navy," King replied, "that Japan could and should be defeated without an invasion of the home islands. Our contention was that blockade and bombardment could bring about Japanese capitulation and that in connection with this course of action, engagement of the Japanese armies in Manchuria by the Soviets would hasten that capitulation.

Roosevelt felt it would take territorial concessions to get Stalin's cooperation against Japan. If Roosevelt had asked King and the JCS for their opinions (and it is uncertain whether he did), King would have said that the President was giving away too much. King thought a sop was enough — perhaps the southern half of Sakhalin Island.

King's attitude toward the Russians had changed with time. It will be recalled that in the summer of 1943 King had been willing to concede Estonia, Latvia, and Lithuania to give Russia some Baltic ports. He was also willing to guarantee Russia access to the open seas through the Kattegat and Skagerrak and through the Bosporus. But King regarded such concessions as a means to guarantee peace after the war, not as a bribe to keep Russia in the war. If the price was too high in the Far East, King was willing to conclude the war against Japan without Russia's help. But whatever the price for Russia's collaboration, it was solely a decision for the President and his political advisors.

Senator Knowland also asked King in June 1951 why the Russians did not invade Manchuria until six days before the Japanese surrender on 14 August 1945. It was a loaded question. Right-wing conservatives, both politicians and writers, had been accusing the JCS (and especially Marshall) of collaborating with the Russians.

King's reply was careful and deliberate: "My expectation was that the Soviets would enter the conflict in the Far East sooner than they did, but perhaps 'Stalin and Company' were getting back at the Allies for not opening up the second front in Europe sooner than they did.

"I would remind you that as the Navy member of the U.S. Joint Chiefs of Staff my job was advisory in nature. I did not attend any of the meetings between Roosevelt, Churchill, and Stalin and consequently I have no first hand knowledge of the decisions reached, policies formulated or agreements made thereof."

In his well-justified zeal to absolve himself from the political consequences of Yalta, King's final statement was not literally correct. King, together with the other members of the CCS, did attend the first plenary meeting on the afternoon of February fourth. It was mostly pro forma. King said nothing. During a recess he did, however, find himself face-to-face with Stalin. Trying to say something appropriate for a conversational opener, King complimented Stalin on the heroism universally displayed by the Russian soldier.

Stalin permitted himself a fleeting smile. "It takes a very brave man," said Stalin, "not to be a hero in the Russian army, Admiral."

Just before the military staff conferences ended, the principals assembled on the afternoon of February tenth for the ritual photograph. Leahy staked out his customary position directly behind Roosevelt, while King stood among his colleagues slightly to the rear. The weather was chilly and many wore overcoats. Roosevelt wore his favorite boat cloak. His wan face reflecting his deteriorating health, Roosevelt wanted to compose himself before the photographers began. Several started taking pictures prematurely. Roosevelt angrily told them to stop. Churchill and Stalin looked the other way.

When the pictures had been taken the group quickly dispersed. The crippled President remained behind, immobilized in his chair. The photographers gathering their equipment ignored the lonely figure. Then Roosevelt's valet appeared with a small wheelchair and placed it next to the President. Roosevelt swung himself into the wheelchair, and the valet pushed him into the palace.

Stroop had been watching from a balcony. "In the meantime, of course, everyone else had departed," Stroop later said. "The patio was deserted. It was very sad, and you were embarrassed for him. You knew that he was embarrassed; he realized his condition. I think all the people who were close to him did. It was obvious that he should not have been at the conference."

King planned to leave immediately for Saki, but just before he left, several Russians entered his room with a package. A commissar stepped forth and made a speech, which, according to King, was intended "to make sure that I got the proper package, for which I thanked him." The Russians opened the package so King could see the vodka, caviar, and fruit inside. King again thanked them and fled to his car.

The caravan drove to a small train depot in the town of Sinferopol. There a special train awaited to take the Americans the remainder of the short journey to Saki. The train remained at the siding until midnight, while inside it the Russians entertained the Americans with food and drink. A Russian vice admiral, who had served as King's host from the beginning, urged King to drink vodka, but King stuck with sherry.

After dinner the reason for the special treatment was made known. The vice admiral handed King a long list of naval equipment that the Russians wanted from the Americans. "Please approve this request and sign it," asked the Russian. King knew he had no authority to approve such a request, nor would he have done so had he the authority. King could only promise to forward the list to the Secretary of the Navy for his sympathetic consideration. The Russian insisted that King sign it immediately, but King continued to refuse. "Whereupon," King later said, "the Russian vice admiral was very grim and seemed to be quite downcast. I assumed that he would be demoted, for which I was sorry. But I couldn't help him."

When the train arrived at Saki in the morning, the airfield was foggy and the aircraft covered with ice. King was anxious to leave but had to wait while the crews melted the ice with heaters. The Russians had provided food and liquor once again; one of King's flag officers got drunk and fell asleep after the aircraft was aloft. Later he awoke and became delirious, yelling that he was about to die. When things calmed down hours later, the officer admitted to King that he was an alcoholic. King kept him anyway. As long as he stayed reasonably sober he was too valuable to lose. "He was a very able man," King later said.

President Roosevelt died on 12 April 1945. King's memoirs of the event are cryptic. "Marshall and I attended when the train pulled into the Washington Station, and we took part in the procession from the station to the White House. The next day the JCS attended the funeral." Afterward the JCS went to Hyde Park for the funeral. "There were hundreds of VIPs," wrote King, "so the JCS couldn't even see the grave. Then we returned to Washington."

King and Roosevelt had rarely spoken in the last months of Roosevelt's tenure. Roosevelt's problems were mostly political, both at home and abroad, so the two men had little in common to discuss. As King was a pragmatic person, he fatalistically accepted that Roosevelt was dying. The war would continue and the Allies would win, with or without Roosevelt. As they were not friends, King would not feel any personal loss. And as for the political implications of Roosevelt's death — well — politics were not among King's concerns. King's sole objective, as always, would be to win the war as soon as possible.

King and Truman had been strangers before Roosevelt's death and remained strangers afterward. Although Truman had chaired a powerful Senate committee investigating war contracts, King had ignored him, even though the committee had discovered serious faults in the Navy's amphibious ship building programs in the early war years. Marshall had been solicitous to the Truman committee — too much so, in King's opinion.

The Big Three at Yalta (U.S. Army photograph)

King and Secretary of State Stettinius waiting for Roosevelt's funeral train in Washington (National Archives 80-G-49019)

When Roosevelt died, King ordered John McCrea (then a rear admiral) back to Washington to serve as Truman's naval aide. Truman, however, wanted a Kansas City friend and shoe salesman, James K. Vardaman, Jr., a reserve lieutenant commander. Vardaman was duly promoted, first to captain and then to commodore, to have rank commensurate with that of Brigadier General Harry Vaughn, the President's military aide.

Because of Truman's former army service, the Navy feared a backlash after years as Roosevelt's favorite. Truman knew so little about war operations that he was considered susceptible to the opinions of those closest to his ear. When it became known that the Army had briefed Truman in the White House, the Navy asked for equal time and got it.

King was such an ineffective speaker that it was decided to have Cooke brief the President. The first rehearsal went badly. "Being perfectly frank," Marine Oman Pfeiffer later said, "I thought it was a horrible exhibition. Cooke didn't seem to know his own mind, he hesitated, he stumbled, he rambled, and his presentation wasn't organized." After more rehearsing, Cooke improved and was pronounced ready.

King and his staff assembled in the White House at the appointed time. Cooke was onstage, with Pfeiffer ready to flip the pages on a chart. The new President seemed unusually diminutive when he entered the room. Perhaps it was the height of the entranceway and the tall Secret Service men surrounding him. "It made me think," Pfeiffer later said, "that I was seeing a lost boy on the way to the guillotine. The President listened to the presentation, and it was apparently effective because none of the dire results which the Navy feared immediately materialized."

Truman's ascension had little effect on strategic planning for the remainder of the war. "The change of presidents," wrote historian Grace Hayes, "meant only the instruction of a new man in a course already for the most part laid out." Nevertheless, things began to change under Truman. Robert Dennison, as an astute member of King's staff, later commented, "Toward the end, when Truman became President, the Joint Chiefs of Staff sort of went down hill because they were no longer needed, or so it was thought then. It became having a luncheon meeting every now and then."

Germany surrendered on May eighth. While the public celebrated V-E Day, King and his colleagues pondered how best to transfer forces from Europe to the Pacific. Even more important was the question of what to do with them when they got there. In early April, King had advised Nimitz by message that the JCS were about to discuss Pacific strategy with the President. Iwo Jima had been seized, Okinawa would fall by mid-June, and MacArthur would announce the liberation of the Philippines in early July. There were two alternatives for later operations, explained King. One was siege or blockade. The other was to invade the home islands. "It is apparent," said King, "that both alternatives have their merits and demerits." King did not express a preference.

The Joint Staff Planners gave their recommendations in early May. It would be necessary, they said, to invade Japan, because the Japanese probably would not surrender otherwise. The greatest argument against invasion was the inevitably enormous American casualties. The planners declined to estimate in numbers what those casualties would be, noting only that heretofore Pacific amphibious assaults had been more costly than protracted European land campaigns.

King was the only member of the JCS to comment on the report. He agreed with the conclusions but rejected the comparisons in casualties, which he felt proved nothing. Nevertheless he approved the planners' report, and his JCS colleagues followed suit. In effect, everyone agreed to the invasion as a basis for planning.

After the war both King and Leahy insisted that they had reluctantly agreed to the invasion for the sake of a unanimous decision. Both said they would have preferred to defeat Japan by blockade and bombing alone, to starve Japan into submission. King even seriously considered a fantastic scheme to spread salt on Japanese rice fields to ruin the crop before it ripened. Yet JCS records do not reveal strong objections by either at any time. When Truman summoned Forrestal, Stimson, and the JCS on 18 June to solicit their opinions, all agreed on the need for an invasion. Based upon what he perceived as their unanimous support, President Truman agreed that the JCS should plan to invade Japan.

The meeting with Truman affirmed what the JCS already had begun. After long jurisdictional arguments between King and Marshall, the JCS had agreed to reorganize the Pacific forces and to make MacArthur and Nimitz jointly responsible for the invasion. On 25 May they had issued the appropriate strategic directive, the last that the JCS would release in the war.

Meanwhile King had lost ships in the Pacific to other than enemy actions, when Halsey had allowed the Third Fleet to blunder into two killer typhoons. The first typhoon, in mid-December 1944, sank three destroyers and damaged many other ships. Some 790 men were killed, scores of others injured, and 150 carrier aircraft were wrecked.

King's first reaction was restrained, consistent with his policy not to bother men in battle. Several days after the typhoon had done its damage, he sent an "eyes only" message to Nimitz and Halsey. "When convenient and not to interfere with major current operations," said King, "I need to know the circumstances which caused operating units of Third Fleet to encounter typhoon which resulted in the loss and crippling of so many combatant ships." Halsey replied by blaming the lack of weather warning, erratic storm behavior, high winds, and low fuel.

Vice Admiral John Hoover headed a subsequent court of inquiry, which reported that Halsey was responsible for the storm damage and loss of lives. But the court also said that Halsey had not been negligent. His mistakes had been errors of judgment, brought on by the stress of war and Halsey's "commendable desire" to keep hitting the Japanese even if he had to steam through a typhoon to keep after them.

The court's report made its way to King almost two months after the typhoon had hit. King agreed with the findings. Halsey remained in the Pacific, and Nimitz wrote a letter to the fleet telling commanders at sea how to avoid typhoons in the future.

Then Halsey did it again. Relieving Spruance off Okinawa on 27 May 1945, Halsey a week later steamed his carrier task force directly into the center of another murderous typhoon. This time the court of inquiry, again under Hoover, was less forgiving. It put the blame squarely on Halsey as well as his carrier commander, John McCain. Privately Hoover thought that Halsey deserved a general court-martial; officially he recommended that serious consideration be given to assigning Halsey and McCain to other duty.

It is hard to reconstruct what happened when the recommendation to relieve Halsey hit Washington in the summer of 1945. Some historians claim that Forrestal wanted either to fire or to retire Halsey. King agreed with the court that Halsey and McCain had been inept in acting upon the weather warnings they had received, and that they should have avoided the second typhoon. Nevertheless, King did not want to discipline Halsey. The war was nearly over, Halsey was a national hero, and King had no stomach for publicly reprimanding Halsey, who certainly would have protested any censure from the Navy Department. Arguments and recrimination would have ruined the Navy's finest hour — victory in the Pacific. King decided to do nothing, and Forrestal went along.

McCain was another matter. His position had been precarious even before the typhoon. Sent by King to the Pacific to spell Mitscher, he had commanded a carrier task group during the Battle of Leyte Gulf in order to gain experience. After forty-eight hours under air attack, McCain had sent an emotional and intemperate message to King, Nimitz, Halsey, Spruance, and Mitscher, bitterly condemning the SB2C dive bomber and appealing for more fighter aircraft. Nimitz thought that he was breaking under pressure. After chewing out McCain, Nimitz told Halsey to retain Mitscher in command of Task Force 38. At the earliest opportunity, said Nimitz, Halsey was to see McCain and then advise Nimitz whether McCain was fit for combat. Halsey later replied that McCain had used poor judgment but should still relieve Mitscher. Nimitz consented. King said nothing, at least not at that moment. Less than a month later, however, McCain wrote King a letter dated 22 December 1944 that indicates that King had intervened in McCain's behalf.

"My dear Admiral King," the letter began. "I needed, without modification or qualification, and of equal value,

"(1) Your assurance that you wished me well, and (2) your statement of confidence in my ability.

"So, I owe to you the maintenance of my self-respect, and such measure of success as I have had in the fighting, and thank you therefor.

"With respect and affection —

"J. S. McCain"

McCain had retained the carrier command, even after the typhoon.

The political leaders of the United States, Great Britain, and the Soviet Union had meanwhile been planning a mid-July meeting in Potsdam, Germany. King, in his usual businesslike way, arranged for two cruisers to transport Truman and his party across the Atlantic. The CCS were told to come almost as an afterthought.

King got underway for Germany on 12 July 1945, once again flying in his private C-54 transport. Dr. Edward Gough, a Navy medical officer, was included in King's party as a precaution. King had been afflicted with an unspecified ailment that would require radiation treatments when he returned, and in the interim he wanted his personal physician nearby.

King arrived at Orly Field, Paris, the next afternoon and was met by Stark, Ghormley, and photographers. The city and its citizens seemed unaffected from the war. That evening the American ambassador entertained King and his party with a lavish dinner at the sumptuous American embassy. King must have been feeling old. He went to bed early. (His staff went out to enjoy the Paris nightlife.)

On the morning of the fourteenth King resumed his journey to

Germany and got a hostile reception: the Red Army had taken over its zone of occupation surrounding Berlin. King's pilot informed the Admiral that he had been ordered to fly within a narrow air corridor. If he strayed the Russians might shoot. The tension eased when a flight of American fighter planes escorted King's plane into Berlin. (The Russians gave Truman the same treatment.)

The contrast between France and Germany was striking. The destruction of war had become increasingly evident from the air and was even more apparent in Berlin. Wrecked buildings, rubble, bomb craters, and ragged refugees were everywhere. King and his party entered Army sedans and, with motorcycle escort, sped between rows of American soldiers standing at attention and onto the road to Potsdam.

Once again the Russians intimidated the Americans by stopping King's convoy for roadblocks and security checks along the way. After annoying delays King finally arrived at the American compound in Babelsberg, a resort city and former movie colony that had escaped damage during the war. Babelsberg's elegant villas and landscaped grounds had been ruthlessly commandeered by the Russians for the Potsdam conferees. Ubiquitous Russian troops made the Americans virtual prisoners. Cooke paddled a canoe on a lake near King's villa and was told he would be shot if he tried it again. It was humiliating, but King and his colleagues acquiesced as they had at Teheran and Yalta.

The CCS confirmed that they had little to discuss. Everyone's thoughts were naturally in the Pacific. The British wanted a part in the defeat of Japan, a subject that the Americans wished to ignore. It would be difficult enough to transfer American forces from Europe to the Far East. Additional British forces would only snarl the pipeline.

The British also began to press for a vote in making Pacific strategy, hitherto an exclusive American function. Such aspirations were not well taken. King and the JCS bluntly reminded the British that the Americans alone would continue to decide what would be done in the Pacific. Although they would consult with the British on matters of general strategy, if the British disagreed, the JCS view would prevail. The JCS would also inform the British about American plans and decisions. Those were the ground rules. If the British did not like them, they could get out of the Pacific war. The British had no choice but to go along.

Meanwhile, the JCS were excluded from the political meetings. Consequently King did not know what was happening, even though Leahy (who was continually at Truman's side) tried to apprise his JCS colleagues of developments. The British chiefs also gave them information passed along from their Foreign Office. Thus it was that King learned secondhand that the Russians intended to declare war against Japan on 15 August. King's isolation was expressed in a letter to Forrestal just before the conference ended. "We — the U.S. Chiefs of Staff," wrote King, "have, at last, made arrangements to get the minutes and the agenda of the 'big 3' meetings. The hitch was the inadequacy — or the reluctance — of State Department subordinates to let us know what is going on, so that we were dependent on such 'bits and pieces' as Admiral Leahy could tell us. The President and Secretary of State had assumed we were getting this information all along."

With so little business at Potsdam, King had time for touring and reviewing troops. He was far more an inquisitive sightseer than a triumphant conqueror. "We went to see the famous square," he wrote in his memoirs, "where the basic government buildings were situated — especially the building where Hitler decided to quit and killed himself with his so-called wife. But I didn't ask to go inside."

King went to the bombproof U-boat construction sites at Bremen and Bremerhaven. The Germans had been building submarines up to war's end. That impressed him. The destruction of German cities did not seem to affect King one way or the other. It was a condition he took for granted. His only comments were about dairy cattle and fertile farms, perhaps because they were such a peaceful, undisturbed contrast to everything else. Churchill had made the same observation at Normandy a year before, as if it were incongruous for people and cities to have suffered so, but not cattle and farms.

Before King returned home he went to southern Germany to see Hitler's "eagle's nest" at Berchtesgaden near the Tyrol. The beautiful valley and surrounding mountains made a spectacular view. War had apparently never touched the people or the countryside. After a lavish meal at a nearby modern hotel, King visited Hitler's mountain retreat in the afternoon. King's physician described the ascent. "The Eagle's Nest was perched upon the very tip of a high peak," Gough later recalled. "The road to the top was a masterpiece of engineering in itself, mile after mile of steep grade cut out of the side of a mountain of rock. At five or six places the road was driven through sheer rock creating tunnels varying in length from a few hundred feet to a half mile, and the ends of the tunnels had huge iron gratings. Eventually we came to a leveled-off expanse for parking and turning. We left our jeeps and entered a well finished tunnel extending twelve hundred feet into the heart of the mountain. Here we came upon an immense bronze door, the entrance to an ornate elevator which rose four hundred feet into Hitler's house.

"The house was fantastically beautiful," Gough continued, "expertly constructed in lovely stone. The lower deck was for his SS bodyguards, while the main floor had a large conference room and a smaller kitchen, dining room, bedroom, and lavatory. Hitler had a beautiful room where he could look out for miles and miles over his domain. It was evident that he never intended to spend much time there — the purpose of the structure was vague — it seemed to have none — and the work and materials entailed must have been appalling. The thought came to mind that he probably wanted to be above his subjects and close to God, in an egotistical way, certainly not in a religious sense. However one looks at it there could only be one conclusion: the idea for something of this nature could only be conjured in the mind of a maniac and fanatic."

King was less mystical as to why Hitler had used it so infrequently. "Probably," King later concluded, "because there was no way to get down once his enemy got him cornered — unless he could fly."

King continued his sightseeing later in the afternoon, cruising upon a lake. ("The loveliest scene that it has ever been my privilege to gaze upon," Gough later remarked.) At a monastery on the lakeshore, King was startled to learn that the monks did not know that Germany had surrendered ten weeks earlier. That evening there was an even more bountiful meal at the hotel. Afterward King went into town while his staff went to a USO show. The Admiral wandered alone down the streets. When it began to rain he stepped into a doorway to keep dry. In time an Army jeep went by, and King hitched a ride to his hotel.

Next morning King began his return home, stopping briefly in Paris to see Forrestal and then continuing via England, the Azores, and Bermuda. Heavy weather thrashed King's aircraft as it approached Washington. The pilot descended through fog and darkness and landed safely. King had been away for eighteen days.

In late 1943 Marshall had entered King's JCS office in the Public Health Building, closed the door, and told King for the first time about the Manhattan Project. Do not discuss the atomic bomb with anyone else, Marshall had warned, and he promised to inform King of its development. By the spring of 1945 Marshall was reporting good progress, and he asked King to assign Captain William S. Parsons to the project as an expert in trigger mechanisms.

During the 17 July JCS meeting at Potsdam, Marshall cleared the room except for the secretariat, then announced the successful atomic bomb detonation in New Mexico. The following day, Marshall again cleared the room and announced Truman's decision to drop the bomb on Japan. Truman later said he had consulted King, as well as other members of the JCS, and had gotten their concurrence before he made the decision. If so, King would never admit it. After the war King declared privately that he "didn't like the atomic bomb or any part of it."

The first bomb was scheduled for Hiroshima on August sixth. King began to tell other members of his staff several days beforehand, although he omitted details. He ordered Neil Dietrich to inform him when the news came in, regardless of the hour. Dietrich was impressed. It had to be something important for King's sleep to be interrupted.

The Nagasaki bomb was dropped on August ninth. The next day King advised Nimitz that Japan was suing for peace and would accept the Potsdam Declaration provided she could retain the Emperor.

Meanwhile there was trouble in Washington about the details of the surrender ceremony. A planning committee chaired by the State Department was about to recommend MacArthur as the sole American representative authorized to sign the surrender document. The Army thought it a splendid idea. The Navy Department was furious. Cooke dispatched Dennison to the committee, but Dennison doubted his own authority to represent the Secretary of the Navy. "That doesn't make any difference," said Cooke. "Just go down and tell them that you're a member, and then get in there and get this thing changed."

Dennison joined the committee, which seemed confused and disorganized. "I carried out my instructions," Dennison later said, "and I stepped on a lot of toes doing it. I had the backing of the people in the Navy, and the other people could not have cared less. Nobody really knew who the hell I was, and they probably didn't care."

His mission accomplished, Dennison returned to King. King relayed the news on to Nimitz that he would represent the United States and that MacArthur would represent the Supreme Commander, Allied Forces. Given this arrangement, all the countries that had fought Japan would have to sign the surrender document. MacArthur would have plenty of company.

Intense diplomatic negotiations continued for the next seventy-two hours. There was every possibility that radical Japanese leaders might attempt a coup d'état. Truman suspended all B-29 attacks, then rescinded the order intending to intimidate the Japanese, then changed his mind again and recalled a thousand bombers already airborne. The atmosphere in King's headquarters was tense, nervous waiting.

Early on the fourteenth, Radio Tokyo announced that the Emperor had decided to surrender. King immediately sent a message to Nimitz ordering him to suspend air attacks forthwith. Nimitz asked about naval gunfire and submarine operations. Cooke read Nimitz's message, then wrote on the margin: "Holding answer for time being."

King sat alone in his office. The phone rang. He answered, listened, spoke briefly, and then hung up. Then he rang for Dietrich.

"Sit down, Neil," said King as his flag secretary entered. It was one of the few times that King used his first name. "I have to go to the White House soon," said King. "The President is going to announce the Japanese surrender." Dietrich said something appropriate in reply.

"Well, it's all over," said King. Dietrich said nothing. "I wonder what I'm going to do tomorrow," said King.

"If you think you had problems during the war," said Dietrich, "it's nothing compared to the problems you're going to have trying to hold everything together now that the war is over."

King did not smile. "I guess there will be something to do here," he said, "but they won't need me." Dietrich tried to cheer him up: King would always be needed. "No, no," said King. Then: "We'll see, we'll see." He paused. "Thank you," said King, and Dietrich left the office.

That evening Truman announced victory over Japan. Cooke drafted a final message to Nimitz: "Suspend all offensive hostile action. Remain alert."

The Second World War was over.

III

After the War

To a Sailor Seeking Retirement Away from the Sea

> . . . Thereafter go thy way, taking with thee a shapen oar, till thou shalt come to such men as know not the sea, neither eat meat savoured with salt; yea, nor have they knowledge of ships of purple cheek, nor shapen oars which serve for wings to ships. And I will give thee a most manifest token, which cannot escape thee. In the day when another wayfarer shall meet thee and say that thou hast a winnowing fan on thy stout shoulder, even then make fast thy shapen oar in the earth and do goodly sacrifice to the Lord Poseidon. . . .
>
> Homer, *Odyssey*, book XI

37

Anticlimax

THE SURRENDER DOCUMENT was signed aboard the battleship USS *Missouri* in Tokyo Bay on Sunday, 2 September 1945. "King was a lost soul when the war was over," recalled Neil Dietrich. "He had served his purpose. He had done what he had set out to do. He had won his part of the war."

King fully intended to retire, and Forrestal fully intended to see that he did retire. Their relationship had become unbearably strained. Aide Alexander S. McDill remembered seeing King tear into Forrestal in a Navy Department corridor, until the Secretary walked silently away. On another occasion McDill showed King a Forrestal order that would have allowed medical officers to determine whether commanders were fit to exercise command in combat. King snatched the paper and stormed out of his office. He returned several minutes later.

"What happened, Admiral?" asked McDill.

"He's not going to send it," said King.

The final blowup arose over the recommendations of a flag selection board convened in mid-1945. As it was the first board to resume normal peacetime selection procedures, King wanted everything done by the book. To King's shock and dismay, Forrestal repudiated the board's selections and even admonished Marc Mitscher, a senior member of the board, for what Forrestal considered the collectively poor judgment of the entire eleven-man board. Forrestal then deleted certain names and added others.

King was outraged. After a furious argument, both went to Truman for a resolution. The President avoided the subject and afterward approved Forrestal's revised list without consulting King.

The matter of King's relief was another divisive issue. At King's initiative (and over the objections of many of his staff), the post of Commander in Chief, U.S. Fleet, was abolished on 10 October 1945. Henceforth the Chief of Naval Operations would be the senior officer in the United States Navy. Who would it be? King championed Nimitz. Whatever King's misgivings about his capabilities, Nimitz had been the senior fleet commander and was entitled to succeed to CNO. Forrestal wanted Edwards. King forced the issue by writing directly to the President on 12 November. "The successful outcome of the war some three months ago," King wrote, "the imminence of my 67th birthday, the advisability of the appointment of a Chief of Naval Operations who will remain in office for some time, and other circumstances, combine to make it appropriate for me to submit, at this time, this my resignation as Chief of Naval Operations, effective at your pleasure and convenience.

"May I commend to your consideration as my successor the officer who has so successfully exercised high command in the Pacific throughout the war and is otherwise eminently qualified, Fleet Admiral Chester W. Nimitz.

"I cannot close this letter without expressing my deep appreciation of your constant consideration and support, nor without saying what hardly needs to be said, that I am ever at your service.

"I am asking the Secretary of the Navy to hand you this letter."

Forrestal received the letter grudgingly. He had no choice other than to forward it to Truman, with the stipulation that Nimitz's tour be limited to two years. "I thought that was improper," King later said, "but it seemed to me when his two years were up that Nimitz was very happy to be relieved."

Forrestal had the last word. King wanted the change of command on 15 January 1946 in order to allow Nimitz a leave period to rest and recuperate. Later King would have settled for 17 December (the fifth anniversary of his return to sea duty) or 30 December (his fourth anniversary as COMINCH). "But Mr. Forrestal got 'mad' about the matter," King later wrote, "and ordered the change of command moved up to December 15th." King did not want to demean himself by asking for a delay, so he acceded to the date mandated by Forrestal.

Honors and recognition began to materialize as King's active service drew to a close. Bowdoin and Harvard had conferred honorary degrees earlier in the summer. More would follow.*

Then there were the farewell dinners. King had last met with his circle of journalists shortly after V-J Day. When the meeting adjourned he asked if he might gather with them one more time. It was done.

* See Appendix VII.

Phelps Adams of the New York *Sun* let him know that a dinner had been arranged at the Statler Hotel. "I think," wrote Adams, "that the enthusiasm with which the fellows are looking forward to this evening with you testifies, far more eloquently than my limited vocabulary possibly could, to the genuine, whole-hearted appreciation and gratitude that all of us feel for the patience, kindness, knowledge and help that you showered upon us throughout all the confusing, rumor-ridden days of the war. It helped us; it helped our papers; and I sincerely believe that it helped America. Mere words and mere thanks are an extremely inadequate and ineffectual reward for your generosity, but if the undying friendship of twenty-six struggling newspapermen is worth anything at all, it is yours, eternally."

The dinner was a great success. Afterwards the correspondents gave King an elaborate scroll, which read:

To Admiral of the Fleet

ERNEST J. KING

an Undistinguished Service Stripe and Promotion to Grand Old Salt of the Alexandria Reserves:

For conspicuous bravery and intrepidity above and beyond the call of duty in performance of which he brilliantly rejected his best professional advice and daringly ignored his own natural instincts, and alone and single-handedly, at a moment when adverse winds of publicity were threatening to sink the whole fleet, exposed himself to a frontal assault by the picked shock troops of the journalistic enemy led by some of the most reprehensible and blood-thirsty Washington correspondents, and from that moment on, never retiring to cover from their incessant salvoes of cross-fire, stormed the enemy in its own defenses and in the decisive and little-known Battle of Virginia conquered and captivated them completely.

(*Signed*)
The Surviving Veterans of the Battle of Virginia

Who are, in order of their appearance:

Glen Perry, *ex-New York Sun*
Bert Andrews, *New York Herald-Tribune*
Ernest Lindley, *Newsweek*
Marquis Childs, *United Features Syndicate*
Alexander (Casey) Jones, *Washington Post*
Mark Foote, *Booth Newspapers*
Joseph Harsch, *Columbia Broadcasting System*

Barnet Nover, *Washington Post*
Roscoe Drummond, *Christian Science Monitor*
Raymond Henle, *American Broadcasting Company*
Lyle Wilson, *United Press Association*
Edward Folliard, *Washington Post*
Walter Lippmann, *New York Herald-Tribune Syndicate*
Phelps Adams, *New York Sun*
Paul Miller, *Associated Press*
Lewis Wood, *New York Times*
Raymond Brandt, *St. Louis Post-Despatch*
Turner Catledge, *New York Times*
James Wright, *Buffalo Evening News*
Dewey Fleming, *Baltimore Sun*
Richard Wilson, *Cowles Publications*
Paul Leach, *Chicago Daily News*
Arthur Krock, *New York Times*
Benjamin McKelway, *Washington Evening Star*
Raymond Swing, *American Broadcasting Company*
William Hillman, *Crowell-Collier Publications*

"It was a sentimental evening," Phelps Adams later wrote, "and it left no doubt that the Admiral, too, had his sentimental side, for he was quite touched by the scroll and the presentation displaying the warmth and esteem in which all of us held him. To others he may have been a 'Sundowner,' a rigid disciplinarian — of himself as well as others — an armor-clad, crusty Old Salt, and — as he himself once put it, son of a bitch; but to the Surviving Veterans of the Battle of Virginia he was — beyond all that — an intensely human being, capable of great warmth and deep friendships, and a delightful companion on any occasion.

"Late in the year," Adams continued, "at the first post-war Gridiron Dinner, he came up to the after-dinner party in the hotel suite I always shared with my friend Harold Brayman, to join our other guests and their wives. Here numerous other guests at the dinner dropped in for a drink and some pleasant conversation. In all, there were, I suppose, sixty or seventy people including Congressmen, Senators, Governors, business leaders and other notables; but on this occasion Ernie King was outstandingly the center of attraction. Seated on the sofa, he had half-a-dozen or more of the wives in a semi-circle at his feet, listening enraptured to some of the untold tales of the war, while Ruth — as hostess — kept his glass brimming with Scotch."

Adams concluded, "And when the party finally began to break up — about 3 o'clock in the morning — he said his 'good nights,' wrapped his scarf jauntily about his neck, donned his cap at exactly the prescribed angle, and — with his shoulders squared, his back ramrod-straight, and his step firm — navigated down the hotel corridor to the elevator, under his own steam, with all the precision of a man who has taken a considerable cargo aboard and is determined nevertheless to bring his ship into port smartly and safely.

"And that is the way I shall always remember him."

Some fifteen of King's personal staff gathered with the Admiral for a final dinner at the Army-Navy Club. "It was very pleasant," Dietrich later recalled. "Admiral Edwards was the toastmaster, and, being rather a genial, easygoing soul, made several pleasant remarks during the course of the meal. The atmosphere was relaxed yet restrained, or to use King's words, 'appropriate for the occasion.' "

Then it was time for King to speak. He rose and stood behind his chair. His remarks were gracious, and he said all the right words of gratitude and appreciation for those who had served with him. "I can forgive anything," King concluded, "except for three things which I will not tolerate — stupidity, laziness, and carelessness. If any of you here have been guilty of any of these, you wouldn't be here now."

In a short while King went home. Several of his staff remained for a nightcap. Those who had known King the longest remarked that it was the first time they had ever seen King betray any sentimental emotion. "If he had been capable of having a tear in his eye." Dietrich later said, "it would have been shed that night."

On 14 December King went to the White House so that Truman could present a gold star in lieu of a third Distinguished Service Medal. Several hundred had assembled for the ceremony, including Leahy, Marshall, Eisenhower, and Nimitz. At 1100 the President arrived, commended King for his service, and then presented the award. It was soon over. The next day Nimitz relieved King in a change-of-command ceremony — brief, very brief, in accordance with the traditions of the naval service.

Among the many tributes that King received or would receive, there were two that were particularly meaningful. One was timely, and the other was late. The first was an illuminated message in beautiful calligraphy, bound in full blue morocco, from the British Chiefs of Staff:

> To Fleet Admiral Ernest J. King, United States Navy.
>
> As your friends and colleagues in the great struggle which has just ended, we, the British Chiefs of Staff, send you our sincere good wishes on the occasion of your retirement from

your post as Chief of Naval Operations of the United States Navy.

Under your leadership as Commander in Chief, the United States Navy has grown, with unprecedented speed, into the most powerful in all the world. We have watched with admiration and heartfelt gratitude the energy and order with which this unequalled expansion has been carried through. We have been inspired by the strategical and tactical skill, and the technical ingenuity, which have contributed so much to the resounding successes of the United States Navy, both in European waters, and, more particularly, in the Pacific.

We are anxious that you should know how deeply we have appreciated, throughout our association in the higher direction of the war, your keen insight, your breadth of vision and your unshakeable determination to secure the defeat of our enemies in the shortest possible time. The intimate cooperation of the United States and British Commonwealth Navies in the European landings, in the war against the U-boats, in all manner of special operations, and latterly in the Pacific, are enduring witnesses of the sense of united effort which you brought to all our deliberations.

Admiral of the Fleet Sir Dudley Pound and Field Marshal Sir John Dill would, we feel sure, have wished to join in this tribute had they been spared to see the completion of their work in the common cause.

ALANBROOKE
CUNNINGHAM OF HYNDHOPE
PORTAL OF HUNGERFORD

The 79th Congress in March 1946, by joint resolution, thanked King and Marshall and provided for a gold medal to be presented by the President in the name of the people of the United States. The section referring to King read:

RESOLVED that the thanks of Congress are hereby tendered to Fleet Admiral Ernest Joseph King for his distinguished leadership, as Commander in Chief of the United States Fleet and Chief of Naval Operations and as a member of the Combined Chiefs of Staff of the United Nations, in planning the expansion, equipment, training, and operation of the United States Navy and in formulating and executing the global strategy that led to victory in World War II; and to the members of the United States Navy, the United States Marine Corps and the United States Coast Guard and to the members of the

Reserve Forces who served under his direction with such heroic devotion and personal sacrifice.

The medal presented to him bore the inscription:

ON BEHALF OF A GRATEFUL NATION.

38

The Final Years

KING'S LIFE came to an end gradually, painfully, and pathetically. Retirement began with an office in the Navy Department, an aide, and a yeoman — all the perquisites of a fleet admiral. At first he was active: writing his memoirs in collaboration with Walter Muir Whitehill; visiting friends and family; making occasional speeches; reading books and writing letters; and traveling to receive awards and attend ceremonies.

King's decline began with a stroke in 1947. Others followed. His activities became progressively curtailed. While his mind remained alert, his speech and writing deteriorated. The once-lean body became crippled and withered. In order to receive the constant attention he needed, King occupied a suite in Bethesda Naval Hospital. In the summertime he went to the naval hospital in Portsmouth, New Hampshire, to escape the heat. He had become an invalid.

The Navy Department became anxious to make plans for King's eventual funeral. George Russell later recalled how he became involved: "Beginning with General Pershing's funeral, the most elaborate of funeral arrangements were made for senior people in the armed forces, including all five-star officers. In order to make the necessary arrangements, somebody had to find out from the officer himself what his wishes might be, or what arrangements he had already made, and I was nominated to go and see Admiral King on this subject. He was then in his office on Constitution Avenue, and after I had made known the purpose of my call, he sat back in his chair and roared with laughter. When he finished laughing, he said to me: 'Well, Russell, I hope this isn't urgent.' "

King died in Portsmouth on Monday afternoon, 25 June 1956, at the age of seventy-eight.

The late Walter Muir Whitehill knew King as well as any man. It was through Walter's encouragement and cooperation that I began to write this book. As my tribute to him, I believe it is both appropriate and fitting (words King would have used) that his description of Admiral King's funeral bring this book to a close.

> On Tuesday noon, the twenty-sixth, King's body was flown in a Navy plane from Portsmouth to Washington, where it was placed in the crypt chapel of St. Joseph of Arimathea in Washington Cathedral. I flew to Washington Thursday afternoon, the twenty-eighth, and drove out to the cathedral in the long light of the June evening. As I passed the Japanese Embassy, which had looked so sad and deserted during the war, the courtyard was well raked and a man-servant stood in the open door awaiting guests. Nearly eleven years had passed since King had disposed of the Japanese fleet. It was a cool sunny early evening. The Bishop's Garden was full of fragrant herbs, roses, delphinium and madonna lilies, and the cathedral grounds were quiet and peaceful. In the massive Norman crypt, King's coffin, covered with a flag, was flanked by an impassive honor guard of six Air Force men.
>
> Washington Cathedral began to fill soon after noon on Friday, June twenty-ninth. The coffin was now in the crossing, with an honor guard, and marines in blue jackets and white trousers. Flag officers in whites, with mourning bands, and generals of the other services, filled the south transept, although the ushers, being young, did not always recognize retired admirals in civilian clothes. At one o'clock the funeral began, the Bishop of Washington using the Book of Common Prayer simply and correctly, without rhetorical flourishes.
>
> Eternal Father, strong to save
> Whose arm hath bound the restless wave
>
> was the only hymn, and by 1:20 the procession was moving out of the cathedral. It went by car to Fifteenth Street and Constitution Avenue, where the main funeral procession formed to march to the Capitol.
>
> My ever-helpful friend, John Heffernan, realizing that I would see more out than in, drove me straight to the Capitol, where he made arrangements to join the "motorcade" to Annapolis. I walked out on the terrace behind the Capitol and

A past and a future admiral. King visits the Naval Academy for his forty-fifth reunion in May 1946 and is greeted by the brigade commander, Midshipman Stansfield Turner. (Courtesy Naval Historical Foundation)

looked down the Mall to the Washington Monument. The day was cool but sunny, one of those rare moments in early summer when Washington is still at its springtime best. In the distance one heard drums and the sound of marching; bands playing funeral marches, "Onward Christian Soldiers" and (with wonderful flourishes of trumpets) "God of our fathers, whose almighty hand." The music came nearer as the procession marched along Constitution Avenue; as it turned into Pennsylvania, and came down toward the Peace Monument, I could see a V-shaped wedge of motorcycle policemen with red headlights, riding very slowly; then the Navy Band, followed by the Battalion of Midshipmen from the Naval Academy in whites with rifles, their officers holding drawn swords with black crape streamers; a company of infantry; the Marine Band, a company of marines, a squadron of airmen, a company of WAVES, WACS, and the like, another band, the national colors, King's five-star flag; then the body on a horse-drawn caisson, followed by cars. As the procession started up Capitol Hill, I went back to John Heffernan's car in the square before the Capitol, and watched it arrive. When the caisson reached the steps of the Capitol, the Navy Band played "Lead, kindly light," as the body was transferred to a motor hearse. The troops dispersed, and some fifty cars formed for the drive to Annapolis.

All along North Capitol Street, New York Avenue, the Baltimore Parkway and Route Fifty to Annapolis traffic was cleared in every direction. As the procession approached Annapolis, carrier planes appeared overhead. When it reached Gate Eight of the Naval Academy at half-past four, the planes flew to and fro in formation during the movement to the Naval Academy Cemetery by College Creek. As the hearse entered the cemetery, the first of a seventeen-gun salute was fired. Midshipmen, Marines, and band were in position by the grave on a lovely tree-shaded hillside where King and his classmates had walked on Sunday afternoons close to sixty years before — the Secretary of the Navy, the Chief of Naval Operations, and honorary pallbearers standing near. As the bearers brought the body from the hearse, the Escort Commander ordered "Present Arms"; the band played four ruffles and flourishes and the hymn "Eternal Father, strong to save" as the body was carried to the grave. The music ceased; the troops came to Parade Rest as the chaplain read the committal, ending with Cardinal Newman's "Lord, support us all the day long" and "May the souls of the faithful departed, through the mercy of

God, rest in peace." Then, as the troops again presented arms, the firing squad fired three volleys, and as the bugler sounded "Taps," the last of the seventeen-gun salute boomed out from across the river. The bodybearers folded the flag, gave it to King's son, and, after a few minutes of quiet conversation, the mourners scattered. Nothing could have been at once simpler and more magnificent, or more appropriate to the man. But to most of the midshipmen at the grave, King — and indeed Nimitz, Halsey, and Hewitt, who were among his pallbearers — must have seemed as distant figures as Dewey, Farragut, or even the sailors of the earliest wars of the Republic. The Class of 1958 is two full generations removed from the Class of 1901, and to a very young man this degree of remoteness borders on that of eternity. So rapidly do great men cease to be people and become instead names, portraits, or statues, curiously familiar, yet personally unknown. The speed of this process has led me to offer this perhaps discursive tribute of affection and respect to a figure of naval history that I had the good fortune, in his last years, to know as a man, rather than as a name.

Acknowledgments

Acknowledgment of Assistance

THE LATE WALTER MUIR WHITEHILL provided the original inspiration for me to write this book, and his friendship, encouragement, and cooperation were very special to me. He was a scholar, a prolific contributor to the arts and letters, and a cultural institution in the city of Boston and the state of Massachusetts. Although Walter died before *Master of Sea Power* was published, he always assured me that he was confident that I could and would do justice to Admiral King.

Llewellyn Howland III was my editor at Little, Brown when I wrote my first book, *The Quiet Warrior: A Biography of Admiral Raymond A. Spruance*. I discovered then how extraordinarily lucky I was to have Louie as my literary counselor, and he also became a wonderful friend. Louie has since formed his own company that buys and sells rare books, but he still generously took time to read and comment upon my King manuscript. His advice was, as always, of inestimable help to me.

Herman Wouk is another friend who gave of himself to help me with King. Although deeply involved in the final stages of his own *War and Remembrance*, Herman Wouk was kind enough to read and assess a preliminary version of my King manuscript. His incisive analysis and trenchant suggestions provided invaluable guidance, for which I shall be forever grateful.

Gerald E. Wheeler is an eminent professor of naval history as well as an author, friend, and colleague. Somehow finding time between his obligations as Dean of the School of Social Sciences at San Jose State University and his own research pursuits into Admiral Thomas C. Kinkaid, he obliged me by reading my manuscript and then sharing his discerning opinions of it with me. So to Gerry Wheeler I also convey my thanks and gratitude.

Robert Emmett Ginna, Jr., became my editor at Little, Brown upon Louie Howland's departure, and Bob's expertise provided the perspective I needed to prepare the manuscript in its final form. Elisabeth Gleason Humez ("Glea" to her associates and appreciative authors) was again my copyeditor. Her meticulous craftsmanship and her skill with the English language are a joy to behold. I am among the legion of her admirers.

Many, many people assisted my research, and I have endeavored to recognize and acknowledge them in the bibliography.

I would like to thank those at the U.S. Military Academy who encouraged me with their good will and moral support, including Brigadier General Frederick A. Smith, Jr., Dean of the Academic Board; and Colonel Thomas E. Griess, Professor and Head, Department of History. Mr. Edward J. Krasnoborski, the department's cartographer, produced the maps that appear on the endpapers. Mr. Egon A. Weiss and his proficient staff at the U.S. Military Academy Library provided the facilities and services that allowed me to work productively away from the distraction and bustle of offices and classrooms. I should also like to thank Marie Capps of the library staff for providing special facilities within the archives when I especially needed them.

Given the many kinds of help I have received, nevertheless only I can be held responsible for the ultimate content of this biography, including whatever errors or omissions there may be.

Finally, and most important, I wish to acknowledge the indispensable contributions of my beloved wife, Marilyn. The thousands of pages of King manuscript, from first draft to final product, came from her typewriter. She served also as my research associate, especially in our dealings with the hundreds of retired naval officers who once served with King. This book is therefore a joint venture between husband and wife.

Thomas B. Buell

Acknowledgment of Permissions to Quote

The author is grateful to the following publishers and people for permission to quote the material cited below.

Forrestal and the Navy by Robert G. Albion and R. H. Connery. © Columbia University Press, New York, 1962. Excerpts from pages 92, 93, 98, 101, 103, and 116.

The Memoirs of General Lord Ismay by Hastings Ismay. © Viking Press, New York, 1960. Excerpt from page 253.

The Grand Alliance by Winston S. Churchill. © Houghton Mifflin, Boston, 1950. Excerpt from page 673.

Triumph and Tragedy by Winston S. Churchill. © Houghton Mifflin, Boston, 1953. Excerpts from pages 146, 147, and 343.

Fleet Admiral King: A Naval Record by Ernest J. King and Walter M. Whitehill. © W. W. Norton, New York, 1952. Excerpts from pages 638, 647, 648, 652, and 653.

Beckoning Frontiers by Marriner S. Eccles. © Sara Eccles. Excerpt from page 336.

A Sailor's Odyssey by Andrew B. Cunningham. © E. P. Dutton, New York, 1951. Excerpts from pages 446 and 612.

The Massachusetts Historical Society for permission to quote "*A Postscript to Fleet Admiral King: A Naval Record*" by Walter M. Whitehill, originally published in the *Proceedings* of the Massachusetts Historical Society, Volume 70, 1950–1953.

Robert L. Dennison, for permission to quote excerpts from pages 70 through 74 and pages 82 and 92 of his oral history.

George C. Dyer, for permission to quote excerpts from pages 203, 220, and 226 through 233 of his oral history.

Cato Glover, Jr., for permission to quote an excerpt from page 35 of his book *Command Performance with Guts.*

Fitzhugh Lee, for permission to quote excerpts from pages 76 and 77 of his oral history.

Robert B. Pirie, for permission to quote excerpts from pages 142, 147, and 148 of his oral history.

Appendixes

APPENDIX I

Cinclant Serial 053 of January 21, 1941

Subject: Exercise of Command — Excess of Detail in Orders and Instructions.

1. I have been concerned for many years over the increasing tendency — now grown almost to "standard practice" — of flag officers and other group commanders to issue orders and instructions in which their subordinates are told "how" as well as "what" to do to such an extent and in such detail that the "Custom of the service" has virtually become the antithesis of that essential element of command — "initiative of the subordinate."

2. We are preparing for — and are now close to — those active operations (commonly called war) which require the exercise and the utilization of the full powers and capabilities of every officer in command status. There will be neither time nor opportunity to do more than prescribe the several tasks of the several subordinates (to say "what", perhaps "when" and "where", and usually, for their intelligent cooperation, "why"); leaving to them — expecting and requiring of them — the capacity to perform the assigned tasks (to do the "**how**").

3. If subordinates are deprived — as they now are — of that training and experience which will enable them to act "on their own" — if they do not know, by constant practice, how to exercise "initiative of the subordinates" — if they are reluctant (afraid) to act because they are accustomed to detailed orders and instructions — if they are not habituated to think, to judge, to decide and to act for themselves in their several echelons of command — we shall be in sorry case when the time of "active operations" arrives.

4. The reasons for the current state of affairs — how did we get this way? — are many but among them are four which need men-

tion; first, the "anxiety" of seniors that everything in their commands shall be conducted so correctly and go so smoothly, that none may comment unfavorably; second, those energetic activities of staffs which lead to infringement of (not to say interference with) the functions for which the lower echelons exist; third, the consequent "anxiety" of subordinates lest their exercise of initiative, even in their legitimate spheres, should result in their doing something which may prejudice their selection for promotion; fourth, the habit on the one hand and the expectation on the other of "nursing" and "being nursed" which lead respectively to that violation of command principles known as "orders to obey orders" and to that admission of incapacity or confusion evidenced by "request instructions."

5. Let us consider certain facts; first, submarines operating submerged are constantly confronted with situations requiring the **correct** exercise of judgment, decision and action; second, planes, whether operating singly or in company, are even more often called upon to act **correctly**; third, surface ships entering or leaving port, making a landfall, steaming in thick weather, etc., can and do meet such situations while "acting singly" and, as well, the problems involved in maneuvering in formations and dispositions. Yet these same people — proven competent to do these things without benefit of "advice" from higher up — are, when grown in years and experience to be echelon commanders, all too often not made full use of in conducting the affairs (administrative and operative) of their several echelons — echelons which exist for the purpose of facilitating command.

6. It is essential to extend the knowledge and the practice of "initiative of the subordinate" in principle and in application until they are universal in the exercise of command throughout all the echelons of command. Henceforth, we must all see to it that full use is made of the echelons of command — whether administrative (type) or operative (task) — by habitually framing orders and instructions to echelon commanders so as to tell them "what to do" but not "how to do it" unless the particular circumstances so **demand.**

7. The corollaries of paragraph 6 are:

(a) adopt the premise that the echelon commanders are competent in their several command echelons unless and until they themselves prove otherwise;

(b) teach them that they are not only **expected** to be competent for their several command echelons but that it is **required** of them that they be competent;

(c) train them — by guidance and supervision — to exercise foresight, to think, to judge, to decide and to act for themselves;

(d) stop "nursing" them;

(e) Finally, train ourselves to be satisfied with "acceptable solutions" even though they are not "staff solutions" or other particular solutions that we ourselves prefer.

ERNEST J. KING

APPENDIX II

Cinclant Serial 0328 of April 22, 1941

Subject: Exercise of Command — Correct Use of Initiative.

Reference: My confidential memorandum, serial 053, dated 21 January 1941 — Subject "Exercise of Command — Excess of Detail in Orders and Instructions."

1. In the three months that have elapsed since the promulgation of the reference, much progress has been made in improving the exercise of command through the regular echelons of command — from forces through groups and units to ships. It has, however, become increasingly evident that correct methods for the exercise of initiative are not yet thoroughly understood — and practiced — by many echelon commanders.

2. The correct exercise of the principle of the initiative is essential to the application of the principle of decentralization. The latter, in turn, is premised on the basic principle known as "division of labor", which means that each does his own work in his own sphere of action or field of activity.

3. What seems to have been overlooked is that the exercise of initiative as involved in "division of labor" (as embodied in "decentralization") not only requires **labor** on the part of those who exercise any degree of command but, as well and even more particularly, on the part of those who exercise initiative. It also seems to have been overlooked that the correct exercise of initiative is applicable not only to operations but to administration and, as well, to personnel and material matters.

4. (a) Initiative means freedom to act, but it does not mean freedom to act in an offhand or casual manner. It does not mean freedom to disregard or to depart **unnecessarily** from standard procedures or practices or in-

structions. There is no degree of being "independent" of the other component parts of the whole — the Fleet.

(b) It means freedom to act only after all of one's resources in education, training, experience, skill and **understanding** have been brought to bear on the work in hand.

(c) It requires intense application in order that what is to be done shall be done as a **correlated part of a connected whole** — much as the link of a chain or a gear-wheel in a machine.

5. In order that there may be clearer understanding — and better practice — in the exercise of initiative, the following paraphrase of certain passages in the reference, together with appropriate additions, are enjoined as a guide upon all those concerned in the exercise of initiative:

". . . . . active operations (commonly called war) require the **exercise** and the utilization of the **full powers and capabilities** of every officer in command status";

"Subordinates are to become "habituated to **think,** to **judge,** to **decide** and to **act** for themselves";

It requires **hard work** — concentration of powers — to exercise command effectively and, frequently, even harder work to exercise initiative **intelligently;**

When told "what" to do — make sure that "how" you do it is effective not only in itself but as an **intelligent, essential and correlated part of a comprehensive and connected whole.**

ERNEST J. KING

APPENDIX III

Executive Order

PRESCRIBING THE DUTIES OF THE COMMANDER IN CHIEF OF THE UNITED STATES FLEET AND THE CO-OPERATIVE DUTIES OF THE CHIEF OF NAVAL OPERATIONS.

By virtue of the power vested in me as President of the United States and as Commander in Chief of the armed forces of the United States and by the Constitution and Statutes of the United States, particularly the Act of May 22, 1917, (U.S.C., title 34, sec. 212), it is hereby ordered that the Commander in Chief, United States Fleet, shall have supreme command of the operating forces comprising the several fleets of the United States Navy and the operating forces of the naval coastal frontier commands, and shall be directly responsible, under the general direction of the Secretary of the Navy, to the President of the United States therefor.

The staff of the Commander in Chief, United States Fleet, shall be composed of a Chief of Staff and of such officers and agencies as appropriate and necessary to perform duties in general as follows:

(a) Make available for evaluation all pertinent information and naval intelligence;

(b) Prepare and execute plans for current war operations;

(c) Conduct operational duties;

(d) Effect all essential communications;

(e) Direct training essential to carrying out operations;

(f) Serve as personal aides.

The Commander in Chief shall keep the Chief of Naval Operations informed of the logistic and other needs of the operating forces, and in turn the Chief of Naval Operations shall keep the Commander in Chief informed as to the extent to which the various needs can be met. Subject to the foregoing, the duties and responsibilities of the Chief of Naval Operations under the Secretary of the Navy will remain unchanged. The Chief of Naval Operations shall continue to be responsible for the preparation of war plans from the long range point of view.

In order that close liaison may be maintained with the Navy Department, the principal office of the Commander in Chief shall be in the Navy Department unless otherwise directed.

FRANKLIN D. ROOSEVELT

THE WHITE HOUSE,

December 18, 1941

(No. 8984)

(F. R. Doc. 41-9587; Filed, December 19, 1941; 12:01 p.m.)

APPENDIX IV

Executive Order

REORGANIZATION OF THE NAVY DEPARTMENT AND THE NAVAL SERVICE AFFECTING THE OFFICE OF THE CHIEF OF NAVAL OPERATIONS AND THE COMMANDER IN CHIEF, UNITED STATES FLEET

By virtue of the authority vested in me by Title I of the First War Powers Act, 1941, approved December 18, 1941 (Public Law 354, 77th Congress), and other applicable statutes, and as Commander in Chief of the Army and Navy and as President of the United States, it is hereby ordered as follows:

1. The duties of the Commander in Chief, United States Fleet, and the duties of the Chief of Naval Operations, may be combined and devolve upon one officer who shall have the title "Commander in Chief, United States Fleet, and Chief of Naval Operations", and who shall be the principal naval adviser to the President on the conduct of the War, and the principal naval adviser and executive to the Secretary of the Navy on the conduct of the activities of the Naval Establishment. While so serving he shall have the rank and title of Admiral and shall receive the pay and allowances provided by law for an officer serving in the grade of Admiral.

2. As Commander in Chief, United States Fleet, the officer holding the combined offices as herein provided shall have supreme command of the operating forces comprising the several fleets, sea-going forces, and sea frontier forces of the United States Navy and shall be directly responsible, under the general direction of the Secretary of the Navy, to the President therefor.

3. The staff of the Commander in Chief, United States Fleet, shall be composed of —

(a) A Chief of Staff, who shall while so serving have the rank, pay, and allowances of a Vice Admiral, and who, in the temporary absence or incapacity of the "Commander in Chief, United States Fleet and Chief of Naval Operations", shall act as Commander in Chief, United States Fleet;

(b) Such deputy and assistant chiefs of staff as may be necessary; and

(c) Such other officers as may be appropriate and necessary to enable the "Commander in Chief, United States Fleet, and Chief of Naval Operations" to perform as Commander in Chief, United States Fleet, the duties prescribed in Executive Order No. 8984 of December 18, 1941.

4. As Chief of Naval Operations, the officer holding the combined offices as herein provided shall be charged, under the direction of the Secretary of the Navy, with the preparation, readiness, and logistic support of the operating forces comprising the several fleets, seagoing forces and sea frontier forces of the United States Navy, and with the coordination and direction of effort to this end of the bureaus and offices of the Navy Department except such offices (other than bureaus) as the Secretary of the Navy may specifically exempt. Duties as Chief of Naval Operations shall be contributory to the discharge of the paramount duties of Commander in Chief, United States Fleet.

5. The staff of the Chief of Naval Operations shall be composed of—

(a) A Vice Chief of Naval Operations, who shall while so serving have the rank, pay and allowances of a Vice Admiral. The Vice Chief of Naval Operations shall have all necessary authority for executing the plans and policies of the "Commander in Chief, United States Fleet, and Chief of Naval Operations" so far as pertains to the duties herein prescribed for the Chief of Naval Operations. In the temporary absence or incapacity of the "Commander in Chief, United States Fleet, and Chief of Naval Operations", he shall act as Chief of Naval Operations.

(b) An Assistant to the Chief of Naval Operations with the title of Sub Chief of Naval Operations, who shall have the rank of rear admiral and while so serving shall receive the pay and allowances of a rear admiral, upper half, and such additional assistant Chiefs of Naval Operations as may be required; and

(c) Such other offices as may be considered to be appropriate and necessary for the performance of the duties at present prescribed for the Chief of Naval Operations.

6. During the temporary absence of the Secretary of the Navy, the Under Secretary of the Navy, and the Assistant Secretaries of the Navy, the "Commander in Chief, United States Fleet, and Chief of Naval Operations" shall be next in succession to act as Secretary of the Navy. In the temporary absence of all of these officers the Vice Chief of

Naval Operations and the Chief of Staff, United States Fleet, respectively, shall be next in succession to act as Secretary of the Navy.

FRANKLIN D. ROOSEVELT

THE WHITE HOUSE,

March 12, 1942.

(No. 9096)

(F. R. Doc. 42-2195; Filed, March 13, 1942; 3:20 P.M.)

APPENDIX V

King's Strategy for the Pacific War

March 5, 1942

Memorandum for the President:

1. The delineation of general areas of responsibility for operations in the Pacific is now taking place, in which it appears that we — the U.S. — will take full charge of all operations conducted eastward of the Malay Peninsula and Sumatra.

2. You have expressed the view — concurred in by all of your chief military advisers — that we should determine on a *very few* lines of military endeavor and concentrate our efforts on these lines. It is to be recognized that the *very few* lines of U.S. military effort may require to be shifted in accordance with developments but the total number should be kept at a *very few.*

3. Consideration of what war activities we (U.S.) should undertake in the Pacific requires to be premised on some examination of our (U.S.) relationship with respect to world-wide war activities — the Pacific being one part of the larger whole.

4. Other than in the Pacific our principal allies — Great Britain and Russia — are already committed to certain lines of military effort, to which our (U.S.) chief contribution in the case of Russia will continue to be munitions in general.

5. As to Britain's lines of military effort:

(a) It is apparent that we (U.S.) must enable the British to hold the citadel and arsenal of Britain itself by means of the supply of munitions, raw materials and food — and to some extent by troops, when they will release British troops to other British military areas.

(b) The Middle East is a line of British military effort which they — and we — cannot afford to let go. This effort should continue to receive our (U.S.) munitions.

(c) The India-Burma-China line of British military effort is now demanding immediate attention on their part — and will absorb its proportion of our (U.S.) munitions — in addition to the munitions which we are committed to furnish to China.

6. The chief sources of munitions for the United Nations are Britain, the U.S. and, to some degree, Russia. The chief sources of man-power for the United Nations are China, Russia, the U.S., and to less degree, the British Commonwealth. The only mobile factors are those available to Britain and to the U.S., because of their use of sea power — navies and shipping.

7. Australia — and New Zealand — are "white man's countries" which it is essential that we shall not allow to be overrun by Japanese because of the repercussions among the non-white races of the world.

8. Reverting to the premise of paragraph 2 — a *very few* lines of military endeavor — the general area that needs immediate attention — and is in our (U.S.) sphere of responsibility — is Australasia, which term is intended to include the Australian continent, its approaches from the northwest — modified ABDA area — and its approaches from the northeast and east — ANZAC area. These approaches require to be actively used — continuously — to hamper the enemy advance and/or consolidation of his advance bases.

9. Our primary concern in the Pacific is to hold Hawaii and its approaches (via Midway) from the westward and to maintain its communications with the West Coast. Our next care in the Pacific is to preserve Australasia (par. 8 above) which requires that its communications be maintained — via eastward of Samoa, Fiji and southward of New Caledonia.

10. We have now — or will soon have — "strong points" at Samoa, Suva (Fiji) and New Caledonia (also a defended fueling base at Bora Bora, Society Islands). A naval operating base is shortly to be set up in Tongatabu (Tonga Islands) to service our naval forces operating in the South Pacific. Efate (New Hebrides) and Funafuti (Ellice Islands) are projected additional "strong points."

11. When the foregoing 6 "strong points" are made reasonably secure, we shall not only be able to cover the line of communications — to Australia (and New Zealand) but — given the naval forces, air units, and amphibious troops — we can drive northwest from the New Hebrides into the Solomons and the Bismarck Archipelago after the same fashion of step-by-step advances that the Japanese used in the South China Sea. Such a line of operations will be offensive rather than passive — and will draw Japanese forces there to oppose it, thus relieving pressure elsewhere, whether in Hawaii, ABDA area, Alaska, or even India.

12. The foregoing outline (of U.S. participation in the war) points

the way to useful lines of U.S. military endeavor in the Pacific, which may be summarized in an integrated, general plan of operations, namely:

Hold Hawaii
Support Australasia
Drive northwestward from New Hebrides.

E. J. KING

APPENDIX VI

Meeting of the Combined Chiefs of Staff, 10 A.M., September 14, 1944, Main Conference Room, Château Frontenac

PRESENT

UNITED STATES	UNITED KINGDOM
Admiral Leahy	Field Marshal Brooke
General Marshall	Marshal of the Royal Air Force Portal
Admiral King	Admiral of the Fleet Cunningham
General Arnold	Field Marshal Dill
Lieutenant General Somervell	General Ismay
Vice Admiral Willson	Admiral Noble
Rear Admiral Cooke	Lieutenant General Macready
Rear Admiral McCormick	Air Marshal Welsh
Major General Handy	Major General Laycock
Major General Fairchild	
Major General Kuter	

Secretariat

Brigadier General McFarland	Major General Hollis
Captain Graves	Brigadier Cornwall-Jones
	Commander Coleridge

J.C.S. Files

Combined Chiefs of Staff Minutes

TOP SECRET

1. APPROVAL OF THE MINUTES OF THE 173D MEETING OF THE COMBINED CHIEFS OF STAFF

THE COMBINED CHIEFS OF STAFF: —

Approved the conclusions of the 173d Meeting. The detailed record of the meeting was approved, subject to later minor amendments.

2. Control of the Strategic Bomber Forces in Europe (C.C.S. 520/4)

The Combined Chiefs of Staff: —

Approved the directive in C.C.S. 520/4 as amended in C.C.S. 520/5. (Amended directive circulated as C.C.S. 520/6.)

3. British Participation in the Pacific (C.C.S. 452/26 and 452/27)

Sir Alan Brooke said that the British Chiefs of Staff were disturbed by the statement of the United States Chiefs of Staff in C.C.S. 452/27 with regard to British participation in the war against Japan. He realized that this paper had been written before the Plenary session on the previous day. He felt that it did not entirely coincide with the proposal put forward at that conference and accepted by the President. For political reasons it was essential that the British Fleet should take part in the main operations against Japan.

Admiral Leahy asked if Sir Alan Brooke's point would be met by the elimination of the words, "They consider that the initial use of such a force should be on the western flank of the advance in the Southwest Pacific." It might be that the British Fleet would be used initially in the Bay of Bengal and thereafter as required by the existing situation.

Sir Andrew Cunningham said that the main fleet would not be required in the Bay of Bengal since there were already more British forces there than required. He agreed to the deletion proposed by Admiral Leahy.

Admiral King also agreed to the deletion of these words which he felt were not relevant to the general case.

Continuing, Sir Andrew Cunningham asked the U.S. views as to the meaning of the term "balanced forces" in the final sentence of paragraph 1 of C.C.S. 452/27. He said that the British Chiefs of Staff had in mind a force of some 4 battleships, 5 to 6 large carriers, 20 light fleet carriers and CVE's and the appropriate number of cruisers and destroyers. This he would regard as a balanced force.

Admiral King stressed that it was essential for these forces to be self-supporting.

Sir Andrew Cunningham said that if these forces had their fleet train, they could operate unassisted for several months provided they had the necessary rear bases — probably in Australia. The provision of bases would be a matter for agreement.

Admiral King said that the practicability of employing these forces would be a matter for discussion from time to time.

Admiral Leahy said that he did not feel that the question for discussion was the practicability of employment but rather the matter of where they should be employed from time to time.

Sir Andrew Cunningham referred to the Prime Minister's statement that he wished the British Fleet to take part in the main operations in the Pacific. Decision with regard to this was necessary since many preliminary preparations had to be made.

Admiral King suggested that the British Chiefs of Staff should put forward proposals with regard to the employment of the British Fleet.

Sir Andrew Cunningham said that the British wish was that they should be employed in the Central Pacific.

Admiral King said that at the Plenary meeting no specific reference to the Central Pacific had been made.

Sir Alan Brooke said that the emphasis had been laid on the use of the British Fleet in the main effort against Japan.

Admiral Leahy said that as he saw it the main effort was at present from New Guinea to the Philippines and it would later move to the northward.

Admiral King said that he was in no position now to commit himself as to where the British Fleet could be employed.

Sir Charles Portal reminded the Combined Chiefs of Staff of the original offer made by the British Chiefs of Staff in C.C.S. 452/18, paragraph 9, which read:

"It is our desire in accordance with His Majesty's Government's policy, that this fleet should play its full part at the earliest possible moment in the main operations against Japan wherever the greatest naval strength is required."

When the British Chiefs of Staff spoke of the main operations against Japan they did not intend to confine this meaning to Japan itself geographically but meant rather that the fleet should take part in the main operations within the theater of war wherever they might be taking place.

Sir Andrew Cunningham stressed that the British Chiefs of Staff did not wish the British Fleet merely to take part in mopping up operations in areas falling into our hands.

Admiral Leahy said that he felt that the actual operations in which the British Fleet would take part would have to be decided in the future. It might well be that the fleet would be required for the conquest of Singapore, which he would regard as a major operation.

The Combined Chiefs of Staff then considered paragraph 2 of C.C.S. 452/27 referring to the use of a British Empire task force in the Southwest Pacific.

Sir Charles Portal said that the Prime Minister had offered the British Fleet for use in the main operations against Japan. By implication this paragraph accepted a naval task force for the Southwest Pacific, and was therefore contrary to the intention he had expressed.

Admiral King said that it was of course essential to have sufficient forces for the war against Japan. He was not, however, prepared to accept a British Fleet which he could not employ or support. In principle he wished to accept the British Fleet in the Pacific but it would be entirely unacceptable for the British main fleet to be employed for political reasons in the Pacific and thus necessitate withdrawal of some of the United States Fleet.

Sir Charles Portal reminded Admiral King that the Prime Minister had suggested that certain of the newer British capital ships should be substituted for certain of the older U.S. ships.

Sir Andrew Cunningham said that as he understood it the Prime Minister and President were in agreement that it was essential for British forces to take a leading part in the main operations against Japan.

Admiral King said that it was not his recollection that the President had agreed to this. He could not accept that a view expressed by the Prime Minister should be regarded as a directive to the Combined Chiefs of Staff.

Sir Charles Portal said that the Prime Minister felt it essential that it should be placed on record that he wished the British Fleet to play a major role in the operations against Japan.

Sir Alan Brooke said that, as he remembered it, the offer was no sooner made than accepted by the President.

Admiral King asked for specific British proposals.

Sir Charles Portal referred once more to the offer made in C.C.S. 452/18 which he had previously quoted.

Admiral Leahy said that he could see no objection whatever to this proposal. He could not say exactly where the fleet could be employed at this moment but there would be ample opportunity for its use provided it was self-supporting.

Admiral King said that the question of the British proposal for the use [of] the main fleet would have to be referred to the President before it could be accepted.

Admiral Leahy said that if Admiral King saw any objections to this proposal he should take the matter up himself with the President. It might not be wise to use the term "main fleet."

SIR ANDREW CUNNINGHAM said that the British Fleet had been offered by the Prime Minister and the President had accepted it. He was prepared to agree to the deletion of the word "main" from paragraph 1 of C.C.S. 452/27.

ADMIRAL KING said that the Prime Minister had also referred to the use of British air power in the Pacific.

GENERAL ARNOLD said that a definite answer with regard to British air help in the war against Japan could not be given now. The amount which could be absorbed would depend on the development of suitable facilities.

SIR CHARLES PORTAL said that it was, of course, impossible to be definite at the moment since the forces available would depend on the length of the war with Germany. What he would ask for was air facilities available in the bases in the Pacific so that the British could play their part. He would put forward a proposal for consideration.

GENERAL MARSHALL said that the best method would be a statement of numbers of aircraft and dates at which they would be available.

GENERAL ARNOLD agreed that this would be preferable.

Referring to paragraph 2 of C.C.S. 452/27, SIR ALAN BROOKE pointed out that this paragraph dealt with the formation of a British Empire task force which was the second alternative put forward by the British Chiefs of Staff if for any reason the support of the British Fleet in the main operations could not be accepted. Since this support had been accepted there would be no British naval forces available for the task force and British land forces could only arrive at a later date. He suggested therefore that this paragraph should be deleted.

ADMIRAL KING asked if it was intended to use the British Fleet only in the main operations and to make no contribution to a task force in the Southwest Pacific.

GENERAL MARSHALL said there were certain objections to forming a British Empire task force under General MacArthur's command at the present time. This had been proposed by General Blamey but if it were carried out between now and February of next year it would cause considerable difficulties from the point of view of land forces since the grouping of formations and the sequence of their movement had already been scheduled in accordance with future operations. The position would be different after March.

SIR ALAN BROOKE agreed that since British land forces would not be available until after Operation DRACULA it would be of no particular value to form a British task force now. The British Fleet could of course play a part in operations in the Southwest Pacific if they were required.

Sir Andrew Cunningham confirmed that there would be no objection to the British Fleet working from time to time under General MacArthur's command.

General Marshall requested that, in order to safeguard his position with regard to the immediate formation of a task force, paragraph 2 of C.C.S. 452/27 be deleted.

Sir Alan Brooke agreed. General MacArthur's plans had already been made and since no British land contribution could at present be made there was no object in retaining this paragraph.

The Combined Chiefs of Staff: —

a. Agreed that the British Fleet should participate in the main operations against Japan in the Pacific.

b. Took note of the assurance of the British Chiefs of Staff that this fleet would be balanced and self-supporting.

c. Agreed that the method of the employment of the British Fleet in these main operations in the Pacific would be decided from time to time in accordance with the prevailing circumstances.

d. Took note that in the light of *a* above, the British Chiefs of Staff withdraw their alternative proposal to form a British Empire task force in the Southwest Pacific.

e. Invited the Chief of the Air Staff to put forward, for planning purposes, a paper containing an estimate in general terms of the contribution the Royal Air Force would be prepared to make in the main operations against Japan. . . .

Extracted from *Foreign Relations of the United States: The Conference at Quebec 1944.* (Washington: G.P.O., 1972, pp. 330–335.)

APPENDIX VII

Decorations, Degrees, and Awards of Fleet Admiral King

United States Naval and Military Service Awards

Navy Cross 1920
Distinguished Service Medal with Two Gold Stars 1926, 1928, 1945
Spanish Campaign Medal 1898
Sampson Medal 1898
Mexican Service Medal 1914
Victory Medal 1918
Atlantic Fleet Clasp 1941
American Defense Service Medal with Bronze "A" 1945
American Campaign Medal 1945
World War II Victory Medal 1945
National Defense Service Medal 1945

Orders and Decorations Conferred by Foreign Governments

Croix de Guerre with Palm (Belgium) 1948
Grand Cross of the Order of the Crown with Palm (Belgium) 1948
Order of Merit, Grande Oficial (Brazil) 1943
Special Class, Order of Pao-Ting (China) 1945
Naval Order of Merit with Diploma (Cuba) 1943
Estrella Abdón Calderón, First Class (Ecuador) 1943
Croix de Guerre (France) 1944
Grand Officier de la Légion d'Honneur (France) 1944
Ouissam Alaouite Chérifien and Certificate (French Morocco) 1943
Knight Grand Cross of the Military Division of the Order of the Bath (Great Britain) 1945

Grand Cross of the Order of George I, with Swords (Greece) 1946
Order of the Crown (Italy) 1933
Grand Cross of the Military Order (Italy) 1948
Order of Orange-Nassau (Netherlands) 1948
Order of Vasco Núñez de Balboa, Grade of Commander (Panama) 1929

Postwar Awards Conferred by American Civilian Organizations

Special Congressional Gold Medal
Masonic Grand Lodge Medal for Distinguished Achievement
Pennsylvania Society Gold Medal for Distinguished Achievement
American Legion Distinguished Service Medal

Honorary Degrees

College of William and Mary, Doctor of Laws, 8 June 1942
Bowdoin College, Doctor of Science, 2 June 1945
Harvard University, Doctor of Laws, 28 June 1945
Northwestern University, Doctor of Laws, 26 October 1945
Princeton University, Doctor of Laws, 22 February 1946
Miami University (Ohio), Doctor of Laws, 2 June 1946
Oxford University, Doctor of Civil Law, 26 June 1946
Columbia University, Doctor of Laws, 21 February 1947

Bibliography

Biographers traditionally seek primary source research material relating to their subject. Fortunately, such material dealing with King (identified and explained on the following pages) is plentiful. King is a wonderful help to the biographer and historian because he preferred to communicate in writing, insisting that reports, recommendations, policy matters, and decisions be reduced to concise, unambiguous written statements. King meant what he wrote, and a single memorandum with King's signature would be the authority for a major wartime operation.

Nevertheless, there are limitations on research material associated with King's CCS and JCS activities. Many of the most important meetings were off the record, forcing one to speculate — on the basis of fragmentary information contained in the memoirs and diaries of the participants — about what went on behind closed doors. In other instances, conference reports are so abridged or otherwise altered that they fail to reflect what actually was said. The historian can be confident only in the final agreements, which were as carefully written as a legal contract. But what led to those agreements is often a mystery.

King explained some of the reasons for these imperfect records in a May 1949 letter to a JCS historian. "The available records of the JCS," wrote King, "at least for the first six months, were rather sketchy until the secretary and his deputies had been trained in extracting the meat or kernel of what the top officers were saying. Even later, the two or three other secretaries would often not get the import or gist of what was being said, because it is hard work to get the sense, and at the same time, keep pace in handwriting." The British, King went on to say, were much more adept in recording conference proceedings.

Another potential limitation is the unwieldy bulkiness of the papers relating to the JCS wartime activities. A researcher would require years of permanent residence in Washington to go through them all. Fortunately for those researchers without such time, Grace P. Hayes, a naval officer and JCS historian in the years immediately following the war, compiled a superb compendium of JCS papers related to the war against Japan, consisting of two volumes totaling 952 pages. "The record of the Joint Chiefs of Staff does exist," wrote Lieutenant Hayes in her introduction, "but in a mass of papers, minutes, memoranda, and reports immense in volume and intricate in detail. While specific data as to JCS actions may be found with relative ease, the broader relationships, causes, and consequences are beyond immediate comprehension. They become apparent only after the searching study and constructive reasoning of the historian have produced a useful synthesis."

Identified by the Historical Section of the JCS as an official history in 1953, it was at first unavailable to most historians because of its secret classification and limited distribution. It has since been declassified and was used extensively by the author, who wishes to thank and commend Grace Hayes publicly for her magnificent scholarship and her priceless contribution to the study of the JCS during the Second World War. It will soon be published by the Naval Institute Press.

A companion work is an unclassified two-volume history on the origins of the CCS and JCS and the development of the JCS committee structure. Written by Vernon E. Davis, the former head of the JCS Historical Division, it was given limited distribution by the JCS in late 1972. It too is a compendium that incorporates outstanding scholarship and is a godsend to anyone doing research on the CCS and JCS during the war. Thus my thanks also to Mr. Davis.

At one time the JCS Historical Division intended to publish a history of the JCS in the war against Germany and Italy, but for a variety of reasons the work was never undertaken. Consequently the author relied upon the authoritative volumes *Strategic Planning for Coalition Warfare 1941–1942*, by Maurice Matloff and Edwin M. Snell, and Matloff's *Strategic Planning for Coalition Warfare 1943–1944*. Louis Morton's *Strategy and Command: The First Two Years* supplemented Hayes. All the above references — Hayes, Davis, Matloff, Snell, and Morton — were supplemented by the State Department's *Foreign Relations of the United States* series, dealing with the principal CCS conferences, together with the British *Grand Strategy* series of official histories.

The text of this biography is without numerical footnotes to avoid distracting the reader, and the bibliography is restricted to a general description of the sources associated with each chapter. A fully annotated copy of the manuscript is available in the Naval Historical Collection of the Naval War College for those interested in the specific sources for each chapter.

The research material used in this biography is identified below.

Primary Unpublished Sources

Author's Collection

This collection is primarily correspondence and interviews with King's associates, friends, and family. More than 450 letters were sent to retired naval officers who once had served with King. Well over two hundred responded, several on cassette tape, providing abundant information on every aspect of King's life and career. Their naval ranks usually were not cited because they changed with time

The author interviewed many people who had been close to King either professionally or personally. These included his son, Ernest J. ("Joe") King, Jr., who in addition to his own reminiscences generously lent the author his family photo albums and permitted the author access to King's service and medical records. King's eldest daughter, Elizabeth King van den Berg, kindly shared memories of her father and family with the author. Five of King's closest friends were especially cooperative in describing his personal life: Rear Admiral and Mrs. Paul E. (Charlotte) Pihl, Mrs. Alfred R. (Betsy) Matter, and Rear Admiral and Mrs. Boynton L. Braun. King's three wartime flag secretaries provided extensive information on his professional activities: retired flag officers Neil K. Dietrich, Howard E. Orem, and George L. Russell. The latter also provided a copy of the unpublished memoirs of Francis S. Low relating to his duty under King from 1939 through the Second World War. Retired Captain Neil Almgren related his service as King's aide from 1949 through 1950.

Through the good offices of war correspondent–author Robert Sherrod, the author contacted retired correspondents Phelps H. Adams and Glen Perry. All three were members of the Surviving Veterans of the Battle of Virginia. The author visited Glen Perry, who generously lent his notes from the evening sessions with King, while Phelps Adams provided a long description of King's first session in his home. These materials, together with Nelie Bull's personal diary of the sessions (described in the Whitehill Collection), were among the most important primary sources for this biography.

The Author's Collection is deposited in the Naval Historical Collection at the Naval War College and is available to qualified researchers upon request.

Whitehill Collection

The late Walter Muir Whitehill used three primary research sources while collaborating with King in writing and publishing King's memoirs. The first source was King's handwritten reminiscences. These were typed by a yeoman and adapted by Whitehill for the text of *Fleet Admiral King: A Naval Record*. King spent nearly four years (1946–1949) writing about his prewar career, which he clearly recalled in lengthy detail. In late 1949 he turned to his wartime career, but by then his health had so deteriorated that his ability to write coherently had become impaired. Nevertheless, his memory remained intact, so that his naval aide and Whitehill together were able to extract the gist of King's wartime recollections through intensive editing.

King's reminiscences, although chronological, are rambling and unstructured, and he wrote whatever occurred to him at the moment. Important material and trivia lay side by side. Characteristically, King's reminiscences are candid — indeed, ingenuous — in such a way that his character, personality, and prejudices are revealed, sometimes unintentionally. He is, however, discreetly silent about his love life.

With official correspondence King was a discriminating writer, but his style was less rigorous when writing informally, typified by numerous exclamation points and vernacular phrases enclosed in quotation marks. Given King's haphazard postwar writing style, which worsened with his advancing age and sickness, the author has occasionally edited or paraphrased King's writing without sacrificing the flavor of his pungent expression.

A second source used by Whitehill was his postwar conversations with King, which usually occurred when the Admiral was a guest at Whitehill's home. Immediately afterward Whitehill would type a record while his memory was fresh, often recapturing King's exact comments on a given subject. These conversations were as revealing as King's written reminiscences.

Whitehill's third source was extracts from King's official papers, which often duplicate material in the Manuscript Division in the Library of Congress. This collection also contains miscellaneous material Whitehill acquired in the research for *A Naval Record*. The most important is a meticulous diary kept by Nelie Bull of the ten meetings between King and the war correspondents in Bull's Alexandria home, beginning with the first on 6 November 1942 and ending with the last on 16 April 1944. (Bull died shortly afterward, and the meetings continued in the home of Phelps Adams.) King was unusually candid during these meetings and revealed his most immediate thoughts and impressions about the war. "I went to one or two of these meetings," Robert Sherrod wrote the author, "and was amazed at King's frankness; he all but laid out next summer's battle plans." Bull's diary and Perry's notes, each kept separately and independent of the other, together substantiate King's attitude and what he said. Consequently they were a primary source of reliable information on what King was doing and thinking about during the war.

The Whitehill Collection now resides in the Naval Historical Collection of the Naval War College, with the kind permission of his wife, Jane Whitehill.

Library of Congress Collection

Most senior naval officers of the past have been notorious for their indifference to their personal papers, especially when compared to army officers. Spruance's papers, such as they were, were stored carelessly in a single cardboard box. Patton, on the other hand, had accumulated fifty file cabinets of personal papers by the time of his death. One reason for this disparity is the Navy's traditional indifference to its own history. The Navy, for example, has never published an official history of the Second World War. Morison's unofficial history, opposed at the beginning of the war by the Director of Naval History, was finally made possible when Morison appealed to his friend FDR, who ordered the Navy Department to cooperate. The Army's Office of Military History, in contrast, has published dozens of its famous "green books" dealing with the Second World War.

King, however, must have had a very early perception that he one day would have a place in history. Unlike most naval officers, he retained records of nearly everything that he wrote or that had been written to him from the time he was an ensign. After King died, his son Joe went to King's Navy Department office and discovered tens of thousands of letters and other documents in King's filing cabinets. Joe King wisely turned these papers over to the Naval Historical Foundation, a private, nonprofit organization which receives gifts for the Secretary of the Navy. The foundation in turn deposited the papers in the Manuscript Division of the Library of Congress, which organized and indexed the material into thirty-seven document containers. The author made extensive use of this collection and considers it essential when conducting research on King.

Franklin D. Roosevelt Library

It is always a pleasure to do research in Hyde Park, because library director Dr. Bill Emerson and his expert staff do everything possible to welcome, aid, and assist visiting scholars and researchers. Given Roosevelt's involvement with the Navy and with wartime strategy, his papers provided important material relating to King of great value to the author. Another important primary source in the library is a series of unpublished reminiscences by Admiral John L. McCrea, Roosevelt's naval aide in the early war years, which the Admiral kindly made available to the author. In addition to his experiences as an aide, McCrea also provides a fascinating account of taking Roosevelt aboard USS *Iowa* on the first leg of the President's journey to Teheran.

When Churchill first visited the White House in December 1941, he brought with him a miniature map room, which intrigued Roosevelt. Roosevelt shortly ordered a map room of his own, in order to display the course of the war and to serve as the White House communication center. Movie star and reserve naval lieutenant Robert Montgomery had been in London and knew the system. With British help, Montgomery established a similar map room for the President, supervised by Roosevelt's naval aide and continually manned by army and naval officers. Roosevelt visited the map room twice daily and received briefings before each major operation. Access was restricted to the President, the JCS, and Roosevelt's naval and military aides. Hopkins was the only other civilian who was routinely admitted. Nevertheless, King's map room was considered even more exclusive.

Roosevelt had cleverly arranged that the Army would handle all outgoing messages and the Navy all incoming messages. Thus either service, should it eavesdrop, would have only an incomplete picture of the President's private communications. On the other hand, Roosevelt monitored all the important Army-Navy messages to keep himself apprised of what his armed forces were doing. Consequently, the White House map room files are a particularly extensive and useful source of information on the conduct of the war.

Navy Department Files

Dr. Dean Allard, head of the Operational Archives Branch of the Naval Historical Center, and his able staff once again provided their consistently splendid assistance to the author. Their most important primary source on King is the recently opened and declassified COMINCH "zero-zero" files. This file contains thousands of messages to and from King's headquarters, many once classified top secret. Among the most important are personal messages between King and his overseas commanders, especially Nimitz. When reading these original messages with King's comments and initials, one can imagine the war as King experienced it, for it was through these messages that King was apprised of what was happening in the world outside his headquarters. There are, however, several unexplained gaps and missing messages, especially on the Battle of Midway once the fighting started. Nevertheless, these message files, together with the official COMINCH letter files, are an inexhaustible source which historians should be able to mine indefinitely.

Another important primary source was the minutes, agendas, and related documents of the King-Nimitz conferences held throughout the war, made available on microfilm to the author. These were supplemented and verified by the rough handwritten notes kept by the conference recorder, on file in King's papers in the Library of Congress.

Naval Institute Oral History Collection

Dr. John T. Mason, Jr., has established an impressive oral history program at the U.S. Naval Institute in Annapolis. The collection continues to grow in importance owing to Jack Mason's skillful and sympathetic interviews of important retired naval officers. He has been particularly attentive to gathering material on King, which he made readily available to the author, consisting of extracts from interviews with some twenty-three retired officers who had associated with King in the past. These oral histories were particularly useful to the author.

Columbia University Oral History Collection

This collection was first sponsored by the Director of Naval History and over the years has accumulated a number of oral histories of prominent naval officers. It was used extensively by the author for his Spruance biography and was equally important in providing material on King. The collection is capably and efficiently supervised by Elizabeth Mason, the wife of Jack Mason. Together they form a first-class team of oral historians who have helped the author in his research for many, many years.

Published Sources

The books listed below were used in varying degrees by the author. The list is not intended to include all published works that might pertain to King. Abbreviations in parentheses indicate references in the bibliographical notes for each chapter, which follow.

Abbazia, Patrick. *Mr. Roosevelt's Navy: The Private War of the U.S. Atlantic Fleet, 1939–1942*. Annapolis: Naval Institute Press, 1975. (*Abbazia*)

Albion, Robert G., and Robert H. Connery. *Forrestal and the Navy*. New York: Columbia University Press, 1962. (*Albion and Connery*)

Alden, John D. *The American Steel Navy*. Annapolis: Naval Institute Press, 1972. (*Alden*)

Arnold, Henry H. *Global Mission*. New York: Harper and Brothers, 1949. (*Arnold*)

Ballantine, Duncan S. *U.S. Naval Logistics in the Second World War*. Princeton: Princeton University Press, 1949. (*Ballantine*)

Blair, Clay, Jr. *Silent Victory: The U.S. Submarine War against Japan*. Philadelphia: Lippincott, 1975. (*Blair*)

Blum, John M. *V Was for Victory: Politics and American Culture during World War II*. New York: Harcourt Brace Jovanovich, 1976. (*Blum*)

Bryant, Arthur. *The Turn of the Tide*. Garden City: Doubleday, 1957. (*Bryant I*)

———. *Triumph in the West.* Garden City: Doubleday, 1959. (*Bryant II*)

Buell, Thomas B. *The Quiet Warrior: A Biography of Admiral Raymond A. Spruance.* Boston: Little, Brown, 1974. (*Buell*)

Butler, J. R. M., and J. M. A. Gwyer. *Grand Strategy*, Volume III. *June 1941–August 1942.* London: Her Majesty's Stationery Office, 1964. (*Butler and Gwyer*)

Churchill, Winston S. *The Gathering Storm.* Boston: Houghton Mifflin, 1948. (*Churchill I*)

———. *Their Finest Hour.* Boston: Houghton Mifflin, 1949. (*Churchill II*)

———. *The Grand Alliance.* Boston: Houghton Mifflin, 1950. (*Churchill III*)

———. *The Hinge of Fate.* Boston: Houghton Mifflin, 1950. (*Churchill IV*)

———. *Closing the Ring.* Boston: Houghton Mifflin, 1951. (*Churchill V*)

———. *Triumph and Tragedy.* Boston: Houghton Mifflin, 1953. (*Churchill VI*)

Coakley, Robert W., and Richard M. Leighton. *Global Logistics and Strategy 1943–1945.* Washington: U.S. Government Printing Office, 1968. (*Coakley and Leighton*)

Connery, Robert H. *The Navy and the Industrial Mobilization in World War II.* Princeton: Princeton University Press, 1951. (*Connery*)

Cunningham, Andrew B. *A Sailor's Odyssey.* New York: Dutton, 1951. (*Cunningham*)

Dyer, George C. *The Amphibians Came to Conquer: The Story of Admiral Richmond Kelly Turner.* Washington: U.S. Goverment Printing Office, 1972. (*Dyer*)

Ehrman, John. *Grand Strategy*, Volume V. *August 1943–September 1944.* London: Her Majesty's Stationery Office, 1956. (*Ehrman*)

Furer, Julius A. *Administration of the Navy Department in World War II.* Washington: U.S. Government Printing Office, 1959. (*Furer*)

Howard, Michael. *Grand Strategy*, Volume IV. *August 1942–September 1943.* London: Her Majesty's Stationery Office, 1972. (*Howard*)

Ismay, Hastings Lionel. *The Memoirs of General Lord Ismay.* New York: Viking, 1960. (*Ismay*)

King, Ernest J., and Walter Muir Whitehill. *Fleet Admiral King: A Naval Record.* New York: Norton, 1952. (*King and Whitehill*)

Leahy, William D. *I Was There.* New York: McGraw-Hill, 1950. (*Leahy*)

Loewenheim, Francis L., Harold D. Langley, and Manford Jones, eds.

Roosevelt and Churchill: Their Secret Wartime Correspondence. New York: Saturday Review Press/Dutton, 1975. (*Loewenheim*)

Lundstrom, John B. *The First South Pacific Campaign: Pacific Fleet Strategy December 1941–June 1942.* Annapolis: Naval Institute Press, 1976. (*Lundstrom*)

Matloff, Maurice. *Strategic Planning for Coalition Warfare 1943–1944.* Washington: U.S. Government Printing Office, 1959. (*Matloff*)

——— and Edwin M. Snell. *Strategic Planning for Coalition Warfare 1941–1942.* Washington: U.S. Government Printing Office, 1953. (*Matloff and Snell*)

Millis, Walter, ed. *The War Reports of Marshall, Arnold, and King.* Philadelphia: Lippincott, 1947. (*War Reports*)

Morison, Samuel E. *History of United States Naval Operations in World War II.* 15 vols. Boston: Atlantic–Little, Brown, 1947–1962. (*Morison, I–XV*)

Morton, Lewis. *Strategy and Command: The First Two Years.* Washington: U.S. Government Printing Office, 1962. (*Morton*)

Pogue, Forrest C. *George C. Marshall: Ordeal and Hope 1939–1942.* New York: Viking, 1965. (*Pogue I*)

———. *George C. Marshall: Organizer of Victory 1943–1945.* New York: Viking, 1973. (*Pogue II*)

Potter, E. R. *Nimitz.* Annapolis: Naval Institute Press, 1976. (*Potter*)

——— and C. W. Nimitz, eds. *Sea Power: A Naval History.* Englewood Cliffs: Prentice-Hall, 1960. (*Potter and Nimitz*)

Reynolds, Clark G. *The Fast Carriers: The Forging of an Air Navy.* Huntington, N.Y.: Krieger, 1978. (*Reynolds*)

Richardson, James O., and George C. Dyer. *On the Treadmill to Pearl Harbor: The Memoirs of Admiral James O. Richardson.* Washington: U.S. Government Printing Office, 1973. (*Richardson*)

Sherwood, Robert E. *Roosevelt and Hopkins: An Intimate History.* Revised edition. New York: Harper & Brothers, 1950. (*Sherwood*)

Smith, Holland M. *Coral and Brass.* New York: Scribner's, 1949. (*Smith*)

Sprout, Harold, and Margaret Sprout. *The Rise of American Naval Power 1776–1918.* Princeton: Princeton University Press, 1967. (*Sprout*)

U.S. Congress, House Appropriations Committee. *Appropriation Hearings 1933–1934.* 73rd Cong., 1st and 2nd Sess., 1933–1934. (*Hearings I*)

———, House Naval Affairs Committee. *Hearings before Committee on Naval Affairs of House of Representatives on Sundry Legislation Affecting the Naval Establishment 1933–1934.* 73rd Cong., 1st and 2nd Sess., 1933–1934. (*Hearings II*)

U.S. Navy Department. *Register of Commissioned and Warrant Officers of the United States Navy and Marine Corps.* Washington: U.S. Government Printing Office, various years. (*Register*)

U.S. Department of State. *Foreign Relations of the United States: The Conferences at Washington, 1941–1942, and Casablanca 1943.* Washington: U.S. Government Printing Office, 1968. (*FRUS 1941–1943*)

———. *Foreign Relations of the United States: The Conferences at Washington and Quebec 1943.* Washington: U.S. Government Printing Office, 1970. (*FRUS Washington/Quebec 1943*)

———. *Foreign Relations of the United States: The Conferences at Cairo and Teheran 1943.* Washington: U.S. Government Printing Office, 1961. (*FRUS Cairo/Teheran*)

———. *Foreign Relations of the United States: The Conference at Quebec 1944.* Washington: U.S. Government Printing Office, 1972. (*FRUS Quebec 1944*)

———. *Foreign Relations of the United States: The Conferences at Malta and Yalta 1945.* Washington: U.S. Government Printing Office, 1955. (*FRUS Yalta*)

———. *Foreign Relations of the United States: The Potsdam Conference.* Washington: U.S. Government Printing Office, 1960. (*FRUS Potsdam*)

Wheeler, Gerald E. *Admiral William Veazie Pratt, U.S. Navy: A Sailor's Life.* Washington: U.S. Government Printing Office, 1974. (*Wheeler*)

Wilson, Eugene E. *Slipstream: The Autobiography of an Air Craftsman.* New York: McGraw-Hill, 1950. (*Wilson*)

Unpublished Sources

Albion, Robert G. "Makers of Naval Policy 1798–1947." Unpublished manuscript ca. 1950, Harvard University Library, microfilm #62-380. This was intended as an official U.S. Navy history of the naval establishment but was abruptly terminated without explanation by the Director of Naval History in 1950. Original ms. was destroyed. Will be published by Naval Institute Press. (*Albion*)

Davis, Vernon E. "The History of the Joint Chiefs of Staff in World War II: Organizational Development." 2 vols. Unpublished official history given limited distribution by the JCS in 1972. The most authoritative source for the creation, development, and organization of the JCS during the Second World War. (*Davis*)

Hayes, Grace P. "The History of the Joint Chiefs of Staff in World War II: The War against Japan." 2 vols. Unpublished official history given limited distribution (50 copies) in 1954 with a Secret classification. Declassified in 1971. Provides a synthesis of all JCS and CCS meetings dealing with the war in the Pacific and indirectly with the war in the CBI and European theaters. It is the most authoritative source readily available to the researcher and will be published by the Naval Institute Press. (*Hayes*)

Published Articles

Clark, J. J. "Navy Sundowner Par Excellence," *U.S. Naval Institute Proceedings* (June 1971).

Davis, Forrest. "King's Way to Tokyo," *Saturday Evening Post* (9 December 1944).

King, Ernest J. "Some Ideas about Organization Aboard Ship," *U.S. Naval Institute Proceedings* (March 1909).

———. "The United States Naval Engineering Experiment Station, Annapolis, Maryland," *Journal of the American Society of Naval Engineers*, vol. 25, no. 3 (August 1913).

———. "Some Ideas about the Effects of Increasing the Size of Battleships," *U.S. Naval Institute Proceedings* (March 1919).

———. Dudley W. Knox, and William S. Pye. "Report and Recommendations of a Board Appointed by the Bureau of Navigation Regarding the Instruction and Training of Line Officers," *U.S. Naval Institute Proceedings* (August 1920).

———. "A 'Wrinkle or Two' in Handling Men," *U.S. Naval Institute Proceedings* (March 1923).

———. "Salvaging U.S.S. *S-51*," *U.S. Naval Institute Proceedings* (February 1927).

Norton, Douglas M. "The Open Secret: The U.S. Navy in the Battle of the Atlantic April–December 1941," *Naval War College Review* (January–February 1974).

Potter, E. B. "The Command Personality," *U.S. Naval Institute Proceedings* (January 1969).

Sanders, Harry. "King of the Oceans," *U.S. Naval Institute Proceedings* (August 1974).

Tate, J. R. "Comment and Discussion," *U.S. Naval Institute Proceedings* (April 1975), pp. 75–77.

Thorndike, Joseph J., Jr. "King of the Atlantic," *Life* (24 November 1941).

Whitehill, Walter Muir. "A Postscript to *Fleet Admiral King: A Naval Record*," *Proceedings* of the Massachusetts Historical Society, vol. 70 (1950–1953).

Bibliographical Notes

Chapter 1: In the Beginning

In the spring of 1946, about six months after his retirement, King agreed to collaborate with Walter Muir Whitehill in order to produce King's autobiography. Some months later King began writing his memoirs. Those dealing with his boyhood and with the Naval Academy were the primary sources for this chapter, supplemented with King's miscellaneous memoranda of recollections and reminiscences. These memoirs contain extraordinary detail, ranging from King's ancestry to his daily activities as a naval cadet.

Charlotte Pihl, Elizabeth King van den Berg, and Joe King provided information on King's early years. Boynton Braun, a native of Lorain, told the author about Lorain and King's family, whom he had known as a boy. Professor Theodore Ropp of Duke University provided information about the political, social, and economic characteristics of Lorain and the surrounding areas of northern Ohio. Mrs. Lucy K. Hatch sent the author letters and photographs that had passed between her mother, Leona Doane, and King.

During the war King frequently wrote to friends in Lorain and often recalled events about his boyhood. The author used several of these letters, which are contained in the Ernest J. King Collection, Library of Congress, Manuscript Division (hereafter cited as LCMD). King was proud that he was a local boy who made good, and he obviously was pleased and flattered by the city's adulation during the war. It would become a continuing love affair between King and the people of Lorain.

King's temper was apparent to everyone at Annapolis, and in later years he wrote to a Navy junior about one of his more spectacular displays. "I was the 'four-striper' that year," wrote King, "and accordingly of some consequence in the battalion. For sail drill I was port captain of the main top. The main topsail yard (and main topsail) of the *Chesapeake* were very large, even somewhat out of proportion to the rest of the yards. When furling sail it was always a race to see who could complete the furling in the quickest time — which handicapped those who were furling the main topsail. On the day in question, while busy furling sail, someone was jiggling the topsail buntwhip which did not lighten the labors of those who were trying to stow the large and unwieldy bunt.

"Your father, standing on the horse-block with his trumpet, directed appropriate remarks to the main topsail yard as to our lack of speed and efficiency. When he had done this for about the third time, I turned on the foot ropes and said, 'We will get the . . . blank, blank . . . topsail furled if you will stop the . . . blank, blank . . . jigging of the topsail buntwhip.' I can see the people on deck now — eyes popping out of their heads — mouths wide open — waiting for the thunder and lightning to strike — me. But what happened was that your father leaped down off the horse-block, ran to the main fife-rail where he stopped the . . . blank, blank . . . jigging of the topsail buntwhip.

"Believe it or not, that ended the incident — no words to me — no report! We could only assume that your father heeded my cry of distress because he sensed it to be genuine — because I spoke in language that voiced an appeal which he understood as coming from one who felt he needed help."

Such episodes undoubtedly confirmed in King's mind that his outbursts were justified if he spoke against a wrong or an injustice. But King's bluntness went to extremes, because of his sense of self-righteousness and an undisciplined temper. Tact and discretion too often lost out to emotional excesses, especially in his early career. Together with his intellectual arrogance and lack of humility, King simply considered that he had more brains than anyone else in the Navy and acted accordingly.

Chapter 2: Learning

King's memoirs do not attempt to conceal his problems with drinking and insubordination during his early years. Without embellishment or apology he states what he did, in a way that typifies King's style of candor. His first years at sea following graduation, described in this chapter, are therefore drawn primarily from these typescript memoirs and from memoranda of conversations between King and Whitehill. The descriptions of the Navy at the turn of the century are from *Alden* and *Sprout.* King's vow to acquire toughness is related in the unpublished memoirs of Francis Low, based upon a conversation he had with King. The author visited and corresponded with Charles A. Focht, who served as a young sailor in King's division aboard *Cincinnati* and still cherished the memories. Other letters between King and his *Cincinnati* sailors are contained in the LCMD.

Chapter 3: Maturing

King seemed compelled to recite instances of his misbehavior in his memoirs, although many did not become published in his book. "Please don't think I was one of those people who was always getting into 'trouble,' " he wrote, "but I must tell you about my incident with A.W. Grant while I was on duty in the Seamanship Department." This narrative was the basis for the description in the chapter of his fight with Grant.

Thus King's typescript memoirs were again the primary source for this chapter, supplemented by memoranda of his conversations with Whitehill. King's concern about his personal appearance were cited both in the memoirs and in an article by Vice Admiral Harry Sanders in the August 1974 issue of the *Naval Institute Proceedings.* The article was illustrated by an after-dinner photo of the official party aboard USS *Augusta* during the Argentia conference in August 1941. All were uncovered save King. "Admiral King was not the only bald or balding guest," Sanders noted, "but he was the only one sensitive enough on the subject to keep his covered."

In his memoirs King never mentioned his feelings about Mattie, except for a brief paragraph relating his long weekend train ride to visit her when they were first married. In the author's conversations and letters with naval officers who had served with King, few told anything (other than rumors) about his private life, even those who had dated his daughters. Consequently, friends and family were the primary source of information on the Kings' husband-wife relationship. Charlotte Pihl was undoubtedly King's closest — perhaps his only — confidant. At the same time she also knew Mattie, for the Kings and the Pihls had socialized as couples. Charlotte Pihl is a remarkably intelligent woman, wise in the ways of people and politics, and extremely perceptive. Numerous and continuing interviews with Mrs. Pihl thus provided an unusually candid insight into King's career, personality, and family life.

Chapter 4: Versatility

King's extraordinary intellectual activities were apparent in his fitness reports. Their format allowed King to cite what he was doing beyond his normal duties. For instance, while executive officer of the Experiment Station at Annapolis, King wrote that he was studying the "science of war, organization, and administration." At Annapolis he also took Naval War College correspondence courses and wrote an article about the Experiment Station in the *Journal of the American Society of Naval Engineers*, August 1913. His studies did not abate when he went to sea in destroyers. Indeed, King directed a correspondence course for the entire flotilla. Just before going to Mayo's staff, King completed one entire series of War College courses and began yet another. These are amazing accomplishments, for the attrition rate was high. Few officers ever finished, because the work was tedious and officers had little time and less inspiration. Despite his strenuous responsibilities as a division commander and commanding officer, King found the time. As King noted in an early 1915 fitness report, he was also reading "in military and naval history, strategy and tactics." Few could match such a performance.

King's typescript memoirs were again long and detailed and again were the most important single source document for this chapter. The author's interviews with King's children, Elizabeth and Joe, provided background on King's family life at Annapolis. Frederick H. Schneider, one of King's post–Second World War aides, supplied information on King's financial affairs. *Wheeler* was valuable for details on Sims and his flotilla when King was commanding *Cassin*.

King assumed that Osterhaus had recommended him to Mayo. Years later King commented, "Mayo was the man for me." Reflecting on why he turned down two other offers from flag officers, King told Whitehill in July 1949, "I was looking for the main chance. Old friends said to me, 'Don't get staff duty just to be on a staff. Look over the fellow you are going to work for.'"

Observed Whitehill: "King did."

Chapter 5: The First World War

There were a variety of sources for King's activities during the First World War. His typescript memoirs contain vivid descriptions of his work on Mayo's staff, his own thoughts about the war, and his opinions of the flag officers of that day. Mayo and Osterhaus were clearly his favorites. The others ranked far below in his esteem. *Wheeler* corroborated King's own version of the inspection of Sims's headquarters in Europe. Leo H. Thebaud wrote the author about his impressions of King as an up-and-coming staff officer.

King's insistence that Mayo was a predominant influence on his own career is intriguing. The two men were unlike both in temperament and in style of command, yet King implies that he modeled himself after Mayo. Perhaps King liked Mayo because he saw in the older man what a flag officer should be. That King could never emulate Mayo apparently in no way lessened King's respect and admiration. Paradoxically, King resented anyone who treated him as he treated others, yet there is little evidence that he tried very hard to be more considerate or patient with other people. Throughout his life King would be a harsh and often intolerant judge of character, but his memoirs are mute on his own self-appraisal — other than when as an ensign he vowed to shed his softness and become a tough naval officer.

Chapter 6: Peace and Command

Primary sources became more diverse and abundant for this chapter. Many retired officers remembered working for King at New London and provided anecdotal information to the author. King's LCMD papers contain scores of letters and other documents relating to his command of the submarine base. His typescript memoirs are again long and explicit.

The official Knox-Pye-King report became lost and disappeared in the Navy Department, King later noted, but he had "arranged" for it to be published in the *Naval Institute Proceedings.* A footnote to the *Proceedings* version stated, "Published by permission of the Navy Department for the information of the service. The Report of the Board has been approved, but the shortage of officers will not permit the recommendations to be carried into effect at present." The board was not identified by name, but everyone knew who they were.

The lowly status of *Bridge* manifested the Navy's attitude toward matters of logistics. The Naval War College taught the subject but once (1926–1927) before the Second World War. Logistics was too dull and tedious to interest naval officers. Ambitious officers served on warships and were unconcerned with the details of providing fuel, food, and ammunition to a distant fleet. King typically wanted to leave *Bridge* and anything else relating to logistics as soon as possible.

King dramatically improved the New London base despite lack of funds, attesting to his innovativeness and ingenuity. A rear admiral inspected in late July 1925 and wrote the kind of report that boosted King on his way to flag rank. The admiral reported, for instance, "The Base shows a progressive increase in efficiency. Levelling of grounds and planting of grass has added to the appearance and prevents flying of dust all over the Base. Large amount of steam piping has been placed in conduits largely constructed by Base Force, with a consequent economy, this with improved operation of power plant has made possible the carrying of load by one boiler instead of two as previously. . . .

"Marked progress has been made in the test of personnel sent to the school, as to mental and intellectual qualifications, with a view to the elimination of those unfit. This has had excellent results and has eliminated men who were not fit for submarines and whose intelligence was such as to make effort to train them a waste of time. . . .

"The curriculum of the school has been improved as experience warranted and now shows a proper balance between practical and theoretical work. . . .

"All enlisted personnel on arrival are required to take the educational courses of the Bureau of Navigation up to the rate they hold. The effect has been excellent, shows those deficient, and improves the efficiency of others. . . .

"The Commanding Officer and personnel are to be congratulated on the excellent appearance of the Base and the progress made since last inspection. There is a general appearance of interest which is very creditable."

Many naval officers did not know what to make of King's work on salvaging *S-51*. Perhaps some were unhappy about the publicity and blamed King. As a submarine salvage was so unprecedented, probably those in Washington could not comprehend what King was doing at sea off Block Island, or what they did know was gleaned from newspapers. A letter to King from Rear Admiral Montgomery M. Taylor in July 1926 is one example of the prevailing ambivalence.

"It is a little late," wrote Taylor, "but I want to congratulate you on your success with the S-51. In spite of the curious articles in the newspapers and the misinformation they spread as to submarines, there is a general idea here that yours is the greater part of the credit. It was a fine piece of work."

King was uncharacteristically modest and more than generous in his praise of his salvage team. "I wish to thank you very much indeed," he replied to Taylor, "for your very kind remarks in your letter of 20 July about the success of the S-51 salvage operations. I am just completing the report and recommendations in regard to the personnel who particularly distinguished themselves and hope that the people in the Department will not be surprised at the perhaps radical recommendations which I have seen fit to make, but I hope that the report will convey some idea of what the individual officers and men actually did."

Having seen brave men perform heroic deeds, King had become emotionally involved and wanted them rewarded. During the Second World War he was isolated in his Washington office from those who were fighting. His attitude changed. As will be seen in later chapters, recognition and awards were grudgingly given under King's regime as COMINCH.

For those seeking additional information on submarines during the 1920s and on the salvage of the *S-51*, the reader is referred respectively to *Blair* and to King's report in the February 1927 *Naval Institute Proceedings*. A more recent source is John C. Niedermair's oral history at the U.S. Naval Institute.

Chapter 7: Aviation Begins

Flag officers during the interwar period were older than they are now. When King first heard (after salvaging *S-4*) that he had received votes from a flag selection board, King regarded himself as "too young" at age fifty to be seriously considered. Most flag officers today are in their mid-to-late forties when promoted from captain. Early or "deep" selection, so common today, was almost never done when King was a captain. Everyone knew he would have to wait until he entered the selection zone with his entire class.

King's memoirs do not mention that Moffet canceled King's first orders to *Lexington* in July 1928. For example, *King and Whitehill*, pp. 206–207, relate King's dismay at being ordered to Washington as Moffet's assistant but imply that King's unhappiness stemmed from his abrupt relief as acting Commander, Aircraft Squadrons, Scouting Fleet. King's service record, however, contains orders and correspondence that reveal that, for at least a few weeks, King thought he would soon command the *Lexington*. This is one instance that illustrates the hazards of relying exclusively on a protagonist's memoirs for accurate information.

Ideally, then, the biographer and historian seek substantiating evidence to find out what happened and why. Although King's typescript memoirs were again a primary source, there were other important primary sources, as well: King's service record; his LCMD papers; the oral history of George van Deurs, a fellow student at Pensacola; letters from King's Pensacola flight instructors; and letters from those who served with him aboard USS *Wright*.

Chapter 8: *Lexington*

The large numbers of officers who served in *Lexington*, either in ship's company or in embarked squadrons, were a primary research source. Those who knew King seemed eager to talk about him. Many responded within days to the author's queries. As certain events seemed to stand out in their memories, their letters often corroborated each other, a fortunate circumstance that reassures a historian seeking accuracy. The aviators' recollections are unusually precise because aviators were required to keep flight logs, which they habitually retained after retirement. Using these to refresh their memories, the *Lexington* aviators remembered King vividly.

Among the many officers who did respond, the author wishes particularly to thank Robert A. Heinlein for his extraordinary time and effort in explaining King and the life aboard *Lexington* for the author's enlightenment. Several oral histories as well were useful, including those of John H. Hoover, Kleber H. Masterson, John J. Ballentine, Fitzhugh Lee, and Gerald F. Bogan.

As in earlier chapters, King's typescript memoirs continued to be valuable. King's paradoxical personal life is conspicuously absent, however. His reminiscence about the desert trip with Mattie is one of the few instances, in hundreds upon hundreds of pages of memoirs, that King even suggests any feelings toward his family. Apparently his family was a very private matter to him. There is no doubt in the minds of his closest friends, Charlotte Pihl and Betsy Matter, that King respected his wife and loved his children. Why, then, did he risk embarrassing them publicly? His marital infidelity and philandering were common knowledge. How King squared such moral conflicts in his own mind is a mystery.

Chapter 9: The New Admiral

King's reactionary political views, expressed in his Naval War College thesis, were not unique among naval officers. Spruance, for example, felt much the same way. The interwar period was frustrating because of public apathy and want of appropriations. Hard-pressed officers became embittered at the democratic processes that denied them support. The naval profession was in their minds a noble calling, unappreciated by civilians. Furthermore, naval officers were deliberately aloof from politics and took pride in not voting. The result was isolation from society and scorn for the civilian way of doing things.

The circumstances of King's promotion to rear admiral were confused in the minds of many retired officers who wrote the author. Many mistakenly assumed that King had been passed over and that Roosevelt had interceded in his behalf. In reality, King was selected early. Retired Vice Admiral Alan R. McCann was secretary of the flag selection board, and he verified that King received a unanimous vote.

Another area of confusion concerns the competition between King and Towers to become Chief of the Bureau of Aeronautics. One knowledgeable retired officer recalled that Towers had already received his orders, which were later canceled in favor of King. All documentary evidence, however, substantiates that King was the only person that Roosevelt nominated. These kinds of contradictions highlight the fallibility of human memory.

King's troubles before the Ayers subcommittee, investigating excess profits in the aviation industry, were related to the author by Admiral Arthur W. Radford, a former chairman of the JCS, who was known for his own skill in dealing with Congress. King himself admitted he was a poor public speaker and inexperienced in the ways of Congress when he headed the bureau. Still, King accomplished a great deal during his bureau tour, all nicely recorded in his final report, "Résumé of the Progress in Naval Aviation during the past three years (May, 1933 to June 1936)," on file in the LCMD.

The primary sources for this chapter included King's typescript memoirs, letters from retired naval officers, *Albion*, interviews with Paul Pihl and Betsy Matter, Navy Department correspondence in the Library of Congress and FDR Library, and the oral history of John J. Ballentine.

Chapter 10: Home Stretch

King's contributions to naval air warfare tactics were substantial. Much of his written carrier doctrine served as a basis for carrier operations during the Second World War. Not everything worked. King's "Experimental Carrier Type Tactics No. 1-39" envisioned six carriers in proximity during flight operations, a concept that did not prove practicable.

As Leahy's retirement as CNO drew near, everyone speculated about his replacement. The fawning and preening in front of Roosevelt aboard *Houston* must have been repugnant to King. "I noted that most of the admirals were trying to please Mr. Roosevelt so hard that it was obvious," King wrote in his memoirs. Rear Admiral Claude Bloch — a fixer — came over to King and asked, "Why don't you go over and speak to the President?"

"I have," King replied. "If he wants to ask me anything, I am right here." King later commented, "I was afraid that he might have thought I was trying to 'grease' him, which I had never done in forty years of service."

J. O. Richardson, then Chief of the Bureau of Navigation, joined with Leahy and Swanson in not recommending King for promotion to four stars. Yet in his memoirs, Richardson gratuitously asserts that he so admired King that he wanted him on the General Board to have him available on short notice should his services suddenly be required. His apologia is suspect, for he implies that King's later ascendancy was all part of Richardson's master plan. Outstanding flag officers who still had a future simply were not sent to the General Board.

King must have been in a foul mood once he had been passed over. His maliciousness toward others is one example. *Lexington* had a wicked, unpredictable roll while underway, but it could also be bad in port. In April 1939 *Lexington* anchored in Hampton Roads, Virginia, following Fleet Problem XX. King's daughter Martha lived at nearby Fortress

Monroe with her Army husband, Fred Smith. A gale was brewing, but King still invited the two for lunch, together with Martha's father-in-law (a major general who commanded the base) and his wife. The four came aboard after a frightening ride in King's barge across stormy waters. "Ernie was delighted," recalled the boat officer, Cato Glover, "and, as the Lex rolled and tossed, the Smiths got greener and greener around the gills. As the guests soon became too seasick to look at food, the Admiral waxed more and more jovial. At long last, he was now proving to the Army that life in the Navy was not all 'beer and skittles.' That performance was almost cruel enough to be sadistic, but it didn't surprise me."

Retired Captain Paul L. deVos told the author about one of King's last nights in command of the carrier force. King allegedly was drinking at the officers' club on North Island and feeling sorry for himself. A drunken junior officer accosted King and called him a has-been on his way to the General Board. King stared at the upstart. Then with dignity and coldness he said, "Young man, stand at attention. You are looking at the future Commander in Chief of the United States Fleet." Everyone laughed at King's presumptuousness.

King spent his last night in command drinking with his staff until five in the morning. Retired Admiral Charles D. Griffin remembered a staff meeting at 0700 with King looking chipper and the staff bedraggled. After the change of command ceremony, King spoke to his staff for the last time. "Don't cheer, boys," he said. "I'll be back."

Chapter 11: Resurrection

One of the minor mysteries of King's resurrection is the circumstances that led Charles Edison to ask for King as a tour guide. Edison's aide, the late Morton Deyo, claimed that he had suggested King to Edison. Yet Edison's aide, Robert H. Rice, told the author that he specifically recalled being told by Edison that it was Roosevelt's idea. In any event, it was the beginning of King's return to power.

King and Stark, if not friends, at least were on good terms. King relates in his memoirs that Stark was almost apologetic when he, and not King, became CNO in 1939. There is solid evidence that Stark admired King's professional competence and knew King was being wasted on the General Board. It was through Stark that King ascended to command of the Atlantic Fleet in 1941, and it was also through Stark that King was so frequently summoned to Washington for consultation and advice. Whether he realized it or not, Stark was setting the stage for King to replace him once war began.

King's familiarity with military history helped him to realize that he had to allow his Atlantic Fleet subordinates to use their initiative. He recalled that Napoleon's marshals were great fighters but had never participated in strategic planning. That was Napoleon's exclusive province. But when the French army was spread across Europe, Napoleon could not be everywhere. The marshals had to think for themselves (as in Spain) and got "messed up," according to King. The same thing could have happened in the Atlantic Fleet if King had not changed his ways.

Although the author used letters from King's staff officers as a primary research source, such letters still had to be carefully evaluated. One staff officer, for example, wrote that the Marines actually did land on St. John Island during Flex 7 despite Holland Smith's objections. His letter contained such details on Smith's behavior and the conduct of the landing that it positively rang with authenticity. Yet Smith's *Coral and Brass*, p. 77, claims that King canceled his order to land on St. John. Further research revealed that Smith was correct and that the staff officer's letter was fantasy.

These kinds of revelations bedevil a historian. What can he believe? He can never — ever — really be sure what happened, and why. But if historians waited until they had incontrovertible proof of past events before writing about them, not much history would ever be written. Liddell-Hart recognized this in his gem of a book, *Why Can't We Learn from History?* No historian in his right mind would ever say that his book was the final word on anything that happened in the past. The art and skill of a historian stem from his ability to discern what probably happened. The author regards Samuel Eliot Morison as a master practitioner. His bibliographical essays in his last two works on the European voyages of discovery in America are masterpieces.

The sources for this chapter, in addition to authentic letters from staff and shipboard officers, include King's typescript memoirs; interviews with George Russell and Neil Dietrich; the memoirs of Frog Low; extensive correspondence in the *1940–1941* file in Box #8 of the King LCMD papers; and the oral histories of Victor H. Krulak and Oman T. Pfeiffer. Other sources included *Abbazia*, *Albion*, *Churchill III*, *Furer*, *Morison I*, and *Smith*. Harry Sanders's fine article, "King of the Oceans" (*Naval Institute Proceedings*, January 1969), is an excellent source for information on King's habits and routine.

Chapter 12: The Atlantic Conference

The sources for the Atlantic Conference included King's typescript memoirs, notes and diaries by Forrest P. Sherman and Ross McIntire, and correspondence and other documents in the *1940–1941* file in Box #8 of King's LCMD papers. Secondary sources include *Abbazia*, *Churchill III*, *Morison I*, and *Pogue I*. The oral history of Olaf M. Hustvedt was useful in reconstructing King's activities in late November and early December 1941, supplemented by the article on King in *Life* magazine, 24 November 1941.

Chapter 13: Taking Command

It is difficult today to comprehend fully the lack of American preparation for the Second World War. How does one visualize how King took command of the fleet from a dirty, empty office in Main Navy with no staff and no organization? He was alone. One can sense the despair that even King felt when he wrote, "Nothing was ready. I had to start with nothing."

Legend has it that when King was summoned by Roosevelt and Knox to become COMINCH, he commented, "When they get into trouble, they call for the sons-of-bitches." Whether King ever said it is speculative. Scores of retired officers who wrote to the author said that he did. John McCrea, Roosevelt's naval aide early in the war, once asked King if he actually had said such a thing. "No John, I didn't," King replied. "But if I had thought of it, I would have said it."

King's decision to live in seclusion aboard *Dauntless* is an interesting contrast to Marshall's way of living. Marshall went home for both lunch and dinner because he could relax with his wife. King's home was a source of tension. He stayed on his flagship. Apparently his family accepted that decision without question, probably because they were accustomed to his long absences at sea over the years.

The uniformed women in the Navy Department and COMINCH headquarters must have been magnificent. All three of King's flag secretaries (Russell, Orem, and Dietrich) praised their performance in conversations with the author. Two other COMINCH staff officers, Bernhard H. Bieri and Henri Smith-Hutton, spoke in their oral histories of their admiration of the women. Given today's emphasis on women's rights, there is an assumption that women some thirty or more years ago were suppressed. That obviously was not true in the Navy Department.

King's memoirs became less useful starting with this period, because his ill health in the late 1940s had begun to degrade his writing. But King's memory was still good, and he had long conversations with Walter Whitehill, which Whitehill meticulously recorded. King's LCMD papers were once again a primary research source. Mrs. Eunice W. Rice wrote to the author about her father, Russell Willson, and his service as King's chief of staff. COMINCH staff officers also wrote to the author about working with King during the first days of the war. Betsy Matter talked with the author about King's reaction to the news about the attack on Pearl Harbor, supplemented with the oral history of Olaf Hustvedt. Harry Sanders's *Proceedings* article was useful as well in describing King's first reaction to the start of the war.

Chapter 14: Opening Moves

The principal source for what was said and done during ARCADIA was *FRUS 1941–1943*, which contains the minutes and the official documents of the conference. It is an imperfect record. The staff secretaries were senior officers and not skilled stenographers. And when hot words were exchanged, the minutes often failed to reflect the temper of the participants. (Note my other comments on these official *FRUS* documents in the introduction to the bibliography.) Still, the *FRUS* series is the best available source of information on the proceedings of the CCS wartime conferences.

One example of the contradictions in the *FRUS* record concerns Churchill's draft telegram to the War Cabinet proposing Wavell as the ABDA supreme commander. The reader will recall that Roosevelt, Hopkins, King, and Marshall edited the telegram before it was sent. *FRUS 1941–1943*, pp. 128–130, states that only Hopkins and Marshall left the room to work on the telegram. Yet a Hopkins memorandum quoted in *FRUS*, p. 277, says that King left the room, as well. Which statement was correct? In this case, it was the latter. A facsimile of the telegram is illustrated on *FRUS*, pp. 277–279. The corrections are obviously in King's handwriting, so King must have left the room with Hopkins and Marshall. A small point, perhaps, but it nevertheless illustrates the inconsistencies in the official record.

The author used a number of other sources to supplement *FRUS*, including *Churchill III*, *Pogue I*, and King's postwar written comments to Colonel C. H. Donnelly of the JCS historical staff.

Turning to events in the Southwest Pacific, *Lundstrom* was by far the best source of detailed information. King's organizational problems with his COMINCH staff are explained in the oral histories of George C. Dyer and Arthur H. McCollum and in correspondence in King's LCMD papers. King's conflicts with Russell Willson were discussed in a letter to the author from Willson's daughter, Eunice Rice. King's personal assessment of Willson, Pye, and many other senior flag officers is contained in a remarkable document prepared by Walter Whitehill. One weekend after the war King and Whitehill had been discussing personalities. Whitehill produced a register of officers and asked King to comment on any he chose. King thumbed through the register and said what he thought about the names he recognized. Whitehill later recorded King's verdicts on his fellow naval officers.

The events leading up to Stark's firing and King's ascension to CNO are described and analyzed in *Albion*. King frequently spoke about Stark's relief to Whitehill and claimed that he was surprised at Roosevelt's decision. There are several sources, including *Davis*, p. 237, that suggest that both King and Stark were ready to step down in favor of each other. Stark lost.

Chapter 15: Organizing for War

The JCS today is so carefully defined and circumscribed by federal law that the contrast to the ad hoc JCS of the Second World War is indeed startling. Before the United States got involved in the war, Roosevelt, Knox, Stimson, Marshall, and Stark obviously could not visualize the kind of organization they would need to fight a world war. So the JCS, as King later said, "just grew like Topsy." *Davis* was the best source for explaining the origins of the JCS and its many organizational developments. King's LCMD papers provided excellent supplementary material. The FDR Library provided correspondence relevant to Harold D. Smith's influence in denying the JCS legal authority. *Hayes* was the primary source for King's new strategy following the collapse of ABDA, supplemented with *Morton*, *Pogue I*, and *Lowenheim*. For those desiring further information on the organization of the Pacific theater under Nimitz and MacArthur, the author suggests *Hayes*, chapter IV, and *Morton*, chapter XI.

Chapter 16: Stopping the Japanese: Coral Sea and Midway

There are many opinions about the wisdom of the Tokyo Raid. Spruance, who commanded the task-force screen, regarded the raid as poor strategy. "The Doolittle raid was a spectacular operation, good for American morale," he later wrote, "but unless it caused the Japanese to retain forces at home which they intended to send to the South Pacific, it did not impress me as particularly valuable from a military point of view." The author agrees with Spruance's assessment. As King was not concerned with public morale, the raid may simply have satiated his desire to draw some Japanese blood. But he could have made the Japanese bleed elsewhere, where it really hurt, as in the Coral Sea. There is a theory that the raid convinced Admiral Yamamato to initiate his disastrous attack on Midway, but if so, that was a lucky aftereffect that was not an original objective. The important question is whether the raid hastened the end of the war. The author thinks not.

King had misgivings about Nimitz, and his confidence in Nimitz was qualified. When the two discussed the performance of senior officers in the Pacific, King often became exasperated. "That fellow is doing all right," was a common Nimitz observation. "You must say more about him than that," King would respond. After the war King told Whitehill of the many times that he had to press Nimitz to be more decisive in dealing with poor performers. King felt that fixers were reluctant to hurt people's feelings because of habits formed by past practices in the Bureau of Naval Personnel.

As discussed in the text, flag officer assignments were a complicated business. George C. Dyer, formerly King's flag secretary, has said that King's one weakness was that he was a poor judge of men, citing Ghormley as an example. Clearly, it is in unfair assertion. However, King did sometimes indulge old friends and drinking buddies. It seemed to his staff, at least, that King sometimes gave them favored assignments. The evidence shows that such cases were the exception.

The minutes of the King-Nimitz conferences were not always satisfactory as an accurate and thorough source of information. King did not expect that they would be. The recorder would be a King staff officer who might not be the same person from one meeting to the next. None was a trained secretary. Whenever King and Nimitz met in San Francisco, they lunched at the Bohemian Club. The conference discussions frequently continued as they ate, and the recorder was usually too far away to hear their conversation and take notes.

The story of the Chicago *Tribune* revelation of Japanese intentions at Midway still attracts scholars. Gina Goren of the Communications Institute, Hebrew University, Jerusalem, recently completed an excellent monograph entitled "Communication Intelligence and the Freedom of the Press," dealing with the frustrated efforts of the Navy Department to prosecute the *Tribune*. The only person ever punished (and it was unofficial) was the unfortunate Commander Seligman. Even though disgraced, unpromoted, and forced into retirement by King, Seligman ironically received a "tombstone" promotion to captain based upon his wartime record. For the most recent account of how Johnston knew about the intelligence messages, see Clyde J. Van Arsdall's comments on pp. 77–79 of the December 1977 *Naval Institute Proceedings*.

There was one other casualty in the aftermath of Midway. The disagreement in mid-May between King and Nimitz as to Japanese intentions had reflected a deeper conflict between their respective intelligence advisors and cryptanalysts in interpreting the Japanese messages. After the battle the ill feelings between Pearl Harbor and Washington intensified, as each claimed credit for having made the Midway victory possible. (See *Potter*, p. 211, and *Blair*.)

Lieutenant Commander Joseph J. Rochefort was regarded by Nimitz as his key cryptanalyst at Pearl Harbor. According to *Potter*, p. 104, Nimitz recommended to King that Rochefort receive the Distinguished Service Medal for his intelligence contributions before the Battle of Midway. King refused Rochefort the medal, because he felt that all the cryptanalysts had simply been doing what they were expected to do. Then, allegedly on the advice of his own cryptanalysts, King transferred Rochefort from Pearl Harbor to the United States to noncryptographic duties. (See *Potter*, p. 211, for one version.) The bitterness of Rochefort's associates toward King remains to this day. The author was unable to confirm whether such bitterness was justified. King's papers make no mention of Rochefort, and further research would be necessary to clarify his role in Rochefort's fall from grace.

The principal sources for this chapter included *Lundstrom*, *Potter*, *Hayes*, memoranda of conversations between King and Whitehill, and King's papers in the FDR Library, the LCMD, and the COMINCH files of the Naval Historical Center.

Chapter 17: Eyes Toward Germany: Operation Torch

If war is fought for political ends, it follows that political considerations often dominate grand strategy. Still, one becomes uneasy with the thoughts that Roosevelt had somehow tied in Operation TORCH with the November 1942 national elections. Yet the evidence is convincing (*Pogue I*, p. 402, and Eisenhower's *Crusade in Europe*, p. 195).

There is no published official record of the King-Hopkins-Marshall meetings with the British in London following the Second Washington Conference. The author relied extensively upon *Matloff and Snell*, *Pogue I*, and *Sherwood* to reconstruct the decision at London that culminated in the agreement on TORCH. These sources were supplemented by memoranda of conversations between King and Whitehill and memoranda from Roosevelt to the JCS in the FDR Library.

The vivid description of King's breakfast at Presque Isle, Maine, on his return from London are from a 15 July 1950 letter from King to Whitehill. King liked to eat well. After the war he could remember almost every menu he had been served while traveling overseas. After the Yalta trip in 1945 he commented, "It seems that we did a great deal of eating." Following naval custom, King's flag lieutenant paid for King's meals from the flag mess treasury that he maintained for the Admiral. "I was always prompt," King later wrote, "to reimburse my flag lieutenant at the end of every month."

Chapter 18: Striking Back: Guadalcanal

The planning and execution of the Guadalcanal campaign was so hectic that conflicting versions are inevitable. Turner's attitude on getting the amphibious command is an example. King remembered Turner's dismay when he got the news; *Dyer*, p. 262, asserts that Turner was delighted. Who can say?

A great deal has been made of the American reaction to the news that a Japanese airfield was under construction on Guadalcanal. *Potter*, p. 115, and *Morison IV*, p. 261, assert that the campaign's objectives and timing were consequently altered by a heightened sense of urgency. In contrast, *Dyer*, pp. 273–276, contends that the airfield was common knowledge and did not materially affect American planning. The King-Nimitz conference notes of 5 July do not substantiate Potter's contention that Guadalcanal was substituted for Santa Cruz during the conference.

Whitehill himself was disturbed by such contradictions and spoke to King about them. "When the Army monograph of the Guadalcanal campaign was nearing completion," Whitehill later wrote, "a copy of the manuscript was sent to Admiral King for comment. He returned it with the criticism that too much space was wasted on low-level planning papers that were of no importance. When it was pointed out to him that the documents he depreciated were all the work of Joint Chiefs of Staff planners, King countered by the irrefutable observation that no use had been made of them in planning the operation, which he and Marshall had had to do in such haste that they had had no time even to look at them; hence they were of no importance in establishing the evolution of the plan. This introduces the disquieting possibility that, without the personal testimony of participants as a guide, the historian may place undue importance upon a seemingly reliable document that is, in fact, nothing more than a red herring."

The most popular version of King's reaction to the news of Savo Island is open to question. According to Forrest Davis (*Saturday Evening Post*, 9 December 1944), when King was awakened he responded, "Why bother me with that? There's nothing I can do about it." This story has often been repeated as an example of King's coldblooded character. Yet George Russell told the author that the story was untrue. Russell himself broke the news, and King responded quite differently, as noted in the text. King could have changed the magazine story. Why didn't he? Perhaps he was too busy to edit every discrepancy. Or was that the image he wanted to portray to the public?

The principal sources for this chapter include *Hayes; Morton;* interviews with Russell, Orem, and Dietrich; memoranda of conversations between King and Whitehill; and messages in the COMINCH files in the Operational Archives, Naval Historical Center. King's own recollection of his reaction to the Savo Island news is contained in an interview with Ira Wolfert in the New York *Times*, 22 October 1945.

Chapter 19: Wars on the Home Front

The makeup and organization of the COMINCH staff came from letters from former staff officers to the author, the oral histories of Robert B. Pirie and Oman T. Pfeiffer, interviews with Neil Dietrich, George Russell, and Howard Orem, and an interview with King's staff readiness officer,

Walter S. DeLany. William R. Smedberg III, King's combat intelligence officer, was particularly helpful through his oral history and his letters to the author. For those who desire more detailed information on the COMINCH organization, the author suggests *Furer*, chapter III.

The association between King and Knox was contained in the reminiscences of John L. McCrea in the FDR Library, LCMD correspondence from King to Knox, an interview with George Russell, and a letter to the author from Walter F. Boone. King's campaign to seize total power in the Navy Department came from many sources: correspondence in the FDR Library and the LCMD; memoranda of conversations between King and Whitehill; the LCMD papers of Frederick J. Horne; and the oral histories of John R. Redman and Paul D. Stroop. The best published source on King's struggle against civilian control is *Albion and Connery*.

Men in power try to eliminate those near the throne whom they perceive as a threat. Horne was just such a threat to King. Horne was too influential (and too valuable) to be fired. King needed him around, but he had to be made less of a challenge to King's authority. King's solution was to give the loyal and faithful Edwards some of Horne's duties and subtly to interpose Edwards between King and Horne.

King struck with a memorandum to Forrestal dated 5 September 1944. "During the past few months," he wrote, "I have been slowly but surely forced to the conclusion that Vice Admiral Horne, Vice Admiral Edwards and I have too much to do to be able to do our work effectively. This is not, I feel sure, because we try to do too much but because the work is growing in complexity and volume with the progress of the war, particularly in those things which require high echelon guidance."

King went on to propose a solution. He would create a Deputy COMINCH–Deputy CNO "whose chief business will be to attend to matters of *military policy* . . ." (italics King's). "If this proposal meets with your approval," King concluded, "it is in order that the concurrence of the President be asked."

Forrestal found it hard to object to a reorganization if King said it was based upon military necessity, and he sent it on to Roosevelt, by then a sick man unwilling to fight King on such matters. It came back to King with the notation, "OK FDR." Horne was understandably upset, and his unhappiness found its way to the press and radio. King felt compelled to write the statement, cited in the text, that Horne had not been demoted, and he purposefully sent a copy of that press release directly to Horne.

Six years later, King told Whitehill the truth. "Horne would have liked to be CNO. Who wouldn't? But I am afraid he was not quite frank with me. I eased him out, finally." King knew what power was all about.

Chapter 20: Roosevelt, Congress, and the Press

The reminiscences of John L. McCrea were the principal source for Roosevelt's routine during the Second World War, including the President's geography lecture to Stimson. The Secretary of War recorded many things in his published diary, but his evening with Roosevelt is not included.

The complex interactions between the Navy Department, FDR, and the Congress are contained principally in *Albion.* The author is pleased that the Naval Institute Press will publish this long-suppressed administrative history of the Navy Department in the near future. It is a reference without which no naval historian ought to be.

King's LCMD papers abound with correspondence between King, the Congress, the press, and the public. Consequently they too were a primary source for this chapter. These were supplemented by letters and interviews with William Smedberg, George Russell, Neil Dietrich, and Howard Orem. Retired correspondents Robert Sherrod, Glen Perry, and Phelps Adams were especially helpful to the author by explaining how King came to meet with his select circle of journalists, the "Surviving Veterans of the Battle of Virginia." Glen Perry's memoranda of these meetings were of inestimable value to the author.

Cornelius Bull's diary of those meetings was probably kept without King's knowledge, and its contents should have been labeled Top Secret. The diary came to King (after Bull's death) from his widow. "Mrs. Bull inquired," wrote King's aide to the Admiral on 15 July 1944, "whether you wished Mr. Bull's 'record of meetings,' and was informed that it would be appreciated if she would send them to this office." This writer and many future historians will be forever grateful to Mrs. Bull for having saved this priceless document for posterity.

Chapter 21: Casablanca

There is a general feeling about King that he was anti-British, and proponents of that argument cite Casablanca as a prime example. *Bryant I* and *Ismay* certainly reflect the antipathy that the British felt at the time.

Howard is more charitable. "The impression was carried away by some British officers," says *Howard*, p. 243, "that [King] had no interest in, and was indeed hostile to, all operations outside the Pacific. That impression was not entirely fair. That Pacific operations should occupy the principal place in his mind and heart was inevitable. On his shoulders rested the ultimate operational responsibility for the conduct of a war unprecedented in complexity and scope against an adversary whose skill and ferocity had astounded the world and who showed as yet no sign of having come to the end of his career of conquest; a war, moreover, to which America's allies could make only a marginal contribution. . . . But on wide issues of world strategy, so long as they did not entrench upon his own particular and huge responsibilities, Admiral King showed himself open-minded. His initial concern at Casablanca was so to clarify the strategic concepts of the Allies as to prevent the uncertainties of European strategic problems upsetting and diverting resources from those projects in the Pacific about which he had no uncertainty whatever, and which he regarded as indispensable for holding the line against Japan."

The approval of C.C.S. 155, which authorized King to begin his Pacific offensive, is covered in some depth in *Pogue II*, pp. 29–30, to which the author invites those readers who seek more details on this phase of the Casablanca Conference. The primary source on the conference was, of course, *FRUS 1941–1943*, supplemented with *Matloff*, *Bryant I*, and *Pogue II;* memoranda by King's aide Ruthven E. Libby, and memoranda of conversations between King and Whitehill as well as Edwards and Whitehill, supplemented with the oral history of Admiral Robert L. Dennison.

King's seminar on his strategic views, which he shared with his inner circle of journalists on 30 November 1942, is recorded in the diary of Cornelius Bull and a report of the meeting from Glen Perry to his New York editor.

Chapter 22: The Battle of the Atlantic

The author used a variety of sources for this chapter, primarily correspondence and other documents in the FDR Library and in King's LCMD papers. Other sources included letters to the author from former staff officers Alan R. McFarland and Harry Sanders, and a letter from Dan Gallery, who captured *U-505*. The memoirs of Frog Low explained how Tenth Fleet was organized, and the oral history of William

Smedberg covered the use of intelligence in the Battle of the Atlantic. Published sources included *Morison I*, *Potter and Nimitz*, *Sherwood*, *Loewenheim*, *Howard*, *War Reports*, and *FRUS Washington/Quebec 1943*.

Chapter 23: After Casablanca: Ships

The discussion of the problems with resource allocation and the decisions on limited objectives in 1943 are primarily from *Hayes*. Charlotte Pihl and Betsy Matter told the author how King would relax with them on afternoons and weekends. Those sections dealing with the problems of ship procurement were based primarily upon correspondence on file in the FDR Library. Supplementary documents came from the COMINCH files in the Naval Historical Center and in King's LCMD papers. Walter DeLany told the author about the reaction to his memorandum on the proposed 1945 shipbuilding program. Other sources included *Albion*, *Albion and Connery*, *Morison X*, and *Blum*.

Chapter 24: After Casablanca: Men

King prided himself on judging people and decided that few could be trusted. "Loyalty is the important thing," King once said. "I got to understand many people. I would look them in the eye and usually understand which man was tricky."

King's dislike for fixers was established early in his career. He liked to recall Mike Trench, a Bureau of Navigation detail officer he had known before the First World War. On one occasion he watched Trench convince an irate ensign that he was lucky to get a job that was the cause of the ensign's original complaint. The young officer left happy and satisfied.

"Mike, how do you do it?" asked King.

"That's easy," Trench replied. "They really don't understand what the hell they want."

The minutes of the King-Nimitz conference are one of the best sources of information on the Navy's wartime personnel policies. Letters in King's LCMD papers were rich with information on every aspect of personnel administration. Other sources included various oral histories; interviews with Howard Orem and Walter DeLany; memoranda of conversations between King and Whitehill; and considerable research and data gathering in the *Register*. For those desiring further information on the Bureau of Naval Personnel, the author suggests *Furer*, chapter VII.

In the author's biography of Admiral Spruance, *The Quiet Warrior*, the author claimed that King personally denied the promotion of Captain Charles J. Moore (Spruance's chief of staff) to rear admiral. That assertion is hereby retracted. On the basis of evidence gathered for this book, it is clear that King had a deep respect for the flag selection system and would not have vetoed Moore's promotion with his vote alone.

Chapter 25: Trident

The problems with the internal organization of the JCS committees are not surprising. At the start of the war joint planning committees did not even exist, for all practical purposes. So there were bound to be difficulties, and there were. The very best source for information on the JCS committee system is *Davis*, vol. 2, which the author used extensively.

Much of the CCS business at TRIDENT was conducted in executive session with no written records. During the 17 May 1943 session the chiefs of staff cleared the room so they could speak freely. When the closed-door bargaining was over, King emerged with the approval he wanted for an offensive in the Pacific. King had met with his journalists and correspondents in Nelie Bull's home both before and after TRIDENT, and he told them beforehand what he intended to do and afterward what had happened. Thus Bull's diary and Glen Perry's reports to his editor were a splendid source of information about TRIDENT that could not be found in the official record.

But the official record did contain much of value, particularly *FRUS Washington/Quebec 1943* and *Hayes*, supplemented with *Bryant I*. Other important sources included King's written comments to the original draft of *Hayes*, together with memoranda of conversations between King and Whitehill. The oral histories of Robert L. Dennison and Charles J. Moore were also important.

Chapter 26: Accountability

Much of the material for this chapter came from correspondence in the FDR Library, the COMINCH files in the Navy Historical Center, and from King's LCMD papers. For additional information on the administration of naval justice, see *Albion and Connery*, pp. 122–124 and 246–247. The story of the sinking of the *Awa Maru* is contained in the April 1974 *Naval Institute Proceedings*, pp. 70–76, supplemented with *Blair*, p. 840, and Vice Admiral Charles Lockwood's memoirs, *Sink Them All.*

Turning to the Pearl Harbor investigations, the principal source was *Pearl Harbor Attack Hearings, Part 39*, supplemented with King's LCMD correspondence. The question of accountability for the Pearl Harbor attack (especially that of Stark and Kimmel) is still controversial today, and it is beyond the scope of this biography to inject the author's own opinions.

Chapter 27: Getting Ready—1943

Admiral John J. Hyland wrote two letters to the author describing his experiences as King's executive pilot. One of his most vivid memories was a flight to Boston. The airport there was closed because of weather, and all intermediate airports including Washington were forecast to go down shortly. Hyland phoned King's aide again and again, as departure time neared, to cancel the trip. It was in vain. "He wants to go," said the aide, "and we're on the way over."

When King arrived, Hyland warned that if they got underway the only alternate field would be in North Carolina.

"I'd like to try," said King, and he climbed into the plane. Hyland took off into the lowering weather and, to his surprise, was just able to land in Boston. As Hyland saw King off the plane, the Admiral routinely thanked him as if nothing unusual had happened. Hyland could not let that pass. "Admiral," he said, "we are lucky as hell to be on the ground in Boston."

King stopped and looked at his pilot. "Hyland, we wouldn't be here if we hadn't started, would we?" Then he walked away.

King later wrote that while he was flying over Iowa a violent storm so buffeted his plane that he got airsick. It was perhaps the only time that King considered landing because of weather. "It was the damndest storm I have ever seen," he wrote, "but we stuck it out."

The principal sources for this chapter included the minutes of the King-Nimitz conferences during the summer of 1943, *Morton*, *Matloff and Snell*, and the oral history of Oman Pfeiffer.

Chapter 28: Aviation

The association between King and Towers has always been a popular topic among naval historians. The evidence suggests that they were once good friends. Towers gave King his first airplane ride before the First World War. When King commanded *Lexington*, Towers commanded the ancient, ugly *Langley*, nicknamed the "covered wagon" because of her flight deck. It was during Prohibition. One day King sent a message to Towers as they passed at sea: MESSAGE CO TO CO: JACK, WHERE ARE YOU GOING IN THAT COVERED WAGON? KING.

The following message came back from *Langley*: WE ARE GOING TO JAMAICA HIC ERNIE HIC WHERE ARE YOU HIC GOING? TOWERS.

King gave a wry smile and told the signalman, "No answer." To a junior officer observer, Robert J. Heinlein, it seemed that King and Towers must have been "intimate friends."

Many historians have also claimed that King prevented Towers from getting a combat command. It was actually Nimitz. "Nimitz and Towers did not agree about anything," King told Whitehill after the war. King also confided to Whitehill that after the war his friends told him that "Towers hated Nimitz and vice versa." King later heard from a mutual friend that Towers eventually regretted his hard feelings toward King during the war.

The decision not to give Towers a combat command evolved from a long series of messages between King and Nimitz in April and May, 1945. The issues are too complex to discuss here, but those desiring further information are invited to read the COMINCH files for those dates, particularly message files numbers 24 and 25 in box #6, Naval Historical Center.

Reynolds was an excellent source for all aviation matters, particularly the Yarnell survey. Most of the primary source material for this chapter came from King's LCMD papers. Other sources included the minutes of the King-Nimitz conferences, *Potter*, memoranda of conversations between King and Whitehill, data from the *Register*, and King's typescript memoirs for the years 1943 and 1944.

The author could not justify a full chapter on submarine warfare because it was truly the "silent service." King's LCMD papers, his official records in the Naval Historical Center, and his own memoirs contain next to nothing on submarines. When the author did find something significant, he wove it into the text of various chapters. In the author's opinion, *Blair* has said the last word on submarine operations during the war, and King is mentioned from time to time. The author invites those readers interested in any aspect of submarine warfare to this splendid book. The author also suggests *Sink 'Em All* by Charles A. Lockwood.

Chapter 29: The Fleet Admiral

Research material on King's gray uniform came primarily from correspondence in King's LCMD papers. The subject of awards and decorations during the war is covered to a degree in *Furer*, p. 301, and in an article by Michael W. Shelton in the August 1978 *Naval Institute Proceedings*. Other sources include memoranda of conversations between King and Whitehill, the minutes of the January 1944 King-Nimitz conference, the oral history of Alan G. Kirk, and conversations with Betsy Matter. Most of the research material concerning five-star rank was contained in King's LCMD papers.

Chapter 30: Quadrant: The First Quebec Conference

It is fascinating to have an insight to King's strategic thinking during the war. During the meetings with war correspondents at Nelie Bull's home in Alexandria, King spoke freely of his assessment of the war and how he felt both about his friends and his enemies. Bull kept a meticulous diary, which the author substantiated through Glen Perry's letters to his New York editor following each meeting. These two sources were once again invaluable to the author.

The test of the Pykrete during the QUADRANT Conference must have been spectacular. The various spectators all have slightly different versions of what happened. No one really seems to remember, for example, who actually fired the shot. Some say Mountbatten, others say a member of the demonstration team. The author's narrative in the text is an amalgamation of all the versions he could find.

The primary source for the proceedings of the conference was *FRUS Washington/Quebec 1943*. Published supplemental sources include *Matloff*, *Howard*, *Bryant I*, *Leahy*, and *Pogue II*. Other sources included memoranda of conversations between King and Whitehill, King's own written recollections, and letters to the author from several retired naval officers who attended the conference as members of King's party.

Chapter 31: Planning and Logistics

The flag secretary is one of the best-informed members of a large naval staff because he sees nearly every piece of correspondence. King's three flag secretaries — George Russell, Howard Orem, and Neil Dietrich — were particularly close to Admiral King. It was extremely fortunate for the author that all three were willing to be interviewed in December 1974. Thanks to their cooperation the author was able to gather extensive information on King's thoughts, habits, and routine, which is reflected in this and other chapters.

Paul Pihl in his conversations with the author was critical of the Navy's logistical planning during the war, and his opinion was substantiated in *Ballantine*. Logistics is a complicated business that King did not understand as well as he should have. This chapter could give only a brief treatment to the topic. For those who desire to read further into the subject, the author recommends *Ballantine*, *Connery*, and both volumes of *Coakley and Leighton*.

The hot debate about who would be the supreme commander in Europe has been related by a number of historians. It is not entirely clear how King first found out that FDR wanted to give the job to Marshall. King told the Alexandria correspondents in December 1943 that he had first heard it from Marshall himself during the First Quebec Conference. Later, in August 1950, King told Whitehill that Knox had been the first to tell him. In any event, the JCS did get the news, one way or the other, at Quebec. King assumed that Leahy and Arnold spoke to the President, as he did, about keeping Marshall in Washington. Leahy typically equivocates in his memoirs, while *Matloff* gives an excellent analysis of events on pp. 274–279. Glen Perry told the author that King had asked him to write editorials about Marshall. Perry's letter to his New York editor, Edmond P. Barnett, on 20 December 1943 confirmed that King had asked Marquis Childs, as well.

Other sources for this chapter included memoranda of conversations between King and Whitehill; letters to the author from members of King's staff; the oral histories of Bernhard Bieri and Royal Ingersoll; the minutes of the King-Nimitz conference in September 1943; and various documents in the King LCMD papers.

Chapter 32: Cairo-Teheran

This chapter opened with King's assessment of the Soviet Union (for the benefit of the Alexandria correspondents) just before the Teheran Conference and was derived from the diary of Cornelius Bull and a letter from Perry to Barnett. The details of the trans-Atlantic crossing in the *Iowa* are from the reminiscences of John McCrea, supplemented by King's written memoirs and extracts from *FRUS Cairo/Teheran*. Roosevelt went by ship rather than aircraft because of poor health. Customarily the President would notify his naval aide of the type of ship he wanted, but he typically would qualify his request. In September 1944 he wrote to Wilson Brown, "Naturally, I do not want to take any ship out of combat service but in these classes it might be possible to find one in the middle of a shakedown period."

The discussions with Eisenhower in Tunis are from King's memoirs, Eisenhower's *Crusade in Europe*, *FRUS*, and the published memoirs of Eisenhower's naval aide, Captain Harry C. Butcher. The chronology is confused as to what happened when Eisenhower returned from his dinner with Roosevelt, but all sources agree on the gist of the conversation.

Primary sources for the First and Second Cairo Conferences and Teheran include *FRUS*, King's memoirs and memoranda of conversations with Whitehill, *Cunningham*, *Bryant II*, and *Pogue II*. King gave his Alexandria correspondents a fascinating account of his adventures at Teheran, which were recorded both by Cornelius Bull and Glen Perry.

Chapter 33: Onward in the Pacific

The long debates that preceded the March 1944 decisions on Pacific strategy are principally contained in *Hayes*. Other sources include *Potter*, the minutes of the King-Nimitz conferences, and the diary of Cornelius Bull. King's apprehensions about a fleet action in the Marianas are revealed in a series of messages between King and Nimitz in the COMINCH message files at the Naval Historical Center. For Spruance's view of his mission at Saipan, see *Buell*, chapter 18.

Chapter 34: Overlord and Anvil

King's relations with Forrestal are from *Albion and Connery*, King's memoirs, conversations by the author with Charlotte Pihl, official correspondence in the COMINCH files at the Naval Historical Center, and the reminiscences of John McCrea. Betsy Matter, Joe King, Elizabeth King van den Berg, John J. Ballentine, Jr., and John A. Moreno told the author about King's concern with his family problems. King's visit to England and Normandy was derived from many sources: King's memoirs and memoranda of conversations with Whitehill, *Matloff*, *Pogue II*, *Bryant II*, and the oral history of Alan G. Kirk. The controversy over the LSTs going to Greece is primarily from the COMINCH message files, the oral history of H. Kent Hewitt, and *Sherwood*.

Chapter 35: Strategic Decisions in the Pacific

King's ideas on Pacific strategy came from *Hayes*, the minutes of the King-Nimitz conferences, and memoranda of conversations between King and Whitehill. *Hayes* and *FRUS Quebec 1944* were the primary sources for the OCTAGON Conference. The Battle of Leyte Gulf had a number of sources: memoranda of conversations between King and Whitehill and of conversations between Whitehill and King aides Alexander S. McDill and Willis R. Denekas; the oral history of William Smedberg; and messages in the COMINCH files, Naval Historical Center. Admiral Jocko Clark has written that King became furious when Halsey went north after the decoy force, but staff officer Malcolm F. Schoeffel had no such recollection. King's opinions of Halsey and Browning are from memoranda of King's conversations with Whitehill, and from the author's conversations with Charlotte Pihl.

Chapter 36: Climax

King wrote rather extensive memoirs about his activities during 1945. As a naval aviator he faithfully maintained a flight log to record his wartime travels. Using the log as a reminder, King would write his postwar memories of those events, which Whitehill later used in *King and White-*

hill. The author found King's memoirs for 1945 equally useful in writing this chapter.

One of the best sources for the Yalta trip was the oral history of Paul D. Stroop. Published sources included *FRUS Yalta*, *Pogue II*, and *Bryant II*. King's correspondence with Senator Knowland is in King's LCMD papers. When King went to Potsdam he was suffering from an illness that would eventually require radiation treatment, but his medical record did not reveal what that illness was. Whatever the illness, it was serious enough for him to take his Navy physician, Edward Gough, and the doctor's memoirs of that trip were a wonderful source of information for many of the details. Other sources for Potsdam included *FRUS Potsdam* and letters from King to Forrestal.

Neil Dietrich told the author about King's reaction to the news that Japan had surrendered.

Chapter 37: Anticlimax

King's unfortunate disagreements about his relief and retirement date are from conversations with Charlotte Pihl, King's written memoirs and memoranda of conversations between Whitehill and King, and between Whitehill and Alexander McDill. Phelps Adams wrote the author about the final dinner with "The Surviving Veterans of the Battle of Virginia," while Neil Dietrich described King's farewell dinner with his staff.

Chapter 38: The Final Years

Paul and Charlotte Pihl, Betsy Matter, and Rear Admiral and Mrs. Boynton Braun told the author about King's activities during retirement. Aides Neil K. Almgren, Frederick H. Schneider, and Willis Denekas provided additional information and details. Walter Whitehill's description of the funeral is from the *Proceedings* of the Massachusetts Historical Society, volume 70, 1950–1953.

Index

Index

ABOUT THE AUTHORS

Thomas B. Buell is a graduate of the U.S. Naval Academy. While at the Naval War College he wrote *The Quiet Warrior: A Biography of Admiral Raymond A. Spruance,* which is also part of the Naval Institute Press's Classics of Naval Literature series.

Commander Buell also taught history at West Point, where he wrote *Master of Sea Power.* These two books received both the Alfred Thayer Mahan Award for Literary Achievement from the Navy League of the United States and the Samuel Eliot Morison Award for Naval Literature from the Naval Order of the United States. Commander Buell is now a writer-in-residence at the University of North Carolina at Chapel Hill.

John B. Lundstrom is curator of American and military history at the Milwaukee Public Museum. He has published three books about the U.S. Navy during World War II, most recently *The First Team and the Guadalcanal Campaign: Naval Fighter Combat from August to November 1942.*

The Naval Institute Press is the book-publishing arm of the U.S. Naval Institute, a private, nonprofit, membership society for sea service professionals and others who share an interest in naval and maritime affairs. Established in 1873 at the U.S. Naval Academy in Annapolis, Maryland, where its offices remain today, the Naval Institute has members worldwide.

Members of the Naval Institute support the education programs of the society and receive the influential monthly magazine *Proceedings* or the colorful bimonthly magazine *Naval History* and discounts on fine nautical prints and on ship and aircraft photos. They also have access to the transcripts of the Institute's Oral History Program and get discounted admission to any of the Institute-sponsored seminars offered around the country.

The Naval Institute's book-publishing program, begun in 1898 with basic guides to naval practices, has broadened its scope to include books of more general interest. Now the Naval Institute Press publishes about seventy titles each year, ranging from how-to books on boating and navigation to battle histories, biographies, ship and aircraft guides, and novels. Institute members receive significant discounts on the more than eight hundred Press books in print.

Full-time students are eligible for special half-price membership rates. Life memberships are also available.

For a free catalog describing Naval Institute Press books currently available, and for further information about joining the U.S. Naval Institute, please write to:

Member Services
U.S. NAVAL INSTITUTE
291 Wood Road
Annapolis, MD 21402-5034
Telephone: (800) 233-8764
Fax: (410) 571-1703
Web address: www.usni.org